THE RANDALL HOUSE BIBLE COMMENTARY

THE RANDALL HOUSE BIBLE COMMENTARY

THE BOOK OF HEBREWS

by

W. STANLEY OUTLAW

FIRST EDITION

RANDALL HOUSE PUBLICATIONS
NASHVILLE, TENNESSEE 37217

All Scripture quotations, unless otherwise indicated, are taken from the *King James Version of the Bible*. Those marked NASB are taken from the *New American Standard Bible*, © Copyright 1960, 1962, 1963, 1968, 1971, 1972, 1973, 1975, 1977 by The Lockman Foundation. Used by permission. Those marked NIV are taken from the *Holy Bible, New International Version*. Copyright © 1973, 1978, 1984, by International Bible Society. Used by permissions of Zondervan. All rights reserved. Those marked NKJV are taken from the *New King James Version*. Copyright © 1982 by Thomas Nelson, Inc. Used by permission. All rights reserved. Those marked RSV are from the *Revised Standard Version of the Bible*, copyrighted 1946, 1952, 1971 by the Division of Christian Education of the National Council of Churches of Christ in the USA. Used by permission.

RANDALL HOUSE BIBLE COMMENTARY, The Book of Hebrews
© Copyright 2005
RANDALL HOUSE PUBLICATIONS
NASHVILLE, TN 37217
ISBN 0892655143
ISBN 0-89265-115-6 (SET)
LIBRARY OF CONGRESS CONTROL NUMBER:
2005935128

General Editor:
ROBERT E. PICIRILLI
Professor Emeritus, Free Will Baptist Bible College
Nashville, Tennessee

Associate Editor:
Harrold D. Harrison
Nashville, Tennessee

ACKNOWLEDGEMENTS

The author expresses thanks to these publishers for permission to quote from the works indicated.

Kistemaker, Simon, *Exposition of the Epistle to the Hebrews,* Copyright © NTC. Excerpts reprinted with the permission of the Baker Publishing Group.

Kent, Homer A. Jr., *The Epistle to the Hebrews,* Copyright © Baker Publishing. Excerpts reprinted with the permission of the Baker Publishing Group.

Lunemann, Gottlieb, *Critical and Exegetical Handbook to the Epistles to the Hebrews* (T. & T. Clark), Copyright © The Continuum International Publishing Group. Reprinted by permission of The Continuum International Publishing Group.

Yeager, Randolph O. *The Renaissance New Testament*, © 1978. Used by permission of the publisher, Pelican Publishing Co., Inc.

PREFACE

Hebrews extensively treats matters that do not receive the same kind of attention anywhere else in the New Testament. Stanley Outlaw, who taught Hebrews many times during his career at Free Will Baptist Bible College, has given us a commentary that is both practical and able in its exposition. Dr. Outlaw knows New Testament Greek well, having also taught that for many years. At the same time, he has a pastor's heart. In this commentary, then, he has capably combined careful exegesis of the text with practical, pious application.

I said that Hebrews deals with some things that are not so thoroughly dealt with in the rest of the New Testament. No other New Testament writer so carefully explains the relationship between the Mosaic system and the person and work of Jesus Christ. Hebrews enables us to understand exactly the meaning of the sacrifices and priestly ministry that helped define Israel, the Old Testament people of God, especially their function to point forward to Him who would be the only finally effective sacrifice and high priest, Jesus Christ.

The possibility of apostasy is a theological issue that has long occupied the Christian church. My colleague, Leroy Forlines (author of the commentary on Romans in this series) has often said that anyone who really wants to know what the Bible teaches about any given subject ought to go first to a place in the Bible where that is the subject under direct discussion—rather than to those places where it is meantioned only in passing. For sure, in Hebrews the discussion of apostasy is at the forefront. Even commentators who do not believe that apostasy is possible, after all, acknowledge that the five major warning passages of Hebrews indicates that it is. We ought to master its teaching on this subject and warn those to whom we minister accordingly. Our desire is that this commentary will contribute to that.

With this volume, the *Randall House Bible Commentary* is one step nearer to completion, leaving just four segments remaining: Matthew, Luke, Acts, and the four writings of John that conclude the New Tetament. Most of these are at one stage or another of preparation and should follow regularly.

As I have observed often, this series is not meant to be highly technical. But neither are the commentaries intended to be merely devotional or "preachy." They are written with the original Greek text in view (and shaping the comments) but with the average user, who does not read Greek, in mind. Therefore the volumes are for any believer who desires careful exegesis of the text of Scripture, written by those who have a high view of Scripture as the inerrant Word of God.

Who then needs such careful exegesis of the Scriptures? The answer is that all serious-minded Christians need this. Of course pastors do; they have to teach the Word to their congregations week after week. But so do Sunday school teachers, who likewise explain and apply the text to their classes every Sunday. And so do the rest of the laity; after all, it is the very purpose of God's revelation of Himself and of His will for us—which we call the Bible—to describe the way that leads to life. And all of us, who are saved by faith and not by works, are under obligation to God to discern and walk in that way.

Robert E. Picirilli
Nashville, Tennessee, 2005

CONTENTS

COMMENTARY ON THE BOOK OF HEBREWS

INTRODUCTION

The Epistle to the Hebrews is one of the most eloquent books in the N.T., both in our English Bible and especially in the Greek N.T. from which it was translated. It is, at the same time, one of the most controversial books of the N.T., and this controversy did not begin in the modern church. It goes back, rather, to the early days of the formation of the N.T. canon, the 27 documents which came to be universally accepted as Scripture by the early church. This controversy extends to a variety of elements about the epistle, including authorship, destination, date, place of writing, as well as doctrinal passages, especially those which seem to emphasize the possibility of apostasy.

Background

There seems to be a logical and a chronological process in the development of the relationship of Judaism and Christianity in the early church which eventually culminated in the writing of Hebrews. First, in the early days of Christianity, after Pentecost, Jewish Christians continued to pray at the Temple (Acts 3:1) and to worship at the synagogues. Though there was only one Temple, there were numerous synagogues in a large city like Jerusalem, and it is likely that some of those synagogues came to be controlled by Christians which led, in essence, to these becoming churches. In many of these synagogues, however, the opposition to Jesus as the Messiah and to Christianity in general became very strong (Acts 6:9). Thus, what had started off as a somewhat harmonious relationship, at least in some quarters, with Christianity viewed as an extension of Judaism, came to an explosive crossroads.

This led to the second step in the development of this relationship between Judaism and Christianity, the stoning of Stephen (A.D. 37). In Acts 6:9-15 Luke records the charges brought against Stephen by leaders of several synagogues, synagogues which appear to have been made up of Hellenistic Jews and proselytes. They charged Stephen with preaching that Jesus would destroy the Temple and change the Mosaic customs (Acts 6:14). Stephen's sermon was cut short when he stressed the presence and activity of God beyond the walls of the Jewish Temple and charged the Jews with continuously resisting the Holy Spirit and murdering "the Just One," Jesus the

Messiah who had been prophesied. Consequently, although we can't be sure, it appears that he had essentially preached what they claimed. Jesus did prophesy the destruction of the Temple (Mt. 24:1, 2) and the fulfillment of, and thus the change of, the law of Moses (Mt. 5:17). The substance of Stephen's sermon indicates that Christians realized that there was no place for the continuation of the sacrificial system, though the Temple was still standing, and that the ceremonial aspects of the law of Moses no longer had importance. Such preaching did not set well with the Jewish leaders; therefore, they stoned Stephen to death in the presence of a notable witness, Saul of Tarsus (Acts 7:58). Luke informs us in Acts 8:1-4 that the resulting persecution of the Jerusalem Christians, led by Saul, brought about their being "scattered abroad throughout the regions of Judaea and Samaria, except the apostles" (Acts 8:1b). Perhaps Christians had become too comfortable, too much at ease, in the seven years or so since Jesus went back to Heaven. It was necessary, therefore, for God to allow this violent upheaval, which produced the next step in fulfilling the Great Commission (Acts 1:8). This scattering of the early Christians from Jerusalem would bring about the conversion of Saul and the beginning of the missionary spread of Christianity "unto the uttermost part of the earth" (see Acts 9-12). Paul's first missionary journey to Cyprus and Galatia (Antioch of Pisidia, Iconium, Lystra, Derbe), with the help of Barnabas and, for a short time, John Mark, created a problem which led to the third step in this development of the relationship between Judaism and Christianity.

This third step is the Jerusalem Council recorded in Acts 15 (A.D. 48). This great historical conference was between the predominantly Gentile church at Antioch of Syria and the Jewish church of Jerusalem. Some believers who were Pharisees had visited Antioch, teaching that circumcision and keeping the law of Moses was necessary for salvation (Acts 15:1, 5, 24), that simply receiving Christ by faith was not enough. The church of Antioch sent Paul and Barnabas, and certain others, up to Jerusalem to get the matter settled. After hearing Peter tell about his experience with Cornelius, and Paul and Barnabas tell about their first journey, James summed up the conference, and the Jerusalem church sent a letter to the Gentile church of Antioch. This official letter confirmed that salvation was by grace through faith in Jesus Christ (Acts 15:11, 23-29) completely apart from any necessity to be circumcised or keep the ceremonial law.

The fourth step in this development of the relationship between Judaism and Christianity is Paul's writing of the Epistle to the Galatians (A.D. 52). Some scholars want to place the writing of Galatians just prior to the Jerusalem Council. It seems more likely, however, that the false-teaching Judaizers would first make their appearance in Antioch of Syria before moving on to the churches of Galatia. Furthermore, the problem in Galatia involved a slight modification in approach from the one dealt with at the Jerusalem Council. While the problem in Jerusalem primarily dealt with the conditions of salvation—that is, how to be saved initially—the problem in Galatia dealt more specifically with the conditions of continuation in the faith—that is, how to stay saved. Paul asks the

Galatians, "Are ye so foolish? having begun in the Spirit, are ye now made perfect by the flesh?" (Gal. 3:3). Then he concludes, "Christ is become of no effect unto you, whosoever of you are justified by the law; ye are fallen from grace" (Gal. 5:4). Paul suggests the possibility of apostasy for those who abandon Christ and return to Judaism. Thus, the problem that Paul confronted in Galatia is getting very close to the problem dealt with in Hebrews.

This leads us to the fifth and final step in the N.T. in dealing with the relationship of Judaism and Christianity, *the writing of the epistle to the Hebrews.* There are some who argue that the apostasy described in Hebrews was not an apostasy from Christianity to Judaism, but rather, an apostasy from Christianity into rebellion and unbelief (Hiebert 87). It is true that the writer of Hebrews never makes any specific charge that the readers are abandoning Christ for Judaism, but that is certainly the picture that is painted by the overall argument of the book. The central theme of the epistle is *the superiority of Christ:* to angels, who were involved in giving the law; to Moses, the human mediator of the law; to Joshua, Moses' successor; to the Levitical priesthood; to the O.T. tabernacle; to the old covenant; and, especially, to the O.T. sacrifices, "For it is not possible that the blood of bulls and of goats should take away sins" (Heb. 10:4). Furthermore, he warns about continuing to sin willfully after having received the knowledge of the truth since "there remaineth no more sacrifice for sins" (Heb. 10:26). There would be no validity in turning from the superior sacrifice of Christ back to the blood of bulls and goats. On this subject the writer concludes, "We have an altar, whereof they have no right to eat which serve the tabernacle" (Heb. 13:10). Though the warnings against apostasy in Hebrews would be equally valid in a general sense—that is, against apostasy from Christianity to mere unbelief—it does appear that this particular audience was in danger of rejecting "the new and living way" through Jesus Christ to turn to the old system of types and shadows, which was insufficient even at its best. Such a tragedy must be prevented if at all possible.

Authorship

In the discussion of the question of authorship of the Epistle to the Hebrews, most commentators emphasize the quotation of Origen of Alexandria from the middle of the third century: "But who it was that really wrote the epistle, God only knows." The uncertainty of this noted churchman on this important subject illustrates the debate about the authorship of Hebrews, which continues to this day. In spite of this uncertainty, which appears in the early days of the church, many would argue strongly for Pauline authorship of the book. Thus, it is appropriate that we first consider the reasons for holding to the Apostle Paul as the author of Hebrews. (1) Our English Bibles (King James Version) read at the beginning of the epistle: "The Epistle of Paul the Apostle to the Hebrews." (2) It was accepted as Pauline, at least in a secondary sense, by the early church fathers. (3) It was written by someone who knew Timothy well (13:23). (4) It was written by someone who had been imprisoned for their faith (10:34; 13:18, 19), and Paul was often imprisoned, including both in Jerusalem (Acts 21:33) and in Rome (Acts 25:11, 12; 28:16). (5) Many of the doctrines in Hebrews are similar to those dealt with by Paul in his known epistles, such as seeing the old covenant as a type and shadow of the new (Rom. 5:14; 1 Cor. 10:1-4; Heb. 8:1-5; 9:8-14); holding that the old covenant was temporary, but the new is permanent (Rom. 7:4-6; 2 Cor. 3:6-18; Heb. 7:17-19; 8:6-8; 10:1-14); that Christ is our mediator at God's right hand in Heaven (Rom. 8:34; Eph. 1:20; Phil. 2:6-11; Heb. 1:2, 3; 10:12, 13; 12:1, 2); and that His death is a propitiatory sacrifice for sin (Rom. 5:8; 8:32; 1 Cor. 5:7; 15:3; Gal. 1:4; 2:20; 1 Tim. 1:15; Heb. 1:3; 2:9; 5:8, 9; 9:11-15; 10:10).

Many excellent preachers and commentators over the years have felt that such evidence as this, both external and internal, is sufficient to accept Paul as the writer of Hebrews, in spite of the fact that his name does not appear anywhere in the text of the epistle. Upon further analysis, however, it appears that much of this evidence is weak, at best, in confirming Pauline authorship of this wonderful book. First, the heading in our English Bible that assigns authorship to Paul does not go back to the earliest manuscripts of Hebrews. The earliest manuscripts of the epistle simply say, "To the Hebrews." Second, it is true that the church of the East, especially the Church of Alexandria, assigned authorship to Paul from an early date, but even so, that assignment was in a somewhat secondary sense. According to Eusebius of Caesarea, Clement of Alexandria, writing about A.D. 200, the epistle was "written by Paul to the Hebrews, in the Hebrew tongue, but was carefully translated by Luke, and published among the Greeks." Origen, the well-known scholar of Alexandria, in his writings somewhere around A.D. 250, said that the thoughts were Paul's, but that "the diction and phraseology belong to someone who has recorded what the apostle said." He mentions that both Clement of Rome and Luke had been suggested in his day as possible authors. Eusebius himself (about A.D. 330) accepted Pauline authorship with the same reservations as Clement and Origen. Beginning with Athanasius, who wrote around A.D. 350, "the ecclesiastical writers of Egypt and Palestine uniformly ascribed it to Paul" (Hiebert 73). The church of the West (centered in Rome), however, was slower in accepting Pauline authorship. Clement of Rome (A.D. 96) clearly quotes from Hebrews in his writings, without giving source or authorship for his quotations. The uncertainty about authorship created some reluctance in the western church toward accepting Hebrews. Jerome (about A.D. 410) and Augustine (about A.D. 420) led the Western church to accept Hebrews as Pauline, though it was obvious that they had reservations as to whether Paul was the direct author. They appear to have felt that the question of authorship needed to be settled in order to enhance the acceptance of this obviously canonical epistle. In A.D. 397 the Council of Carthage referred to "the thirteen Epistles of the Apostle Paul, one Epistle of the same writer to the Hebrews," while the Council of Hippo in A.D. 419 dropped this strange way of referring to Hebrews and simply referred to "fourteen epistles of Paul." Thus, we can see that the acceptance of Hebrews as Pauline in the early church came through a somewhat agonizing process.

Third, it is true that in Hebrews 13:23 the writer mentions "*our* brother Timothy." Though this reference does show that the author was one who knew Timothy well and thus was in the "Pauline" camp, this is not the normal way in which Paul referred to him, though a similar reference can be seen in 1 Th. 3:2. But in 1 Tim. 1:2 Paul refers to Timothy as "*my* own son in the faith" (lit. "my genuine child"), and in 2 Tim. 1:2 he refers to him as "*my* dearly beloved son." The reference in Hebrews 13:23 seems to lack the intimacy that Paul usually expressed in relation to Timothy.

Fourth, while the writer of Hebrews had been imprisoned for his faith in Christ (10:34; 13:18, 19), many of the early apostles were imprisoned for their faith (Acts 5:17-42; 12:1-11); therefore, the fact that the writer of Hebrews had been so imprisoned in no way makes certain that it was Paul.

Fifth, though several doctrines in Hebrews are similar to those dealt with by Paul in his known epistles, they are common doctrines of the faith which were addressed in the recorded sermons in the book of Acts, and are also discussed by James, Peter, and John in the other epistles as well as Revelation. Furthermore, there are also other doctrines, especially the priesthood of Christ according to the order of Melchisedec, which do not appear at all in the known writings of Paul.

The weakness of these arguments for Pauline authorship certainly does not completely eliminate the possibility that he wrote Hebrews, but it does call that position into question.

On the other hand, there are several arguments against Pauline authorship that make this position even less tenable, the first three of which are, in my opinion, the strongest. *First*, the style and vocabulary used in the epistle are quite different from Paul's known writings in the N.T. Though this difference in style is somewhat evident even in our English Bibles, the difference becomes much more obvious when Hebrews is considered in the Greek N.T. It was especially this difference in style which caused Clement of Alexandria to propose Luke as the translator into Greek of an original copy of Hebrews written by Paul in the Hebrew (Aramaic) language, and for Origen to suggest that the thoughts of Hebrews are Paul's but the style someone else's.

Second, the Epistle to the Hebrews is anonymous; there is no reference to Paul as the author anywhere in the text of the document. This is completely contrary to the credentials Paul presents for his letters in 2 Th. 3:17, "The salutation of Paul with mine own hand, which is the token in every epistle: so I write." Paul here was specifically addressing the problem of a false epistle written in his name (2 Th. 2:2), and thus he presents the presence of his name in the text of his writings as a means of ascertaining their genuineness. Some proponents of Pauline authorship have joined Clement of Alexandria in suggesting that Paul omitted his name because of his audience, Hebrew Christians who did not always see eye to eye with the apostle. Though Paul was certainly willing to be accommodating to prove his faithfulness as a Hebrew (see Acts 21:20-26), to avoid identifying himself as the author of such a powerful epistle does not fit at all the integrity, boldness, and determination of the man characterized in the book of Acts and in his known writings.

Third, the writer of Hebrews claims to be a second-generation Christian who faithfully subscribed to the gospel "which at the first began to be spoken by the Lord, and was confirmed unto us by them that heard him" (Heb. 2:3). Such an admission of dependence on the original apostles for revelation about the person and work of Christ seems contrary to Paul's position in Gal. 1:15—2:10. He contends that his three years in Arabia prepared him to preach the same gospel as preached by those in Jerusalem, so much so that, when he finally communicated his message to James, Peter, and John some 14 years later, they "added nothing" to him (Gal. 2:6). This certainly does not make the writer of Hebrews' admonitions any less inspired or authoritative, even as Luke suggests in the introduction to his Gospel (Lk. 1:1-3), but it does seem to be contrary to the position claimed by the Apostle Paul.

To these three strong arguments against Pauline authorship could be added: *fourth*, the uncharacteristic way of referring to Timothy (for Paul) as "our brother Timothy" (13:23), as compared to Paul's description of Timothy as "my own son" (1 Tim. 1:2); *fifth*, unique doctrinal expositions in Hebrews, such as Christ's priesthood according to the order of Melchisedec, which are not found in Paul's known epistles; *sixth*, the writer of Hebrews' practice of quoting only from the Septuagint, the Greek version of the O.T., whereas Paul quotes from both the Hebrew and the Greek O.T. in his known epistles; and *seventh*, the absence of any evidence in the epistle that the writer had experienced the kind of dramatic conversion to Christianity as Paul, a conversion from a fanatical persecutor of the church to one of its most devoted adherents (Donald Guthrie 20).

If Paul is not the likely author of Hebrews, then who is? A number of suggestions have been made and defended over the years. *Clement of Rome* has been suggested by some because of his prominence as a second-generation Christian (Heb. 2:3), and because he is the earliest witness to direct quotations from the epistle (about A.D. 96). *Luke* has been promoted as the author because of the beauty of his Greek style, as witnessed by the Gospel of Luke and the book of Acts in the N.T., and its similarity to that found in Hebrews. Both Calvin and Delitzsch point to Luke as the likely author of Hebrews. About A.D. 200 Tertullian suggested *Barnabas* as the likely writer of the epistle, and arguments could be made for him because of his early association with Paul; his nickname as "the son of consolation," encouragement, or exhortation (see Heb. 13:22); the fact that he was a Levite, thus familiar with the Levitical system of worship; and the fact that he was from Cyprus, which might explain the Hellenistic flavor of the epistle. *Apollos* was apparently first suggested by Martin Luther because of Luke's description of him as an eloquent Jew from Alexandria, Egypt, who was "mighty in the scriptures," convincing the Jews publicly "that Jesus was Christ" (Acts 18:24, 28). Thomas Hewitt follows Selwyn in pointing to *Silas* as the likely author of the Epistle to the Hebrews (29). Most Bible scholars identify Silas with the Silvanus mentioned in 1 Th. 1:1; 2 Th. 1:1, and 1 Pet. 5:12, with Silas being his Hebrew name and Silvanus the Latin equivalent. It does seem in the above references that Silvanus is associated with the writing of the epistles. Silas is suggested both because of his known association with Paul and a supposed similarity between the style of 1 Peter and Hebrews, a similarity which appears unlikely on the surface. Out of all these suggestions, Luke seems to be the most appealing. He was certainly a close companion of the Apostle Paul, from his own personal witness in the book of Acts. He was perhaps the only N.T. writer who was Greek rather than Jewish, and that fact, as well as the evident eloquence of the Greek style of Luke and Acts, well qualifies Luke as the author of Hebrews. I am also struck by Luke's statement in Lk. 1:2, "Even as they delivered them unto us, which from the beginning were eyewitnesses," as compared with the writer of Hebrews' statement concerning the great salvation "which at the first began to be spoken by the Lord, and was confirmed unto us by them that heard *him*" (Heb. 2:3).

We must therefore conclude that the question of the authorship of Hebrews cannot be permanently and satisfactorily settled this side of eternity. But it is important to notice that this in no way lessens the authenticity and inspiration of the book. It is obvious, because of its widespread acceptance as Scripture in the earliest days of the church, that the quality and inspiration of its content were clearly evident, in spite of questions from the beginning about authorship. This quality of content is what made some, such as Origen, Jerome, and Augustine, willing to attach Paul's name to the epistle in spite of their lingering doubts. We must also remind ourselves that anonymity of a Biblical document in no way lessens its authority and inspiration. If so, such O.T. books as Judges, Ruth, Kings, Chronicles, Esther, and Job would be in question. Though there is uncertainty about the authorship of each of these O.T. documents, there is no uncertainty about their inspiration or canonicity. Furthermore, even though we may be uncertain about the author of Hebrews today, it is clear from the epistle itself that the writer and the readers knew each other well, and were well aware of each other's identity (see Heb. 6:9, 10; 10:32-34; 12:4; 13:7, 17, 22, 23).

Destination

The oldest manuscripts of the epistle merely say, "To the Hebrews." It appears from statements made in the epistle that it was addressed to a particular congregation of Jewish Christians, not to Jewish Christians in general. He reminded them of earlier persecution they had endured for the name of Christ, including physical, emotional, and financial suffering in the loss of property (10:32-34). He knew, however, that this suffering had not yet resulted in martyrdom (12:4) in this particular congregation. He did expect to see them again soon, most likely in the company of Timothy (13:19, 23). Such specific information surely points to a specific congregation of Jewish Christians, or, at the very least, a specific group of congregations in a given location. Most commentators in the early church held that Hebrews was written to Jewish Christians in Palestine, or in Jerusalem in particular. There are several arguments in favor of this destination. (1) Since Jerusalem is where the gospel was first preached, there would be time for early growth followed by spiritual lethargy (5:11-14); (2) Jerusalem/Palestine would be the most likely place for an all Jewish church; (3) Since the Temple was located in Jerusalem, the prominence given to the Levitical service would seem appropriate, and certain statements would seem more understandable in that context (13:12, 13). There are some problems, however, with the Jerusalem/Palestine destination. (1) The unwavering use of the Septuagint (LXX) might seem strange to the church in Jerusalem. (2) The statement that this church had "not yet resisted unto blood" (12:4) would not fit in light of the early deaths of Stephen and James, the brother of John. (3) The salutation, "They of Italy salute you" (13:24), is more difficult to explain if written to the Jerusalem church.

The other most frequently suggested destination for Hebrews is the Christian Jews of the churches of Rome. There are several arguments which favor this position. (1) The earliest evidence of the epistle is in quotations in the writings of Clement of Rome about A.D. 96. (2) The greeting in Heb. 13:24, "They of Italy salute you," is best explained if the epistle is being addressed to Christians in Rome, or at least in Italy. The way this greeting is worded implies that the writer is passing on greetings from Italian Christians who were then somewhere outside Italy, but were saying "hello" to the folks back home. (3) Luke's record in Acts 28:17-31 reveals some successful evangelism by Paul, as a prisoner under house arrest, toward the Jews in Rome. After they heard Paul's presentation of the gospel of Jesus Christ, Luke says, "Some believed the things which were spoken, and some believed not" (Acts 28:24). Lenski thinks this means that at least half of them were immediately converted, and that three or four of the seven Jewish synagogues in Rome became Christian churches (14). Paul's rebuke of the Roman Jews for their unbelief, using the words of Is. 6:9, 10, somehow does not sound that optimistic. The passage does, however, validate the fact that a number of Roman Jews did embrace Jesus as their Messiah and Savior. Assuming that there were already a number of Jews who were part of the existing Roman church, it does seem that there would have been enough Christian Jews in Rome to make a Roman destination for Hebrews a good possibility.

Date

The date of Hebrews, as with most other books of the Bible, is somewhat dependent on the decision about authorship and destination. Because of the prominence given to the discussion of the Levitical ritual in the book, it seems likely that it was written before the Temple was destroyed in A.D. 70. Though it is true that the writer makes no direct reference to the Temple itself, but rather to the O.T. tabernacle, it seems unlikely that no hint would be given of the destruction of the Temple, where the sacrifices had been offered for hundreds of years, if that great historical event had already occurred. Furthermore, the Jewish wars in Palestine, which eventually led to the destruction of the Temple and the entire city of Jerusalem, began about A.D. 66. It seems likely that Hebrews would have been written before these events as well. Whether the destination is considered as Palestine or Rome, or even some other place, the destruction of the Temple in Jerusalem would change forever the thinking of both Jewish and Gentile Christians.

The reasoning given here for the date of Hebrews will be based on the assumption that the epistle was probably written to Jewish Christians in Rome. Two references in the book itself are significant in narrowing the possibilities for the date. In 10:32 the writer says, "But call to remembrance the former days, in which, after ye were illuminated, ye endured a great fight of afflictions." Then in 12:4 he states further, "Ye have not yet resisted unto blood, striving against sin." The earlier time of affliction experienced by this congregation might well refer to that under the Roman Emperor Claudius, which occurred in A.D. 49, when Claudius "commanded all Jews to depart from Rome" (Acts 18:2), thus creating the occasion of the meeting of the Apostle Paul with Aquila and Priscilla in Corinth. Though both unbelieving Jews and Jewish Christians would have fallen under this edict, the persecution which resulted was evidently mild, and by the time Paul wrote to the Roman Church, about A.D. 58, Priscilla and Aquila had been able to return to Rome (Rom. 16:3). Nero had succeeded Claudius as emperor in A.D. 54. But a tragic event had a dramatic effect on Christians in Rome, and all over the Roman Empire for that matter. In July of A.D. 64 the city of Rome burned. It appears that Nero himself may have been responsible for the devastating fire. However, in order to direct the accusations and attention away from himself, he blamed Christians for the burning of Rome, and as a result numerous Christians, both Jewish and Gentile, were arrested for their faith, many of them being executed. Ancient tradition says that both Peter and Paul were executed during this period of time (between A.D. 64-68). Since the statement in Heb. 12:4 about not yet having "resisted unto blood" could not have been made after July of A.D. 64, it must be assumed that the date of writing would be a little earlier. The tone of the epistle, however, seems to suggest that pressure and persecution toward Christians were already increasing. On this basis I would suggest a date of writing for Hebrews in the early part of A.D. 64.

Theme and Purpose

The purpose of the writer of the Epistle to the Hebrews can be expressed in four observations. (1) He writes *to warn them about the possibility of apostasy from their faith in Christ.* These warnings are issued at least five times throughout the book (2:1-4; 3:7—4:16; 5:11—6:20; 10:19-39; 12:18, 19). Such warnings are especially grave in light of the fact that apostasy from Christ is irremediable (6:4-6; 10:26-31). Once that line of total abandonment of Christ has been crossed through continuous and willful rebellion, there is no turning back; in fact, there is no desire to turn back since the Holy Spirit has departed. (2) He writes *to warn them about their lack of spiritual growth,* their spiritual sluggishness, which is one of the reasons apostasy looms in the distance (5:11-14; 10:19-25). He implies that they have lost the spiritual motivation they once had and have actually gone backward to the point that they need a thorough review of the basics of Christianity. Some have become quite irregular in their attendance for worship, fellowship, and Bible study with other members of the congregation. (3) He writes *to warn them about their attitude toward persecution for their faith in Christ,* the other reason that has caused them to be in danger of apostasy (10:32-39; 12:3-15). They have faced persecution in earlier days, and have faithfully persevered, but the determination of some is beginning to fade, either because the persecution is promising to become more intense or because their endurance is wearing out. Perhaps they were eager for the sprint, but they are having some hesitation about the marathon. (4) This leads to the fourth statement of purpose, which is the primary theme of the epistle: he writes *to emphasize the superiority of Christ in all respects.* This theme, more than any other, runs throughout the epistle, from beginning to end. It forms the basis for this commentary's outline of the Epistle to the Hebrews. The writer presents the superiority of Christ in relation to the revelation under the old covenant; His superiority to angels, to Adam, to Moses, to Joshua, to Aaron, to Abraham, to Levi, to the Old Testament priesthood, Tabernacle, covenant, and sacrifices; and finally the superiority of faith under the new covenant. In connection with this primary theme, the writer of Hebrews gives special attention to our Lord's role as High Priest, the only book of the N.T. which carries such an emphasis.

HEBREWS

THE OUTLINE OF HEBREWS

I. The Superior Revelation of the Son in Relation to the Prophets and Angels, 1:1—2:18
   A. Superiority to the Prophets, 1:1-3
   B. Superiority to the Angels, 1:4—2:18
      1 Superiority to the angels by inheritance, 1:4
      2. Proofs from the Old Testament, 1:5-14
         a. In His relation to the Father, 1:5-7
         b. In His authoritative position, 1:8-14
      3. First warning: against neglecting such superior revelation, 2:1-4
      4. The necessity and propriety of the humiliation of the Son, 2:5-18
         a. To attain man's intended destiny, 2:5-9
         b. To experience and conquer suffering and death, 2:10-18
            (1) By making the captain of our salvation perfect, 2:10-13
            (2) By Jesus' partaking of flesh and blood as we do, 2:14-18

II. The Superior Leadership of Christ in Relation to Moses and Joshua, 3:1—4:16
   A. The Superiority of the Son to Moses, 3:1-6
      1. As a builder to a house, 3:1-4
      2. As a son to a servant, 3:5, 6
   B. Second Warning: Against Neglecting the Leadership of the Son, 3:7—4:16
      1. Israel's failure to follow Moses, 3:7-19
         a. Substantiated from Psalm 95:7-11, 3:7-11
         b. Need to exhort one another against unbelief and sin, 3:12, 13
         c. Steadfastness demanded of partakers of Christ, 3:14, 15
         d. Rebellion and unbelief kept Israel from entering Canaan, 3:16-19
      2. Possibility of failure to enter God's promised rest, 4:1, 2
      3. Proofs that a rest still remains, 4:3-10
         a. The basis of God's promised rest is the Sabbath, 4:3, 4
         b. Israel failed to enter the Promised Land, 4:5, 6
         c. A rest remained after Joshua took Israel into Canaan, 4:7, 8
         d. A rest remains for God's people today, 4:9, 10
      4. Helps in entering God's perfect rest, 4:11-16
         a. The example of Israel's unbelief, 4:11
         b. The power of God's Word, 4:12
         c. The knowledge of God's omniscience, 4:13
         d. The intercession of Christ as our High Priest, 4:14-16

III. The Superior Intercession of the Son as High Priest in Relation to the Levitical Priesthood, 5:1—10:39
   A. The Priesthood of Christ a New Type of Priesthood, 5:1-10
      1. The requirements of the O.T. priesthood, 5:1-4
         a. His background, 5:1a
         b. His purpose, 5:1b
         c. His compassion, 5:2, 3
         d. His divine call, 5:4

2. The essential qualifications met by Christ, 5:5-10
   a. His divine call, 5:5, 6
      (1) As the only-begotten Son, 5:5
      (2) As a priest after the order of Melchisedec, 5:6
   b. His priestly compassion, 5:7, 8
   c. His redemptive purpose, 5:9, 10

B. Third Warning: Against Failure to Progress Through Christ as High Priest, 5:11—6:20
1. Lack of spiritual understanding and discernment caused by lack of spiritual progress, 5:11-14
   a. Difficulty in understanding the new priestly order, 5:11
   b. Absence of progress from the first principles, 5:12
   c. Those who need milk described, 5:13
   d. Those who can take strong meat described, 5:14
2. Possibility of renouncing true faith without a return to spiritual progress, 6:1-8
   a. The foundation which must be built upon, 6:1-3
   b. The serious consequences of total apostasy, 6:4-6
   c. This truth illustrated from nature, 6:7, 8
3. Encouragement to faithful endurance and progress through depending upon Christ as High Priest, 6:9-20
   a. The writer's faith in the Hebrews, 6:9
   b. Their past work for Christ, 6:10
   c. The writer's desire that their hope and faith continue until the end, 6:11, 12
   d. The patience of Abraham toward God's promises, 6:13-18
      (1) God backs up His promise with an oath, 6:13-15
      (2) The reason for God's oath to Abraham, 6:16-18
   e. Jesus as our priestly forerunner, 6:19, 20

C. Reasons for the Priesthood After Melchisedec Replacing the Levitical Order, 7:1-28
1. Superiority of Melchisedec to Abraham, 7:1-10
   a. Melchisedec identified as a type of Christ, 7:1-3
   b. Superiority of Melchisedec explained, 7:4-10
      (1) In receiving tithes from Abraham, 7:4-6a
      (2) In blessing Abraham, 7:6b, 7
      (3) In a living priesthood as opposed to a dying priesthood, 7:8
      (4) In receiving tithes from Levi through Abraham, 7:9, 10
2. Superiority of the order of Melchisedec to the order of Aaron, 7:11-28
   a. Because a change of priesthood calls for a change of law, 7:11-19
      (1) Perfection lacking in the Levitical priesthood, 7:11, 12
      (2) The new priest from Judah, not Levi, 7:13, 14
      (3) The new priest after the order of Melchisedec, 7:15-17
      (4) The law of the priesthood now null and void, 7:18, 19

b. Because Christ's priesthood was instituted by an oath, 7:20-22
c. Because of the permanence of Christ's priestly order, 7:23-25
d. Because of the moral perfection of Jesus Christ, 7:26-28

D. The work of Christ as High Priest, 8:1—10:39
1. Tabernacle and priesthood a type of Christ's work as High Priest, 8:1-5
a. The main point emphasized, 8:1, 2
b. Tabernacle and priesthood point to Christ, 8:3-5
2. Work of Christ based on a new covenant, 8:6-13
a. The necessity of the new covenant, 8:6, 7
b. The Scriptural background of the new covenant, 8:8-12
(1) With regard to its objects, 8:8, 9
(2) With regard to its nature, 8:10-12
c. The realization of the new covenant, 8:13
3. Old and new covenants contrasted, 9:1—10:18
a. In relation to the tabernacle and its furniture, 9:1-5
b. In relation to tabernacle divisions and priestly access, 9:6-10
c. In relation to a better tabernacle, sacrifice, and covenant, 9:11-15
d. In relation to the inauguration and dedication of the covenants, 9:16-28
(1) The old covenant inaugurated, 9:16-22
(2) The new covenant inaugurated, 9:23-28
e. In relation to a permanent sacrifice, 10:1-18
(1) Yearly repetition points to an inadequate sacrifice, 10:1-4
(2) The psalmist points to an obedient sacrifice, 10:5-10
(3) Christ's position points to a sufficient sacrifice, 10:11-14
(4) Remission of sins points to a finished sacrifice, 10:15-18
4. Fourth warning: against neglecting the new way to God through Jesus Christ, 10:19-39
a. The basis of the new and living way, 10:19-21
b. The duties of the new and living way, 10:22-25
(1) The duty of true worship, 10:22
(2) The duty of steadfastness, 10:23
(3) The duty of mutual consideration, 10:24, 25
c. The consequence of forsaking the new and living way, 10:26-31
(1) The definition, 10:26a
(2) The result, 10:26b, 27
(3) The contrast, 10:28, 29
(4) The judgment, 10:30, 31
d. Encouragement to patience in the new and living way, 10:32-39
(1) By remembering past sacrifices, 10:32-34
(2) By remaining faithful until Christ's return, 10:35-38
(3) By positive identification with those who persevere, 10:39

IV. The Superiority of Faith Under the New Covenant, 11:1—13:17
  A. Faith Illustrated From Old Testament History, 11:1-40
    1. Faith defined for all time, 11:1, 2
    2. Specific examples of faith related, 11:3-38
      a. In the early days of Biblical history, 11:3-7
        (1) Creation, 11:3
        (2) Abel, 11:4
        (3) Enoch, 11:5, 6
        (4) Noah, 11:7
      b. Abraham and his family, 11:8-19
        (1) In his call and sojourn in Canaan, 11:8-10
        (2) In their reception of the promised seed, 11:11, 12
        (3) In realizing that their citizenship was not of this world, 11:13-16
        (4) In offering Isaac, the promised seed, 11:17-19
      c. Isaac, Jacob, and Joseph, 11:20-22
      d. Moses, 11:23-29
        (1) From birth to his flight to Midian, 11:23-26
        (2) During the exodus from Egypt, 11:27-29
      e. In the fall of Jericho: Joshua and Rahab, 11:30, 31
      f. Others too numerous to relate, 11:32-38
        (1) Many who experienced earthly victory, 11:32-35a
        (2) Many who experienced earthly defeat but eternal victory, 11:35b-38
    3. The connection of their faith with ours, 11:39, 40
  B. Faith Progressing Toward Consummation, 12:1-29
    1. Jesus as our source and our example, 12:1-4
    2. Divine discipline a means of Christian growth, 12:5-13
      a. It confirms that one is a true son of God, 12:5-8
      b. It is better than what our earthly parents gave us, 12:9, 10
      c. It produces good results in the end, 12:11-13
    3. A proper attitude develops good priorities, 12:14-17
      a. To pursue peace and holiness and avoid bitterness, 12:14, 15
      b. To note the tragic example of Esau, 12:16, 17
    4. Fifth warning: against the more severe consequences of departing from Mt. Zion, 12:18-29
      a. The threat to Israel at ancient Sinai, 12:18-21
      b. The awesome position of the New Testament believer, 12:22-24
      c. The solemn consequences for those who turn away from Christ, 12:25-29
        (1) Warning about God's final revelation, 12:25-27
        (2) Admonition concerning God's coming kingdom, 12:28, 29
  C. Final Admonitions for Those Who Are Living by Faith, 13:1-25
    1. Attitudes and actions that reflect the teachings of Christ, 13:1-9
      a. Brotherly love and hospitality, 13:1, 2
      b. Suffering believers, 13:3

c. Christian marriage, 13:4
d. Provision of material needs, 13:5, 6
e. Respect for Christian leaders and an unchanging Christ, 13:7, 8
f. Doctrinal steadfastness, 13:9

2. Willingness to stand with Christ against opposition, 13:10-16
a. The Old Testament sin offering: a type of Christ, 13:10, 11
b. Jesus: the fulfillment of the sin offering, 13:12-14
c. Appropriate Christian sacrifices, 13:15, 16
d. Submission to church leaders, 13:17

V. Conclusion, 13:18-25
A. Prayer for the Writer, 13:18, 19
B. Prayer for the Readers, 13:20, 21
C. Closing Admonitions, 13:22-25

I. THE SUPERIOR REVELATION OF THE SON IN RELATION TO THE PROPHETS AND ANGELS (1:1—2:18)

Those who followed the Lord under the old covenant had great respect for both prophets and angels. God spoke through the prophets both orally and in writing. They were His flaming spokesmen throughout O.T. history. In like manner, the angels were frequently seen as mediating in the communication of God's Word to man. The writer of Hebrews first demonstrates Christ's superiority in relation to these two instruments in the construction of the O.T.: one human, the other supernatural.

A. Superiority to the Prophets (1:1-3)

Our writer first looks at the human instruments in delivering God's Word to his people. Men who served in the role of prophet spoke many things in serving as God's voice, which were not written down as Scripture. These words, however, refer to that which was written, inspired, and infallible.

1 God, who at sundry times and in
divers manners spake in time past
unto the fathers by the prophets,
2 Hath in these last days spoken
unto us by *his* Son, whom he hath
appointed heir of all things, by
whom also he made the worlds;
3 Who being the brightness of *his*
glory, and the express image of his
person, and upholding all things by
the word of his power, when he
had by himself purged our sins, sat
down on the right hand of the
Majesty on high.

The subject of this first sentence in Hebrews is "God," and the main verb which goes with it in v. 2 is "hath spoken." What a marvelous fact: God has spoken! Whatever else may be said, this is wonderful in itself. The God and Creator of the whole universe has chosen to reveal Himself to us lowly creatures. The writer in v. 1 is speaking about the Old Testament; in v. 2 he refers to the N.T. "At sundry times" (Greek *polumeros*) points out that the O.T. was given "in many parts," segment by segment, over a long period of time. The earliest books, written by Moses, originated around 1400 B.C., while the latest books were written about 400 B.C. Often there were also long stretches of time in between various segments of the O.T. In sharp contrast, the N.T., from Matthew to Revelation, was composed over a period of about 50 years, with James perhaps the earliest (A.D. 45) and Revelation the last (A.D. 95; Thiessen 85). "In divers manners" (Greek *polutropos*) means "in many ways." This speaks of the variety of modes or methods used in the communication of the O.T. Certainly He often spoke to the writers in a voice, with different levels of dramatic display. But He also used more unique ways. To Moses He spoke from the burning bush (Ex. 3:1-10), or the words were written in stone by "the finger of God" (Ex. 31:18). He appeared to Abraham as a mysterious visitor (Gen. 18:1-22), to Jacob in a wrestling match (Gen. 32:24-32), and to Joshua as the angel with the drawn sword (Josh. 5:13-15). To Balaam He spoke through a donkey (Num. 22:22-35). Later to Elijah He spoke by fire, but also by "a still small voice" (1 Kg. 19:11, 12). Isaiah saw Him as "the Lord sitting upon a throne, high and lifted up" (Is. 6:1), and Ezekiel saw "a wheel in the middle of a wheel" (Ez. 1:15, 16). In contrast, the N.T. was given with much less variety, and primarily in connection with Christ's life on earth and in the succeeding ministry of the apostles.

"In time past" refers to the time when O.T. revelation was given, in the age of the ancients that preceded the coming of Christ. "The fathers" were the recipients of that revelation, especially the spiritual leaders, and "the prophets" were the spokesmen and the writers. In this context the word *prophet* would include all the O.T. writers, whether they were primarily identified by that term in their day or not. "By the prophets" is more literally "in the prophets" (Greek *en*). God not only spoke *through* them, He was actually *in* them. God dwelled in them; their entire lives were controlled and overshadowed by the Spirit of God (see Mt. 10:20; 2 Cor. 13:3).

Verse 2 describes the N.T. revelation in sharp contrast. Almost every word and phrase in verse 2 stands in contrast with verse 1. The new revelation was given "in these last days"; the old was given "in time past." The new was given to "us," the believers under the new covenant, including the writer; the old was given "unto the fathers." But the greatest contrast of all is that the new was given (literally) "in *his* Son"; the old came "in the prophets." The subject and the verb, however, dramatically tie the two verses together, "God . . . hath spoken." There may be major differences in the old and new revelation with regard to *when*, and *how,* and *who*, but there is absolutely no difference in the ultimate source of Scripture; it is God Himself.

"In these last days" in v. 2 is more literally "upon the last of these days." The phrase is based on the Septuagint translation of "the last days" in the Hebrew O.T. The Hebrew people thought of God's work with Israel in relation to the age of the patriarchs, the age of Moses, and the age of the prophets. All this was to be followed by the age of the Messiah, "the last days," the last period of time, however long that may be, which will culminate with the eternal state when God will permanently dwell with His people (see Is. 2:2; Dan. 10:14). It is obvious that the N.T. writers use this and similar terms to refer to the entire church age, from beginning to end (Acts 2:17; Jas. 5:3; 2 Tim. 3:1; 1 Pet. 1:20; 2 Pet. 3:3; 1 Jn. 2:18; Jude 18). Some argue that this terminology reflects the fact that the N.T. writers expected Christ to return soon, even in their lifetime (Meyer 72). To some extent there is no problem with that. In Mk. 13:32 our Lord Himself said that even He did not know the day of His coming. The doctrine of the Second Coming is taught in such a way that each generation of believers can honestly look for His return in their lifetime. As N.T. Christians we are always living "in the last days" until He does return.

Our writer says that at the beginning of this period called "these last days," God has spoken to us "by *his* Son." This phrase contrasts with "by the prophets" in v. 1, and, as there, here also "by" is more literally "in." It is clear, however, that there is something far greater in God speaking "in *his* Son" than merely "in the prophets." Note also that "his" is in italics, which means that it was not in the original. There is no question, of course, that it does mean God's Son, but when there is no article in front of a Greek word, *quality* is being stressed rather than *identity*. The quality or attribute of being a "Son," in contrast to being merely a "prophet," is being emphasized.

If N.T. revelation is, as our writer declares, that which God has spoken through His Son, then any further revelation is impossible. This passage serves as a condemnation of the claims, down through the ages, of all the cultic religious practitioners who have based their new doctrines on some further word of prophecy revealed only to them (also Rev. 22:18, 19; Dt. 18:18-20). Nothing could be more perfect than this final word given by God in His Son (Lenski 33).

It is this beloved Son "whom he hath appointed heir of all things." Commentators debate about when this appointment occurred, in time or in eternity, and about whether His inheritance relates to His eternal Sonship or only applies to Him as the incarnate Son of God. With regard to the time of appointment, it seems that all of God's decrees and appointments likely took place in eternity (Eph. 1:4; Rev. 13:8; 17:8). The fact that He was appointed as heir prior to His work in creation, in the expressed order of v. 2, would also seem to prove this position. Meyer (75) and others think that this inheritance refers to the dignity of the eternal Son of God, to His identity in relation to the Father from eternity. But I agree with Lenski who sees the reference to the incarnate Son receiving the inheritance upon the completion of His redemptive work. As Lenski (34) points out, "God made His Son the heir of all things, not according to His deity which could inherit nothing, but according to His humanity which could and did inherit all things."

God has appointed Christ as the heir of "all things," and this can be taken in the most absolute sense, even our Lord's restoration to the exalted and visible position that He had before He came to earth. The emphasis, however, should be placed on the fulfillment of promises made. In His victorious position as heir, Christ has fulfilled God's desire for Adam to have dominion over all creation (Gen. 1:28), for Abraham to bless the world and for his seed to be as the dust of the earth (Gen. 12:1-3; 13:15, 16; Rom. 4:13), and for David's heir to occupy the throne forever (2 Sam. 7:12-16). God expressed this poetically through the psalmist when He invited his Messianic Son, "Ask of me, and I shall give thee *the* heathen *for* thine inheritance, and the uttermost parts of the earth *for* thy possession" (Ps. 2:6-8; see Westcott 8).

God appointed His Son to such an inheritance because He was the one "by whom he also made the worlds." The Son is presented as Creator also in Jn. 1:3; 1 Cor. 8:6; and Col. 1:16. The preposition by (Greek *dia*) here refers to Christ's mediating role in creation. God the Father is the direct agent of creation, God the Son is the mediating agent, and God the Holy Spirit is the activating agent. This same relationship of the members of the Trinity is also true in the spiritual creation, which occurs when an individual is saved. God the Father initiated the process (Jn. 3:16), God the Son mediated it by His incarnate work (1 Tim. 2:5; Heb. 8:6), and God the Spirit activates and applies Christ's provision (Jn. 3:5-8). This seems to be the working order of the Trinitarian Godhead in everything.

The object of the Son's creative activity here is "the worlds" (Greek *aion*). The phrase literally means "the ages," and our English word *eon*, meaning "an indefinitely long period of time; an age," is derived from the Greek. The two other Greek words most commonly translated "world" are *kosmos*, emphasizing the world as orderly (see Mt. 16:26), and *oikoumene*, emphasizing the world as inhabited (see Mt. 24:14). Because of the root meaning of the word, a time element is likely included. However, in this context, and in light of the use of the plural (the only other plural is Heb. 11:3, another reference to creation), the ultimate meaning is best seen as all-inclusive, meaning "the universe." God the Son made, not only the world with its order, or the world with its inhabitants, but, even more than that, He made the world and everything that goes with it. He made it and He sustains it in time.

In outlining Hebrews, it is somewhat difficult to decide what to do with 1:3. It is definitely a transition verse. It clearly continues the thought of v. 2 in telling us more about the Son who has been appointed heir of all things. But it also forms a transition to v. 4 in pointing to the exalted position our Lord now holds, which demonstrates that He is "so much better than angels." Since, however, it does continue to describe the attributes of the Son from v. 2, I am leaving v. 3 with that section.

This blessed Son of God introduced in v. 2 as "heir of all things" is further described in v. 3 with regard to both His nature and His work. In His relation to the Father the Son is "the brightness of his glory, and the express image of *his* person." The first phrase describes the Son more in His outward manifestation, while the second phrase defines Him in His inner being. "Brightness" (Greek *apaugasma*) points to the source of the Son's being and His eternal connection with the Father. The word can bear the idea of reflection or radiation, but radiation seems more appropriate in describing the Son's relationship to the Father. The "glory" is that of the Father Himself. In the O.T. God often appeared in the form of a bright shining light. So He appeared to Moses in the continually burning bush in the desert (Ex. 3:2), as a guide to all Israel in the cloud by day and the pillar of fire by night (Ex. 13:21, 22), and in meeting with Moses and the priests between the cherubims on top of the mercy seat (Ex. 25:22; 40:34-38; 1 Sam. 4:4). Moses had the remarkable experience of viewing some part of the essence of God's glory (Ex. 33:18-23); then after his second 40 days with God on Sinai, Moses' own face reflected such brightness of the presence of God that the Israelites begged him to wear a veil (Ex. 34:29-35).

What the writer of Hebrews is describing here is what the Son was prior to His incarnation and what continued in His essential being after the incarnation. If you had personally seen Jesus on earth, this "brightness" would not have been visible; but on at least one occasion, on the Mount of Transfiguration, He took the veil away, and in the presence of the inner circle of disciples He "was transfigured . . . and his face did shine as the sun, and his raiment was white as the light" (Mt. 17:2).

In His relation to the Father, the Son was also "the express image of his person." "Express image" is only one word in the original (Greek *charakter*), one to which our English word "character" bears some connection. It is said that "character" is what you are, while "reputation" is what people think you are. In a person of integrity one expects the two to be the same. In the original, the word could refer to the mark left upon a coin, which determined its value as well as the stamp or tool which made that mark. In what the writer is saying here, the Father could be viewed as the stamp and the Son as the impression that is left. The two would, of course, be identical. However, all such earthly illustrations have their limitations when attempting to describe the persons of the Godhead.

"Person" (Greek *hupostasis*) refers to the essence of the Father, the most basic characteristics which make Him God. The original word literally means "that which stands under," and it describes what is foundational or essential in whatever is being defined. The newer translations usually use "being" or "essence" to translate the word into English since, theologically, each member of the Godhead is seen as having a separate personality, but all three persons of the Godhead share the same essence.

In continuing with the work of the Son, the writer views Him as "upholding all things by the word of his power." "Upholding," literally "bearing" (Greek *phero*), assigns to the Son the role of sustainer of all creation. In v. 2 He is seen as Creator. Contrary to the teaching of deistic heresies, however, Christ is also seen as the one who continues to sustain all existence. Ancient mythology viewed Atlas as bearing the world on his shoulders, but only as a passive burden. Our Lord bears the entire universe actively and aggressively, assuring us that ultimately His perfect goal for all things will be accomplished. "All things" includes the universe and all that is in it, especially man, the primary object of God's attention. It is the same "all things" of which the Son is the heir in v. 2. (The article in the original—"the all things"—shows this previous reference.)

The means of His sustenance of the universe is "by the word of his power." "Word" (Greek *hrema*) does not refer to the written word, but to the spoken word. In Hebrews 11:3 our writer will proclaim that "the worlds were framed by the word of God," and that is certainly true to the account of Moses: "God said, Let there be light: and there was light" (Gen. 1:3). Throughout all six days of creation, God commanded and it happened. The same is also true of the continuation of the universe. The sun, stars, planets, and man only continue at the word of God, and one day He and the Son will give their spoken command, and time will be no more (1 Th. 4:16; Rev. 10:6; 14:15). With such results from His spoken word, it is easy to see why the writer calls it "the word of his power." "Power" (Greek *dunamis*) is an appropriate description of the spoken word of the Son which accomplishes so much. Alfred Nobel, the Swedish inventor of dynamite, evidently drew the name for his new, powerful explosive from this Greek word. But dynamite carries only a thimble full of power in comparison to that which our writer assigns to the Son.

One may not think it possible that the glorious, powerful Son of God would be willing to humiliate Himself to become our Savior. But our writer declares, "When he had by himself purged our sins." This is the first reference he has made to Christ's work as High Priest. The idea of purification or cleansing is based upon the fact that sinful men cannot otherwise worship or commune with an absolutely holy God. The writer likely has in mind the symbolism of the Day of Atonement (Lev. 16) when purification was made by the high priest for the sins of himself and of the nation as a whole. When Hebrews refers to a specific sacrifice, it is always to the sacrifice of the Day of Atonement, the only day during the year when the high priest entered the Holy of Holies. "When he had purged" in the original implies that the work is completed (Greek aorist participle). In contrast to the Levitical priests who kept repeating the sacrifice of the Day of Atonement, as well as all the other sacrifices, Christ's sacrifice for our cleansing will never need to be repeated. Though the O.T. priests offered animal sacrifices, which proved to be ineffective, Christ made cleansing for us "by himself" (Greek middle voice). He served as both the priest and the sacrifice. "Our sins," the sins of believers in particular, but of all the world in general (1 Tim. 4:10; 1 Jn. 2:2), were purged, cleansed, and removed by our Lord's self-sacrifice on the cross.

What Christ did next fulfilled prophecy and clearly declared that His act of atonement was complete: He "sat down on the right hand of the Majesty on high." This act of Christ was a direct fulfillment of Ps. 110:1. It is the act of the Divine King, the Heir to the Davidic throne (2 Sam. 7), taking His position of authority and power. At the same time the fact that He "sat down" declares that the work of redemption is complete. It demonstrates the same truth dramatically exhibited in Christ's statement from the cross, "It is finished" (Jn. 19:30).

"The Majesty" refers to the throne of God the Father in His sovereign reign over all things in Heaven and in earth (1 Chr. 16:31; Ps. 97:1; Is. 52:7). The Son's exalted position is "on the right hand" of the Father, the position of highest dignity and honor. "On high" either tells where he sat (Westcott 15, Lenski 41) or where the Father's throne is located (Alford 12, Morris 15). The Greek word order favors the latter position. The result is the same either way. In a similar way Paul repeats the familiar theme that the Father has set Christ "at his own right hand in the heavenly places" (Eph. 1:3, 20; 2:6; 3:10; 6:12).

There is also debate among commentators as to the literalness of this declaration. Westcott (15) and Lenski (40) want to erase any sense of space or time in this declaration, giving "the right hand of the Majesty on high" a figurative sense emphasizing dignity and authority. But Alford's view seems to be preferable in seeing the statement as a Scriptural description of Heaven (15), and Heaven must always be interpreted as a literal place, though various contexts may change the definition. If there were not some literal sense in describing Christ's present position, then we would not be looking forward to His Second Coming. Since the Son is truly and fully God, there is a sense in which He is everywhere, and can thus be with us in our church meetings (Mt. 18:20); but there is also a real sense, a local sense, in which the incarnate Son is not here, and we look for His return in victory, riding the white horse (Rev. 19). In this sense Christ said to His disciples, "It is expedient for you that I go away: for if I go not away, the Comforter will not come unto you; but if I depart, I will send him unto you" (Jn. 16:7).

B. Superiority to the Angels (1:4—2:18)

The human agents in the communication of the O.T. were "the prophets." Both the Scriptures and Hebrew tradition affirm the involvement of supernatural agents, the angels, evidently acting in a mediatorial role, in the revelation of God's Word to man (Acts 7:53; Gal. 3:19).

1. Superiority to the angels by inheritance (1:4)

4 Being made so much better than the angels, as he hath by inheritance obtained a more excellent name than they.

In v. 4 the writer tells us why the Son has been exalted to His high position on the right hand of the Father: "Being made so much better than the angels." More literally, "being made" is "having become." This phrase should be contrasted with "being" in 1:3. The first part of v. 3 describes the characteristics that the Son has always had in relation to the Father. Verse 4 tells us about the exalted position which the incarnate Son has obtained as a result of His earthly work. Because of His earthly work of purification and atonement, the Son has become "so much better than the angels."

"Better" is used here in the epistle for the first time, but certainly not the last. It is the key word of the epistle and is used 13 times. The key word is clearly in line with the theme of the superiority of Christ: Christ is "better" than everyone and everything. Though the word *better* may not be used in some passages, it is clearly implied. In Christ we have a better revelation (1:2); He is better than angels (1:4), better than Adam (2:5-9), better than Moses (3:3-6), better than Joshua (4:8), better than Aaron (5:1-4), better than Abraham (7:1, 2), better than Levi (7:9, 10). Furthermore, He introduces a better covenant (7:22), a better tabernacle (8:2), better promises (8:6), a better sacrifice (9:12-14), a better faith (11:1, 39, 40), and a better kingdom (12:28).

The writer compares Christ to the "angels" at this point because they were the supernatural agents in communicating the word in the O.T. (Acts 7:53; Gal. 3:19), just as the prophets were the human agents (1:1). All this makes his argument, in this section, that we have a better revelation in Christ.

"As he hath by inheritance obtained" is more literally, "He has inherited." The original here communicates the idea of completed action accompanied by continuing result (Greek perfect tense). The emphasis in this context is on the continuing result. What He has inherited is His forever as a result of His earthly work of redemption as the incarnate Son of God. Specifically, what He has inherited that makes Him better than the angels is "a more excellent name than they."

The "name" which the writer has in mind is the name "Son" mentioned back in 1:2. It is true that others are called sons of God in Scripture. The angels are referred to by that title in Job 1:6 and 2:1, Israel in Dt. 14:1, and Hos. 11:1, Solomon in 2 Sa. 7:12-14, and believers in Gal. 3:26, 27. But in each of these cases the title is used in an entirely different way than when it is applied to Jesus Christ, the incarnate Son of God. John calls Him "the only begotten Son" (Jn. 1:18; 3:16). The term used by

John to describe the Sonship of the eternal Word means that He is "the only one of his kind" (Greek *monogenes*). As believers, we become sons of God only in and through Jesus Christ (Gal. 3:4-7; Rom. 8:14-17). However, our writer is not so much emphasizing the eternal Sonship of the Word as that position which He earned and inherited as a result of His incarnation and redemptive work. Special and blessed creatures though they are, angels have never been called the sons of God as our Lord is.

2. Proofs From the Old Testament (1:5-14)

The writer now proceeds to defend his argument concerning the superiority of the Son over angels, using seven quotations from the O.T. The quotations can be divided into two groups: (1) the first four quotations (vv. 5-7), which contrast the Son's relation to the Father with the Father's relation to the angels; (2) the last three quotations (vv. 8-14), which emphasize the Son's authoritative position over all things, including the angels.

a. In His relation to the Father (1:5-7)

5 For unto which of the angels said he at any time, Thou art my Son, this day have I begotten thee? And again, I will be to him a Father, and he shall be to me a Son?
6 And again, when he bringeth in the firstbegotten into the world, he saith, And let all the angels of God worship him.
7 And of the angels he saith, Who maketh his angels spirits, and his ministers a flame of fire.

The writer introduces the first quotation in v. 5 with the title of Son still very much in his mind. He asks his readers rhetorically, "For unto which of the angels said he at any time, Thou art my Son, this day have I begotten thee?" Though no answer is given, the answer is obvious: He has never said this to any angel. Angels collectively, and in an entirely different manner, may be called "sons of God" (Job 1:6; 2:1), but no individual angel is ever addressed as the Son of God. This title, in the manner it is used, belongs exclusively to the only begotten Son. This first quotation is from Ps. 2:7. Jewish interpreters at all times have recognized the second psalm as Messianic.

Psalm 2 seems to have three parts. In the *first part*, the heathen, the unsaved of the world, rebel "against the LORD, and against his anointed" (Ps. 2:2). The title "Messiah" in Hebrew means "the anointed one." In Greek the equivalent term is *Christos* or Christ. In the *second part* of Psalm 2 the Lord's three-fold response is given. (1) He will laugh at the foolishness of even thinking that a mortal could possibly prevent the will of God from ultimately being accomplished (2:4). (2) He declares that the Messiah will be crowned regardless of what wicked men may do (2:6, 7). (3) He warns them of the destiny of those who rebel when He will "break them with a rod of iron" (2:9). In the *third part* of the psalm the writer gives inspired advice in light of the divine determination of the Messiah, "Kiss the Son, lest he be angry, and ye perish *from* the way, when his wrath is kindled but a little" (2:12). God's Messianic King will be crowned; therefore, the best action that anyone could take is to fall in line and by faith make Him your King and your Savior.

There is also some debate as to when God said this to His Messianic Son. The declaration (Ps. 2:7) does not refer to what has been called "the eternal generation" of the Son (Lenski 46), though the Father/Son relationship, or at least what is communicated by it, has always existed in the relation of these two members of the Godhead. The Scripture writers apply this quotation, in part or in whole, to Christ's baptism (Mk. 1:11); His transfiguration (Mk. 9:7); His resurrection (Acts 13:33; Rom. 1:4); and His exaltation to His priestly intercessory ministry (Heb. 5:5). It appears, therefore, that the prophecy was meant to point to Christ's entire incarnate ministry, climaxing with His present victorious position at God's right hand. Barnes (33) observes, "He is treated and addressed as a Son. In his original existence this was so. In his incarnation this was so. When on earth this was so; and in his resurrection, ascension, and exaltation to the right hand of God, he was treated in all respects as a Son, as superior to all servants, and to all ministering spirits."

The writer further establishes Christ's right to the title of "Son" by a quotation from 2 Sam. 7:14. He says, "And again, I will be to him a Father, and he shall be to me a Son." In its original context God made this promise to David with immediate application to Solomon as the first step in the fulfillment of the Davidic Covenant. Though God did not allow David to build Him a house, the Temple, as he had wanted, He did promise him an heir on his throne forever (2 Sam. 7:13). This promise found its perfect fulfillment in Christ, and it is in this manner that the writer of Hebrews applies it.

There is quite a debate among commentators about the third quotation, with regard to the connection of the word "again" to the rest of the sentence. Our translation reads, "And again, when he bringeth in the firstbegotten into the world, he saith, And let all the angels of God worship him." As we have it here, "again" serves to add this quotation as further evidence in the writer's arguments for the superiority of the Son over angels. This would seem appropriate since he has just used the same word, "again," in the preceding quotation from 2 Sam. 7:14 for the same purpose. If we take it this way, "When he bringeth in the firstbegotten into the world" would be best applied to the birth of Christ, the beginning of His incarnate life on earth (so also Chrysostom, Calvin, Owen, Bengel, Stuart). At this point the prophetic command was fulfilled, "And let all the angels of God worship him." Luke's birth account (Lk. 2:8-14) clearly demonstrates the praise and worship of the angels at Christ's birth. Others who take "again" in this same manner prefer to see the occasion as a continuation of our Lord's exaltation to the Father's right hand following the resurrection and the brief period on earth (Morris 18).

Most commentators, however, prefer to take "again" with the verb and read, "When he again bringeth his firstbegotten into the world." With this placement of "again" they feel strongly that the application is to the return of Christ to the earth for the reception of His glorious kingdom. Angels will accompany Him in His return (1 Th. 4:16; Rev. 19:11-14) and will thus fulfill the command to worship Him (Lunemann 87,

Alford 17, Conybeare and Howson 791, Delitzsch I:71, Westcott 21, Barnes 35, Lenski 50). Though the majority take this latter approach, it seems to me that the quotation of the O.T. command for the angels to worship Christ would call for the time of their original introduction to the incarnate Son, and that would be at His birth when "the Word was made flesh, and dwelt among us" (Jn. 1:14). It may indeed extend to His exaltation and Second Coming, but the occasion of His birth deserves primary application.

Our writer here calls the Son the "firstbegotten" (Greek *prototokos*) or the "firstborn." Elsewhere the term is used at Christ's birth (Lk. 2:7); in relation to creation in general (Col. 1:15) and the church in particular; with regard to our present sanctification (Rom. 8:29) and to our future resurrection (Col. 1:18; Rev. 1:5). The writer of Hebrews, however, uses the term in a more absolute sense. The meaning here is the same as the Hebrew idea of the firstborn Son. In this position the incarnate Son of God has all the dignity and privileges that accompany it, including the fact that God the Father "hath appointed [him] heir of all things" (1:2). "World" (Greek *oikoumene*) refers to the "inhabited world," of which the angels are a part. Here we have a very specific word (emphasis on the beings who populate this world), whereas in verse 2 the broader word "worlds" stressed the time element ("ages") and was broad enough to include the entire universe.

The quotation, "And let all the angels of God worship him," comes from Dt. 32:43 in the Septuagint. The Massoretic text (the Hebrew text of the O.T. as we now know it) does not have this last line, but a Hebrew manuscript found among the Dead Sea Scrolls at Qumran does have it (Bruce 16, note 75). A statement with very similar wording, especially as it reads in the Septuagint, is found in Ps. 97:7. The Hebrew text of this passage says "worship him, all ye gods," but the word translated "gods" (Hebrew *elohim*) can, in this context, refer to pagan gods, rulers, or angels. The Son's superiority to angels is clearly demonstrated by the Father's command to them to worship Him.

In v. 7 the writer continues contrasting the relation of the Son to the Father as opposed to the relation of the angels. The angels are commanded to worship the Son in v. 6, and here they are presented as His messengers sent forth like wind and fire to do His bidding. The writer declares, "And of the angels he saith, Who maketh his angels spirits, and his ministers a flame of fire" (compare Ps. 104:4). The contrast is with v. 8, not with v. 6. The Father has sovereign control over these supernatural servants, whom He makes to carry out His will, though certainly with no objection on their part. In line with Hebrew parallelism, the verse might be translated, "Who maketh his angels *winds*, and his ministers a flame of fire" (see NASB, NIV). The word for "spirit" (Greek *pneuma*) can also mean "wind," and in this verse "wind" is clearly more of a parallel to "flame of fire" in the second phrase than is "spirit." The psalmist is describing the function of the angels. The word "angel" itself (Greek *angelos*) means "messenger," and one of the primary functions of angels is carrying forth the Word of God to men. In speeding forth to do God's bidding, they are like the wind in its quickness. In forcefully carrying out God's commandments, they are like "a flame of fire" in its power, and in this latter function they are merely "his ministers" (Greek *leitourgos*), His officials sent forth to administrate His orders (Lenski 53).

b. In His authoritative position (1:8-14)

8 But unto the Son *he saith*, Thy throne, O God, *is* for ever and ever: a sceptre of righteousness *is* the sceptre of thy kingdom.
9 Thou hast loved righteousness, and hated iniquity; therefore God, *even* thy God, hath anointed thee with the oil of gladness above thy fellows.
10 And, Thou, Lord, in the beginning hast laid the foundation of the earth; and the heavens are the works of thine hands:
11 They shall perish; but thou remainest; and they all shall wax old as doth a garment;
12 And as a vesture shalt thou fold them up, and they shall be changed: but thou art the same, and thy years shall not fail.
13 But to which of the angels said he at any time, Sit on my right hand, until I make thine enemies thy footstool?
14 Are they not all ministering spirits, sent forth to minister for them who shall be heirs of salvation?

While the angels are only His messengers and His ministering officials, the exalted position of the Son is entirely different. In vv. 8, 9, to bring the Son's position out in contrast, the writer quotes Ps. 45:6, 7. While the previous quotation was spoken in reference to the angels, this one is spoken in regard to the Son. Our writer says, by way of contrast, "But unto the Son he saith, Thy throne, O God, is for ever and ever." Some (Westcott 25) want to translate the first phrase of the quotation, "Thy throne is God" or "God is thy throne" (Greek *ho thronos sou ho theos*), rather than taking "God" to be the title of address for the Son, as in KJV, NASB, NIV, etc. Certainly the motive of some of the modern theologians would be to deny the deity of the Son, but with Westcott that is not the case. His objection for taking "God" as vocative, as a direct address to the Son, is that the person originally addressed in the psalm was a Davidic king who would not have been called "God" (Hebrew *elohim*). Delitzsch (I:77), however, maintains that Ps. 45 is not merely Messianic in type, with an immediate reference to the current Davidic king, but is "a directly prophetico-Messianic Psalm." It seems appropriate, therefore, to take the quotation as the Father addressing the Son and calling Him "God." To God the Son He says, "Thy throne . . . *is* for ever and ever." In contrast to the relatively short reign of the Davidic kings, the kingdom of Christ, who is the ultimate fulfillment of the Davidic Covenant, will never end.

The psalmist adds further, with regard to the reign of the Son, "A sceptre of righteousness is the sceptre of thy kingdom." A scepter was the ancient symbol of kingly authority, often literally held in the king's hand as he sat on his throne and issued authoritative decrees. The Son's scepter is "a sceptre of righteousness" (Greek *euthutes*), which literally refers to "straightness." There is nothing crooked about this Messianic King. His judgments are honest; His dealings are forthright. You can always depend on His word.

In v. 9 the psalmist describes further the reign of the King: "Thou hast loved righteousness, and hated iniquity." The Hebrew uses the present tense for the verbs (love and hate), but the Septuagint, from which our writer quotes, uses the past (aorist tense), indicating "the completed work now seen in its glorious issue" (Westcott 26). In His rule the Messianic Son is extremely biased. He never straddles the fence, nor is He vague in His rulings. His judgments are so clear, and His instructions so plain, that we can always know where we stand with Him. He will have no problem in separating the sheep from the goats in the day of judgment (Mt. 25:31-46). As His children, we, too, should feel very strongly about good and evil, about right and wrong, about righteousness and iniquity. Because of these attributes ascribed to the Son, "Therefore God, even thy God, hath anointed thee with the oil of gladness above thy fellows." "Therefore" is literally "because of this." Though "God" could again be taken as a vocative (direct address), in light of the action described it is best to take it here as the subject. The psalmist is referring to God the Father. Though the Son is truly God, yet as the Son of man He told Mary Magdalene, "I ascend unto my Father, and your Father; and *to* my God, and your God" (Jn. 20:17). At the consummation of our Lord's earthly work, God the Father "hath anointed" the Son. Though earthly Davidic kings were anointed with literal oil, the heavenly Son of David, seated at the Father's right hand, was to be anointed "with the oil of gladness." In applying the prophecy, the writer of Hebrews views the Son as having already been anointed in His present exalted position at God's right hand. As a result of His victorious earthly ministry and His present position of authority, great rejoicing is certainly in order. This anointing has placed the Son in a position "above thy fellows." Lenski (56) identifies the "fellows" (Greek *metochoi*) referred to as the saints of God; but, in light of the context, it seems certain that he has in mind the angels, since they are the ones to whom He is being compared (Hagner 34, Hewitt 58, Lunemann 95).

The writer continues the thought introduced in v. 8, "Unto the Son he *saith*." The quotation from Ps. 45:6, 7 in vv. 8, 9 has shown the Son to be superior to the angels in His exalted position at God's right hand. Here, in vv. 10-12, he quotes Ps. 102:25-27 in presenting the superiority of the Son over all that He has created. The angels, of course, are part of that creation. The creation itself is subject to change, but the Son, as a member of the eternal Godhead, will never change in His essential being.

In v. 10 the writer uses "and" to show that he is giving an additional quotation with reference to the Son. The quotation of Ps. 102:25-27, as usual with our author, is from the Septuagint. In the Hebrew text of this psalm, God's personal name, Jehovah or Yahweh, is used throughout. The Septuagint regularly uses the Greek word *kurios*, translated by KJV as "Lord," for God's personal name. Our writer, quoting the Septuagint, has this name in Ps. 102:25, though it is not in the original (see Ps. 102:25 in KJV). This fits well with the practice of the N.T. writers in identifying the incarnate Son with the Jehovah (literally the Hebrew verb "to be" or "I am") of the O.T. Psalm 102 is the prayer of the distraught, exiled Israel for deliverance, and that deliverance is ultimately fulfilled in the Messianic King, Jesus Christ.

The writer has already credited the Son with both creating (1:2) and sustaining (1:3) the universe and all that is in it. That truth is reiterated here by the psalmist; both the "earth" and the "heavens" are the work of His hands. Some of the Greek philosophers maintained that matter is eternal. But that is contrary to the teaching of Scripture. God is both eternal and immutable, but the world that He made is not. The psalmist emphasizes, "They shall perish; but thou remainest; and they all shall wax old as doth a garment; And as a vesture shalt thou fold them up." The metaphor of a garment communicates two truths about the material universe: (1) it gets old; (2) it will be changed (Morris 19). Any garment made of physical material, no matter how good, will grow old and will eventually need changing or replacing with a new one. The Scriptures are consistent in calling for the ultimate renewal and recreation of this universe, not necessarily its annihilation (see Is. 51:6, 16; 65:17; 66:22; 2 Pet. 3:13; Rev. 21:1). Our God, whether we refer to the Father or, as here, to the Son, stands in complete contrast. With great joy and consolation the psalmist declares, "But thou art the same, and thy years shall not fail." Our writer is going to make an even more lengthy case for this truth in Heb. 12:25-29 with the use of a quotation from Hag. 2:6.

In his final quotation, from Ps. 110:1, the writer returns to the method of introduction which he used in 1:5: "But to which of the angels said he at any time, Sit on my right hand, until I make thine enemies thy footstool?" The obvious answer is the same as in v. 5: God the Father never said this to any angel, and He never will! Psalm 110 is one of the most frequently used Messianic passages by N.T. writers. The command to "sit" is given in continuous action, "Keep sitting," indicating some period of time before the intended goal will be accomplished. Though our Lord Himself indicated that He did not know the time of His return (Mk. 13:32), there are indications that He did know that it would be a lengthy period of time (see Mt. 25:14; Acts 1:7). Premillennialists feel that the climax of this victorious reign will be seen in an earthly millennium (Rev. 20:1-10). Amillennialists interpret the same passage figuratively and see it as being fulfilled currently in Christ's heavenly reign at the Father's right hand. Jesus Himself revealed the Messianic importance of Ps. 110:1 in His question to the Pharisees in Mt. 22:41-46. He challenged them to examine the reason that David called his own Messianic Son "Lord" in this passage. If they had come to the right conclusion, they would have accepted Jesus Christ, who "was made of the seed of David according to the flesh" (Rom. 1:3), as their Messiah and Lord.

The image of Christ's enemies being made His footstool comes from the ancient tradition of kings placing their feet on the necks of vanquished enemies (see Jos. 10:24). The message clearly communicated is that of ultimate and complete victory. According to Paul's application of this passage, the last enemy to be destroyed will be death (1 Cor. 15:24, 25).

The writer's application of the quotation from Ps. 110:1 to the immediate subject of our Lord's superiority to angels can be seen by reminding ourselves of the constant position of angels in Scripture. They are always seen standing and serving God, ever ready to carry out His orders at a moment's notice (Dan. 7:10; Lk. 1:19; Rev. 8:2). Thus, he concludes, "Are they not all ministering spirits, sent forth to minister for them who shall be heirs of salvation?" These words are our writer's final application of these O.T. passages to prove his point that Christ is far superior to the angels. The word used for "ministering" (Greek *leitourgikos*) is from the same root as the word ministers in 1:7, in the quote from Psalm 104:4. Like there, it describes an officiant performing his service. They are being "sent forth" (the original has continuous action) "to serve" (Greek eis *diakonia*), literally "for service." Their missions are urgent and protracted, and they will continue in this role until the Father's goal for the Son has finally been attained. But in this capacity they do not minister to the Son, for He is at the Father's right hand. Their ministry is directed toward those "who shall be heirs of salvation." Since our salvation is eternal, from the moment we receive it (Heb. 5:9), it is not surprising that it can be presented in Scripture from a past, present, and future point of view. In the past we received it; in the present we possess and enjoy it; and in the future we will realize its final and full application. The writer is here emphasizing the future aspect (see also 9:28). In 1:4 he spoke of the "inheritance" which our Lord has received; and here, as with Paul, he sees us as "heirs of God, and joint-heirs with Christ" (Rom. 8:17).

Summary (1:1-14)

As stated in the introduction, one of the themes of Hebrews is the superiority of Christ. Here in chapter 1 that theme is emphasized with regard to the superior revelation that we have through Jesus Christ. In showing this superior revelation, the writer first explains the superiority of the Son to the prophets, the human agents by which God's Word was delivered in the O.T. In ancient times God spoke at different times and in different ways through those faithful servants, but in this new dispensation God's revelation has been much more specific and much more focused through one primary person, God's incarnate Son. The Son was the very radiation of God the Father, the "spitting image," as we would say. The Son, the second person of the Triune Godhead, possessed all the qualities that characterized the Father. In this capacity He performed the great priestly sacrifice when He "by himself purged our sins"; then He demonstrated that His redemptive work was complete by taking His seat "on the right hand of the Majesty on high" (1:1-3).

In the second part of chapter 1, the writer moves forward with the theme of the superior revelation in Christ by contrasting the Son with the angels, the supernatural messengers which God created to perform His will. He does this through a series of seven quotations from the O.T. The first four give a contrast between the Son and angels with regard to their relation to the Father. He makes clear that He has in mind the Son in His incarnation rather than in His eternal relation to the Father, since He "by inheritance obtained a more excellent name than they." To make his case, he quotes Ps. 2:7 to show how the Father called Christ the Son whom He had begotten; 2 Sam. 7:14 to show again the Father-Son relationship; Dt. 32:43, from the Septuagint, to reveal the angels worshiping the Son at His birth; and Ps. 104:4 to demonstrate the role of angels as God's messengers (1:4-7).

In the final three quotations the writer emphasizes the superior position of the Son in relation to angels. He quotes Ps. 45:6, 7 to demonstrate Christ's authoritative reign over all other creatures, especially the angels. Then he moves to Ps. 102:25-27 to present Christ in His marvelous role as the Creator of the universe, and to show that the material universe is growing older, winding down, while God the Son, like God the Father, doesn't change at all. Finally, he quotes Ps. 110:1 as God's invitation to the Son to take His position at the right hand of the Father until every enemy has been defeated. While Christ is all of these things—Son, King, God, Eternal and Immutable—the angels, great as they are, are "ministering spirits, sent forth to minister for them who shall be heirs of salvation" (1:8-14).

Application: Teaching and Preaching the Passage

The fact that the God of all creation would communicate with us, the lowly, rebellious, fallen objects of His creation, is most remarkable. The writer of Hebrews starts out by emphasizing that marvel, even under the old covenant when God spoke at many different intervals over a period of a thousand years, using many different methods of communication: direct and indirect, in types and symbols, in dreams and in visions, through men and through angels, and on one occasion even through a donkey. But His communication under the new covenant was even more marvelous because it was on the basis of one single person, God's own Son, Jesus Christ, and it was given to us over an extremely short period, relatively speaking, of about 50 years. What a wonder that Almighty God has freely given us His Word! Let us read it and heed it in our lives every day (1:1, 2).

There is a three-fold contrast between the old covenant and the new covenant in 1:1, 2. The contrast is in relation to: (1) their nature—the old, fragmentary and incomplete; the new, perfect and final; (2) the agents used—the old came through the prophets, weak and sinful men; the new through God's perfect Son; (3) the dispensations described—one was "in time past," the other "in these last days."

In presenting the new dispensation in 1:2, 3, we have an interesting description of our Redeemer. (1) The title which He bears—"Son," in direct contrast to God's servants, the prophets. (2) The inheritance which He received—this refers to His kingdom to which He was appointed back in eternity, but which became a reality through the actions of the Son in this dispensation, "in these last days." (3) The creation which He mediated—all three persons of the Trinity were involved in the creation: God the Father created through the mediation of His Son and through the effective accomplishment of the Holy Spirit. (4) The nature of His being—"the brightness of *his* glory, and the express image of his person"—He was the true and exact radiation of the Father. (5) The continued sustaining of the universe—"upholding all things by the word of his power"—contrary to evolution, the entire universe, and all that is in it, is both created and sustained by the presence and power of the triune God. (6) The sacrifice which He made—He "by himself purged our sins"—one of the primary points emphasized throughout this epistle. (7) The completeness which was signified—He "sat down on the right hand of the Majesty on high." The O.T. priests always carried out their ministry standing. They never sat because the ministry was never complete; their sacrifices had to be repeated every year. However, from the cross Jesus cried, "It is finished" (Jn. 19:30), signifying the eternal efficacy of His sacrifice and leading to the sitting position of His present and continuing ministry.

In 1:4-14, the writer shows the superiority of God's Son, Jesus Christ, to the angels through a series of seven quotations from the Old Testament. We may summarize the ministry of angels as follows: (1) They have a deep interest in the affairs of men, rejoicing over the salvation of even one soul (Lk. 15:10), and representing the interests of God's little ones, both spiritually and physically, before the Father in Heaven (Mt. 18:10). (2) They have a special interest in God's provision for man's redemption, announcing the coming birth to both Joseph (Mt. 1:20) and Mary (Lk. 1:26-38), and announcing the birth event itself to the shepherds (Lk. 2:8-14); Peter indicates that the angels have a great admiration and curiosity about the gospel plan of redemption (1 Pet. 1:12). (3) They had an ongoing ministry in the life of Christ, after His temptation (Mt. 4:11), after His agony in Gethsemane (Lk. 22:43), in announcing His resurrection to the disciples (Lk. 24:3-9; Jn. 20:11-13), as well as prophesying His imminent return at His ascension (Acts 1:10, 11). (4) They are involved in protecting God's people from threatening danger, as when a host of angels protected the prophet Elisha from the king of Syria (2 Kg. 6:13-17), or when the psalmist promised deliverance from evil because "he shall give his angels charge over thee, to keep thee in all thy ways. They shall bear thee up in *their* hands, lest thou dash thy foot against a stone" (Ps. 91:11, 12). (5) They are involved in delivering God's people from danger that they are already in, as when they delivered Lot and his family from Sodom (Gen. 19:1, 15, 16), Daniel from the lion's den (Dan. 6:22), the apostles from imprisonment (Acts 5:17-20), and Peter as he "was sleeping between two soldiers, bound with two chains: and the keepers before the door kept the prison" (Acts 12:6-9). (6) Finally, they bear the souls of saints who have died in Christ to their rest in Heaven (Lk. 16:22; see Barnes 51).

In Heb. 1:8, 9 the writer quotes Ps. 45:6, 7, originally spoken in prophetic anticipation of the Messiah, and now applied to God's Son, Jesus Christ. In these two verses several things are claimed about Messiah: (1) He is "God," not just an earthly king, and is addressed by the psalmist as such. (2) He has a "throne," a "sceptre," and thus a "kingdom." (3) The duration of His kingdom, in contrast with that of earthly kings, is "forever." (4) The nature of His kingdom is one of "righteousness," for He loves "righteousness" and hates "iniquity." (5) He did not inherit this kingdom, as most earthly kings do, but was appointed and "anointed" by God Himself as King. (6) His anointing was superior to all other kings as He was anointed "with the oil of gladness" above His companions, whether kings or angels. He is, thus, "King of kings, and Lord of lords" (Rev. 17:14; 19:16).

In 1:10-12 the writer quotes Ps. 102:25-27 in contrasting the ever-changing face of the world that God created with the immutability of God Himself. One day, perhaps soon, God will bring the world as we know it, the world that He still controls, to a conclusion. Then He will "fold them up" as a garment that is being put away after serving its purpose, but God Himself does not and will not change. The psalmist declares, "But thou art the same." In applying this principle of God's immutability, we note that the Triune God is "the same" with regard to: (1) being the Creator and Sustainer of the universe; (2) all the attributes of the Godhead, including omnipotence, omniscience, and omnipresence, love, truth, light, etc.; (3) the one plan of salvation, that is, by grace through faith in Jesus Christ; (4) the fact that He is the judge of both believers and unbelievers, and that, as such, there is a day of accountability approaching. These four things are, of course, only representative of His immutability. In response to Moses' inquiry about His name, God replied, "I AM THAT I AM: and he said, Thus shalt thou say unto the children of Israel, I AM hath sent me unto you" (Ex. 3:14). Thus, God's personal name, Yahweh or Jehovah, means "I AM," and speaks both of His eternality, with regard to time, and His immutability, with regard to His being or attributes. The writer reaffirms this characteristic in relation to God's Son when he later declares, "Jesus Christ the same yesterday, and to day, and for ever" (13:8).

In 1:13 the writer quotes Ps. 110:1 and applies it to Jesus Christ. From that we learn: (1) In His present ministry of intercession on our behalf, He continues to "sit," that is, the battle that He is fighting is still based on His completed work at Calvary, and the victory will be His with no great further struggle, for the war has already been won. (2) But in this present dispensation, Christ still has "enemies," the world of men who oppose Him, as well as Satan and all his angels. (3) These enemies will be made to become Christ's "footstool," implying the completeness of the victory which will be won. (4) The ultimate victory is in the hands of God the Father ("until I make"), and it is He who guarantees the victory. (5) In the meanwhile Christ rules and reigns in His present kingdom from His exalted position at the Father's "right hand."

3. First warning: against neglecting such superior revelation (2:1-4)

1 Therefore we ought to give the more earnest heed to the things which we have heard, lest at any time we should let *them* slip.
2 For if the word spoken by angels was stedfast, and every transgression and disobedience received a just recompence of reward;
3 How shall we escape, if we neglect so great salvation; which at the first began to be spoken by the Lord, and was confirmed unto us by them that heard *him*;
4 God also bearing *them* witness, both with signs and wonders, and with divers miracles, and gifts of the Holy Ghost, according to his own will?

This is the first of several warnings, combined with admonitions, that occur throughout the epistle (see also 3:7—4:16; 5:11—6:20; 10:19-39; 12:18-29). It is also the first negative note that the writer has sounded in relation to his readers. It is clear, however, that he sees real danger lying before them, but he certainly does not see their position as hopeless. None of them have yet committed apostasy, but if they keep on in the direction that at least some of them are going, the consequences will be both severe and eternal.

"Therefore," literally "because of this," refers back to the proofs that the writer has given to show that Christ is superior to the angels. "We ought" translates an impersonal verb (Greek *dei*) which literally means, "It is necessary." The warning that he is about to give is absolutely obligatory for the Hebrew recipients. "To give heed" is expressed in continuous action. Constantly they must give their closest attention to the inspired instructions from God's Son and His inspired apostles. The writer strengthens his exhortation by urging the attention to be "the more earnest" or "more abundant."

These inspired instructions are referred to as "the things which we have heard." This would include whatever part of the N.T. had been written at that time, as well as the Gospel message as it had come to them orally. Since few copies of the Scripture would have been available, the message would have come to most by way of the ear rather than the eye. The phrase is literally "the things which were heard" (aorist passive). The Gospel message was made clear to the hearers in the past. Now it is time to take action and make application. The consequences of failing to give constant and more abundant attention to the instructions of the N.T. will be severe.

The writer warns, "Lest at any time we should let *them* slip." Our effort to pay close attention to the Word must never relax. We must never allow our relation to the written Word or to our living Lord to become casual; if we do, the likely result would be that "we should let *them* slip." This verb (Greek *pararreo*) is used of things which slip away, such as a ring from the finger, or something or someone which takes the wrong course, like a crumb of food going down the windpipe, or an inappropriate subject slipping into a conversation (Westcott 37). The tense of the verb in the original (Greek aorist) does not indicate a slipping that is in process, but one that is so serious that it is completed. A process may indeed be involved but the writer is here looking at the completed and fatal result. In every generation there are always multiple opportunities to turn our attention away from the Word of God. Such trends come and go, but the Word of God remains firm. It is to that Word that we must remain anchored lest we let the ship of our salvation drift into uncharted waters.

In v. 2 he reminds us of the seriousness of neglecting the O.T., and the Law of Moses in particular: "For if the word spoken by angels was stedfast, and every transgression and disobedience received a just recompence of reward." The broader term for "word" (Greek *logos*) is used here because the law "spoken by angels" also became the written and established Word of God, forming the basis for the rest of the O.T. This contrasts with "word" in 1:3 (Greek *hrema*) where the Son's sovereign utterance, His spoken word, is the meaning.

The mediation of angels in giving the law, though quite logical, is not made clear in the law itself. Hints of it, however, do appear in the O.T. (see Dt. 33:2; Ps. 68:17), and N.T. statements make it clear (see Acts 7:53; Gal. 3:19). It seems to have been firmly held in the traditional teaching of Judaism (Lunemann 102).

This law "was stedfast" or, literally, "became firm" or "established" in being written down as the law of God and carrying appropriate and severe punishments for disregarding it. Thus, the writer adds, "And every transgression and disobedience received a just recompence of reward." "Transgression" (Greek *parabasis*) refers to any active violation of the stated law of God, doing what the law forbids, while "disobedience" (Greek *parakoe*) refers to an absence of adherence to God's law, neglecting to do what the law commands (Hewitt 62).

Under the O.T. law, whoever was found guilty of violating it or neglecting it "received a just recompense of reward." The governing principle of O.T. law was "eye for eye, tooth for tooth, hand for hand, foot for foot" (Ex. 21:24; Mt. 5:38). Thus the law was "just" in that the punishment was custom designed to fit the crime. "Recompence of reward" (Greek *misthapodosia*) refers to due wages given in return for something. The word can be used either in an unfavorable sense for an appropriate punishment for some crime, as here, or in a favorable sense for an appropriate reward, as in 10:35 and 11:26 (Lunemann 103).

The writer of Hebrews frequently makes his point more emphatic through an interrogative rather than a declarative statement. He asks, "How shall we escape, if we neglect so great salvation?" The answer is so obvious that it does not need to be provided. There can be no possibility of escaping the most severe judgment of God if we turn away from the salvation that has been provided in Christ. Note that the writer includes himself in the warning. No Christian is exempt, no matter who he may be. If apostasy is a possibility for any Christian, it is a possibility for all Christians. He does not say, "If we reject," but rather, "If we neglect." He is referring to apathy and indifference toward that which has already been received, not refusal and rejection of that which is just being presented. The gospel message is referred to as "so great salvation" because it provides eternal deliverance from the spiritual bondage of sin.

He goes on to explain the process in the delivery of the gospel message of salvation: "which at the first began to be spoken by the Lord, and was confirmed unto us by them that heard *him*." The original is expressed in such a way as to put strong emphasis on the beginning, the origin, of the message of salvation. The origin of the gospel was in the earthly ministry of Jesus Christ (compare Mk. 1:1). Other than the birth stories and His visit to the Temple in Jerusalem when He was twelve, the central content of the gospel is found in the actions and instructions of our Lord in His brief ministry of three and one-half years at the most. Thus, the beginning was defined and specific. "To be spoken" is in continuous action, indicating that the message was given over a period of time during His earthly ministry.

Now the writer points to the second step in the communication of the Gospel: "and was confirmed . . . by them that heard *him*." The writer is describing the original disciples or apostles, especially those whom God would use in writing the N.T. But we must also remember that the gospel message was preached orally for at least 20 years before the first Gospel was written (from the crucifixion/resurrection in A.D. 30 to the Gospel of Matthew about A.D. 50). Then, when it was written down, the source of information was never second hand. Matthew and John were both eyewitnesses, and Mark, according to ancient church tradition, got his information from Peter (see 1 Pet. 5:13). Luke says that he was writing about "those things which are most surely believed among us, Even as they delivered them unto us, which from the beginning were eyewitnesses" (Lk. 1:1, 2). Luke also tells us that, when the apostles voted to place Matthias in Judas' position, they strictly required that he must have been an eyewitness to Jesus' ministry from John's baptism to the present (Acts 1:21-26). In fact, a key word of Acts, which relates the history of the growth and progress of the early church, is "witness" or "witnesses." There was, therefore, no question about the truth of the message, for it had indeed been "confirmed," established, made sure, by those who first had the information.

The writer says that this message was confirmed "unto us." He apparently places himself in the second generation of Christianity, one step removed from the original hearers and proclaimers. As a writer of an inspired N.T. book, this certainly gives us no problem, for, as we saw above, Luke does the same thing (Lk. 1:1, 2). It does, however, create great difficulty for those who feel they must insist that Hebrews was written by Paul. Paul's own words would seem to eliminate him from using such terminology since he clearly claims to have received his message directly from the risen Christ (Gal. 1:15—2:9; 1 Cor. 15:1-4). (See the discussion in the introduction for more details about the problem of authorship.)

The assurance of the authenticity of the N.T. message is threefold: (1) in its original announcement—by the Lord Jesus while on earth; (2) in its convincing proclamation—by the apostles; (3) in its divine attestation—by God the Father (Westcott 39). Our writer describes this attestation in v. 4: "God also bearing *them* witness, both with signs and wonders, and with divers miracles, and gifts of the Holy Ghost, according to his own will." The heart of the gospel message of salvation was the proclamation of the Resurrection of Christ. No one can be asked to believe that a man died, was buried, and rose again after three days without clear and convincing evidence. One of the greatest evidences in any court of law is an eyewitness, and human courts send men to prison, and even execute them, on the basis of nothing more than being convinced that the witness was telling the truth. But our writer tells us that God gave us more than this when He confirmed the proclamation of the Gospel message with divine attestation: "God also bearing *them* witness." The word translated "bearing witness" (Greek *sunepimartureo*) is a double compound, a word that has two prepostiions added as prefixes. The word by itself means "to bear witness" or "testimony." The first preposition added (Greek *epi*), literally "upon," means that God's testimony through miraculous demonstrations is added to confirm the testimony of the apostles. The second preposition (Greek *sun*), meaning "with," emphasizes the fact that the two testimonies are complementary, God's and the apostles', that they are partners in accomplishing the same goal.

The writer seems to indicate that he wants us to take the following list of divine witnesses individually (by presence of Greek particle *te*), rather than together, although the first two are listed as partners on numerous occasions (Westcott 40). "Signs" (Greek *semeion*) refer to dramatic events that are obviously meant, due to the context or the situation at hand, to confirm something. The act or event does not have to be something out of the ordinary. The circumstances under which it occurs may make it a "sign." Some of the plagues on Egypt were like this. The plague of locusts, for example, was not an unfamiliar event to the Egyptians, but its timing and intensity revealed it to be at the direct hand of God. John consistently uses this word in his Gospel to refer to the miracles of Christ.

"Wonders" (Greek *teras*) is never used alone in the N.T. It is usually used as an accompaniment of "signs" (in the Synoptics, John, Paul, and especially in Acts 1-15). In the Synoptics and in 2 Th. 2:9 the pair is used of the powers of evil. "Wonder" always describes something remarkable, marvelous, far out of the ordinary, an object of special amazement.

God's confirmation also came about by means of "divers miracles" (Greek *poikilai dunameis*). "Miracles" here literally means "powers." The word is used to describe a miraculous act that is an obvious manifestation of the omnipotence of God, a powerful demonstration that is far beyond the normal ability of man. The word is often used in the Synoptic Gospels for the miracles of Christ. Our writer calls the confirming miracles of the apostles "divers" (different, various) because of their number and their variety.

God's fourth and final means of confirmation were "gifts of the Holy Ghost." The word translated "gifts" here (Greek *merismos*) is, literally, "distributions," translated "gifts" in this context since it is obvious that the gifts of the Spirit are the things which are being distributed. In the N.T. the Holy Spirit is both the Gift and the Giver. In this phrase some commentators think that the gift of the Spirit Himself is meant (Westcott 40; Alford 31), referring to the Holy Spirit as the Gift which God gives (Greek objective genitive). But the use of the plural "gifts" appears to eliminate that possibility. It seems better to take it to mean the gifts which the Holy Spirit gives (Lenski 70, Greek subjective genitive). The gifts of the Spirit are listed in Rom. 12:3-8 and 1 Cor. 12:4-11; such lists are usually not exhaustive, only exemplary. Here in Hebrews, however, the writer is not speaking about gifts intended for the practical benefit of the church as a whole, but rather gifts that were primarily intended for the confirmation of the message of salvation.

Another important truth to keep in mind is that gifts that were given specifically for purposes of confirmation may very well be discontinued when the need for supernatural confirmation is no longer present. Some modern Christians insist that anyone who doubts the continuation of all the gifts listed in the N.T. is doubting the power of God. But that is not necessarily true. Moses was given three special signs to confirm his authority to the elders of Israel (Ex. 4:1-

9), but no one would argue that these signs were intended to continue beyond the time and purpose for which they were designed. Their passing certainly did not detract from the power of God for future generations. That first generation of Christianity needed special confirmation, especially in the dramatic transformation from the old to the new covenant. In light of the gross misinterpretation of the Messianic promises of the O.T. by the Jewish teachers of N.T. times, only undeniable works of a supernatural nature (healings, miraculous languages, resurrections) could convince people of the truth of the gospel message. But if that first generation had something that we do not have today, we must remember that we also have something that they did not have, the completed Word of God, including the wonderful authority of N.T. revelation. All of these elements of confirmation (signs, wonders, miracles, gifts) were given "according to his own will"; that is, according to the will of God the Father.

4. The necessity and propriety of the humiliation of the Son (2:5-18)

Though the thought of the superiority of the Son to angels will fade into the background after v. 5, we see that he has not lost that thought since he renews it again in 2:16. The reason that this subject occupies a secondary position for the next several verses is that he turns his primary attention to the need for the Son, as the Second Adam, to obtain God's ideal and original goal for man, the goal of the complete subjugation of this earth and all that is in it.

a. To attain man's intended destiny (2:5-9)

5 For unto the angels hath he not put in subjection the world to come, whereof we speak.
6 But one in a certain place testified, saying, What is man, that thou art mindful of him? or the son of man, that thou visitest him?
7 Thou madest him a little lower than the angels; thou crownedst him with glory and honour, and didst set him over the works of thy hands:
8 Thou hast put all things in subjection under his feet. For in that he put all in subjection under him, he left nothing *that is* not put under him. But now we see not yet all things put under him.
9 But we see Jesus, who was made a little lower than the angels for the suffering of death, crowned with glory and honour; that he by the grace of God should taste death for every man.

Since 1:4 the writer has been showing us various ways in which the Son is superior to the angels. In 2:1-4 he has warned about neglecting and turning away from the revelation of "so great salvation" which originated with the Lord Himself while He was here on earth. Now he moves to another reason for the Son's superiority to angels: "For unto the angels hath he not put in subjection the world to come, whereof we speak." There seems to have been a belief among the Jews that the present world was placed by God under the control of angels. Some interpreters argue that the Scriptures back this idea up in such passages as Dan. 4:13; 10:13, 20,

21; 12:1; Mt. 18:10; Rev. 1:20; 9:11; 16:5 (Alford 31). But as Delitzsch (I:103) points out, the description of the work of angels in all of these passages merely fits in with the explanation of their role as seen in Heb. 1:14, as "ministering spirits . . . for them who shall be heirs of salvation." John MacArthur (52) also subscribes to this point of view, that the present world is under the control of angels, citing passages that relate to Satan's dominion over this present world (Jn. 12:31; 14:30; Eph. 6:12). But passages like these do not refer to the world as God originally created it, but rather to the world that came to be as a result of the fall of Adam in Eden.

The key to understanding this verse and this entire section of Hebrews hangs, to some extent, on understanding what the writer means in v. 5 by "the world to come." It seems to me that most commentators misunderstand what the writer is talking about here. Most think that he is referring to the future, from the writer's point of view, either to the present kingdom over which Christ reigns at the Father's right hand (Alford 32) or to the eternal state, the future new Heaven and earth at the return of Christ (Delitzsch I:102; Lenski 72); or to the millennial reign of Christ on earth at the end of this age (Pink 96; MacArthur 52). Lenski admits that "world" (Greek *oikoumene*), as used here, usually refers to this present inhabited world. But he feels that the phrase "to come" (Greek *ten mellousan*), modifying the "world," alters the meaning and points to the eternal world of the future.

It seems to me, however, that, in this context, the writer is clearly referring to the present created world. The confusion, no doubt, comes from the fact that he says "the world to come," and, if we think from the N.T. point of view, or from our present point of view, we would naturally conclude that he is referring to the future. In this context, however, the writer appears to mean "the world that was to come," speaking from God's point of view before He created this present world. If we were looking with God at the world that He was about to create, we would call it "the world to come." That this is his meaning I believe is made clear by his quotation in Ps. 8:6-8, in which the Psalmist David refers back to God's original purpose for man in Gen. 1:26 (Evans 72; Hughes 82; Turner 54; Stedman 37; so also Chrysostom and Theophylact, according to Alford 32). Hughes partially subscribes to this point of view when he says, "But it is also now present, in that the Messiah has indeed come, in the person of the incarnate Son, and by his coming has inaugurated the era of fulfilment. By his life, death and resurrection (2 Cor. 1:20) he has performed all that was needful for the redemption of fallen man and his world" (82). More precisely, Turner observes that the writer is referring to the present world over which Adam was to have dominion (54). When God was about to create man, He said, "Let us make man in our image, after our likeness: and let them have dominion over the fish of the sea, and over the fowl of the air, and over the cattle, and over all the earth, and over every creeping thing that creepeth upon the earth" (Gen. 1:26). Unfortunately, because of Adam's fall, that intended dominion was never completely realized, the very point which the writer of Hebrews is making. But that perfect dominion has now been guaranteed in the work of Jesus Christ, the Second Adam. It is this world "whereof we speak," the world that was never subjected to angels, but was, in the beginning, made subject to Adam and his descendants, and because of the fall was only successfully brought under subjugation by the work of the incarnate Son of God.

The way the writer refers to this O.T. quotation seems strange to us today: "But one in a certain place testified, saying," and then he gives the quotation from Ps. 8:6-8. Two things may help us understand why he refers to the O.T. in this manner. First, we must remember that the ancient Scriptures were not divided up into chapters and verses, as we now have them, until the 1500s. Second, since he was writing to Hebrew people, he would expect them to know where a familiar passage of Scripture is found without making more than general reference to it. His method of referring to this passage certainly should not be taken as an indication of a lack of scriptural knowledge on his part. His scholarship and familiarity with the O.T. are shown by his numerous quotations to prove the various points that he presents. Throughout the seven quotations the writer has referred to in chapter 1, he does not give any indication even as to the book where they are found. In other places he refers to the human author in quoting a passage (Moses, for example, in 7:14; 8:5; 12:21). In quoting Ps. 95:7-11 (Heb. 3:7-11) he refers to "the Holy Ghost" as the divine author; but, when he refers to the same passage again in Heb. 4:7, he mentions David as the human author.

Now, to continue to make his point of the superiority of Christ to angels, the writer quotes Ps. 8:6-8. Psalm 8 is titled "a psalm of David." Like many O.T. passages that have Messianic significance, there was a more immediate purpose in the mind of the original writer when he, under inspiration, composed the passage. Indeed, it was not necessary for Scripture writers to understand fully the depths of the meaning of their words or their future application. With regard to Psalm 8, it appears that David originally spoke about the amazing care, trust, and responsibility which God committed to man from the very beginning (Gen. 1:26-28), even though, from man's point of view, we can seem very small and insignificant. His were the very thoughts you would expect from a young shepherd as he sat out under a clear, star-filled sky, thinking deep thoughts about his relationship with the Lord.

David asked, and the writer of Hebrews quotes: "What is man, that thou art mindful of him? or the son of man, that thou visitest him?" The deists, who were often prominent in the early days of America (Benjamin Franklin, Thomas Jefferson, etc.), said that God created the universe, but then left it to operate on the basis of natural laws that He ordained. They would never see Him interfering with or caring about the lives of His creatures. In the midst of his overwhelming feeling of smallness, the psalmist too wondered why God would care. "Man" and "the son of man" are two different ways of referring to human beings, the highest order of God's creation, and the only ones made in His own image. (Such poetic repetition is in line with the common use of parallelism in Hebrew poetry.) The psalmist does not agree with the deists. As hard as it may be to understand, though God is so big and we are so small, He does care, and the psalmist knows the writings of Moses well enough to know that.

Psalm 8:6 questions why God would ever care about small, feeble, paltry man. But Ps. 8:7, 8 replies by telling just how much God does care, beginning with "Thou madest him a little lower than the angels." The words refer to original creation. To understand the meaning, we may add two words for clarification: "*Yet* thou madest him *only* a little lower than the angels." "Yet" provides the contrast which the psalmist intends between his previous observation about man's seeming insignificance in relation to God and his presentation of the true picture, according to the account of creation. "Only" brings out the fact of man's rank in the created order: "only a little lower than the angels." Some commentators have wanted to translate "a little lower" (Greek *brachu ti*) with regard to time, "For a little while lower" (NASB), rather than "a little lower," which indicates rank. But there is no reason for this since both the psalmist and the writer of Hebrews, in quoting him, do mean to indicate man's rank in the order of creation. Even though he applies the same phrase a little later to Christ, he is still speaking of rank in the created order since Christ took upon Himself the true nature of man.

David further describes God's unbelievable care for mankind: "Thou crownedst him with glory and honour." In Gen. 1:26 Moses tells us, "And God said, Let us make man in our image, after our likeness." Out of all the wonderful creatures that God made, only man was made in His image. He immediately gave Adam a visual aid in understanding man's high position when He had him examine all the animals to see that they were not like him, that there was no suitable companion for him among the animals. Note that God did this before He made Eve as Adam's companion in marriage (Gen. 2:18-22). How different this is from the humanist's fanciful story of man's orgin through evolution!

The psalmist further describes the trust that God placed in the hands of man: "And didst set him over the works of thy hands: Thou hast put all things in subjection under his feet." This thought also reflects Gen. 1:26: "Let them have dominion over the fish of the sea, and over the fowl of the air, and over the cattle, and over all the earth, and over every creeping thing that creepeth upon the earth." God's original intention was for man to have complete dominion, in the fullest sense of the word, over all other aspects of His creation.

The writer of Hebrews clearly realizes that the psalmist is referring to Gen. 1:26 and the account of creation. He shows his wise understanding of both David and Moses when he observes, "For in that he put all in subjection under him, he left nothing *that is not* put under him." The writer of Hebrews correctly perceives that there was absolutely nothing in the created order of things that was exempt from this command for total dominion. We must stress, however, that that was God's *original* intention for man, not what actually happened. The sad truth is that the tragedy of Genesis 3 stands in the way of man's realization of his divinely intended goal. Adam, through his rebellion and disobedience, fell from his perfect position, and he and Eve and all their descendants justly reaped the promised consequences of their fall, immediate spiritual death as revealed in their alienation from God (Gen. 2:17; 3:8), and ultimate physical death as manifested in the oft-repeated phrase in Genesis 5, "And he died" (Gen. 5:5).

Thus, on the one hand, we have God's ideal goal for man, as stated in Psalm 8, based upon Moses' declaration in Gen. 1:26. On the other hand, we have reality, as we know it today, by just looking and listening concerning the daily manifestations of the failure of Adam and his descendants to exercise dominion. Accordingly, the writer concludes, "But now we see not yet all things put under him." If this was apparent in our writer's day, it seems even more clear today, with the abundant presence of immorality, rebellion, and disobedience. There are so many characteristics presently evident from Paul's description of "the last days" when "perilous times shall come" (2 Tim. 3:1-5), that an excellent case can be made for believing that those days are upon us. His charge is so unarguable that he is not even concerned about giving evidence or examples. He knows that his reading audience will fully concur. Perhaps the greatest illustration of all, however, with regard to man's failure to subdue his environment is the ever prevailing presence of "the grim reaper." In spite of the wonderful advances of modern medicine, and the blessing of complete or near complete victory over numerous fatal diseases, death always finds another door. As God promised, all of man's life he battles with the earth to pull his living from the soil, and the earth only reluctantly yields her life-giving fruit. Then the earth claims final victory when, in death, man's body is returned to the ground (Gen. 3:19).

In light of this failure of Adam and his descendants, we are dramatically introduced to the Second Adam in these words, "But we see Jesus, who was made a little lower than the angels." This is the first occurrence of our Lord's human name in the book, and the use is intentional. The eternal Son of God was not always "Jesus"; that is the name of the incarnate Son. Since this epistle emphasizes the redeeming and priestly work of Christ, our writer delights in frequent use of our Lord's human name (3:1; 6:20; 7:22; 10:19; 12:2, 24; 13:12). It is in this role only, as the incarnate Son, that He becomes our Savior. The writer deliberately applies a key phrase from Ps. 8:5 to Jesus, observing that He, too, like the original Adam, was made "a little lower than the angels." When the phrase was applied to the first Adam, it appeared to place him in an exalted position, "a little lower than the angels." But when that same phrase is applied to the incarnate Son, it appears to humiliate Him in contrast to the relation with the Father which He had throughout eternity. But the primary purpose of the phrase, as applied to Christ, is to say that He was truly and fully human.

The Authorized Version, by its positioning of the comma, seems to place the phrase, "for the suffering of death," with the preceding statement, "made a little lower than the angels." That would appear to mean that the phrase states the specific purpose for which Jesus was made a little lower than the angels. However, "for" (Greek *dia*) means "because of," not "in order that." Thus most interpreters feel that it is better to apply the phrase to the following statement about Christ, "crowned with glory and honour." He was crowned with glory and honor because of the suffering of death. Such was the Father's appropriate reward for the obedience and sacrifice of His incarnate Son (Bruce 39;

Lenski 76; Gaebelein 26; Delitzsch I:111). Elsewhere the exaltation takes place after the humiliation (see Phil. 4:9; Heb. 12:2; Jn. 13:31), and that seems the most logical way to take the meaning here. Christ's final victory when death is completely destroyed will yet be manifested at His Second Coming (1 Cor. 15:24-26).

The writer describes Christ's redemptive work as occurring "by the grace of God." Jesus did not die for men because they had earned it or deserved it. "Grace" refers to "unmerited favor." Men do not deserve the great benefit that Christ provided for them through His death and resurrection. If Christ had waited until we earned such favor, He would never have died. Yet in His great love (see 1 Jn. 4:10) it was the Father's will that He "should taste death for every man." The word *taste* is in no way meant to lessen the horrible fact of Christ's death (see also Mt. 16:28 and Jn. 8:52). To the contrary, it is likely that the use of this word intensifies the meaning of His redemptive act. He "tasted" death in its complete and most awful manifestation. He did not just devour it, as a hungry dog does his food, with hardly any awareness of its flavor. He did not just nibble at it and spit it out. He experienced the cup of death to its fullest and bitterest extent (Westcott 46).

The writer makes clear the identity of the recipients of the benefits of Christ's death: it was "for every man." "For" (Greek *huper*) means "for the benefit of," not "in the place of"—although there are some things that one cannot do for another's benefit without taking his place, and Jesus' death for us was such a thing. Christ died, not just for mankind in general, but, more specifically and emphatically, for each and "every man" as an individual. "Every man" (Greek *pantos*) is masculine, not neuter. If it were neuter, it would refer to every thing, which would include angels, and that would contradict Heb. 2:16 (Lunemann 116). Though Christ's redemptive work will ultimately result in the restoration of all creation, even the material world, to its former glory (see Rom. 8:19-23), that is not what the writer is stressing here; rather, he is placing emphasis on the personal objects of Christ's work. No one is excluded except those who exclude themselves by refusing Christ. The provision has already been made. The debt has been paid in full. All that is left is for the pardon to be accepted. Arthur Pink (110), in an attempt to defend his view of limited atonement, maintains that "for every man" should be translated "for every one," referring to "every one of those who form the subjects of the whole passage—every one of 'the heirs of salvation' (1:14), every one of the 'sons' (2:10), every one of the 'brethren' (2:11)." It is difficult, however, to see how "every one" makes this statement about the scope of Christ's atonement any more limited than "every man." "Every one" includes each and every individual as much as "every man" does. Pink's interpretation makes a great deal of reading between the lines necessary. It is better to take the writer at his word, and also to see this statement in line with other passages in the N.T. concerning the universal atonement of the death of Christ (Mk. 10:45; Jn. 3:16; 1 Tim. 2:6; 2 Pet. 3:9; 1 Jn. 2:2). Pink also argues that, if "every one" means every single individual, then everyone should be saved, everyone should go to Heaven, since Jesus tasted death for all, without exception (110). But Pink willingly ignores the clear condition for salvation which is emphasized throughout the N.T., including the epistle to the Hebrews. That clear condition is faith. Though Jesus clearly died for all, the benefits of His death do not apply to those who do not accept it by faith (Jn. 1:12; 3:16, 18, 36; Acts 16:31; Rom. 4:3-5; 10:9, 10; Eph. 2:8, 9). In Hebrews the writer warns against "an evil heart of unbelief" (3:12); he also declares, "We which have believed do enter into rest" (4:3), and he urges them to be "followers of them who through faith and patience inherit the promises" (6:12). So it is throughout the epistle: faith is the sole condition of salvation, and without it no one will be saved even though Christ provided salvation for them through His death and resurrection. Perhaps the Apostle Paul puts it best when he points to Jesus Christ as "the Saviour of all men, specially of those that believe" (1 Tim. 4:10).

b. To experience and conquer suffering and death (2:10-18)

In vv. 5-9 the writer has pointed out how Jesus Christ came to obtain man's destiny as the second Adam. The first Adam, because of the fall, failed to have dominion over all of God's creation as God originally intended (Gen. 1:26). Perhaps the most pointed example of man's failure to have dominion is in the permeation of death throughout society. Each time we have a funeral, we are reminded of this failure. In light of this, God sent Jesus, His Son, to experience and conquer suffering and death on behalf of all mankind.

(1) By making the captain of our salvation perfect (2:10-13)

10 For it became him, for whom *are* all things, and by whom *are* all things, in bringing many sons unto glory, to make the captain of their salvation perfect through sufferings.
11 For both he that sanctifieth and they who are sanctified *are* all of one: for which cause he is not ashamed to call them brethren,
12 Saying, I will declare thy name unto my brethren, in the midst of the church will I sing praise unto thee.
13 And again, I will put my trust in him. And again, Behold I and the children which God hath given me.

At the end of v. 9, Jesus, the incarnate Son, is the one who tasted death for every man. But v. 10 calls for a change of subject. Here the writer is referring to God the Father. "For it became him" refers to that which was fitting or proper for God the Father in the work of salvation. Though similar statements could be made about the eternal Son (Heb. 1:2), "for whom *are* all things, and by whom *are* all things" in this verse must of necessity refer to the Father. This phrase is more literally translated, "Because of whom . . . and through whom are all things." "All things" calls our attention back to v. 8, in the quotation from Psalm 8:6. The reference is to all the works of God's hand. When God created all things, He did so for His own sake and through the power of His own hand. He was both the reason and the means of creation, both the cause and the agent. "In bringing many sons into glory" is our writer's way in this verse of describing the action of God the Father in redemption. "Many sons" stands in contrast to "for every man" in v. 9. Christ's death potentially provided the means of salvation for every single individual, but the actual realization of salvation, by man's own choosing, will be experienced only by "many sons" (Lenski 79). In previous verses the writer has presented Christ as the eternal Son (1:2, 5, 8), and now, through the redemptive work of the Son, the Father wills to bring other sons "into glory." The "glory" which these sons will share is the same glory which was given to the Son, in v. 9, as a result of His tasting death for every man.

The "bringing" (Greek aorist participle) of the many sons into glory took place at the same time that the Father sought "to make the captain of their salvation perfect through sufferings" (Westcott 48). That Jesus was to be made "perfect" does not mean moral perfection, since the incarnate Son was never morally imperfect. It points rather to the attainment of a goal specified by the context. Here it refers to His qualification for His role of Redeemer and High Priest of mankind. The eternal Son became the incarnate Son (Jn. 1:14) so that He might feel as we feel when He experienced all of our circumstances, enduring all the sinless infirmities of humanity (hunger, thirst, weariness, etc.). In our own day, to say that someone is not qualified for a specific job is no reflection on that person's moral character. He could, in fact, be well qualified for many other roles, but not for this specific one. The eternal Son, the almighty, all-knowing, ever-present second member of the Divine Trinity, could not in that role obtain redemption for man. Thus, He willingly became a man so that He might become "the captain of their salvation."

"Captain" (Greek *archegos*) can also be translated author, leader, pioneer, pathfinder, etc. It speaks of one who starts something, who blazes a trail which others will follow. The term does not tell us everything about the work of Christ, but it does tell of one very important aspect of His work: the means through which God the Father would make our Captain perfect is "through suffering." This "suffering," which led to His ultimate perfection, to His full qualification for His redemptive task, involved all the sinless aspects of human suffering. It began with His birth of humble parentage in Bethlehem, and included such circumstances as Herod's attempt to kill the baby, Satan's three major tests of His character at the beginning of His ministry, efforts of the Jewish leadership to take His life, and finally, His arrest, mock trial, beating, and crucifixion.

"For" in v. 11 advances the argument a step farther. Jesus Christ took upon Himself a true human nature. As mankind suffers in its humanity, so Christ has taken upon Himself that role as Son of Man. We suffer, and He suffers, though His suffering has much deeper meaning than ours. His suffering was vicarious, suffering in the place of and for the benefit of others.

"He that sanctifieth and they who are sanctified" is, literally, "The one who is sanctifying and those who are being sanctified." The emphasis on continuous action (Greek present participles) is important here. The work of sanctification is a continuing work. "To sanctify" means to set apart for special and sacred purposes, to make a person pure and holy in the image of God. In Scripture the doctrine of sanctification unfolds in three steps. *Initial* sanctification takes place in the purifying work of the Holy Spirit at the time of salvation (2 Cor. 5:17). *Progressive* sanctification takes place throughout the life of a Christian (Rom. 8:28, 29); it is also referred to as "growing in grace" (2 Pet. 3:18). This is the element of sanctification that the writer stresses in this verse. *Final* sanctification will become a reality only when we see Christ (1 Jn. 3:2); at that time the process of changing us into His image will be complete. Christ is here presented as the sanctifying agent who continues to do His purifying work in our hearts as our relationship to Him grows; and as a result we, the objects of His work, are "being sanctified," growing progressively more like Him as we mature in our Christian walk (Westcott 50)

The writer declares that both Christ and Christians, both the agent and the objects, are "all of one." Who is the "one" that both we and Christ are from? It cannot be Abraham (Bengel, so Lunemann 125), for that would not be inclusive of all humanity. Lenski (85) thinks that it must refer to Adam since saying that we all come from God would include angels, for whom Christ provided no redemption. However, Lenski is ignoring the context. The writer is not speaking about angels any more than about animals, which were also created by God. He is speaking only of Christ and saved human beings. The most obvious source from which both Christ and Christians come is God the Father. Jesus Christ came from God the Father because He is His Son, and we came from the Father physically through creation and spiritually through the new birth (Delitzsch 121; Lunemann 125; Bruce 45; Westcott 50).

The writer further stresses our common fellowship with the Son: "For which cause he is not ashamed to call them brethren." "For which cause" refers to our common origin. Since Christians and Christ both come from God, though admittedly in somewhat different ways, we are in the same family. Therefore, "he is not ashamed to call them brethren." If we are children of the same Father, then it is only logical that Christ can relate to us as brothers. The fact that He is willing to look upon us as brothers speaks of a closer relationship to Him and thus enhances His work for us as our High Priest.

In v. 12 the writer backs up his claim that Christ is not ashamed to call us "brothers" with three quotations from the O.T. The first quotation is from Ps. 22:22, evidently written by David during the difficult days of suffering when Saul was pursuing him in the wilderness. The N.T. writers saw David, in his role as the king of Israel, as the type of the greater King Jesus who was to come, the ultimate heir to the throne of David. The fact that Ps. 22 was considered clearly Messianic is shown in its being quoted or referred to four times in the account of the crucifixion of Christ: (1) when the Roman soldiers divided His garments (Mt. 27:35; Ps. 22:18); (2) when the passersby mocked Christ on the cross (Mt. 27:39; Ps. 22:7); (3) when they continued to mock His trust in the Lord (Mt. 27:43; Ps. 22:8); and, finally, (4) on the very lips of our Lord Himself when He questioned why God had forsaken Him (Mt. 27:46; Ps. 22:1). This last quotation was considered so important that the Gospel writer recorded the words in Aramaic, the language which Jesus regularly spoke.

The quotation cited in this context is meant to show us that the Divine Messiah-King is most willing to bring Himself to our level. The words come from the mouth of David's heir: "I will declare thy name unto my brethren." The "name" is the personal name of Jehovah or Yahweh ("I AM"—Ex. 3:14), which God's Son knows better than any other. Since the "name" of God in the O.T. stood for the fullness of God's character and attributes, to "declare His name" would mean to describe and illustrate His covenant relationship to His people. Christ did that throughout His earthly ministry for those whom He was willing to call His "brethren." These brethren would include believers of all ages, those under the old covenant as well as those under the new, since Jesus' ministry and death brought salvation to all. An illustration of this very relationship of our Lord with His immediate disciples is seen in Jn. 20:17 where He commissions Mary Magdalene, "Go tell my brethren."

The quotation continues: "In the midst of the church will I sing praise unto thee." The "church" (Greek *ekklesia*) in the original quotation would refer to the worshiping congregation of Israel with whom King David gladly and humbly participated (2 Sam. 6:12-19). The word *church* appears in the O.T. quotation because our writer always quotes from the Septuagint, the Greek translation of the O.T. The truthful application of this typical prophecy was borne out in Jesus' regular and faithful participation in public worship with the common people, both in the Temple (Lk. 2:40-50) and in the synagogue (Lk. 4:16-32). Thus Jesus, like David, fulfilled the promise, "I will sing praise unto thee."

The quotations cited in v. 13 are from Is. 8:17, 18. As David's words pointed to the fulfillment of Christ's role as King, so Isaiah's words pointed to the fulfillment of Christ's role as Prophet. In the first quotation (Is. 8:17, as always from the Septuagint), Christ in His role as Prophet says, "I will put my trust in him." Jesus, in His incarnate ministry on earth, led faithful believers in placing their faith and trust in God. In his humanity Christ constantly depended on strength and guidance from the Father. Think of the occasion when Satan cast his worst temptations at Christ (see Mt. 4:1-11), when Jesus faithfully quoted God's Word to rebuke the devil, and when it was over "angels came and ministered unto him" (Mt. 4:11); or when He uttered His agonizing cries in Gethsemane and prayed, "Father . . . not as I will, but as thou *wilt*" (Mt. 26:39). In many other situations Christ demonstrated His absolute trust in the Father.

If Jesus, like Isaiah, led others in trusting God, in like manner He gave thanks for His disciples as for His "children": "Behold I and the children whom God hath given me." The Gospel accounts of Christ's life on earth clearly show that He held both a brotherly and a fatherly relation with His followers. In His ability to intercede for us, He, too, had to place His trust in God; but in His ability to sustain us in time of need, He is our fatherly provider. One of the most outstanding places where Jesus prayed for His disciples as for children was in His high priestly prayer in John 17. In 17:9 He prayed for His immediate disciples ("I pray for them: I pray not for the world"), and in 17:20 He prayed for all of His future disciples, including us ("Neither pray I for these alone"). It is this priestly care that the writer of Hebrews is emphasizing at this point. Like Isaiah of old, the prophetic Messianic type, Jesus also recognized that only God can produce children. The Messiah gives thanks for the children "whom God has given me." Again, the similarity to Christ's own words in the closing days of His ministry is surely more than coincidental. In Jn. 17:6 He mentions "the men which thou gavest me out of the world." Isaiah's physical children were a gift of God, but the true spiritual children, the believers, are just as much a product of God's work. God uses us as His instruments in producing both, but the children are indeed a gift of God.

(2) By Jesus' partaking of flesh and blood as we do (2:14-18)

14 Forasmuch then as the children are partakers of flesh and blood, he also himself likewise took part of the same; that through death he might destroy him that had the power of death, that is, the devil;
15 And deliver them who through fear of death were all their lifetime subject to bondage.
16 For verily he took not on *him the nature of* angels; but he took on *him* the seed of Abraham.
17 Wherefore in all things it behoved him to be made like unto *his* brethren, that he might be a merciful and faithful high priest in things *pertaining* to God, to make reconciliation for the sins of the people.
18 For in that he himself hath suffered being tempted, he is able to succour them that are tempted.

The writer now goes back to his main subject, which he introduced in 2:9, 10: the subject of Christ's becoming a man so that He might be the Captain of our salvation. "Forasmuch then," literally, "since therefore," makes this previous connection. The idea of referring to believers as "the children" is a continuation from the quotation of Is. 8:18 in the previous verse. The word used here for "the children" (Greek *paidia*) views believers as being loved and cared for. It might be translated "dear children." The declaration that the children "are partakers" is, more literally, "have partaken" or "have become partakers." The word indicates a partaking that began in the past and continues to the present (Greek perfect tense). The word itself describes a group of participants who have partaken of something that is common to all (Greek *koinoneo*). He is referring, of course, to that human nature which all men have possessed ever since Adam. This humanity is described as "flesh and blood," in some manuscripts "blood and flesh." This order ("flesh and blood") also appears in Eph. 6:12; when "blood" is placed up front, it may stress its priority as the highest symbol of life (Lev. 17:11). The more usual order, "flesh and blood," occurs several times in the N.T. (Mt. 16:17; 1 Cor. 15:50; Gal. 1:16). Whichever is first, the two expressions together stand for a person's true humanity, without any intention of discounting the importance of the soul or spirit (Lenski 89).

If humanity can best be described as partakers of "flesh and blood," Christ must duplicate that fact in His life if He is to be our Redeemer. The writer emphasizes that duplication by using the term "likewise." As all men since Adam had partaken of this nature, Christ must do the same. But a different word is used here to say that Christ "took part" (Greek *metecho*). In contrast to the word used for mankind's obligatory partaking of true human nature, this word indicates that Christ's partaking of the same nature was fully voluntary. He had no personal obligation to become a man, or to provide redemption for us. Rather He willingly did it because of the love of the Father and Himself for lost mankind (Westcott 52).

The last statement in this verse, combined with v. 15, emphasizes two of the main purposes of the incarnation: (1) to destroy the one who had the power of death, and (2) to provide freedom for those who cowered under the threat and fear of death. Paradoxically, the means of destroying the one who had the power of death was "through death." Note that he does not say "through *his* death," but (literally) "through the death." Of course, there is no question that it was *His* death, but here the writer places the emphasis on death itself, on the fact that death became the means of destruction for both death and the devil. In the 1860s, through his brilliant research, French scientist Louis Pasteur discovered one of the most valuable facts in medical history. He discovered the preventive and healing power of immunization, the process of taking a specially treated and weakened form of the actual germ, which was causing a disease, and inoculating the patient for either prevention or cure. Afflictions which have been cured or prevented by immunization include smallpox, diphtheria, measles, snakebite, etc. The truth of this great discovery existed long before Pasteur's work. The process works because it is part of God's great creation plan. In a real sense we can say that Jesus Christ used this same process in providing our redemption. He destroyed death through death, and thus he immunizes all believers from the dreadful and eternal effects of the most terrible disease of all, spiritual death.

Christ died on the cross and rose victorious over the grave so that "he might destroy him that had the power of death, that is, the devil." Some might question the writer's declaration concerning the destruction of Satan since, according to other Scriptures, he still seems to be doing his dastardly work. Paul refers to him as "the prince of the power of the air" (Eph. 2:2), and he warns the Ephesians against "the wiles of the devil" (6:11). Peter records that he as "a roaring lion, walketh about, seeking whom he may devour" (1 Pet. 5:8). The devil's ultimate destruction is still future. Paul reveals to us that Christ's present reign will continue until every enemy has been put under His feet. Then he explains, "The last enemy *that* shall be destroyed *is* death" (1 Cor. 15:25, 26). Since the ultimate destruction of death and Satan is yet in the future (see also Rev. 20:1-3, 10), instead of "destroy" (Greek *katargeo*) here, we might better translate, "put out of commission" (Lenski 88), or "render powerless" (NASB). Paul marks the certainty of this ultimate fulfillment, however, by declaring that Christ "hath abolished death, and hath brought life and immortality to light through the gospel" (2 Tim. 1:10).

In the death and resurrection of Christ the devil has been robbed of his most potent weapon, the threat of death: not only physical death, but, most of all, spiritual and eternal death. The "hornet," the "scorpion" of death is still with us for a while, but his "stinger" has been pulled (1 Cor. 15:55). "Him that had the power of death" is, literally, "the one having" (Greek present participle). In one sense, he had the power of death but is no longer in control; and, in another sense, he still has it until the last enemy is destroyed (Westcott 53). It is also important to realize that "the power of death" primarily refers to the power of spiritual and eternal death. It is this meaning that the Scripture almost always emphasizes when speaking about death as the penalty of sin. For example, in the first such reference in Scripture, God said to Adam concerning the tree of knowledge, "In the day that thou eatest thereof thou shalt surely die" (Gen. 2:17). If God primarily meant physical death, the warning did not occur as God said, for Adam actually lived to be 930 years of age (Gen. 5:5). It is obvious that God primarily referred to spiritual death, separation from God, as the penalty of sin (Rom. 6:23; 1 Cor. 15:22; Rev. 21:8). In this sense Adam died immediately when he disobeyed God's command, and the signs of his death were evident in his failure to meet God for fellowship "in the cool of the day" (Gen. 3:8). Thus we understand our Lord's statement to Martha after the death of Lazarus, "Whosoever liveth and believeth in me shall never die" (Jn. 11:26). Physical death is only a secondary by-product. From the point of view of scriptural teaching, spiritual life and spiritual death are the real thing (1 Jn. 3:14).

The "power" (Greek *kratos*) the devil wields with regard to death refers to absolute and potentially destructive power. Such was the power that Satan, the evil one, held over all mankind prior to the death and resurrection of Christ. Our writer makes no attempt to prove that the devil has such power. After all, he was writing to Hebrew Christians who knew all about the story of the fall in Genesis 3. However, Satan does not possess this power directly, but rather indirectly through the entrance of sin into the human race. In a similar way Jesus did not challenge the devil's claim to "all the kingdoms of the world" in the temptation account. Satan rules over the realm of life and death, and the realm of the world's ownership, by usurpation. It is a realm that he controls through no right of his own, but rather through the choice of Adam and his heirs (Rom. 5:12). But Christ has won that right of control back to Himself through the power of His death and resurrection (Westcott 53).

The writer of Hebrews identifies the one who holds the power of death as "the devil" (Greek *diabolos*). This is the Greek name of the wicked one used by the writers of the N.T. The word refers to one who "casts something at, by, or through someone." Thus, the name "devil" highlights Satan's wicked role as "the accuser." Paul uses the same term to mean "slanderers" with regard to what should not be true of deacon's wives (1 Tim. 3:11). In Revelation there is great rejoicing at the end of time because "the accuser of our brethren is cast down" (Rev. 12:10). Though the same Greek word is not used there, the devil is identified in his pernicious work as the accuser. Satan in the role of accuser is described in some detail in his appearances before God in Job 1 and 2; compare Zech. 3:1, 2. If he could, he would turn almighty God against His own children. The Hebrew name, used constantly in the O.T., is Satan. This name pictures the wicked one as "the adversary, the opponent, the enemy."

He always stands in opposition to our serving God, and he would do his best to destroy our faith and turn us away from God. Though some N.T. writers use this term also, the writer of Hebrews never does. Interestingly, Rev. 12:9 puts the various names used for the wicked one together in one statement so that the identity of the person described should not be in doubt.

In 2:15 the word translated "deliver" (Greek *apallasso*) means to change from one state or attitude to another, and in that sense to deliver, release, or set free from the previous condition (Delitzsch I:134). The objects of this deliverance, through Christ's death and resurrection, are those "who through fear of death" were in bondage. It is better to see this phrase more as a limitation than merely a description, especially in light of v. 16, where our writer will explain that angels, who are not subject to death as we are, are excluded from the benefits of Christ's death. Therefore, although it involves a limitation, its inclusion is nonetheless very broad: the entire human race. The fear of death may be more powerful to some than to others, but to every human being it is a reality. The miserable existence for mankind through this fear of death is heightened by the time involved. Those so affected "were all their lifetime" in this condition. This phrase actually translates an action rather than an abstraction: literally, "were during all their living." There is never a moment that man lives when he can be completely free from this paralyzing fear. Even in the midst of his happiest moments, if he will be realistic, this awful fear is in the back of his mind.

And what a fear it is! It makes all of mankind "subject to bondage." Unredeemed man deals with this terrible bondage in different ways. Some treat it philosophically, expressing willingness to accept their fate unflinchingly. Some seek the explanation of false religion, always with vague and unsatisfying solutions to the problem. Others choose outright denial or avoidance of the subject. But all such "solutions" deal only with the symptoms, not with the disease. Christ, through His own death and resurrection, guaranteed the death of death, immediately in relation to the primary meaning of death—that is, spiritual death—and ultimately in relation to physical death, which is only the secondary culprit (Rom. 7:24; 8:15; 2 Tim. 1:10). Joseph Tong, a Romanian pastor, illustrates the truth of this Scripture well in a story about a fellow pastor during the days of severe communist persecution in Romania. An arrogant military commander reminded the pastor that his very life was in his hands, that he could have him executed with only a word. God gave the Romanian pastor wonderful grace, and he replied, "Sir, do you know what happens to a Christian when he dies? He goes to glory. Sir, you cannot threaten me with glory." For those who know Christ, we are no longer subject to the threatening fear and bondage of death.

In v. 16 "verily" (Greek *depou*) is strongly emphatic, introducing the writer's declaration with regard to the purpose of Christ's death. He has said much up to this point concerning the ministry of angels in God's plan of revelation and redemption. There is disagreement here in translating the negated verb, "he took not on" (Greek *epilambanomai*). Our translators, in consideration of the broader context of Christ's incarnation, supplied the words "*him the nature of*," to make this declaration apply to that also (so also some modern interpreters, e.g. Morris 29). But the writer has introduced the narrower purpose of Christ's coming in vv. 14, 15, to destroy the devil and give life and spiritual freedom to those who had lived in fear of death. Thus, it is better to take the more natural meaning in the context, "He took not on angels," to say, "He did not help angels." To "take on" in this context means "to help" (NASB; NIV; Lenski 92; Westcott 54; Lunemann 131). NIV translates, "For surely it is not angels he helps, but Abraham's descendants." In spite of the exalted estate of angels in God's plan, the writer, in line with both Peter and Jude (2 Pet. 2:4; Jude 6), declares that God made no provision for their redemption in Christ's death. His purpose rather was "to help," "to redeem" "the seed of Abraham." The writer does not mean to say that Christ died *only* for "the seed of Abraham," the Jews, but that He died especially for them. He says this because he is writing to the Hebrew believers in this church who are considering abandoning Christ under duress of severe trials (Lunemann 131, Lenski 92). At times N.T. writers point to "the seed of Abraham" in a broader sense, referring to all the children of faith (Gal. 3:28, 29), but that is probably not the meaning here (but see Westcott 55).

In 2:17 "wherefore" points to the declaration in v. 16. If Christ would "help" the Hebrew people, if He would provide redemption for them, and the rest of mankind as well, He must "be made like unto his brethren." "It behoved him" states the absolute necessity of the incarnation if eternal redemption would be possible. It does not mean that He was coerced into doing what He was not willing to do (see Jn. 10:17, 18). It means, rather, that if He would bring redemption to mankind willingly, there was only one method by which it might be attained: He had to become one of them. In this there was no choice. The extent of His incarnation is measured in the words "in all things" (Greek *kata panta*). This does not mean that there could be no exception to this likeness, such as His sinlessness (see 4:15), or His unique virgin birth (Mt. 1:23). The writer is merely saying that Christ was truly and fully human, that He was able to experience the depth of human passions and the frustrations of human limitation.

The purpose of this similarity between Christ and us was that "he might be a merciful and faithful high priest in things pertaining to God." Of all the N.T. writers, only this one presents Christ in the role of priest or high priest. But for Him it is our Lord's main function. Christ becomes the perfect fulfillment of all the goals of the O.T. priesthood, so inadequately met by the officeholders themselves. In John 17 Christ speaks as fulfilling this role, though He is not referred to as high priest there. The priestly office called for the priest to minister toward the people and toward the Lord. They served as mediators to bring together sinful man and a holy God. Such efforts of the O.T. priests were weakened by the sinfulness of the men who held the office. Christ bore no such inadequacies, but He also fulfilled this double role. In regard to His relationship to men, He is "merciful." Sharing our feelings, He is able to exercise compassion toward our needs; and in taking those needs to His heavenly Father, He is "faithful" (Lenski 94). We can believe implicitly that He will always represent our best interests.

The area of His redemptive concern is narrow. It is "in things pertaining to God." His ministry is primarily concerning our spiritual needs. That does not mean that He does not care about the whole person, but it does mean that He knows that the primary need of mankind is spiritual, not physical, emotional, or financial. Thus Jesus refused to show interest or provide help to the man who wanted his brother to divide the inheritance with him (Lk. 12:13, 14). The writer, in fact, narrows our Lord's priestly purpose even further: "to make reconciliation for the sins of the people." "To make reconciliation" (Greek *hilaskesthai*) might be better translated "to expiate the sins of the people." The writer presents the act of expiation in continuous action (Greek present infinitive), emphasizing the ongoing effectiveness of Christ's death to those who receive the benefit. We must be careful to avoid any idea that God was somehow internally affected by Christ's death on the cross, that any essential attribute of God was somehow changed. The expiation had to do with our sins, not with any shortcoming on God's part. God's attitude of love and His demand for holiness have never changed. He has always loved us with an everlasting love, but His absolute holiness would allow no ongoing relationship with us in our sins. The necessary reaction of God to our sinfulness is His wrath (Mt. 3:7; Rom. 1:18). Through Christ's substitutionary death our sins were actually paid for and the wrath of God has been turned away (Rom. 5:9; 1 Th. 5:9). Through faith in Christ His absolute righteousness is applied to us so that a holy God is able to look with favor on us and exercise toward us the love that has been there all along. It is not God who has changed; it is the sinner who has been changed by the sacrifice of Christ (Westcott 57; Lenski 95; Morris 30).

Christ made this expiation "for the sins of the people." "The people" in the context of Hebrews refers to the entire nation of Israel. That does not mean that Christ's death did not include Gentiles, but here the writer's immediate concern is about the nation of Israel. If Israel, God's own covenant people, needed this expiation for their sins, then how much more the Gentiles, who previously were not a people (see Rom. 9:24-26).

Furthermore, Christ as our High Priest is able to continue to provide for us beyond the mere point of salvation, "for in that he himself hath suffered being tempted, he is able to succour them that are tempted." Christ's entire ministry involved a series of temptations, from Satan's three efforts at the beginning of His ministry right on to His emotional sufferings in Gethsemane, as well as the sufferings of the cross itself. Some are bothered by the idea that Christ was tempted, perhaps because they wish to avoid the idea that He had any inclination toward sin. The truth is that His temptation was even worse than ours. As sinners, we often yield before experiencing the entire force of the temptation. As the sinless sufferer, He did not yield and thus received the whole weight of everything Satan could throw at him (MacArthur 71). We should also note that the word translated "tempt" (Greek *peirazo*) can also be translated "test." Because He experienced our sufferings without yielding to our sin, He is a very sufficient High

Priest, "able to succour them that are tempted." The old English "to succor" means "to help." His continuous and sufficient provision is for "those who are being tempted." As long as we are in this life, we are always in a battle with the world, the flesh, and the devil. But as our temptations are continuous and troublesome, so His help is always continuous and effective.

Summary (2:1-18)

The writer begins chapter 2 with his first of five warnings throughout the epistle. Each of the warnings is of the most serious nature. This first one is against neglecting the superior revelation they have received. He makes an emphatic contrast between the word spoken by angels, the O.T. law, and the Word "which at the first began to be spoken by the Lord": that is, the gospel message. He implies that the punishment would be much more severe for disregarding the gospel, the message of the N.T., than for disregarding the commandments of the law, though that in itself was severe (2:1-4).

He goes on to discuss the necessity and propriety of the humiliation of Christ. To make his point about the necessity of the incarnation, the writer employs a unique approach. He quotes from Psalm 8, which was itself based on the creation account in Genesis, concerning God's original design for man to have dominion over all of God's creation. Then he points out that it is obvious that man has never attained that design. At that point the writer makes a dramatic declaration, "But we see Jesus." Thus, he presents Jesus Christ in the role of the Second Adam who came to succeed where the first Adam failed. Jesus would gain this dominion over the world that God made, the world which was so drastically affected by the fall, by tasting "death for every man," by meeting death on its home court, so to speak, and defeating it with a complete and absolute victory (2:5-9).

However, in order to face and defeat death in such a convincing manner, the eternal Son of God had to become a man, had to become a partaker of "flesh and blood." He became "the captain of our salvation" in order to lead the way by means of His own suffering and death, not just as an example for us in suffering, but as a substitutionary atonement so that we may have eternal life. By becoming one of us, He understood our needs and was identified with the family of men even to the extent that He was "not ashamed to call them brethren." Thus, when He became one of us and faced and overcame death through the power of His resurrection, He not only destroyed death but He also rendered powerless the one who had controlled death and continuously imprisoned mankind with its fear, the devil himself. When the Son of God took upon Himself another nature, it was not the nature of angels, but it was the nature of man. In His ministry He did not provide salvation for angels, though there were fallen angels as well; He instead provided eternal salvation exclusively for mankind (2:10-16). In addition to providing salvation for us through His identification with us in suffering and death, He also became our High Priest to present His own sacrifice to God on our behalf. Having presented His own sacrifice for us, He continues to minister on our behalf to help us live for Him day by day (2:17, 18).

Application: Teaching and Preaching the Passage

In 2:1 the writer says that we should listen carefully to and apply the gospel message we have heard "lest at any time we should let *them* slip." Here are some of the reasons that might cause us to "let *them* slip": (1) by failing to understand the importance of these gospel truths; (2) by being too involved with our career or education; (3) by devoting ourselves primarily to the fleshly pleasures of this world; (4) by procrastinating about spiritual decisions which need to be made immediately.

In 2:3 the writer warns further against neglecting "so great salvation." A number of things make this salvation "so great": (1) The author is great—Jesus Christ, the eternal Son of God. (2) The present effects are great—the joy of daily fellowship with Jesus as our High Priest as well as fellowship with our brothers and sisters within the church. (3) The eternal consequences are great—to live eternally with Christ where all the evil things of this life are passed away. (4) The evidence is great—such great truths need to be carefully substantiated, and they have been in the infallible record of the Word of God along with the continuing witness of the Holy Spirit in our lives.

Human nature has often been honored throughout history by great heroes like Wycliffe, Luther, Washington, Lincoln, etc. But human nature was never so highly honored as when the eternal Son of God became Jesus of Nazareth, indeed became one of us. (1) He took our nature, not the nature of angels. (2) He was pure and holy, while we are defiled. (3) He performed wonderful works. (4) He accomplished a marvelous redemption through His human nature. (5) In His human nature He was exalted to the right hand of God in Heaven. (6) According to Acts 17:31, God will one day soon "judge the world in righteousness by *that* man whom he hath ordained" (Barnes 64).

The writer says in 2:9, "But we see Jesus"; we may ask, how do we see Him? (1) the fact of His humiliation—"made a little lower than the angels"; (2) the extent of humiliation—"for the suffering of death"; (3) the purpose of His humiliation—"that he . . . should taste death for every man"; (4) the basis of His humiliation—"by the grace of God"; (5) the reward of His humiliation—"crowned with glory and honour."

In 2:10 the writer says, "For it became him," that is, it was proper or fitting or appropriate that He did what He did in His incarnation and earthly mission. (1) It "became" His wisdom—to devise such a plan of salvation. (2) It "became" His holiness—the only way a holy God could forgive the sins of wicked men. (3) It "became" His power—in the miraculous concentration of the sufferings of Christ in those six awful hours on the cross without eternally destroying Him. (4) It "became" His love and grace—John noted it this way in 1 Jn. 4:10, "Herein is love, not that we loved God, but that he loved us, and sent his Son *to be* the propitiation for our sins" (Pink 114).

Also in 2:10 the writer says that God made "the captain of their salvation perfect." Thus, He is "perfect" or complete: (1) in His example in suffering; (2) in His sympathetic ministry as our High Priest; (3) in the perfect redemption provided through His death and resurrection.

In 2:12, 13 we note the terms used to refer to those whom Christ redeemed. We are called: (1) brethren, which speaks of our fellowship with Him and of His becoming one of us; (2) church, which describes our corporate worship, the "called out ones," in our praise and our singing, led by none other than Christ Himself; (3) children, which identifies our family relationship with God through His Son, and of our having been begotten by Him.

In 2:14 there are several things that might be emphasized about the incarnation: (1) the *wonder* of it—the marvel that the eternal God would become a man; (2) the *necessity* of it—it was absolutely the only way of redemption; (3) the *nature* of it—He became a partaker of "flesh and blood"; (4) the *accomplishment* of it—"He also himself likewise took part of the same"; (5) the *purpose* of it—"that through death he might destroy him that had the power of death, that is, the devil."

In 2:15 the writer calls attention to "the fear of death" or the dread of death. With regard to death, we fear: (1) the suffering leading to death which we may endure—but Jesus, who suffered beyond what any of us will endure, is our sympathetic High Priest (Heb. 2:18; 4:14-16); (2) the thought of the end of our present existence, the separation from our loved ones—but the joys of the eternal presence of Christ will fill that void (Rev. 14:13); (3) the loneliness of that last journey—those who love you most cannot go with you, but those who know Christ won't have to make this final trip alone (Jos. 1:5; Lk. 16:22; 2 Cor. 4:8, 9; Phil. 1:23); (4) the imagined darkness of the tomb—but our real being, our soul or spirit, won't be there (2 Cor. 5:8); (5) the unknown aspects of the other world—but if we know Him, that's all we need to know, because He has prepared a place for us (Jn. 14:1-3); (6) the thought of facing the judgment of an all-knowing God—but, if we are in Christ, God will not see our sin, but rather His righteousness; (7) the wrath and condemnation of God for those who are unprepared—but the truth about that is that no one has to face God unprepared; for those who do, in spite of God's warnings, it will indeed not be pleasant.

II. THE SUPERIOR LEADERSHIP OF CHRIST IN RELATION TO MOSES AND JOSHUA (3:1—4:16)

Through Jesus Christ, who willingly became one with us as a partaker "of flesh and blood" (2:14), we have a wonderful helper in our struggles in the flesh and in the spirit. This great helper is so much better than angels in every way, even though angels have frequently been God's instruments in bringing help our way, especially in mediating the giving of the law of Moses. It would be natural for the Jewish Christian to think about Moses himself, the human agent in presenting the law to Israel. Thus, the writer turns his attention to a comparison and contrast between Moses and Jesus; and, since Moses died before Israel entered the Promised Land, he also contrasts Jesus with Joshua in attaining the perfect rest.

A. The Superiority of the Son to Moses (3:1-6)

The writer points out that Jesus is superior to Moses, God's human instrument in giving the law to Israel, in at least two ways: as a builder is superior to the house he has built, and as a son is superior to a servant, no matter how great that servant may be.

1. As a builder to a house (3:1-4)

1 Wherefore, holy brethren, partakers of the heavenly calling, consider the Apostle and High Priest of our profession, Christ Jesus;
2 Who was faithful to him that appointed him, as also Moses *was faithful* in all his house.
3 For this *man* was counted worthy of more glory than Moses, inasmuch as he who hath builded the house hath more honour than the house.
4 For every house is builded by some *man*; but he that built all things *is* God.

In using "wherefore" as a connector with the previous chapter, the writer reminds us of all that he has said about Jesus in chapters 1 and 2: the one through whom He has spoken "in these last days" (1:1, 2), and the one who has become so much better than angels by actually becoming one with us and completely identifying Himself with us. He addresses the recipients here as "holy brethren." In doing so, the author identifies himself with the readers, but he also to some extent identifies them and himself with Christ who, in His intercessory ministry, was not ashamed to call them "brethren" (2:12). And in addressing them in this manner, he clearly acknowledges the position from which he addresses them, as a fellow-partaker in the common salvation through the ministry of Christ. Contrary to the presuppositions of some commentators (like Pink, MacArthur), there is no evidence that the writer has more than one audience in mind; that audience consists solely of people whom he considers to be in Christ, even as he. They are "holy," both because of their justification in the perfect work of Christ, and through their progressive movement toward the realization of the image of Christ in their own personal lives (Rom. 8:29). The latter, practical aspect is probably what is most in mind here.

He furthermore describes his audience as part of redeemed society by addressing them as "partakers of the heavenly calling." As a "partaker" (Greek *metochos*), each recipient shares equally in the benefits provided to the group as a whole. The blessing in which this group partakes is "the heavenly calling." It is a "calling" since none of us comes to Christ of his own unaided initiative. Jesus declared, "No man can come to me, except the Father which hath sent me draw him" (Jn. 6:44). The calling is described as "heavenly," either because of its ultimate goal, which is to live in Heaven, or because of its immediate source, which is from Heaven. In fact, the two ideas may be combined (Delitzsch I:154; Alford 57).

The writer admonishes his audience to "consider the Apostle and High Priest of our profession." The word used in the exhortation, "consider" (Greek *katanoeo*), literally means "to think down." The writer is asking his audience to cast themselves on Jesus for help in their spiritual lives, knowing full well who He is and what He is able to do for them in their times of distress. He is not advising uninformed dependence on Christ, but rather a fully educated deliberation. He sees Christ here in a double role of completeness and perfection.

"Apostle" (Greek *apostolos*) means "one who is sent." Christ fulfills the role of apostle by being sent from Heaven to bring God's message and ministry to us. When He went back to Heaven, Christ sent the earthly apostles to carry out His message and ministry on the basis of the same pattern which He had established in coming to represent the cause of the Father on earth (Jn. 20:21). That Jesus is our "High Priest" emphasizes His ministry in the opposite direction, as our Divine Mediator, representing our desperate cause before a holy Father who hates our sin but who also dearly loves His Son. What a perfect combination! As our "Apostle" He represents God's will to us, and as our "High Priest" He represents us before the heavenly Father. He fulfills these two roles in relation to "our profession." "Profession" (Greek *homologia*) is more literally "confession." When we confess Christ as our Lord and Savior, we thus employ Him in this doubly perfect role in presenting God to us and presenting us to God. And lest we not know for sure to whom the writer refers in this great ministry, he clearly and emphatically identifies Him as "Christ Jesus."

In v. 2 the writer makes clear that his purpose is to compare and contrast Jesus, in His redemptive and intercessory role, with Moses, the great man of Sinai. The first description of Moses brings in a favorable comparison between the forensic master of Sinai and the blessed Savior from Heaven. First, both Christ and Moses were "appointed" to their respective ministries. Neither of them initiated his ministry at his own will. Knowing, as only He could know, the full implications of His ministry through the cross, Christ prayed even in Gethsemane for the bitter cup to pass, but He submissively added, "Not my will, but thine, be done" (Lk. 22:42). It was clearly the Father's initiative to send His obedient Son to the cross (Jn. 3:16). God also called Moses from the desert of Midian to serve in his remarkable role in leading Israel out of Egypt, and Moses too, no doubt in a different way, was reluctant to accept his call (Ex. 3). But in both cases, once "appointed," Jesus and Moses were "faithful" to the ministry which God gave each of them. In this respect both Jesus and Moses compare favorably. But from there the comparison ends and the contrast begins. The realm in which Jesus and Moses were faithful was "in all his house." The writer's use of the word "house" is suggested by Num. 12:7. In each case "house" stands for the place of ministry to which each person was appointed. Moses was appointed to minister, in a very outward way, to the nation of Israel, the chosen nation of God. Christ, on the other hand, was appointed to minister to and for the people of God of all ages, whether under the new covenant or the old. The ministry of Christ is much broader than that of Moses since it includes a ministry to those in the present and future, from the viewpoint of His death, and to those who lived in the past as well.

Now our writer emphasizes two great contrasts between Christ and Moses. The first reason that Jesus is better than Moses is pointed out in v. 3. Here Christ is presented as "he who hath builded the house." In John's great prologue he declared about Christ, "All things were made by him; and without him was not any thing made that was made" (Jn. 1:3). If Christ is the great builder of all things in general, He is certainly the builder of the spiritual house of His people. In the O.T., this house was Israel; and in the New Testament, it is Christ's church. From that point of view, Christ was the builder of the house. Moses, on the other hand, was merely part of the "house." Indeed, he was a very important part, and the role to which God appointed him was a unique role; nevertheless he was still just part of God's great house. The simplicity of the illustration is both wonderful and practical. We boast greatly on the beauty of some particular house, but when we really think it through it is the builder who deserves the credit, not the house itself.

The illustration which began in v. 3 is completed in v. 4. Houses do not build themselves. Unthinking people may sometimes get caught up so much in glorying over a beautiful house that they forget to direct the deserved attention toward the builder. But God's Word always points to the proper way of looking at truth, even a simple truth like this one: "every house is builded by some man." This obvious, though often ignored, truth applies whether the house is literal or figurative, whether a material house or a spiritual house. The verb used here is action in progress: "Every house is being built by some one" (Greek present tense). The truth is universal and for all time. The other significant truth in this verse is also frequently ignored, especially in our day: "But he that built all things is God." Here the writer uses completed action (Greek aorist tense). If we apply the truth to original creation, then it is affirmed in Genesis 1 and 2. But it applies equally to the world as we know it today, for God is the Creator and Sustainer of everything for all time, and since Jesus Christ is *very* God, He, too, deserves the glory of that role (Heb. 1:2, 3).

2. As a son to a servant (3:5, 6)

5 And Moses verily *was* faithful in all his house, as a servant, for a testimony of those things which were to be spoken after;
6 But Christ as a son over his own house; whose house are we, if we hold fast the confidence and the rejoicing of the hope firm unto the end.

Now the writer points to the second reason Jesus is better than Moses. He again reminds us that Moses himself was faithful to the task which God gave him. Faithfulness is not how Jesus and Moses were different. They were different, in this case, in how they related to the Father. In spite of the importance of Moses to the Jewish people and in Hebrew tradition, and his importance to God in His plan, he was, nevertheless, "a servant." Man's approach tends to exalt those who hold roles of leadership almost to the point of deification, but God does not do this, even with His greatest leaders. He certainly gives them appropriate honor, and asks us to do so as well (Rom. 13:7), but He does not exalt them to the point of making everyone else insignificant—neither in O.T. Israel nor in the N.T. church. "Servant" (Greek *therapon*) refers to a free servant who serves of his own accord, not to a bondslave (Greek *doulos*), which refers to one forced into service (Lenski 107; Westcott 77). Paul, however, often willingly claims the latter title for himself (Rom.1:1), indicating his desire to be totally submissive to the will of Christ in every way.

The specific role in which Moses served was as God's mouthpiece to His people, "for a testimony of those things which were to be spoken after." The writer evidently again refers to the same context where God says about Moses, "With him will I speak mouth to mouth" (Num. 12:8). God communicated personally with Moses, and He expected Moses to communicate His Word accurately and faithfully to the people of Israel, and Moses was very faithful in doing so.

It is a great privilege to be a servant of God on any level, and certainly on the level that Moses worked. But there is no comparison between the privileges of a servant and those of a "son." The writer again stresses a double superiority for Christ. Not only does he hold the honor and power of Sonship, but as God's only-begotten Son He is "over his own house." In the O.T. He was the head of Israel, the people of God; and in the N.T. He is the head of the church, and the church itself is His body (Eph. 1:22, 23). With the phrase, "whose house are we," the writer identifies himself with the people of God under the new covenant. When we are saved, we do not have to await the final outcome to begin to experience the benefits. However, that does not mean that the final outcome, from the human side, has been settled. Though all things are certain in the mind of our all-knowing God, even the identity of the names written in God's book of salvation (Rev. 17:8), they are not certain from the human point of view. It is from man's side that the writer now speaks: "If we hold fast." "If" (Greek *ean*) indicates the uncertainty from man's point of view, but it also suggests probability. "Hold fast" (Greek aorist subjunctive) is expressed as one act, indicating the action of grabbing hold of something and not turning loose. This does not mean that human effort keeps us saved any more than human effort saved us in the beginning. But it does mean that, as free moral agents, we always have a choice in the matter. Salvation is a wonderful gift prepared by God on the basis of the blood of Jesus Christ. He offers that free gift to all who hear the gospel. If they respond, He will enable them to come. But the Scripture nowhere teaches that He will compel them to come. And, once they have come, the Scripture does not teach that He will compel them to stay.

Calvinistic interpreters explain that this statement does not mean to imply any uncertainty in the security of genuine Christians, merely that the sign of genuine Christianity is perseverance. For them, the fact that one does not persevere reveals that he was never saved (MacArthur 83). But that is not what the writer says. If he had wanted to make this a statement of concession, rather than condition, he could have used a different word for "if" (Greek *ei*). In that case we might translate, "Since we will hold fast." But the writer, under inspiration, chose to use the word for "if" which implies a real possibility of not holding fast. Furthermore, he gives no indication that their lack of perseverance will prove that they were not genuine any of the time. That idea is read into this and other passages by those who have already decided their view on the basis of other passages of Scripture.

The object to be held so vigorously is "the confidence and the rejoicing of the hope." "Confidence" (Greek *parresia*) communicates the idea of boldness which produces a confidence in the reliability of a person or thing. Such confidence easily joins in partnership with "rejoicing" (Greek *kauchema*) or boasting or glorying. The ultimate object of such boastful confidence is "the hope" which finds its basis in the finished work of Christ. Though we do not believe that Christ will keep one contrary to his own will, we do believe very firmly that He can and will keep all those who keep their trust in Him. That is why we are urged to grab hold and never turn loose. In modern English our use of the word "hope" is very anemic. If someone says, "I hope this will happen," it implies some amount of uncertainty. In the N.T. the word "hope" (Greek *elpis*) is very strong, built on the same root as the word "faith" (Greek *pistis*). It actually adds an element to faith. Faith merely says, "I believe," but hope takes it a step further in saying, "I believe and expect." Hope adds and emphasizes the element of eager, confident expectation. Of course, the only way to hold on to such wonderful hope is "firm unto the end." Jesus laid down a divine principle for all time when He declared, in the Olivet Discourse, "He that shall endure to the end, the same shall be saved" (Matt. 24:13). That principle always applies, whether we refer to the destruction of Jerusalem in A.D. 70, to the Second Coming of Christ, or to any other time in our own lives. The N.T. books were all written in a historical context. That context is crucial to understanding Hebrews. In the face of increasing persecution, the writer was fearful that some of the Jewish believers would turn back to the old ritualistic and powerless religion. He knew that such an unwise choice would have fatal consequences. It was not his job, nor ours, to determine whether they were truly saved. Everything that he said implies that he assumed they were. His job was rather to warn them not to go back. If they could not turn back, there would be no need for such a warning; but if they could, it would be worse than criminal to fail to do so.

B. Second Warning: Against Neglecting the Leadership of the Son (3:7—4:16)

The writer issues the second of five warnings in Hebrews by reviewing Israel's sad record in the wilderness. Like those ancient Israelites, the readers, too, could fail to enter the Promised Land. God's ability to take them all the way is not in question; the issue is their willingness to depend on the leadership of the Son.

1. Israel's failure to follow Moses (3:7-19)

In the book of Numbers there is a record of at least ten different rebellions on the part of Israel. Through God's remarkable power, they had been delivered from Egypt as a result of the ten plagues. God had parted the Red Sea so that they were able to walk through on dry ground. In the wilderness He provided their every need; He brought them to the very border of Canaan, the Promised Land. In spite of all this, their rebellion persisted until God rejected them. The writer of Hebrews warns that God will still deal the same way with persistent rebellion today.

a. Substantiated From Psalm 95:7-11 (3:7-11)

7 Wherefore (as the Holy Ghost saith, To day if ye will hear his voice,
8 Harden not your hearts, as in the provocation, in the day of temptation in the wilderness:

9 When your fathers tempted me, proved me, and saw my works forty years.
10 Wherefore I was grieved with that generation, and said, They do alway err in *their* heart; and they have not known my ways.
11 So I sware in my wrath, They shall not enter into my rest.)

If Israel could fail to reach Canaan, the earthly Promised Land for Israel, so could these modern Hebrew Christians fail to reach the heavenly land of promise. However, if they, and we, continue to rely on Jesus Christ, the ultimate destination of that eternal rest is assured.

To prove his point about the possibility of going back on the Lord, the writer now turns to the well-known warning of Ps. 95:7-11. Our writer does not seem to be bothered by taking such a warning from a psalm that definitely implies it is addressed to the true people of God, for the psalmist says in the verse just before our quotation begins, "For he *is* our God; and we *are* the people of his pasture, and the sheep of his hand" (Ps. 95:7). This confirms that our writer addresses an audience whom he considers composed of genuine Hebrew Christians.

"Wherefore" connects the quotation, with the admonition that has just been given about holding fast, with the admonition that follows (v. 12): to "take heed." That the "Holy Ghost" or Holy Spirit is cited as the author of the psalm reminds us that every book in the Bible, O.T. and N.T., has double authorship. There is always a human author, though his identity is sometimes unknown, as in this epistle. Then there is always the divine author, the Holy Spirit. God is always the ultimate author, because the Bible is God's Word. The Holy Spirit, the third person of the Trinity, is often seen as the communicator of God's will to man. When the same writer refers again to the same psalm in 4:7, he ascribes the psalm to David, and he perceives no conflict at all.

When there is danger of turning away from the Lord, the time to hear and heed the warning "to hold on" is today. The writer stresses the initial word of the quotation to point up the urgency of getting things settled with God immediately. Whenever Scripture writers urge spiritual conversion or spiritual renewal, they never promise it for tomorrow. Getting right with the Lord can only be promised by any preacher for today. Our writer continues to admonish his audience, "if ye will hear his voice." This is the same word for "if" as used in v. 6, implying a likely possibility or even probability. On the other side, however, is the potential for refusing to hear God's voice. The writer obviously fears this possibility. The Scripture knows of no irresistible grace, as spoken of by Calvinistic interpreters. To "hear" God's voice, in the language of Scripture, is to obey His voice, to heed His warning, and to awake from any consideration of departing from Christ in the face of increasing persecution.

The psalmist continues to warn, "Harden not your hearts." The Scripture presents the hardening process from three different points of view. Each of these points of hardening can be found in the story of Pharaoh in Exodus. (1) Pharaoh hardened his own heart against God (Ex. 8:15, 32; 9:34). (2) The Lord hardened Pharaoh's heart (Ex. 4:21; 9:12; 10:1, 20, 27; 11:10; 14:4, 8). (3) Pharaoh's heart was hardened (Ex. 7:7:14, 22; 9:7, 35). What applied to Pharaoh in response to the words of Moses can still happen to Christians today (Westcott 81). The logical order is as follows: In our own self-will we refuse to listen to the Word of God; after continued refusal to respond, God brings on us a supernatural hardening that makes refusal ever easier; the final result of the process culminates in a totally passive response to the call of God. In relation to salvation, the process of hardening could go on for many years. It appears that the rate of its progress and the nature of its conclusion are directly related to the attitude of the individual in question. God's hardening process never keeps those from believing who truly want to believe.

As usual in Hebrews, the quotation from Psalm 95 is from the LXX (the Septuagint). The Massoretic text (the Hebrew O.T.) varies from the quotation here by referring to the two most notable trials of Israel in the wilderness. Thus, the Hebrew text of the psalm says, "As at Meribah, as in the day of Massah in the wilderness." These two great acts of unbelief sum up the entire 40 years of rebellion in the wilderness (Num. 20:1ff.; Ex. 17:1ff.). As the disobedient Israelites sneered at the blessings of God in the wilderness, even when God brought water for them out of the rock, so the Hebrew Christians were considering turning away from the living God. Such a hardening is always a "provocation," an act of willful rebellion against the clear manifestation of the hand of God, and such will always be a fateful "day of temptation" or testing for the people of God. We cannot regard God's Word with contempt without suffering the consequences.

The word translated "tempted" in v. 9 (Greek *peirazo*) can also mean "tested" in a good sense. But here clearly the bad sense is meant; therefore, "tempted" is proper. The Lord charged, furthermore, that the purpose of the Hebrew "fathers" in the wilderness was that they "proved me, and saw my works." They did not mind putting God to the test over and over again, yet in the next crisis they were as skeptical as they had been at the beginning. Their faith did not grow in spite of the fact that they had viewed some of the greatest works that God ever did before anyone on the face of the earth. The seriousness of this kind of unbelief would be bad enough if it continued only for a brief period of time, but it was made much worse in that such testing and proving continued over the entire period of "forty years." Some think that the writer of Hebrews here would compare the 40 years in the wilderness to the similar period of almost 40 years since Christ went back to Heaven (Delitzsch I:171; Alford 66). Once again these Hebrew believers had the opportunity to see God demonstrate His power among them for almost four decades.

In v. 10 the psalmist points to the expected response to such willful rebellion against the Word of God. "Wherefore" connects God's response with the conduct of the Israelite fathers. The phrase "I was grieved," might be translated somewhat stronger, "I was angry." A holy God cannot remain untouched by man's sinful disobedience. "That generation" is literally "this generation." By using the near demonstrative pronoun, the psalmist applied the illustration of Israel in the wilderness to his own generation, just as the writer of Hebrews, by quoting the passage, is applying it to his generation. God's basic principle of responding to faith or to unbelief has not changed, whether we are speaking about Israel or the church.

God's anger was caused by the nature of their sin, which is of the worst sort. God declared, "They do always err in *their* heart." In Scripture the heart does not represent the emotions, as we often think in our day. The heart represents the total person, the summation of all that a person is: thoughts, feelings, and will (Morris 34). Israel's sin of unbelief was not superficial, not merely a sin or ignorance or emotion. Knowing full well what God wanted of them, they rejected God's will and demanded their own way. The error of the heart is then manifested outwardly, "And they have not known my ways." This cannot mean that the Israelites disobeyed God merely because they did not know what He wanted. Through Moses God had made His way abundantly clear to them. They knew in their minds, but they rejected God's way in their hearts. They did not know God's way in the sense that they did not acknowledge and do it. The sin of apostasy is always a sin against light. God may have compassion on genuine ignorance, but He cannot tolerate open rebellion against His will (1 Sam. 15:21, 22).

God is a longsuffering God. He had repeatedly proven His patience with Israel. He had dealt with individual rebellions numerous times, dealing appropriately with the individuals involved in each case. There is an end, however, even to the longsuffering of God. Concerning their rebellion, God said, "So I sware in my wrath." God is the God of all truth. He cannot lie; therefore, He does not need to swear about something which He promises. When He swears, He does so for emphasis to His audience. He wants to stress the fact that there are no exceptions to what He is saying. Later on, the writer points out that God swore in establishing the Abrahamic Covenant "that by two immutable things" (His Word and His oath) He might affirm the certainty of this covenant (Heb. 6:18). In response to this final rebellion of Israel in the wilderness, God swore, "They shall not enter into my rest." The "rest" for Israel was primarily the land of Canaan. But this same writer points out later on that Abraham knew from the beginning that a greater rest awaited those who were faithful to God, "for he looked for a city which hath foundations, whose builder and maker is God" (11:10). For Israel Canaan always stood as a typical picture of the promised eternity with God for those who obey Him by faith and follow His ways.

b. Need to exhort one another against unbelief and sin (3:12, 13)

12 Take heed, brethren, lest there be in any of you an evil heart of unbelief, in departing from the living God.
13 But exhort one another daily, while it is called To day; lest any of you be hardened through the deceitfulness of sin.

The quotation from Ps. 95:7-11 ended with Heb. 3:11. The writer now makes application of the quotation to his readers. He admonishes them to "take heed": literally, "Keep on taking heed." The imperative is expressed in continuing action (Greek present tense). The danger always lies out there for those who are following God's way. The devil is always busy, who, "as a roaring lion, walketh about, seeking whom he may devour" (1 Pet. 5:8). Furthermore, such severe warnings are not addressed to those who are merely intellectual adherents to the faith, who are not true Christians. They are rather addressed to "brethren," people whom the writer considers as true companions in the faith of Christ. In spite of the obvious meaning of this term in this context, John MacArthur, who has his own plan of dividing the epistle up for three different audiences, insists that the term here does not refer to true Christians, but rather "to racial brothers, unbelieving Jews, as the term does throughout the book of Acts" (92). True Christians, according to MacArthur, are addressed as "holy brethren," as in Hebrews 3:1. This is a rather technical way of dividing up a book which, I suspect, few readers would catch without MacArthur's help. There is no need for such hermeneutical gymnastics if we are willing to accept the clear warning of the writer. The seriousness of this warning demands individual attention on the part of each one of these Hebrew believers.

Thus, the writer says, "Lest there be in any of you." Without careful attention to this matter, any one of the recipients could be in danger. When we are referring to matters of faith, no one is immune to the attacks of Satan, whether they be apostles, prophets, preachers, teachers, or laity. Though there are many passages that promise great security in Christ, an important part of that security is being aware of and attentive to the dangers. In that spirit Paul warned, "Let him that thinketh he standeth take heed lest he fall" (1 Cor. 10:12). The word translated "take heed" is the same word in the same tense (continuous action) as used here by the writer of Hebrews. Our vigilance is an important part of our security in Christ.

Without such vigilance on the part of each individual, any one of them could have "an evil heart of unbelief." The writer fears the very problem which caused God to abandon the Israelites in the wilderness. In the original the order is literally "a heart evil of unbelief." We might think of many wicked actions and attitudes which might cause others to think of a person as having an "evil heart." But from God's point of view the attitude that causes a heart to be more wicked than any other is the stubborn attitude of unbelief. Unbelief always refuses to obey. Attitude and action are tied hand in hand. The phrase here could be taken to mean "an evil heart which comes out of unbelief," "an evil heart with reference to unbelief," or "an evil, unbelieving heart." Though each idea might contribute to the fullness of the meaning, the latter one is probably the best (Lenski 117; Gaebelein 36; NIV).

Entertaining such an evil heart of unbelief will eventually result "in departing from the living God." The word translated "departing" (Greek *aphistemi*) gives us our English word "apostasy," the act of leaving or withdrawing from a position or a doctrine once held. The tense of the verb (Greek aorist infinitive) indicates a definite and decisive departure. These Hebrew Christians were in danger of committing apostasy, of once for all turning their backs on the Christ who had saved them in the face of increasing persecution for that cause. The writer characterizes such a departure as an abandonment of "the living God." He sees God as "living," not in contrast to the deadness of the law, nor with the deadness of the pagan gods of the Gentile world, but rather in reference to His active response in punishing rebellion and rewarding obedience (Lunemann 154). Our God is a God who cares, who always sustains a living relationship with His people.

Scripture certainly promises us that the power of God will continue to work in our salvation. Though that is true, however, He also expects that we employ our own initiative individually and collectively in obeying Him and resisting sin. "But" (v. 13) contrasts the positive action which must be taken with the apostasy which will result if no action is taken. As a group, Christians are admonished to "exhort one another daily": literally, "Keep on exhorting (encouraging) one another each day." The proper Christian life is a social life, a life lived in regular and joyful contact with one another. This would include the regular meetings of the congregation, but it goes much further than that. It also involves the important daily contacts that we have with one another in our work and in other social settings. Christians should always be encouraging one another. Our lives for Christ cannot be lived in isolation.

In the next phrase we see the preacher in the writer of Hebrews. Several times in the book he will quote a verse or passage from the O.T., and then isolate and emphasize a word or phrase from that quotation. Here he says, "While it is called To day," drawing the word "to day" from Psalm 95:7. By emphasizing "today" he stresses both the urgency and the opportunity of the situation. It is urgent because time for repentance will soon be exhausted. God's patience is running out, and our lives will too soon be gone. But "today" also speaks of opportunity to correct a wrong path that has been chosen, to reverse a negative attitude that has developed, to right a wrong that has been committed. "Today," as all days, will soon come to an end; we must act now before the darkness of apostasy falls upon us.

The writer knows that action must be immediately taken when a spirit of rebellion and unbelief begins to set in. Such an urgent and immediate response is called for "lest any of you be hardened through the deceitfulness of sin." When a person first becomes a Christian, his heart is tender and naturally responsive to God's Word. Initially, young Christians often seem more dedicated than those who have been saved much longer. Ideally, that responsive condition should continue and even increase throughout a believer's life. Unfortunately, however, the Christian is not immune to the work of Satan and to the attraction of the world around him. When God saves us, He does not remove the sinful nature. As long as we remain in the physical body, the sinful nature will also remain. If we grow in the Lord as we should, and the process of progressive sanctification moves along as it should, we will become more and more like Christ (Rom. 8:28, 29), and the old nature becomes more subdued. But if we don't care for our souls as we should, if we don't pray, study the Scriptures, and worship faithfully with fellow believers, we, too, are subject to the "deceitfulness of sin." Sin, in its great variety of manifestations, has an amazing ability to deceive anyone, including Christians. Sin always promises more than it can deliver. It always gives only partial truth. It never paints the full picture; it never reveals the final end of its product. When the prodigal started on his journey, he was unable to see the hog pen from his glowing, naive perspective. But James draws the picture clearly when he says, "Then when lust hath conceived, it bringeth forth sin: and sin, when it is finished, bringeth forth death" (Jas. 1:15). The adulterer never thinks of the awful disease, or of the hurt to his wife and children. The liar never thinks of the snowball effect, of one lie leading to another. The gambler always thinks that he will win with the very next turn of the wheel or throw of the dice. The social drinker certainly does not plan to become a drunkard. But that is how sin deceives, gradually luring people into its net.

c. Steadfastness demanded of partakers of Christ (3:14, 15)

14 For we are made partakers of Christ, if we hold the beginning of our confidence stedfast unto the end;
15 While it is said, To day if ye will hear his voice, harden not your hearts, as in the provocation.

The word "partakers" stands first for emphasis in the original: "Partakers of Christ we have become." In 3:1 the writer addressed his audience as "partakers of the heavenly calling." Those who have been called and who have responded to the Gospel message now share with Christ because we are His body, and He is our head (Eph. 5:23, 30). "We are made" is more literally, "We have become" (Greek perfect tense), stressing an act which is past but has continuing results. The idea is that we have become partakers and still are partakers of Christ. The salvation which these Hebrew Christians had experienced some time back was still as good "today" as it ever was. If salvation is a gift of God (Eph. 2:8, 9), then it does not gradually fade until it disappears. The only thing that could take us out of Christ once we have become united with Him is for Him to withdraw the gift of salvation from us. He will do that only if we abandon Him, if we turn from our faith to unbelief. John MacArthur insists that the writer means that we are partakers of Christ only if we continue in the faith (93). Continuation is always the test of genuineness (Jn. 8:31; 1 Jn. 2:19). But that is not the natural implication of any of these passages. It is much more simple and natural to take the meaning to be that continuation as a "partaker of Christ" is determined by our personal continuation in the faith. The writer does not say that we were never partakers if we don't continue. MacArthur and others are reading that into this passage from preconceived notions based on other passages of Scripture.

The condition laid down here is, "If we hold the beginning of our confidence stedfast until the end." This is the same form of construction used in v. 6 above. "If" again indicates a probability but allows for a possible failure to continue. For most believers the beginning of their Christian life was very special; to that "beginning" the writer now asks us to cling. Though the depth of emotion may vary, depending on individual personalities and circumstances, the early stages of a Christian's faith are often the strongest and most joyful. At the beginning we are unhampered by the complexities of future experience. Part of the joy is caused by the newness of the experience. But if Satan can, he will rob us of that joy and lead us away from the simple faith with which we started. However, we do not have to allow that to happen. With proper vigilance, prayer, and study of Scripture, we can progressively grow in the Lord to the point that our experience with Him becomes all the sweeter as time goes by.

Our author refers to this early stage of Christian life as the beginning of our "confidence" (Greek *hupostasis*). In 1:3 the writer used the same word to refer to Christ's "person" (KJV) or "being" (NIV). In defining faith in 11:1 the writer uses the word to mean "substance" (KJV) or "being sure" (NIV). The word literally means "that which stands under" and thus gives support to something. In this context it refers to the beginning of our certainty in Christ, our assurance, or our "confidence" in him (Bruce 67). The writer specifically chose the word in contrast with "departing" (Greek *aphistemi*) in v. 12 (Lenski 121). Those who do not heed the warning given here will depart, but those who hear and obey will stand fast, will continue to manifest their confidence in the power of Christ. This initial confidence must be held "stedfast unto the end." "Stedfast" speaks of the manner with which this confidence is held, while "unto the end" speaks of the duration required. For a Christian there is never a time to turn back. In giving the same principle, Jesus said, "No man, having put his hand to the plough, and looking back, is fit for the kingdom of God" (Lk. 9:62).

As in v. 13, the writer in v. 15 again emphasizes the urgency of the hour. They must give serious attention to their vacillation. By quoting Ps. 95:7, 8 again, he points to the example of the Israelites in the wilderness. If they could turn back in their hearts after seeing all of God's miracles in coming out of Egypt and in the wilderness, then these present-day Israelites, these Hebrew Christians, could do the same.

d. Rebellion and unbelief kept Israel from entering Canaan (3:16-19)

16 For some, when they had heard, did provoke: howbeit not all that came out of Egypt by Moses.
17 But with whom was he grieved forty years? *was it* not with them that had sinned, whose carcases fell in the wilderness?
18 And to whom sware he that they should not enter into his rest, but to them that believed not?
19 So we see that they could not enter in because of unbelief.

In vv. 16-19 the writer continues to emphasize Israel's apostasy, as referred to in Ps. 95:7-11, as a reminder to his present Hebrew audience. There seems to be unanimous agreement among recent commentators and translators that both parts of v. 16 should be taken as a question rather than a declaration, and, as a result, "some" (Greek *tines*) should be translated "who" (Greek interrogative pronoun rather than indefinite pronoun; see Bruce 68; Barnes 90; D. Guthrie 109; Hewitt 84; Clarke 822; Lenski 122; Westcott 87). The same Greek word can be translated either way. Since most ancient manuscripts had no punctuation marks, only the context can tell whether a statement is a declaration or a question. Thus, the translation would best read, "For who, when they heard, did provoke? Indeed, did not all those who came out of Egypt by Moses?" For his present purposes, the writer is overlooking the exception of Caleb and Joshua (see Num. 14:6-10; 32:10-13). Paul makes the same point in a slightly different way in 1 Cor. 10:5.

Two more arguments favor this approach. (1) It seems better to say that "all provoked God" in the wilderness than to say only "some" did, when almost all the adults 20 years old and above did, except for Caleb and Joshua. The latter appears to be too much an understatement. (2) Since vv. 17 and 18, with a similar construction, must be translated as questions it seems likely that verse 16 should also be taken as a question. Basically the entire nation turned their backs on God in the wilderness, and they paid dearly for that rebellion by failing to enter the land of promise.

In vv. 17, 18 the writer carries the point further with more questions. He asks, "But with whom was he grieved forty years? *was it* not with them that had sinned, whose carcases fell in the wilderness?" The questions continue to be based on the earlier quotation from Psalm 95:7-11. The fact that "he was grieved" here was not so much a grief of sorrow, but more a grief of outrage, of anger. "Them that had sinned" would again include the entire nation that had come out of Egypt with few exceptions, notably Caleb and Joshua. The rebellion of Israel was not just one rebellion; rather it was a long series of rebellions which led to a fatal climax. Any rebellion against God is serious, but continuous rebellion leads to apostasy, and apostasy, total and final rebellion against God, is unforgivable. The writer will explain this in further detail in chapter 6 and in chapter 10.

Still going back to Ps. 95, he again asks, "And to whom sware he that they should not enter into his rest, but to them that believed not?" God's anger and grief were so severe against rebellious Israel that He swore never to change His mind about their fate. As always, it was not God who abandoned them, but they who abandoned God. God's grief and His oath were both against them that believed not (literally: "those who disobeyed"). Disobedience is always refusal to believe (Lenski 123).

Having completed his explanation, the writer makes his pointed application in 3:19: "So we see that they could not enter in because of unbelief." The present audience must realize that these rebels were their forefathers. If God would not tolerate their rebellion and unbelief, neither will He tolerate theirs. Only those who continue in faith will enter God's rest. It is never merely how we start, but rather always how we finish.

Summary (3:1-19)

In chapters 1 and 2 the writer has shown our Lord's superiority to the angels, highly exalted creatures though they are. In chapters 3 and 4 he continues with the theme of the superiority of Christ. In these chapters he shows how and why Christ is superior to Moses, the greater lawgiver, as well as to Joshua, Moses' immediate successor. Both Jesus and Moses were faithful to their calling, but the faithfulness must be viewed from an entirely different perspective. Jesus is better than Moses in at least two respects: first, as a builder is to the house which he has built. The "house" in this contrast is God's people, the nation of Israel. Moses was Israel's great leader through a period of some 40 years, but while he was their leader, he was at the same time part of the house which God created. A house may be a beautiful thing to behold, but the builder of the house deserves the compliments (3:1-4). But Jesus is also better than Moses in the sense that a son is better than a servant. As God's true servant, no one could hold a higher position than Moses nor be more dedicated than Moses to the mission to which he was called, that is no other servant like Moses. Jesus, however, was not the servant of God; He was rather the Son of God, and there is no just comparison that can be made even between the highest servant and that one who is God's only Son (3:5, 6).

At this point the writer issues his second serious warning to the Hebrew Christians, a warning against neglecting the leadership of God's Son, Jesus Christ. The basis of his warning is a lengthy quotation from Ps. 95:7-11, which, coincidentally, is in Hebrews 3:7-11. Using the words of David, he reminds the Hebrews how Israel's persistent rebellion in the wilderness cost them the possession of the Promised Land of Canaan. God was so frustrated with Israel that He swore that they would never enter the rest that He had planned for them in Canaan (3:7-11). Thus the writer sees crossing over Jordan into Canaan as a type of the challenge which we have today to cross over into the heavenly land of promise. If Israel's unbelief could cause them to come short of the reward, so can unbelief and sin on the part of these Hebrew readers. In light of this possibility, they need to constantly exhort one another toward faithfulness and persistence in reaching the eternal goal (3:12, 13).

When we read Israel's history in the wilderness in the book of Numbers, we see a constant record of ups and downs, of going a few steps forward, then threatening to completely return to Egypt from which they came. The writer stresses here, as throughout the epistle, that how we began this race for the Lord is not as important as how we end the race. Though they had started with Christ some time ago, a spiritual sluggishness had developed which he implies here and discusses in more detail at the end of chapter 5. But the backsliding has not yet turned into apostasy; there is time yet to turn around. In his desire to see them make an about-face the writer brings home this warning by especially emphasizing the word "today" from the quotation of Psalm 95:7. It is time to stop this spiritual fading from the vibrant position they once had occupied in their relation with the Lord, and the only appropriate time to make such a turnaround is today (3:14, 15).

Sad to say, it was almost the entire nation of Israel who was banned from the Promised Land in that first generation out of Egypt, all those who were above 20 years of age. Only Caleb and Joshua, in faith and obedience, stood in contrast to the unbelief and disobedience of the rest of Israel (Num. 14:21-30). If God was angry with that generation of Israelites because of their persistent unbelief, He will be no less angry with these modern-day Hebrews who were wrestling with the same choices (3:16-19).

Application: Teaching and Preaching the Passage

Note that there are four different titles used for our Lord in 3:1, each one with a distinct significance. (1) He is our Apostle. This title may seem a bit strange since we commonly associate it with the original twelve apostles, or with Paul, whom Jesus called into His service. An "apostle" is, literally, "one who is sent," especially one sent to deliver a special message. Jesus Himself explains it best in Jn. 20:21 when He admonished His disciples, "As *my* Father hath sent me, even so send I you." Thus, we see Jesus was the original Apostle, sent by the Father to bring us the message of redemption. Then He commissioned and sent the original apostles with that same message of redemption. (In an even looser sense of the word we all are apostles sent forth to proclaim the great commission from our Lord.) (2) Jesus is our High Priest. It is that office which the writer of Hebrews emphasizes more than any other office of Christ, and he certainly emphasizes that office for our Lord more than any other book of the N.T. As an Apostle, Christ was sent from the Father to deliver a message to us; as our High Priest, He is sent back to the Father to intercede for us. With these two titles the writer dramatically describes Jesus' two-fold ministry, a ministry from Heaven to earth as well as a ministry from earth to Heaven. (3) Jesus is the name of the person who is this great Apostle and High Priest in our behalf. That is His human name, the name that His mother and father gave him at the command of the angel. Jesus is the Greek equivalent of the Hebrew Joshua or Jehoshua, the name borne by the successor of Moses, later mentioned in 4:8. In whatever language, Jesus means "Jehovah is Savior" or "Jehovah will save." It is His human name that especially emphasizes His ability to understand our struggles and trials, thus putting Him in a position to be our sympathetic High Priest. (4) The name Christ (Greek *christos*) does not appear in all the manuscripts in v. 1, but is in all of them in v. 4. The word Christ literally means "the anointed one." It refers to the anointing which officially began the service of the priest (Ex. 30:30), king (2 Sam. 2:4; 5:3), and prophet in the O.T. While the priest and king were literally anointed with the holy oil, the prophet was figuratively anointed with the presence of the Holy Spirit in his life. In connection with 3:6, to please our Lord we must walk closely, consistently, courageously, and constantly in the faith and practice of the gospel (Henry 901).

With regard to the sin of the Israelites (3:7-11), we note: (1) the circumstances of their sin—in the wilderness; (2) the nature of their sin—they tempted and provoked God; (3) the persistence of their sin—for 40 years; (4) the root of their sin—they erred in their hearts and did not know His ways; (5) God's patience and resentment of their sin—He was grieved with that generation; (6) the irreversible doom for their sins—God swore in His wrath, "They shall not enter into my rest."

In 3:12-14 the writer calls attention to Israel's example of failure: (1) He cautions them with a warning—"take heed, brethren." (2) He compels them with his address—"lest there be in any of you an evil heart of unbelief, in departing from the living God." (3) He counsels them with an exhortation—"exhort one another daily, while it is called To day." (4) He comforts them with encouragement—"we are made partakers of Christ."

Note that there are six appeals in chapter 3 marked by the commands or exhortations in the chapter: (1) consider (v. 1); (2) hear His voice (v. 7); (3) harden not your hearts (v. 8); (4) take heed (v. 12); (5) exhort (v. 13); (6) hold fast (v. 14).

One of the master tricks of Satan is deception. He practiced on Eve in the Garden of Eden, and because she succumbed to his deception, she disobeyed God and ate from the forbidden tree. In Jn. 8:44 Jesus, in warning the Pharisees concerning their hypocrisy, declared, "Ye are of *your* father the devil, and the lusts of your father ye will do. He was a murderer from the beginning, and abode not in the truth, because there is no truth in him. When he speaketh a lie, he speaketh of his own: for he is a liar, and the father of it." Here in 3:13 our writer reminds us that a hard heart concerning spiritual things comes through "the deceitfulness of sin." Satan deceives us concerning sin when he convinces us that: (1) delay in sin is not dangerous; (2) the consequences of sin are not serious; (3) the definition of sin is uncertain; (4) the condemnation of sin is unjust; (5) the appeal of sin is enticing; (6) the remedy for sin is too difficult.

In 3:15 the writer emphasizes "To day" from his earlier quotation of Ps. 95:7. Thus, we may declare that: (1) Today is the time for all unsaved people to repent and believe in Christ. (2) Today is the time for all backsliding people to awake to spiritual renewal in Christ; (3) Today is the time for those who have heard God's call to service to answer in person. Furthermore, "today" indicates a sense of: (1) Priority—what must have our first attention; other things in our lives may need consideration, but spiritual matters should come first. (2) Urgency—what must have immediate attention; time is quickly running out. (3) Limitation—you can only make that needed spiritual decision today; tomorrow is, at best, uncertain. (4) Opportunity—today you can get right with God; circumstances may change to the extent that such an opportunity never occurs again.

The *progression* of sin can be seen in 3:16-18. Sin begins with a provocation. Provocation, when persisted in, produces sin in all of its ugly manifestations. When sin is continued, it creates a life and attitude of rebellion, even against the voice of God, and when rebellion against God is continued, it results in apostasy (see Jas. 1:13-15). An aspect of progression can also be seen in the sin of unbelief which the writer stresses in 3:19. Unbelief often begins as a question; a question left unanswered becomes a doubt; a doubt which is not resolved often results in disobedience; and; disobedience, when persisted in, turns into full-fledged unbelief.

2. Possibility of failure to enter God's promised rest (4:1, 2)

1 Let us therefore fear, lest, a promise being left us of entering into his rest, any of you should seem to come short of it.
2 For unto us was the gospel preached, as well as unto them: but the word preached did not profit them, not being mixed with faith in them that heard *it*.

"Rest" is the key word in the writer's warning to the Hebrew church in chapter 4. The word has been drawn from his quotation of Ps. 95:7-11 in the preceding chapter. In 3:11 he quoted Ps. 95:11, "I sware in my wrath that they should not enter into my rest." Since the writer is using a physical and historical lesson from Israel's past to emphasize a spiritual and eternal truth for his readers, it is important to understand what he means by the word "rest" as it applies to them. For the Israelites in the wilderness, the rest was Canaan. But even for them the earthly rest was only a type and a promise of the ultimate heavenly rest. Thus, for his readers the rest that he has in mind is their eternal rest in Heaven after this life is over (Westcott 92, 98; Lenski 130; Lunemann 170, 176; Kent 84, Bruce 73, 78; Whedon 67; Alford 77; Delitzsch I:197; Barnes 98; Pink 197). In chapter 11 the writer confirms this idea of a future rest when this life is over by affirming that Abraham, already dwelling in earthly Canaan, "looked for a city which hath foundations, whose builder and maker is God" (11:10), and that he and his descendants "desire a better *country*, that is, an heavenly" (11:16). This same idea is reflected in Revelation 14:13, "Blessed *are* the dead which die in the Lord from henceforth: Yea, saith the Spirit, that they may rest from their labours; and their works do follow them." The hymn writer, Samuel Stennett, reflected this view when he wrote,

On Jordan's stormy banks I stand,
And cast a wishful eye
To Canaan's fair and happy land,
Where my possessions lie.
("On Jordan's Stormy Banks," 1787)

Other interpreters, however, feel that the present rest which the writer points to is the rest found only in salvation by grace through faith, the rest found in Jesus when we have ceased from wrestling, thrashing, and striving in our own self-effort toward salvation (MacArthur 96; Morris 43; Jensen 34; Morgan 58; Archer 31; Yeager 157). MacArthur resorts to his strange position of dividing Hebrews up as being addressed to three different audiences. He believes that the material from 3:7 through chapter 4 is addressed to "informed but unresponsive Jews," not to those who had actually been saved. Concerning this rest, he says, "Applied to God's rest, it means no more self-effort as far as salvation is concerned. It means the end of trying to please God by our feeble, fleshly works. God's perfect rest is a rest in free grace" (96). Others who want to stay away from Canaan as a type of the heavenly rest, but who do feel that those described here are saved, suggest that the writer has in mind a certain plateau in the believer's life, a certain level of sanctification, when he quits struggling with sin and rests peacefully and victoriously in Christ (Thomas 48). Hewitt, taking this position, says, "The rest of Canaan is a type of consecration rest, that is, of the rest which comes from a surrender of the mind, will and heart to God's power and influence which enables the believer to conquer sin" (92). Making the rest refer to this present life is often favored by Calvinistic interpreters who prefer to steer away from the idea of a warning about falling short of Heaven and of ultimate and final salvation. It appears to me, however, that this is exactly what the writer has in mind.

"Therefore" in 4:1 connects the warning with the closing observation in chapter 3. If the original Israelites who left Egypt for the Promised Land failed to enter because of their unbelief, the same danger still remains for these present-day Hebrew Christians. The fact that the writer makes application to the current believers suggests that the promised rest was broader than the mere entrance into earthly Canaan. Canaan stood as a figure for the ultimate home of all believers in the presence of our Lord in Heaven.

"Let us fear" emphasizes the urgency of the situation. God has done His part in providing eternal salvation through His Son, but proper concern must be exercised on our part. "Fear" refers to the exercise of concern and care in the evaluation of the genuineness and fervency of our faith. John says, "Perfect love casteth out fear" (1 Jn. 4:18), referring to fear as a lack of trust, a persistent uncertainty about God's promises. When we truly love Christ, that kind of fear disappears. The psalmist, however, declared, "The fear of the Lord is the beginning of wisdom." This is the kind of fear that our writer admonishes here, the concern that God means what He says about those who fail to meet the conditions of His promises. The fact that such concern is to be considered universal among all believers is shown by the writer's inclusion of himself in this warning by his use of the pronoun "us." This is not merely a concern for a certain group of persecuted Hebrews in a certain locality, but it must be a concern for all believers, both then and now, both Hebrew and Gentile.

The "promise being left" is the one to which the writer indirectly referred in 3:11: namely the promise of God to give Israel "rest" in Canaan. Since that generation failed to fulfill the promise, as God meant it to be fulfilled, that promise still stands for us today. The promise specifically is that of "entering into his rest." It seems obvious from the broader context that the writer has more in mind in his use of the word "rest" than mere entrance into earthly Canaan, for that promise would only have applied to those who left Egypt under Moses and the next generation who successfully entered Canaan under Joshua. Since entrance into an earthly Canaan did not fulfill God's promise, He must have in mind a greater fulfillment, the entrance into heavenly Canaan where God's children will be with Him forever.

The present generation of Hebrews must be careful lest "any of you should seem to come short of it": that is, the promise of entering God's rest. Commentators disagree on the meaning of the word translated "seem" (Greek *dokeo*). If "seem" is correct, the meaning is that there should not be even the appearance of turning away from the fulfillment of God's promise in Jesus Christ. That is, indeed, all that our human author could conclude apart from direct divine revelation with regard to the status of these Hebrew believers. God never asks us to judge anyone's eternal destiny. That is a task reserved for the infallible judgment of an all-knowing God. Furthermore, their ultimate, eternal destiny could not then be determined since they were yet in the process of living their lives either in faith or in unbelief. But there were some undesirable symptoms that had appeared in some of them which indicated growing uncertainty with regard to the Christian faith. From such appearances they must flee with all haste (so Westcott 93; Barnes 95; Morris 39).

Others take the meaning as "think" rather than "seem." Thus: "lest any one of you should think that he has fallen short of it." As a result of persecution by the Romans, and especially because of pressure from unbelieving Jews, some of the Hebrew Christians had begun to think that following Christ as the promised Messiah was the wrong choice. They were now thinking of renouncing that choice and returning to Judaism. Our writer vigorously condemns such thinking (Lenski 126). It appears more natural to the context to take the first meaning, "seem," as the correct interpretation.

"For" (Greek *gar*) in v. 2 applies the warning in v. 1 both to the author and his readers. The possibility of turning away in unbelief, even after having made a start in the Christian walk, is still apparent. Translators wrestle with whether to translate "the gospel preached" (KJV, NIV) or "the good news preached" (NASB). The word "gospel" itself means "good news," but many feel that the term "gospel" has become theologically entrenched by common usage both in the N.T. and in church history so that it can only refer to the N.T. message of salvation through Christ. Thus, those with strict dispensational concerns would insist that the common term "gospel" should not be used for both Old and New Testament messages. But surely the writer of Hebrews was as aware as we are of the common application of the verb which he chose (Greek *euaggelizomai*), yet he used it anyway. Perhaps he was reasoning that salvation by faith is the essence of the gospel, whether in the Old Testament or the New. Paul was thinking the same way in Rom. 4:3 when he wrote, "For what saith the scripture? Abraham believed God, and it was counted unto him for righteousness." Thus, it appears there is no justification for avoiding the translation "the gospel preached" since there is no difference in God's method of salvation. Whether under the old or new covenant, salvation is always a matter of faith in God's promise, at whatever present stage of fulfillment.

With regard to Israel in the wilderness, the writer observes, "But the word preached did not profit them." How close men can be to salvation, and yet turn from it! In the case of the O.T. apostates, the "word preached" (literally, "the word of hearing" or "the word which they heard") was Moses' message proclaimed, throughout the exodus experience, that God would supply their needs and bring them to the Promised Land. But the book of Numbers records a continuing series of at least ten rebellions by groups and individuals against God's Word. The final rebellion was at Kadesh-barnea, on the very border of the land itself—so close, and yet so far away (see Num. 13:16—14:45; 32:8). The reason they failed was the reason people always fail with regard to God's promise of salvation. It was not "mixed with faith in them that heard it." This is the first time that the word "faith" (Greek *pistis*) occurs in Hebrews, but our writer uses it a total of 32 times by the end of the epistle. Only Paul in Romans uses it more frequently, a total of 40 times. Though its meaning varies according to context, here, as often in the N.T., it refers to a right response to God's message, a response of trust demonstrated in action (Morris 40).

3. Proofs that a rest still remains (4:3-10)

The writer now wants to demonstrate the fact that a rest still remains for God's people today: that is, the heavenly rest which believers will enjoy when life amid the sin and sorrow of this earth is over. He offers three proofs that such a rest is still available: (1) that the basis of a continuing rest is God's original Sabbath rest; (2) that Israel failed to enter the Promised Land, and in fact died in the wilderness; (3) that a rest remained even after Joshua took Israel into Canaan. After examining these three proofs, the writer concludes that a rest still remained for his Hebrew audience. That conclusion still applies to Christians today.

a. The basis of God's promised rest is the Sabbath (4:3, 4)

3 For we which have believed do enter into rest, as he said, As I have sworn in my wrath, if they shall enter into my rest: although the works were finished from the foundation of the world.
4 For he spake in a certain place of the seventh *day* on this wise, And God did rest the seventh day from all his works.

In vv. 3 and 4 the writer points to God's creation Sabbath, at the end of His six days of creative activity, as the basis for the promised rest to Israel and the continuation of that promise for us today. The law of Moses placed a strong emphasis on keeping the Sabbath. The Sabbath was important as a day of physical rest from the hard labor of the other six days of the week as well as a time for genuine worship and praise to God and for spiritual refreshing. In addition to these two key reasons for the Sabbath, we learn from the writer's emphasis that the Sabbath also had an important, symbolic meaning for God's people. It symbolizes the eternal rest which we will have with the Lord after the labors of this life are over.

The "we" who are entering God's rest in v. 3 are more specifically defined by "which have believed," referring to our initial exercise of saving faith as the beginning of our entrance into God's rest. We might expect the writer to emphasize the continuity of our faith ("we who are believing"), but that is not what he wants here. Faith is the sole condition for entering God's rest, and those who have it must be separated from those who do not have it. Though saving faith must continue, it always has a beginning. It is that historical reality of faith which the writer wishes to stress. In contrast to this past and completed act of believing, our entrance into God's rest is placed in the present: "we do enter," or "we are entering." In a true sense, the Israelites began their entrance into the Promised Land when they left Egypt.

The writer sees the entire exodus as a picture of the Christian life. The departure from Egypt corresponds to our initial act of faith. Their trip through the wilderness, along with all of its tests, struggles, and victories, pictures our entire life in the Lord. Their entrance into Canaan, or failure to do so, pictures our final entrance into God's rest and our heavenly home. Just as the trip to Canaan was a process, so is our entrance into the heavenly rest (Westcott 95; D. Guthrie 112; Hagner 69; Morris 40). The fact that you start does not mean that you will finish, but it is also important to note that only those who start will finish. Only those "who have believed" will one day inherit God's promise. Sometimes the present tense is used in the N.T. to express the certainty of something that will actually happen in the future, especially promises of our Lord's Second Coming (Jn. 14:3, 18; Mt. 17:11; 1 Cor. 3:13; Col. 3:6). Indeed, there may be an element of that in the present tense here, because our actual entrance into God's rest is future (Bruce 73), but the main emphasis in this context seems to be on the fact that the process of entering begins with the true act of faith.

The writer is not describing an entrance "into rest" in general, but rather our entrance "into *the* rest" (article present in the Greek): that is, into God's rest—the rest being discussed in this passage. Some interpreters, like John MacArthur, want to make God's rest primarily, if not exclusively, present. He says, "It means no more self-effort as far as salvation is concerned. It means the end of trying to please God by our feeble, fleshly works. God's perfect rest is a rest in free grace" (96). But such an approach sacrifices the obvious parallel that our writer intends between the Christian life of faith and the exodus of the Israelites from Egypt. In referring to God's rest, he is not referring to the departure from Egypt, which is parallel to our act of faith in Christ, but rather to the arrival in Canaan, which is parallel to our final rest in going to be with the Lord. The word for "rest" (Greek *katapausis*) refers to a cessation of labor, a completion of effort. Though we do truly rest by faith in Christ's completed work of redemption when we are saved, that is not the rest that the writer is emphasizing in this context. He is stressing the completion of our earthly journey of faith and our arrival in the very presence of Christ.

Characteristically our author backs up his idea with a reference to Scripture: "As he said, As I have sworn in my wrath, if they shall enter into my rest." "He said" is literally "He has said" (Greek perfect tense), stressing the certainty of the truth of God's word, the guarantee of its fulfillment. God's passionate feeling about their rejection of Canaan is demonstrated both in His oath and in His anger. "If they shall enter into my rest" should be translated, as it was when Ps. 95:11 was first quoted in Hebrews 3:11, "They shall not enter into my rest."

Up until this point the writer has been using the Israelites' entrance into Canaan as the parallel to our entrance into God's heavenly rest. Here he introduces a second illustration: "although the works were finished from the foundation of the world." This second illustration is God's own rest from His work of creation. It is God's will that His children ultimately share with Him in this ideal rest which He entered after the six days of creation, the Sabbath rest. In fact, His works were so completely finished at that time that the names of His true children were "written in the book of life from the foundation of the world" (Rev. 17:8); and the kingdom of His eternal rest which He will give to those who will stand on His right hand at the judgment was, in fact, prepared for them "from the foundation of the world" (Mt. 25:34).

The writer refers to the source of his declaration that God's works are finished. He says, "For he spake in a certain place of the seventh *day* on this wise." It was not necessary for the writer to be more specific for Hebrew believers who knew the O.T. well. However, it must be remembered that the Bible had not been so nicely and minutely divided in ancient days and that scrolls were not as easy to manipulate as our convenient modern-day Bibles. The quotation is from Gen. 2:2, "God . . . rested on the seventh day from all his work." Scripture concludes the account of each of the first six days of creation with the statement, "And the evening and the morning were" the first day, second day, etc. But this formula is not applied to the seventh day. It is as if the seventh day is left open. God's rest from His creation work, which He took at that time, is still awaiting us. As believers in worship, we enjoy a bit of that rest each week, but we await the day when that rest becomes permanent with Him (Bruce 74; Morris 41).

b. Israel failed to enter the Promised Land (4:5, 6)

5 And in this *place* again, If they shall enter into my rest.
6 Seeing therefore it remaineth that some must enter therein, and they to whom it was first preached entered not in because of unbelief.

The writer emphasizes again the quotation from Ps. 95:11, which he first recorded in 3:11. In the context of an oath the word translated "if" (Greek *ei*) should be taken as a negative. As in the original quote in 3:11, it should read, "They shall not enter into my rest." From the time of creation God has been finished with His creation work and He wants those who love Him to participate with Him in that rest. Those who join Him in that final rest, however, must continue to trust Him throughout their lives. For those who persistently rebel against His Word, His declaration to Israel still applies, "They shall not enter into my rest."

In v. 6 the writer explains why that rest is still available. The fact that there is yet room in God's eternal rest is demonstrated in that the generation of Israelites to which the Promised Land was first offered rejected the offer and "in their hearts turned back again into Egypt" (Acts 7:39), as well as by the fact that God's original Sabbath has always been a sign of the promise of God's covenant, especially to Israel (Ex. 31:17). When God's offer of redemption is rejected by some, He always willingly and openly turns to others who will respond to the invitation (Mt. 22:8-10; Acts 13:46).

Our translators followed the Latin Vulgate in using the word "unbelief" here. But in the original the word is not the one (Greek *apistia*) translated that way, but rather the word for "disobedience" (Greek *apeitheia*). Unbelief is the state of mind, while disobedience is the outward manifestation of that state of mind (Westcott 97). The two words are logical partners, but they should not be confused any more than faith and works should be confused. Thus, it was because of their disobedience and rebellion, the open and outward demonstration of their lack of faith, that the original generation did not enter Canaan.

c. A rest remained after Joshua took Israel into Canaan (4:7, 8)

7 Again, he limiteth a certain day, saying in David, To day, after so long a time; as it is said, To day if ye will hear his voice, harden not your hearts.

8 For if Jesus had given them rest, then would he not afterward have spoken of another day.

In 4:7 our writer exhibits a homiletical element as he isolates one word from his quotation of Ps. 95:7. "He limiteth a certain day" means that the Scripture writer points to and specifies a certain day, but he does not mean to say that the psalmist was pointing to one particular day out of all of the days of history. He means, rather, that he is pointing to and specifying any day which is called "today" and only while it is called "today." Some commentators think that the expression, "saying in David" should probably be taken only as a common Hebrew manner of referring to the psalms as a whole, including psalms that were not necessarily written by David (Westcott 97). David apparently wrote almost half of the 150 psalms, by far more than any other single composer. But most of his psalms are in books one and two, through Psalm 72. However, the Septuagint (LXX), the ancient Greek translation of the O.T., which the writer of Hebrews always quotes, does assign the 95th psalm to David (Lunemann 174). Notice also that the writer of Hebrews, in quoting the same O.T. passage in 3:7, says there, "The Holy Ghost saith," while here he says, "saying in David." He obviously feels no problem in referring to the divine author of Scripture in one place and then referring to the human author for the same quotation in another. All Scripture has both a divine and human author. God Himself gave the Scripture, through various means and circumstances, but He always used a human author whom He protected and inspired in the recording of His Word.

Our inspired preacher emphasizes the part of Ps. 95:7 which meets his purpose, "To day, after so long a time; as it is said, To day if ye will hear his voice, harden not your hearts." The fact that an opportunity to enter God's rest still remains is drawn from the emphasis on the word "today." Such an opportunity obviously existed when the psalmist wrote this to his generation, over 400 years after the opportunity to enter the Promised Land was rejected by those original Israelites under Moses. Now the writer of Hebrews exhibits his faith in the relevance of Scripture as he applies the invitation to his own generation of Jewish believers. But "after so long a time" looks back to Moses' day, not to David's. For his purposes, the writer sees only two generations: that of Moses and his own (Lenski 135). "Today" is always the day of salvation, and only today. Nowhere does God ever promise salvation for tomorrow. Paul, in like manner, admonishes, "Now *is* the accepted time; behold, now *is* the day of salvation" (2 Cor. 6:2).

Some may question the logic of the writer concerning the fulfillment of God's promised rest to Israel. Did not Joshua, who succeeded Moses, take that next generation into Canaan? Did not that have some part in fulfilling God's promise? The writer supplies the answer in 4:8: "For if Jesus had given them rest, then would he not afterward have spoken of another day." This is one of two places in the KJV where the translators, translating literally, use the name "Jesus" when it does not refer to the Lord Jesus Christ. (The other is in Stephen's review of Israel's history in Acts 7:45.) The name "Joshua" in Hebrew (literally, *Jehoshua*) means "Jehovah (Yahweh) will save." The name "Jesus" in Greek (literally, *Iesous*) also means "Jehovah (Yahweh) will save." However, the context in both references makes it clear that Joshua, Moses' successor, is meant. Newer translations have made the change for clarification (NASB, NIV, NKJV, etc.).

It is certainly true that Joshua did take the next generation of Israelites into Canaan. This did bring fulfillment to certain aspects of the Abrahamic Covenant (Gen. 12:1-3), but it did not fully satisfy the spiritual elements of that Covenant, and it did not give the full and permanent rest that God had in mind for His people. Thus, the writer reasons, "Then would he not afterward have spoken of another day." Through David, in Ps. 95:7-11, God did speak of another day of rest which remains open to those who come to God by faith. Through the inspiration of the Spirit of God, David saw that day of rest for his generation, and through the same Spirit the writer of Hebrews sees the promise of that full rest for his generation. Because of the continuing relevance of the Scriptures, that same promise applies to us who have come to God by faith in His Son today. Indeed in dealing with Abraham later in chapter 11, the writer indicates that he always saw the fulfillment of the covenant in more than mere physical and financial blessing. Even after Abraham was in Canaan he "he looked for a city which hath foundations, whose builder and maker is God" (11:10), and "they that say such things declare plainly that they seek a country" (11:14). The entrance into Canaan, therefore, even under Joshua's victorious leadership, served only as a type of the grander rest which God had in mind for His children through faith in Christ.

d. A rest remains for God's people today (4:9, 10)

9 There remaineth therefore a rest to the people of God.
10 For he that is entered into his rest, he also hath ceased from his own works, as God *did* from his.

The writer arrives at his well-reasoned conclusion in v. 9: "There remaineth therefore a rest to the people of God." Follow his steps of reasoning from the preceding verses: (1) The basis for God's promised rest was His own rest from His creative activity on the seventh day, the Sabbath. (2) The original generation under Moses did not enter the Promised Land. (3) The next generation under Joshua did not fulfill the perfect idea of God's rest either. (4) This is shown by the fact that David still spoke of the availability of God's rest in his day. (5) That leads him to the conclusion that this rest is yet available for us today through faith in Jesus Christ. The word for "rest" (Greek *sabbatismos*) is different from the one he has used previously (Greek *katapausis*). The word here is fuller; it means "a Sabbath rest," and is used, no doubt, as a reminder of his point in v. 4 that God's own Sabbath rest after the six days of creation was a type of the eternal rest He wants us to share with Him through Jesus Christ. "The people of God," as the writer uses it, applies specifically to the believing remnant of the nation of Israel. God always extends His covenant, the Abrahamic Covenant, through them. Paul explains the idea of the extension of God's covenant in Rom. 1:16, "I am not ashamed of the gospel of Christ: for it is the power of God unto salvation to every one that believeth; to the Jew first, and also to the Greek."

"For" (Greek *gar*), in v. 10 connects this statement with the thought in v. 9, the fact that a rest is still available for us today. "He that is entered" might be translated, "He who has entered," referring to a completed act (Greek aorist tense). For the word "rest" the writer changes back to the more common word (Greek *katapausis*) used in the preceding verse, indicating that here he means them as synonyms.

For the sake of interpretation, it is very important to decide whether the writer is referring to a future rest in Heaven, after the struggles and trials of this life are over (Kent 88; Bruce 78; Lenski 137; Lunemann 175; Westcott 98; Barnes 103), or rather to a rest here and now by faith in Christ, having abandoned our useless efforts to be saved by our own good works. Most of those who want to make the primary application of the rest to this life grant that there is also some future significance (MacArthur 104; Morris 43). But it is highly questionable whether the writer has in mind any present application of his idea of rest. He is, after all, addressing Jewish believers who are beginning to face severe persecutions for their Christian faith. Some are apparently beginning to wonder if the struggles and trials are really worth it. The writer wants them to look beyond the present sufferings to the inexpressible joys in the presence of the Lord (Rom. 8:17, 18; Mt. 25:21, 23). In this verse, as in v. 4, he reminds these Jewish believers, who loved the Sabbath so much, that the very idea of the Sabbath was a beautiful symbol and type pointing toward our future and eternal rest with God. When that day comes, and only when that day comes, will the individual believer have "ceased from his own works, as God *did* from his." In creating this great universe and its inhabitants, God labored during the six days of creation. It was only when He was finished with this earthly scene, when His creative activity was complete, that He rested. In like manner we must continue to work and to exercise care in our Christian walk until our earthly journey is complete.

In this last phrase a different pronoun is used to describe God's work than for the believer's work. It is literally "his own" (Greek *idios*) work, emphasizing the fact that God's work in creation was absolutely personal and independent of all assistance. In applying the idea of the parallel between our final rest and God's Sabbath rest, Barnes (102) makes several appropriate observations: (1) Heaven is a place of cessation from wearisome toil; (2) Heaven will be like a Sabbath; (3) the Sabbath (the Lord's Day) here should be like Heaven; (4) they who do not love the Sabbath on earth are not prepared for Heaven; (5) the modern disregard for the Sabbath is a sad commentary as to widespread unreadiness for Heaven.

4. Helps in entering God's perfect rest (4:11-16)

In the following verses, through the end of chapter 4, the writer lays out at least four different aids or helps to make sure that we enter God's heavenly rest. These four helps are: (1) the example of Israel's unbelief (4:11); (2) the power of the written Word of God (4:12); (3) the knowledge of God's omniscience (4:13); (4) the intercessory ministry of Christ as our High Priest (4:14-16). If we use these helps as believers in Christ, we can be sure that we will enter God's heavenly rest when we pass from this earthly scene. Truly the Lord is able to keep us secure in our profession of faith in Him, but He does use spiritual and logical means of keeping us, and we are free to refuse to rely on those means of grace. He can and will keep us by His grace, but He will not keep us contrary to our own wills. Nowhere does the Scripture teach that God's grace for salvation is irresistible.

a. The example of Israel's unbelief (4:11)

11 Let us labour therefore to enter into that rest, lest any man fall after the same example of unbelief.

The first help for believers in entering God's eternal rest is the example of Israel's unbelief. We learn from examples, even from bad examples, and such is the admonition here. We must take extra care and caution that we enter God's rest since we can see that some, who had abundant opportunity, failed to do so. "Therefore" sets 4:11-16 apart and at the same time connects it with the preceding concern about entering the rest which the Lord has reserved for us. "Let us labor" (Greek *spoudazo*) is literally "Let us endeavor," "make every effort," "try hard." We might expect the admonition to be expressed in continuous action to point to the need for constant effort, but this is completed action (Greek aorist), further emphasizing the need for immediate and determined attention. The writer is obviously concerned for believers since he includes himself in the common exhortation. Entrance into "that rest," the one pointed out in v. 9, is still available for us, and that is our concern. The possible fall (Greek *pipto*), which we are warned about, is also expressed in completed action (Greek aorist), emphasizing a deadly, disastrous, and terminal fall (Lenski 139). The writer's desire is for all of us, not just his Hebrew audience, to heed the warning presented to us in the Biblical example of Israel's failure to enter Canaan's rest. We must not follow that "same example of unbelief." Again, as in v. 6, "unbelief" is "disobedience."

b. The power of God's Word (4:12)

12 For the word of God *is* quick, and powerful, and sharper than any twoedged sword, piercing even to the dividing asunder of soul and spirit, and of the joints and marrow, and *is* a discerner of the thoughts and intents of the heart.

The writer points to a second help to ensure that we enter God's rest, the wonderful, guiding, sanctifying power of the Word of God. If we rely on God's Word, we can certainly make it through this life of trial to God's rest in Heaven. Though the "word" is the same (Greek *logos*) as that which John 1:1 applies to the personal and eternal Son of God, it seems clear that the meaning here is not the "word" personified. There is some question whether the idea of calling the eternal Son "the Word," "The Logos," had developed this early in Christian theology. Hebrews was apparently written prior to A.D. 70, while John wrote his Gospel some 20 years later. But even if such thinking did already exist in the apostolic tradition, the context here makes it clear that the written and spoken Word is meant. Because of John's usage of *logos*, no doubt, many of the Greek and Latin fathers (e.g., Eusebius,

Athanasius) applied this verse to the personal, rather than the written, Word of God (see Westcott 101), and that tradition has been preserved by a few more recent commentators (Morgan 58, 59). But the description given here applies much better to the written and spoken Word than to the personal Word of God, His eternal Son (Archer 32; Thomas 50; Alford 82; Westcott 101; Lenski 140). In addition to this, the word in question (Greek *logos*) is used commonly throughout the N.T. to refer to the written and spoken Word of God. In this verse, then, the "Word" has its broadest sense: whether the O.T., which the writer of Hebrews freely quotes; or the word of the apostles, the N.T., which was still being formed under the guidance of inspiration; or the preached word when men filled with the Spirit of God deliver their exhortations based squarely on the written Word to the congregation (see Jn. 12:48; Dt. 18:18, 19).

The writer now uses five terms to describe the impact of the written and spoken Word of God. The Word of God is "living" (Greek *zao*): that is, it is not dead nor will it ever die; it endures when other things fade away. Jesus declared, "Heaven and earth shall pass away, but my words shall not pass away" (Mt. 24:35).

The Word of God is "powerful" (Greek *energes*); it is effective (Philem. 6); it is fully capable of doing what God wants done. The Lord declared concerning His word, "It shall not return unto me void, but it shall accomplish that which I please, and it shall prosper *in the thing* whereto I sent it" (Is. 55:11). Note the similarity of the original word to our English word "energy" or "energize." God's Word, when it is read or preached, demonstrates that kind of power.

Furthermore, the Word of God is "sharper than any twoedged sword." The Roman soldier normally carried a sword with two cutting edges to do its work both coming and going. Paul made a similar comparison in describing the Christian's armor, patterned after that of the Roman soldier. The Christian is to bear "the sword of the Spirit, which is the word of God" (Eph. 6:17). But God's Word not only cuts like a double-edged sword, removing the dross and defending the faith, perhaps from a more personal point of view, it also is "piercing even to the dividing asunder of soul and spirit, and of the joints and marrow." A native Chinese brought back a N.T. to the missionary. When reminded that it was not necessary to return the little book, that it was his to keep, the Chinese man said, "I don't want to keep it; every time I read it, it kicks me." All of us who are Christians have experienced the penetrating force of the Word of God, both in coming to Christ as well as in the ongoing sanctification process.

The writer emphasizes the depth of the piercing power of the Word even to the dividing of "soul and spirit." Some have tried to use this verse, along with 1 Th. 5:23 (see the discussion of this verse in the commentary on 1 Thessalonians), to prove that man is composed of three parts: body, soul, and spirit (Pink 217). This view is called *trichotomy*, while the view maintained by others, that man is composed of only two parts, is called *dichotomy*. It seems more likely that, in both cases, the writers are not arguing that point. Paul in Thessalonians is merely trying to stress what makes up the whole person, for sanctification and preservation, while the writer of Hebrews means to emphasize the depths to which God's Word penetrates, dividing even that which technically cannot be divided. When viewed separately, the body is the material part of man; the soul is the seat of life and emotions, of self, the earthly part; while the spirit is the higher part of man that responds to God, the immortal part of man. In the unregenerate man the soul, the self, rules, and the spirit is enslaved, but in regeneration the spirit is enthroned. Following conversion we are not ruled by our earthly nature, but by our spiritual nature (Lenski 141; 1 Cor. 2:14). There are passages, however, where the idea of soul seems also to include spirit (Gen. 2:7; Ps. 16:10; Mt. 10:28; 16:26, etc.).

The writer goes further to show how deeply God's Word penetrates into a person's being, "even to the dividing of the joints and marrow." These elements form part of the bone structure of a man. While "soul and spirit" emphasize the spiritual part of a person, "joints and marrow" emphasize the physical part. There is absolutely no part of a person that the Word of God cannot touch.

Finally, the Word of God is "a discerner of the thoughts and intents of the heart." The word translated "discerner" (Greek *kritikos*) means a judge or a critic. Jesus declared, "He that rejecteth me, and receiveth not my words, hath one that judgeth him: the word that I have spoken, the same shall judge him in the last day" (Jn. 12:48). If we don't allow God's Word to be our judge, our critic, while we live, then it will certainly become our judge in the day of judgment. Furthermore, God's Word is able to judge not just the externals, which may be evident to all men, but also that which is internal, even "the thoughts and intents of the heart." These two words include both the emotions or affections as well as the motives, reasoning, or purposes in a person's life. How dramatically the writer declares the penetrating, convicting power of the Word of God!

c. The knowledge of God's omniscience (4:13)

13 Neither is there any creature that is not manifest in his sight: but all things *are* naked and opened unto the eyes of him with whom we have to do.

Some maintain that v. 13 is still describing the spoken or written Word of God (Lenski 145). But the wording is much better applied to God in a more personal way, particularly to His attribute of omniscience (Westcott 104; Barnes 103; Bruce 105; Delitzsch I:215; Pink 219; Alford 86). This is the third help which the writer points to as an aid to entering God's rest. Westcott and Delitzsch point out that the nature of the two personal pronouns in the phrases "*his* sight" and "the eyes of *him*" as well as the meaning of the last phrase, "with whom we have to do," all call for a personal reference to God rather than to His spoken and written Word. It is also a very logical move from speaking about God's Word in v. 12 to God's omniscience in v. 13, especially as it further illustrates God's penetrating power and knowledge in our lives. Knowing that God sees everything we do, down to the smallest detail, should help us in being more open to Him in confessing our fears and weaknesses and depending on His strength.

Indeed, God's all-seeing eye covers all of creation: "Neither is there any creature that is not manifest in his sight." "Creature" (Greek *ktisis*) can refer either to the act of creation itself (Rom. 1:20) or to the product of His creation, to any created thing (Rom. 1:25). In this context, of course, the writer primarily has in mind mankind, the sole object of creation which was made originally in God's own image (Gen. 1:26). He first puts it negatively. There is not one single one of God's created beings "that is not manifest in his sight." But he follows this with a positive and a two-fold declaration of God's omniscience: "all things are naked and opened" to God's eyes. As men we can only see the outward appearance of our fellow man, only what he chooses to present to us, whether good or bad; but when God looks at us, He sees everything. The fine moral clothing with which we dress up our disobedience is stripped away, and there is nothing left except what we really are; we stand "naked" before Him.

The psalmist described the absoluteness of God's omniscience when he declared the impossibility of escaping His presence, whether in Heaven, in Hell, beyond the sea, or even in the darkness: "The darkness hideth not from thee; but the night shineth as the day: the darkness and the light *are* both alike *to thee*" (see Ps. 139:7-13). Jesus also declared, "Nothing is secret, that shall not be made manifest; neither *any thing* hid, that shall not be known and come abroad" (Lk. 8:17). The writer takes this all-seeing atttribute a step further when he says that we stand "opened" to His eyes. This word (Greek perfect passive participle of *trachelizo*) literally means "having been opened," "standing opened." The root of the word used here refers to the neck (Greek *trachelos*). Some think that it refers to the practice of a wrestler who triumphantly grabs his opponent by the hair of the head and thrusts his head back, exposing his face and neck to the cheering crowd in his shame and defeat or thrusting the defeated enemy prostrate to the ground (Westcott 104). Others think that the writer is painting a picture with a more Biblical brush as he depicts the action of the priest who, in offering the lamb as a sacrifice, pulls his head back to expose his neck to the sharp blade of the knife (Barnes 105). Though it is difficult to prove what the writer specifically had in mind, I prefer the latter interpretation, especially in light of the prominence of the priests and the sacrifices in Hebrews. What a graphic picture our writer has presented of the complete exposure we face as we stand before God!

Regardless, the point is that we stand naked and opened before the eyes of him "with whom we have to do." Though the meaning seems fairly evident, the words are a bit cumbersome in the original, literally: "to whom for us the account." The NIV translates, "To whom we must give account," and that is the meaning that most commentators agree upon, which seems appropriate in the context. We will not stand before men, who can be so easily deceived, but rather before God, who sees and knows everything (Gal. 6:7). The writer hopes that reminding the Hebrews about the all-seeing eyes of God will encourage them when they are being persecuted and warn them against any continuation in the spiritual sluggishness into which some had fallen.

d. The intercession of Christ as our High Priest (4:14-16)

14 Seeing then that we have a great high priest, that is passed into the heavens, Jesus the Son of God, let us hold fast *our* profession.
15 For we have not an high priest which cannot be touched with the feeling of our infirmities; but was in all points tempted like as *we are, yet* without sin.
16 Let us therefore come boldly unto the throne of grace, that we may obtain mercy, and find grace to help in time of need.

The fourth help or aid the writer gives us for entering God's rest is the intercession of Jesus Christ as our High Priest, as our man in Heaven. He already introduced Christ as seated "on the right hand of the Majesty on high" (1:3), as "a merciful and faithful high priest" (2:17), and as our "Apostle and High Priest" (3:1). But having reintroduced the theme here of Christ as our High Priest, he will continue with this theme (with some detours) at least through chapter 10 (Barnes 107; Westcott 105). The verses here (4:14-16) serve as a transition from his description of Christ's superiority to Moses and Joshua to the superiority of His priesthood in contrast with that of Aaron and the Levitical order.

In the phrase, "Seeing that we have a great high priest," our translators supplied "seeing" to suggest the idea of cause: "Since we have a great high priest." "Great" describes the dignity of His office and is meant to present Him beyond all comparison in the priestly office. First, He is our great High Priest because of His location, the place where He ministers. He has "passed into the heavens." On the Day of Atonement, the tenth day of the seventh month in ancient Israel, and only on that day, the high priest entered the Holy of Holies of the tabernacle with sacrificial blood to sprinkle on the Mercy Seat in the very presence of Almighty God (Num. 16). It seems obvious that the writer has this offering in mind as he presents the present position of our High Priest.

"Passed into" is more literally "passed through" (Greek *dierchomai*), based on the picture of the O.T. priest as he parted the inner veil on the Day of Atonement and proceeded into the Holy of Holies. "Is passed" (Greek perfect tense) means "having passed" and indicates a completed act that carries continuing results. The O.T. priest repeated this act every year, but our High Priest has taken this position on our behalf until He comes again. "The heavens" stand in contrast to the veil which the Levitical priest passed through. Paul spoke of being caught up into the presence of God in the third heaven (2 Cor. 12:2); others have spoken of seven heavens. Regardless how one counts them, the writer means to say that Christ passed beyond all the nearer heavens to the right hand of God to intercede for us. As Paul declared, He "ascended up far above all heavens, that he might fill all things" (Eph. 4:10).

Second, Jesus is our great High Priest not only because of His *location*, but also because of His *title*, His identity. He is "Jesus the Son of God." "Jesus" is the name given to Him by His parents at the command of the angel Gabriel (Mt. 1:21; Lk. 1:31) at His incarnation, when "the Word was made flesh, and dwelt among us" (Jn. 1:14). It is the name that identified Him as a true man, as one able to feel our needs and sympathize with our situations. Because He is Jesus, He understands our troubles and can effectively communicate them to the Heavenly Father. But He is also "the Son of God." He became Jesus when He was born of the virgin, but He has been the Son of God from all eternity. As the man Jesus, He understands our needs; but as the Son of God, He possesses the power to meet those needs, because "in him dwelleth all the fulness of the Godhead bodily" (Col. 2:9).

On the basis of having such a great High Priest, the writer exhorts, "Let us hold fast *our* profession." "Hold fast" (Greek *krateo*) is used again in 6:18 with reference to "laying hold of the hope set before us." There the writer emphasizes completed action (Greek aorist), stressing the act of firmly grabbing hold of something. Here he uses continuous action (Greek present), "Let us keep holding fast," stressing the fact that an ongoing effort is required in the Christian life. "Holding fast" is the opposite of "falling away" in 6:6.

"Profession" (Greek *homologia*) is better taken as "confession" (as in 3:1), referring to that confession of Christ which we made when we first believed. The word literally means "speaking alike" or "speaking in agreement with." God says that we are sinners, and that Jesus Christ, His Son, died for our sins. When we confess, we acknowledge that God is right; we agree, both in the confession of our sins and in the confession of Christ in faith, with all that the Scripture teaches about Him. The Scripture repeatedly stresses the importance of public confession (Mt. 10:32, 33; Rom. 10:9, 10; 1 Tim. 6:12). John declares, "Every spirit that confesseth that Jesus Christ is come in the flesh is of God" (1 Jn. 4:2), and "Whosoever shall confess that Jesus is the Son of God, God dwelleth in him, and he in God" (1 Jn. 4:15). Those who follow Jesus, our great High Priest, into Heaven must hold faithfully to this confession.

"For" in v. 15 introduces the reason we should be able to successfully "hold fast our confession," expressed both negatively and positively. Negatively, it is because "we have not an high priest which cannot be touched with the feeling of our infirmities." He could have said, "We have a high priest who can be touched," but that would not catch our attention nearly so well. The writer also probably used this negative expression because he was anticipating a problem in the minds of his readers. They might question whether the sinless Son of God could truly sympathize with the struggles they were facing and the weaknesses which so often dragged them down. He answers the question before it can be asked. Furthermore, the negative expression highlights the positive reason which follows.

"To be touched with the feeling" (Greek *sumpatheo*) literally means "to suffer with" someone, to feel as they do in their struggles. Our English word "sympathize" finds its origin in the word used here. Our Lord, because He became "Jesus" through the incarnation, because He was "made like unto *his* brethren" (2:17), is able to understand how we feel in the midst or our trials and struggles. Someone who has always been rich, and never been poor, might have difficulty in truly understanding how poor people feel. Paul saw the appropriateness of this very illustration when he said, "For ye know the grace of our Lord Jesus Christ, that, though he was rich, yet for your sakes he became poor, that ye through his poverty might be rich" (2 Cor. 8:9). He doesn't just sympathize with our struggles from a distance, as an outward observer, but He sympathizes with them because He has Himself endured them (Westcott 106). As a result of the incarnation Jesus is able to sympathize with our infirmities (Greek *astheneia*). This does not mean our sins, because Christ certainly does not sympathize with those; rather, He forgives them. "Infirmities" refers to those sinless weaknesses which are characteristic of all true human beings, even Jesus Christ. Jesus at times grew tired (Jn. 4:6); He became hungry (Mt. 4:2), and thirsty (Jn. 19:28); He was sometimes discouraged (Jn. 6:67), sad (Jn. 11:35), lonely (Mt. 26:40), and disillusioned (Mt. 26:50; Yeager 175). In men these sinless weaknesses sometimes lead us into sin, but Christ resisted that.

Even so, He was "in all points tempted like as *we are*." Some might question "in all points" with the thought that some temptations that we face today did not even exist when Jesus was on the earth. In looking at our Lord's three temptations, following the order of the Gospel of Luke, He was tempted to turn stones into bread (Lk. 4:1-4), to worship Satan in exchange for the kingdoms of the world (Lk. 4:5-8), and to cast Himself from the pinnacle of the Temple to attract the crowds (Lk. 4:9-12). By analyzing these three temptations, and comparing them with Gen. 3:6, in the Serpent's temptation of Eve, and 1 Jn. 2:16, where John lists "all that is in the world," we may conclude that temptations are of a common lot from the beginning of time to the present day. The "lust of the flesh" refers to the *natural appetites* (turning stones into bread); the "lust of the eyes" refers to the *desire for possessions and wealth* (kingdoms of the world); and the "pride of life" refers to the *desire for fame and recognition* (pinnacle of the temple). I suggest that this Biblical summary of temptation explains "in all points" in which Jesus was tempted. He was tempted in every area of human struggle which we will ever face, and thus He is able to fully sympathize with our needs in similar struggles today and to the end of time. In the similar passage in 2:18 the writer used completed action (Greek aorist tense), "being tempted," to express the fact of His temptation. In "tempted" here (Greek perfect tense) he pictures the temptation as a process which continued throughout His life, but is now complete with His death, resurrection, and ascension to His present position of intercession (Lenski 150).

Because Jesus' temptation was accomplished in this manner, it was, indeed, "like as we are," fully qualifying Him as our sympathetic High Priest, but with one grand and glorious exception: "yet without sin." The sinlessness of Christ is strategic to the plan of redemption. If He was not sinless, He was no better than we are. He certainly could not help with our failures if He had failed Himself. As Alford (89) points out, in facing the same temptations that we face, He victoriously overcame them in their origin, in their process, and in their result. The sinlessness of Christ is also emphasized in 2 Cor. 5:21; 1 Pet. 2:22; and 1 Jn. 3:5.

In verse 14 the writer pointed out the position of our great High Priest in Heaven and identified Him by both His human and divine nature. In v. 15 he stressed His ability to sympathize with our weaknesses because of His similar experiences. "Therefore" in v. 16 connects these observations with the writer's exhortation to the Hebrews to take full advantage of this great help which is available for us. "Let us come" (Greek *proserchomai*) is commonly used in Hebrews, always with the idea of approaching God in worship (7:25; 10:1, 22; 11:6; 12:18, 22). It is expressed with continuous action, "Let us keep on coming," to emphasize the need for constant dependence on Christ as our High Priest. The word is frequently used in the Septuagint (LXX), the Greek version of the O.T., with this as well as other applications.

In this exhortation the writer has us approaching "the throne of grace." The fact that this *throne* is the antitype to that which was pictured by the mercy seat in the O.T. tabernacle seems obvious in light of the context here in Hebrews, though Alford (90) doesn't think so. As he suggests, this throne is the throne of God, but that is what the mercy seat, the place in the tabernacle where God appeared between the cherubim (Ex. 25:22), represented (Bruce 86). It is appropriately called the throne of "grace" because it is the source of our undeserved supply of strength for facing the struggles and trials of life. It is the throne of grace during this dispensation, and we must take full advantage of it, for it will become the throne of judgment for all who have neglected it when our Lord returns in glory (Rev. 20:11-15; Westcott 108).

We should come before this throne of grace "boldly," literally "with boldness" (Greek *meta parresias*). The boldness refers to both our courage, through Jesus Christ, in coming before God's awesome presence, as well as our confidence that we can freely confess all of our weaknesses to one who is more than willing to supply our need. The purpose of our coming is twofold: "that we may obtain mercy, and find grace." "Mercy" is God's compassion toward those in distress; "grace" is God's favor toward the undeserving. In His mercy God withholds the punishment that we justly deserve, but in His grace He grants His favor and His strength that we may victoriously live for Him. We are sinful and need mercy; we are feeble and need grace (Barnes 109).

Notice also the difference in the verbs used for the reception of God's two kinds of love: we "obtain" or receive mercy, but we "find" grace. Perhaps the difference is chronological. In our weakness and failure we can only reach up and receive mercy and pardon, but with that encouragement, we can seek and find God's grace for living the Christian life. Mercy especially emphasizes forgiveness for the past, and grace emphasizes strength for the present and for the future.

This mercy and grace are always supplied by our loving Father and His beloved Son "in time of need," or more literally, "for timely help" (Greek *eis eukairon boetheian*). God's timing and our timing do not always agree. It may seem sometimes that God is not going to come through in our struggles, but ultimately He always does, just at the right time. God didn't keep Paul and Silas from being beaten and imprisoned in Philippi, but He sent an earthquake to open the prison doors as well as the hearts of the Philippian jailer and his household (Acts 16:19-33). God didn't keep persecution from coming to these

Hebrews, but He did and will supply mercy and grace to help them and us overcome.

Summary (4:1-16)

On the basis of the writer's reminder to the Hebrews in chapter 3 that Israel failed to enter God's perfect rest because of their unbelief, he starts chapter 4 by making this same application to them. If Israel could fail to enter the earthly rest of Canaan, these Hebrew Christians, who were their descendants, could also fail to enter the ultimate Promised Land of rest—Heaven itself (4:1, 2).

The writer then proceeds to demonstrate the certainty that a rest still remains for God's people. First, he points to the basis of the idea of a promised rest. It comes from the fact that God made the earth in six days and rested on the seventh. God's Sabbath rest was established, not because the Lord Himself was tired and needed rest, but as a distinct symbol that His creative work was complete. Thus, the idea of the Sabbath rest, which was established by God at creation (Gen. 2:3), and commanded by Moses in the Law (Ex. 20:8), stands as a symbol and a goal for God's people today. Just as God rested after His work was done, so we can look forward to our eternal rest after our work on this earth is done (4:3, 4).

Another reason that a rest still remains for God's people is that original Israel which came out of Egypt did not enter the Promised Land of Canaan because of their rebellion and unbelief. Concerning that generation God said that they would not enter into His rest (Ps. 95:11). Since God did not allow that original generation to enter in, that means His goal of a promised rest for His people was left unfulfilled (4:5, 6).

The third reason as to why a rest still remains is the fact that Joshua still did not perfectly fulfill God's goal for a rest for His people when he took the next generation of Israelites into Canaan after the death of Moses. We know that such a rest is still open because of the quotation from Ps. 95:7-11 which the writer recorded in 3:7-11.

When David spoke to the Israelites of his time, he used the word "today" in warning them against hardening their hearts with regard to entering God's rest. For the writer of Hebrews "today" is still with us, and this time reference indicates that God's promise of a rest for His people is still with us as well (4:7, 8). Thus in 4:9 the writer gives his conclusion to his arguments about God's present-day rest based on the two O.T. types of Sabbath rest and Canaan rest: "There remaineth therefore a rest to the people of God." Just as God ceased His creative work on the seventh day, the Sabbath, so we will cease our labor when this life is over, but until then we must continue to trust in Christ our Savior and work for the advancement of His kingdom (4:9, 10).

Now that he has established the premise of a rest remaining for God's people, the writer concludes the chapter by giving four different helps or aids to ensure that we will enter God's rest. The first help is the example of Israel's unbelief. If ancient Israel failed to enter Canaan because of their unbelief, the same possibility existed for the original readers of Hebrews, and for us. We must therefore be warned and on guard. Second, he points to the written and spoken Word of God as a powerful and piercing motivator to push us on toward that heavenly rest. Third, if the penetrating power of the written and spoken word is not enough, we are reminded of the all-seeing eyes of a personal God who misses absolutely nothing about our lives, not about our behavior nor even the innermost thoughts of our hearts and minds. Fourth, there is the tremendous privilege of having God's only beloved Son, Jesus Christ, as our High Priest.

Though Jesus now sits at the right hand of the Father on the throne of grace, the heavenly mercy seat, He once walked this earth in human flesh and faced the same struggles and trials, many of them from the devil himself, which we all face today. He was different, however, in one very important matter: in the midst of all those temptations, He never sinned. He completed His course without a single blemish. Because of this, we should constantly and confidently go to Him with every need in our lives, expecting to receive in great abundance God's mercy for forgiveness and God's grace for strength at just the right time in every situation (4:11-16).

Application: Teaching and Preaching the Passage

There are three things to keep in mind concerning the promised rest. (1) It is possible for those who are offered this promised rest to fall short of it. If it were not possible to fall short of the promised rest, such a warning would not be given. (2) It is an awful circumstance to seem to come short of that rest or to actually come short of it. There are always preliminary indications that should heighten our awareness that things are not going well in our spiritual lives. It is also the responsibility of brothers and sisters in Christ to call our attention to spiritual lethargy, just as the writer of Hebrews is doing, since others can sometimes discern such failings better than the person experiencing them. (3) The means to avoid falling short of that rest is to have the proper fear or respect for the possibility of falling. The Apostle Paul warns, "Let him that thinketh he standeth take heed lest he fall" (1 Cor. 10:12). Knowing that there is a real possibility of failing to enter that eternal rest should make us constantly watchful against the spiritual enemies that would destroy our souls (4:1).

Several observations can be made concerning the statement, "The word preached did not profit them" (4:2). (1) The primary purpose of preaching the Word is always that we might profit from it. (2) Unfortunately, many in every generation, and in almost every audience, do not profit from hearing the Word preached. Such was the teaching of the parable of the sower, perhaps Jesus' most famous parable (Mt. 13:3-23). Some of the Gospel seed fell by the wayside, some on stony places, some among thorns, and some on the good ground, producing genuine fruit. Three out of four did not respond to the Word in faith. (3) The primary cause when we do not profit from hearing the Word is unbelief, as was the case with ancient Israel (Henry 906). Unbelief and disobedience are constant spiritual partners, just like faith and works. James said, "Be ye doers of the word, and not hearers only, deceiving your own selves" (Jas. 1:22).

Notice also that the "gospel" (Greek *euangelion*) was preached to Israel in the wilderness just as to the Hebrews by our writer. The word "gospel" means "good news," and it is basically the same in every generation. Since the fall of Adam, every man who is saved was saved by grace through faith (Hab. 2:4; Rom. 1:17; Eph. 2:8, 9). In the O.T. they looked forward to the cross in types and prophecies; in the N.T. those types and prophecies were fulfilled in Jesus' birth, life, death, resurrection, and ascension. Thus, because the basis of salvation is the same in both dispensations, the warning about failure (Israel in the wilderness) and the encouragement from success (e.g. the faith of Abraham) were applicable to the writer's Hebrew audience, as well as to the modern-day church (4:2).

God's promise for a rest for His people was implied by: (1) the original Sabbath rest when God rested, not because He was tired, but because His creative work was finished; (2) the continual observance of the Sabbath on the basis of God's original blessing of the seventh day and the command to remember the Sabbath day in the law of Moses (Ex. 20:8); (3) the proposal of Canaan as a typical rest for those who believe; (4) the certainty of another rest beyond Sabbath rest and Canaan rest.

There are four helps for entering God's rest in 4:11-16: (1) the example of Israel's unbelief (4:11); (2) the effectiveness of the Word of God (4:12); (3) the awareness of God's omniscience (4:13); and (4) the intercession of Jesus as our High Priest (4:14-16).

The Word of God: (1) convicts us of sin (4:12); (2) converts the soul (Ps. 19:7); (3) cleanses the conscience (Jn. 15:3); (4) consecrates the life (Jn. 17:17); (5) corrects the wrong (2 Tim. 3:16); (6) confirms the right (Jn. 8:31); (7) comforts and encourages the heart (Ps. 119:11; Thomas 60). We must give the Word of God: (1) careful consideration; (2) continual meditation; (3) close application.

God's Word is highlighted: (1) It is quick or alive—it endures and is relevant in every generation (Mt. 5:18; 24:35). (2) It is effective or energetic—it accomplishes the purpose for which it is sent (Is. 55:11). (3) It is convicting of even our most hidden sins—it cuts and penetrates to the deepest part of our being (Jer. 23:29). (4) It is a critic and a motivator with regard to all of our plans and intentions, whether good or bad (2 Tim. 2:16, 17).

With regard to Christ as our High Priest, the writer points to: (1) possession of Jesus as our High Priest proclaimed—"Seeing then that we have a great high priest" (4:14); (2) persistence in our confession demanded—"Let us hold fast *our* profession" (4:14); (3) dependence on God's provision of mercy and grace—"Let us therefore come boldly" (4:16). In both Hebrew and Greek the word "test" and "tempt" are identical. The meaning must be determined by the context. If the motivation is evil, as from Satan or evil men, then it is a temptation (Mt. 4:1); but if the motivation is good, as from God or good men, then it is a test or a trial (Gen. 22:1; Jas. 1:13, 14). Sometimes the same events in our lives are a temptation to defeat or destroy us from the devil's point of view, but a test or trial to strengthen us from God's point of view.

III. THE SUPERIOR INTERCESSION OF THE SON AS HIGH PRIEST IN RELATION TO THE LEVITICAL PRIESTHOOD (5:1—10:39)

A. The Priesthood of Christ a New Type of Priesthood (5:1-10)

The writer has introduced the idea of Christ as our High Priest several times earlier in the epistle. In 1:3 he referred to the historic occasion "when he had by himself purged our sins." In 2:9 he pointed to the one who became a man "that he by the grace of God should taste death for every man." In 2:17 he described Jesus as "a merciful and faithful high priest in things *pertaining* to God." The present discussion of Christ as our compassionate priest was introduced in 4:14-16. Since we are advised to come boldly to His priestly throne where He now sits in the heavens (4:16), it is necessary that the writer delve more deeply into the characteristics and qualifications of Jesus as our High Priest.

1. The requirements of the O.T. priesthood (5:1-4)

In Hebrews 5:1-4 the writer outlines various requirements for the O.T. priest under the law of Moses. "For" at the beginning of 5:1 indicates that he is continuing to explain the declaration about Jesus as our great High Priest in 4:14-16. Jewish believers would naturally be concerned about what happened to the O.T. teaching about the high priest in their move from Judaism to Christianity. In 5:5-10 the writer shows how Christ met these requirements and thus fulfilled the purpose and function of the O.T. priesthood.

The number of requirements outlined here from the O.T. high priesthood depends on how we divide them. Some writers see only two (Bruce 88), while others see three (MacArthur 119) or four (Barnes 110). For the sake of understanding, it is best to make the division as detailed as possible. Thus, the writer points to these requirements for an effective high priest: (1) his background; (2) his purpose; (3) his compassion; and (4) his divine call. Though it is true that many of the O.T. priests between Aaron and Christ did not fulfill this ideal, including the priests of Jesus' day, these were still the requirements which God sought in the priesthood.

a. His background (5:1a)

1a For every high priest taken from among men is ordained for men in things *pertaining* to God.

First, the priest must be "taken from among men." In Israel's history the high priest was to come from Aaron's family, who was from the tribe of Levi. Thus he was indeed one of them and should be able to understand their thinking. Though the writer of Hebrews does not take the time to make individual application of each of these requirements to the life of Jesus Christ, it is obvious that this is what he desires in the mind of his readers. Knowing the gospel story, they understood the importance of the incarnation for Christ's priestly ministry, the fact that "the Word was made flesh, and dwelt among us" (Jn. 1:14). The writer has already given his understanding of the incarnation in 2:5-18. In 2:5-9 in particular he pointed out that Jesus

Christ, as the Second Adam divinely appointed as man's representative, succeeded where the first Adam had failed. Hebrews 2:9 sums up his view of the incarnation: "But we see Jesus, who was made a little lower than the angels for the suffering of death, crowned with glory and honour; that he by the grace of God should taste death for every man." Like Aaron, Jesus Christ was "taken from among men." Aaron was in every respect one of the brethren, and so was Christ.

b. His purpose (5:1b)

1b That he may offer both gifts and sacrifices for sins.

The second requirement relates to the *purpose* of his ministry. The O.T. prophet and the N.T. apostle were sent by God with a message to man. The priestly ministry was the very opposite. He went to God on behalf of the needs of his fellowman, which he understood because he was one of them. Though our writer leaves it unsaid at this point, his readers knew that Christ performed this aspect of the priestly ministry in His life, death, resurrection, ascension, and His present, continuing ministry.

Paul, writing to the Ephesians a little earlier, pointed to God's power toward us "Which he wrought in Christ, when he raised him from the dead, and set *him* at his own right hand in the heavenly *places*" (see Eph. 1:19-23). But the writer of Hebrews also points out that one of the main functions of the priest was that he "may offer both gifts and sacrifices for sins." The present tense "is ordained" apparently indicates that the sacrifices were still going on at the time, and thus that the Temple was still standing. By emphasizing "both gifts and sacrifices for sins," the writer may be pointing to the different types of offerings described in detail in Leviticus 1-5. We usually enumerate them in five different offerings under two categories. The Dedicatory Offerings were: (1) the whole burnt offering, emphasizing the desire for complete dedication to God; (2) the meal or grain offering, emphasizing thanksgiving for physical provisions; (3) the peace offering, emphasizing thanksgiving for a spiritual relationship with God. The term "gifts" refers to the Dedicatory Offerings. But then there were two types of Sin Offerings: (1) the sin offering itself, which was offered for sins in general; and (2) the trespass offering, an offering made for the violation of the rights of others. These offerings are referred to as "sacrifices for sins." Other writers think, however, that the writer's meaning is not intended to be so specific, but rather by "gifts and sacrifices for sins" he simply means to sum up the whole sacrificial system of ancient Israel (Bruce 89). Our Lord, of course, offered the greatest sacrifice that could ever be made when He offered Himself on the cross.

c. His compassion (5:2, 3)

2 Who can have compassion on the ignorant, and on them that are out of the way; for that he himself also is compassed with infirmity.
3 And by reason hereof he ought, as for the people, so also for himself, to offer for sins.

The third requirement for the O.T. high priest was *compassion*. Here, and probably almost always in the epistle, the great Day of Atonement is in view, when the priest, once a year, entered the Holy of Holies to ask forgiveness for his sins and the sins of the entire nation (see Lev. 16). A priest who is so different from us that he could not possibly understand the difficulties we face in real life would be little help to us. Our Lord's compassion has already been described in 4:15, "For we have not an high priest which cannot be touched with the feeling of our infirmities; but was in all points tempted like as *we are, yet* without sin." There the word infirmities (Greek *astheneia*) is used in the plural, referring in context to the sinless weaknesses which are a common lot of all human beings, including Jesus Christ, the weaknesses of growing tired, being hungry, being thirsty, being lonely, etc. Christ was able to sympathize, to feel with them, because He also experienced such sinless weaknesses Himself in His full experience of humanity. Here the writer is speaking directly about the O.T. high priest, not specifically about Christ. However, he limits his ability to sympathize with sinners to "compassion on the ignorant, and on them that are out of the way." He is obviously conscious of the limits to sympathy and forgiveness for sins which are committed willfully, as acts of persistent rebellion against God. He has in mind such instruction as given in Num. 15:27-31:

> And if any soul sin through ignorance, then he shall bring a she goat of the first year for a sin-offering. And the priest shall make an atonement for the soul that sinneth ignorantly, when he sinneth by ignorance before the LORD, to make an atonement for him; and it shall be forgiven him. Ye shall have one law for him that sinneth through ignorance, *both* for him that is born among the children of Israel, and for the stranger that sojourneth among them. But the soul that doeth *ought* presumptuously, *whether he be* born in the land, or a stranger, the same reproacheth the LORD; and that soul shall be cut off from among his people. Because he hath despised the word of the LORD, and hath broken his commandment, that soul shall utterly be cut off; his iniquity *shall be* upon him.

God warned Israel about a sin which could not be forgiven (Bruce 91). Christ taught about the same (Mt. 12:22-37), and Hebrews will discuss this more fully in chapters 6 and 10.

The O.T. priest was able to be sympathetic with sinners coming for forgiveness "for that he himself also is compassed with infirmity." "Infirmity" (Greek *astheneia*), used in the singular, is the same word used in the plural with reference to the sympathy of Christ in 4:15. There, however, it may refer only to the sinless weaknesses which are common to all humanity, Jesus Christ included. Here, in reference to the Levitical priests, the word takes on a deeper meaning, as is clear in the next verse: "And by reason hereof he ought, as for the people, so also for himself, to offer for sins." The instructions of Leviticus 16 about the Day of Atonement are very clear. The high priest was first to enter the Holy of Holies with the blood of a bullock for his own sins. He would then enter a second time with the blood of a goat for the sins of the people of Israel. Finally, he would send a scapegoat into the wilderness symbolically bearing away the sins of Israel. It is to this action on the Day of Atonement that the writer of Hebrews is referring. Leviticus 16:6 says, "And Aaron shall offer his bullock of the sin offering, which *is* for himself, and make an atonement for himself, and for his house."

Some might think that a sinner priest could be more sympathetic to the appealing sinners than the sinless Christ. Not so, for as the writer has already mentioned in 4:15, our Supreme Savior and High Priest was "in all points tempted like as *we are, yet* without sin." Even if the Levitical high priest was good and sincere, and many of them were not, as a sinner himself he would not suffer the full weight of temptation. Such an impact could only be experienced by one who never gave in, no matter how unbearable the trials had become.

d. His divine call (5:4)

4 And no man taketh *this* honour unto himself, but he that is called of God, as *was* Aaron.

The fourth requirement of the O.T. priest related to his *divine* call. This call of Aaron is indicated in Ex. 28:1-3 as details are given about the garments in which he was to serve. This call is dramatically reaffirmed in God's judgment on Korah and the 250 princes who followed him in Numbers 16. Then in Numbers 17 God's call is symbolized for future generations in Aaron's rod which budded and was to be stored in the Ark of the Covenant (see Num. 17:9, 10). God's subsequent judgment on Saul (1 Sam. 13:8ff.), and later on Uzziah (2 Chr. 26:16ff.), for invading the priestly office stresses the importance of God's call for the priestly office. Aaron's call, of course, applied to his descendants who succeeded him in the office. But for Christ there must be a new call, for His priesthood is from a different order and thus marks a new and different dispensation.

2. The essential qualifications met by Christ (5:5-10)

In Heb. 5:5-10 our author shows that Christ fulfilled these requirements for the priesthood, dealing with them in reverse order. Thus he deals first with the divine call as it relates to Christ (vv. 5, 6), then with the priestly compassion (vv. 7, 8), and, finally, with the redemptive purpose of his ministry (vv. 9, 10) (Westcott 121). His true humanity, which stood out in the enumeration of the priestly requirements above, would be included in his application of priestly compassion to Christ in vv. 7, 8.

a. His divine call (5:5, 6)

The divine call of Christ as our High Priest is explained in 5:5, 6. Jesus Himself spoke in another context of the inappropriateness of one appointing himself to an exalted position. When the Jews accused Him of making Himself to be better than Abraham, He said, "If I honor myself, my honor is nothing; it is my Father that honoreth me; of whom ye say, that he is your God" (Jn. 8:54). The writer of Hebrews also upholds this idea and lays the O.T. foundation for our Lord's call to be our High Priest.

(1) As the only-begotten Son (5:5)

5 So also Christ glorified not himself to be made an high priest; but he that said unto him, Thou art my Son, to day have I begotten thee.

The writer uses the official title "Christ," not the human name "Jesus," to give even greater emphasis to our Lord's submission and obedience to His heavenly Father. To take such a position for Himself would be glorifying Himself. In Jesus' own high priestly prayer in Jn. 17:5, he prayed, "And now, O Father, glorify thou me with thine own self with the glory which I had with thee before the world was." Even there Jesus asked the Father to grant Him this position of glory; He did not dare, in the proper order of things, to take it for Himself. This is the first time in Hebrews that the writer applies the term "high priest" directly to Christ, and he is the only writer in the N.T. to do so. But the appropriateness of such a role is clear from the facts given in the four Gospels. It is also necessary for the benefit of potential Jewish believers to explain what happened to the role of the O.T. priest, which was so strategically important throughout Hebrew history.

Our author appeals to two commonly acknowledged Messianic psalms to cite the basis for Christ's call to the office of high priest. The one who issued this divine call is described as "he that said unto him." In the context of the psalm, the speaker would be God the Father and the recipient would be His Messianic Son.

The first basis of the priestly call comes from Ps. 2:7, "Thou *art* my Son; *this day* have I begotten thee." This verse is quoted in two other places in the N.T. in relation to Christ's ministry. Hebrews has already used the verse in Heb. 1:5 to show the unquestioned superiority of the Son to any angel. The Apostle Paul used it in his sermon at Antioch of Pisidia (Acts 13:33) as a prophecy fulfilled in the resurrection of Christ. It appears that the inspired interpreters of the O.T. Word saw this passage as an overall prophecy of the total ministry of Christ inclusive of His role as the exalted Son who is our Prophet, Priest, and King. But our writer sees it as part of Christ's call to His priestly ministry.

(2) As a priest after the order of Melchisedec (5:6)

6 As he saith also in another *place*, Thou *art* a priest for ever after the order of Melchisedec.

The writer refers to the second O.T. Messianic quotation in what is to us a mysteriously vague fashion, "As he saith also in another place." This strange way of referring to passages which we today identify with more specific references is a potent reminder that our present division of the Biblical text into chapters and verses did not occur until the sixteenth century. It also reminds us that the Scriptures were not nearly so available to the general public as they are today.

The citation comes from Ps. 110:4. Barnes (114) mentions six evidences that this psalm is Messianic: (1) It is a psalm of David, yet he speaks of one who is superior to him, whom he calls "Lord" (v. 1). (2) The one of whom he speaks is also distinguished from Jehovah in v. 1. (3) In his own time David would have applied this terminology to no one but God. (4) In the future David would have applied this terminology to no one except Messiah. (5) It is specifically applied by the Lord Jesus to Himself in Mt. 22:43, 44. (6) The general scope of the psalm throughout fits the application to the Messiah.

The term "priest" rather than "high priest" is used in this quotation. In this situation, however, that is all that is needed. Other than Christ Himself, Melchisedec is the only priest in this order. He was, therefore, of necessity both priest and high priest. The sole historical appearance of Melchisedec is found in Gen. 14:18-20. He is identified as the King of Salem, Priest of the Most High God, who met Abraham with bread and wine and blessed him, and then received tithes from Abraham. (We will say more about possible identifications of Melchisedec in connection with chapter 7.)

The importance of Ps. 110:4 as part of the basis of Christ's call as High Priest is twofold: (1) Melchisedec was both a priest and a king; and (2) Melchisedec's priesthood, contrary to that of the Levitical priests, never ended. There was never a person in the history of ancient Israel who served as both priest and king. The priests were from the tribe of Levi, and the kings of the Davidic line were from the tribe of Judah. But, like Melchisedec, Christ our High Priest is both a Priest and a King. Furthermore, His priesthood is "forever." After Aaron there were some good priests who sincerely tried to minister to the needs of the people, though some were scoundrels—like the sons of Eli, or even the sons of Samuel, or, for that matter, the priests of Jesus' day. But even if the priest was good, there was one great shortcoming: he died. This is not so with the priesthood of Christ. It is one that never comes to an end. He is truly a Priest upon whom we can always rely. Thus, His priesthood is "after the order of Melchisedec," not after the order of Aaron. We never read of Melchisedec dying. Every time we turn to that reference in Genesis, he is still there, carrying out his blessed ministry as the priest-king who so generously and mysteriously served Abraham.

b. His priestly compassion (5:7, 8)

7 Who in the days of his flesh, when he had offered up prayers and supplications with strong crying and tears unto him that was able to save him from death, and was heard in that he feared;
8 Though he were a Son, yet learned he obedience by the things which he suffered.

In Heb. 5:7, 8 the writer next shows how Jesus met the priestly requirement of His true humanity and His genuine compassion. "Who" does not refer to Melchisedec, the nearest antecedent, as a superficial reader might think, but rather to "Christ" who is the main antecedent back in v. 5. "In the days of his flesh" points to the incarnate Christ in His earthly ministry prior to His death and resurrection. This is that state of existence which our Lord began at His birth when "the Word was made flesh, and dwelt among us" (Jn. 1:14). The phrase is meant to describe Christ in His human nature, prior to glorification.

Paul declared in 1 Cor. 15:50, "Flesh and blood cannot inherit the kingdom of God." What Paul meant, of course, is flesh as it now stands, subject to corruption. In another sense, however, Christ had a fleshly body even after the resurrection. To the astonished disciples after the resurrection Christ declared, "Behold my hands and my feet, that it is I myself: handle me, and see; for a spirit hath not flesh and bones, as ye see me have" (Lk. 24:39). We too have the promise that our glorified bodies will be similar, for again Paul said, "Who shall change our vile body, that it may be fashioned like unto his glorious body" (Phil. 3:21). But the phrase in the text points to Christ before His death on the cross, and the exact time to which the writer refers is very clearly during our Lord's suffering in the Garden of Gethsemane.

The time of intense prayer accompanied by deep emotional stress in Gethsemane is described in these words: "When he had offered up prayers and supplications with strong crying and tears." In using the phrase "offered up" in regard to "prayers and supplications," our writer implies that worship before God, when properly rendered, is in itself a spiritual sacrifice. Notice that the writer adds to the intensity of the occasion by doubling up the words: "prayers and supplications" as well as "strong crying and tears." The word "prayers" (Greek *deesis*) refers to the most general type of petition in which our needs are expressed. The verb form means "to ask," or "to beg." The term "supplications" (Greek *hiketeria*) is a stronger word referring to a plea for help in defense from the worst enemy or the worst calamity. The word pictures an ancient custom of presenting an olive branch to the one hearing the petition to deepen the sense of urgency for the needed help.

The writer further intensifies the appeals for help by describing the external emotions involved: "With strong crying and tears." Christ's prayer in Gethsemane was not a silent prayer. Luke points out that He went on from the three disciples who accompanied Him inside the garden "about a stone's cast." In other words, He went beyond them a distance far enough that His prayer could not have been heard by them had it not been uttered with some volume. The Gospel account of Gethsemane does not record any tears, but this detail may well have been passed along by one or all of the three eyewitnesses, and it certainly is natural to assume that such intense prayer, offered in the throes of such wrestling over a moment that would mean so much to our redemption, would be accompanied by tears. Christ is said to have shed tears on only two other occasions: (1) at the tomb of Lazarus (Jn. 11:35), and (2) over the city of Jerusalem (Lk.19:41). Luke describes most powerfully Jesus' suffering in Gethsemane. He says, "And being in an agony he prayed more earnestly: and his sweat was as it were great drops of blood falling down to the ground" (Lk. 22:44).

Our Lord's prayer was prayed "unto him that was able to save him from death," obviously God the Father. When Peter drew his sword to defend Jesus at His arrest, as he said he would, Jesus gently rebuked him and declared that He could call and the Father would send twelve legions of angels to rescue Him (Mt. 26:53). His death was by no means obligatory. Concerning His absolute control of His life, Jesus Himself declared, "No man taketh it from me, but I lay it down of myself" (Jn. 10:18). When Andrew and Philip brought some Greeks to Jesus, He saw this as an additional sign that His hour of suffering and redemption was at hand. He said, "Now is my soul troubled; and what shall I say? Father, save me from this hour: but for this cause came I unto this hour" (Jn. 12:27).

The result of Jesus' prayer in Gethsemane is this: "And was heard in that he feared." Some have been concerned about saying that Christ was praying about the cross in Gethsemane. They feel that it would be straining the meaning to say that Christ was heard when He prayed to the one who was able to save Him from death in light of the fact that He was crucified shortly thereafter. Because of this, MacAuthur says that Jesus was not praying about the cross in Gethsemane, but rather about the resurrection, that He was not asking to be saved from dying per se, but to be saved "out of death," that is, to be raised from the dead. To MacArthur this approach better explains Christ's answered prayer, for indeed He did rise from the dead on the third day. (So also Pink 246, Pentecost 453, and others.) This approach, however, does not go well with Jesus' subsequent concession, "Nevertheless not my will, but thine, be done" (Lk. 22:42).

Still others, wrestling with this same problem, have said that Satan was trying to kill Jesus in Gethsemane that night, before He got to the cross, thus foiling God's plan of complete redemption, which would include the ultimate destruction of Satan. This view is connected with the statement in Lk. 22:44, "And being in an agony he prayed more earnestly: and his sweat was as it were great drops of blood falling down to the ground." Thomas Hewitt suggests this approach when he says, "If Christ had died in the Garden, no greater calamity could possibly have fallen on mankind" (100). The fact, however, that God has absolute authority over Satan would seem to make such an effort unlikely (Job 1, 2; Mt. 8:29-32). The problem is easily solved by simply analyzing exactly what Jesus prayed in Gethsemane: "Father, if thou be willing, remove this cup from me: nevertheless not my will, but thine, be done" (Lk. 22:42). The simplest and most direct identity of "this cup" in the Gospel account is Jesus' redemptive suffering and death on the cross (so also Lenski 163, Westcott 127, Morris 50, etc.). Jesus Christ was not shrinking from the fact of death, for in His omniscience He certainly knew that He would be raised. He feared, dreaded, and shrank from two things, I believe, with all His being: (1) the knowledge that all the sin of all the world would be placed upon His holy person on the cross (2 Cor. 5:21); and (2) the fact that, once sin had been placed upon Him in His vicarious death, the absolutely holy Father would have to turn His back on Him for an awful moment (Mt. 27:46). In a way that we, as sinful beings, cannot possibly understand, Jesus dreaded and shrank from that cup of bitter suffering on the cross. As we see from the Gospel accounts, He did not ask absolutely to be saved from death. The implication is that He was asking that, if there was any other way to redeem fallen mankind apart from this horrible choice, that is what He wanted. But He made it clear that He was willing to die if this was necessary for redemption. And, thus, as Paul declared, He "became obedient unto death, even the death of the cross" (Phil. 2:8).

We should keep two things in mind about prayers like this. (1) A prayer for deliverance from suffering may be heard even when we are not delivered from that suffering. And (2) though God may not answer our prayer exactly as we would like, in His wisdom and sovereignty He may grant an answer somewhat different and far better than what we literally prayed for (Barnes 116).

Furthermore, the intense prayer of Christ in Gethsemane was heard "in that he feared": literally, He "was heard from his godly reverence." His godly fear and submission to the Father's will was the source of the guarantee of answered prayer. Solomon declared, "The fear of the LORD *is* the beginning of wisdom" (Pr. 9:10). Our Lord had that perfect reverence, that perfect trust, that what He asked of the Father, He would do.

Because of His eternal relationship with the Father, one might expect that the eternal Son would not have to experience the depths of suffering that is the lot of so many in this world. But the very opposite is true: "Though he were a Son, yet learned he obedience by the things which he suffered." There is some difficulty in deciding whether this statement should be taken with what goes before (Bruce 103), emphasizing the significance of all His sufferings, including Gethsemane, or with what follows (Westcott 128), introducing the perfection of His redemptive priesthood. Perhaps it is best seen as an appropriate link between both ideas. His Sonship must include His incarnation since this is in the midst of a description of His earthly ministry, but the reference to His Sonship obviously points back to His eternal relation with the Father.

In the face of such a relationship with the Father, we might expect that there was nothing to be learned, no progress to be made. But the writer declares, "yet learned he obedience." This thought is in line with Luke's information about His childhood: "Jesus increased in wisdom and stature, and in favour with God and man" (Lk. 2:52). "Obedience" has a definite article before it: "the obedience." The presence of the article emphasizes and identifies this obedience in its broadest terms as that which characterized the entire life of the Son. Of course, it in no way implies that He was ever rebellious or disobedient, either in thought or in action. But to become qualified for His role as our redemptive High Priest, He must actually experience obedience in the midst of trials and temptations of the severest sort.

And He specifically learned this obedience "by the things which he suffered." "By" (Greek *apo,* literally "from") points to the source rather than the means of His learning, though the two ideas are closely aligned. The suffering of Christ extended throughout His entire life, though these climactic sufferings of His agony in Gethsemane, betrayal, arrest, trial, and crucifixion would be far more intense than the poverty (2 Cor. 8:9), homelessness (Mt. 8:20), criticism, and rejection in His earlier life and ministry. His life of suffering was preparatory to the redemptive suffering in His death. Paul, in like manner, declared that the incarnate Son of God "became obedient unto death, even the death of the cross" (Phil. 2:8; see also Gal. 3:13; 2 Cor. 5:21).

c. His redemptive purpose (5:9, 10)

9 And being made perfect, he became the author of eternal salvation unto all them that obey him;
10 Called of God an high priest after the order of Melchisedec.

The difference between Jesus and the Levitical priests was twofold: (1) He had no need to make a sacrifice for Himself before He made an offering for others; (2) His sacrifice was permanent, never needing repetition. The writer declares the result of these final sufferings, culminating in His death on the cross: "being made perfect," or "having been made perfect" (Greek aorist passive participle). As in v. 8 where no lack of obedience was implied, so here no lack of moral perfection is suggested. The verb (Greek *teleioo*) points to the idea of completeness in attaining a set goal; and the goal, in this context, was becoming fully qualified to be our High Priest. This offers a contrast between Christ's priesthood and those priests from the line of Aaron (Westcott 129). Since their sacrifices in no way brought perfection, they had to be regularly repeated. But He "became the author of eternal salvation." "Author" (Greek *aitios*) has as its root meaning "cause," and in this context it is an action noun, "the one who causes." This "salvation" which Jesus produced or caused is "eternal," everlasting, never-ending because it is based on the permanent sacrifice of Christ which is valid for all time. Unlike the Levitical sacrifices, it never needs repetition (Bruce 105). The writer of Hebrews emphasizes things eternal throughout the epistle: "eternal judgment" (6:2); "eternal redemption" (9:12); "eternal inheritance" (9:15); and "the everlasting covenant" (13:20). His repeated use of this word brings out one of his main points: the contrast between the temporary nature of the old covenant and the permanence of the new. Our Lord caused this eternal salvation for us when He completed His suffering on that Friday afternoon so long ago, when He declared from the cross, "It is finished" (Jn. 19:30). The divine approval of His accomplishment was demonstrated early on the following Sunday morning when He defeated death once and for all in His glorious resurrection.

This wonderful accomplishment of eternal salvation applies "unto all them that obey him": literally, "to all those who keep on obeying him" (Greek present participle). It is not by chance that our writer stresses that the one who learned to obey (v. 8) brought salvation to all those who obey Him (Morris 50). In the divine order of salvation, grace is the cause; the blood of Christ is the basis; faith is the condition; and works (obedience) are the evidence. This connection between grace, faith, and works is clearly demonstrated in Eph. 2:8-10. Salvation is, indeed, by faith alone (see Rom. 3:28; 4:3), but Scripture knows of no saving faith except that which produces works or obedience (see Jn. 14:15, 21; Jas. 2:17, 20, 26).

However, MacArthur also points to a needed clarification when he says, "Whoever does not believe does not truly obey, no matter how moral, well-meaning, religious, and sincere" (125). It is always saving faith which produces works, never the other way around. There is an exact parallel between 2:10 and 5:9 where we have (1) the same agent, God; (2) the same means, suffering; (3) the same verb (Greek *teleioo*), "to bring to a certain goal"; (4) the same object, the captain or the author (the cause), and (5) the same beneficiaries, "many sons" or "all them that obey him" (Lenski 166).

In v. 10 our author comes back to where he started in v. 5 with his first, and perhaps, his most important point in comparing and contrasting Jesus Christ in His High Priestly ministry with the Aaronic priesthood. He says that Christ was "called of God an high priest after the order of Melchisedec." The word "called" (Greek *prosagoreuo*) appears only here in the Greek N.T. It "expresses the formal and solemn ascription of the title to Him to whom it belongs" (Westcott 130). God's call of His Messianic Son as "an high priest after the order of Melchisedec" was formally and prophetically recorded when David wrote Ps. 110, with the call after this new order seen there in vv. 1 and 4 especially. It was v. 4 that our author quoted as part of the basis of Christ's call in Heb. 5:6, but he had already noted the Messianic significance of Ps. 110:1 by his quotation in 1:13.

B. Third Warning: Against Failure to Progress through Christ as High Priest (5:11—6:20)

In these verses our writer diverts from the subject of Christ and His High Priestly ministry in order to rebuke these Hebrew believers for their lack of spiritual growth (5:11-14) and to issue a severe warning with regard to the real possibility of apostasy (6:1-8) from faith in Christ. He is careful, however, to give them a message of encouragement equally as strong as the warning about apostasy (6:9-20). He sees his audience at a strategic turning point in their spiritual lives with the possibility in view that some of them might return to their old way of life under Judaism—which was, at the moment, less subject to persecution than was their new life in Christ. He will not come back again to the subject of Melchisedec until 7:1.

1. Lack of spiritual understanding and discernment caused by lack of spiritual progress (5:11-14)

a. Difficulty in understanding the new priestly order (5:11)

11 Of whom we have many things to say, and hard to be uttered, seeing ye are dull of hearing.

There are three possibilities with regard to the antecedent of "whom" in this verse. In looking to the preceding context, the writer could refer to Melchisedec, mentioned at the end of v. 10; or to Christ, who has been the subject of the entire paragraph back to 5:5; or, preferably, to Christ as High Priest after the order of Melchisedec. Indeed, as 5:10 suggests, the compound title is what the writer has in mind. The pronoun "we" is best taken in an editorial sense, meaning the writer and other apostolic and local church leaders (see also 2:5).

The writer's immediate concern is twofold: (1) the amount of material that needs to be covered, and (2) the difficulty in the presentation. Thus, he says, "We have many things to say, and hard to be uttered." A subject can be difficult to present for at least three reasons: (1) the teacher is not very informed about the subject or is not verbally or graphically expressive; (2) the subject itself is very difficult for even the most intelligent person to comprehend; or (3) the recipients of the teaching are themselves, for whatever reasons, very slow to learn, very inept. In this case, the third reason is involved, as is clear when he says, "Seeing ye are dull of hearing." He is clearly giving this as the reason for the difficulty of presentation. "Dull"

(Greek *nothros*) means slow, lazy, sluggish. The same word in 6:12 is translated "slothful." In this context, of course, he is not referring to physical hearing impairment, but rather to spiritual. It is also important to note that "ye are" is literally "Ye have become" (Greek perfect of *ginomai*). By this he suggests that the spiritual sense of hearing of the Hebrews had, at one time, been more keen than it was now. They were not just stagnant in their spiritual growth; they had actually gone backward from where they once had been.

b. Absence of progress from the first principles (5:12)

12 For when for the time ye ought to be teachers, ye have need that one teach you again which *be* the first principles of the oracles of God; and are become such as have need of milk, and not of strong meat.

"When for the time" (Greek *chronos*) is literally "because of the time." If our writer is addressing his audience shortly before the destruction of the Temple in A.D. 70, that means that the Gospel of Christ's kingdom had been preached 37 or 38 years (assuming the crucifixion to have taken place in A.D. 30). If these Hebrew Christians were located in Palestine, that means that they had known Christ for much of this period. If the audience is made up of Hebrew Christians converted under Paul's ministry during his first Roman imprisonment (Lenski 19), they have still been Christians long enough to grow in the Lord into reasonable spiritual maturity (from about A.D. 60 to 63 until the time of this writing), a period of five to seven years. By this time they "ought to be teachers."

"Teachers" (Greek *didaskalos*) includes teachers in an informal sense, not just those who have the gift of teaching (Eph. 4:11), like bishops or pastors who must be "apt to teach" (1 Tim. 3:2). Here he means teachers as Paul describes in 2 Tim. 2:2, "And the things that thou hast heard of me among many witnesses, the same commit thou to faithful men, who shall be able to teach others also." Every Christian who has any degree of maturity ought to be able to teach others, at least on an individual basis, about the Gospel of Christ. But the Hebrew Christians in this congregation had not so matured.

Instead, they "have need that one teach you again which *be* the first principles of the oracles of God." "One" (Greek *tina*), taken here as an indefinite pronoun, was interpreted by some ancient commentators as an interrogative pronoun. In that case we would read, "Ye have need to be teaching you *what* are the first principles." The problem, however, was not that they did not know what they were; rather, they did not embrace them and live by them as they once did. Thus, they need some forceful reminders, which the writer proceeds to give (Westcott 133).

"The first principles" (Greek *ta stoicheia tes arches*), or "the rudiments of the beginning," refer to the basic rudiments or tenets of any matter, the ABC's, so to speak, of any given subject. In our educational system we first learn the basic facts of the subject, whether in relation to language, history, math, science, etc. With regard to language, we first learn the alphabet, then simple words, then how to put those words into sentences, and so forth. The "first principles" are such basic truths of the Gospel of Christ. Furthermore, these basic tenets or rudiments are from "the oracles of God," or "the sayings of God." In Stephen's sermon in Acts 7:38 this word (Greek *logion*) is used of what Moses received at Sinai, and Paul uses it in a similar way in Rom. 3:2. Though the writer of Hebrews could have in mind the message of early Christian revelation, the N.T., which was still in the process of coming together, he is most likely referring to the O.T., especially as it related to the coming of Christ. When we read the sermons of Peter, Stephen, and Paul in the book of Acts, we see them preaching about Christ from O.T. passages. It is to these O.T. "oracles" that our writer is referring. This would have included relating the Gospel story and showing how it fulfilled the O.T. prophecies concerning the coming of Messiah. Of course, these Hebrews still remembered the first principles as to mental awareness, but they no longer embraced them, taught them, or rejoiced in them, as they once did. Their spiritual condition had become unstable.

Because of this, they had "become such as have need of milk, and not of strong meat." This charge toward this Hebrew congregation would likely call forth a more emotional response from them than anything the writer has said up to this point. And, we can be sure, that is exactly what the writer is hoping for. He hopes to awaken them from their lethargy and drive them to repentance and renewal. As in v. 11, the writer indicates the backward drift of his readers. Once again, the charge indicates that they had once experienced a different and greater level of maturity than at the present. The writer is stressing a process which has now become a continuing state (Greek perfect tense). The nature of the Christian walk is such that we never stand still. If we are not going forward, we are going backward. "If the dark things do not become plain then the plain things will become dark" (Hewitt 101).

"Milk" is used figuratively for the rudiments, the first principles of the Christian faith. "Strong meat" or solid food is used figuratively for the more difficult, more advanced truths of God's Word. Some of the early church fathers said that milk referred to Jesus' humanity, including His resurrection and ascension, while solid food was the more mysterious teachings about His Godhead (Westcott 133). But it seems best to make the contrast more general, with milk referring to the fundamental truths about Jesus Christ from the O.T. and strong meat (solid food) referring to the deeper, more complex truths with regard to the person of Christ.

Paul uses a similar contrast in 1 Cor. 3:1-3 where he indicates the need to continue giving the Corinthians milk rather than meat because of the divisive spirit which was so prevalent among them. Bruce (108) even thinks that the writer of Hebrews may have based his thoughts on 1 Cor. 3:1ff., which he sees as a possibility because he leans toward Apollos as the writer of the epistle. His reasoning is based especially on the knowledge that Apollos had a significant ministry and influence at Corinth (Acts 19:1; 1 Cor. 1:12; 3:4-7). Peter uses the idea of milk in a more general sense as a figure of the nourishing Word of God (1 Pet. 2:2), but he does not make a contrast between the milk and meat of the word as Hebrews and 1 Corinthians do.

c. Those who need milk described (5:13)

13 For every one that useth milk *is* unskilful in the word of righteousness: for he is a babe.

Though we don't know exactly how long this Hebrew congregation had known Christ, it is obvious that it had been long enough in the writer's eyes for them to have gained a level of spiritual maturity far beyond where they stood at the time of this epistle. Spiritual growth comes by discipline, not just by the time that has elapsed. Christians who have not grown past the milk content of the Word of God will always be the ones in danger of being drawn back into the old way of life. "Every one that useth milk" is literally "everyone who is partaking of milk," emphasizing the spiritual infancy on the part of the readers. "Unskilful" (Greek *apeiros*) means "inexperienced," referring to one who has not acquired skill in any given activity because he has not practiced the art. In this case, they are unskillful in "the word of righteousness." "Word" (Greek *logos*) does not have a definite article in the original; consequently most commentators do not think that it is referring to the Word of God as a whole, but rather to more specific or smaller parts of the Word, to given doctrines or teachings. In that case, "righteousness" is best taken in an adjectival sense to describe the Word. Thus we should understand "word of righteousness" to mean "right teaching" or "proper doctrine" (Westcott 134; Lenski 172; Delitzsch I:263). Not only are the Hebrews unskillful in the entire body of God's Word, they are also inept as relates to individual and important parts of it, particularly to those parts of the O.T. that related to Christ and His coming, and to elements of the Gospel accounts that they had received, at least verbally if not yet in written form.

The writer draws the only logical conclusion that he can as to the cause of this continuing milk diet for any individual: "For he is a babe." The Apostle Paul demonstrated the meaning of a "babe" when he declared, "When I was a child, I spake as a child, I understood as a child, I thought as a child: but when I became a man, I put away childish things" (1 Cor. 13:11). The word "child" in this verse is the same in the original as "babe" here (Greek *nepios*). Barnes, however, adds about this Hebrew congregation, "It does not mean that they were not true Christians, but that they had not the experience or knowledge requisite to enable them to understand the higher mysteries of the Christian religion" (120).

Contrary to most interpreters, MacArthur (134) maintains that these "babes" are not Christians at all, but individuals who have heard the gospel preached, and are very interested in the teachings about Christ, but are still living on the outer edges of Judaism, lacking the courage to sever themselves from the old traditions. I believe, however, that Barnes, and most other commentators, are correct in seeing these "babes" as immature Christians who have not grown in the Lord as they should have, or who have, at least in some cases, actually retrogressed in their walk with Christ.

d. Those who can take strong meat described (5:14)

14 But strong meat belongeth to them that are of full age, *even*

those who by reason of use have their senses exercised to discern both good and evil.

"Them that are of full age" could also be translated "those who are perfect" or "those who are complete" (Greek *teleios*). Paul makes this same contrast between babes and full-grown men when he declares, "Till we all come in the unity of the faith, and of the knowledge of the Son of God, unto a *perfect man*, unto the measure of the stature of the fulness of Christ: That we *henceforth* be no more children, tossed to and fro, and carried about with every wind of doctrine" (Eph. 4:13, 14). Though this process, which theologically we call sanctification, will continue throughout our Christian lives, we can soon come to the place of sufficient maturity to feed on "strong meat" or "solid food," the deeper truths of God's Word which go beyond the milk diet of newborn infants. In a similar way in our natural physical lives, we keep growing for a lengthy period of time, but under normal circumstances we move from the milk diet of infancy after a relatively brief period. So should it be in the Christian walk. The writer is not describing some sort of super-Christian, one far beyond the normal expectation in the Christian walk, but rather what is expected of each Christian who follows Christ and becomes a student of His Word. The phrase "by reason of use" could be translated "because of their condition." The key word in question (Greek *hexis*) refers to the culminating result of a process of conditioning in their Christian lives. The word implies a period of rigorous spiritual discipline which has produced this ideal state. In the realm of athletics, we refer to the training period as "conditioning," and when the process has produced its beneficial results, the well-trained athlete arrives at that ideal condition. To obtain such results, the conditioning must be habitual, not merely now and again.

Such a conditioning process, of necessity, involves only those who "have their senses exercised": literally, "their senses having been exercised" (Greek perfect passive participle). In the natural body the five major senses are seeing, hearing, smelling, tasting, and feeling. In the spiritual nature of the believer there are similar senses that, when enhanced by the Word and the Holy Spirit, become more sensitive to our inner spiritual needs and to the challenges of the evil world around us. Just as our physical senses can become dull, or even disappear, due to age or disease, even so our spiritual senses can be affected by a lack of normal growth in the Christian life.

The word translated "exercised" (Greek *gumnazo*) is the root from which our English word "gymnasium" is derived. Just as we work physically at the gymnasium to arrive at a desired physical condition, so we must work in the spiritual gymnasium of our study about the deeper truths of God's Word in order to become a perfect, complete, or full-grown man or woman in the Lord.

Those who are of full age as a result of such habitual spiritual exercise will be able "to discern both good and evil." Because of the immediate context and the fact that the words for "good" (Greek *kalos*) and "evil" (Greek *kakos*) used here by the writer normally point to outward or external appearance, not to good and evil in an inner or moral sense, many commentators restrict the meaning to the ability to discern what is milk and what is strong meat in the Word of God (Westcott 136; Lenski 173). I agree, however, with other interpreters who feel that this is an unnecessary restriction (Bruce 109; MacArthur 134; Hewitt 102; Morris 52; Clarke 831). Even moral judgments must be made, at least initially, on our evaluation of things, events, people, behavior, etc. as they appear externally. Besides, limiting this spiritual maturity to the ability to discern the difference between "milk" and "strong meat" does not go far enough in preparing us to face the actual threats of the world, the flesh, and the devil.

Perhaps the writer uses the external words for good and evil in order to be all-inclusive. The discernment certainly includes the ability to discriminate between milk and strong meat in God's Word, but it goes deeper than that in enabling us to make right moral and theological choices that affect our daily lives. Those who have become of full age are "not in danger of being imposed on by false doctrine, pretensions of hypocrites, or by being deceived by the subtleties of Satan" (Clarke 831). "They have an exact or right judgment in all things. When different viewpoints are placed before them, they can at once distinguish the good from the evil, the right from the wrong" (Hewitt 102).

Though the writer expresses doubts about the ability of these Hebrew Christians to understand the deeper truths of the Word of God, especially about the difficult subject of the new order of Christ's priesthood following the model of Melchisedec, he will, nevertheless, proceed with that subject in chapter 7. Sometimes reluctant babes must be dragged toward adulthood. If they are ever to become anything more than infants in Christ, constantly under the threat of returning to the old life, they must dine on something more than milk. Therefore, after continuing through chapter 6 with further details of the severe warning which he started in 5:11, he will come back to this most important subject of Christ's eternal priesthood.

Summary
(5:1-14)

The writer turns from contrasting the superior leadership of Jesus Christ with that of Moses and Joshua, the two greatest national leaders of Israel, to contrasting His priesthood with that of the ancient Levitical priesthood headed by Aaron, the brother of Moses. In order to show that the priesthood of Christ was new and different, it is necessary for him to list some of the key requirements for the O.T. priesthood. He mentions four different requirements of the Levitical priest. (1) As to his background, he is taken from among men, thus able to understand and sympathize with their needs. (2) As to his purpose, his ministry is for the benefit of man as he relates to God, especially with regard to making atonement for sin and ministering to the people's spiritual needs in general. (3) As to his compassion, he has the same physical and emotional weaknesses as his brothers, including the need for atonement for his sin; thus he is well able to completely sympathize with and minister to their needs. (4) As to his divine call, it is important to remember that Aaron did not choose himself as the initial high priest of the nation of Israel. Such an important office would have questionable credibility if the man occupying it was self-appointed. Instead, Aaron was called of God to serve in this office as a mediator between God and man in ancient Israel (5:1-4).

The writer's main point in going over the qualifications and characteristics of the Levitical priest was to lay the foundation for showing that Jesus Christ's priesthood was based on similar characteristics, though He will be shown to be a Priest of an entirely different order. Since the most important requirement mentioned in vv. 1-4, at least as far as our writer's present purpose is concerned, was the fact that Aaron was called by God to his position as the high priest of Israel, that is where he starts in describing the priesthood of Christ. In other words, he outlines the qualifications of Christ in a somewhat reverse order to his discussion in 5:1-4.

First, the writer shows that the priesthood of Christ was not self-initiated, just as Aaron was not self-appointed as high priest. He uses as the basis of the call of Christ as High Priest two O.T. passages. The first is from the highly Messianic second Psalm 2, "Thou art my Son; this day have I begotten thee" (Ps. 2:7), while the second is a quotation from Ps. 110:4, "Thou *art* a priest for ever after the order of Melchisedek."

The second qualification of Christ as High Priest is His sincere identification with and compassion for humanity, as illustrated by the well-known incident from the Gospels in the Garden of Gethsemane. That notable incident summed up the sufferings of Christ prior to the cross and completed His full qualifications to become the redeemer of humanity in the awful event that was about to take place, the crucifixion.

This leads the writer to the third qualification of Christ as our High Priest: His redemptive purpose. Without specifically mentioning the crucifixion, he describes how He became "the author of eternal salvation unto all them that obey him." When He was made "perfect," that is, when His qualifications and His ultimate obedience had been completely satisfied, He was able to become our Savior. In contrast, however, to the Levitical priest who had to repeat the offerings of the Day of Atonement every year, along with all the other gifts and sacrifices which he offered on a daily basis, our Lord's supreme sacrifice is good for all time and will never need to be repeated since He is a Priest of an entirely different order, the order of Melchisedec (5:5-10).

The introduction of the subject of Christ's new priestly order, following the O.T. model of Melchisedec, brings the writer to the point of issuing his third severe warning to his readers. He expresses some degree of reluctance in proceeding with the discussion of this High Priesthood because the spiritual perception of this Hebrew congregation has actually gone backward. For whatever cause or causes, they are not as sensitive to spiritual teaching as they had been in earlier days. By this time, in fact, they should be able to teach others, at least in an informal sense, about Jesus Christ and His priestly ministry. Instead, they actually need to be reminded about the very rudiments of Christianity, the place where they had started evidently some years ago.

Rather than being ready to go on to "strong meat" or solid food material with regard to the person and work of Christ, such as His priesthood according to the order of Melchisedec, they actually need to return to baby food, to the milk doctrines of their early Christian profession. Only Christians who have habitually exercised their spiritual senses by using them on a regular basis will be able to digest the deeper truths of the Word of God and to discern what is right or wrong in the daily issues which confront them, both inside the church and outside in the world in which they live (5:11-14).

Application: Preaching and Teaching the Passage

A lesson might be taught on the four qualifications of the priesthood of Aaron: (1) his roots—"taken from among men" (5:1); (2) his compassion—"for that he himself also is compassed with infirmity" (5:2); (3) his atonement for sin—"also for himself" (5:3); (4) his divine call—"as *was* Aaron" (5:4).

The author's purpose, of course, in mentioning these qualifications of the Levitical priests, was to compare and contrast the ministry of Jesus Christ as the High Priest of the new dispensation. Jesus parallels each of the above qualifications, but in each case He also varies from the qualification or characteristic of the priesthood in an important way. (1) Whereas the Levitical high priest was "taken from among men," Christ, the eternal Son of God in Heaven, took upon Himself true humanity and experienced the fullness of identification with the needs of man "in the days of his flesh" (v. 7). (2) Whereas the high priest of Israel felt compassion because he too was "compassed with infirmity" and had to make an offering for his own sins, Jesus Christ, the sinless Son of God, enhanced His compassion for sinful man as "he learned obedience by the things which he suffered" (v. 8). (3) Whereas the earthly high priest had to make atonement for his sins and those of the people by ineffective animal sacrifices repeated every year, Christ as our High Priest "became the author of eternal salvation unto all them that obey him" (v. 9). (4) Whereas Aaron was called and anointed as Israel's high priest, Jesus Christ was called as our eternal High Priest under a different order, the order of Melchisedec (v. 10).

The writer brings out the importance of the Messianic psalms when he describes Christ's call as our eternal High Priest on the basis of two quotations from the psalms. The first aspect of His call stresses His strong relation to the Father, before whom He appears as our High Priest: "Thou *art* my Son; this day have I begotten thee" (Ps. 2:7). The second aspect of His call stresses the new order from which His priesthood is derived: "Thou *art* a priest for ever after the order of Melchisedek" (Ps. 110:4). These two aspects, His special relationship with God and the new and eternal order of His priesthood, highlight the effectiveness of His priestly ministry in relation to believers. Both of these, Psalm 2 and Psalm 110, should be read and examined in detail to understand these verses which our writer quotes as making up Christ's call to His eternal priesthood.

Regarding the words, "And was heard in that he feared" (5:7), some controversy has developed about Jesus' prayer in Gethsemane when He cried, "O my Father, if it be possible, let this cup pass from me: nevertheless not as I will, but as thou *wilt*" (Mt. 26:39). Matthew, who gives more details, says that Jesus prayed these same words three times. Since the writer of Hebrews says that His prayer was heard, a variety of interpretations have been associated with the meaning of "this cup" in the Gospels. (1) Some say that it meant His physical death on the cross in and of itself, that, like most real human beings, He was afraid to die. But this idea is contrary to the whole tenor of Jesus' words in preparation for His death, especially His prophecy of His voluntary sacrifice (Jn. 10:17, 18). (2) Some say that it refers to Satan's attempt to physically destroy Christ in Gethsemane, illustrated by Luke's comments about His agony in the Garden to the extent that "his sweat was as it were great drops of blood falling down to the ground" (Lk. 22:44). But too much must be assumed about the details to embrace this view. (3) Some say that "this cup" referred to the death itself, not to the crucifixion, and that He indeed was delivered from death through the resurrection; therefore, His prayer was heard. (4) Some say that it refers to His coming sufferings on the cross, not just the idea of physical death (as stated in view # 1), but the idea of all that was involved in His death, His bearing the sins of the world and the awful forsaking of the Father because He became sin for us (2 Cor. 5:21). I believe that this final interpretation is the most obvious and correct view. With regard to the problem of our writer's statement that His prayer "was heard," we merely need to note that His entire prayer in Gethsemane included very plainly and repeatedly, "Not my will, but thine, be done" (Lk. 22:42).

Though Jesus was God in the flesh, He demonstrated His complete reliance on the Father by His devotion to prayer throughout His ministry. His prayers often lasted all night, and on most occasions He sought a private place for prayer where He could give His uninterrupted attention to thanksgiving, worship, and supplication. If the sinless Son of God felt such a deep need for prayer, how much more should we who are sinners saved by grace.

As we analyze our Lord's ministry in the Gospels, we find that He prayed (1) about the direction of His ministry in its early stages (Mk. 1:35); (2) about the choosing of the twelve disciples as He began to organize His ministry (Lk. 6:12); (3) about the culminating events of His ministry on the Mount of Transfiguration (Lk. 9:28); (4) for Peter as he was about to face a severe trial in his denial of Jesus (Lk. 22:32); and (5) about drinking the "cup" of His suffering on the cross as He agonized about it in Gethsemane (Mt. 26:39, 42, 44). To this last powerful prayer the author refers in Hebrews 5:7.

There are those who make light of grown men weeping. There is nothing wrong with weeping when there is due cause. We note that our Lord set an example about weeping in His earthly ministry. There never lived a truer man than Jesus Christ, the incarnate Son of God. If it was all right for Him to weep on certain occasions, it would certainly be proper for sinful, frail human beings to weep when the sufferings and woes of this life make it appropriate. We note that Jesus wept on at least three different occasions: (1) At the tomb of Lazarus Jesus wept in sorrow for His dearest friends, but even more over the limited faith of His disciples about His power over death (Jn. 11:35). (2) He wept over the widespread unbelief of the city of Jerusalem, especially as He foresaw the awful suffering that would soon come her way because of her rejection of God's Son (Lk. 19:41). (3) According to the author of Hebrews, He "offered up prayers and supplications with strong crying and tears" as He agonized in Gethsemane about His coming suffering on the cross. Solomon said long ago that there is "a time to weep, and a time to laugh; a time to mourn, and a time to dance" (Eccl. 3:4). It is most appropriate that a well-balanced Christian exercise all these emotions as the case may dictate.

Some have questioned what the writer means when he says, "For when for the time ye ought to be teachers" (5:12). Among the gifted people God has given the church for the "perfecting of the saints" Paul lists "pastors and teachers" (Eph. 4:11). In the qualifications of the bishop or pastor Paul says that he must be "apt to teach" (1 Tim. 3:2). But the writer of Hebrews surely does not mean that God expects all believers to become preachers and teachers in this formal sense. He rather is speaking about teaching in a much more informal sense. Paul refers to this type of teaching, which all mature Christians ought to be qualified for, when he challenges Timothy, "The things that thou hast heard of me among many witnesses, the same commit thou to faithful men, who shall be able to teach others also" (2 Tim. 2:2). But these Hebrew Christians were not even able to do this type of teaching, that is, effectively sharing their faith, because they had receded into a state of spiritual infancy. If they cannot be awakened, even more serious spiritual consequences await.

In the modern-day church, just as in this Hebrew congregation, there are many believers who either have never grown past the state of spiritual infancy, or who, like these readers, have actually backtracked in their status of spiritual maturity to the point that they are once again babes in their understanding. Even in the physical realm, a tiny baby is cute and admired by everyone, but a big baby is nothing less than disgusting. This is true in the spiritual realm as well. The causes of this kind of immaturity in the church need to be identified, analyzed, and evaluated, and effective solutions for changing the situation need to be formulated. Some of the most obvious causes of immaturity are: (1) failure to make our relationship with Christ a top priority; (2) lack of spiritual discipline in our Christian lives; (3) failure to faithfully read and study the written Word of God; (4) a tendency to depend on our own abilities rather than on the omnipotent hand of God; (5) failure to pray and worship God on a daily basis, as Daniel did in Daniel 6.

2. Possibility of renouncing true faith without a return to spiritual progress (6:1-8)

In spite of the writer's concern about the spiritual infancy of this group of Hebrew Christians, a spiritual infancy which is actually the result of a relapse from a greater level of maturity, he drives them on in an effort to regain the ground that has been lost. His concern for their spiritual advancement is twofold: (1) to enhance their ability to comprehend deeper truths in God's Word through the profitable exercise of their spiritual senses, and (2) to warn them about the irremediable consequences of continuing in their downward road of spiritual regression. Because of these concerns, he seeks to lead them on to spiritual progress.

a. The foundation which must be built upon (6:1-3)

1 Therefore leaving the principles of the doctrine of Christ, let us go

on unto perfection; not laying again the foundation of repentance from dead works, and of faith toward God,
2 Of the doctrine of baptisms, and of laying on of hands, and of resurrection of the dead, and of eternal judgment.
3 And this will we do, if God permit.

"Therefore" connects the writer's attempt to lead his readers into deeper spiritual truths with the entire rebuke about their lack of progress in 5:11-14. As a good teacher of God's Word, he is not satisfied to abandon them to their present inclination toward a diet of spiritual milk, but he seeks to take them forward toward spiritual maturity and the resultant stability which it will bring. "The principles of the doctrine of Christ" is literally "the word of the beginning of Christ." This phrase refers back to "the first principles of the oracles of God" in 5:12, the rudiments of the Gospel message in its most elementary presentation. Indeed, there is nothing wrong with this elementary presentation of the basic Gospel message. It is, in fact, where all of us must start when we are "born again" (Jn. 3:3, 5) through the effects of the Word and the Spirit. But to remain in this spiritual infancy, with a continuing diet of milk rather than solid food, will not make one strong and properly balanced, prepared to withstand the sure assaults of Satan.

The participle "leaving" is expressed as completed action (Greek aorist tense) because the writer is viewing the departure as one act, "Having left the word of the beginning of Christ." "Leaving" can have two different interpretations: (1) we leave something that is bad for us in the sense of forsaking it or abandoning it; or (2) we leave something that is beneficial to us by using it to take a higher position, as the bottom rung of a ladder is used to climb higher. We can't reach the higher rungs on a ladder without first stepping on the bottom rung, but if we don't leave that rung and climb on, we will never get to the top of the ladder and the higher position which is our goal. Commentators take either one or the other of these views, largely depending on how they interpret the six principles which are listed in this verse and the next. (I will give further explanation below in connection with the discussion about these principles.)

As a result of completing this departure from the elementary principles about Christ, the writer exhorts his readers, "Let us go on unto perfection." The "we" ("us") that is used here is not merely an editorial "we," because the writer must, of necessity, involve his audience in the process if it is to be at all successful. This moving forward from first principles to perfection must be a cooperative effort between the writer, the Hebrew Christians, and the Holy Spirit. "Let us go on" may be translated more literally, "Let us continue being carried along" (Greek present passive voice), or "Let us continue going on" (Greek present intensive middle). In the first case the emphasis is on total surrender for all parties, the abandonment of all existing resistance to the Word and the Spirit as they take us to the desired level of maturity. In the second case the emphasis is on the cooperative effort that must be involved in order to attain the maturity which is being sought after. KJV translators followed the latter approach, which is perhaps more natural, but there is an element of both ideas involved, both self-surrender and a genuine spirit of cooperation. Note that in either case the work is viewed as a process, a project that will continue for some period of time. No one moves from spiritual infancy to spiritual maturity overnight; therefore, the readers must be committed to perseverance in the struggle which lies ahead. "Perfection" (Greek *teleiotes*) corresponds with "them that are of full age" (Greek *teleios*) in 5:14, coming from the same root in the original. Both words refer to the end result, the desired goal, in any given context. In this context, the goal is spiritual maturity which will produce stable Christian lives.

But if they are to go on to perfection the readers must also avoid something else, which the writer expresses almost as a command: "Not laying again the foundation." The negative participle, "not laying," is expressed in continuous action (Greek present), stressing the long period of time during which these Hebrew Christians have been working on the elementary principles about Christ. The addition of the word "again" places a double emphasis on the need to avoid repeating an activity which, though good in itself, has taken long enough already.

The word "foundation" is emphasized (in front of the verb in the Greek order). The writer is clearly viewing the principles which he is about to name as the foundation of a building. Anyone even slightly acquainted with the process of building a house knows the importance of the foundation. Without a solid foundation, the strength of the rest of the house will be questionable. On the other hand, a builder who never leaves the foundation to continue building the house above it will never accomplish his purpose. Foundations are built primarily to place houses on. The "foundation" and "the principles of the doctrine of Christ" are the same, and the writer is about to enumerate them more specifically.

There is some range of interpretation among commentators with regard to these six principles. (1) Some view them as totally Jewish and thus something that must be abandoned, forsaken, if these Hebrew readers are to make any progress toward Christ (Pink 279; MacArthur 138; Dods 335). These interpreters usually view the readers, at least at this point, as unsaved. MacArthur (135) says, "The writer is specifically talking to Jews who had heard the gospel and not accepted Christ as Savior and Lord." Most of those who hold this view would interpret "leaving" to mean "forsake" or "abandon." These unsaved Jews must abandon their attachment to Judaism and follow Christ into salvation. (2) Some view the principles described as having a Jewish flavor but also fitting into the principles of the Christian Gospel (Hagner 87; Bruce 112; Whedon 76; Morris 53; Clarke 831). Many of these commentators would see the readers as Christians, though immature, who are still holding too much to ancient Jewish traditions. (3) Other interpreters see the principles mentioned here as describing the basic elements, the rudiments, the fundamentals of N.T. Christianity (Westcott 142; Lenski 175; Barnes 124; Delitzsch I:266; Archer 39). Those who hold to this position understand "leaving" in the first part of the verse to mean "building upon," not "abandoning." I believe this third view best fits the context. The exhortation that they should not be "laying again the foundation" confirms this point of view, and the six principles that are listed certainly seem to be in line with this approach.

The six principles listed give a more detailed explanation of the "foundation" already mentioned. These six principles can be divided into three pairs. (1) The first pair, repentance from dead works and faith toward God, point to the inward requirements of salvation. (2) The second pair, the doctrine of baptisms and laying on of hands, describe the outward confession of salvation. (3) The final pair, the resurrection of the dead and eternal judgment, emphasize the ultimate conclusion of our salvation. Like lists of this kind often are in the Bible, the six-fold enumeration is probably not intended to be all-inclusive. The fact that the three pairs seem to represent the *inward, outward, and final manifestation* of the basic elements of Christianity supports this understanding.

The first pair, "repentance from dead works" and "faith toward God," describe the negative and positive requirements for salvation. "Repentance" (Greek *metanoia*) means "after thinking" or "a change of mind." In the Bible it refers to a genuine change of both mind and heart when the new birth takes place in an individual's life. "Dead works" refer to those efforts of outward conformity to the law and of Jewish traditions which, in first century Pharisaism, were seen as the primary means to salvation. All works, no matter how outwardly impressive, which are done apart from the life-giving Spirit, are completely useless before God. If this were written to Gentiles, they might be admonished to turn "to God from idols to serve the living and true God" (1 Th. 1:9), but as Jews they are urged to turn from their empty formalism to a living "faith toward God," a complete surrender and confident trust in the One who gave His only-begotten Son for our salvation. These do not represent two different requirements for salvation, but one that may be presented either negatively, as a turning from the old way of life whatever it may have been, or positively, as a turning to God and all that the Scriptures teach about Him. Thus, in the N.T., some salvation passages point to repentance as the way to salvation (Lk. 13:3, 5; Acts 2:38), while others speak of faith or "believing" as the way to Heaven (Jn. 3:16; Acts 16:31; Rom. 10:9, 10). Most passages do not mention both repentance and faith (but see Mk. 1:15) since each one of them, when performed as the Scripture defines them, of necessity includes the other.

The second pair in the list of first principles appears in v. 2. The word "foundation" (v. 1) is still connected: thus the foundation "of the doctrine of baptisms, and of laying on of hands." This second pair covers the outward confession of the Christian's salvation. Perhaps the word "doctrine" or teaching is used with these last four because these involve instructions which must be given after a person becomes a Christian, while the first two give initial and essential requirements for entrance into the Christian life. It is clear, however, that these last four doctrines are part of the foundation, the rudiments, the first principles of the Gospel. There is some disagreement about the meaning of "baptisms" because of the use of the plural and because the word used here (Greek *baptismos*) is not the usual word for N.T. baptism (Greek *baptisma*, as in Eph. 4:5; Col. 2:12). In the two other places where this word occurs (Heb. 9:10; Mk. 7:4), it refers to the Levitical washings or purifications of the O.T. As a result, at least four different views have been postulated regarding the meaning of "baptisms" here. (1) Some say that it is a direct reference to the Levitical washings, not to Christian baptism at all. The five other doctrines mentioned are remnants of Judaism these Hebrew readers have not been able to turn loose (Pink 280; Clarke 831; MacArthur 139). (2) Some think that baptisms refer to the two major types of baptism taught in the N.T.: baptism in water (Mt. 28:19; Mk. 16:16) and baptism by the Holy Spirit (Mt. 3:11; Mk. 1:5). Albert Barnes takes this position (126). (3) Some say that baptisms refer to the actual multiple water baptisms of the individual believers that made up this body of Christians. Each one had been baptized once, but the group together involved numerous baptisms (Lenski 177). (4) Finally, another group of commentators says that baptisms appear in the plural to indicate the different types of baptism that these Hebrew Christians need instruction about. This would, of course, center on Christian baptism, as commanded by Jesus in the Great Commission (Mt. 28:19), but the instruction would include defining and contrasting baptism into Christ with the Levitical washings or purification system of the O.T.; the baptism of John the Baptist, which some disciples still embraced at least 25 years after the crucifixion (Acts 19:1-5); as well as the baptism of the Holy Spirit which was introduced to the church on the Day of Pentecost (Acts 1:5; 2:1-4, 38). Commentators holding this position include Westcott (145), Lunemann (228), Delitzsch (I:274), and Alford (106). This last view seems to be most likely. It is hard to believe that, in a list of Christian basics, the word baptism would not, at the very least, include the idea of Christian baptism. The fact, however, that the word is used in the plural, and the word in the original refers elsewhere to the Jewish washings, would seem to suggest a contrast between the different types of baptism as suggested above. The need for this would be understandable with these Hebrew readers.

The second member of this pair relating to the outward confession of salvation is "laying on of hands." The act was introduced in the O.T. when those making sacrifices laid their hands on the head of the animal to symbolically identify themselves with the animal whose blood was about to be shed as an atonement for their sins. In the N.T. it was used by both Christ (Mk. 5:23) and the apostles (Acts 19:11; 28:8) in healing the sick, and by Jesus Himself in blessing the little children (Mt. 19:13). It is mentioned on several occasions with regard to ordination for service: of the seven lay leaders in the early church (Acts 6:6), of Paul and Barnabas as they were sent out for service (Acts 13:3), of Timothy's ordination and his gifts for service (1 Tim. 4:14; 2 Tim. 1:6), and with regard to ordaining other church leaders (1 Tim. 5:22).

Perhaps the most significant references to the laying on of hands are to Peter and John laying hands on the new Samaritan believers after they had been baptized so that they might receive the Holy Spirit (Acts 8:16, 17), and to Paul performing a similar act for the same reason on the twelve disciples at Ephesus who had only known the baptism of John (Acts 19:5, 6). Thus, the laying on of hands in the N.T. was associated with the open confession of the Christian life and the reception of the

Holy Spirit as well as with ordination for service in God's kingdom. Although the Holy Spirit soon indwelt believers instantaneously after the initial act of faith, without the need for laying on of hands (see Acts 10:44-48; Rom. 8:9), it still remains significant as an act of blessing as well as ordination for service to this day.

The final pair, which relates to the culmination of the Christian life, is the doctrine "of resurrection of the dead, and of eternal judgment." Eschatology (doctrine of the last things) becomes much clearer in the N.T. Though the idea of the "resurrection of the dead" and of eternal life was taught in the O.T. (Jesus quoted Ex. 3:6 to the Sadducees in Mt. 22:32), that body of inspired literature was more concerned with the development and the deterioration of the nation of Israel as God's vessel to bring Messiah into the world.

The Sadducees, a religious/political group in first century Israel, were composed mostly of individuals of the priestly order. They had become so naturalistic that they denied the resurrection of the body (Mt. 22:23). But Jesus clearly declared the certainty of a bodily resurrection and of eternal judgment for both the righteous and the wicked (Jn. 5:28, 29). It was the preaching of the resurrection which got the early apostles in trouble with the Sadducees (Acts 4:1-3). Paul boldly preached the resurrection to the Athenians on Mars Hill (Acts 17:32) and divided the Pharisees and the Sadducees at his arrest in Jerusalem by declaring that doctrine. And it was Paul in 1 Cor. 15:12-19 who proclaimed the doctrine of the resurrection, both of Christ and of believers, as the central teaching of the N.T. church.

The N.T. also points to several different phases of God's judgment (Mt. 25:46; 2 Th. 1:4-10; Rev. 20:11-15). Though Christians do not agree on the time of these judgments, we do agree on their certainty. "Eternal judgment" here describes its consequences, not the duration of the judgment itself. The word used for judgment (Greek *krima*) looks to the final result, not the process of judgment. Thus, these six principles covering the whole spectrum of Christian doctrine are representative of the rudiments of Christianity in the early church.

Having described the foundation of the doctrine of Christ, with which the Hebrews should have been most familiar, the writer declares his intention in Hebrews 6:3 to take them to higher ground, "And this will we do, if God permit." "This" refers back to the phrase in v. 1, "Let us go on unto perfection." He interrupted that chain of thought by enumerating the six principles of the Christian foundation, but he is now ready to proceed with this pressing matter of spiritual growth through the knowledge of and dependence upon Christ's priesthood after the order of Melchisedec. Again, "we" indicates that this must, indeed, be a cooperative effort between the writer, his readers, and, most of all, the Holy Spirit of God. He uses the future tense to underline his determination to bring his goal into fruition. He does not use the conditional statement "If God permit" because he has doubts as to whether this is the will of God; but, rather, to acknowledge his surrender to God in this and all matters and his complete dependence on God for the accomplishment of His purpose. The Apostle Paul used a similar expression with regard to his plans to stay awhile with the Corinthians on his next visit (1 Cor. 16:7), and James strongly admonishes believers to constantly consider God's will in all the plans that we make (Jas. 4:13-15).

b. The serious consequences of total apostasy (6:4-6)

4 For *it is* impossible for those who were once enlightened, and have tasted of the heavenly gift, and were made partakers of the Holy Ghost,
5 And have tasted the good word of God, and the powers of the world to come,
6 If they shall fall away, to renew them again unto repentance; seeing they crucify to themselves the Son of God afresh, and put *him* to an open shame.

Before looking at the detailed interpretation of this passage—perhaps one of the most controversial in the entire epistle, if not in the entire N.T.—it is appropriate to summarize and evaluate the different approaches to the passage. My research reveals at least seven different positions which have been taken by commentators with regard to the individuals described here. (1) *They are professors of salvation, but not actual possessors of salvation* (MacArthur 142; Henry 62; Hagner 92; Kistemaker 162; Archer 40; Bruce 118; Morris 55, 56; Pink 285; Trapp 674; Gaebelein 264; Gill 707; Edwards 512; Calvin 138; Owen 72; Hughes 222; Gouge 396; Ironside 79; Murray 209; Newell 185; Seiss 157; Ridout 105; Pettingill 62; Stedman 75; Bengel 619; Brown 293; Meyer 114; Saphir 261; George Guthrie 220). (2) *They are "regenerate" but not "elect"*; though a genuine work of the Holy Spirit has taken place in their lives, they can and will fall away since they are not included among God's elect (Alford 113; Jamieson 543). (3) They are genuinely saved people who receive a serious warning about apostasy as a preventive measure, but the whole thing is hypothetical since other N.T. passages teach that a true Christian is eternally secure (Hewitt 108; Barnes 128, 129; Thomas 74; Lange 115; Erdman 70; Roddy 69; Robinson 81; Wiersbe 65; Kent 113). (4) They are saved people, but the writer is speaking about loss of rewards, not loss of salvation (Yeager 202; Draper 153; Henrichsen 79). (5) The sin of apostasy spoken of here involves *a special situation which could not be repeated today* (Wuest 118). (6) They are saved people who are on the verge of apostasy, but *even if they proceed into apostasy, they could come back to God,* not through any human effort, but only by the power of the mighty Spirit of God (Whedon 78, 79; Carter 95; Westcott 150; Harless and Hofmann according to Delitzsch I:290). (7) They are saved people who are seriously backslidden in their spiritual lives, and if they continue to the point of apostasy, *they will be eternally lost since they have committed the sin against the Holy Ghost* (Lunemann 239; Lenski 180, 181; Delitzsch I:288; Moffatt 79; Moulton 128; Dods 298; Evans 134; Lane 94; Schneider 51; Turner 105; Wiley 194; Ellingworth 317, 325; Picirilli 220; Ashby 174; Crowson 70).

Having enumerated seven views on this passage, it is appropriate to provide a more detailed description of each view, along with an evaluation. (1) *Those described here are professors of salvation in Christ, but not genuine possessors of that salvation.* MacArthur, perhaps following Pink, imagines that the writer addresses three different groups in the epistle. In the introduction to his commentary (xi-xv) MacArthur describes these three groups as (1) Hebrew Christians; (2) Hebrew non-Christians who were intellectually convinced but not genuinely saved; and (3) Hebrew non-Christians who were not convinced of the truth of Christianity. He maintains that most of the epistle is written for the encouragement of the Hebrew Christians who were struggling with the persecution of Jewish unbelievers as well as with remnants of the practice of the old covenant which they had grown up with. But the most controversial passages in the book, which warn the readers about going back from Christ to the point of final apostasy, are addressed to the second group made up of unsaved Jews who are only intellectually convinced that Jesus Christ is the Messiah and the Savior of the world. Passages which apply to this second group include 2:1-3a; 6:4-6; 10:26-31; and 12:15-17. Concerning the warning here in chapter 6, MacArthur (146) explains,

> Because they believe the warning is addressed to Christians, many interpreters hold that the passage teaches that salvation can be lost. If this interpretation were true, however, the passage would also teach that, once lost, salvation could never be regained. If, after being saved, a person lost his salvation, he would be damned forever. There would be no going back and forth, in and out of grace. But Christians are not being addressed, and it is the opportunity for receiving salvation, not salvation itself, that can be lost.

What MacArthur observes about a person being finally and eternally lost after he becomes an apostate is certainly accurate. A careful and literal reading of the passage will produce that conclusion, and that is the position of this commentary. His attacks on an "in and out, back and forth" view of salvation do not apply to those who are sometimes referred to as Reformed Arminians (Ashby 137), those whose views go back to the original views of Jacobus Arminius rather than to some of his later disciples. But MacArthur's criticism is appropriate with regard to those who hold such an "in and out" salvation position, and there are some who fall under the broad description of Arminianism who do hold this position.

MacArthur's third group in Hebrews is Hebrew non-Christians who were not convinced. He applies Hebrews 9:11, 14, 15, 27, 28 to this group. These passages in chapter 9 relate to Christ's redemption through the shedding of His blood. MacArthur can't imagine the writer saying to believers, "It is appointed unto men once to die, but after this the judgment" (9:27). But it makes perfectly good sense if he is addressing Hebrew Christians who are on the brink of crossing the line of no return by turning from the blood of Christ to the old ways of Jewish forms and observances.

MacArthur maintains that discerning these three groups in the epistle is the key to understanding its interpretation. But it seems likely that the average reader, indeed even the most educated reader, could not be sure which group is being addressed without MacArthur's guidance. Herein lies the weakness of such an approach, for it borders on what might be legitimately described as hermeneutical gymnastics. MacArthur, however, to his credit, does maintain that the group that is warned about apostasy is being warned about the sin against the Holy Spirit, which, as Jesus declared, is completely without forgiveness. With that position I certainly agree. But it seems highly unlikely that such artificial divisions as are applied by MacArthur will stand the scrutiny of closer examination.

Several commentators, while holding to this same position—that those referred to in 6:4-6 were professors but not possessors—do hold to a variation. They maintain that those who commit this sin of falling away from Christ could possibly be reclaimed and led back to genuine salvation (Henry 62; Hagner 92; Bruce 118; Bengel 619; Brown 293; Meyer 114; Saphir 261; D. Guthrie 220). Though the writer says, "It is impossible . . . to renew them again unto repentance," these commentators say that this refers to man, not to God. Bruce, for example, states, "We know, of course, that nothing of this sort is ultimately impossible for the grace of God, but as a matter of human experience the reclamation of such people is, practically speaking, impossible" (118).

But it seems better to accept the Scripture at face value. Men can never bring anyone to repentance in the first place (Jn. 6:44); it seems obvious, therefore, that the writer is applying the impossibility to both God and man. This variation is similar to the sixth view described below; however, those who propose that position about the possibility of renewal believe that the apostates were actually saved, while those referred to here maintain that they were not truly saved.

The second view of this passage claims that *these were "regenerate" but not "elect."* My original thought was to include this view as a variation of view two, professors but not possessors, but that does not seem to be a good fit. Other writers have suggested that Calvin considered this view as an explanation of this passage, but I have found no recorded evidence of that. Alford and Jamieson are the only commentators I have been able to substantiate with this view. Alford explains,

> One landmark of exegesis then must be to hold fast the simple plain sense of the passage, and recognize the fact that the persons are truly the partakers of the spiritual life, regenerate by the Holy Spirit. Elect of course they are not, or they could not fall away, by the very force of the term: but this is one among many passages where in the Scripture, as ever from the teaching of the Church, we learn that 'elect' and 'regenerate' are not convertible terms. All elect are regenerate: but all regenerate are not elect. The regenerate may fall away, the elect never can (113).

Jacobus Arminius lists the decrees of God in relation to the salvation of sinful men as: (1) to appoint Jesus Christ as the Savior, Redeemer, Mediator, Priest, and King through His own death; (2) to save those from mankind who repent of their sins and believe in Christ, and persevere in this faith to the end, but to leave in sin and under wrath those who refuse to repent and believe; (3) to administer in a sufficient and efficacious manner the means which were necessary for repentance and faith; (4) to save and damn certain particular persons. Concerning this fourth decree, Arminius (I:653, 654) says,

> The decree has its foundation in the foreknowledge of God, by which he knew from all eternity those individuals who would, through his preventing grace, believe, and, through his subsequent grace would persevere, according to the before-described administration of those means which are suitable and proper for conversion and faith; and, by which foreknowledge, he likewise knew those who would not believe and persevere.

This quotation shows that true Arminians believe in the doctrines of election and predestination, simply because the Bible teaches them (Eph. 1:4, 5; Rom. 8:28, 29). Paul says, "All things work together for good to them that love God, to them who are the called according to *his* purpose. For whom he did foreknow, he also did predestinate *to be* conformed to the image of his Son, that he might be the firstborn among many brethren" (Rom. 8:28, 29).

Election and predestination are based on the absolute foreknowledge of an all-knowing God. God's foreknowledge is always correct; it can never be wrong about anything, including who will be saved and who will be lost. But God's sovereign and absolute foreknowledge works in coordination with man's free will. God, through the Holy Spirit, woos, draws, and influences, but He never coerces, especially as it has to do with man's salvation.

The words of Arminius also show that Alford's view about all the elect persevering, but not necessarily all the regenerate, could fall under the spectrum of Arminian theology. If "divine election" in Scripture is intended to apply only to those who actually go to Heaven, and it seems to me there is evidence that it should be applied that way, then Alford's view on that point is, at least, worthy of consideration. In other words, not all the truly saved persevere and are finally saved; but God only "elects" (to find salvation) those whom He foreknows will persevere.

The third view with regard to Hebrews 6:4-6 is *the hypothetical position*. Those who hold this view say that the ones addressed are truly saved people, and the warning given is an actual description of fatal and final apostasy; but the warning is hypothetical: if it could happen to a Christian, this is indeed the way it would happen. Hewitt (108) says,

> The writer by the use of the phrase *if they shall fall away* does not say that the readers or anyone else had fallen away. He is putting forward a hypothetical case . . . If it were possible for them after their great experiences to reject completely and finally the grace of God found in the great work of Christ they would be guilty of committing 'the unforgivable sin', and it would be impossible *to renew them again unto repentance*. There is no suggestion in the context that the sin against the Holy Spirit, which Jesus regarded as unpardonable, and the mysterious 'sin unto death' (cf. 1 Jn. 5:16) is ever committed by true Christians.

Thomas adds, "The passage is apparently a supposed case to correct their wrong ideas" (74). Barnes' (128) gives three reasons the writer uses this strange warning against a sin which, Barnes says, cannot be committed: (1) It would show the greatness of the sin of apostasy. (2) Such a statement might be one of the most effectual means of preserving from apostasy. (3) The means used by God to preserve His people from apostasy have been entirely effectual, for there is no evidence that one has ever fallen away who was a true Christian (133, 134).

It is interesting to note that Barnes' modern editor, Robert Frew, thinks that Barnes interpretation of this passage is not a good one at all, and he has a lengthy note to that effect (134). In my opinion, however, Frew gets further away from the truth in attempting to maintain that those described here were merely professors, not possessors, and that the five descriptive phrases do not define truly saved people. Though I strongly disagree with Barnes' position on the passage, he at least recognized the uselessness of trying to say that these Hebrews were not saved; ultimately, his position is no better than Frew's and is embraced for the same reasons: both of them believe that other passages clearly teach that a genuinely saved person cannot become lost after he has been saved (Jn. 10:27-29; Rom. 8:38, 39; 1 Jn. 2:19).

Of all the views listed, this approach (hypothetical) may be the worst with regard to the integrity of Scripture. It suggests that we cannot always take seriously God's warnings, that He may actually be playing games with us. It appears to make God operate on the premise: "What they don't know won't hurt them; it may actually be good for them." That approach is not even ethical for sinful men, say nothing about a God who honors truth at the highest level, who Himself said, "Thou shalt not bear false witness." This view proposes that, though we cannot actually fall, God was telling the Hebrews that they could fall as a means of scaring them into spiritual maturity. It attacks the heart of one of God's most outstanding attributes, His veracity. It has God, as it were, posting signs along the spiritual highway of life: "Bridge Out, Detour," when the bridge is not actually out. This view is worthy of nothing more than to be tagged as a cop-out, a trumped-up explanation contrived to avoid the obvious truth of this passage of Scripture.

The fourth view on Heb. 6:4-6 says that they are saved people, but the writer is not speaking about loss of salvation, but rather about *loss of rewards*. Yeager correctly points out the dilemma which the Calvinist puts himself in when he argues that these supposed apostates were not really saved, though they had been called by the Spirit and had, indeed, followed His leading to the very brink of salvation, but then have turned back into irremediable apostasy. He says that, when they do this, they are denying "effectual call" and "irresistible grace." Yeager, who is himself a Calvinist, also cannot accept the position that those described here could become true apostates. He says (202),

> The Arminian on the other hand reasons that the writer here describes a truly regenerate person, who then "falls away" to ultimate damnation. This interpretation also proves too much - like throwing out the baby with the bath water - since it teaches that the sinner has only one real chance to be saved, and that if he rebuffs the Holy Spirit in the first encounter he can never again be

brought to the point of repentance and faith.

The passage teaches the Arminians' view that the context is to the believer, but it does not teach that "falling away" means ultimate damnation. The believer can never lose his salvation but he can lose everything else about his experience except his salvation. To "fall by the roadside" (*parapipto*) is to fall into a permanent condition of stunted spiritual growth that renders the "baby" totally fruitless and unable to ever again grow in grace.

Yeager correctly points out that those described here must be seen as true Christians for at least two reasons. (1) The five characteristics used to describe their spiritual experience cannot legitimately be taken as depicting people who are mere professors, not true possessors of salvation. Those who come to such a conclusion must ignore the obvious meaning of the characteristics individually and collectively. (2) The context of the passage, clearly building upon the thought of 5:11-14 where the writer is addressing immature believers, demands that the recipients of these warnings be taken as genuine believers.

It seems to me, however, that there are at least two errors in Yeager's conclusion that the writer has in mind loss of reward, not loss of salvation. First, he misinterprets the Arminian view as giving a sinner only one chance to be saved. He seems to feel that the Arminian view leaves no room for a backslider, that a Christian who falls back into sin immediately becomes an apostate, with no hope of repentance. We believe that backsliders can repent and be forgiven and restored (1 Jn. 1:9). But Arminians do not believe that the writer is describing mere backsliders, but rather individuals who have abandoned Christ completely. Second, Yeager's contention that the writer is describing loss of reward rather than loss of salvation just does not agree with the language used in the passage. When the writer says in 6:4-6, "*It is* impossible . . . to renew them again unto repentance," that certainly does not appear to be declaring loss of reward for those in this position. Repentance is a condition of salvation, not a condition for rewards. If a person cannot repent, then he cannot meet one of the essential requirements for salvation. To the Jewish leaders who self-righteously pointed to recent tragedies as examples of the judgment of God, Jesus warned, "Except ye repent, ye shall all likewise perish" (Lk. 13:3, 5). The inability to repent surely means more than loss of reward; it must be no less than eternal forfeiture of salvation.

The fifth view maintains that the sin of apostasy spoken of here involves a special situation which *was limited to the first century and could not be repeated today*. In my research I found only one commentator, Kenneth S. Wuest, who held to this position. Wiersbe (65) also mentions the view as embraced by some, though he thinks that it is unacceptable. Wuest (118) explains this approach,

> Of course, it should be plain that this sin cannot be committed today. There is no temple in Jerusalem, there are no sacrifices to leave and to return to, no attesting miracles being performed, there is no question as to the closing of the old dispensation and the opening of the new. This sin is not

> the same as the rejection of Christ by the sinner today. It is not only a rejection of Christ, bad as that is. This sin involves the relative merits of the first and near testaments, the abandonment of the type for the reality, the sin of the crucifixion of the Messiah by His own people.

Such a position is not worthy of serious consideration. It appears all too obvious that it is an approach specifically designed to explain away a passage which the author considers extremely difficult to align with his foregone conclusions about eternal security and the possibility of apostasy. If this explanation is allowed, it could be used to set aside almost any commandment or instruction, both in the Old and New Testaments, which we do not like, or which does not fit in well with our theology. It is, in fact, similar to a more recent effort to discredit passages of Scripture which condemn homosexuality and other sins by saying that the writer was merely reflecting the culture of his day, and that a more enlightened position is called for which is not so hard on sin, which places more emphasis on love than on judgment. If the integrity of Scripture is to be preserved, such attempts to avoid the clear implications of a Biblical passage cannot be tolerated.

The sixth view says that these are saved people who are on the verge of apostasy, but that, if they do fall from grace, *it is not necessarily final.* In spite of the fact that the passage plainly states, "*It is* impossible . . . to renew them again unto repentance," these interpreters say that the statement does not need to be taken in the most absolute sense. Delitzsch (I:288), though opposing this approach, explains the view of such commentators as Ebrard, Harless, and Hofmann, when he says:

> Such a man is not therefore irrecoverably fallen; he may possibly, by the might of grace, regain his hold again, tear asunder the web of deceit, and again recover himself out of the snare of the devil (2 Tim. 2:26). We must guard as much against making the apostolic warning a rack of despair, as against making it a pillow of carnal security (288).

Those who hold to this position suggest that the latter part of Heb. 6:6 should be translated, "While they are crucifying to themselves the Son of God afresh," rather than, "Seeing they crucify" (KJV), or "Because they are crucifying." Though "while" is a possible interpretation of the participle used in the original, it is really not in line with the gravity of the sin described, with the use of the word "impossible," nor with the tense of the participle translated, "If they shall fall away" (Greek aorist tense), which presents the idea of a complete and final fall.

Whedon, following this interpretation, adds that such apostates are "beyond human reach, but not beyond God's reach" (78, 79). He compares this situation to the teaching of Jesus about rich men in Mt. 19:23-26: "Verily I say unto you, That a rich man shall hardly enter into the kingdom of heaven. And again I say unto you, It is easier for a camel to go through the eye of a needle, than for a rich man to enter into the kingdom of God." However, Jesus somewhat mollifies His statement by adding, "With men this is impossible; but with God all things are possible."

Whedon thinks that the same principle could be applied here, that, though men could not "renew them again to repentance," God can. But the truth is that men never can bring other men to repentance; that is always something that God alone can do. Jesus Himself declared, "No man can come to me, except the Father which hath sent me draw him" (Jn. 6:44). The fact that a man cannot bring another man to repentance is a truth that is too obvious, both logically and theologically, for the writer of Hebrews to mean that. It is much better to accept the fact that the impossibility of renewing these apostates is without condition or qualification.

The seventh view says that *those to whom this severe warning is issued are truly saved people who are seriously backslidden, and if they continue in this downward spiritual direction to the point of apostasy, they will have crossed the line of no return, and will, thus, be eternally lost.* Since there is only one sin which cannot be forgiven, the sin against the Holy Spirit, this then must be at least one manifestation of this awful sin. In Mt. 12:31, 32 and Mk. 3:28, 29 Jesus accuses the Pharisees, who were certainly unsaved, of being at least on the edge of committing this sin because of their constant and willful rejection of divine truth in His teachings and in His works. They instead claimed that His teachings and works came about through the power of Satan rather than the power of God. But in Lk. 12:10, Jesus issued the same warning to His disciples in giving them instructions about the importance of public confession of the name of Christ, even under the stress of persecution. Therefore, the sin against the Holy Spirit can be committed by both unsaved people, who constantly and willfully reject the obvious truth of the Gospel, and by saved people who also constantly and willfully turn their back on Christ to the point of final apostasy. It is about this sin that these Hebrew Christians are being warned.

Hewitt refers to Westcott in defense of his position that the passage is only hypothetical, that it does not say anyone ever has or ever will commit this sin of apostasy (111). But he misinterprets Westcott's position on this passage. It is true that Westcott does use the term "hypothetical," but by this he merely means that these Hebrew Christians had not yet committed the sin of apostasy, and with this position I firmly agree. If the writer's Hebrew audience was already guilty of the sin of apostasy as described in this passage, by his own definition there would be no point in warning them about it, for it would be "impossible to renew them to repentance." But Westcott clarifies his use of the term "hypothetical" when he adds, "But though the case is only supposed it is one which must be taken into account. It is possible for us to see how it can arise. The state of a man may become such as to make the application to him of the appointed help towards the divine life not only difficult but impossible" (165).

Westcott then goes on to point to other similar warnings (Heb. 3:12; 10:26f.; 1 Jn. 5:16), and he specifically identifies the sin here described with the sin against the Holy Spirit in Mt. 12:31, 32. It is obvious, therefore, that he does not view the passage as "hypothetical" in the sense that Hewitt and others take it (see the discussion above).

Now we turn to the exposition of the passage. "For" (v. 4) connects the severe warning issued in Heb. 6:4-6 with what has been said about the need to "go on to perfection" in vv. 1-3. His design in these verses is to emphasize the dire consequences of not being able to take these Hebrew Christians beyond the foundational principles of the Christian life that they have started with. Since 6:4-6 is one long sentence, it would be easy to miss the sense of the whole thing. "It is impossible" finds its completion in verse 6. Thus, we should read, "It is impossible . . . to renew them again unto repentance." As discussed above, some commentators have suggested that this impossibility of renewing to repentance is merely on man's part, but that no one, regardless of their spiritual condition, is beyond the power of the grace of God. There is no indication, however, that this impossibility is to be limited in any way. Those who have fallen away after having all these spiritual experiences are beyond the reach of both God and man, because they have committed the sin against the Holy Spirit.

Those who cannot be renewed to repentance are described in great detail by the use of five phrases (participles in Greek). It is helpful to see them all together in this fashion: "It is impossible to be renewing again to repentance those who have experienced the following: [1] were once enlightened, [2] tasted of the heavenly gift, [3] were made partakers of the Holy Ghost, [4] tasted the good word of God, and the powers of the world to come, and [5] then have fallen away from [abandoned] these experiences." In the original, one article joins all five of these descriptive participles, indicating that all five are being used to describe the same group of people. The first four statements describe the spiritual experience of these Hebrew Christians, and the fifth statement describes the apostasy itself.

As I have noted, some commentators, like MacArthur and Pink, say that, regardless of their appearance, these four descriptions do not really apply to a true conversion experience. But if someone was trying to describe in detail what happens to a person when he is converted, it would be difficult to come up with better words than those used here. Barnes (128, 129) gives three reasons why these descriptions should be taken as applying to those who are genuinely saved: (1) This is the most obvious meaning to most readers unless there is some theory to defend. (2) The context demands it since the writer is addressing true Christians in an effort to keep them from apostasy. (3) This is in accord with the proper meaning of the phrases used to describe their spiritual experience (128, 129).

The first description is of "those who were once enlightened." The same word (Greek *photizo*) is used in Heb. 10:32, where the KJV translates, "But call to remembrance the former days, in which, *after ye were illuminated*, ye endured a great fight of afflictions." This passage occurs at the conclusion of a warning similar to this one. It seems clear that the writer in that passage is addressing people whom he considers to be true Christians, people who had even been subjected to severe suffering for the name of Christ.

Paul uses the same root in 2 Cor. 4:6 when he says, "For God, who commanded the light to shine out of darkness, hath shined in our hearts, *to give the light* [Greek *photismos*] of the knowledge of the glory of God in the face of Jesus Christ." Again it is clear that the word is used in the context of truly saved people who have come out of darkness into the light of our Savior, Jesus Christ (see Jn. 1:8, 9). To add strength to the definiteness of these experiences, our writer adds the word "once" (Greek *hapax*), which he probably intends to be taken with all five participles, just as the article mentioned above; thus: "once enlightened, once tasted, once were made partakers," etc. In addition to this, all five participles express completed action (Greek aorist). Surely no one could have these 5 experiences and not have been truly saved!

The second phrase is *those who "have tasted of the heavenly gift."* Some who argue that these are not genuine Christians emphasize the word "tasted" (Greek *geuomai*) (MacArthur 142), suggesting that those described had merely nipped at Christianity, never really swallowing and digesting Christ as their Savior. Though the word may occasionally be used in this manner (see Mt. 27:34), that is not its normal meaning in real life or in the Scripture. Those who are ill often complain that they ate their food but did not enjoy it because they were unable to taste it. We often compliment our host or hostess with comments about how good the food tasted. Thus, "taste" usually means "to fully experience with a sense of genuine joy or pleasure." The psalmist invited those who did not know the Lord to "taste and see that the LORD *is* good" (Ps. 34:8). Just prior to the Transfiguration, Jesus declared, "There be some standing here, which shall not taste of death, till they see the Son of man coming in his kingdom" (Mt. 16:28). But the strongest passage of all is Heb. 2:9 where the writer says, "But we see Jesus, who was made a little lower than the angels for the suffering of death, crowned with glory and honour; that he by the grace of God should taste death for every man." Jesus certainly did not merely nibble at death. He fully experienced suffering and death, even to its bitterest depths, so that we might be saved. Thus, when the Hebrews tasted the heavenly gift, or the good word of God, or the powers of the world to come, they did not merely nibble at them, but they fully experienced them and were genuinely converted.

What these Hebrews tasted of, in this case, was "the heavenly gift." In some passages in the N.T. the Holy Spirit is referred to as God's gift to the church (Acts 2:38; 10:45; 11:17), but it seems unlikely that the writer has the Spirit in mind here since He is mentioned in the next phrase. In Jesus' interview with the Samaritan woman at Jacob's well, He said, "If thou knewest the gift of God, and who it is that saith to thee, Give me to drink; thou wouldest have asked of him, and he would have given thee living water" (Jn. 4:10). In a similar manner, Paul views the gift of righteousness through faith in Christ as the only means of salvation and justification (Rom. 5:15-17). So here the writer of Hebrews is referring to salvation in Jesus Christ as God's gift to his readers. It is called the "heavenly" gift because it came from Heaven, not from men, just as Paul said to the Ephesians, "For by grace are ye saved through faith; and that not of yourselves: *it is* the gift of God" (Eph. 2:8).

The third descriptive phrase is "were made partakers of the Holy Ghost." Again, some commentators have tried to picture the word "partakers" (Greek *metochos*) as merely meaning "in association with" or "participating with" (MacArthur 142; Pink 285), not true partakers of the Holy Ghost, as genuine Christians would be. But the same word is used by the same writer in Heb. 3:14 where he says, "For we are made partakers of Christ, if we hold the beginning of our confidence stedfast unto the end." As He returned to Heaven, Jesus promised His disciples, "Ye shall be baptized with the Holy Ghost not many days hence" (Acts 1:5). After the promise was fulfilled on the Day of Pentecost, Peter invited others to participate, instructing them to repent and be baptized in the name of Jesus so that they might "receive the gift of the Holy Ghost" (Acts 2:38). The only work that the Holy Spirit performs in relation to the unsaved is the work of reproof or conviction (see Jn. 16:8-10), and surely being made "partakers of the Holy Ghost" in this passage means more than mere conviction. These, indeed, were believers, immature though many of them were, who had experienced the indwelling of the Spirit, as do all believers (Rom. 8:9).

The fourth phrase is that they "have tasted the good word of God." The word "tasted" carries the same connotation as in v. 4, to both experience and enjoy whatever is being taken in. In this case it is "the good word of God." "Word" (Greek *hrema*) is not the same as that used in 4:12 (Greek *logos*). There the writer was speaking about the Word of God as a whole, the complete message of the Gospel; here he is referring to a specific utterance or group of utterances from the Lord. In this context he most likely has in mind those utterances of the Gospel which relate to salvation, those utterances in particular which marked their confession of faith (as Acts 2:38; Rom. 10:9, 10). It is called "the good word" because of the message which it contained, the message of salvation, and because of the result it produced. "Good" (Greek *kalos*) emphasizes not only the inner truth and unblemished character of the Word, but also the beauty of the Word in its promises. The psalmist referred to this when he said, "How sweet are thy words unto my taste! *yea, sweeter* than honey to my mouth!" (Ps. 119:103).

The fourth phrase adds that they also had tasted "the powers of the world to come." "Powers" (Greek *dunamis*) is often used for the miraculous works of Christ in the Gospels (Mt. 11:20; Mk. 6:2; Lk. 19:37), as well as for miracles performed by the apostles in the early church (1 Cor. 12:10; 2 Cor. 12:12; Gal. 3:5). It may refer to that miraculous type of power as it was witnessed and experienced by the Hebrew Christians. The word is also used in a more general sense as when Paul says, "I am not ashamed of the gospel of Christ: for it is the *power* of God unto salvation to every one that believeth; to the Jew first, and also to the Greek" (Rom. 1:16). Here Paul uses the word *power* to describe the life-changing effects of the gospel when a person comes to Christ, and that indeed is one of the greatest miracles that can ever happen. "The world to come" is literally "the coming age." In Heb. 2:5 a similar phrase (though not identical in the original) referred to the created world, the present inhabited world, which God in creation placed under the dominion of mankind, not under the dominion of angels. From the perspective of the O.T. dispensation, "the world to come" referred to the age of the Messiah, the period after Messiah has come, and that is the way it was often used among ancient Jewish writers. But from the perspective of the Messianic age itself, the period of the new covenant after Christ has come, it refers to the next dispensation after this life is over, the heavenly one. As with all believers, when we are saved we experience "a foretaste of glory divine." The Hebrews had truly experienced that miraculous and life-changing power of Christ in their lives; a taste of Heaven had come down; the world to come had invaded this present world as a result of their faith in Christ (see Rev. 21:1-5).

"If they shall fall away" is the fifth phrase describing the characteristics and condition of those the writer is defining as apostates. The participle can legitimately be translated with an "if" (Greek conditional participle), since the readers to whom the warning is issued have certainly not yet taken this final step. If they had, there would be no point in the warning. It might be better, however, to see it translated as parallel with the other four participles in the series, which it is, gramatically. Thus, we would read: "It is impossible for those who were once enlightened . . . and who tasted . . . and who became partakers . . . and who tasted . . . and who fell away." The first four participles mark the genuine spiritual conversion which these Hebrews had experienced, while the fifth participle expresses the tragic result of those who have abandoned Christ and the Christian way. The verb "fall away" (Greek *parapipto*) expresses an action which is viewed as final and complete (Greek aorist tense). The word refers to one who has fallen away from the right path. This is not describing an act like Peter's when he denied Christ under great stress, confusion, and fear, and then repented when he realized what he had done (Mt. 26:75). This is more like the act of Judas who willfully and knowingly betrayed his trusted Friend and, though he apparently felt some remorse at the outcome (Mt. 27:3, 4), persisted in his rebellion to the point of taking his own life (Mt. 27:5). Though Peter's sin and Judas' sin bear some outward similarities, they are different in their original intent, their persistent development, and their final outcome.

We now find the completion of the long thought started in v. 4: It is impossible "to renew them again unto repentance." "To renew them again" (Greek *anakainizo*) is an infinitive expressing action in progress (literally, "to be renewing them again"), emphasizing the impossibility of bringing apostates back to their former state in spite of repeated and persistent efforts. This is also one of the strongest phrases in the whole passage indicating that these were genuine Christians, not mere professors who really did not possess salvation in Christ.

If these potential apostates had never known true repentance, how could there even be any consideration for bringing them back to the same? The word itself, "to renew," implies bringing something or someone back to a condition previously known or experienced. To strengthen that meaning the writer adds the word "again" and places it up front (in the original) for the sake of emphasis.

The condition to which an apostate cannot be again renewed is "repentance" (Greek *metanoia*), referring to a genuine and inward change of mind which manifests itself in an outward change of thought and conduct. It has already been mentioned in 6:1 as one of the two initial acts which mark the beginning of the Christian life: repentance from dead works and faith toward God. As discussed in that context, when the N.T. speaks about salvation, it often mentions either faith alone or repentance alone since one of them, when performed as the Bible teaches, always includes the other. Here, then, since repentance refers to a change of heart and mind, we can say that the writer points to *the psychological result of apostasy*. In Heb. 10:26 the writer points to the same irreconcilable sin, but there he describes it from a slightly different standpoint, saying that for such there is "no more sacrifice for sins"; and thus stating *the soteriological result of apostasy* (soteriology is a theological term referring to the doctrine of salvation). In Heb. 6:6 the writer points out how apostasy affects a person from the inside, leaving him with no desire to come back to Christ, no inner will to abandon the path to perdition which he is traveling. In Heb. 10:26 he points out how apostasy affects a person from the outside, leaving him without any provision for salvation. Since he has rejected the only way of redemption, there is no way he can come back in repentance unless Jesus Christ makes another trip to Calvary, and we can be sure that will never happen.

Since the sin is clearly designated as being unforgivable in both places—in Hebrews 6 by claiming that it is "without repentance," and in Heb. 10:26 by claiming that it is "without sacrifice"—and since Jesus Christ forcefully declared the sin against the Holy Spirit to be the only unforgivable sin (Mt. 12:31, 32; Lk. 12:10), it seems necessary to conclude that the sin described here is indeed that awful sin which dooms those who commit it to an eternal existence apart from God.

Verse 6 concludes with two reasons why the sin which he has described does not allow for repentance: "seeing they crucify to themselves the Son of God afresh, and put him to an open shame." In contrast to the five preceding phrases in 6:4-6 which expressed completed action (Greek aorist tense), these two participles are given in continuous action (Greek present tense), indicating the constant and unchangeable result for the individual who has committed apostasy. Because the participles are expressed in continuous action, some have tried to suggest that the writer is saying that they cannot be renewed to repentance "while" or "as long as" they keep crucifying the Son of God, thus taking the participles to be *temporal*. But this interpretation seems highly unlikely since it would then offer a contradiction to the warning that the sin is "without repentance," and would, thus, basically destroy the seriousness of the sin. The KJV translators took the writer to be indicating the cause for the sin being "without repentance" or unforgivable by their translation, "seeing." Other English translations get the correct idea of *cause* across by using the word "since" (NASB, NKJV), or "because" (NIV).

The two expressions as to why the sin of apostasy is unforgivable both identify the apostate with that rebellious crowd that demanded the crucifixion of Christ. First, "They crucify to themselves the Son of God afresh." According to history, Pontius Pilate, the Roman procurator or governor of Judaea, was one of the most cruel leaders of all time. Yet, cruel as he was, he saw the hypocrisy of the Jewish leaders and perceived the innocence of Jesus of Nazareth. The Scripture records numerous efforts which he made to release Jesus, but in spite of this they stubbornly demanded His crucifixion, which only the Roman governor could order. From the cross Jesus Christ prayed, "Father, forgive them; for they know not what they do" (Lk. 23:34). However, in the context of this prayer, it is clear that it was prayed for the Roman officials who were carrying out the crucifixion.

Concerning his awful sin as a persecutor of Christians wherever he could find them, Paul declared, "I obtained mercy, because I did *it* ignorantly in unbelief" (1 Tim. 1:13). Like Paul, the Roman soldiers were unaware of whom they were crucifying. But that cannot be said of the Jewish leaders who demanded His crucifixion. They knew what they were doing. These persistent rebel apostates identify themselves when *they crucify "the Son of God afresh."* Their crucifixion is, of course, figurative, but by their attitudes they manifest that they would have been in that crowd of rebels and would have cried aloud for His crucifixion if they had been there. The writer adds that they do this crucifying of Christ "to themselves," perhaps suggesting the realm or the sphere within which this crucifixion occurs: within themselves. It also might be taken in the sense of "for themselves," that is, "for their own interest," or as NIV translates, "to their loss" (Greek dative of disadvantage). The writer adds to the weight of the sin by using the title, "the Son of God." When they demanded the crucifixion of Jesus of Nazareth, they were demanding the death of the Divine Mediator who became a man through the virgin Mary, and though He was fully and truly man in every sense, He was yet "the Son of God."

The writer adds further emphasis to the awful sin of these apostates: by their rejection they "put *him* to an open shame." The root word is used in Mt. 1:19 when the Scripture says that Joseph, though not knowing the details about Mary's pregnancy at the time, was not willing to make her "a publick example." Here the compound word (Greek *paradeigmatizo*) strengthens that meaning. Crucifixion, by its very nature, exposed the victim, not only through the shame of the nature of the death itself, but also through being literally stripped naked for all the world to behold the awful agony of his suffering. Those who become apostates declare their agreement with the original rebels who treated the Savior of the world, the Son of God, in such a despicable manner.

c. This truth illustrated from nature (6:7, 8)

7 For the earth which drinketh in the rain that cometh oft upon it, and bringeth forth herbs meet for them by whom it is dressed, receiveth blessing from God:
8 But that which beareth thorns and briers *is* rejected, and *is* nigh unto cursing; whose end *is* to be burned.

The writer now turns to an illustration with which these Hebrew Christians would be very familiar, living as they did in the largely agricultural economy of Palestine. We must be careful to note that he is not speaking about two different pieces of ground, but rather one piece of ground that has the potential of responding in two different ways. Thus, he illustrates, "For the earth which drinketh in the rain that cometh oft upon it, and bringeth forth herbs." Jesus Himself often used the natural earth, and its potential to produce good fruit, to illustrate various lessons which He wanted to teach. In His most familiar parable of all, the parable of the sower, He illustrated four different responses to the gospel seed, when it is sown, by pointing to four different types of soil. In Mk. 4:26-29 Jesus illustrated the wonderful cooperation between God and man in the production of a harvest. The man sows the seed and then goes his way. Though he may do a little plowing and fertilizing along the way, it is God's good earth that produces the fruit. Even though the man may not understand the process, he nevertheless reappears at harvest time to reap the benefit of God's miracle of growth. The obvious application to spiritual fruit is clear.

Jesus illustrates the Lord's patience in waiting for fruit in Lk. 13:6-9 when the dresser of the vineyard asks for one more year to dig about and fertilize the fig tree. "If it bear fruit, well," he says, "and if not, *then* after that thou shalt cut it down." The writer of Hebrews points to a similar lesson here. The immaturity and fruitlessness of these Hebrew Christians were coming to be a serious problem.

The fact that one single piece of earth is in the mind of the writer is illustrated in the original by the fact that three participles are connected with this word by a single article: "drinketh . . . bringeth forth herbs . . . beareth thorns." "The rain" represents all the spiritual blessings which the Lord had bestowed upon the Hebrews to enable them to produce a good spiritual harvest. "Herbs" (Greek *botane*) refer to all the general varieties of beneficial vegetation which are good as food for mankind, and in the parable they point to the spiritual harvest which God rightfully expected. These herbs, this spiritual harvest, is "meet for them by whom it is dressed." "Meet" means "useful" or "suitable." "By whom" is more literally "because of whom," referring not only to the owner of the land, but to all of his dependents as well. "It is dressed" refers to the human cultivation of the piece of land and its produce. Though man's cooperation in growing a crop in the natural realm, or in winning men to Christ and edifying them in the spiritual realm, is very important, the human aspect is played down here, though it is present. The human element is not emphasized because God's part is so much more significant in the production of a good crop, whether natural or spiritual.

Such a piece of ground which produces good fruit, as the Lord has ordained, "receiveth blessing from God." For the literal piece of ground, this blessing would include God's favor which would guarantee the continuation of the rain and sunshine for future productivity. For the believer, to whom the writer is pointing, it refers to the continuation of God's enhancement of His spiritual gifts so that spiritual results may increase. The lesson is similar to that of the vine and the branches in Jn. 15:1-6. For those branches that continue to abide in the vine, the husbandman prunes them that they may bring forth more fruit; that is, that the believer may be even more productive in the many varied types of fruit in the Christian life.

On the other hand, Jesus says, "If a man abide not in me, he is cast forth as a branch, and is withered; and men gather them, and cast *them* into the fire, and they are burned" (Jn. 15:6). In like manner, the writer of Hebrews says in v. 8, "But that which beareth thorns and briers *is* rejected." If this same piece of land, or this same drifting believer which the land represents, does not respond to God's gifts which are designed to produce good fruit, then there is a point of total abandonment. Notice, however, that God's beneficial rain keeps falling often upon it, and the human workers continue to cultivate the ground, just as with the land which produces good fruit in v. 8. No man becomes an apostate overnight. But this passage indicates that there is a point of no return, a point where even God's patience runs out. Some would object that to claim God's total rejection because the land bears "thorns and briers" would suggest a salvation by works, not by grace through faith. But a departing believer at some point becomes an unbeliever, and that point of apostasy can only be determined by an all-knowing God.

Furthermore, the writer has already pointed out the intimate connection between persistent rebellion, sin, and unbelief in his description of Israel in the wilderness in Heb. 3:15-19. James declares, "Faith, if it hath not works, is dead, being alone" (Jas. 2:17), and Paul completes his great statement about salvation being by grace through faith as a gift of God (Eph. 2:8, 9) by proclaiming, "For we are his workmanship, created in Christ Jesus unto good works, which God hath before ordained that we should walk in them" (Eph. 2:10). Just as faith is evidenced visibly by good works, so unbelief is evidenced visibly by evil works, even by the production of "thorns and briers" in the face of all of God's good blessings.

The fact that this apostasy is a process, not instantaneous, is further indicated by the writer's description of it in three steps. He says that the land that bears thorns and briers is (1) *rejected,* (2) *and is nigh unto cursing,* (3) *whose end is to be burned.* "Rejected" (Greek *adokimos*) refers to being disapproved, disqualified, or rejected as a result of testing. In another prominent use of the same word, Paul says, "I keep under my body, and bring *it* into subjection; lest that by any means, when I have preached to others, I myself should be a castaway" (1 Cor. 9:27). (See the discussion of this in the commentary on 1 Corinthians, pp. 133, 134.) In all the places this word is used in the N.T. (2 Cor. 13:5-7; Rom. 1:28; Tit. 1:16; 2 Tim. 3:8), including the two mentioned here, it appears to refer to total, complete, and final abandonment.

The writer also says that such land is "nigh unto cursing." Yeager argues that the land is not, in fact, cursed, but that it is only near that point, and that a complete curse or abandonment cannot possibly occur because the Bible teaches eternal security (209). But it would seem better to suggest that the writer describes the curse as being "near" because those to whom the warning is issued have not already committed apostasy. Some of them may be on the verge, the very brink of it, but they have not yet crossed that line of no return.

Finally, the writer says about such land, "whose end *is* to be burned." In this harsh context, he certainly does not have in mind a mere purging, a burning for the purpose of purification (as in 1 Cor. 3:13-15), but rather a burning as indicative of total rejection of the land, as the Orientals and Romans often did (Barnes 136). This is a burning of utter desolation, as of a land destroyed by volcanic forces (Westcott 153).

In connection with the discussion of this most severe warning by our writer concerning the possibility of total, final, irremediable apostasy, it seems appropriate to define one or two terms. First, in my view, a clear distinction must be made between a backslider and an apostate. A backslider is a genuine child of God who has drifted, to a lesser or greater extent, away from perfect fellowship with the Lord. He is not eternally lost until he crosses that point of no return, that point where he becomes an apostate.

David, writing under inspiration, viewed himself as a backslider in spite of his awful sins of adultery and murder. He prayed, "Cast me not away from thy presence; and take not thy holy spirit from me. Restore unto me the joy of thy salvation; and uphold me *with thy* free spirit" (Ps. 51:11, 12). Furthermore, John assures us that, though we should not sin (1 Jn. 2:1), "If we confess our sins, he is faithful and just to forgive us our sins, and to cleanse us from all unrighteousness" (1 Jn. 1:9).

This is not to suggest that there is no danger in backsliding. Anyone who thinks this should look at the example of David who, though forgiven for all eternity, suffered greatly and continuously on this earth for the remainder of his life. You do, indeed, reap what you sow (Gal. 6:7). And, most fearful of all, remember that backsliding is the road to apostasy. There is, indeed, a spiritual point of no return.

The other term or phrase which we should discuss is the oft-made statement that a Christian can *lose* his salvation, a term often emphasized by those who ridicule our position. Let me say boldly, and without apology, I do not believe that we can *lose* our salvation. The word "lose" implies an accident. People lose their wallet, their purse, or their keys, implying something that was completely unintentional, not in any way a willful act, or an act of rebellion. Surely our salvation by grace through faith in an all-wise, all-powerful Savior is more secure than that!

I believe that our brothers who espouse the teaching of eternal security misinterpret the passages from which they draw that doctrine. But, at the same time, I do believe that those passages teach security, the security of *the believer.* I believe that it is better for us to say that we believe that a Christian can *forfeit* his salvation (a stronger word than "lose," implying at least some participation on the part of the one who forfeits, though this word also includes a loss), or even better, we believe that a Christian can commit apostasy or apostatize, a word which communicates a willful act of departing from what was once fondly and faithfully embraced. Apostasy is an act of willful, rebellious departure from God, in spite of His persistent efforts through Scripture, preaching and teaching the Word, inner conviction by the Holy Spirit, and life's circumstances, of which God is in charge, to bring him back to Himself. The apostate crosses a theological line of no return when he willfully abandons the Savior he has once known and, in doing so, he commits the only unforgivable sin, the sin against the Holy Spirit. Since the Holy Spirit has been withdrawn, there is no chance of future salvation since Jesus Himself declared, "No man can come to me, except the Father which hath sent me draw him" (Jn. 6:44).

3. Encouragement to faithful endurance and progress through depending upon Christ as High Priest (6:9-20)

In this section our writer leaves, for the time being, the negative emphasis that included a strong warning about the possibility of total and final apostasy. He expresses confidence in the readers' perseverance and points to the example of those who have persevered before them, even in the face of great obstacles, such as Abraham, the father of the Hebrew people. But beyond the good example of Abraham, he ultimately encourages them to place their hope in Jesus Christ, who is not only their Savior, but also their High Priest according to the order of Melchisedec. That point will bring him back to where he left off in 5:10.

a. The writer's faith in the Hebrews (6:9)

9 But, beloved, we are persuaded better things of you, and things that accompany salvation, though we thus speak.

"But" introduces a contrast in both words and tone to the severe warning about the possibility of apostasy in the previous verses. The writer addresses his readers as "beloved," the only time the word is used in the entire epistle; by doing so, he markedly softens the harsh warning he has just given. He in no way, however, intends to take back the warning, or to mollify the severity of the consequences of apostasy. "We are persuaded" actually stands up front in the original, indicating the thought that the writer wants to emphasize. The meaning is, "We have been persuaded" (Greek perfect tense), and the implication is that, not only have we been persuaded, but we still are. It indicates some struggle in thought on the part of the writer which has resulted in a settled conclusion.

The object about which the writer has been persuaded is "better things of you." "Better" stands as the key word of the book of Hebrews, used some 13 times throughout the epistle. Here the "better things" offer a contrast with the worst things in v. 8, where the potential apostates are like the unproductive land which "*is* rejected, and *is* nigh unto cursing; whose end *is* to be burned." When he says "of you" or "about you," he does not mean to indicate that he is now somehow addressing a different group from those who received the warning about unsatisfactory spiritual growth and the potential for final apostasy in 5:11—6:8, as MacArthur, Pink, and others suggest. Though these warnings apply to this same group, the writer wants to motivate them to flee from the cliff's edge, and he does so by honestly emphasizing the higher expectations that he has of them.

These "better things" are further explained as "things that accompany salvation." "Better things" and "things that accompany salvation" are connected by one article in the original, indicating that they are both meant to refer to the same things. These things would include, in particular, a renewal of spiritual growth, an increasing dependence on Christ's priestly ministry, a continuation of the love they had previously manifested toward one another, as well as continued patience in tribulation. By pointing to "things that accompany salvation," the writer in no way means to imply that the potential apostates referred to in 6:4-6 were not saved (MacArthur 152). He is rather encouraging this entire Hebrew church to increase in the spiritual characteristics mentioned above, things that indeed do accompany salvation. The question is not whether they are now saved, for they certainly are, as is unquestionably indicated in the description given in 6:4, 5. It is rather a question of whether they will continue on the upward road to Heaven rather than lapse further toward the eternal precipice of apostasy.

By adding the words "Though we thus speak," the writer again emphasizes the contrast between the previous words of warning and the present words of encouragement. This phrase also clearly indicates that he has the same group in mind in both places. The warning is for these Hebrew Christians, who are lacking in spiritual growth, and he is serious about that warning. But these words of encouragement are for this same group, and he fully believes that the positive message will carry the day.

b. Their past work for Christ (6:10)

10 For God *is* not unrighteous to forget your work and labour of love, which ye have shewed toward his name, in that ye have ministered to the saints, and do minister.

"For" points to the major part which God Himself must play in bringing these delinquent Hebrew Christians out of their lethargy and back onto the road of vibrant spiritual growth. The writer is not able to issue the encouraging word which he just gave in v. 9 merely out of confidence that he has in them; it comes rather from their dependence on God, and that "God *is* not unrighteous to forget your work and labour of love."

In a similar manner, other passages emphasize God's righteousness or faithfulness in relation to believers. He is faithful to forgive our sins when we confess them (1 Jn. 1:9); He is faithful in not allowing us to be tempted above what we are able to bear (1 Cor. 10:13); He is faithful and able "to keep that which I have committed unto him against that day" (2 Tim. 1:12), etc. The fact that God is a just and righteous God gives us the certain confidence that He will always act in accordance with His attributes, and that, most of all, He will always act in accordance with the promises of His Word. He will not "forget." The O.T. is especially replete with declarations that God will not forget us or our work in His behalf (see Am. 8:7; Is. 49:14-16); furthermore, if God does not forget even one sparrow, which is worth such a small amount (Lk. 12:6), how much more will He not forget us.

God will not forget "your work and labour of love." More details are given about these works in 10:32-34, the persecutions they had endured, both personally and through coming to the aid of other Christians who were also suffering, including the writer himself, as well as the confiscation of their personal property because of their faith. But work, by itself, is not a sure sign that a person is a true Christian. The work of the Pharisees of Jesus' day was quite impressive with regard to its volume and its detail (they even tithed their garden herbs—Mt. 23:23), but it was all motivated by the flesh; they sought the praise of men rather than the praise of God (Mt. 23:5). But the work of these

Hebrew Christians was genuine because it was truly motivated by love.

Some recent translations, following a different Greek text, read here, "Your work and the love you have shown" (NIV, NASB). The meaning is basically the same. The only work that will receive God's approval and His reward is that which is done unselfishly from a heart of love. Similar to this passage, Paul, writing to the Thessalonians, remembers their "work of faith, and labour of love" (1 Th. 1:3).

The writer points out further that this is work and love "which ye have shewed toward his name." As mentioned above, the Pharisees did their works to be seen of men; that is, their motive was self-glorification. But Jesus admonished, "Let your light so shine before men, that they may see your good works, and glorify your Father which is in heaven" (Mt. 5:16). The Hebrews were obeying this admonition when they "shewed" (Greek *endeiknumi*), displayed, or demonstrated the work and love that had been so evident in their lives in the past.

Indeed, these were works performed from the highest motives, for they were done "toward his name." To say that their services were done "toward his name" rather than "toward him" makes their work more intimate, more personal. The word "name" carries with it all the attributes, all the detailed characteristics of the person whose name it is. The O.T. presents numerous names for God, and each one is filled with special meaning. Toward that name of God and His Son, Jesus Christ, they performed their works of love. Jesus said, "Whosoever shall give to drink unto one of these little ones a cup of cold *water* only *in the name* of a disciple, verily I say unto you, he shall in no wise lose his reward" (Mt. 10:42). Merely doing a work does not bring a reward; more important is why and how that work was done.

The writer describes the means or manner of their work and labor of love with phrases (Greek participles): "in that ye have ministered to the saints, and do minister"; both use the same verb (Greek *diakoneo*). The first, "ye have ministered," describes action in the past, completed action (Greek aorist); while the second, "and do minister," expresses action which is continuing at the present time (Greek present). In some respects this is an amazing revelation. These Christians who are earlier described as being so sluggish, so in need of a spiritual awakening, are yet manifesting signs that they are really saved. This is certainly a strong indication that we are looking at real Christians, not people who only outwardly profess Christ without really knowing Him in their hearts.

This past and continuing ministry is "to the saints." The Hebrew equivalent is used often to refer to God's people in the O.T. The word (Greek *hoi hagioi*) literally means "the holy ones," and it refers to those who are chosen and set apart to be God's and to serve Him. But we must be careful to note that the word, as used in the N.T., refers to *all* Christians, not to some special person who has been elevated to sainthood by an earthly church.

"Saints" is used only once in the Gospels, to refer to those mysterious figures who rose from the dead in connection with the crucifixion of Christ (Mt. 27:52). Its more specific N.T. usage begins in Acts 9:13 when Ananias spoke of the "saints at Jerusalem" whom Saul of Tarsus had so recently persecuted. From there it is used throughout the Epistles and Revelation to refer to all of God's people who have been set apart for His service.

We notice that the work of love which these Hebrews did toward His name was done to and for His saints. But that is certainly in line with the teaching of Scripture elsewhere. In connection with His dramatic picture of the final judgment, Jesus declared, with regard to the works of those who stood before Him, "Inasmuch as ye have done *it* unto one of the least of these my brethren, ye have done *it* unto me" (Mt. 25:40), and John says that our love for God in Heaven is realistically demonstrated by our love for our fellow believer on this earth (1 Jn. 4:12, 20). Interestingly, the writer emphasizes perhaps the three greatest Christian graces in this and the next two verses: love, hope, and faith.

c. The writer's desire that their hope and faith continue until the end (6:11, 12)

11 And we desire that every one of you do shew the same diligence to the full assurance of hope unto the end:
12 That ye be not slothful, but followers of them who through faith and patience inherit the promises.

"And" (Greek *de*) presents a contrast and might be translated "but" (NASB). The contrast is between their past and present ministering and the assurance that both this and other matters will receive their attention in the future. "We desire" expresses a deep, emotional longing for their success in these areas by both the writer and those who were with him at the time. Verses 9 and 10 expressed confidence and encouragement to the Hebrew readers as a whole, but here he addresses the individuals, "We desire that every one of you." For the whole congregation to make progress, it must begin with individuals. As each one succeeds individually, the entire church will in like manner demonstrate success in the neglected areas.

This way of addressing them might also suggest that some had been more negligent than others with regard to their spiritual growth and their fading hope. His desire for each one of them as individuals was that "you do shew the same diligence." "You do shew" is expressed in continuous action (Greek present) and might be translated, "We desire. . . that you keep on showing." The good Christian qualities which they had demonstrated in the past and the present must continue in the future, and this demonstration needs to be broadened into other areas which were the cause of even more concern.

What the writer wants them to demonstrate is "the same diligence" or "the same zeal" which they had shown toward their work of love, particularly their past and present ministering to the saints which had been mentioned in v. 10. It is sometimes easier to earnestly devote ourselves to outward labor for an excellent cause than to analyze and evaluate the inner spiritual condition of our heads and hearts. These Hebrew Christians were long on ministering, which was good and a true sign of their genuine conversion, but they were showing some signs of waning with regard to matters of the heart: hope, faith, and perseverence.

Consequently, the writer pushes them "to the full assurance of hope."

Hebrews 10:22, using the same word (Greek *plerophoria*) speaks of the "full assurance of faith," and Col. 2:2 mentions the "full assurance of understanding." When something is fully assured, whether hope, faith, or understanding, it means that there is an overflowing abundance of that quality, that it is demonstrated so well in the individual's life that there is no doubt as to its genuine presence. The quality which the writer wishes to see abundantly manifested in their lives is hope. In Scripture hope is an even stronger quality than faith, because it includes faith and then goes beyond it. Hope fully believes that a promise of Scripture will come to pass; then it eagerly awaits and expects the fulfillment of that promise.

The duration of this full assurance of hope which the writer is longing for in the lives of his readers is "unto the end" (Greek *telos*). The end here is not so much the long range conclusion of the N.T. dispensation (Mt. 28:20), the consummation of the age, but rather the more immediate end or goal during which time this full assurance of hope is needed; that is, the end of the Christian's life on this earth (Lenski 194; Barnes 138), or particularly the end of the present trials and struggles which were testing their faith to the breaking point, however long they might last (Westcott 156).

In v. 12 the writer expresses the result to be realized, both positively and negatively, if the Hebrews do become as diligent in their assurance and hope as they had been in their ministering to the saints. First, negatively, "That ye be not slothful." He used this same word in 5:11 (Greek *nothros*) when he charged that they had already become "dull of hearing." Now he fears that this dullness, slothfulness, or sluggishness will spread to broader parts of their Christian lives and eventually swallow them up completely if it is not stopped by positive action.

Positively, in contrast to this slothfulness, the writer encourages them with an admonition to become "followers of them who through faith and patience inherit the promises." "Followers" (Greek *mimetes*) or imitators is used only here in Hebrews, but Paul uses it five times in his writings (1 Cor. 4:16; 11:1; Eph. 5:1; 1 Th. 1:6; 2:14). It suggests the idea of becoming thoroughly familiar with a person who has been a positive example and modeling oneself after that person in one's own life. It becomes obvious from the following verses that the examples he has in mind are faithful heroes from the O.T.

"Faith" (Greek *pistis*) refers to the confidence and trust that these heroes had in God and the promises He had made with regard to the future, and "patience" (Greek *makrothumia*) or longsuffering refers to the circumstances and struggles under which that faith was manifested. Two different words are translated "patience" in our English New Testament. The one used here refers to enduring what people have done to you, being slow in allowing your emotional temperature to rise under such circumstances, having a "long fuse." The other word (Greek *hupomone*) literally means "to stay under," and refers to bearing up under the ills that come upon us (see 2 Th. 1:4; Jas. 1:3; Rev. 13:10). David was an example of the former when he was pursued by Saul, while Job was an example of the latter when he suffered in the throes of devastation and disease (Lenski 195).

The beautiful result of such trust and perseverance is that these heroes of the past "inherit the promises." When you are an heir, you look with hope toward the promise of the inheritance, but when the inheritance becomes yours, that hope has been fulfilled. "The promises" refer to all the Messianic commitments of the Old Testament. Some of them were more temporal and some more eternal. Some bore immediate consequences, and others looked to the future; but they all, in some way, pointed to the ultimate fulfillment of all God's redemptive promises in the person of His Son, Jesus Christ. It seems obvious that this encouragement to look to the heroes of the faith is a suggestion of that which is developed more fully in chapter 11.

d. The patience of Abraham toward God's promises (6:13-18)

In vv. 11, 12 the writer has exhorted the need for perseverance "unto the end," and has promoted such perseverance by pointing to the examples of those who have been successful with regard to such promises in the O.T. Now he turns to a more specific example in the person of Abraham.

(1) God backs up His promise with an oath (6:13-15)

13 For when God made promise to Abraham, because he could swear by no greater, he sware by himself,
14 Saying, Surely blessing I will bless thee, and multiplying I will multiply thee.
15 And so, after he had patiently endured, he obtained the promise.

"For" connects the example given here with the encouragement to become followers or imitators of those who persevered in v. 12, the most appropriate example being Abraham: "When God made promise to Abraham." God's promises to Abraham were repeated several times, and the repetitions themselves must have been reassuring. God made the promise originally in connection with the call to Abraham to leave Ur of the Chaldees and go to Canaan. The promise involved a land, a nation, and a blessing to Abraham that would include "all families of the earth" (Gen. 12:1-3). The Lord renewed the promise after Abraham separated from Lot (Gen. 13:14-17), and again after he met with Melchisedec as he returned from his successful battle against the kings of the East (Gen. 15:4-6). The passage to which the writer refers here is the final renewal of the promise to Abraham after he offered Isaac on the altar (Gen. 22:15-18), no doubt the most momentous demonstration of the faith of Abraham.

The writer identifies this occasion when he says, "Because he could swear by no greater, he sware by himself." The ancient tradition of oath taking was appropriate and morally acceptable on proper occasions, especially when official transactions were being affirmed. What Jesus condemned in the Sermon on the Mount was the pernicious habit of the Pharisees in swearing about almost everything they said, to the point that the oaths became meaningless, and especially about their practice of placing their approval on falsehoods depending on the nature of the thing by which they swore (see Mt. 5:33-37). The Bible places its approval on legal oaths by the fact that God Himself used such an oath and that Jesus placed Himself under such an oath in His reply to the Jewish high priest (Mt. 26:63, 64). When someone affirms the truthfulness of a promise given in a legal oath, the common practice is for the person to place his hand on something greater than himself. In our society that thing upon which people swear has usually been the Bible as an emphatic symbol of God's approval of the statement or the promise.

When the writer says, "He sware by himself," the preposition "by" (Greek *kata*) literally means "down upon," giving a graphic picture of the hand being placed "down upon" the greater object upon which the oath is taken (Lenski 197). But a peculiar circumstance is created when God wishes to place Himself under an oath, as He did in this example from Gen. 22:16. Since nothing and no one is greater than God, God must swear by Himself. It would never do for Abraham, or any other human being, to demand an oath from God, but here God willingly placed Himself under a legal oath in order to make His promise even more secure.

In v. 14 the writer briefly quotes the promise from Gen. 22:17, "Saying, Surely blessing I will bless thee, and multiplying I will multiply thee." He only quotes the first part of the promise since his emphasis is on the oath which made the promise doubly secure, at least from a human point of view. "Surely" appropriately translates the intensity which is reproduced from the Hebrew (infinitive absolute in Hebrew) by doubling the main verb (with a participle in Greek): "Blessing I will bless thee." The continuous action of the participle adds to this intensity.

The same technique is repeated in the last phrase, "and multiplying I will multiply thee." Of course, the quotation comes from the Septuagint, the Greek version of the O.T., from which the writer of Hebrews typically quotes. In the preceding verse, Gen. 22:16, the Lord prefixed the promise with His oath when he said, "By myself have I sworn . . . because thou hast done this thing, and hast not withheld thy son, thine only *son*."

Having quoted the promise, the writer of Hebrews makes his point in v. 15: "And so, after he had patiently endured, he obtained the promise." "And so" indicates that the writer is making his conclusion. In v. 12 he urged the Hebrews to be followers or imitators "of them who through faith and patience inherit the promises." Now he has called attention to Abraham in his long wait for Isaac as a prime example. Some 25 years passed between Abraham's entrance into Canaan when he was 75 years old (Gen. 12:4) and the birth of Isaac (Gen. 21:5) when he was 100 years old. When the writer of Hebrews refers to the oath and the promise given in Gen. 22:16, 17, immediately after the offering of Isaac, more years had passed (we are not sure of Isaac's age at that time). Thus, the writer says, "After he had patiently endured."

The Holy Spirit is kind in offering this evaluation of Abraham, since, from a human point of view, Abraham appeared at times to grow a bit impatient. Since Sarah was already 65, well past the age of child bearing, when they arrived in Canaan, Abraham seems to have originally thought of Lot, his nephew, as a possible heir (Gen. 12:5). Then he promoted Eliezer, his trusted servant, as his heir (Gen. 15:2), then his son Ishmael by Hagar the Egyptian (Gen. 17:18, 19). But God is gracious and merciful in His evaluation of our lives. Perhaps this is primarily because He sees the perfect life of His Son, Jesus Christ, who died in our place. Though Abraham lived before Christ's birth, life, death, and resurrection, yet he was still saved by faith (see Gen. 15:6), a faith that was made effective only in the coming of Christ. This Scriptural tendency to overlook the weaknesses and the lapses of believers will be illustrated in more detail in chapter 11.

After all of this time, then, from his entrance into Canaan until the offering of Isaac, "He obtained the promise." There was a sense in which Abraham had already received the promise several years earlier at the birth of Isaac (Gen. 21:1-5). But the fact that the oath and the promise to which the writer of Hebrews refers came in connection with the offering of Isaac shows the importance of that event. Though God certainly knew what Abraham would do, it was the actual fulfillment of this complete act of submission on the part of Abraham that established him forever as "the father of the faithful." At this point, then, the Lord now reaffirmed, with both an oath and a promise, the future fulfillment of other parts of the Abrahamic Covenant (see Gen. 22:15-18), including the multiplying of Abraham's seed as well as the fact that his seed would, in the coming of Christ, bless "all the nations of the earth."

There is no contradiction when the writer later cites Abraham as "not having received the promises" (see Heb. 11:13 and 11:39, 40). Many of the Messianic promises of the O.T. had immediate as well as ultimate fulfillments. The immediate fulfillment to Abraham was in the birth of Isaac, the necessary link to the ultimate fulfillment in Jesus Christ. But Abraham, and the other patriarchs, did not see that most blessed completion of the promise in the birth of Jesus Christ our Savior. In that sense they did not obtain the promise (Bruce 129, 130).

Some other commentators, however, maintain that the promise which Abraham obtained after much endurance was the promise of Heaven and of eternal life which he received at his death (Delitzsch I:309; Lenski 199). Abraham truly did look for the fulfillment of God's promises beyond this earth in the presence of the Lord (Heb. 11:10, 14-16), and those promises indeed were fulfilled as was affirmed by Jesus Christ Himself (Mt. 8:11; 22:32; Jn. 8:56). But in this context the writer of Hebrews seems to be referring to the temporal promises which Abraham saw fulfilled after much endurance as an example for the Hebrews to follow with regard to their endurance of persecutions in their Christian lives.

(2) The reason for God's oath to Abraham (6:16-18)

16 For men verily swear by the greater: and an oath for confirmation *is* to them an end of all strife.
17 Wherein God, willing more abundantly to shew unto the heirs of promise the immutability of his counsel, confirmed *it* by an oath:
18 That by two immutable things, in which *it was* impossible for God to lie, we might have a strong consolation, who have fled for refuge to lay hold upon the hope set before us.

The writer offers a fuller explanation as to why God saw fit to bring Himself down on the level of man and willingly place Himself under an oath. Such is the common practice of men, then and now. An important part of a witness giving his testimony in court even in modern times is the swearing in by a court official. When men are placed under such legal oaths, they are expected to tell the truth, and if they lie even after being placed under oath, they make themselves subject to prosecution and punishment. The reason for such a practice in the courts of men is understandable because of the fallible character of men.

In making such oaths, the writer explains, "men verily swear by the greater." In Christian society the hand is traditionally placed on the Bible, symbolically signifying that the witness is pledging to tell the truth under the all-seeing eyes of the Lord and, at the same time, placing himself under God's judgment if he does not tell the truth. The Bible, representing the person of God Himself, is the thing greater or the one greater in the courts of men.

The result of such "an oath for confirmation is to them an end of all strife." When a witness is sworn in, it is accepted, without contradictory evidence, that he is telling the truth; the oath gives "confirmation" (Greek *bebaiosis*) or assurance of his truthfulness. "Strife" (Greek *antilogia*) means "contradiction, dispute, or argument." There might have been some debate prior to the oath as to the truthfulness of the witness, but swearing him in makes it more likely that truth will come from his mouth. The oath is meant to settle that argument.

"Wherein" at the beginning of v. 17 means "because of" (Yeager 220) or "in connection with" (Lenski 201): that is, because of or in connection with this traditional practice of taking an oath to assure truthfulness, God did what He did with Abraham. None of us would dare make such a request of God, that He should confirm His promise by an oath; such a demand would be most inappropriate from fallen man. But that is what makes what God did even more assuring: He voluntarily placed Himself under an oath.

He did so because He was "willing more abundantly to shew unto the heirs of promise the immutability of his counsel." It is probably best to take the adverb "more abundantly" (Greek *perissoteros*) with "to shew" rather than with "willing." God was willing to show or demonstrate more abundantly, more clearly, the certainty of His promise (see NIV). The objects of the oath and the affirmation were "the heirs of promise," not just Abraham, but all those who are the spiritual seed of Abraham, both Jews and Gentiles (see Rom. 4:10-13). Thus, it certainly included these Hebrew Christians who were Abraham's seed both physically and spiritually.

What God wanted to show or demonstrate more clearly was "the immutability of his counsel." How wonderful it is that we serve a God who sticks with His eternal plan, not a God who capriciously alters His purposes with the appearance of every bump in life's road! Because of the disobedience of man, and the Lord's determination to allow human free will, God's plans may sometimes appear to be delayed or even detoured, but we recognize that even these delays and detours were part of God's eternal purpose. God's "counsel" (Greek *boule*) is His purpose to multiply Abraham's seed and make him a blessing to all the world (Gen. 22:17, 18), the ultimate Messianic promise which found its ultimate fulfillment in God's Son, Jesus Christ, the Savior of the world.

As the means of making the certainty of His promise even more clear, God "confirmed *it* by an oath." The word translated "confirmed" (Greek *mesiteuo*) means "to mediate or intercede between two parties." The noun form means "a mediator," used of Jesus Christ in 1 Tim. 2:5. In this context the oath itself serves as the mediator between God, who made the promise, and the heirs of that promise.

The writer continues to explain the added assurance provided when almighty God, because of His love for us, did this unique thing: "That by two immutable things, in which *it was* impossible for God to lie, we might have a strong consolation, who have fled for refuge to lay hold upon the hope set before us." The "two immutable things" to which the writer refers are God's promise and His confirming oath to Abraham. If God in His very nature is immutable (Mal. 3:6), then all that He is and all that He says is also immutable.

Since "it was impossible for God to lie," His promise would have been sufficient without the addition of an oath. But these promises are doubly important because they affect not only Abraham and the nation that came from him, they affect the entire world for both time and eternity. For that reason God willingly placed Himself under oath in order to emphatically affirm the certainty of the Messianic promises.

The reason He offered these two immutable things, His promise and His oath, was so that "we might have a strong consolation." "We" would include the writer, the Hebrew recipients, and all "the heirs of promise" (v. 17) who need assurance about salvation and eternal life. "Strong" (Greek *ischuros*) refers to absolute strength, the kind that can only come from God. The word "consolation" (Greek *paraklesis*) is best taken in its more positive and aggressive meaning of "encouragement" in this context (Westcott 161). God has graciously given us these two immutable things, His promise and His oath, so that we might have strong encouragement to continue to pursue the course of salvation to its final goal.

This strong encouragement is given to those "who have fled for refuge to lay hold upon the hope set before us." The idea of those "who have fled for refuge" comes from the instructions about the cities of refuge under the Mosaic Law (Num. 35:9-34). In the O.T. picture, those who were guilty of serious crimes, subject to the pursuit of the avenger, could come to these appointed cities and cast themselves upon the mercy of the court and thus find some measure of safety and relief.

Such is our case: we are fully guilty of all the accusations of sin in our lives. We have fled for refuge "to lay hold upon the hope." Both the fleeing and the laying hold are expressed as completed actions (Greek aorist tense). The fleeing was an act of desperation; all other supports have been abandoned. The laying hold of was with a firm and determined grasp, one that will not let go. The object to which we have fled and grasped hold upon is "the hope set before us." Hope is faith magnified. With hope we believe the promise, but beyond that, we eagerly and patiently await its fulfillment (see Rom. 8:24, 25). Hope keeps us going when suffering and discouragement make us want to give up. As is always the case with hope, it is "set before us" (Greek *prokeimai*). In Philo and Josephus the word pictures the goal of a race or a contest, or the prizes contended for in the contest (Delitzsch I:318). It is that mark toward which we run, that prize of the high calling which we pursue (Phil. 3:14) with full determination that we will not quit until the goal, our heavenly reward, has been reached.

e. Jesus as our priestly forerunner (6:19, 20)

19 Which *hope* we have as an anchor of the soul, both sure and stedfast, and which entereth into that within the veil;
20 Whither the forerunner is for us entered, *even* Jesus, made an high priest for ever after the order of Melchisedec.

This "hope" which has been set before us as a prize at the end of a race successfully run is now presented as even more secure. It is this hope that "we have as an anchor of the soul." "Anchor" (in the singular) is used only here in the entire Bible. But the anchor as a symbol of hope often appeared on Christian rings in the early church and frequently appeared in the company of the drawing of or the spelling of "fish," a well known early Christian symbol (Westcott 162). As an anchor holds a ship steady, especially in a time of storm, so hope centered in the person and work of Christ holds the "soul," the inner spiritual life of the believer, steady in the storms of life.

The hope which serves as the anchor of our souls is "both sure and stedfast." The two adjectives are similar in meaning, but the doubling up is intentional to add emphasis to the writer's description of the stability of our hope in Christ as our firm anchor. Some commentators want to make the adjectives ("sure and steadfast") go with "anchor" (Barnes 142; Alford 123; Lenski 204; Lunemann 255), but it is probably better to take them with "hope" as the main subject of the thought (NASB; Hewitt 115; Westcott 162; Bruce 131). Ultimately it makes little difference since our hope in Christ is, indeed, our anchor, and under this imagery any description applied to our hope must, of necessity, also apply to our anchor.

Furthermore, this hope as our anchor "entereth into that within the veil." "Entereth" is expressed in continuous action (Greek present participle): hope, as our soul's anchor, continues to enter the veil in connection with the ongoing intercessory ministry of Jesus Christ (see Heb. 1:3) as long as we continue to live for Christ on this earth. The "veil" (Greek *katapetasma*) refers to the inner veil of the O.T. tabernacle which separated the Holy Place from the Holy of Holies (see Ex. 26:31-34). Within that veil, inside the Holy of Holies, was the Ark of the Covenant, with the two tables of the law; as a covering on top of the Ark was the solid gold Mercy Seat. In O.T. times God's presence appeared above this mercy seat, between the cherubim (Ex. 25:17-22).

Though the writer of Hebrews uses the imagery of the Holy of Holies here, an imagery with which these Hebrew Christians were thoroughly familiar, he is actually referring to Heaven itself, of which the O.T. inner sanctuary was only a type (see Heb. 8:1, 2). This inner veil in the Herodian Temple of Jesus' day, the equivalent of the veil in the ancient tabernacle, was torn in two at the crucifixion of Christ (Mt. 27:50, 51), thus signifying the opening of the true residence of God to all men on the basis of the shed blood of Christ. We note with interest that anchors normally extend downward into the depths of the sea to hold a ship steady, but this anchor, which is our eternal hope in Jesus Christ, extends upward into Heaven with the design of eventually pulling us up into His Presence.

Within this veil, according to v. 20, "the forerunner is for us entered, *even* Jesus." As our Lord goes into this heavenly sanctuary, not the earthly one, He goes as our "forerunner" (Greek *prodromos*). The word is not used elsewhere in the N.T., but John the Baptist certainly fulfilled that role when he came to prepare the way for the coming Messiah, as Isaiah had prophesied (Mt. 3:3). Greek literature often used the word of those who were sent before an invading army to gather information for the benefit of that army, just as Moses sent the twelve spies into Canaan (Num. 13:1-16) and as Joshua later sent two spies into Jericho (Jos. 2:1). The word is used in the Septuagint in Is. 28:4 for the firstfruits of the fig tree. Thus, Jesus Christ has gone before us to prepare the way for us to follow Him into that eternal Promised Land and to be the firstfruits of a subsequent abundant harvest (1 Cor. 15:20, 23; Clarke 835).

As our forerunner He has entered the heavenly sanctuary "for (Greek *huper*) us," that is, in our behalf, or for our benefit. This phrase is used in a similar way in Heb. 2:9 and 9:24. The writer gives special emphasis to the name "Jesus," the human name given to the eternal Son of God when He "was made flesh, and dwelt among us" (Jn. 1:14). It was the name given to Him by Joseph and Mary at the command of the angel of the Lord. The name means "Jehovah will save," because "he shall save his people from their sins" (Mt. 1:21). Thus, the writer stresses this human name to emphasize the work which our Lord, as our High Priest, had completed prior to His entrance into the heavenly sanctuary.

When he says that Jesus was "made an high priest," he does not mean to imply that He only became a high priest upon His entrance into Heaven (Lenski 206). His entire ministry had been a priestly ministry, but especially His death, resurrection, and ascension to His present position "on the right hand of the Majesty on high" (1:3). His priestly ministry is "forever," as the writer has stated already in 5:6 on the basis of the quotation from Psalm 110:4. But it is not the O.T. priesthood after the order of Aaron; it is rather a new priesthood "after the order of Melchisedec." As our eternal high priest, Jesus made atonement (1:3; 9:11-14; 10:12); He makes intercession (2:17, 18; 4:14-16; 7:25), and He is making preparation for us to be with Him forever (Jn. 14:2; Heb. 9:28).

Under the law of Moses the high priest entered the Holy of Holies on the Day of Atonement with the blood of an animal sacrifice, and then he came back out to the waiting people. Jesus Christ entered the heavenly sanctuary on the basis of His own blood, and one day we will join Him in that home He has prepared for us (Jn. 14:3). With this reference to "the order of Melchisedec," our author has brought us back to the subject which he left in 5:10, and in the next chapter he will explain that priestly order of Christ in detail.

Summary (6:1-20)

In 5:11-14 the writer warned his Hebrew readers about their lack of spiritual growth in light of the length of time they had been Christians. He suggested that they had become so anemic in their Christian profession that they needed to study again the first principles of the Gospel message. They had come to need a milk diet composed of these simpler things rather than a strong meat diet of the deeper truths of God's Word—including the teaching he wanted to give them about Christ as a high priest according to the order of Melchisedec. On the basis on this warning issued in chapter 5, the writer, in the first part of chapter 6, emphasizes the possibility of renouncing true faith in Christ because of this lack of spiritual progress. He names six of the essential doctrines of Christianity which make up the principles or the rudiments of the beginning of the Christian faith. These essential doctrines are like the foundation of a house. They must, indeed, be there if the house is to stand, but just as importantly the rest of the house must be built upon this necessary foundation.

Having enumerated these first principles, the writer expresses his determination to lead them in continuing to build upon these rudiments in order to regain their previous level of spiritual maturity (6:1-3). If the writer is not successful in stirring up such needed spiritual growth, dire consequences can be expected.

To stress the depth and genuineness of the spiritual experience of his Hebrew audience, he gives a five-fold description of what had happened to them in their relationship with the Lord. They had come to the light of the Gospel, received the gift of salvation and the blessings of the Holy Spirit, and had personally experienced God's Word and miracles in their lives. When people have had such life-changing experience, and then willfully turn away from that relationship with the Lord, they commit a sin resulting in the withdrawal of the Holy Spirit. The resulting inability to repent identifies them with the Jewish leaders who rejected Christ and had Him nailed to the cross (6:4-6).

Turning aside from knowing Christ in this way to follow their own inclinations, they are like a piece of land, once fruitful in response to the blessings of Heaven, that has completely stopped producing good fruit and now grows nothing but thorns and briers. Such land is on the verge of being rejected and burned, and such Christians are on the verge of total and final apostasy (6:7, 8).

In spite of such a severe warning about apostasy, the writer expresses faith in his Hebrew audience that they will awaken from their slothfulness and demonstrate "better things" with regard to their spiritual maturity. Both their past and present ministry to fellow believers calls for such faith on the part of the writer. They are encouraged, therefore, to follow heroes of the faith from Biblical history who have inherited the promises through perseverance in the face of severe difficulties (6:9-12).

Such an example to follow was Abraham, the father of the Hebrew people. They ought to find being faithful somewhat easier when they realize the two-fold commitment which God made to Abraham after he demonstrated his willingness to offer his only son, Isaac, in absolute submission to the will of God. God not only promised Abraham that He would completely fulfill His covenant made with him earlier, but He went even further: He brought Himself down on man's level by placing Himself under an oath in His own name. God's promise alone would surely have been enough, but He was willing to swear by Himself, since no one is greater than God, in order to assure men, including these Hebrews, of His absolute faithfulness to His promise (6:13-18). With the assurance of both God's promise and His oath to Abraham, the writer points his readers to the firm hope which he, they, and we can have by looking to Jesus, our new Priest after the order of Melchisedec, who has entered the heavenly tabernacle so that we soon may follow (6:19, 20).

Application: Teaching and Preaching the Passage

A message might be developed from 6:1 on the basis of the word "leaving." (1) Some things in life need to be left in the sense of abandoning them, forsaking them, departing from them, even as Paul "put away childish things" when he became a man (1 Cor. 13:11). (2) Some things need to be left in the sense of building upon them, even as a builder does with the foundation of a house, and such is the meaning in this passage.

A lesson could be built from 6:1 on the Biblical use of "perfection": (1) perfection in relation to our conduct toward others—Mt. 5:43-48; (2) perfection in relation to spiritual maturity—Heb. 5:11—6:1; (3) perfection with regard to its completion—1 Jn. 3:2.

A lesson could be taught on the basis of the six principles of the doctrine of Christ listed in 6:1, 2. They can be dealt with in pairs: (1) the beginning of the Christian life—repentance and faith; (2) the official initiation of the Christian life—baptism and laying on of hands; (3) the conclusion of the Christian life—resurrection and eternal judgment.

A message might be developed around the theme: "If God permit," from 6:3: (1) God's permission with regard to prayer—Mt. 26:36-46; (2) God's permission with regard to our practice—Heb. 6:3; (3) God's permission with regard to our plans—Jas. 4:13-17.

A lesson can be taught on the four spiritual experiences which describe salvation from 6:4, 5. Salvation is: (1) a process of enlightenment; (2) receiving it as a gift from Heaven; (3) partaking of the Holy Spirit; (4) experiencing God's good Word or utterance and the life changing powers of the coming age. (If a person can have all of these spiritual experiences without truly knowing the Lord, as the disciples said in Mt. 19:25, "Who then can be saved?")

This would be a good place to develop a message about the sin against the Holy Spirit on the basis of 6:4-6: (1) What is the sin against the Holy Spirit? (2) Can it be committed today? (3) Who can commit this sin? (4) What are the consequences of committing the sin against the Holy Spirit?

From 6:7, 8 one can build a message on the blessings of God: (1) they come often; (2) they produce fruit when rightly received; (3) they benefit many people; (4) all true blessings are from God; (5) it is a serious matter to reject or misuse God's blessings.

A message could be drawn from 6:9-12 on the basis of the writer's encouragement of the Hebrews in the face of the severe warning he had given them: (1) the writer's personal faith in them—v. 9; (2) God's remembrance of their work, past and present—v. 10; (3) the successful models for them to follow—vv. 11, 12.

A message on assurance can be developed from God's twofold commitment to Abraham: (1) the context of His commitment—the offering of Isaac; (2) the content of His promise—the nation of Israel and the Messiah; (3) the certainty of His oath—its nature described.

On the basis of the writer's statement in 6:15, "After he had patiently endured," a historical outline can be developed bringing out the statement's irony on Abraham's part as well as sovereignty on God's part: (1) the stop in Haran after the original call in Ur—Gen. 11:31—12:5; (2) his hopes for Lot—Gen. 13:5-13; (3) his suggestion about Eliezer of Damascus—Gen. 15:1-4; (4) he presents his son, Ishmael, to God—Gen. 17:18-20; (5) he finally laughs in faith after the birth and offering of Isaac—Gen. 21, 22.

Finally, a message can be built on the theme of hope from 6:18-20: (1) Hope in Christ is a refuge, a shelter from the storms of life. (2) Hope always looks forward to fulfillment; it is set before us. (3) Hope in Christ is our spiritual anchor, our security in changing times. (4) Hope reaches beyond earth into Heaven where Jesus has gone as our Forerunner. (5) Hope finds its ultimate fulfillment in the person of Jesus Christ as our High Priest.

C. Reasons for the Priesthood after Melchisedec Replacing the Levitical Order (7:1-28)

In 5:11 through 6:20 the writer has given his third warning, a warning against failure to make progress through Christ as High Priest. In concluding that warning he emphasized God's two-fold commitment to Abraham after he offered Isaac when He backed up His sure promise with an oath in reaffirming the Abrahamic Covenant. Now in chapter 7 he continues with another aspect of the story of Abraham in building his case for the superior intercession of Jesus Christ. He does this in 7:1-10 by showing the superiority of Melchisedec to Abraham, and then in 7:11-28 by showing the superiority of the priestly order of Melchisedec to the priestly order of Aaron.

1. Superiority of Melchisedec to Abraham (7:1-10)

Abraham was, without a doubt, the single greatest hero to the Jewish people. He was the father of the nation of Israel, for from him descended the other great patriarchs, Isaac, Jacob, and Joseph, and it was from Jacob that the twelve tribes of Israel came through his sons. If some other individual is actually greater than Abraham, then that person needs to be identified. Indeed, in 7:1-10 the writer does identify such a person, the mysterious Melchisedec, and explains his superiority.

a. Melchisedec identified as a type of Christ (7:1-3)

1 For this Melchisedec, king of Salem, priest of the most high

God, who met Abraham returning from the slaughter of the kings, and blessed him;
2 To whom also Abraham gave a tenth part of all; first being by interpretation King of righteousness, and after that also King of Salem, which is, King of peace;
3 Without father, without mother, without descent, having neither beginning of days, nor end of life; but made like unto the Son of God; abideth a priest continually.

Melchisedec, who is very important to our writer's argument, is mentioned in only two places in the O.T. The historical reference, reflected here, is found in Gen. 14:18-20. The only other reference to Melchisedec, outside of this discussion in Hebrews, is in Psalm 110:4 when David prophesies concerning his Messianic Son, "Thou art a priest for ever after the order of Melshizedek." This verse has already been quoted in Heb. 5:6 as one of the two scriptural evidences of Christ's call as a High Priest. Now the writer goes back to the historical reference in Gen. 14:18-20 to further explain Melchisedec's identity.

Three different views have been proposed concerning Melchisedec's identity: (1) Some ancient Jewish writers have suggested that he should be identified with Shem, the son of Noah, but this is little more than pure speculation; furthermore, it seems certain that Abraham lived too many years after the flood for Shem to still be living, even if he did live to be 600 years of age (Gen. 11:10, 11). (2) A second view would have Melchisedec to be a Christophany, an appearance of Jesus Christ in preincarnate form (several in the orthodox church, according to Lunemann 262). There certainly are Christophanies in the O.T. (Gen. 18:1-33; Ex. 3:1, 2), but this does not appear to be one of them. The historical description of Melchisedec in Gen. 14:18-20 does not appear to be a Christophany at all. This view is especially based on Hebrews 7:3, which will be dealt with below. (3) The third view is that Melchisedec, though a real, historical figure, is seen by the writer of Hebrews, as well as by David in Ps. 110, as a type of Christ, especially a type of His continuing priesthood in contrast to the temporary priesthood of the line of Aaron (most recent interpreters).

In Hebrews 7:1-3 the writer proposes Melchisedec as a type of Christ (1) in relation to his name, (2) in relation to his political position (King of Salem), (3) in relation to his religious position (Priest of the Most High God), and (4) in relation to his genealogy.

"For this Melchisedec" in 7:1 continues the thought of 6:20: the Melchisedec after whose priestly order Jesus has entered the heavenly Holy of Holies as our forerunner. Though his readers were Jews and thus very familiar with the workings of the Levitical priesthood, even they might not be as familiar with the priestly order of Melchisedec. The writer, therefore, reviews the historical identity of Melchisedec.

Melchisedec held a political/governmental position as "king of Salem." Salem from ancient times has been identified with Jerusalem. The name is derived from the Hebrew word "Shalom," which means "peace." The word was used in Israel in both ancient and modern times as a greeting, much like our "Hello." Melchisedec also held a religious position. He was "priest of the most high God." As a priest he would serve as a mediator between God and men, just as the Levitical priests did. He would lead in the worship of "the most high God," and offer sacrifices to Him. Though no word is given about his appointment to this office, it evidently came directly from "the most high God" (Hebrew *El Elyon*). This name for Jehovah is used by Balaam in Num. 24:16 and by Moses in his farewell song in Dt. 32:8. This mysterious person who serves as such a dynamic type of Christ is both a king and a priest, just as our Lord.

Melchisedec "met Abraham returning from the slaughter of the kings." Thus, the writer identifies Melchisedec in the historical context of Gen. 14:18-20. When Abraham received word that four kings from the East, led by Chedorlaomer, king of Elam, had taken his nephew Lot and others from the cities of the plain, he pursued them with his neighbors and his own 318 trained men. When Abraham returned from his amazing victory over these fierce kings Melchisedec met him with "bread and wine" (Gen. 14:18). The writer makes no attempt to connect this supply of bread and wine with the Lord's Supper. His focus is more narrow (Bruce 135). What he does emphasize are the two things which indicate Melchisedec's superiority to Abraham, and these are the things which Moses emphasized as well in the original account in Genesis.

First, when Melchisedec met Abraham, he "blessed him," and the one who blesses is always understood as being superior to the one receiving the blessing. In response to that blessing, Abraham gave a tenth part of all, that is, all the spoils of battle, the second thing which demonstrated Melchisedec's superiority to Abraham. At this point the writer indicates the fact that he sees Melchisedec as a type of Christ, a picture-prophecy of Christ's eternal priesthood. To make the type clear he interprets or translates the meaning of the great king's name. He says, "first being by interpretation King of righteousness." The meaning of the Hebrew name *Melchisedec* is "King of righteousness"; in his very name this ancient and mysterious king pointed toward the coming of Christ who was made "*to be* sin for us, who knew no sin; that we might be made the righteousness of God in him" (2 Cor. 5:21).

The type continues in the meaning of Melchisedec's political or governmental position: "and after that also King of Salem, which is, King of peace." This is again a matter of translation from the Hebrew, since the word "Salem," derived from the word "shalom," means "peace." The order is significant. Righteousness is the foundation of our faith in Christ, not ours but His. In the next chapter of Genesis, Scripture declares about Abraham, "He believed in the LORD; and he counted it to him for righteousness" (Gen. 15:6).

As a result of Christ's righteousness in our lives, we have peace, for as this verse says He is *first* King of righteousness and *then* King of peace. What Melchisedec was, in a relative sense as a type of Christ, Jesus was in the most perfect sense as the divine antitype (Bruce 135; Westcott 172). This same order is seen in Paul's declaration that the kingdom of God is "righteousness, and peace, and joy in the Holy Ghost" (Rom. 14:17) as well as in this writer's declaration that God's discipline "yieldeth the peaceable fruit of righteousness" (12:11; see also Eph. 4:13).

Our author continues to explain Melchisedec as a type of Christ in v. 3. With regard to his genealogy, he declares that Melchisedec was "without father, without mother, without descent, having neither beginning of days, nor end of life." This is a classic example of an argument from silence. The writer of Hebrews is building his case on the fact that there is no ancestry for Melchisedec recorded in Gen. 14:18-20 or elsewhere. There is also no record of his birth and no record of his death. As far as the Bible is concerned, every time we look at it, Melchisedec is simply "there," serving as the priest-king, just as he was in Abraham's day.

If we are right about the true identity of Melchisedec, he was a normal person who did indeed have a father and mother, a line of ancestry, and a day of birth and death. But the point that our author is making is that, in connection with his priesthood, there is absolutely no record of such information.

The validity of this point becomes clear when we realize the importance of such a genealogy to the Levitical priests after the order of Aaron. The priests of Israel were to come exclusively from Aaron and his family (Ex. 28:41; 29:44). When this appointment was challenged by Korah and his cohorts in Num. 16:1-3, the Lord ordered a sign of confirmation, Aaron's rod that miraculously budded, to be placed in the Ark of the Covenant as a continuing reminder to Israel. Many years later in the return from Babylon, those who claimed they were priests could not serve because they could not prove their genealogy (Ezra 2:61, 62).

Jesus Christ was a Priest from an entirely different order. His priesthood, therefore, did not depend on such a genealogy. With regard to the time of service, the Levitical priesthood was again quite limited. They officially entered the priestly service at 25 years of age (Num. 8:24), though they did not perform regular services as priests in the tabernacle until 30 years of age (Num. 4:3), and that priestly service promptly came to an end when they were 50 years of age (Num. 8:25). The Levitical priesthood, therefore, was limited not only by the death of the priests, but even more by the rules which governed its operation. This priesthood was specifically designed for temporal and earthly purposes, but Christ's priesthood, after the order of Melchisedec, had no such limitations.

The nature of the final statement of Heb. 7:3 is most significant in identifying the purpose of Melchisedec. In confirming Melchisedec's absence of any genealogy, of any date of birth or date of death, the writer declares, "But made like unto the Son of God; abideth a priest continually." He does not say that he *was* the Son of God, but rather that he was "made like unto the Son of God." Melchisedec was the original model of which Jesus Christ is the perfect fulfillment. He was a type of Christ, specifically in relation to his ongoing priesthood, a priesthood neither inherited from someone before him nor passed on to some successor. He stands in contrast to the Levitical priests who served only for a relatively short period and then passed off the scene.

b. Superiority of Melchisedec explained (7:4-10)

In the first three verses of chapter 7, the writer dealt with the historical information about the encounter of

Melchisedec and Abraham in Gen. 14:18-20. On the basis of that passage he pointed out how Melchisedec was a type of Christ. Now in 7:4-10 he continues to look at this meeting of the priest-king and the father of the Jews with a view to explaining the superiority of Melchisedec to Abraham. He emphasizes four ways in which Melchisedec stands out as superior.

(1) In receiving tithes from Abraham (7:4-6a)

4 Now consider how great this man *was*, unto whom even the patriarch Abraham gave the tenth of the spoils.
5 And verily they that are of the sons of Levi, who receive the office of the priesthood, have a commandment to take tithes of the people according to the law, that is, of their brethren, though they come out of the loins of Abraham:
6a But he whose descent is not counted from them received tithes of Abraham.

"Now" (Greek *de*) introduces a different approach to the subject of Melchisedec and Abraham. "Consider" (Greek *theoreo*) is expressed in continuous action (Greek present tense), implying ongoing contemplation. The writer asks his audience to give this important subject of the new order of Christ's priesthood, as seen in the type prefigured in Melchisedec, very careful attention. Some of them are apparently considering returning to dependence on the Levitical priesthood instead of the priesthood of Christ. They need to see the picture more clearly before making such a devastating decision. They need to see "how great this man *was*."

From the historical text of Genesis, the writer reviews the things that demonstrate Melchisedec's greatness, "unto whom even the patriarch Abraham gave the tenth of the spoils." The presence of "even" here heightens the contrast between Abraham and Melchisedec. As great as Abraham was, he still acknowledged by his action the priest-king's superiority. In the original the title "patriarch" is placed at the end of the sentence, thus adding a further contrast by stressing the personal importance of Abraham. The word "patriarch" depicts a chief or beginning father, the one who is the head of a line. Abraham is referred to as such because he is the father of the nation of Israel, God's chosen people in the O.T.

The fact that Abraham "gave the tenth," the tithe, was completely voluntary, which makes the recognition of Melchisedec's superiority even more significant. There is no evidence that Abraham was responding to any commandment, either written or oral. The word used for "the spoils" (Greek *akrothinion*) indicates the firstfruits. Though the tenth came from the entire booty which Abraham and his confederates had recovered, Abraham saw that the tithe consisted only of the very best, the uppermost of the heap (Lunemann 265). It is significant that this is the first time tithing is mentioned in Scripture. There is no indication where Abraham got the idea. As God's foremost servant at the time, and the father of God's chosen people, it seems safe to assume that he was directly led by the Lord to take this action. Two principles stand out about tithing in this first reference: (1) Abraham "gave a tenth part of all";

thus, the tithe should be based on all of our profits in labor or in business. (2) The tithe which we give to God should represent our very best, not that which is left over or not used for other purposes.

The writer presents a contrast in vv. 5, 6 (Greek *men/de*) between the priests of Israel on the one hand, who were descendants of Abraham through Levi, and Melchisedec, on the other hand, who was not from the line of Abraham at all. The writer of Hebrews feels the need to deal with a problem that he perceives may occur to his Jewish readers: if receiving a tithe and giving a blessing signifies superiority on the part of Melchisedec as related to Abraham, what does that same thing, especially the well-known practice of tithing in Israel, say about the Levitical priests in relation to the rest of Israel? Are the Levitical priests, indeed, superior to the other Israelites?

In v. 5 the contrast begins: "And verily they that are of the sons of Levi, who receive the office of the priesthood, have a commandment to take tithes of the people according to the law." "Verily" (Greek *men/de*) emphasizes the first part of the contrast. Not all Levites were priests, rather only those from the family of Aaron (Ex. 28:1; Num. 18:1-7). But all the Levites did serve in the tabernacle in some manner, and thus they received tithes from their brothers as their means of support. The tribe of Levi did not receive an inheritance of a specific section of the Promised Land, as did the other twelve tribes. In lieu of the inheritance, God gave them 48 cities scattered throughout the other tribes (Num. 35:6, 7; Jos. 21:1-41) to enhance their service to Israel. In addition to that, He commanded all the rest of Israel to tithe to the Levites in general, and the Levites to tithe to the priests, the family of Aaron, for their support (Num. 18:21-32).

"Receive" is expressed as continuous action in the original (Greek present participle), thus indicating that the priestly service was still going on when Hebrews was written. The word here translated "office of the priesthood" (Greek *hierateia*) emphasizes the actual service of the priests more than the office itself (Westcott 176), for it was for their service to the people of Israel that the tribe of Levi received tithes (Num. 18:21). Thus, it was on the basis of the "commandment to take tithes" that the tribe of Levi received tithes, not on the basis of any personal superiority on their part, for those from whom they received tithes were "their brethren." This irony the writer emphasizes: "though they come out of the loins of Abraham." Both the tribe of Levi and the rest of Israel equally traced their background to Abraham; therefore, the fact that all the tribe of Levi received tithes did not indicate any personal superiority on their part.

Such was not the case, however, with Melchisedec. In v. 6 our writer emphasizes the second part of the contrast: "But he whose descent is not counted from them received tithes of Abraham." The fact that Melchisedec received tithes from Abraham was not based on any existing law or commandment. There is absolutely no kinship between Melchisedec and Abraham, and thus there is also no relationship to the priests of the house of Aaron or the tribe of Levi, who were descendants of Abraham. The fact that Abraham tithed to Melchisedec voluntarily, completely free from any commandment, enhances the writer's argument of the superiority of the priestly order of Melchisedec. "He received tithes" (Greek *dedekatoken*) indicates the permanent significance of the act (Greek perfect tense); its importance still stands.

(2) In blessing Abraham (7:6b, 7)

6b And blessed him that had the promises.
7 And without all contradiction the less is blessed of the better.

In the last part of v. 6 the writer emphasizes the second primary reason for the superiority of Melchisedec to Abraham, the fact that Melchisedec "blessed him." This action, like the receiving of tithes, also stresses its continuing and permanent significance (Greek perfect tense). The writer heightens Melchisedec's superior position when he stresses that he blessed "him that had the promises." To the Hebrew mind Abraham, the father of the nation of Israel, would occupy the highest position among men. Yet Abraham's position in relation to Melchisedec is clearly revealed in the inspired account of Gen. 14:18-20.

Consequently, v. 7 adds: "And without all contradiction the less is blessed of the better." The word translated "contradiction" (Greek *antilogia*) means "debate, argument to the contrary." The writer is stating a universal principle, an obvious truth recognized by all reasonable men at all times. As great as Abraham was, he was not the priest-king who by his life and actions pointed directly toward the future priestly order fulfilled finally and completely in Jesus Christ (Lenski 217). It is true that Jas. 3:9 refers to the use of our tongues to "bless God," obviously without any suggestion of our superiority to God. But James is using "bless" with a different connotation, actually amounting to something like "praising God." The blessing bestowed by Melchisedec, on the other hand, indicated a granting of favor, a bold but undeniable claim that he represented God, that he stood in His place; and Abraham acknowledged the truth of this claim by receiving the blessing and paying the tithes.

(3) In a living priesthood as opposed to a dying priesthood (7:8)

8 And here men that die receive tithes; but there he *receiveth them*, of whom it is witnessed that he liveth.

Though the two primary arguments for Melchisedec's superiority to Abraham are seen in his receiving a tithe and giving a blessing, a third aspect contrasts a dying priesthood with a living one. Once again the contrasting balance in the two parts of the statement are suggested in the original (Greek *men/de*). This balance can be indicated in English by translating, "On the one hand . . . but on the other hand." On the one hand we have the presence of dying men in the Levitical priesthood, but on the other hand we have the living priesthood of Christ after the order of Melchisedec. "Here" indicates the familiarity and proximity of the Levitical priesthood to the Hebrew readers, but it also seems to suggest that this priesthood was still being experienced at the time.

"Men that die" is literally "dying men." In this manner the frailty of the

Levitical priesthood is described. No sooner has the bright light of their service appeared at the age of 30 than it begins to fade, and almost in the twinkle of an eye, at the age of 50, another priest has passed from the scene. Many of them were good men who conscientiously performed their duties, but all too quickly their ministry came to an end. "But there" introduces the contrast. In contrast to the Levitical priesthood, which was "here" and now, which the readers personally witnessed on a regular basis, that continuing priesthood of Melchisedec was "there," referring perhaps to both the historical record of Abraham's encounter with Melchisedec (Gen. 14:18-20) and to David's later reference to the continuing priesthood according to the order of Melchisedec (Ps. 110:4). In the example more familiar to these Hebrew readers, dying men receive tithes; but, in that less familiar but even more important example, one who is a continuing priest received Abraham's tithes.

The important fact concerning this latter priesthood is this: "Of whom it is witnessed that he liveth." "It is witnessed" is literally "it is being witnessed" or "it is being testified" (Greek present), clearly indicating the ongoing presence of the witness. In contrast to the dying Levitical priests, the testimony of Scripture is that he liveth. The Scripture indicates the continuing priesthood after the order of Melchisedec in two ways: (1) in the continuing record of Melchisedec's priesthood in Genesis and in Psalms; and (2) in the continuing ministry of Jesus Christ as our High Priest at God's right hand, the antitype of the model seen in Melchisedec. In Heb. 7:16 and again in 7:24 the writer stresses this continuing and eternal priestly ministry of our Lord (Hagner 106).

(4) In receiving tithes from Levi through Abraham (7:9, 10)

9 And as I may so say, Levi also, who receiveth tithes, payed tithes in Abraham.
10 For he was yet in the loins of his father, when Melchisedec met him.

"As I may so say" is used to introduce a statement which is both unique and of special importance. It serves to highlight and emphasize the following statement. It does not mean, as suggested by some (Lunemann 269; Hewitt 119), that the statement is not to be taken literally. If it were not taken literally the validity of the observation would be called into question (Lenski 220).

"Levi also, who receiveth tithes, payed tithes in Abraham." What the writer is suggesting here actually relates to the important theological doctrine of *imputation*. "To impute" means to "put onto one's account." It implies that someone has done something through someone else, or has received benefit or blame from the actions of another.

Scripture refers to three major acts of imputation (Unger 520): (1) of Adam's sin being imputed to the human race (Rom. 5:12-21); (2) of the sin of the human race being imputed to Christ (Is. 53:5, 6; 1 Pet. 2:24; 2 Cor. 5:21); (3) of the righteousness of Christ being imputed to the believer (Rom. 5:17-19; 2 Cor. 5:21; 1 Cor. 15:22; 1 Pet. 2:24). Paul points to the idea when he writes to Philemon about any wrongdoing on the part of the runaway slave, Onesimus, "Put that on mine account"

(Philem. 1:18). Thus our writer's thoughts about Levi tithing to Melchisedec through the actions of his great-grandfather, Abraham, would be quite understandable to the Hebrew mind.

In v. 10 the writer further explains his point: "For he was yet in the loins of his father, when Melchisedec met him." Levi preexisted in Abraham both physically or naturally, as Augustine suggested, and by the counsels of God (Delitzsch I:347). In these important circumstances where imputation occurred (Adam, Christ, Abraham), Scripture makes it clear that God, in His wisdom, appointed the person as an official representative. Paul puts it concisely, "As in Adam all die, even so in Christ shall all be made alive" (1 Cor. 15:22). As we have inherited death in Adam and life in Christ, so Levi inherited all the implications of Abraham's tithing to Melchisedec and being blessed by Melchisedec.

"The loins of his father" draws us back to v. 5. The only other similar reference in the N.T. is Peter's declaration at Pentecost concerning David's prophecy of the resurrection of Christ, who was "the fruit of his loins, according to the flesh" (Acts 2:30). Levi, of course, stands both for himself and for the priests of Israel who came from him—whom the writer is preparing to discuss in the coming verses. As Melchisedec was superior to Abraham, in blessing Abraham and receiving tithes from him, so the priestly order of Melchisedec, perfectly fulfilled in Jesus Christ, is superior to the priestly order of Aaron, the descendants of Abraham through Levi.

In a broader sense, all of us inherit both blame and blessing as consequences of the actions of our forefathers, but we thank God that we can establish our own independent relationship with Him. Ancient Israel excused their wrongdoing by quoting a proverb, "The fathers have eaten sour grapes, and the children's teeth are set on edge" (Ezek. 18:2), but God countered such excuses with His plain declaration, "All souls are mine; as the soul of the father, so also the soul of the son is mine: the soul that sinneth, it shall die" (Ezek. 18:4). In our personal relationship with Him, God deals with us as individuals, not collectively. Though we are sons of Adam and thus have inherited our sinful nature from him, through Christ's death and resurrection we can claim His righteousness to obtain good standing with God and the promise of eternal life.

2. Superiority of the order of Melchisedec to the order of Aaron (7:11-28)

In 7:1-10 the writer has established the personal superiority of Melchisedec to Abraham on the basis of the fact that Melchisedec blessed Abraham and Abraham, in turn, tithed to Melchisedec. He has further demonstrated that Melchisedec's superiority to Abraham must, of necessity, be applied to Levi, the patriarchal ancestor of Aaron, from whom all the priests of Israel descended. In the rest of chapter 7, the writer moves on to apply this established truth to the entire Levitical priesthood. If Melchisedec is personally superior to both Abraham and Levi, then the priestly order of Melchisedec is also superior to the priestly order of Levi. In these verses he explains the monumental consequences of these conclusions.

a. Because a change of priesthood calls for a change of law (7:11-19)

First, the writer makes a connection between the inadequacies of the Levitical priesthood and the inadequacies of the law. If the Levitical priesthood is lacking, then the law itself must be examined, for the two Hebrew institutions stand or fall together.

(1) Perfection lacking in the Levitical priesthood (7:11, 12)

11 If therefore perfection were by the Levitical priesthood, (for under it the people received the law,) what further need *was there* that another priest should rise after the order of Melchisedec, and not be called after the order of Aaron?
12 For the priesthood being changed, there is made of necessity a change also of the law.

"Therefore" (Greek *oun*) refers to the conclusion reached in the previous section, that the priesthood of Melchisedec is superior to the Levitical priesthood. On the surface it appears that the clause, "If therefore perfection were by the Levitical priesthood," should be taken as expressing a condition contrary to fact (Greek second class condition): "If perfection had been by the Levitical priesthood [but it wasn't], then what need would there be for another priesthood to arise?" [Answer: There wouldn't.] But it is possible to take this construction as assumed true (Greek first class condition), with some interpreters (like Lenski 221): "If we assume that perfection was by the Levitical priesthood, then what need was there for another priesthood to arise?" [Answer: The need is this, showing the falseness of the assumption.] This way, which I think is correct, assumes for the moment that the Levitical priesthood did bring perfection. This would, indeed, be the opinion of most Hebrews, even Hebrew Christians. The result and meaning is the same either way.

The superiority of Christ's priesthood was not a well-developed doctrine at this point in their Christian profession. If it had been, they would not even be considering a return to the Levitical practices. The writer must convince them that such an abandonment of Christ would be foolish and would bear eternal consequences. He accomplishes this by asking them a question, "What further need *was there* that another priest should rise after the order of Melchisedec?" In this way he causes them to question a position that had been dear to them, that the Levitical priesthood was sufficient to meet their needs and was a more appealing alternative than suffering persecution for Christ.

"Perfection" (Greek *teleiosis*), in this context, refers to right standing before God, the condition in which we are completely acceptable to Him (Morris 66). As Gentile believers, it is easy for us to see the shortcomings of the Levitical priesthood, but for Hebrew Christians who had depended on it all their lives such a conclusion could not be reached without some struggle. The "priesthood" (Greek *hierosune*) refers to the priestly office in the abstract in contrast to the priestly service mentioned in v. 5. There appears to be no significant difference, however, in the two ideas. The office and the service went together.

The writer connects priesthood and law in his parenthetical comment, "For under it the people received the law." "Under it" (Greek *ep' autes*) is better taken as "on the basis of it" (Westcott 180; Alford 135). "It" refers back to the Levitical priesthood. On the basis of the priesthood the law was given, especially the law as it related to the priestly service. As our law would be useless without the enforcement of the police, so the Levitical law would be useless without the ministry of the priests.

We might think that the law formed the basis for the priesthood, but our writer sees it the other way around. Sacrifices were offered, with God's blessings, before the law was given at Sinai (Gen. 8:20, 21; 15:9, 10; 22:13; Ex. 12:1-10). Priesthood, therefore, came before law and formed the basis for the law. "Received" indicates that the law had been given in the past and still stands in the present (Greek perfect), another indication that the priestly service was still active.

This new priesthood finds its sole embodiment in Jesus Christ who now sits "on the right hand of the Majesty on high" (1:3), performing His priestly ministry for us "after the order of Melchisedec." He is "another priest," of an entirely different order. The word used for "another" means "another of a different kind" (Greek *heteros*), certainly not another successor in the long line of descendants from Aaron. The inadequacy of the Levitical priesthood is emphasized in the fact that our new priest would "not be called after the order of Aaron." The basis, of course, for the writer's premise about the need for a new priest comes from his quotation of Ps. 110:4 back in 5:6. David's inspired reference to the priesthood of Melchisedec implies the coming of a new priestly order. He will remind us of that basis again in v. 17.

Having established the need for a new priesthood, the writer, from a Jewish point of view, now makes an even bolder declaration. Based on the conclusion that he has just presented, he says, "For the priesthood being changed, there is made of necessity a change also of the law." "For" (Greek *gar*) refers back to the main thought in v. 11, the need for a new priesthood (Westcott 282). It is certainly logical that there could not be a change of priesthood without having a change of law, since the priesthood formed the basis for the law.

The reference to the priesthood "being changed" (Greek *metatithemi*) may sound somewhat mild, but the word has strong connotations for this writer as indicated in later references. The same word is used in 11:5 to describe the fact that Enoch was "*translated* that he should not see death," and in 12:27 it describes God's last great earthquake which will accomplish "the *removing* of those things that are shaken . . . that those things which cannot be shaken may remain." In both of these usages the writer points to a removal of the objects described. He is suggesting the removal of the entire Levitical priesthood and its replacement with another priesthood "after the order of Melchisedec."

Since the priesthood and the law are intertwined, the former as the basis of the latter, there cannot be a change of one without a change of the other. It is a "necessity" (Greek *anagke*); it is demanded because of the relationship of priesthood and law. The noun "change" (Greek *metathesis*), used in the last phrase concerning the law, is from the same root as the verb used concerning the priesthood. If there is a removal of the priesthood, we must expect a removal of the law as well. The fact that the "law" which he has in mind is not limited to laws governing the Levitical priesthood is indicated by later references, as in 7:18, 19 and 8:7, 13 (Lunemann 272; Hagner 107). He is describing a change in nothing less than God's covenant with His people, a change from the old covenant to the new one.

(2) The new priest from Judah, not Levi (7:13, 14)

13 For he of whom these things are spoken pertaineth to another tribe, of which no man gave attendance at the altar.
14 For *it is* evident that our Lord sprang out of Juda; of which tribe Moses spake nothing concerning priesthood.

"For" (Greek *gar*) introduces v. 13 as giving the cause for the necessity of the change of both law and priesthood. "He of whom these things are spoken" refers back to v. 11, the things that relate to David's call (Ps. 110:4) for "another priest . . . after the order of Melchisedec." Note that the writer points to "He of whom" these things are spoken. We have moved from many priests under the Levitical order to one permanent priest under the order of Melchisedec, "a great high priest that is passed into the heavens" (4:14).

"Pertaineth" indicates the permanent place He has held, from the time of His birth, in a different tribe (Greek perfect tense). It means "has partaken," and it describes Christ's voluntary assumption of His human nature (Westcott 182). Unlike us, He chose the circumstances of His birth. That choice involved "another tribe." As in v. 11, "another" indicates "another of a different kind," for Jesus Christ did not come from the tribe of Levi, the priestly tribe, at all.

The yet unnamed tribe from which Jesus came was one "of which no man gave attendance at the altar." This is why the old system of law, given at Sinai, must be removed. Those laws could not govern someone who was not a Levitical priest, not from the house of Aaron. "Gave attendance" (Greek *prosecho*) describes a sincere devotion to priestly ministry, to which no one from this tribe had ever served. The specific service which the writer has in mind was that which was rendered "at the altar" (Greek *thusiasterion*), the large altar where the sacrifices of Israel were offered in the outer court outside the main sanctuary.

In v. 14 "for" continues to give the cause introduced in the previous verse for the necessity of a change of priesthood and law. The writer is explaining more fully why the laws relating to the Levitical priesthood cannot be applied to the priesthood of Christ. Thus he emphasizes, "It is evident that our Lord sprang out of Judah." "*It is* evident" (Greek *prodelos*) means that it is clearly set forth before the eyes as an undeniable fact. Though the N.T. references concerning Jesus' coming out of Judah are not that frequent, that fact is, nevertheless, very clear. Following the legal genealogy of Joseph, Matthew traces the lineage of Christ back through Judah (1:3) to Abraham, the father of Israel. Luke, apparently following the bloodline of Jesus' mother Mary, also traces His lineage through Judah (3:33) all the way back to Adam.

When the wise men sought the place of the birth of the Christ child in Jerusalem, the chief priests and scribes informed them of the well-known fact (Mic. 5:2) that the Messiah was to be born in Bethlehem of Judah (Mt. 2:6). Other passages, making essentially the same point, predicted that the ruler of Israel would come from the tribe of Judah (Gen. 49:10), and from the line of David (2 Sam. 7:12-16). This Davidic connection was clearly pointed out at His birth (Mt. 1:1, 6; Lk. 1:32; 3:31; Rom. 1:3). Thus John identifies the one who is able to open the seven-sealed book as "the Lion of the tribe of Juda, the Root of David" (Rev. 5:5; see also Ps. 132:11-18; Jer. 23:5-8).

The writer of Hebrews places strong emphasis on the true humanity of Christ as well as on His full deity (1:3). He speaks of Jesus here as "our Lord," and again in 13:20 as "our Lord Jesus." Thus, he claims Christ as his own, along with all other believers, freely acknowledging Him as the sovereign ruler of our lives. The title is especially drawn from the full reading of Ps. 110:1, to which the writer has already alluded in 1:3.

The word "sprang" can also be translated "arose." It is used of the rising of the sun and the stars, as well as the rising of plants from the ground or the budding of a branch on a tree. Our writer obviously chose the word to reflect Messianic prophecy, for the O.T. pictured Him as "the Sun of righteousness" who would "arise with healing in his wings" (Mal. 4:2), as the "Star out of Jacob" (Num. 24:17), and as a rod and a Branch "out of the stem of Jesse" (Is. 11:1). Using this same imagery, Zacharias, the father of John the Baptist, described the Messiah as "the dayspring from on high" (Lk. 1:78).

The tribe of Judah is one "of which tribe Moses spake nothing concerning priesthood." The Hebrew Christians in his audience would know this truth very well. Moses recorded Jacob's prophecy of Judah as the one who would hold the scepter (the symbol of rule and authority in government) "until Shiloh [Messiah] come" (Gen. 49:10), but he said nothing about a priest from Judah. In His infinite wisdom, God ordained, in relation to imperfect men in Israel, that the authority of government and the authority of the church be separated, but in Jesus Christ, the sinless Son of God, all three O.T. titles can be combined (Yeager 245): He is the Great Prophet (Dt. 18:15, 18; Mt. 12:41), the Great Priest (Ps. 110:4; Mt. 12:6), and the Great King (2 Sam. 7:12-16; Mt. 12:42).

(3) The new priest after the order of Melchisedec (7:15-17)

15 And it is yet far more evident: for that after the similitude of Melchisedec there ariseth another priest,
16 Who is made, not after the law of a carnal commandment, but after the power of an endless life.
17 For he testifieth, Thou *art* a priest for ever after the order of Melchisedec.

If Jesus Christ is to be a priest, he must operate under a set of rules or laws different from those for the Levitical priesthood. The laws of the priesthood given under Moses pertained to priests from the house of Aaron, from the tribe of Levi, and those certainly could not apply to Jesus Christ, from the tribe of Judah. Verse 15 confirms: "And it is yet far more evident: for that after the similitude of Melchisedec there ariseth another priest." Commentators differ on what "it" refers to in this verse. Some think the writer is looking back to the imperfection of the Levitical priesthood brought out in v. 11 (Westcott 183), or to the need for a change of law from v. 12 (Alford 137).

Perhaps it is best to see the author as looking back in a more general sense to the entire argument of vv. 11-14. Thus, he includes all of the above and more: (1) the imperfection of the Levitical priesthood; (2) the need for a new priest of a different order; (3) the accompanying change of law which is derived from a change of priesthood, and (4) the fact that the new priest is Jesus Christ from the tribe of Judah, not from the tribe of Levi (Lenski 226; Morris 68).

"Evident" (Greek *katadelos*) is a stronger word than in v. 14; two additional modifiers strengthen the phrase: it is "far more evident." The readers must realize that the Levitical priesthood, as far as God is concerned, is completely invalid. It has been replaced for all time by an effective priest of a new order. For them to consider returning to the old priesthood, which was so deficient, makes no sense at all. They must see this at all cost.

What makes this so clear is "for that after the similitude of Melchisedec there ariseth another priest." The words "for that" might be translated "if" (NIV) or "since" (Greek first class condition) in that the writer is stating a fact, a statement of reality. If another priest of a different order has been appointed, as is proven by the priestly ministry of Christ, then the obsolescence of the Levitical priesthood should be clear. "Similitude" (Greek *homoiotes*) refers to likeness, comparative similarity. Our Lord's priesthood is, in the ways that have already been outlined, like that of Melchisedec who blessed Abraham, the father of Israel, and received tithes from him. Melchisedec is the type, the model, of which Jesus Christ is the perfect fulfillment, the antitype.

"Ariseth" stresses the certainty and the immediacy of this priesthood (Greek present tense). The establishment of this new priesthood is now taking place. From God's standpoint the old priesthood and the old sacrifices ceased when Jesus died on the cross, when the veil of the Temple was split in two (Mt. 27:51); but with men the transition was slower. The process was already well on its way, but the transition would be made evident to all when God allowed General Titus and the Roman armies to destroy Jerusalem and the Temple in A.D. 70, only about six years after Hebrews was written. The new priesthood was arising like the sun upon a new day. "Another priest," as in v. 11, means "another of a different kind," another priest of an entirely different order, not after the order of Aaron.

Verse 16 continues to describe this other priest of a different kind. He is one "who is made," or "who has become," indicating that he has become such a priest, and ever shall so remain (Greek perfect tense of *ginomai*). "Who" is singular in contrast with the Levitical priests, who were many, a fact emphasized in v. 23.

In the following description of the two different kinds of priesthood, every word in the two phrases offers a contrast. He has become a priest "not after the law of a carnal commandment, but after the power of an endless life." In these two phrases "law" stands over against "power," "commandment" stands over against "life," and "carnal" contrasts with "endless." The order of the phrases in the original is interesting: "not after a law of a commandment carnal, but after power of life endless." The adjectives "carnal" and "endless" are placed at the ends of the phrases for emphasis.

The first phrase describes the Levitical priesthood: "the law of a carnal commandment." "Law" is the broader term, referring to the Mosaic system as a whole. "Commandment" is more narrow, the particular manifestation of the law concerning a specific subject, in this case the Levitical priesthood and its operation. The commandment is "carnal" (Greek *sarkinos*), not because it is evil in any way, but rather because it is of this world, not heavenly; it is temporal, not eternal, and it is external rather than internal.

On the other hand, the priesthood of Christ, after the order of Melchisedec, is "after the power of an endless life." "Power" (Greek *dunamis*) is internal and energetic, in contrast to "law," which is external and powerless in itself. The writer may be emphasizing the resurrection in particular. Paul says that Jesus Christ was "declared to be the Son of God with power, according to the spirit of holiness, by the resurrection from the dead" (Rom. 1:4). "Life" is active, productive, effective, in contrast with "commandment" which, though its purpose is good, is in itself dead and useless. As our High Priest, our Lord has life in Himself (Jn. 1:4; 11:25; 14:6)

Furthermore, this life is "endless" (Greek *akatalutos*), indestructible, indissoluble, in contrast with the commandment which is "carnal," earthbound, external, temporary. Some think that this "endless life" is derived from the eternal existence of the Son (Pink 389; Lunemann 275), but perhaps in this context the "endless life" is that possessed by Jesus Christ, the God-man and our eternal priest, after the resurrection (Alford 138; Delitzsch I:356): the victorious life that He now has as our risen Savior and High Priest.

This does not mean that His priestly ministry itself did not begin before the resurrection, for it was in His office as Priest that he offered Himself upon the cross for our sins (see 1:3). Though His sacrifice on the cross was final and complete in itself, so that He cried victoriously from the cross, "It is finished" (Jn. 19:30), yet it was essential in His priestly function to present that sacrifice before the throne of God in Heaven, the true Holy of Holies (see Jn. 20:17), as the writer will point out (9:12, 23, 24).

The Scriptural authority of this other priest who possesses "the power of an endless life" is again emphasized in v. 17. "For" (Greek *gar*) again introduces the cause, as it so often does. "He testifieth" can be translated, "It is being testified of *him*," that is, the Scripture continues to offer this testimony of the new priesthood embodied in Jesus Christ. The Scriptural testimony is, "Thou *art* a priest for ever after the order of Melchisedec." The writer of Hebrews likes to take O.T. texts and preach on them, so to speak. He first quoted Ps. 110:4 in 5:6 as part of the Scriptural basis for the call of Christ to be a priest. Here he emphasizes it again in contrasting the priesthood according to the order of Melchisedec with the Levitical priesthood, and he will quote it again in

v. 21 in stressing the origin of Christ's priesthood on the basis of an oath. This quotation describes both the permanence of His priesthood (it is "for ever") and the character of His priesthood (it is after the order of Melchisedec, not after the order of Aaron).

(4) The law of the priesthood now null and void (7:18, 19)

18 For there is verily a disannulling of the commandment going before for the weakness and unprofitableness thereof.
19 For the law made nothing perfect, but the bringing in of a better hope *did*; by the which we draw nigh unto God.

For (Greek *gar*) introduces vv. 18, 19 as an explanation of the thought emphasized in vv. 11-17: that a powerless priesthood and a powerless law called for replacement, and that replacement was prophesied in David's presentation of a new priesthood according to the order of Melchisedec. The form used in the original indicates that v. 19 is needed to complete the thought of v. 18 (Greek *men/de*). The verb translated "there is" must be understood with the second clause as well, that is, "On the one hand, there is a disannulling of the commandment . . . but, on the other hand, there is the bringing in of a better hope. . . ."

The necessary connection between an imperfect priesthood and an imperfect law was first suggested in v. 12. The priesthood formed the basis for the law, but the law also gave authority to the priesthood. They were so intimately connected that if one becomes invalid, so must the other. Thus the writer boldly declares the "disannulling" (Greek *athetesis*), the setting aside, of the law as it relates to the priesthood. The same word is used again in 9:26 in connection with the putting away of sin. The word "commandment," rather than "law," limits his consideration to the law as it relates to the priestly service. His concern for the law is broader, as he will indicate later; but, in this context, he is dealing with the law as it related to the Levitical priesthood.

Some might call attention to God's promise to Aaron and his sons of "an everlasting priesthood throughout their generations" (Ex. 40:15; see also Jer. 33:18; Hagner 112). But a covenant is formed by two parties, though they may not be at all equal parties, as in the case of God and Israel. The covenant may become invalid from two different perspectives: (1) if one or both of the parties fail to live up to the conditions of the covenant, or (2) if the need for the covenant has been fulfilled. For both reasons, the law establishing the Levitical priesthood has been annulled.

In the case of the Levitical priesthood, and for that matter the law as a whole, both the priests themselves and the nation of Israel as a whole failed to live up to the terms of the covenant. Furthermore, the need for the covenant of law and priesthood was fulfilled in the coming of Christ. Such was Jesus' position in relation to the law. He declared, "Think not that I am come to destroy the law, or the prophets: I am not come to destroy, but to fulfil" (Mt. 5:17).

From the perspective of the Hebrew Christians, the commandment relating to the priesthood was the commandment "going before," that is, it predated in time both the introduction by David of a new priesthood according to the order of Melchisedec (Ps. 110:4), as well as the coming of Jesus Christ to fulfill that prophecy.

We may note that Paul argues, from a different perspective, that the covenant of grace or faith actually preceded the covenant of law by some 430 years (Gal. 3:17ff), and on that basis he explains that grace and faith must prevail over law. Of course, both points are valid, each reflecting a legitimate point of view (Yeager 250).

"For" (Greek *dia* with acc.) means "because." The cause of the setting aside of the commandment relating to the priesthood was "the weakness" (Greek *asthenes*) and "unprofitableness" (Greek *anopheles*) thereof. These are two adjectives used as nouns. Like the priesthood that formed its basis (v. 11), the law was completely ineffective with regard to the desired result: the establishing of an inner and eternal relationship with God. Both the law and the priesthood were formal, external, and primarily earthbound. They were "our schoolmaster *to bring us* unto Christ" (Gal. 3:24), but now that schoolmaster is no longer needed (Gal. 3:25).

The first clause in v. 19 is parenthetical, inserted as an explanation of the weakness and unprofitableness of the priestly commandment. The writer declares, "For the law made nothing perfect." As in this entire discussion, "the law" in the immediate context concerns the law of the priesthood, but it ultimately includes the entire Mosaic system, which the writer makes abundantly clear in the discussion to follow. The law is the whole body, of which the commandment is a part.

"Made perfect" (Greek *teleioo*) is used in its noun form in v. 11 in reference to the Levitical priesthood. Here it has the same meaning as it is applied to the law, for, indeed, the law and the priesthood stand or fall together. One cannot endure without the other. Neither the law nor the priesthood of the old covenant were able to make men acceptable before a holy God. Though they served as the God-ordained substitute for the time, that is all they were. They stood as completely insufficient apart from Christ's personal sacrifice and priestly ministry. This lack of complete satisfaction included every area, for the law made "nothing" perfect. There was nothing that the law touched where complete satisfaction was attained.

Verse 19 returns to the main thought, the completion of the contrast from v. 18. "Bringing in" (Greek *epeisagoge*) stands in contrast with "disannulling" in v. 18. One institution was being declared invalid because it did not produce permanent results (nor was that ever intended in God's overall plan), while the other institution was being introduced because of its permanent effectiveness.

"A better hope" stands in contrast with "the commandment going before" in v. 18. We must remember that "hope" in the N.T. is a strong word, implying trust in the fulfillment of a promise along with an earnest expectation for the same. This is the fourth and final context in which our writer mentions the word hope (see 3:6; 6:11, 18, 19). "Better" is his favorite word throughout, a key word of the epistle, used some 13 times (1:4; 6:9; 7:7, 22; 8:6 (twice); 9:23; 10:34; 11:16, 35, 40; 12:24). The writer is firmly convinced that everything under the new covenant is better than that under the old; thus the new covenant must replace the old. By implication he suggests that there was hope under the law, for it did, indeed, serve its purpose for the time. But that hope was only temporary and transitory, while this hope is eternal.

Most commentators feel that it is best to take the verb in the first clause of v. 18 as also implied in the main clause of v. 19. Thus, we would read, "For, on the one hand, there is an annulling of the commandment . . . but, on the other hand, there is a bringing in of a better hope." On the basis of ("by which") this better hope in the sacrifice of Christ and His continuing priestly ministry "we draw nigh unto God." Under the law "drawing nigh" or "coming near" was used of the priests' worship as they approached the presence of the Lord in the tabernacle (see Ex. 19:22; Lev. 10:3; also of Moses at Sinai in Ex. 24:2). James picks up the same imagery when he admonishes believers, "Draw nigh to God, and he will draw nigh to you" (4:8). In the O.T. God's presence was hidden by veils and curtains, but in the N.T. those veils have been torn away, and we are all priests with the privilege of approaching God's throne directly on the basis of the shed blood of Christ (1 Pet. 2:5, 9; Rev. 1:6; 5:10; 20:6).

b. Because Christ's priesthood was instituted by an oath (7:20-22)

20 And inasmuch as not without an oath *he was made priest*:
21 (For those priests were made without an oath; but this with an oath by him that said unto him, The Lord sware and will not repent, Thou *art* a priest for ever after the order of Melchisedec:)
22 By so much was Jesus made a surety of a better testament.

Since v. 11 the writer has been emphasizing the superiority of the order of Melchisedec to the order of Aaron. In vv. 11-19 he has pointed out that a change of priesthood of necessity calls for a change of law. The Levitical priesthood must be replaced because it could not give those who worshiped under it a right standing before God. Now in vv. 20-22 he stresses the importance of becoming priest by an oath. One of the priestly orders under discussion did, but the other did not.

Verse 20 explains, with regard to the priesthood of Christ, "And inasmuch as not without an oath *he was made priest*." The writer uses "and" to introduce another step in his argument, as he has already in v. 15 and will again in v. 23. He has pointed out that Jesus was called under oath in 5:6, and this oath was again stressed in v. 17 of this chapter, the oath from Ps. 110:4 which he is about to quote again in v. 21. On this basis he explains that Jesus' priesthood was "not without an oath." A somewhat stronger word is used for "oath" here than in 6:16, 17. There the simple word for "oath" is used (Greek *orkos*), but here the more complex word which literally means "the act of taking an oath" or "a sworn statement" (Greek *orkomosia*).

The last phrase in this statement, "*He was made priest*," is in italics, meaning that it is not in the original. The translators felt that it was needed to complete the sense. It is easy to see that it was correctly drawn from the first part of v. 21. All of v. 21 is parenthetical, justifying the declaration of v. 20 that Christ's priesthood originated under an oath. Thus, the direct connection of v. 20 is with v. 22. We might read, literally, "And since his priesthood was not without an oath, by such Jesus became a surety of a better covenant."

In v. 21 the writer makes a parenthetical explanation of v. 20. He declares, "For those priests were made without an oath." "For" (Greek *gar*) introduces v. 21 as giving the cause of the statement made in v. 20. The two clauses in v. 21 are set in balanced contrast to each other (Greek *men/de*), giving the idea of "on the one hand"/"on the other hand," "those priests" as opposed to "this" (priest). The Levitical priests were given authority for holding their office and performing their service by the law, but the Scripture does not record that they took an oath. The construction the writer uses here again suggests that the Levitical priests were still practicing in the Temple in Jerusalem as he wrote. The statement literally says, "For those (O.T. priests) are having become priests apart from the taking of an oath" (Greek perfect), suggesting a priesthood instituted in the past but continuing to the present (Lunemann 280).

The writer emphasizes the contrast between Jesus as a priest and those O.T. priests in the next phrase, "But this with an oath by him that said unto him." "This" means "this man" or "this priest," in reference to Christ. The word oath again means "oath-taking," as in v. 20. "By him" refers to God the Father, the one who through the psalmist prophetically placed the coming Christ under oath to serve in the new priestly order. "By him that said" is literally "by him who is saying," emphasizing that the oath is still there in Scripture for all to see. It is not a dead oath that only belongs to history, but rather a living oath that is part of the living and inspired record. This oath was spoken by God the Father "unto him," that is, to the eternal Son in anticipation of His coming incarnation.

The writer makes the statement stronger by including the oath which God the Father spoke prophetically to the Son when "the Word was made flesh, and dwelt among us" (Jn. 1:14). The full oath, from Ps. 110:4, is: "The Lord sware and will not repent, Thou *art* a priest for ever after the order of Melchisedec."

The Levitical priesthood was temporary and transitional. Contrary to the thinking of many of the Jewish leaders of Jesus' day, it was never intended to be permanent. Just as with Abraham (Heb. 6:13ff), God the Father placed Himself under oath as He uttered the statement that instituted the Melchisedecan priesthood.

With added emphasis, the psalmist affirmed, "He will not repent." There are some passages that speak of repentance on God's part, as when He repented of the creation of man because of his wickedness (Gen. 6:6), when He repented that He had made Saul king over Israel (1 Sam. 15:10, 11), when He repented of His judgment against David and the city of Jerusalem (2 Sam. 24:16), or when He explained that He would repent or turn from His wrath when wicked people themselves repent of their sinfulness (Jer. 18:8). In each of these cases, however, the Scripture speaks of an outward change on God's part, a change only from man's point of view. God's eternal decrees and His ultimate purposes never change. His nature and attributes do not change. He may appear to change on the outside, but His inward and eternal determinations will always be accomplished (see Rom. 11:25-29). His eternal decrees regarding Christ's priesthood still apply today, including Ps. 110:4: "Thou art a priest for ever after the order of Melchisedec."

Now the writer completes the statement begun in v. 20 before the parenthetical explanation of v. 21: "By so much was Jesus made a surety of a better testament." "By so much" refers us back to v. 20 and reemphasizes the fact that our Lord became a priest by an oath, in stark contrast with the Levitical priests who took no oath when they served. He uses our Lord's human name, "Jesus," because it is only in His incarnation that He can serve as our High Priest, and in the original he places the name at the end of the sentence to give it additional emphasis.

"Was made" points to a past accomplishment as well as continuing service (Greek perfect of *ginomai*). "Surety" (Greek *egguos*) refers to a guarantee, a commitment that what has been promised will indeed take place. Though this is the only time this word occurs in the N.T., it comes from the same root as the verb "draw nigh" in v. 19. As we draw near to God in our worship on the basis of the better hope which our Lord has made possible, He also stands near the Father, even at His right hand (compare 1:3), to ensure the fulfillment of all divine promises. Note that He is not a surety, a guarantee, of men to God but rather of God to men (Lunemann 281).

Through the divine oath our Lord has become a guarantee "of a better testament." The word translated "testament" (Greek *diatheke*) occurs 21 times in the N.T., translated "testament" seven times and "covenant" 14 times in the KJV. The Septuagint (the Greek version of the O.T.) uses this word to translate the Hebrew word for covenant (*berith*), which originally referred to the act of "cutting" the words of the covenant in stone (Unger 224).

The writer of Hebrews takes advantage of the more complex Greek word which carries both a legal meaning ("testament" or "will") and a theological meaning ("covenant"; Hagner 113). Most recent translations use "covenant" here, in preparation for the discussion of the new covenant in chapter 8, while the idea of a "testament" or a will is brought out by the writer in his discussion in chapter 9 (vv. 15-18, 20). There are at least four common points between a covenant and a testament: (1) They both depend entirely on the desires of the author. (2) They aim to transfer wealth or blessings. (3) They may establish conditions which must be met. (4) They designate specific persons as recipients (Lenski 234). This covenant or testament is "better" than the priestly covenant in the Mosaic ritual, both because this priest serves under an oath and because He sits at God's right hand as our unfailing guarantee of the fulfillment of God's promises.

c. Because of the permanence of Christ's priestly order (7:23-25)

23 And they truly were many priests, because they were not suffered to continue by reason of death:
24 But this *man*, because he continueth ever, hath an unchangeable priesthood.
25 Wherefore he is able also to save them to the uttermost that come unto God by him, seeing he

ever liveth to make intercession for them.

The writer now explains his third argument for the superiority of the order of Melchisedec, and of Jesus as its continuing Priest, to the order of Aaron. He begins the statement with "and" to show the parallel between v. 23 and v. 20, which also began with "and." In v. 23 he continues, "They truly were many priests, because they were not suffered to continue by reason of death." Our writer sets v. 23 in a well balanced contrast with v. 24 (Greek *men/de* clauses). The emphatic contrast is, on the one hand, between the "many priests" of v. 23 and, on the other hand, "this man," the one priest, Jesus Christ, in v. 24. It is clear that he is speaking about the office of high priest, not priests in general, from v. 26. Though the Lord did speak of "an everlasting priesthood" for Aaron and his sons (Ex. 40:15), that promise was for the office, not for the individual, and even that came with conditions which ultimately were not met.

"They were" is literally "they are having become": that is, the multiplication of O.T. high priests started in the past and continues into the present (Greek periphrastic perfect). Again, the words leave the clear implication that the high priest was still serving in the Temple in Jerusalem even as the writer addressed his audience.

The plurality of high priests is to be viewed in succession; one dies and is succeeded by another. According to Josephus, there were 83 high priests between Aaron and the destruction of Jerusalem in A.D. 70 (Hagner 112). The cause of the multiple high priests is all too clear, "They were not suffered to continue by reason of death." "They were not suffered to continue" is literally, "They are being hindered from continuing." This situation still prevailed; high priests were still dying or waiting to die.

With few exceptions, all men, including the priests, have died since the fall of Adam (Gen. 3:19). Death as the unwelcome visitor is so regular for the entire race of men that we have come to expect it. But even if the death of the high priest was expected, it nevertheless demonstrated a serious hindrance to the effectiveness of the Levitical priesthood. It made this priesthood less than desirable, especially when something far better is available.

That better Priest is introduced by contrast in v. 24, "But this *man*." He is only one High Priest in contrast with the many priests of the line of Aaron. His priesthood is better "because he continueth ever." The two causal clauses of vv. 23, 24 stand in stark contrast. The Levitical priests were many because they were constantly dying, ever subject to the frailties of the descendants of Adam. But the priesthood of Christ is always available because, though He died, He arose victorious over death on the third day and now "death hath no more dominion over him" (Rom. 6:9). The statement reflects Jesus' declaration in Jn. 8:35, "The servant abideth not in the house for ever: but the Son abideth ever" (see also Jn. 12:34). The verb here is the same as in John (Greek *meno*).

As a result of His continuous abiding in the office of high priest, He "hath an unchangeable priesthood." The word "unchangeable" (Greek *aparabatos*) refers to that which cannot be invaded or violated. His priesthood is unchangeable because it cannot be invaded or assaulted by any enemy, including death itself (Westcott 191).

"Wherefore" introduces v. 25 as stating the wonderful result of the continuing priesthood of Christ. Because of this continuing priesthood and His divine power "he is able also to save them." In 2:18, concerning those who are being tempted, the writer has already declared, "He is able to succour them" or help them. Here he emphasizes our Savior's ability to finish what He started. Paul said it this way, "He which hath begun a good work in you will perform *it* until the day of Jesus Christ" (Phil. 1:6). "Also" is used to emphasize this further explanation of the benefits of Christ's continuing priesthood.

"To save them" is "to keep on saving them" (Greek present tense), not referring to the initial act of salvation, which is instantaneous (Jn. 3:3, 5; 2 Cor. 5:17; 1 Jn. 5:12), but to the ongoing process of salvation which we sometimes refer to as sanctification. These two aspects of salvation are described dramatically by the same writer in 10:14, which, translated literally, reads, "For by one offering he hath perfected for ever them that are sanctified." Though Christ's provision of salvation was finished when He died at Calvary (Jn. 19:30), His actual work of salvation in our lives is a continuing process. Justification begins the work of salvation, solely on the basis of the merits of Christ; sanctification completes the work on the same basis.

Our heavenly High Priest takes this salvation for each Christian to the greatest extent, even "to the uttermost" (Greek *eis to panteles*). Commentators debate whether the emphasis here is (1) time, telling us how long He saves us (Yeager 259; Hewitt 125); or (2) degree, telling us how completely He saves us (Barnes 166; Alford 143; Westcott 190; Lenski 238). Agreeing with the latter emphasis, Delitzsch states, "Christ is able to save in every way and in all respects, *unto the uttermost*; so that every want and need, in all its breadth and depth, is utterly done away" (I:371). The idea of degree, of salvation in its most perfect sense, is also that which is in line with the present context (see vv. 11, 19). That does not mean, however, that there is no time element in the phrase at all. If our Lord were not able to save us with regard to time until we meet Him in eternity, then His salvation would not be complete. But it is the broader emphasis of degree, extent, or completeness, that is being stressed.

Note, however, that a limitation is placed on this complete salvation. It is only for those "that come unto God by him." As God's work in saving us was expressed in continuous action, so is the description of those whom He saves. This salvation applies only to "those who keep coming (Greek present) to God by him." The continuous action expressed in this verse is very relevant to the problem he was addressing with his audience. At least some of them were considering returning to what they thought of as the safety of Judaism with the idea of escaping the temporal persecution which was increasing toward Christians. Those who were entertaining such thoughts must realize that their salvation is not complete if they do not continue their dependence on Christ as their High Priest.

The idea of coming "unto God by him" certainly stresses personal faith in Christ, but it also emphasizes the importance of our continuing worship and devotion to God (see 4:16; 7:19). The wording is again reminiscent of the approach to the altar in worship in the O.T. by the priests as well as the people (Ex. 19:22; Lev. 10:3). In John's Gospel, Jesus stressed the fact that it was only through Him that we are able to come to God (Jn. 10:9; 14:6).

The reason for the availability of complete salvation for those who continue in faith and worship is: "seeing he ever liveth to make intercession for them." In sharp contrast to the O.T. priests who were always dying, Jesus, as our High Priest, "ever liveth." That is why they were "many" and he is "this man," the only one. To John on Patmos Jesus declared, "*I am* he that liveth, and was dead; and, behold, I am alive for evermore" (Rev. 1:18). The primary reason that He lives and sits at the right hand of the Father is "to make intercession for them," also expressed in continuous action: "to be making intercession for them" (Greek present tense).

This subject is especially on Paul's mind in Romans 8 when he emphasizes the intense intercession of the Holy Spirt "with groanings which cannot be uttered" (Rom. 8:26, 27) and subsequently points to Christ who, at God's right hand, "maketh intercession for us" (Rom. 8:34). A prayer of intercession is an intense prayer for the needs of others, whatever those needs might be. No doubt as a prophetic type of this effective intercession of God's Son, Jesus Christ, before the throne of the Father, the O.T. points out that Aaron, the original high priest, was to "bear the names of the children of Israel in the breastplate of judgment upon his heart" when he entered the Holy of Holies (Ex. 28:29). Such intercession as that was both personal and impressive, but it cannot begin to measure up to the individual intercession each Christian experiences in his continuing worship and service for Christ.

d. Because of the moral perfection of Jesus Christ (7:26-28)

26 For such an high priest became us, *who is* holy, harmless, undefiled, separate from sinners, and made higher than the heavens;
27 Who needeth not daily, as those high priests, to offer up sacrifice, first for his own sins, and then for the people's: for this he did once, when he offered up himself.
28 For the law maketh men high priests which have infirmity; but the word of the oath, which was since the law, *maketh* the Son, who is consecrated for evermore.

In 7:26-28 the writer gives a fourth reason for the superiority of the order of Melchisedec over the order of Aaron, and of Jesus Christ, the High Priest who holds that position. The priesthood of Christ is infinitely better not only because He lives forever, but also because He is morally superior to the Levitical priests. Indeed, His moral character is not merely better than theirs, it is absolutely perfect.

"For" introduces v. 26 as a further explanation of our Lord's ability "to save . . . to the uttermost," as described in v. 25. "Such" looks forward in the verse to the description in some detail of the kind of priest the writer has in mind. This kind of high priest "became us" (Greek *prepo*), meaning that it was fitting, suitable, proper, and even necessary, that we have such a priest as described here to meet our needs. Nothing less could satisfy the requirements of a holy God. The continuous action from the past (Greek imperfect tense) suggests that this has been the need of sinners all along. The Levitical priests who served God's purpose as a type of that greater Priest who was to come never really met God's strict requirements. We desperately need such a priest as is found only in the Lord Jesus Christ. In 2:10 the writer pointed out what was proper or becoming for God; now he describes what is proper or becoming for us.

The writer now uses five words or phrases in succession to describe the human nature of Christ in His relationship with those to whom He ministers as High Priest. First, He is "holy" (Greek *hosios*), a word that occurs only here in the N.T. The usual word for "holy" (Greek *hagios*) refers to holiness in the most absolute sense, internal holiness. This word describes a relational holiness, a holiness which is especially manifested in His dealings with men (Westcott 193).

Second, He is "harmless" (Greek *akakos*), literally "without evil." There is nothing within Him that would ever do damage to those to whom He ministers. Only goodness issues from His person, and during His whole earthly ministry He "went about doing good" (Acts 10:38).

Third, He is "undefiled" (Greek *amiantos*), meaning "without a stain." In His contact with this evil world no impurity ever tainted His character.

Fourth, He is "separate from sinners." "Separate" literally means "having been separated," emphasizing the fact that His separation began in the past, at His incarnation when the Word became flesh, and continues to the present (Greek perfect tense).

The writer has gone to great effort to show that Jesus is one of us with respect to His sympathy with our frailties and His genuine participation in human nature (2:10-14; 4:14-16), but here he needs to stress His difference from us. Even in 4:15, when he was describing how Jesus was "in all points tempted like as *we are*," he stressed the fact that He remained "without sin." Throughout His ministry He freely mingled with sinners and ministered to their needs (Lk. 15:1, 2), but in all of this He never participated in their sins in thought or act. He is able to be both the sacrifice for our sins and our eternal High Priest because there was never the least taint of sin in His life and character. Though none of us can attain the perfect balance our Lord demonstrated in this matter, we can at least seek to model His example of separation from sin and love for sinners.

Jesus, however, was not only "separated from sinners" in His life, but also in His office (D. Guthrie 168). As the O.T. high priest separated himself from sinners through the purification of sacrifices on the Day of Atonement and came before the presence of God in the Holy of Holies (see Lev. 16), so Jesus Christ as our High Priest has entered the heavenly Holy of Holies on the basis of His own sacrifice and His own personal holiness.

The writer refers to this position when he declares the fifth characteristic of our High Priest who *was* "made higher than the heavens." He has previously referred to this exalted position of our Lord whom he described as seated "on the right hand of the Majesty on high" (1:3; see also 1:13; 4:14). This position which Christ assumed at His ascension, which reflects Ps. 110:1, is mentioned several times in the N.T. (see Mt. 22:44;

Acts 2:33, 34; 5:31; 7:55, 56; Rom. 8:34; Eph. 1:20; Phil. 2:9; Col. 3:1). In this close proximity to the Father, He now effectively intercedes on our behalf.

While v. 26 describes the perfect moral character of our High Priest, v. 27 describes the perfection of the sacrifice which He made. The writer first approaches it from a negative standpoint: "Who needeth not daily, as those high priests, to offer up sacrifice." Interpreters are not all agreed as to the point of the word "daily" (Greek *kath' hemeran*). It seems obvious that the primary emphasis here is on the Day of Atonement, given the added qualification that these sacrifices were "first for his own sins, and then for the people's." This is the exact description of the sacrificial procedure on the Day of Atonement as found in Leviticus 16. That the writer is fully aware of this once-a-year sacrifice for sin is evident from subsequent discussion (see 9:7; 10:1).

The problem then is how to apply the word "daily" to sacrifices that only occur once a year. Some have suggested that the solution is found in connecting the word "daily" only with "needeth," not with "to offer up sacrifice." He does not say that the high priest offered up sacrifices for sins daily, but that he needed to because of his daily sins (Lenski 243; Yeager 262). With a slightly different emphasis, others think "daily" should be taken with the ministry of Christ, not with the sacrifices of the high priests. As He daily ministers in our behalf, He has no need to offer sacrifices since His one sacrifice is complete (Westcott 196; Bruce 157; D. Guthrie 169).

Perhaps the best solution, and the one that takes the words more at face value, is that the writer includes in his thinking the special sacrifices for sin (as described in Leviticus 4 for the priest himself, for the whole congregation, for a ruler, and for any one of the common people), which might occur on a daily basis, even though he is emphasizing the Day of Atonement, the only day of national repentance in Israel, as the symbol and summation of all sacrifices for sin (Lunemann 287; Kistemaker 207; Bruce 157). As to a sacrifice for His own sins, Jesus did not need to give any attention at all, since He was the sinless, virgin-born Son of God.

As to atonement for the sins of the people, the writer emphasizes, "For this he did once, when he offered up himself." "This" refers back to the sacrifice "for the people's" sins in the preceding clause. With regard to the two-fold contrast with the Levitical high priest on the Day of Atonement: first, Jesus as High Priest had no need for a sacrifice for personal sins; and second, His sacrifice of Himself for the sins of the people needed no repetition. This sacrifice he did, he made, only once, using a word (Greek *ephapax*) that is more emphatic than the simpler one in 6:4; 9:26, 28 (Greek *hapax*). While the latter word means "once," the former means "once for all"; it appears again in 9:12 and 10:10 to stress the finality of Jesus' sacrifice and its application in the heavenly Holy of Holies at God's right hand.

This final and complete payment for our sins was made "when he offered up himself," the first time the writer has referred to His offering up of Himself. As he pursues our Lord's redemptive actions through the rest of the book, he will refer in more detail to His personal sacrifice of Himself, especially in 9:11ff. and 10:5ff. "He offered up" (Greek *anaphero*) depicts the act of placing the sacrifice on the altar. It is the same word used in continuous action earlier in the verse for the repeated offerings of the high priest on the Day of Atonement. Here it is expressed in completed action (Greek aorist tense) since Christ's sacrifice needs no repetition.

In v. 28 "for" (Greek *gar*) introduces a conclusion and a summary of what has been discussed in vv. 11-25. His declaration that "the law maketh men high priests which have infirmity" reviews a fact first mentioned in 5:2, 3. This verse expresses more concisely the three dramatic contrasts (Greek *men/de* clauses) emphasized in vv. 18-21, and vv. 23, 24. "The law," the Mosaic code especially as it related to the Levitical system, of necessity used in the role of high priest men who were sinners through and through. Many of them were good men, men who were saved by their faith in God's promises, though they were surrounded by "infirmity," sinful weaknesses of the flesh and of the mind. They merely served as types of the Great High Priest who was to come.

In contrast, "the word of the oath, which was since the law, *maketh* the Son, who is consecrated for evermore." The three-fold contrast in the two clauses is between "the law" and "the word of the oath, men and the Son," and men with "infirmity" and the Son who is "consecrated for evermore." "The word of the oath" refers back to v. 21 and the oath which was quoted from Ps. 110:4. That oath, which was the sign and prophecy of a new priesthood, "was since the law" because it was given through David. The fact that it was after the giving of the law shows the divine dissatisfaction with the priesthood under the law. As in 1:2, there is no definite article in the original ("Son" rather than "the Son"), thus emphasizing the quality of being a "Son," though indeed God's only Son, in contrast with the quality of being mere "men."

The men who served as high priest under the law were many, but there is only one Son, and He is "consecrated for evermore"; "consecrated" might also read "perfected" or "completed." The verb indicates that this consecration, perfection, or completion was made in the past with results that continue to the present (Greek perfect tense). That fact is further confirmed by the adverb "for evermore." This perfection of the Son was mentioned earlier in 2:10 and 5:9 and also is suggested in vv. 11 and 19 of this chapter. As discussed before, this consecration or perfection refers to His full qualification for the office of High Priest. He has met those qualifications through His earthly life, death, and resurrection, and now He has ascended to God's right hand to serve as our Mediator forever.

Summary (7:1-28)

The writer first mentioned Christ's new priesthood according to the order of Melchisedec in 5:9, 10. But he dropped the subject temporarily to issue a severe warning to his audience about their lack of spiritual growth and the dire consequences—even final and total apostasy—that could result. In 7:1 he picks up that subject once again and carries it throughout chapter 7.

In order to show the superiority of Christ's priesthood after the order of Melchisedec to the Levitical priesthood, the writer first seeks to prove Melchisedec's superiority to Abraham (7:1-10). Abraham was, after all, the father of the entire nation of Israel, including his great-grandson, Levi, as well as Levi's great-grandson, Aaron. He first explains the historical reference to Melchisedec from Genesis 14, and points out how Melchisedec is a type of Christ (7:1-3). Then he discusses four different ways in which Melchisedec is superior to Abraham (7:4-10). Melchisedec is superior to Abraham in that he received tithes from Abraham (7:4-6a); then he in turn placed a blessing upon Abraham (7:6b-7). Furthermore, Melchisedec, and the priesthood after his order, is better because he lives, both in the historic Scripture record as well as in his sole successor, Jesus Christ. On the other hand, Aaronic priests, the sons of Abraham, who later received tithes, die (7:8). Finally, Melchisedec is not only superior to Abraham, but he is also superior to his great-grandson, Levi, the father of the priestly line of Israel, since Levi was biologically and spiritually in Abraham when he tithed to Melchisedec (7:9, 10).

Having shown Melchisedec's superiority to Abraham, the writer then seeks to demonstrate in more detail the point suggested in vv. 9, 10, that the priestly order of Melchisedec is far superior to the priestly order of Aaron, the first high priest of Israel and the great-grandson of Levi (7:11-28). He does this by discussing four ways in which the priestly order of Melchisedec is superior to the priestly order of Aaron. His first point is that a change of priesthood of necessity carries with it a change of law (7:11-19). If there was no need for a change of priesthood, then God would not have supplied another priest in the person of His Son, Jesus Christ. The fact that He did supply such a priest, as the Hebrew readers should know, suggests the ineffectiveness of the Levitical order. Furthermore, this new priest is not from the tribe of Levi at all, but rather from the tribe of Judah. He could not possibly serve in the role of the traditional priesthood since Moses never gave any authority or instructions with regard to a priest from the tribe of Judah. His priesthood must come from an entirely different order, the order of Melchisedec, which finds its Scriptural basis in Ps. 110:4, "Thou *art* a priest for ever after the order of Melchisedec." In light of the presence of this new priesthood which finds its authority on a different foundation, the old order and the old law which governed it must be set aside.

Secondly, he argues that the order of Melchisedec is superior to the order of Aaron because it was instituted with an oath, the oath given by the Lord Himself in Ps. 110:4 (7:20-22). No such oath was ever mentioned when Aaron or his sons assumed their position. God through David prophesied the coming of the new priesthood when he mentioned the Lord's oath that pointed forward to such a fulfillment.

Thirdly, this new priesthood in Jesus Christ is superior to the Levitical order because it is permanent (7:23-25). The Levitical priesthood was occupied by "many" different priests over the course of the years, some 83 in all down to the destruction of the Temple in A.D. 70. In sharp contrast, our Lord is the sole successor to the ancient priesthood according to the order of Melchisedec. Like the type, Melchisedec, who lives on in the Scripture record of Genesis 14, so the antitype, Jesus Christ, lives on literally at God's right hand in Heaven. Thus He is able to "save us to the uttermost" when we keep coming to God by Him.

Finally, Christ's priesthood after the order of Melchisedec is superior because of the moral perfection of the Priest Himself. Ancient Israel might take some comfort in sympathy from their priests since they were sinners like themselves and must, because of that, offer a personal sacrifice for sin on the Day of Atonement and throughout the year in the other sacrifices for sin (Lev. 4). But that comfort would be short-lived when they realized the ineffectiveness of this priesthood because of the moral imperfections of its priests as well as their physical frailties. Because of the personal purity of Jesus Christ, His absolute sinlessness, and because of the qualifications for His priesthood through His experience on earth, He has become our "consecrated" or perfected High Priest in Heaven forever.

Application: Preaching and Teaching the Passage

A type of Christ is a person, event, or thing which points in one or more ways to the coming of Christ. The person, event, or thing that offers the prophetic picture is called the type, while the fulfillment of that prophetic picture is called the antitype. A few popular types found in the O.T. are God's slaughter of the animals to provide skins for clothing for Adam and Eve because of their sin (Gen. 3:21), Noah's ark and the flood (Gen. 6-8), the offering of Isaac (Gen. 22), the life of Joseph (Gen. 37-50), the Hebrew passover (Ex. 12), the tabernacle (Ex. 25-40), the various kinds of offerings and sacrifices (Lev. 1-5), Jonah as a type of the resurrection, and the story of Hosea as a type of redemption. Some Bible teachers point to many other O.T. situations which they feel offer types or pictures of Christ, though the idea is sometimes overused. The safest types, no doubt, are those which the N.T. specifically points to as types, like the one under discussion here, but I would not be surprised to find out in Heaven that God intended many other things as picture-prophecies of coming events in His kingdom, especially of God's Son, Jesus Christ.

A good teaching or preaching outline from 7:1-3 can be presented by showing the four ways in which Melchisedec is a type of Christ. The historic account of the meeting of Melchisedec and Abraham should be carefully read and analyzed (Gen. 14:18-20), from which the writer draws his conclusions. Melchisedec was a type of Christ: (1) in his name—its Hebrew meaning is "King of Righteousness"; (2) in his political position—he was "King of Salem," which means "King of Peace"; (3) in his religious office—he was Priest of the Most High God; (4) in reference to his genealogy—he had none, which especially stands out in light of the importance of genealogies to the Aaronic priests.

In 7:4-6 four things are emphasized which show the surpassing eminence of this mysterious figure, Melchisedec: (1) the very name of the one to whom he is superior—"even Abraham"; (2) the important title which belonged to Abraham—"the patriarch"; (3) the fact that Abraham voluntarily gave him a tenth part of the spoils; (4) the fact that Melchisedec in turn blessed Abraham and Abraham gladly received the blessing.

This passage of Scripture offers a wonderful opportunity to teach about the subject of tithing. We note several things about tithing. (1) In its origin (this is the first reference to tithing in Scripture) tithing was voluntary. Nothing required Abraham to tithe to

Melchisedec. He did it freely out of respect for Melchisedec's exalted position. Our giving should always be done willingly, "for God loveth a cheerful giver" (2 Cor. 9:7).

(2) Tithing was an acknowledgment of the blessing which Abraham received from Melchisedec. Our generous giving also acknowledges that "every good gift and every perfect gift is from above."

(3) The second person in the O.T. who pledged a tithe or a tenth was Jacob, as he was leaving the land of Canaan to visit his pagan uncle Laban (Gen. 28:19-22). His pledge was in regard to Bethel, where he had his dream of personal communication with God. He promised to build God a house at Bethel (which means "house of God") and give his tithes for its support. One of the main reasons we also give is to support God's work, both in the local church and in ministries outside the church.

(4) Under the law the Lord commanded the Levites to receive tithes from Israel for the support of their ministry. They did not receive an inheritance with the other tribes, and their main duty in life was priestly service to the worshiping community (Num. 18:20-24). In like manner N.T. Christians give their tithes and offerings to support the ministry of the church, for those who "preach the gospel should live of the gospel" (1 Cor. 9:14).

(5) Though God is always good to us, far beyond what we deserve, Scripture makes a direct connection between the abundance of blessings in our lives and our generosity in giving. The Lord challenged Israel concerning their lack of response in this area and invited them to participate in these words, "Prove me now herewith, saith the LORD of hosts, if I will not open you the windows of heaven, and pour you out a blessing" (Mal. 3:10). In like manner, Paul reminded us, "God is able to make all grace abound toward you" (2 Cor. 9:8).

(6) Jesus commended the Pharisees' adherence to tithing, but He strongly criticized them for their lack of attention to even more important heart matters like judgment, mercy, and faith. He concluded, "These ought ye to have done [tithing], and not to leave the other undone" (judgment, mercy, and faith) (Mt. 23:23). It would be possible for an individual to be very faithful in his giving, and other formal and outward things of the Christian life, and yet die unsaved and spend eternity in Hell. As important as giving is, it must truly come from a heart that loves God to be of any value at all.

(7) The N.T. principle of giving is according to one's ability (see Acts 11:29; 2 Cor. 8:12-15; 9:6-8). Logically, that means all giving should start with the tithe, the minimum obligation under the O.T. law. But many Christians whom God has blessed in a special way should do more than that; I have heard that J.C. Penny came to the point that he gave 90% of his income to the Lord's work.

Those who are not familiar with Scriptures may find the principle emphasized in vv. 9, 10 difficult to grasp—the principle of headship, representation, and imputation. The principle is based on a declaration of God, not by the person himself or by some other man, that the individual is the head of a particular race or nation. In such a case the actions of that individual are counted as applying to the race or nation that has a physical or spiritual connection with him, so that those who have this connection receive either the blessing or the curse of those actions: that is, the blessing or the curse is imputed to them. Three prime examples are emphasized in Scripture: (1) the application of the sin of Adam in the Garden of Eden to the entire human race (see Gen. 2:17; Rom. 5:12; 1 Cor. 15:22, 45-47); (2) the application of Abraham's act of tithing to Melchisedec to his descendants, specifically to Levi and the priests of Israel that came from his line (Heb. 7:9, 10); (3) the application of Christ's righteousness and His payment of the penalty of our sins on the cross to those who are in Him by faith (see 1 Cor. 15:22, 45-47; 2 Cor. 5:21; 1 Pet. 3:18; Gal. 2:20; Eph. 2:5, 6; Jn. 1:11, 12).

In Heb. 7:11 the writer makes reference to the lack of perfection on the part of the Levitical priesthood which caused the need for a new priesthood as promised through David in Ps. 110:4. The words "perfected," "perfection," and "made perfect" occur frequently throughout the book. Perfection, as used in Hebrews, always has the idea of completeness in relation to a specific goal. The references in Hebrews can be divided up into at least three categories. First, the Levitical Priesthood was lacking in perfection with regard to: (a) the priesthood itself (7:11), (b) the law upon which it was based (7:19), and (c) the sacrificial system (9:9; 10:1). Second, Jesus Christ was made perfect as our High Priest with regard to: (a) the sufferings which qualified Him to serve (2:10; 5:8, 9), (b) the oath which gave authority to His priesthood (7:28), and (c) the sacrifice which never needed repeating (9:9-12). Third, believers themselves have now been perfected through the righteousness of Christ with regard to: (a) the need for continuation until the goal is complete (6:1; 10:14), (b) the noble company which we join as believers (11:40; 12:23), and (c) the evidence of our faith in a life of obedience to His will (13:21).

In turning to the broader scope of the N.T., this perfection for believers, according to Pink (382) is manifested in: (a) righteousness (2 Cor. 5:21); (b) peace (Rom. 5:1); (c) light (Jn. 1:18; 1 Jn. 2:8); (d) access to God (Heb. 10:19, 22; Eph. 2:18); (e) unveiling of the future state (Jn. 14:1-3; Rev. 1:19); (f) joy in our personal lives (Rom. 14:17; 1 Pet. 1:8), and (g) glorying in the Lord (1 Cor. 1:29-31).

Every part of 7:16 stands out in contrast. The contrast is between "the law of a carnal commandment" and "the power of an endless life." It is the contrast between the old Levitical priesthood and God's new priest, Jesus Christ, who is modeled after the ancient order of Melchisedec. But the contrast is not only in the two phrases, but also in each word of the phrases: (a) "law" is contrasted with "power," (b) "commandment" stands in contrast with "life," and (c) "carnal" is seen in contrast with "endless." See the commentary for details about each word.

Hebrews 7:25 is perhaps the most outstanding verse in the chapter. The subject is the ministry of Christ as our High Priest. The verse explains: (1) the power of His ministry—"wherefore he is able"; (2) the content of His ministry—"to save," that is, "to keep on saving"; (3) the extent of His ministry—"to the uttermost"; (4) the condition (limitation) of His ministry—those "that come unto God by him," that is, "those who keep on coming to God by Him"; (5) the reason for His ministry—"seeing he ever liveth to make intercession for them."

In 7:26-28 Christ is described as our High Priest in relationship to: (1) His personal character—"holy, harmless, and undefiled"; (2) His relation to sinners—"separate from sinners"; (3) His present position—"made higher than the heavens"; (4) His permanent sacrifice—"this he did once, when he offered up himself"; and (5) His favored relationship with God—not "men . . . which have infirmity," but "the Son, who is consecrated [perfected] for evermore."

D. The work of Christ as High Priest (8:1—10:39)

The writer goes into much more detail about the priestly work of Christ in chapters 8—10. In chapter 7 he has introduced us to the idea of Christ as High Priest according to a different order, the order of Melchisedec. Now he wants to show us how the O.T. institutions were types and shadows of better things under the priestly ministry of Jesus Christ. Thus we will see in these chapters a contrast between the old and new tabernacle, the old and new covenant or testament, the old and new sacrifice, and the old and new way to God. He concludes chapter 10 with another strong warning about the severe and eternal consequences of turning away from the superior work of Christ to that which is manifestly inferior, the totally ineffective service of the Levitical order.

1. Tabernacle and priesthood a type of Christ's work as High Priest (8:1-5)

In the first five verses of chapter 8 the writer emphasizes the main point, which is drawn from the previous discussion and will be expanded in subsequent discussion in chapters 8—10. Those O.T. institutions—like tabernacle, priesthood, and sacrifices—were never meant to be an end in themselves. They were merely types and shadows which pointed toward a perfect fulfillment in the coming of Christ.

a. The main point emphasized (8:1, 2)

1 Now of the things which we have spoken *this is* the sum: We have such an high priest, who is set on the right hand of the throne of the Majesty in the heavens;
2 A minister of the sanctuary, and of the true tabernacle, which the Lord pitched, and not man.

"Now" (Greek *de*) marks the transition from the writer's detailed discussion about Christ as High Priest according to the order of Melchisedec to further explanations of His priestly ministry. The subject will still be our Lord's work as High Priest, but he is moving on to other aspects of that ministry. The sum (Greek *kephalaion*), appears at the front of v. 1 in the original for emphasis. The word can mean a sum or a summary of a subject which has just been addressed. However, the same word can also mean, "This is the main point," and in this context that is the meaning that fits best. The statement that the writer makes in the latter part of v. 1 and in v. 2 is not a summary of what has been said in chapter 7, but rather an announcement of the subject on which he will elaborate in chapter 8. The word looks forward rather than backward. Most commentators agree on this approach (Westcott 212; Lenski 248; Alford 146; D. Guthrie 170; Yeager 265; see also NIV, NASB).

In line with this, "Of the things which we have spoken" is literally "About the things which are being spoken." The writer is making a transition from his discussion of Christ's priestly order to further details of His work as High Priest: "Now this is the main point about the things which are being spoken." The main point is: "We have such an high priest, who is set on the right hand of the throne of the Majesty in the heavens." "Such" (Greek *toioutos*) "an high priest" also looks forward to the discussion of Jesus' redeeming work as Priest in the following verses, perhaps all the way through 10:18. His redeeming and intercessory work is made possible by the fact that He "is set on the right hand of the throne of the Majesty in the heavens." "Who is set" might be translated "who sat." This seated position of our Lord's present ministry was first introduced in 1:3. It is again emphasized in 10:12 and 12:2. As mentioned earlier, this position stresses the fact that Christ's work is finished, His sacrifice is permanent, and His intercessory ministry is eternally effective.

The fact that His seated position is at "the right hand of the throne" of God the Father confirms His authority and power. His work of redemption has been approved by the Father, as is shown by His resurrection and ascension to His present position. The ministry of the Levitical priests of the O.T. was always carried out from a standing position. They never sat down while performing their ministry in the tabernacle because their work was never finished. The annual sacrifice for sins for the nation of Israel on the Day of Atonement had to be repeated again each year. This contrast between the standing position of the O.T. priests and the seated position of our Lord is pointed out in more detail in 10:11, 12. He sits as the King/Priest at the right hand of the throne "of the Majesty in the heavens" (see 1:3).

Though He sits because His redemptive work is complete, He still serves for He is "a minister of the sanctuary." The word translated "minister" (Greek *leitourgos*) is used in the Septuagint (LXX) to refer to the service of various officials, including, of course, the service of the priests. Paul uses it of his own ministry of service (Rom. 15:16) as well as the service of civil authorities (Rom. 13:6). (Our English words "liturgy" and "liturgical" come from this root.) From His seated position Christ is a minister "of the sanctuary" (Greek *ta hagia*). The word literally means "the Holies," and in this context it refers to the main part of the tabernacle, the Holy Place and the Holy of Holies. But the emphasis here is on the Holy of Holies since in Heaven these have become one.

The writer adds a further designation in apposition with the previous one: Jesus' place of ministry is not only "the sanctuary," but is also "the true tabernacle." Hebrews always refers to the "tabernacle," the original tent of worship which Moses and the Israelites pitched in the wilderness, never to the Temple, whether of Solomon, Zerubbabel, or Herod. In his description of this tabernacle he never refers to the Outer Court, only to the Holy Place and the Holy of Holies (see especially 9:1-10). This is due, no doubt, to the fact that the writer of Hebrews is dealing with the finished work of Christ. The sacrifices of the ancient altar are no longer needed, and the place where it was located is not even mentioned.

Christ's present ministry does not take place in the ancient tabernacle but rather in "the true tabernacle." "True" (Greek *alethinos*) means "genuine," the real thing. The apostle John especially liked the word, representing Christ as the true light (Jn. 1:9), the true bread (Jn. 6:32), and the true vine (Jn. 15:1).

The reason that the tabernacle in which Christ presently ministers is the true one is because it is the one "which the Lord pitched, and not man." The reference is, of course, to our Lord's present ministry in Heaven. He is not referring to some visible tabernacle which happens to be located in Heaven, but rather to Heaven itself, as 9:24 makes abundantly clear. The earthly tabernacle was set up by Moses and his assistants, but the heavenly tabernacle is not touched by human hands (Is. 42:5). When John says, "The Word became flesh, and dwelt among us," the word "dwelt" (Greek *skenoo*) is the verb form of "tabernacle." The O.T. tabernacle was the appointed place where God appeared to man. When Jesus came, that tabernacle was no longer needed, for God dwelt in His fullness in the person of Jesus Christ. Now that Christ has made His priestly sacrifice in our behalf, He continues His priestly ministry of intercession in the very presence of God, the true tabernacle of which the O.T. one was only a picture, a prophecy of better things to come.

b. Tabernacle and priesthood point to Christ (8:3-5)

3 For every high priest is ordained to offer gifts and sacrifices: wherefore *it is* of necessity that this man have somewhat also to offer.

4 For if he were on earth, he should not be a priest, seeing that there are priests that offer gifts according to the law:
5 Who serve unto the example and shadow of heavenly things, as Moses was admonished of God when he was about to make the tabernacle: for, See, saith he, *that* thou make all things according to the pattern shewed to thee in the mount.

"For" (Greek *gar*) in v. 3 introduces the first explanation of the main point which the writer emphasized in vv. 1 and 2. He will expand his explanation throughout chapters 8, 9, and 10. The first phrase, "Every high priest is ordained to offer gifts and sacrifices," is an exact reflection of the writer's previous definition of the O.T. priesthood in 5:1. The primary function of the O.T. priesthood was "to offer," literally "for the purpose of offering." Though there were other peripheral duties of the priesthood, this was the main one.

The verb reflects the repeated and ineffective sacrifices under the O.T. system (Greek present tense). The "gifts and sacrifices" cover all the offerings made, but especially those made on the Day of Atonement. Some of the offerings were "gifts" of praise and thanksgiving to God, while others were "sacrifices" for sins, both for the priest and for the people. When the writer defined the priesthood in 5:1-4, his emphasis was on his call or appointment to the office. Here the emphasis is on the offering or sacrifice to be made. If Jesus Christ is a Priest in the fullest sense of the word, He must fulfill this priestly duty as well. Thus, the writer declares, "Wherefore *it is* of necessity that this man have somewhat also to offer." For the O.T. priest the "necessity" (Greek *anagkaios*) was a matter of his duty, of the full performance of his office, but for Christ it was a divine necessity to open the way of access to God and provide forgiveness for the sins of men (D. Guthrie 171).

The writer purposely uses indefinite terms at this point, "this man" and "somewhat" or "something," since he will give details about these matters in his subsequent explanation. He has already defined, however, what He has to offer in 7:27 when he declared, "For this he did once, when he offered up himself." But he will provide further definition along this line in 9:14 ("the blood of Christ"), in 9:26 ("the sacrifice of himself"), and in 10:10 ("the body of Jesus Christ"). The writer uses vagueness at this point to create a sense of anticipation for the fuller description to come. "To offer" is expressed as completed action (Greek aorist) in obvious contrast to the continuous offering of "gifts and sacrifices" by the O.T. priests in the first phrase of the verse. When Christ offered Himself, it was an offering that would never need repeating.

Thus our Lord's priestly ministry must involve a different sacrifice, offered in a different sanctuary. The writer explains in v. 4, "For if he were on earth, he should not be a priest." As the writer has explained earlier, He would not and could not be an earthly priest, both because their ministry had proved ineffective (7:11, 12) and because He was not even from the right tribe to serve as an earthly priest (7:13, 14). In His earthly ministry, Christ regularly visited the Temple as a whole and the outer precincts of the Temple to worship, pray, and teach people whom He met there (Lk. 22:53). He never once entered the inner sanctuary of the Temple where only the Levitical priests could minister. On earth He was a layman, but in Heaven He is a Priest.

Consequently, the conditional sentence in v. 4 is one that is assumed untrue (Greek second class condition): "If He were on earth {which He is not], he would not be a priest." The reason Jesus could not serve as an earthly priest was: "Seeing that there are priests that offer gifts according to the law." There cannot be two divinely appointed priestly orders on earth. If the first order, the Levitical order, had been effective, there would be no need for another priestly order (7:11, 12). But the very fact that David prophesied about another priestly order (Ps. 110:4), the priestly order of Melchisedec, strongly implied the failure of that order of priests. "Gifts" is the abbreviated form of "gifts and sacrifices" in v. 3 and includes both ideas. These gifts are "according to the law," that is, they are offered under the authority of the law and according to the specifications of the law.

In v. 5 the writer points out that it is these priests "who serve unto the example and shadow of heavenly things." The word translated "serve" (Greek *latreuo*) is commonly used of worship or priestly service (Bruce 165). The writer uses it again in this manner in 9:9, 14; 10:2; 12:28; 13:10. Once again, the usage strongly indicates that the service was still going on at the time of this writing (Greek present tense). This priestly service under the O.T. was never meant to be an end in itself. These earthly institutions—the priesthood, the sacrifices, and the tabernacle itself—all served, and were serving at the time, as an "example" (Greek *hupodeigma*) of a fuller manifestation in Heaven. The word refers to a copy of the real thing, a model offered for imitation, a sketch, tracing, or outline (Lenski 255). The same word is used in 9:23 in the same sense, translated "patterns." The use of the word "shadow" (Greek *skia*) furthers this idea. The priests were imperfect models of the Greater Priest who was to come. When an individual stands in bright sunlight, his body will cast a shadow, an outline, but the shadow is not the real thing. It is only a dark outline pointing to the real thing.

These earthly institutions served as examples and shadows "of the heavenly things." They had a real purpose and their proper use was essential for the times, but when the real thing appears, the model or sketch must be set aside. An architect's drawings are quite important in the process of building the house, but when the house is complete, the drawings are set aside. "The heavenly things" (Greek *epouranios*) refer to the fulfillment of these earthly institutions in Heaven itself. It speaks of things that are in the very presence of God. Paul especially likes to use the term in his epistle to the Ephesians (see Eph. 1:3, 20; 2:6; 3:10; 6:12) where he means God's awesome and exalted presence, His right hand where our Lord presently sits.

As further evidence of the fact that the O.T. institutions were intended as sketches, outlines, or models of the real thing, the writer refers to God's instructions to Moses in the book of Exodus, "As Moses was admonished of God when he was about to make the tabernacle." "Admonished" (Greek *chrematizo*) is used when authoritative directions are given, especially those which involve a divine oracle. The word is used in the birth story of Christ when the wise men were warned by God to avoid Herod in their return home (Mt. 2:12) and when Joseph was warned by God about the danger of Archelaus, the son of Herod, which resulted in his making their home in Galilee (Mt. 2:22). The writer's point is that God's instructions to Moses "when he was about to make the tabernacle" were very precise. The warning was originally given before the details about the construction of the tabernacle were laid out. Though the actual quotation is from Ex. 25:40, the same instructions, almost word for word, were first spoken in Ex. 25:9.

The importance of this admonition is emphasized by its repetition in Ex. 26:30 and 27:8. The writer quotes the admonition, "See, saith he, *that* thou make all things according to the pattern shewed to thee in the mount." The admonition to see means "to see to it," "to closely observe that the desired goal is accomplished." And this meticulous concern about the details of the tabernacle did not just apply to certain sections, or to the tabernacle in its broad design. Moses, rather, was instructed to "make all things" in strict obedience to God's instructions. He was told specifically to follow "the pattern shewed to thee in the mount."

The word "pattern" (Greek *tupos*) can have several different meanings. (1) Some think that it merely means the vivid description which God gave Moses, recorded in the instructions given in Exodus (Westcott 216). (2) Others think that it refers to a drawing, a sketch, a blueprint, a tracing, or an outline (Lenski 255; Kistemaker 220). (3) Still others see it applying to a scale model, a miniature copy of the end product, either real (Bruce 165) or in the form of a vision (Barnes 174). (4) Finally, some have suggested that the pattern might refer to a vision of Heaven itself which the Lord revealed to Moses on Sinai. Bruce (165) and Lenski (255) mention this as a possibility. The inclination to think of something visible comes from the fact that the pattern was one which God "shewed" to Moses on Mt. Sinai. However, it does not seem that "shewed" has to be taken in its most literal sense. According to common understanding, we might say that we have shown someone how to build something when we have done nothing more than give them verbal or written instructions about the construction. Certainly nothing more than this is specified in the text of Exodus. There is no clear reference to any scale model or drawing and there is certainly no indication that Moses was given some supernatural vision of Heaven itself. This point of view would also explain the care taken in giving the details in Exodus 25—30 in preparation for the construction, and then repeating those details, almost verbatim, when the completed tabernacle was set up in Exodus 36-40.

2. Work of Christ based on a new covenant (8:6-13)

In 8:1-5 the writer has pointed out that Christ is the true High Priest who is presently interceding for us in the true tabernacle "on the right hand of the throne of the Majesty in the heavens." He pointed out that the O.T. priests and tabernacle were types and shadows of the ministry of Jesus Christ. Now he emphasizes the fact that this new priesthood and new tabernacle call for a new covenant.

a. The necessity of the new covenant (8:6, 7)

6 But now hath he obtained a more excellent ministry, by how much also he is the mediator of a better covenant, which was established upon better promises.
7 For if that first *covenant* had been faultless, then should no place have been sought for the second.

"But" completes the contrast which was introduced in v. 4 (Greek *men/de* clauses). He is not on earth but in Heaven where He is ministering in our behalf. This wonderful and effective ministry of Christ is "now," in contrast with the O.T. ministry which was in the past and which it has replaced. It is a ministry that Jesus Christ "hath obtained" (Greek *tugchano*), has come to possess through His work in His life, death, and resurrection. The verb emphasizes a past act with continuing result (Greek perfect tense): once He had obtained it, that ministry continues to the present.

His redemptive work has resulted in "a more excellent ministry." In this verse the writer again stresses, as he does throughout the epistle, the overall theme of the superiority of Christ. "Ministry" (Greek *leitourgia*) comes from the same root as "minister" in v. 2. Both words refer to the service of divine worship and priestly intercession. The word in v. 2 points to the person who is serving, while the word here emphasizes the office in which He serves.

The means or the cause of this more excellent ministry is indicated in "by how much also he is the mediator of a better covenant, which was established upon better promises." "Mediator" (Greek *mesites*) refers to someone who stands in the middle, who brings parties at variance with each other to reconciliation. The writer presents Christ in this role again in 9:15 and 12:24. The word is used in Gal. 3:19, 20 concerning the mediation of the law through angels and through Moses. In the papyri the word was used in business for an arbitrator who sought to bring two groups or individuals to an agreement (Bruce 167). In this case, however, the parties are by no means equal, for we have on the one hand a righteous God and on the other hand an offending an offensive sinner. One party is completely holy, with no blemishes whatsoever, while the other party stands in spiritual ruin, whose "righteousnesses *are* as filthy rags" (Is. 64:6). Such a reconciliation demands a special mediator, one who not only understands both parties, but who is Himself a partaker of the nature of both parties, the God-man, Christ Jesus.

Job longed for such a mediator in his complaints against God, one who would stand as a "daysman [same word as here in LXX] betwixt us, that might lay his hand upon us both" (Job 9:33). Our Lord is that Mediator, perhaps to a far greater extent than Job could ever have hoped. In this role Paul observes that there is "one mediator between God and men, the man Christ Jesus" (1 Tim. 2:5).

In His more excellent ministry Jesus serves as the mediator of "a better covenant" (Greek *diatheke*). This "better covenant" or "better testament" has already been mentioned in 7:22, where Jesus was said to be the "surety," the guarantee of the better "testament" (KJV) or "covenant" (NIV). The offices of surety and mediator are complementary to one another. A "covenant" is a promise, an agreement, a commitment which is formed between two parties, not necessarily on an equal basis, which may have conditions and limitations. A "testament" is a will, a document that states the terms of inheritance and specifies the heirs of the estate. A covenant may not require a death for its inauguration, but a testament or a will never takes effect apart from the death of the testator (Heb. 9:16). The Hebrew term (*berith*) and the Greek term were evidently broad enough to include both ideas, but in English two different words are demanded. This causes a problem for translators in this section of Hebrews. Though here in 8:6 and back in 7:22 "covenant" may be the better choice, clearly in 9:16 "testament" is the meaning. In any case, we have both a better covenant and a better testament through the work of our Savior, Jesus Christ.

Furthermore, the new covenant is better because it "was established upon better promises." "Established" (Greek *nomotheteo*) looks back to its point of enactment, the point at which this better covenant became legal or was in force, that is, at the point of Christ's death and resurrection. (The same word was used in 7:11 with regard to the people receiving the law.) But as it is used here it also emphasizes the fact that this better covenant has been enacted and remains in force to the present (Greek perfect tense), just as the previous covenant of law was enacted and remained in force until it was set aside by the new covenant. The "better promises" are outlined in some detail in the quotation from Jeremiah which follows.

For (v. 7) introduces the writer's argument for the replacement of the old covenant. The Jews held the covenant of law, the Mosaic covenant, in high regard, as they indeed should, for it had been given to them from the hand of God. Unfortunately, however, they had misinterpreted the purpose of the law. Paul, who had himself been a Pharisee and knew better than most how they thought, emphasized their gross misuse of the law. They must realize that "by the works of the law shall no flesh be justified" (Gal. 2:16), and that, "If righteousness come by the law, then Christ is dead in vain" (Gal. 2:21). He went on to argue that the covenant of faith, God's covenant with Abraham, preceded the law by 430 years (Gal. 3:17). The covenant of law was never intended to replace the covenant of promise. Thus, it would be a serious mistake for these Hebrew Christians to consider returning to a system that was never intended to bring salvation.

The writer points out, "If that first *covenant* had been faultless, then should no place have been sought for the second." As in 7:11 and 8:4, "If" introduces a statement that is contrary to fact (Greek second class condition). If the first covenant had proven to be without fault, there would have been no need for another covenant; but since it was not faultless, then a new covenant was necessary. Though the word *covenant* is not in the original (as AV indicates by italics), it is correctly understood from v. 6. Though the Abrahamic covenant of faith, promise, and grace was actually first chronologically—as Paul argues and I have noted above—in the present context, the Mosaic covenant, the covenant of law, was "first" in relation to the new covenant which came through Jesus Christ.

The argument which the writer uses here concerning the insufficiency of the old covenant has already been used earlier regarding the Levitical priesthood (see 7:11), as well as regarding the "rest" of Canaan in Joshua's day (see 4:8). Note that in each of these cases the writer's premise is based on his quotation of O.T. Scripture: for the insufficiency of Joshua's rest, Ps. 95:7-11; for the insufficiency of the Levitical priesthood, Ps. 110:4; and now, for the insufficiency of the old covenant, the passage from Jeremiah which we are about to consider. It was God, of course, who sought the place "for the second" in His declaration through Jeremiah.

b. The Scriptural background of the new covenant (8:8-12)

Jeremiah's prophecy about the new covenant (Jer. 31:31-34), which the writer quotes to prove that God sought a place for a second covenant, can be divided into two parts. He first emphasizes the objects of the new covenant, the house of Israel and the house of Judah, and then he describes the nature of the new covenant.

(1) With regard to its objects (8:8, 9)

8 For finding fault with them, he saith, Behold, the days come, saith the Lord, when I will make a new covenant with the house of Israel and with the house of Judah:
9 Not according to the covenant that I made with their fathers in the day when I took them by the hand to lead them out of the land of Egypt; because they continued not in my covenant, and I regarded them not, saith the Lord.

"For" introduces the writer's explanation of the insufficiency of the old covenant by quoting the promise of the new covenant from Jer. 31:31-34. He introduces the quotation with an observation, "Finding fault with them." "Finding fault" (Greek *memphomai*) comes from the same root as the word "faultless" (Greek *amemptos*) in v. 7, and by this the writer emphasizes the connection. But in v. 7 he blames the first covenant, while in v. 8 he blames the people: the fault is "with them." The obvious solution is that both are true.

The covenant of law was fine when used for the purpose intended. It stated God's high expectations for His people and pronounced severe judgments for those who failed to adhere. It was especially designed to bring the Israelites to the point of frustration with their own righteousness and their own abilities, to recognize that they could not, in themselves, meet God's standards of holiness. When they came to this realization, they were to cast themselves in faith upon the Lord for His gifts of mercy and forgiveness (see Dt. 7:9-11; Prov. 3:5, 6). The Day of Atonement emphasized for the nation God's mercy and forgiveness for those who would put their trust in Him. The purpose of the law, in a word, was to make sin "exceeding sinful" (Rom. 7:13). The major problem with the covenant of law was that it had the power to condemn, but not the power to make alive (see Rom. 7, especially 7:5-10; Hagner 122). A new covenant was needed for that. But as v. 8 points out there was also a serious problem with Israel's disobedience. The fault was not only a problem with the covenant itself; more than that, it was a problem with the people. While they delighted in their claim of the covenant of law and of their national pride in it, they actually practiced wholesale disregard of it. They had persisted in this disobedience even to the point where God carried out His final judgment against them (see Dt. 28:63-68) by sending them into the captivity of pagan nations: first, of Israel into Assyria in 722 B.C., and then of Judah into Babylon in 586 B.C. Jeremiah was in the midst of experiencing the captivity of Judah when he wrote these words from the Lord which the writer of Hebrews quotes here. Jeremiah and the remnant of Israel needed a word of hope in that day, and the present audience needs to realize that what Jeremiah prophesied has now come to pass.

Jeremiah wrote: "Behold, the days come, saith the Lord, when I will make a new covenant with the house of Israel and with the house of Judah." The writer does not identify Jeremiah; he is more concerned that his readers realize that the message is from "the Lord," the source of ultimate authority (D. Guthrie 174). "The days come" is a familiar phrase in Jeremiah, occurring more than ten times there. As usual in prophecies which related to time, it is somewhat indefinite. It is clear, however, that the writer of Hebrews firmly believes that those days have arrived.

The prophecy called for "a new covenant." The fact that God called for a new covenant in the days of Jeremiah, some 600 years earlier, implied that there were serious problems with the old covenant. The new covenant had now come in the person of God's Son, Jesus Christ. "New" (Greek *kainos*) means new in contrast to the old covenant which preceded it. But in 12:24 he uses a different word for "new" (Greek *neos*) which means intrinsically new, new in its own being as compared to the old which is worn out and in need of replacement (Westcott 220). Thus, this new covenant is totally new. It will not do at all for these Hebrew Christians to return to that which has been replaced both as the fulfillment of divine prophecy and on the basis of the shed blood of God's dear Son. Jesus Himself pointed to the fact that He was introducing a new covenant in His inauguration of the Lord's Supper (Mt. 26:28; Mk. 14:24; Lk. 22:20; 1 Cor. 11:25).

This new covenant was "with the house of Israel and with the house of Judah." The prophecy emphasizes both Israel and Judah to let us know that the covenant is with the nation as a whole, not part of it. Israel had not been a whole nation since the division occurred under Rehoboam, the son of Solomon, over a thousand years earlier. The northern ten tribes, called "Israel" after the division, never officially returned from captivity, but no doubt many of them did return when Judah began its return from Babylonian captivity about 538 B.C.

The interpretation of Jeremiah's prophecy brings us, of necessity, into commentators' viewpoints on eschatology. Some choose to reveal little or nothing about their viewpoint, however, by saying that the writer's application is limited to Hebrew Christians which make up his immediate audience (D. Guthrie 175). Some say that Israel and Judah should be taken in the broadest sense, as a symbol of the people of God without racial or national distinctions. Lenski (263) says, "Right here we have the universality of the N.T. Lost among the Gentiles and turned Gentile, the gospel goes out to all nations to bring the N.T. in Christ's blood to all." He does admit, however, that "the writer is dealing with former Jews and, thus, does not stop to bring out the universality of this final testament." Those who take this position are amillennial, like Lenski, or postmillennial, like Barnes (176). They refer for clarification to such passages as Rom. 2:28, 29 and 9:6. These interpreters do not expect any national conversion of Israel in the future.

Still others believe that the application in this context applies only to the Jewish people in the reception of the Gospel of Christ, but that this does not prohibit the expectation of a future return and conversion of Israel on the basis of other passages of Scripture (Bruce 179; Alford 151; Pink 445; MacArthur 212). These interpreters may be amillennialists, but more often are premillennialists. MacArthur, a premillennialist, points out that all of God's covenants were made with Israel, and that Gentiles share in those covenants as they come under the umbrella of God's chosen people (213).

Though the writer's present concern is with his Jewish audience and their relation to the Gospel of Christ, which he sees as the beginning of the new covenant, this does not mean that there are not other aspects in the complete accomplishment of the new covenant in the future. Other passages, such as Rom. 11:25, 26, seem to point to a future national conversion of literal Israel. Though some modern-day Jews may not know to which tribe they belong, surely God does, and Scripture suggests that saved remnants from those tribes will one day come together to form the nation of Israel, most likely in the closing events of the last days involving the tribulation and the millennium (see Rev. 7:4-8). God's original covenant with Abraham, the father of the nation of Israel, was never annulled.

Though its accomplishment has been delayed because of Israel's rebellion and rejection of His Son, it will yet be perfectly and finally fulfilled when the literal nation of Israel joins her Gentile brothers and sisters in the kingdom of God, for "the gifts and calling of God *are* without repentance" (Rom. 11:29). Thus, in this passage in Hebrews, God through Jeremiah refers to both Israel and Judah because the new covenant is with the nation as a whole, not just part of it.

In v. 9 the Lord continues to explain this new covenant negatively: it is "not according to the covenant that I made with their fathers." That it was "not according to" that first covenant means that it was not like it. It was vastly different from the Mosaic covenant, and He will specify at least three ways in which it is different in the remainder of His declaration through Jeremiah. It was the covenant that He "made with their fathers," that is, that generation of Israelites who first received the law at Sinai. But the obligation to obey that law rested upon each succeeding generation until the coming of Christ.

He further defines the time frame when that covenant was given. He declares that it was "in the day when I took them by the hand to lead them out of the land of Egypt." "In the day" does not necessarily refer to one particular day. It refers, rather, to that whole period of God's dealing with Pharaoh, the supreme ruler of Egypt, from Moses' bold challenge, "Let my people go" (Ex. 5:1, 2), through all the ten plagues, the celebration of the Passover, the exodus from Egypt, the crossing of the Red Sea, the arrival at Sinai, and the reception of the law. From a stricter point of view, however, there were two specific occasions when the Mosaic covenant was formalized. The first one was in Ex. 24:1-8 when the law was inaugurated and dedicated. The writer of Hebrews will refer to this passage more directly in 9:18-21. The second occasion was when the law was dedicated for the new generation of Israelites about to enter Canaan in Dt. 29:1-9 (see 29:1 in particular).

The Lord highlights His tender guidance of Israel by emphasizing the manner of His relationship with them. He declares, "I took them by the hand." He led them as a doting father leads an immature child. He was well aware of their spiritual ignorance heightened by long years of slavery and abuse. He was very tolerant of their doubts and rebellions to a point, for He was leading them "out of the land of Egypt" where they had been since the time Jacob and his family joined Joseph there under much better circumstances. The Scripture presents Egypt as a type of the world, and thus it emphasizes God's people coming out of Egypt, not going into it (see Gen. 13:1-4; Num. 11:4-6; Is. 30:1-3; Hos. 11:1; Mt. 2:15; Acts 7:37-39).

The Lord now gives the reason the new covenant is not at all like the old one: "because they continued not in my covenant." "They" (Greek *autoi*) is emphatic in the original. The people of Israel made a start with regard to the Mosaic covenant, but the problem was that "they continued not in my covenant." Like us, they had a free will. God never coerces people into serving Him. As far as His part is concerned, in any of the great covenants He has made, God is always faithful. But when man makes his choice not to continue in God's covenant, there will always be an appropriate response from God. All of God's covenants require continuation from men. Even this new covenant which the Lord promised by Jeremiah requires continuation. Jesus said to the Jews that had believed on Him, "If ye continue in my word, *then* are ye my disciples indeed" (Jn. 8:31). Picturing Himself as The True Vine, Jesus declared, "If a man abide not in me, he is cast forth as a branch, and is withered; and men gather them, and cast *them* into the fire, and they are burned" (Jn. 15:6).

In this case, because Israel did not continue in the Mosaic covenant, God said, "I regarded them not." Just as "they" was emphatic in the previous clause, so "I" (Greek *ego*) is emphatic here. If we do not continue in God's Word, we can expect a direct and unpleasant response from Him. Under normal circumstances our God is a caring, loving God who is deeply concerned about the welfare of His children. However, even God has His limits.

At least ten separate rebellions can be defined in the book of Numbers. Though hurt by Israel's defiance, God persisted in His regard for Israel far longer than any of us would. But the tenth rebellion, the rebellion led by the majority of the spies against the courageous challenge of Caleb and Joshua, crossed the line of no return. At that point God abandoned Israel to wallow for 40 years in the fruits of her disobedience (see Num. 14:20-38). The next morning some of those Israelites attempted to recant from their rebellion. But Moses announced in the name of the Lord, "Go not up, for the LORD *is* not among you; that ye be not smitten before your enemies" (Num. 14:42). Subsequent generations of Israelites were, by and large, no better, though the spiritual temperature of the nation did fluctuate from time to time.

(2) With regard to its nature (8:10-12)

10 For this *is* the covenant that I will make with the house of Israel after those days, saith the Lord; I will put my laws into their mind, and write them in their hearts: and I will be to them a God, and they shall be to me a people:
11 And they shall not teach every man his neighbour, and every man his brother, saying, Know the Lord: for all shall know me, from the least to the greatest.
12 For I will be merciful to their unrighteousness, and their sins and their iniquities will I remember no more.

While vv. 8, 9 defined the primary object of the new covenant, the reunited nation of Israel, vv. 10-12 describe the nature of that covenant. The Lord points to three characteristics of this new covenant: (1) It is an inner, spiritual relationship, not one which is merely formal and external (v. 10). (2) It includes a universal and innate knowledge of the Lord (v. 11). (3) It emphasizes genuine and total forgiveness (v. 12). "For" (Greek *hoti*) introduces the description of this covenant. Since it is different from the covenant that God made with the fathers of Israel, those differences must be specified. These are the "better promises" mentioned in v. 6.

Again, the one-sided aspect of this covenant, just as with all of God's covenants, stands out. He declares, "This *is* the covenant that I will make."

It is not a mutual agreement between God and Israel. God Himself makes it, and imposes His terms and conditions on the objects of the covenant. They do not have to accept those terms and conditions, but if they do not they must face devastating and eternal consequences.

The O.T. often spoke of "cutting a covenant," perhaps emphasizing the fact that the substance of the covenant was written or "cut" in stone. The N.T. uses several synonyms to describe the institution of a covenant; in fact three different words are used in 8:8, 9, and 10. The verb used in v. 10, "I will make" (Greek *diatithemi*) means to arrange or ratify a covenant or will, from the same root as the noun "covenant" itself. God is saying that He will draw up a covenant, will establish it, bring it into effect "with the house of Israel." Here He does not have to specify Israel and Judah since He has already emphasized that the divided nation is again one.

God will establish this new covenant "after those days," referring back to "the days" which were to come in v. 8. The terms of this covenant will take effect after those days have set in, when the Messianic era has been inaugurated, the same period referred to as "these last days" in 1:2. The writer of Hebrews is clearly applying the Lord's declarations in Jeremiah to the Gospel era. He is challenging these Jewish believers not to forsake this new and far superior covenant for the old and ineffective one that it had replaced. As discussed earlier, I believe that this new covenant was established with the death, resurrection, and ascension of Christ to His present position at God's right hand. But I also believe that it awaits its complete fulfillment when the nation of Israel turns to Christ at the end of the age, when Paul predicts that "all Israel shall be saved" (see Rom. 11:25-29).

This new covenant emphasizes an inner relationship with God in contrast with the more external relationship under the law: "I will put my laws into their mind, and write them in their hearts." "I will put" (though a Greek participle) is properly taken, as our translators have, as parallel to the main verb, "I will write." The two clauses form parallel descriptions of the inner nature of the new covenant (Lenski 265).

The "laws" are God's moral requirements in both the Old and New Testaments. They are the outward manifestations of the holiness of God. Under the Mosaic system, however, there was no inner motivation for obedience. Under the new covenant that motivation has come in the person of the Holy Spirit who indwells and guides all believers (Rom. 8:9). This inner motivation of our new life in the Spirit is described in some detail in Romans 8. God sent His Son to live and die for us "that the righteousness of the law might be fulfilled in us, who walk not after the flesh, but after the Spirit" (Rom. 8:4).

The marvelous result of this inner working of God's Spirit is manifested. Under this new covenant God will place these laws in their "mind" (Greek *dianoia*), the seat of thought, reasoning, and understanding; and write them in their "hearts" (Greek *kardia*), the Biblical seat of intimacy, feeling, and emotion. In combination with the will, these summarize human personality, the inner soul of man.

As a result of this inner, spiritual relationship with the Lord and His Word, He promises, "I will be to them a God, and they shall be to me a people." Even under the old covenant God had made this promise if Israel obeyed (Ex. 6:7; Lev. 26:12). In the midst of God's punishment of the northern ten tribes through Assyrian captivity, God commanded Hosea to name his son, Lo-ammi, "not my people," emphasizing the Lord's rejection of Israel for her unbelief and disobedience. But in the next breath the Lord prophesied, "In the place where it was said unto them, Ye are not my people, *there* it shall be said unto them, *Ye are* the sons of the living God" (Hos. 1:10). The perfect fulfillment of this apparently awaits that day when Heaven comes down, when "the tabernacle of God is with men, and he will dwell with them, and they shall be his people, and God himself shall be with them, *and be* their God" (Rev. 21:3).

The second aspect of the nature of the new covenant is seen in v. 11. It points to a universal and innate knowledge of the Lord: "And they shall not teach every man his neighbor, and every man his brother, saying, Know the Lord." The characteristics of this new covenant are obviously meant to be a contrast with the old covenant. Under the old covenant, knowing the Lord could mean different things. When the Scripture says about young Samuel that he "did not yet know the LORD," the meaning is, as the statement goes on to say, "Neither was the word of the LORD yet revealed unto him" (1 Sam. 3:7). Samuel already had a living relationship with God, but he had not yet become God's prophetic vessel to his generation. On the other hand, when the Scripture says that the wicked sons of Eli "knew not the LORD," it is a judgment on their spiritual and moral character (1 Sam. 2:12). They had no relation with the Lord whatsoever (Bruce 174).

The writer of Hebrews has already pointed out the manner of O.T. revelation in 1:1 as being "at sundry times and in divers manners," that is, in different parts and in different ways. Under the old covenant God spoke now to one prophet, then to another, now through a dream, then through a vision, or directly, or through a writing, and all of this over a period of more than 1,000 years. Under the new covenant of the gospel of Christ that revelation has been completed. Again, as the writer has already said, God "hath in these last days spoken unto us by *his* Son" (1:2). Because of this completed revelation and the coming of the Holy Spirit at Pentecost, the knowledge of God and His Word is now more natural and more universal within the community of believers.

Thus, the Lord explains, "For all shall know me, from the least to the greatest." Even under the old covenant the Holy Spirit existed and operated, for He is, indeed, the third person of the eternal Trinity. He certainly did not come into being on the Day of Pentecost. But in the O.T. His operation was selective, not universal, and periodic, not continuous; while in the N.T. every believer possesses the Spirit (Rom. 8:9). In the O.T. worshipers usually came to God through some human mediator, but in the N.T. we can go directly to God through Jesus Christ (1 Tim. 2:5). In a similar way John declares, "Ye have an unction from the Holy One, and ye know all things" (1 Jn. 2:20), and, "The anointing which ye have received of him abideth in you, and ye need not that any man teach you" (1 Jn. 2:27).

However, we still live in a world where the majority of those around us are unbelievers, and only believers have this knowledge that comes under the new covenant. As Paul explains, "The natural man receiveth not the things of the Spirit of God" (1 Cor. 2:14). Even this aspect of the inner and innate knowledge of God will become more universal when Christ comes to reign on earth at the end of time (Rev. 5:10; 11:15; 20:1-6). Perhaps Isaiah had this in mind when he promised, "They shall not hurt nor destroy in all my holy mountain: for the earth shall be full of the knowledge of the LORD, as the waters cover the sea" (Is. 11:9; Yeager 282). Men often were close to God even under the old covenant, as is indicated by the exalted spiritual and poetical expressions in Psalms and Proverbs, but under the new covenant such knowledge is available to all who genuinely trust Christ.

The third and final characteristic of this new covenant is complete forgiveness of sins. All of these aspects of the nature of the new covenant are obviously "better promises" than those under the old covenant, but this one is the best of all. Pink (458) says that it is the foundational mark of the new covenant: "For I will be merciful to their unrighteousness, and their sins and their iniquities will I remember no more." "Merciful" (Greek *hileos*) points to God's favor and forgiveness in spite of our guilt, in spite of the fact that we deserve punishment. But this does not mean merely overlooking our sin, pretending that it never happened. God's favor is based on the payment of the penalty for sin by Jesus Christ, forgiveness based on propitiation (Rom. 3:24, 25; 1 Jn. 2:1, 2).

The severity of our need is indicated by the use of three different words to describe our offenses. "Unrighteousness" (Greek *adikia*) refers to wrongs done to God, violations of His laws and commandments. The word is actually in the plural, pointing to multiple offenses which make up the whole. "Sins" (Greek *hamartia*) point to missing the mark in our lives, especially the mark of glorifying God (Rom. 3:23), and "iniquities" (Greek *anomia*) refer to lawlessness, acts committed in defiance and rebellion against the known will of God. (Some manuscripts do not have this third term.)

The Lord's forgiveness goes even further than being merciful, withholding the punishment which we justly deserve. He promises, "Their sins and their iniquities will I remember no more." In His essential being God is omniscient. He knows everything all the time. That he will not "remember" our iniquities does not limit his knowledge of them. What God is promising is that He will not hold our sins and iniquities against us. When He forgives us on the basis of the shed blood of Christ, our sins are "covered," (Ps. 32:1); they are removed from us "as far as the east is from the west" (Ps. 103:12); they are cast "into the depths of the sea" (Mic. 7:19).

God's mercy and forgiveness come in response to genuine repentance on the part of the sinner. When David committed the awful sins of adultery and murder, he realized that mere rituals and ceremonies would not do. He prayed to the Lord, "Thou desirest not sacrifice; else would I give *it*: thou delightest not in burnt offering. The sacrifices of God *are* a broken spirit: a broken and a contrite heart, O God, thou wilt not despise" (Ps. 51:16, 17).

c. The realization of the new covenant (8:13)

13 In that he saith, A new *covenant*, he hath made the first

old. Now that which decayeth and waxeth old *is* ready to vanish away.

The quotation from Jer. 31:31-34 has extended from vv. 8-12. "In that he saith" still refers to the Lord as the speaker, not to Jeremiah who was only the human instrument. Now that he has concluded the quotation, the writer makes a very brief but pointed conclusion, and he does so by using a technique that he repeats several times throughout the epistle. He takes one word from the extended quotation and drives it home: the word "new," drawn from Jer. 31:31 as quoted in v. 8.

When one speaks of something as "new" in contrast to something that is already in existence, he is strongly implying that the thing already in existence is old, out of date, useless. That is the point that the writer is making in reference to the Mosaic covenant. When the Lord spoke through Jeremiah of a new covenant, "he hath made the first old." "He hath made . . . old" (Greek perfect tense) indicates that the first covenant had already become old in Jeremiah's day, and that status would continue with no hope of renewal or modification.

Now (Greek *de*) introduces a continuation of the application, emphasizing the coming doom for the old covenant: "That which decayeth and waxeth old is ready to vanish away." "Decayeth" (Greek *palaioo*) "and waxeth old" (Greek *gerasko*) translate words that are almost synonyms. The first indicates the process of becoming old, often with the connotation of becoming useless (Bauer 606), while the second one is the more general word for "growing old." The continuous action (Greek present tense: "that which continues to decay and grow old") further emphasizes the aging process in relation to the old covenant. If it was already old in Jeremiah's day, some 600 years earlier, it must be thoroughly decrepit during this time shortly before A.D. 70.

A covenant that is in such a state "*is* ready to vanish away" (Greek *aphanismos*). A word from the same root is used in Mt. 6:19 with reference to the disappearance of earthly treasure when attacked by moth and rust, and in Jas. 4:14 in describing our lives as like a vapor which "vanisheth away." Such is the status of the old covenant. It, too, must be set aside since it has served its useful purpose and is no longer functional or effective. Though it was once good as a type and a shadow of better things to come, it makes absolutely no sense to return to it, as some of these Hebrews were considering, when the real thing is now in effect.

The dissolution of the old covenant implies the dissolution of all that went with it: the priesthood, the sacrifices, the tabernacle, and the later Temple, which was evidently still standing. Jesus Christ had prophesied this when He declared about the Temple, "There shall not be left here one stone upon another, that shall not be thrown down" (Mt. 24:2), and then He had declared more specifically, "This generation shall not pass, till all these things be fulfilled" (Mt. 24:34). The Jewish leaders, charging Stephen with blasphemy and capital crimes, claimed they had heard him say "that this Jesus of Nazareth shall destroy this place, and shall change the customs which Moses delivered us" (Acts 6:14). Paul also spoke of the new testament or covenant and the old testament or covenant in 2 Cor. 3:6, 14. Thus, the coming of the new covenant in Jesus Christ should be no surprise to these Hebrew Christians since it had been predicted by God Himself in Jeremiah and had been proclaimed by Christ and the preachers of the early church.

Summary (8:1-13)

In chapter 8 the writer begins to emphasize Christ's work as High Priest, and this emphasis continues through the end of chapter 10. The fact that Jesus Christ is currently serving as our High Priest at God's right hand in Heaven—which is the true tabernacle—is the main point which connects chapter 7—His priesthood according to the order of Melchisedec, with chapters 8—10, which give the details of Christ's priestly work (8:1, 2). If Christ were still on earth, He would not be carrying on a priestly ministry, because the Levitical priests had done that for hundreds of years, and were evidently still doing that at the time of the writing of Hebrews. But that ancient priesthood, and the tabernacle in which they ministered, were never intended to be ends in themselves. They served as "the example and shadow" of the true tabernacle, Heaven itself, and of Jesus Christ, our eternal High Priest, who ministers there.

It was for that reason that the Lord kept stressing to Moses in Exodus about the need to construct the tabernacle exactly as he had been shown on Sinai (8:3-5). If the tabernacle and its ministry pointed directly to the ministry of Christ, then every division and every piece of furniture pointed to some aspect of the priestly work of the Messiah.

The writer is not merely introducing us to a new tabernacle and a new priesthood, he is introducing us to a completely new covenant, a covenant that had been prophesied some 600 years earlier through the prophet Jeremiah (8:8-12). In pointing this out, the writer quotes Jer. 31:31-34, which gives the Scriptural background for this new covenant. He first emphasizes the objects of this new covenant, "the house of Israel . . . and the house of Judah." This revealed the fact that the nation of Israel would once again be reunited, a prophecy which has not yet been completely fulfilled. Judah did return from Babylonian captivity in 538 B.C., but that return did not immediately bring about the new covenant. Though there was never any further problem with idolatry, one of the main sins that had led them into captivity, there soon developed another problem which was even more insidious, the combined problem of formalism and self-righteousness.

Thus, the Lord used Jeremiah to describe the nature of the new covenant with the nation of Israel, involving three special features in contrast to the old covenant of Moses. First, it was based on a direct heart relationship with God Himself, not a formal relationship involving a priestly mediator from the line of Aaron. It also included a personal and universal knowledge of God. These first two characteristics of the new covenant were at least partially fulfilled in the coming of the Holy Spirit to the infant church on the Day of Pentecost (Acts 2). However, perfect fulfillment of these terms of the new covenant evidently awaits the development of the last days of this era, including the personal return of Christ to this earth. The third and final characteristic of the new covenant is complete forgiveness of sins, which is especially emphasized in the fact that Christ's sacrifice for sin never has to be repeated, as did the annual sin offerings of the Day of Atonement (8:10-12).

Now that this new covenant has been described in detail, the writer insists that the time of its inauguration has now arrived. The Lord would not have spoken of a "new covenant" if the first one was not becoming old, even in Jeremiah's day. When something becomes old, it must be replaced, and that is exactly what has happened through the life, death, resurrection, and ascension of Christ to His present priestly position (8:13). If such is the case with the new covenant, in contrast with the old, it will certainly not do for these Hebrew Christians to consider returning to the old ways in the face of increasing persecution of Christianity.

Application: Teaching and Preaching the Passage

In Heb. 8:1-3 we have the High Priestly ministry of Jesus Christ described. The writer speaks of: (1) The *nature* of His ministry—"We have such an high priest." In these verses the writer is emphasizing the chief point of his argument about Christ as our High Priest. He is connecting what he has said in chapter 7 about the new order of Christ's priesthood after that of Melchisedec with what he says in chapter 8 about the new location of His ministry. In Jesus Christ we have "such an high priest" who is able to meet all of our needs, both for salvation and for sanctification. His ministry is complete in all the ways in which the ministry of the O.T. priests was incomplete.

(2) The *basis* of His ministry—He is "set on the right hand of the throne of the Majesty in the heavens." One of the main reasons His ministry is so effective is the basis or position from which He operates. From 1:3 we learn that He took this position at God's right hand in Heaven only after "he had by himself purged our sins." This seated position declared that His redemptive work was finished. On the basis of this authority the Christian church is commanded to evangelize the world (see Mt. 28:18-20).

(3) The *place* of His ministry—in "the true tabernacle, which the Lord pitched, and not man." Though Jesus made many trips to Jerusalem and to the Temple during His earthly ministry, He never once entered the inner sanctuary, the Holy Place and the Holy of Holies. There were Levitical priests from the family of Aaron who carried on that ministry. But that earthly sanctuary, along with its priests and sacrifices, was only "the example and shadow" (v. 5) of the real thing. Our Lord now carries on that ministry in Heaven.

(4) The *purpose* of His ministry—"that this man have somewhat also to offer." The writer will go into much more detail in chapters 9 and 10 about the sacrifice of Christ. But he suggests here in v. 3 in a dramatic understatement that, since the O.T. priests offered gifts and sacrifices, "*it is* of necessity that this man have somewhat also to offer." That "somewhat" was, of course, nothing less than Jesus Christ Himself, through "his own blood" (9:12) and His own body (10:10).

In v. 5 the writer points out that the O.T. priests and tabernacle served as "the example and shadow of heavenly things." To prove his point, he quotes Ex. 25:40 in v. 5, "See . . . *that* thou make all things according to the pattern shewed to thee in the mount." This verse emphasizes the importance of types in the O.T. In fact, the word here translated "pattern" is the very source of our English word "type" (Greek *tupos*). There are numerous types—persons, places, things, or actions—that give a picture-prophecy of things to come in the N.T., especially things related to the life and ministry of Jesus Christ: (1) The priests served as a type of Christ and His priestly ministry. (2) The tabernacle pointed toward Heaven, the place of our Lord's ultimate ministry. (3) The veil in the tabernacle pointed to the incomplete status of the O.T. ministry (see 9:8; Mt. 27:50, 51). (4) The various types of sacrifices pointed to the final and complete sacrifice of Christ for our sins. (5) Likely all seven primary articles of furniture in the tabernacle pointed in one way or another to the coming of Christ: the brazen altar and laver in the outer court; the golden candlestick, the table of showbread, and the altar of incense in the Holy Place; and the Ark of the Covenant and the mercy seat in the Holy of Holies. Preachers and teachers may at times go to extremes on types in the O.T., but there is no doubt that the principle of types is proper, as is clearly shown in this passage of Scripture.

Several things are pointed out about the old covenant, the covenant of the law, in what the writer says and in the quotation from Jer. 31:31-34: (1) the people with whom it was made—the house of Israel (vv. 8, 10); (2) the time when it was made—"when I took them by the hand to lead them out of the land of Egypt" (v. 9); (3) the problem with the old covenant—it was not faultless (v. 7); (4) the judgment under the old covenant—"because they continued not in my covenant, and I regarded them not" (v. 9); (5) the replacement of the old covenant called for—that which "waxeth old *is* ready to vanish away" (v. 13).

Throughout the epistle to the Hebrews the writer draws a word or a phrase from an O.T. quotation and emphasizes it, "preaching" about it to drive it home. From Jer. 31:31-34 he draws the word "new" in regard to the new covenant which the Lord predicted (see v. 13). This covenant is new: (1) in relation to its sacrifice—Christ Himself, not the blood of bulls and goats; (2) in relation to its mediator—Jesus, not the Levitical priests; (3) in relation to the place of ministry—the heavenly tabernacle, not an earthly one; (4) in relation to replacing the old covenant—see v. 13; (5) in relation to the characteristics of the covenant.

There are three primary characteristics of the new covenant described by the Lord in Jeremiah: (1) an inner, heartfelt relationship with the Lord, in contrast to the more external relationship under the old covenant (v. 10); (2) a universal knowledge of the Lord that permeates the Christian community through the indwelling Holy Spirit (v. 11); and (3) complete forgiveness of sins based upon the permanent sacrifice of Christ on the cross (v. 12). These are the "better promises" of the new covenant mentioned in v. 6.

3. Old and new covenants contrasted (9:1—10:18)

In chapter 9 the writer continues the subject of the work of Christ as High Priest started in 8:1, which continues through the end of chapter 10. In chapter 8 he stressed the fact that the O.T. priesthood and tabernacle were never meant to be an end in themselves but were rather "the example and shadow of heavenly things" (8:5). Then, in the last part of the chapter, he introduced the idea of the new covenant based on the lengthy quotation from Jer. 31:31-34. The prediction of that new covenant by the Lord Himself indicated, of necessity, the passing of the old covenant. Now, here in chapter 9, he goes into much greater detail in contrasting the old covenant with the new, in relation to the tabernacle and its furniture, divisions, priestly access, the sacrificial system, and the initiation of the two covenants.

The writer's purpose in contrasting in some detail the old and new covenants is to show the unquestionable superiority of the new one. He first reminds his Hebrew audience of something with which they would be quite familiar, the articles of furniture in the two different rooms of the inner sanctuary.

a. In relation to the tabernacle and its furniture (9:1-5)

1 Then verily the first *covenant* had also ordinances of divine service, and a worldly sanctuary.
2 For there was a tabernacle made; the first, wherein *was* the candlestick, and the table, and the shewbread; which is called the sanctuary.
3 And after the second veil, the tabernacle which is called the Holiest of all;
4 Which had the golden censer, and the ark of the covenant overlaid round about with gold, wherein *was* the golden pot that had manna, and Aaron's rod that budded, and the tables of the covenant;
5 And over it the cherubims of glory shadowing the mercy seat; of which we cannot now speak particularly.

The writer is continuing his emphasis on the new covenant which he brought out through the quotation from Jer. 31:31-34 and his declaration in 8:13 that the introduction of something new indicates the replacement of that which is old. He uses "then verily" (Greek *men oun*) to stress his continuation of thought. "The first *covenant*" refers to the Mosaic covenant, designated in the previous chapter as the old covenant (see 8:13); the KJV correctly supplies the word "*covenant*" from this obvious connection. The covenant made at Sinai was first in a chronological sense in relation to the new covenant in Jesus Christ which was now replacing it.

This first covenant, the covenant at Sinai through Moses, "had also ordinances of divine service." "Had" may be taken as a simple past tense, referring back to the time when the ordinances were originally given (Lenski 273), or it may be taken to imply the invalidation or abrogation of those ordinances (Westcott 242; Alford 155). Probably the simple past connotation is the best way to understand it. "Also" stresses the fact that both covenants were parallel in this respect, operating on the basis of clearly defined "ordinances." "Ordinances" (Greek *dikaioma*) is used in several different ways in the New Testament. It refers to righteous judgments, righteous conduct, and righteous declarations. In this context the writer has in mind righteous declarations.

These ordinances were rules of operation for the priests as they conducted "divine service" or worship in the tabernacle. That first covenant not only had such ordinances—righteous rules of conduct for the priestly service—but that service was also conducted in "a worldly sanctuary." In this context "sanctuary" (Greek *to hagion*) refers to both rooms of the inner tabernacle, the Holy Place and the Holy of Holies. The writer never refers to the Outer Court or its furniture in this epistle. It is initially surprising to see this sanctuary described as "worldly" (Greek *kosmikos*), but the writer is making no moral pronouncements about the ancient tabernacle. He is rather describing it as "belonging to this world," the earthly tabernacle in contrast to the heavenly one where our Lord carries on His High Priestly ministry (see 8:2, 5; 9:11, 12). There is a definite article in the original ("the worldly sanctuary"), emphasizing that it was the one and only tabernacle in Israel's history. Remember that our writer, in his discussion of the two covenants, always refers to the tabernacle in the wilderness, never to the Temple in Jerusalem. The Temple, however, was a replica of the tabernacle, with all of its divisions, though on a grander scale.

"For" in v. 2 indicates the continuation of the description of the "worldly sanctuary" introduced in v. 1. "Tabernacle" (Greek *skene*) refers to the two inner compartments—the Holy Place and the Holy of Holies—as a whole. Then the writer proceeds to divide the compartments on the basis of the furniture located in each one. The O.T. tabernacle was always set up with the entrance on the east side; as the priest entered he was moving from east to west. (Hebrews never mentions the Outer Court of the tabernacle, where the large altar for sacrifices and the laver for washing were located; see Ex. 27:1-7; 30:17-21.) That this tabernacle "was made" (Greek *kataskeuazo*) means more than its simple construction; the word indicates preparation, placing in readiness, being fitted for service. It pictures the tabernacle being set up and the articles of furniture placed in their proper positions (Alford 157).

As the writer proceeds to look into the two inner rooms with their contents, "the first" was the Holy Place. On the south side of that sacred room was "the candlestick" or lampstand (Ex. 26:35). It was made of pure gold with three lamps coming from each side of the main branch of the lamp, making seven lamps in all (Ex. 25:31-39). The Hebrew word for candlestick or lampstand is "menorah." The seven lamps of the menorah burned pure olive oil (Ex. 27:20). The Temple of Solomon had ten of these lampstands, five on each side of the Holy Place (1 Kg. 7:49; 2 Chr. 4:7). Next, located on the north side of the Holy Place, was "the table," overlaid with pure gold, which held the twelve loaves of bread. It measured two cubits (36 inches) long, one cubit (18 inches) wide, and one and one-half cubits (27 inches) high (Ex. 25:23-30). Solomon's Temple also had ten tables, five on each side of the Holy Place (2 Chr. 4:8) Placed on the table just mentioned, in two rows of six each, was "the shewbread" (Ex. 25:30, Lev. 24:5-9), literally "the setting forth of the bread" (Greek *he prothesis ton arton*). The bread was changed each sabbath, and only the High Priest and his sons were to eat this bread, as they served in the Holy Place.

This first room of the inner part of the tabernacle "is called the sanctuary" (Greek *hagia*), or the Holy Place. The word in the original is used without the definite article, thus placing a greater emphasis on the character of the room as "holy." Note that, based on the context, the word "sanctuary" in v. 1 refers to both of the inner rooms of the tabernacle, while the same word in v. 2 refers to the first room, the Holy Place, as distinguished from the second room, the Holy of Holies. The verb "is called" (Greek present tense) indicates that the terminology was still used at the time of the writing of Hebrews.

The writer continues to lead us into the O.T. tabernacle from the entrance on the east side toward the west. In v. 2 he described the Holy Place. Now he says, "And after the second veil." The first veil (see Ex. 26:36; 36:37, 38) formed the entrance to the first room of the main sanctuary. It separated the Holy Place from the Outer Court. This "second veil" separated the Holy Place from the Holy of Holies. Its construction and hangings are described in Ex. 26:31-33. The second veil marked the entrance to "the tabernacle which is called the Holiest of all." Though the Holy of Holies was part of the same tent as the Holy Place, our writer views it as a separate one in light of the division of the room by the veil. That veil was all important. It was the veil which the Jewish high priest parted only one day each year, on the Day of Atonement (see Lev. 16).

In Solomon's Temple the veil was formed by two doors made of olive wood (1 Kg. 6:31-35). Notice that by the time of the building of the temple the Holy of Holies was also called "the oracle" (1 Kg. 6:5, 31), a name emphasizing that this was where God met and communicated with the high priest under the O.T. worship. It was also that veil that was miraculously divided from top to bottom at the time of Christ's death on the cross (Mt. 27:50, 51). That rending of the veil signified the end of the old covenant of law and the initiation of the new covenant of grace (see 9:8).

Verse 4 continues to describe the part of the tabernacle which was "after the second veil," the Holy of Holies, by observing that it "had the golden censer." Controversy developed from the earliest days over the identity of this article of furniture. "Censer" (Greek *thumiaterion*) may refer to the vessel used by the high priest for bearing coals of fire from the altar on the Day of Atonement to burn incense inside the Holy of Holies (see Lev. 16:12, 13). Or it may mean "altar of incense," referring to the golden altar of incense itself, which was used to burn incense each morning while the high priest dressed the lamps, and each evening as he lit the lamps again (Ex. 30:1-10).

The Septuagint uses the word to refer to the censer, and this is apparently the meaning adopted by our translators. Barnes (188) and Alford (161) maintain this view. But numerous early writers, including Philo, Josephus, Clement of Alexandria, and Origen, take the word to refer to the altar of incense; so do many modern commentators (Westcott 246; Lenski 276; D. Guthrie 180; Calvin 196). It seems unlikely that the writer, in giving this rather detailed notation of the articles of furniture in the sanctuary, would omit one of the primary articles, the golden altar of incense.

However, that approach creates another problem. Why does our writer place the altar of incense in the Holy of Holies rather than in the Holy Place "before the veil," as it was in the original tabernacle (Ex. 30:6)? This problem is probably the main reason for taking the word to refer to a "censer." The best solution is found in noting the stress which the O.T. places on the *function* of the golden altar of incense in relation to the Holy of Holies, especially on the Day of Atonement. Moses was instructed to place this altar "before the vail that *is* by the ark of the testimony, before the mercy seat that *is* over the testimony, where I will meet with thee" (Ex. 30:6; 40:5). In like manner, in Solomon's Temple, we are told that "the whole altar that *was* by the oracle [the Holy of Holies] he overlaid with gold" (1 Kg. 6:22). Thus, though the golden altar was technically located in the Holy Place, it was *functionally* associated with the Holy of Holies, especially on the Day of Atonement when the high priest took coals from the altar and burned incense inside the Holy of Holies "that the cloud of the incense may cover the mercy seat that *is* upon the testimony, that he die not" (Lev. 16:13). Indeed, the writer does not say that the golden altar was "*in* the Holy of Holies," but that it "had" it, an expression that can be understood as meaning relationship, not necessarily physical location. This close association is strengthened by the fact that the high priest placed blood from the sin offering on the horns of this altar on the Day of Atonement, just as he sprinkled blood on the mercy seat inside the veil (see Ex. 30:10; Lev. 16:14, 15). Lunemann (317) takes the unfortunate position that the writer of Hebrews simply made a mistake about the location of the golden altar because he apparently did not live near Jerusalem. Such an approach to this or any other passage of the inspired Scripture is unacceptable.

The writer further describes the contents of the Holy of Holies. It had "the ark of the covenant overlaid round about with gold." The Ark was a rectangular box which measured two and one-half cubits in length (45 inches) by a cubit and one-half in width (27 inches) by a cubit and one-half high (27 inches). Moses said that it was overlaid with gold "within and without" (Ex. 25:11). It was called "the ark of the covenant" because it contained the tables of stone on which were written "the words of the covenant, the ten commandments" (Ex. 34:28). It was often called "the ark of the testimony" (Ex. 25:22) because these commandments clearly expressed God's "testimony" or will for both faith and obedience for Israel, His chosen people. The original Ark was first brought to Jerusalem by David and placed in a special tabernacle he had constructed for it (2 Sam. 6:17). When Solomon completed the Temple, he had the priests bring the Ark from the city of David to its proper place in "the oracle of the house, to the most holy *place, even* under the wings of the cherubims" (1 Kg. 8:1-6).

According to Jewish tradition, the Holy of Holies of the Temple which was constructed after Babylonian exile, later elaborately modified and enlarged by Herod the Great (and which stood in Jesus' day), contained absolutely nothing (Bruce 188). The Ark and its contents were apparently destroyed when Nebuchadnezzar and his army burned the Temple and destroyed Jerusalem in 586 B.C. (2 Kg. 25:8-10).

The contents of the Ark of the Covenant in the original tabernacle included "the golden pot that had manna, and Aaron's rod that budded, and the tables of the covenant." God instructed Moses and Aaron to lay up "before the Testimony, to be kept," a "pot" containing an omer (about 2 quarts) of manna for a witness of God's provision in the wilderness (Ex. 16:32-34). In like manner, "Aaron's rod that budded," which was a sign of his priestly authority (Num. 16:1-3), was to be brought "before the testimony, to be kept for a token against the rebels" (Num. 17:10).

The main content, from which the Ark received its name, was "the tables of the covenant," which the Lord commanded to be placed inside the Ark (Ex. 25:16). The pot of manna and Aaron's rod are only mentioned here in Hebrews and in the original references noted above. When Solomon placed the Ark in the newly constructed Temple in Jerusalem, "the two tables of stone, which Moses put there at Horeb," were the only contents of the Ark (1 Kg. 8:9).

"And over it" (v. 5), that is, over the Ark of the Covenant were "the cherubims of glory shadowing the mercy seat." The two "cherubim" (plural of cherub in Hebrew) or angelic figures were formed as one piece with the mercy seat. They faced each other with their wings outspread, thus "shadowing" the mercy seat (Ex. 25:18-20). In the Temple of Solomon, however, the cherubim stood wing to wing, "and their faces were inward" (2 Chr. 3:11-13).

Cherubim are first mentioned in Scripture as guardians of Eden after the fall of Adam and Eve (Gen. 3:24). They are called cherubims of glory because the bright and glorious presence of the Lord appeared over the mercy seat between the cherubim (Ex. 25:22; 2 Sam. 6:2; 2 Kg. 19:15; Rom. 9:4).

"The mercy seat" (Greek *hilasterion*) was actually a lid or a covering over the Ark of the Covenant (Ex. 25:17, 21), and the word itself means "a covering" (Westcott 249). Below the mercy seat, inside the Ark, was the covenant of the Lord with instructions for life and judgments for disobedience. Above the mercy seat was the awesome presence of a Holy God. How appropriate that mercy stands between the demands of the law and the wrath of God!

The word translated "mercy seat" is used by Paul to describe Christ as "a propitiation through faith in his blood" (Rom. 3:25), and a word from the same root is twice used by John to picture Christ as "the propitiation for our sins" (1 Jn. 2:2; 4:10). Hebrews has already used the verb form of this word in 2:17 to say that our Lord became like us "to make reconciliation for the sins of the people."

With this impressive description of the sanctuary and its furnishings concluded, the writer adds, "of which we cannot now speak particularly," referring back to all the pieces of furniture which he has named, not just the mercy seat. "Particularly" (Greek kata *meros*) literally means "according to part," that is, to speak in detail, part by part about each subject. He could go into much greater depth about each article and its symbolism, but such a sidetrack, delightful as it might be, would not accomplish his purpose. He will, however, go on to emphasize the significance of the division of the tabernacle and the absence of continuous and personal access to the presence of God under the Levitical system.

b. In relation to tabernacle divisions and priestly access (9:6-10)

6 Now when these things were thus ordained, the priests went always into the first tabernacle, accomplishing the service *of God.*

7 But into the second *went* the high priest alone once every year, not without blood, which he offered for himself, and *for* the errors of the people:
8 The Holy Ghost this signifying, that the way into the holiest of all was not yet made manifest, while as the first tabernacle was yet standing:
9 Which *was* a figure for the time then present, in which were offered both gifts and sacrifices, that could not make him that did the service perfect, as pertaining to the conscience;
10 *Which stood* only in meats and drinks, and divers washings, and carnal ordinances, imposed *on them* until the time of reformation.

Though the writer does not wish to speak in detail about the typical significance of the articles of furniture, although he certainly could, he does want to stress the significance of the divisions of the tabernacle: "Now when these things were thus ordained." "Now" connects us with the preceding discussion and points to forward progress on the same subject. "These things" refer back to the whole discussion about the tabernacle and its furnishings in 9:1-5. "Were ordained" (Greek *kataskeuazo*) is the same word translated "was made" in v. 2; and, as there, it carries the connotation of preparation for service. The verb points to the preparation originally done when the tabernacle was first built during Moses' day and suggests that such preparation and performance of service continued, once started (Greek perfect tense; see Yeager 291). "Thus" carries us back to the description of the preparation, especially the enumeration of the articles of furniture in the tabernacle, in vv. 1-5.

Once the tabernacle was set up and the articles of furniture put in place, the divine purpose began to be carried out: "The priests went always into the first tabernacle." "The priests" included all those in active service from the age of 30 through 50 (see Num. 4:3). Because their numbers had multiplied to the extent they could not all serve at once, David divided them into 24 courses so that they could rotate their turns of service (1 Chr. 24:1-19). Zacharias, the father of John the Baptist, was serving in one of these rotations ("the course of Abia," Lk. 1:5) in the Temple when the angel Gabriel gave him the message about his son's coming birth.

As in v. 2, "the first tabernacle" refers to the Holy Place. Into the Holy Place these priests went "always"; that is, they entered it daily on a continuous basis, day after day, in performing their duties. Their entrance into the Holy Place daily was for the purpose of "accomplishing the service *of God*." "Service" (Greek *latreia*) is the same word which was rendered "divine service" in v. 1. The three primary daily or regular duties of the priest inside the Holy Place were: (1) dressing the lamps in the morning and lighting them in the evening (Ex. 27:20, 21; 30:7, 8); (2) burning sweet incense on the golden altar while servicing the lamps (Ex. 30:7, 8); (3) changing the twelve loaves of bread on the table of showbread each Sabbath (Lev. 24:5-9).

"But into the second *went* the high priest alone once every year" (v. 7). There is a four-fold contrast (Greek *men/de* clauses) between v. 6 and v. 7. (1) With regard to the *place of service,* the contrast is between "the first tabernacle" in v. 6 and "the second" in v. 7; (2) With regard to the *person doing the service*, the contrast is between "the priests" in v. 6 and "the high priest alone" in v. 7; (3) With regard to *frequency of service,* the contrast is between the regular and daily use of the Holy Place and the much rarer use of the Holy of Holies. The contrasting words are "always" in v. 6 and "once every year" in v. 7; (4) With regard to the *presence of blood in the service,* the contrast is between the bloodless ministry throughout the year in the Holy Place and the high priest's entrance into the Holy of Holies "not without blood."

The occasion to which v. 7 refers is the annual Day of Atonement (see Lev. 16:11-19), celebrated on the 10th day of the 7th month of each year (Lev. 16:29). The Day of Atonement was not a festival, as many of the holy days were, but rather a time of mourning, fasting, and repentance over sin. Though the priest entered the Holy of Holies only on this one occasion each year, he actually entered two separate times on this day, bearing the blood from the sacrifices "which he offered for himself, and *for* the errors of the people." This emphasis on the offerings of the Day of Atonement has already been mentioned in 5:3 and 7:27. The priest first sacrificed a bullock for his own sins, entered the Holy of Holies with its blood, and sprinkled the mercy seat seven times. He then repeated that act with the blood of the goat for the sins of the people.

The writer expresses the people's sins with the word "errors" (Greek *agnoema*), meaning "sins of ignorance." Though this word does not appear again in the N.T., the same thought was mentioned earlier in 5:2. Sins of ignorance reflect the Lord's definition in Leviticus and Numbers of sins that are forgivable (see Lev. 4:1, 2, 13, 22, 27; 5:15-19; Num. 15:22-29), in contrast with presumptuous sins which could not be forgiven (Num. 15:30, 31; Dt. 17:12, 13) and resulted in that person's being "cut off from among his people."

A sin of ignorance obviously means more than a sin committed unknowingly. If that is the only kind of sin that is forgivable, then all of us are surely in trouble. The phrase is technical, referring to sins that arise through the weakness of the flesh and the passion of the moment (Hagner 128), sins that are acknowledged, confessed, and abandoned. Presumptuous sins, on the other hand, are sins that are not acknowledged or confessed, but are, rather, persisted in as acts of rebellion against the known will of God. This distinction between sins that may be forgiven and those that may not be will be emphasized again in 10:26-31.

The writer sees a divine message in this division of the O.T. sanctuary into two rooms, the Holy Place and the Holy of Holies: "The Holy Ghost this signifying." The Holy Spirit, the third person of the Trinity, is the instrument of Divine revelation, whether through the spoken word, the written word, or symbols and actions. The tabernacle, with its furniture and divisions, had such a message. The writer sees this division into two rooms as "signifying," as showing or demonstrating, the specified truth.

"This" points us forward to the truth which the Holy Spirit signified in the division of the O.T. sanctuary, "that the way into the holiest of all was not yet made manifest, while as the first tabernacle was yet standing." Jesus Christ declared Himself to be "the way, the truth, and the life," the exclusive means of approaching the Father (Jn. 14:6). One of the commonly used names for followers of Christ in the early church was followers of "the way" (Acts 9:2; 19:9, 23; 22:4; 24:22). "The way" which the writer mentions here points to that same idea. It speaks of access to God (Rom. 5:1, 2). "The holiest of all" refers to the antitype, not the type, to Heaven itself, of which the Holy of Holies in the O.T. tabernacle stood as a symbol (Alford 164). The same words had the same meaning in 8:2, where it was translated "the sanctuary." As long as we had an earthly sanctuary with its veil and its divisions, the clear way to Heaven "was not yet made manifest." Certainly O.T. people will be in Heaven through that approach to God, but it was never intended to be permanent. That approach was indirect, through a priest, and infrequent, only once a year.

"The first tabernacle" means the same thing as in v. 6, the Holy Place of the O.T. tabernacle. The writer sees the tabernacle in its two divisions: the first (v. 6) is the Holy Place, and the second (v. 7) is the Holy of Holies. "Yet standing" (literally "having a standing") refers to the physical existence of the divided sanctuary, as well as to its Divine status. It was the presence of the inner veil that created the division of the O.T. tabernacle. This shows the awesome significance of the declaration at the very moment of Christ's death on the cross, "Behold, the veil of the temple was rent in twain from the top to the bottom" (Mt. 27:51). No doubt the Jewish priests attempted repairs on the earthly "veil," but its standing was no longer valid. As Jesus Himself had prophesied, the Lord ordained the permanent destruction of that Temple and that veil by the hands of General Titus and the armies of Rome in A.D. 70 (Mt. 24:1, 2, 34), though that event had apparently not yet occurred when Hebrews was written. In the O.T. only the High Priest could enter the earthly Holy of Holies, but because of Jesus' death and entrance into the heavenly sanctuary (v. 12), we can now follow Him and enjoy direct access to God through Him (see 10:19-21).

"Which" in v. 9 refers back to "the first tabernacle" in v. 8 and all that the writer has said about it. As long as there was a first tabernacle, a veil, and a second tabernacle, it was a sure sign that the way to God was not open. The true tabernacle has no such divisions. That whole structure "*was* a figure" (Greek *parabole*), the word commonly translated "parable" in the Gospels, but here meaning that the tabernacle with its divisions was a type or an illustration.

Commentators do not agree on the meaning of the phrase "for the time then present." In itself, the phrase simply means "the present time," and in this context that could be taken to mean the present time in relation to the O.T. tabernacle and its service, or the present time in relation to the ministry of Christ in the true tabernacle in Heaven—either "the time *then* present" (KJV; NASB), referring to the O.T., or "the time *now* present" (NIV), referring to Christ's current ministry. According to the first approach, the tabernacle with its divisions was a figure and a reminder for those who worshiped under the O.T. system that the way was not complete, but that "the time of reformation" (v. 10) was on its way (Westcott 252). According to the second approach, the O.T. tabernacle was an illustration for us today, for the time now present, that perfect or complete worship of God is only possible on the basis of the life, death, and present ministry of Christ (Bruce 195; Hagner 134). The true meaning of the tabernacle and its divisions can only be understood in light of the coming of Christ. It is difficult to choose between the two approaches since both meanings are valid. There was certainly a message in the tabernacle for those who used it and were blessed by it, but that message is obviously much clearer to us who have the light of N.T. revelation.

In that tabernacle "were offered both gifts and sacrifices." "Were offered" (Greek present) is literally "are being offered," again strongly implying the existence of the Temple at the time of writing. The reference to "gifts and sacrifices" has already occurred in 5:1 and 8:3. The writer probably has in mind the two different types of offerings under the O.T. system, as described in Lev. 1—5. Some offerings were gifts of thanksgiving and dedication, while others were offerings for sin.

Though these were proper for that time, it is obvious that they "could not make him that did the service perfect," including both the priests who ministered as well as the people who came to God through them. This inability of the Levitical system to "make" the worshiper "perfect" or complete was previously defined in 7:11 and was especially "pertaining to the conscience." As v. 10 emphasizes, the Levitical system placed more emphasis on that which was outward. It did little to ease the pangs of conscience associated with the guilt of sin. Inner peace of mind, which comes with forgiveness, was regularly interrupted by the daily and yearly repetition of sacrifices for sin. The importance of conscience is also stressed in 9:14; 10:2, 22, and 13:18.

Verse 10 further defines the imperfect "gifts and sacrifices" mentioned in v. 9. "Only" goes with the word "ordinances" which appears at the end of the clause and is in apposition to "gifts and sacrifices" in the previous verse. The same word was used in 9:1. These gifts and sacrifices under the old covenant were only "carnal" ordinances, "ordinances of flesh," regulations that were purely external, earthly, relating to the body. "Carnal" does not mean that the ordinances were bad, or wrong, just that they were limited to externals. They were temporary and transitory (see the similar use in 7:16).

Under the old covenant these ordinances were manifested "in meats and drinks, and divers washings." The "meats" refer to the offerings in general, both sin offerings and dedicatory offerings, both animal sacrifices and grain offerings, as described in Leviticus 1—5. "Drinks" likely refer to various instructions as in the Nazarite vow (Num. 6:3), or to ministering priests (Lev. 10:9), as well as the drink offering itself (Lev. 23:13, 18, 37). "Divers washings" would include all the different cleansings prescribed for both priests and people in connection with worship and sacrifice (Ex. 29:4; Lev.11:25, 28ff.; 16:4, 24ff.; Num. 8:7; 19:17, etc.).

Such ordinances were "imposed *on them* until the time of reformation." God "imposed" them on the Israelites at Sinai. Their obedience to God's law was obligatory as a condition of keeping that covenant. In response to the Lord's demands, Israel promised, "All that the LORD hath spoken we will do" (Ex. 19:8). Their obligation to those earthly ordinances, however, was limited: only "until the time of reformation." "Reformation" (Greek *diorthosis*) refers to that which is straight or correct. It points to the proper order of things, the perfect arrangement which is meant to replace that which was temporary and preparatory (Yeager 296). The fulfillment of this "time of reformation" was in the total ministry of Jesus Christ, including His birth, life, death, resurrection, and ascension to His priestly position at God's right hand. It corresponds to the new covenant prophesied by Jeremiah which the writer already referred to in 8:8-12. This period, in which we are now living as Christians, should not be confused with the time of "the regeneration" (Mt. 19:28) referred to by Jesus Christ, or to "the times of restitution" referred to by Peter (Acts 3:21). Both of these refer to the dispensation of time which will begin with the return of Christ to this earth.

c. In relation to a better tabernacle, sacrifice, and covenant (9:11-15)

11 But Christ being come an high priest of good things to come, by a greater and more perfect tabernacle, not made with hands, that is to say, not of this building;
12 Neither by the blood of goats and calves, but by his own blood he entered in once into the holy place, having obtained eternal redemption *for us*.
13 For if the blood of bulls and of goats, and the ashes of an heifer sprinkling the unclean, sanctifieth to the purifying of the flesh:
14 How much more shall the blood of Christ, who through the eternal Spirit offered himself without spot to God, purge your conscience from dead works to serve the living God?
15 And for this cause he is the mediator of the new testament, that by means of death, for the redemption of the transgressions *that were* under the first testament, they which are called might receive the promise of eternal inheritance.

In the latter part of chapter 8 the writer stressed the importance of the new covenant prophesied by Jeremiah. In 9:1-10 he has discussed the tabernacle of Moses' day, going into some detail about the divisions and their significance and the placement of various articles of furniture. Now in 9:11-15 he emphasizes the fact that the new tabernacle, sacrifice, and covenant which have been introduced through the coming of Jesus Christ are far better, in every way, than those which the Israelites experienced under the law of Moses. In this section he gradually puts the tabernacle and the covenant in the background and moves on to a greater emphasis on the supreme sacrifice under the new covenant, the blood of Jesus Christ Himself.

"But" (v. 11) introduces a contrast between the new tabernacle and sacrifice involving Christ's own blood and the old tabernacle and sacrifices which were just discussed. Though the writer often uses the name "Jesus," which stresses the humanity of our Lord, here he appropriately uses His official title as "Christ" (Greek *christos*), the Messiah of Israel, the Anointed One, in connection with the discussion of His High Priestly ministry. He sees Him as being come an high priest, as "having arrived" (Greek *paraginomai*) in that position on the basis of His finished work.

His priestly ministry is in connection with good things to come. Some commentators and translators, on the basis of a different manuscript reading, see this as "the good things that are already here" (NIV; Westcott 255), the good things which they were already enjoying in relation to His priesthood according to the order of Melchisedec. It is better, however, to stick with the reading which we have as expressing an even broader idea. Even the present blessings of Christ's priestly ministry could be viewed, from the perspective of these Hebrew Christians standing at the threshold of the new era, as largely "good things to come." They would be able to reap even greater benefits from this ministry in the future if they laid aside the temptation to abandon Christ in the face of increasing persecution. Even so, the writer is pointing beyond the temporal sphere to the even greater eternal hope and joy with Jesus Christ in Heaven (Hewitt 146; Lenski 288).

The writer now points to the dual means which Christ used in establishing His position as High Priest. In relation to *the place*, it is the heavenly tabernacle; and in relation to *the sacrifice*, it is His own blood (v. 12). First, he introduces the place: "By a greater and more perfect tabernacle." As mentioned above, "by" (Greek *dia*) should be taken as "by means of" both here and in v. 12. The "tabernacle" which He used to establish His priestly ministry was not that earthly one with its divisions. It was, rather, "the true tabernacle" described in 8:2, the antitype of which Moses' earthly tabernacle was a pattern or a model (8:5).

Many of the ancient church fathers tried to make this tabernacle refer to the body of Christ, His humanity. Westcott strains to adapt this view by suggesting that His body is the church (255). But such an idea seems foreign to the context. As 9:24 makes clear, when Christ entered this tabernacle, He went "into heaven itself."

The writer describes this tabernacle as "greater and more perfect" in contrast to the limited and temporary tabernacle of Moses. The two adjectives should be taken together. It was "greater" because it was "more perfect," and it was more perfect in that it satisfied all the goals of bringing us into the very presence of God, not just once a year symbolically through a human priest, but directly, continuously, and personally through God's own Son (see Eph. 2:4-6).

Since this tabernacle is Heaven itself, unlike the tabernacle of Moses constructed by Bezaleel and Aholiab, it was "not made with hands, that is to say, not of this building." "Building" (Greek *ktisis*) properly means "creation" or "created thing." Though Heaven itself is God's handiwork, it is not of this created order, and in this context it is certainly not created by men, as was the O.T. tabernacle.

In v. 12 the writer goes on to describe the second means by which Christ accomplished our redemption and took His position as our High Priest. In v. 11 he pointed to the location, not on earth, but in Heaven. Now in v. 12 he defines the nature of the sacrifice. He first declares negatively, "Neither by the blood of goats and calves." He has in mind the sacrifices of the Day of Atonement when the O.T. priest first offered a bullock for his own sins (Lev. 16:11) and then a goat for the sins of the people (Lev. 16:15).

The blood of these animal sacrifices was never effective in itself. It only postponed God's judgment on sin by pointing, as a type, to the accomplishment of true redemption in the sacrificial death of Jesus Christ (see 8:5). In contrast to this, our Lord's accomplishment of our redemption was "by his own blood." Some claim that the reference to "blood" is merely a symbol of His death, and suggest that we translate, "By his own death." They seem to want to remove the blood from our redemption, to make the Christian religion less gory. But such efforts cannot be tolerated. The shedding of blood implies a sacrificial and substitutionary death. The shed blood of Christ was efficacious in paying for our sins because of who Christ was and because of the sinless life that He lived. In contrast to the blood of goats and calves, John saw Jesus as "the Lamb of God, which taketh away the sin of the world" (Jn. 1:29), and also as "the Lamb that was slain" (Rev. 5:12).

By means of this shed blood Jesus "entered in once into the holy place." Some commentators are too materialistic at this point. The writer does not say that "he entered" *with* (Greek *meta*) His blood, but rather that He entered *by* (Greek *dia*) His blood. Lenski (293) explains,

We discard the idea that at the time of his death Jesus took his blood into the heavenly Sanctuary before God. One is disturbed to read what Bengel, Stier, Delitzsch, and others say about Christ's blood; such things as that the blood of Christ shed was received back into his body, that it was received into heaven, or that the blood which was left in Christ's dead body was increased and renewed. These distressing conceptions center particularly on the Lord's Supper, in connection with which some speak of "the glorified blood" that is now given us to drink in the Sacrament. Where does Scripture speak of Christ's "glorified blood"?

We must be careful not to contradict one of Jesus' most significant statements from the cross. In His final declaration, He exclaimed, "It is finished" (Jn. 19:30). He meant that the plan of salvation was now complete, the debt of sin had been paid. The writer of Hebrews is not talking about something additional which Christ did to accomplish our redemption but about the means or basis upon which He took His present position as our High Priest in Heaven.

"Once" (Greek *ephapax*) is a strong word meaning "once for all." The writer is contrasting the offering of Christ with that of the high priest on the Day of Atonement. That offering had to be repeated every year, but Christ's one offering is good for all time. "The holy place"—literally, "The Holies"—refers to the heavenly Holy of Holies, that is, Heaven itself (see 9:24), where Christ now sits at the Father's right hand (1:3). The writer clarifies: "Having obtained eternal redemption *for us*." "Having obtained" (Greek aorist) describes something which Jesus had already accomplished before He entered the heavenly Holy of Holies (Lunemann 329; Yeager 300; Bruce 200). Some interpreters (like Westcott 259; Alford 169) regard this as completed only upon Christ's entrance into the heavenly Holy of Holies (thus taking it to mean "He entered the Holy Place and obtained eternal redemption"). But this seems inconsistent with the Scriptural declaration that Christ's redemptive work was finished on the cross. He did not enter Heaven to complete our redemption. Instead, He entered Heaven on the basis of His completed work, by means of its accomplishment.

In contrast to the repeated sacrifices of the ancient Day of Atonement, Jesus obtained "eternal redemption" for us. The writer likes to speak of things "eternal" (Greek *aion*) or "everlasting." He refers to eternal salvation (5:9), eternal judgment (6:2), eternal redemption (9:12), the eternal Spirit (9:14), eternal inheritance (9:15), and the everlasting covenant (13:20).

"Redemption" (Greek *lutrosis*) refers to the act of paying a price for deliverance from bondage, a ransoming. A similar word is used in Mk. 10:45 where Jesus declared, "The Son of man came not to be ministered unto, but to minister, and to give his life a ransom for many." "Ransom" (Greek *lutron*) there refers to the price which was paid in the act of redemption. A compound word for "redemption" is used in 9:15 (Greek *apolutrosis*), adding the idea of separation from bondage on the basis of the price paid (see also Rom. 3:24); and another compound is used in 1 Tim. 2:6, there translated "ransom" (Greek *antilutron*), emphasizing the substitutionary aspect ("instead of") of the price paid.

In v. 13 "for" advances the explanation of the efficacy of the blood of Christ in contrast to the blood of the sacrificial animals of the O.T. "If" (Greek *ei*) introduces a condition assumed true (Greek first class condition), and might well be translated "since." The "if" clause of v. 13 is followed by the conclusion clause in v. 14. "The blood of bulls and of goats" presents the offerings of the Day of Atonement, as in v. 12 (Lev. 16). The more specific term "bulls" is not intended to be different from the "calves" of v. 12.

To the sacrifices of the Day of Atonement, the writer adds "the ashes of an heifer sprinkling the unclean" (see Num. 1:1-22). The ashes of this heifer, burned without the camp, were set aside to be mixed with water for the specific purpose of sprinkling for purification those who had come in contact with a dead body. God's demand for such ceremonial cleansing was a reminder of His holiness as well as His desire for spiritual purity on the part of His people. The reference to these two types of offerings under the old covenant is intended as a summary of the whole sacrificial system.

Those O.T. sacrifices "sanctifieth to the purifying of the flesh." The writer presents a two-fold contrast in vv. 13, 14: (1) there is a contrast between the blood of animals and the blood of Christ, and (2) there is a contrast between the external purification of the body and the inner purification of the conscience. In this context "sanctifieth" (Greek *hagiazo*) is basically synonymous with "purge" in v. 14, both words referring to the cleansing efficiency of what is being discussed. This is supported by the fact that the noun "purifying" (Greek *katharotes*) is from the same root as the verb "purge" in the next verse. The contrast is between "the flesh,"—the body, that which is external—in v. 13, and "the conscience"—the spiritual intellect, the inner man, in v. 14.

In v. 14 the writer highlights the contrast with the declaration, "How much more shall the blood of Christ." The writer habitually makes such contrasts in Hebrews. We should give more earnest heed to the word spoken "by the Lord" than to those spoken by angels (2:1-4); through His oath to Abraham, the Lord made His promise "more abundantly" certain (6:17); the truth that Christ is a priest after the order of Melchisedec is "far more evident" (7:15); He has also obtained "a more excellent ministry" than the Levitical priests (8:6); this priestly ministry is conducted in a "more perfect tabernacle" (9:11); and believers should be faithful to the Christian assembly "so much the more" as the day of reckoning approaches (10:25). Here "the blood of Christ" stands in sharp contrast to the mere animal sacrifices of the Day of Atonement and all the other Levitical offerings. There is a contrast in the *value* of the blood, for this is "the precious blood of Christ" (1 Pet. 1:19), as well as in the *voluntariness* of the sacrifice (Lenski 298). No animal ever volunteered to be a sacrifice, but Jesus declared about His life, "No man taketh it from me, but I lay it down of myself. I have power to lay it down, and I have power to take it again" (Jn. 10:18).

The sacrifice of His blood was made "through the eternal Spirit." Some commentators think that this refers to the Holy Spirit (Kent 172; Kistemaker 252) who certainly aided Christ in other aspects of His ministry: at His baptism (Mk. 1:10); in the temptation (Lk. 4:1); and in various aspects of His ministry (Lk. 4:14). The reference, however, is probably not to the Holy Spirit, but rather to the spirit of Christ Himself, His Divine nature (Alford 171; Bruce 204; Lenski 298; Westcott 261). To try to make this refer to the Holy Spirit would contradict the declaration of Jn. 10:18. Jesus Christ, in His own person, was in complete control of this sacrifice. With just a word from the Son, the Father would have immediately sent "twelve legions of angels" to deliver Him (Mt. 26:53). But our Lord "offered himself." Contrary to the O.T. offerings, He was both the priest and the sacrifice. The Levitical requirements specified that the various offerings be "without spot" (Num. 19:2) or "without blemish" (Ex. 12:5; Lev. 1:3, etc.). This, of course, referred to external blemishes, physical imperfections. But Jesus Christ, as our supreme sacrifice, offered Himself "without spot" in every sense of the word: physically, morally, and spiritually. No other person would dare challenge his enemies with such a bold declaration, "Which of you convinceth me of sin?" (Jn. 8:46).

Those O.T. sacrifices were essential for that time and place, but they only provided purification of the flesh, the outside of the person who brought the offering. Our writer declares, however, that our Lord's sacrifice has the power to "purge your conscience," the inner man, the totality of the person originally created in the image of God. The application of the blood of Christ specifically results in the cleansing of the inner man "from dead works," that is, all human efforts to please God apart from faith in Christ (Alford 171; Kent 173). Apart from the regenerating power of the blood of Christ, all such efforts are useless, whether performed in strict obedience to the law of Moses or merely in allegiance to moral law in general. The dead works here are the same as in 6:1. The Pharisees of Jesus' day were astute in the practice of such dead works (see Mt. 23:3-33), and these Hebrew Christians were their descendants, both spiritually and physically. The ashes of the red heifer purified O.T. people when they had come in contact with a dead body, but the blood of Christ goes much deeper than that. It separates us from those useless efforts to save ourselves, those dead works that could never bring true cleansing.

But the Lord does not save, sanctify, and cleanse us merely to sit and enjoy our new spiritual status. He saves us, rather, "to serve the living God." The continuing service referred to here (Greek present tense) is that of worship and praise to God. All true service for God, regardless of the content, is performed out of a heart of love toward Him, never out of legalistic allegiance to a set of laws, rules, or regulations. Furthermore, it is service rendered to "the living God," in sharp contrast to "the dead works" from which our consciences have been purged by the blood of Christ. Though Paul used a different word in the original, he put forth a similar thought when he pointed out that the Thessalonians had "turned to God from idols to serve the living and true God" (1 Th. 1:9). The service of praise, thanksgiving, and submission is the most natural outcome of the cleansing power of the blood of Jesus Christ.

In vv. 11-14 the writer has emphasized the fact that Jesus Christ has entered a "more perfect tabernacle"—the one in Heaven, not on earth—and He has entered that tabernacle on the basis of a sacrifice superior to that of bulls and goats—the sacrifice of Himself, the shedding of "his own blood." In v. 15 he explains, "And for this cause," that is, because of His superior sacrifice confirmed in the heavenly tabernacle, He is now "the mediator of the new testament." This thought was already introduced in 8:6. As a "mediator" (Greek *mesites*) Jesus Christ, through His substitutionary atonement, has brought sinful men together with a Holy God. As a result the N.T. church, whether made up of Jews or Gentiles, must approach this Holy God under the terms of "the new testament" or "new covenant" prophesied long ago in Jer. 31:31-34, quoted by our author in 8:8-12.

The translators of the Septuagint translated the Hebrew word for "covenant" (*berith*) with the Greek word (*diatheke*) which commonly means "testament" or "will." They used this word because of the strictly one-sided nature of a Biblical covenant, just as the terms of a will are determined solely by the person who is making the will (Kent 173); he may well make requirements of the beneficiaries as conditions for receiving the inheritance, but that is completely in his hands. Our English translators normally use the word "covenant" because of the broader emphasis of the O.T. term, picturing a one-sided contract between two or more parties which may involve terms and conditions.

But here the English translators used the word "testament" because of the desire to stress the two-fold ideas of an inheritance and the necessity of a death to activate the will. This emphasis in v. 15 is preparing us for the details given in the rest of the chapter, vv. 16-28, where the writer continues to explain the terms and reasons for a "new testament." This new testament or will was activated "by means of death," that is, because a death has occurred.

In this context the writer wants to emphasize that this death of Jesus Christ, which involved the shedding of His own blood, was for the purpose of "the redemption of the transgressions *that were* under the first testament." "Redemption" (Greek *apolutrosis*) is not the same word as in v. 12; this one adds the idea of separation to that of a price made for deliverance from bondage. The ransom which Christ paid for our deliverance has separated us from the bondage we knew. "Transgressions" (Greek *parabasis*) views sin as a deviation from God's standard, a direct and willful violation of His commands.

"Redemption of the transgressions," then, means the ransoming of those who were deeply in debt to a Holy God because of these violations and deviations. When the writer specifies that these sins were "under the first testament," he does not mean to exclude the application of Christ's death to those of us under the new testament. Other passages in Hebrews make that abundantly clear (see 2:9). He is, rather, pointing out to these Hebrew Christians the ineffectiveness of the old sacrifices, the blood of bulls and goats or the ashes of a heifer. The death of Christ not only covers us who live under the new covenant, but it also covers the ancestors of these Hebrews, since the O.T. sacrifices served only as types and shadows of the better sacrifice which was to come (see also Gal. 3:19; Rom. 3:24-26).

Though this writer, as well as other writers in the N.T., makes it abundantly clear that Jesus died for all, the actual benefits of Christ's death only apply to those "which are called," that is, those who have heard God's invitation and have responded by faith on the basis of Christ's blood. The verb indicates that the call was issued in the past, but that it continues to have its effect in the present (Greek perfect tense).

We should be careful to note that there is a more general call which God sends forth, as is indicated in some of Jesus' parables (see Mt. 22:1-14; Lk. 14:16-24). Jesus refers to this general call when He observes, "Many are called, but few are chosen" (Mt. 22:14). In both these parables the king, through his servants, issued a broad call to all his subjects, to which they were free to respond. The majority, however, made excuses and did not accept the gracious invitation to the banquet which had already been prepared. The writer of Hebrews refers in this passage to those who do respond. He has in mind God's successful call, His effectual call. Peter acknowledged this in his sermon at Pentecost when he declared, "For the promise is unto you, and to your children, and to all that are afar off, *even* as many as the Lord our God shall call" (Acts 2:39). Paul adds detail when he explains that "all things work together for good to them that love God, to them who are the called according to *his* purpose" (Romans 8:28). Because of His foreknowledge, God is certain about who will respond to His call (see Rev. 17:8; also 13:8 in NASB); but from the human side, we are completely free to accept His call of grace and receive eternal salvation through the blood of Christ, or to reject that call and justly receive God's eternal condemnation. The certainty of God's knowledge in no way indicates coercion. Though we cannot respond to God's call apart from divine help (Jn. 6:44), we have the free will to reject that help, as is clearly indicated by the parables referred to above.

Those who respond in faith to God's call through Jesus Christ "receive the promise of eternal inheritance." Now we see why the writer wanted to direct our attention to the more narrow conception of the "covenant" as a "testament" or a will. What we have in Christ on this earth is certainly wonderful: peace, forgiveness, fellowship, etc. At times in Christian history, however, living the Christian life has not been all that enjoyable (see 1 Cor. 15:19, 32; 2 Cor. 11:21-33). But we look forward to the certain fulfillment of all the benefits promised to us in our Savior's will, here spoken of as our "eternal inheritance."

d. In relation to the inauguration and dedication of the covenants (9:16-28)

The writer continues to emphasize the point introduced in v. 15. For this new testament to become valid, a death must occur. He demonstrates his point by contrasting the dedication of the first testament or covenant with the dedication of the new one.

(1) The old covenant inaugurated (9:16-22)

16 For where a testament *is*, there must also of necessity be the death of the testator.
17 For a testament *is* of force after men are dead: otherwise it is of no strength at all while the testator liveth.
18 Whereupon neither the first *testament* was dedicated without blood.
19 For when Moses had spoken every precept to all the people according to the law, he took the blood of calves and of goats, with water, and scarlet wool, and hyssop, and sprinkled both the book, and all the people,
20 Saying, This *is* the blood of the testament which God hath enjoined unto you.
21 Moreover he sprinkled with blood both the tabernacle, and all the vessels of the ministry.
22 And almost all things are by the law purged with blood; and without shedding of blood is no remission.

Many commentators, for the sake of consistency, attempt to use the word "covenant" even in vv. 15-17 (Westcott 265). They see it as confusing to translate the same Greek word (*diatheke*) as "covenant" in most of its occurrences, and "testament" only in these two or three verses. Lenski recognizes the two different ideas, but insists that we should translate only "covenant" throughout (305). Lunemann (336) makes a good point in arguing for visualizing and verbalizing the different ideas. He says,

> It is, however, to be observed that while for us, since we are obliged to employ a twofold expression for the reproducing of the diversity of sense, the transition from the one notion to the other appears abruptly made, this transition for the author, on the other hand, might be an imperceptible one, inasmuch as in the Greek one and the same word included within itself both significations.

In order for us, as English readers, to grasp the double implications of the Greek word, it seems better to me to vary from the more usual "covenant" to "testament" or "will" in vv. 15-17 (Kent 175; Bruce 213). This makes the point clear: "For where a testament *is*, there must also of necessity be the death of the testator." The idea of the death of Messiah was a problem for many Jewish believers, perhaps even more so for the first readers of Hebrews who had not been eyewitnesses of the events of the Gospels (see 1 Cor. 1:18-24). The writer relies on a well-known truth to bring home his argument, a truth readily admitted in any and all societies.

Like a covenant, a testament or a will is one-sided. The one making the will, "the testator," is in complete control. He alone determines the heirs, the inheritance which each one receives, and the terms and conditions of the will. Unlike a covenant, however, the activation of a will demands "the death of the testator" himself. The language of the original is actually a bit more technical as it declares, literally: "Where there is a will, the death of the testator must be brought out" (Hughes 371). The writer seems to describe the scene, still true in our modern society, where the official death certificate, the proof of death, must be presented to make the will legal. Our writer has already pointed out that God the Father has appointed the Son "heir of all things" (1:2). Furthermore, as children of God through the power of the Spirit, we are "heirs of God, and joint-heirs with Christ" (Rom. 8:17).

In v. 17 the writer reiterates the truth introduced in v. 16: "For a testament *is* of force after men are dead." "Of force" (Greek bebaios) in this context means "confirmed" or "established." A will never takes effect until the maker of the will has died. The plural "men" is used in line with the statement as a general truth, applicable to all. To further drive home the point, the writer expresses the thought from the opposite perspective: "Otherwise it is of no strength at all while the testator liveth." If the death of the will-maker is what activates the will, then the will cannot take effect apart from that death.

Our writer is straining to bring the truth home to a people who have been reluctant to accept it, and who, now under persecution, are manifesting some inclination to give in to their doubts, to consider the idea of the cross a stumbling block. That "it is of no strength" (Greek *ischuo*) means that the will has not taken effect, has not been executed, "while the testator liveth." Though there are some comparisons between a will in our culture and the new covenant through Jesus Christ, it is a wonderful fact that there also are several contrasts. Our Testator did die, as required to activate the testament; but He did not stay dead, and we have become joint-heirs with Him. Furthermore, the material inheritance which we might receive on this earth, no matter how large, is still limited; but our riches in Christ are sufficient to meet all our needs forever.

In v. 18 the writer proceeds to illustrate the principle he has explained in vv. 16, 17. Since a death is needed to make a will effective, he applies that principle also to the O.T. covenant in its inauguration. The writer of Hebrews, so well aware of the capabilities of the Greek vocabulary, moves easily between the idea of a covenant in v. 15 to a testament in vv. 16 and 17, and now back to a covenant in v. 18. This means that we too should stress the characteristics which a testament and a covenant have in common, rather than differences which could be magnified. Thus, the writer illustrates the necessity of a death, which involves the shedding of blood, by turning to Moses' dedication of the covenant of law in Ex. 24: "Whereupon neither the first *testament* was dedicated without blood." These Hebrew Christians, who seemed to be having reservations about the blood of Christ, needed to see that the foundation principle of shedding of blood started under the old covenant, that the new covenant merely advances a principle which was based on the types and shadows explained in the old.

"Whereupon" (Greek *hothen*) introduces the following statement as a justification of the principle explained in vv. 15-17. Though the word *testament* does not actually appear in this verse, as indicated by the italics, it is correctly supplied from the preceding verses. The writer actually picks up on the thought of "the first *testament*" from v. 15. The verb "was dedicated" (Greek *egkainizo*) is used in the Septuagint to mean "renew" (1 Sam. 11:14) and "dedicate" (1 Kg. 8:63). Thus, the meaning points to the dedication or inauguration of something that is new, as was the first covenant which Moses inaugurated in Ex. 24:1-8. But the point that the writer especially wants to call attention to is that the first covenant was not dedicated "without blood"—and thus not without a death.

Verse 19 gives the details of that dedication to make the point clear: "For when Moses had spoken every precept to all the people according to the law, he took the blood of calves and of goats, with water, and scarlet wool, and hyssop, and sprinkled both the book, and all the people." Commentators point out that there are several differences between what our writer records about that dedication and the account of Moses in Ex. 24:1-8 (Hughes 376; Kistemaker 257). In particular, Moses mentioned the blood of oxen, not "the blood of calves and of goats." Furthermore, he did not refer to "water, and scarlet wool, and hyssop," and Moses said that he sprinkled the altar which he had built at the foot of Sinai as well as "all the people," but he did not specifically mention sprinkling "the book." The solution to this problem, however, is not complicated.

The blood of calves and of goats was offered on the Day of Atonement, as the writer mentioned earlier (9:11), and the ox and the calf are from the same family and might be used interchangeably. In fact the Septuagint, the primary O.T. source in Hebrews, actually uses the word "calf" in the account of the dedication of the covenant (Ex. 24:5). Though the offering of a goat is not mentioned there, it was certainly one of the common sacrifices under the old covenant and might very well have been included. Scarlet wool, hyssop, and water are all mentioned in connection with the cleansing of a leper (Lev. 14:4-7), as well as in connection with the ashes of the red heifer, used in ceremonial cleansing of those who had come in contact with the dead (Num. 19:6, 7); thus, they were evidently common elements used in connection with blood sacrifices. Though the record in Exodus does not specifically mention Moses' sprinkling the book, it does mention that "he took the book of the covenant, and read in the audience of the people" just prior to his sprinkling the people with blood (Ex. 24:7). It is thus logical to suppose that Moses also sprinkled the book with blood just as he did the altar and the people. Finally, Josephus, the Jewish historian who was a contemporary with Christ, produced an account of Moses' dedication of the first covenant very similar to that which the writer of Hebrews gives here (Josephus, *Antiquities* 3.206). It seems obvious, therefore, that the writer's account, like that of Josephus, was based on a solid Hebrew tradition.

Verse 20 gives a paraphrase of Moses' solemn declaration on the occasion of the inauguration of the first covenant: "This *is* the blood of the testament which God hath enjoined unto you." The exact words of Moses in Ex. 24:8 are, "Behold the blood of the covenant, which the LORD hath made with you concerning all these words." It seems probable that Jesus patterned His statement after these words of Moses when He inaugurated the new covenant as He celebrated the Passover with His disciples at the Last Supper. As He offered them the cup, symbolizing His blood which was about to be shed, He announced, "This is my blood of the new testament, which is shed for many for the remission of sins" (Mt. 26:28). The writer of Hebrews, no doubt, saw the connection and thus emphasized these words in his observations about the old covenant.

Yeager (310) presents a strange idea at this point, maintaining that the Israelites should have refused God's covenant of law, and should have requested a furtherance of God's covenant of grace instead. He claims that it was pure arrogance which caused them to respond to Moses' reading of God's commandments with the pledge, "All the words which the LORD hath said will we do" (Ex. 24:3). It seems to me that Yeager is seeing something in this passage that is not there. Though their declaration might have been naive, nothing in the passage in Exodus indicates that the Lord was displeased with their pledge of allegiance to His instructions. Contrary to Yeager's reasoning, there is room for a commitment to obedience in the covenant of grace. Jesus Himself said to His disciples, "If ye love me, keep my commandments" (Jn. 14:15).

In v. 21, to further emphasize his point about the importance of blood under the old covenant, the writer refers to other occasions: "Moreover he sprinkled with blood both the tabernacle, and all the vessels of the ministry." In Exodus 24, at the inauguration of the old covenant, the tabernacle had not yet been built. But when Moses dedicated Aaron and his sons to the priestly ministry, several animal sacrifices were offered; from these Moses took blood and anointed the horns of the brazen altar, sprinkled blood around the altar, and touched their right ears, thumbs, and big toes with blood. Finally, he sprinkled Aaron and his sons and their garments with holy anointing oil and with blood (Ex. 29:1-21).

Subsequently, Moses "took the anointing oil, and anointed the tabernacle and all that was therein, and sanctified them" (Lev. 8:10). The two passages make clear that the tabernacle and its vessels were indeed sprinkled with both the holy anointing oil and with blood.

Anointing with oil was also mentioned when the tabernacle was set up and dedicated. God said to Moses, "Thou shalt take the anointing oil, and anoint the tabernacle, and all that *is* therein, and shalt hallow it, and all the vessels thereof: and it shall be holy" (Ex. 40:9). Josephus, again, reflects this same Hebrew tradition concerning the sprinkling of the tabernacle and its vessels with blood (*Antiquities* 3.206).

Verse 22 sums up the point of vv. 18-21. "And almost all things are by the law purged with blood." In Leviticus 1—5, Moses describes the different types of offerings, the dedicatory offerings in 1—3, and the sin offerings in 4, 5. Chapter 1 explains the whole burnt offering, a voluntary offering expressing complete dedication to God. Chapter 2 points to the grain offering, an offering expressing thanksgiving to God for His material blessings. Chapter 3 defines the peace offering, an offering expressing thanksgiving to God for His spiritual blessings. Chapter 4 records details about the *sin offering*, an offering made for priests, rulers, individuals, or the whole congregation of Israel, for sins of a general nature. Finally, chapter 5 describes the *trespass offering*, an offering made for more specific sins, especially for sins which violate the rights of others.

Of these five major offerings, only the grain offering was bloodless; all the others required a blood sacrifice. This explains why the writer uses the term "almost" in this first clause. His use of the word "purged" suggests application to the offerings of purification or dedication. In addition to these major offerings, other specific offerings used purification with water (Ex. 19:10; Lev. 15:5; 16:26, 28; 22:6) and with fire (Num. 31:22, 23). "Almost" goes only with the first clause (Lenski 310), not with both clauses in v. 22, as some commentators suggest (Kent 177).

Now our writer observes, "And without shedding of blood is no remission." As explained above, most of the dedicatory offerings demanded a blood sacrifice, as did *all* the types of offering for the forgiveness of sin, without exception. Some have seen an exception in the poor's offering for sin, which, in cases of extreme poverty, allowed the offering to be composed of "the tenth part of an ephah of fine flour" (Lev. 5:11). But even that does not imply an exception inasmuch as it was offered clearly as a substitute for the lamb, two turtledoves, or two young pigeons which the impoverished offerer could not afford.

The writer has made his case to the Hebrew congregation which he is addressing. They should not be repelled by the offering of the blood of Messiah since the whole covenant of law, from its initiation, was filled with the shedding of innocent blood as a type of that greater sacrifice to come. The word translated "shedding of blood" (Greek *haimatekchusia*) is found nowhere else in Greek literature and may have been coined by the writer (Lenski 311). However, the two words from which this word was formed (Greek *haima*—"blood" and *ekchuno*—"to shed" or "to pour out") are used together in Matt. 26:28, "This is my blood of the new testament, which is shed for many for the remission of sins." "Remission" (Greek *aphesis*) literally refers to "a sending away," which is what God does with our sins when He forgives them. The word appears again in 10:18. In other occurrences in the KJV it is sometimes translated "remission" and sometimes "forgiveness." David reflects this thought when he observes, "As far as the east is from the west, *so* far hath he removed our transgressions from us" (Ps. 103:12); in like manner Micah states about the Lord, "Thou wilt cast all their sins into the depths of the sea" (Mic. 7:19). The same idea was visually demonstrated on the Day of Atonement when the scapegoat was sent away into the wilderness, symbolically bearing the sins of Israel (Lev. 16:20-22).

(2) The new covenant inaugurated (9:23-28)

In vv. 16-22 the writer has established the importance of the principle of shedding blood for the cleansing of sin by pointing back to the dedication and inauguration of the first covenant, the covenant of Moses. By referring back to the O.T., he showed how animal sacrifices had been freely used in initiating the ministry of the law, the tabernacle, and the priesthood. The Lord explained the significance of shedding of blood for purification and redemption, rather than some other element, when He declared, "The life of the flesh *is* in the blood: and I have given it to you upon the altar to make an atonement for your souls: for it *is* the blood *that* maketh an atonement for the soul" (Lev. 17:11). Now the writer turns to the beginning of the new covenant and shows that the same principle is carried through with, however, some major differences.

23 It *was* therefore necessary that the patterns of things in the heavens should be purified with these; but the heavenly things themselves with better sacrifices than these.
24 For Christ is not entered into the holy places made with hands, *which are* the figures of the true; but into heaven itself, now to appear in the presence of God for us:
25 Nor yet that he should offer himself often, as the high priest entereth into the holy place every year with blood of others;
26 For then must he often have suffered since the foundation of the world: but now once in the end of the world hath he appeared to put away sin by the sacrifice of himself.
27 And as it is appointed unto men once to die, but after this the judgment:
28 So Christ was once offered to bear the sins of many; and unto them that look for him shall he appear the second time without sin unto salvation.

Verse 23 concludes: "*It was* therefore necessary that the patterns of things in the heavens should be purified with these." "Therefore" (Greek *oun*) is merely advancing the previous thought concerning the importance of blood for purification and remission under the old covenant. He is doing more, however, than just repeating the thought of v. 22. There is a balanced contrast between the two clauses of this verse (Greek *men/de* clauses), one that is not reflected in our English translation. Translators often indicate this contrast by inserting, "On the one hand" at the beginning of the first clause, and, "On the other hand," at the beginning of the second clause. Here the contrast is brought out by the presence of "therefore" in the first clause and the contrasting conjunction "but" at the beginning of the second clause.

"Necessary" (Greek *anagke*) goes with both clauses. The requirement of shedding blood, established under the old covenant, applies also under the new covenant. The O.T. tabernacle and priesthood were "patterns" (Greek *hupodeigma*) "of things in the heavens." The same word was used in the singular in 8:5, there translated "example," to make basically the same point with regard to the priesthood. "With these" refers back to "the blood of calves and of goats" mentioned in v. 19, the animal sacrifices used in the dedication and inauguration of the O.T. tabernacle.

Now the writer makes the contrast: "But the heavenly things themselves with better sacrifices than these."

"Purified" goes with both clauses, referring to the cleansing of both the earthly and the heavenly sanctuaries. Though it might be easy to see the need for the cleansing of the earthly tabernacle, since it was made with human hands, it is more difficult to see the need for cleansing the heavenly sanctuary where the very presence of the Holy God dwells. The solution is seen, however, in realizing that the cleansing applies to the sinners who would enter both sanctuaries, and to their sins which have been washed away, symbolically in O.T. animal sacrifices but actually in the shed blood of Jesus Christ.

Leviticus 16:16 explains, "He shall make an atonement for the holy *place*, because of the uncleanness of the children of Israel, and because of their transgressions in all their sins." Hughes (380) points out the same truth in relation to the heavenly tabernacle: "Moreover, the unapproachability of heaven to sinful man argues the need for the purification, not of heaven, but of the sinner: to redeemed mankind, cleansed from sin and sanctified by the Holy Spirit, heaven, previously closed, now lies open" (so also Kistemaker 262; Lenski 313). This new openness of Heaven will be further emphasized in 10:19-25.

While animal sacrifices might suffice for the symbolic and ceremonial purification of the O.T. tabernacle, "the heavenly things themselves"—that is, God's dwelling place in Heaven where Jesus Christ is now seated at the Father's right hand (1:3)—can only be occupied by sinners who have undergone a more literal and actual purification "with better sacrifices than these." The writer uses the plural, "better sacrifices," merely to refer to the general principle in contrast to "the blood of calves and of goats" used in the earthly tabernacle. That better sacrifice is, of course, fulfilled in the singular, once for all offering of the blood of Christ for the forgiveness of our sins.

When our Lord was on earth He often came to the outer portion of the Temple in Jerusalem where He prayed, worshiped, and taught, but He never entered the inner sanctuary. There was an abundant supply of Levitical priests to make those sacrifices. Thus, our writer explains, "For Christ is not entered into the holy places made with hands." "For" advances the thought from the better sacrifice of v. 23 to the better sanctuary in v. 24. "Christ" is the official title of the Son of God, connecting Him with the Messianic prophecies of the O.T., both in type and in word. "The holy places made with hands" refers to the Holy of Holies, including the one in the original tabernacle as well as those in the later temples in Jerusalem, including the Temple of Jesus' day. The same point was made in v. 11.

Those earthly sanctuaries were only "figures of the true." In a similar way, the writer referred to the tabernacle and its accompaniments in 9:23 as "the patterns of things in the heavens." "Figures" (Greek *antitupos*) refers to those things which are copies of the original. According to Acts 7:44, Moses was to make the tabernacle according to the "fashion" (Greek *tupos*) which he had seen on Sinai; and Heb. 8:5, referring to the same passage (Ex. 25:40), states that Moses was to make the tabernacle according to the "pattern" (Greek *tupos*) which he had seen in the mountain. In those passages what Moses saw in the mountain—evidently a verbal and/or visual presentation of the true tabernacle—was the "type"; and the tabernacle (by implication) was the "antitype." This use of antitype is in line with the meaning here in Heb. 9:24.

In 1 Pet. 3:21, the only other N.T. passage where the word for antitype is used, baptism is "the like figure" (Greek *antitupos*) to the flood of Noah's day. As the waters of the flood saved Noah and his family, so the waters of baptism, figuratively speaking, save those who come to Christ by faith. Here baptism, which represents salvation "by the resurrection of Jesus Christ," as Peter emphasizes in the last part of the verse, is the antitype, while the flood is the type. Thus, the customary view of type as the figure or picture and antitype as the fulfillment does not find consistency in these passages. That view is confirmed in Rom. 5:14 and 1 Pet. 3:21; but the opposite is seen in Acts 7:44, Heb. 8:5, and 9:24, where the figure or picture is viewed as the antitype and the fulfillment as the type.

This leads some authorities to conclude that the terms are ambiguous in the N.T., even somewhat interchangeable in meaning (Bauer 76; Morris 91; Westcott 271; Hughes 382; Alford 180), depending on the context. However, Yeager's view seems more satisfying. He says, "The two words do not refer to the real/unreal, heavenly/earthly, or physical/spiritual distinction, but to that which is first (*tupos*) and that which is made after it (*antitupos*)" (315). This idea brings all the references together: Adam is the type, Christ is the antitype (Rom. 5:14); the heavenly tabernacle is the type, and the earthly tabernacle, which came later, is the antitype (Acts 7:44; Heb. 8:5; 9:24); the waters of Noah's flood, which provided salvation for him and his family by bearing the ark, are a type, while the water of baptism, which represents salvation in Christ, is the antitype. Though this idea is a bit different from the normal view of type and antitype, it does serve to bring more consistency to the N.T. references.

In any case, Jesus Christ, as our Savior and High Priest, entered "the true" (Greek *alethinos*), the genuine, tabernacle, which, as the writer makes clear, is "heaven itself." His purpose for entering Heaven, the real tabernacle which has no divisions, was "now to appear in the presence of God for us." This refers, of course, to Christ's ascension into Heaven (see Acts 1:9) and taking His seat at the Father's right hand (see Acts 2:33, 34; Rom. 8:34; Eph. 1:20; Phil. 2:9-11; Col. 3:1; Heb. 1:3; 8:1; 10:12; 12:2). "To appear" states the purpose of our Lord's ascension to this exalted position, focusing on the beginning of His priestly ministry (Greek aorist tense), while "now" stresses the fact that it continues from that notable beginning to the present time. "In the presence of God" literally means "before the face of" [Greek *prosopon*] God. The location of our Lord's priestly ministry speaks of the influence and power which He possesses. What is most meaningful to believers is that this powerful ministry is also a personal ministry; it is "for us," for our benefit and advantage. Referring to at least one aspect of this ministry, John declares, "If any man sin, we have an advocate with the Father, Jesus Christ the righteous" (1 Jn. 2:1; see also Rom. 8:34 and Heb. 7:25).

In vv. 25-27 the writer stresses again the once-for-all effectiveness of the death of Christ (see previously in 7:27,

28; 9:12). The verb "appears," in v. 24, speaks not only of the *beginning* of Christ's session at the Father's right hand but also of its *permanence*, in contrast to that of the O.T. Levitical priests: "Nor yet that he should offer himself often." "Nor" indicates that v. 25 is continuing a second negative contrast to that mentioned in v. 24. There the negative point was that Christ did not enter an earthly Holy of Holies, but into Heaven itself. Here the point is that He did not repeatedly offer Himself, as the Levitical high priest did with his sacrifices on the annual Day of Atonement.

The offering of Himself refers to our Lord's death on the cross, as it did in v. 14 (Westcott 273; Hughes 384), not to His presentation of Himself for His High Priestly ministry at the Father's right hand (Alford 181; Lenski 316; Morris 92). This is confirmed by the fact that Christ's having been "once offered" in v. 28 is viewed as parallel to dying in v. 27.

In this light, the last part of v. 25 must be viewed as an abbreviated statement. Christ did not offer Himself often "as the high priest entereth into the Holy Place every year with blood of others." The full story, according to Leviticus 16, is that, on the annual Day of Atonement, the high priest offered two offerings on the brazen altar in the Outer Court of the tabernacle: a bullock for his own sins (Lev. 16:11) and a goat for the sins of the nation (Lev. 16:15). From both offerings the high priest took blood inside the veil, into the Holy of Holies, and sprinkled the Mercy Seat for temporary atonement, until the next year when the same procedure had to be repeated.

The writer of Hebrews, however, does not mention the priest's offering of a sacrifice for himself or the fact that the offering was actually made on the brazen altar, and then the blood was presented in the earthly Holy of Holies. His purpose in emphasizing only the priest's entrance into the Holy of Holies was to bring out the annual repetition of the Day of Atonement, in pointed contrast to the once-for-all sacrifice of Christ. "As the high priest entereth" gives evidence once again that the priestly service was still occurring as this epistle was being written (Hughes 383).

"The holy place" actually refers to the Holy of Holies, as in v. 12. This entrance into the earthly Holy of Holies by the Levitical high priest was made "every year with the blood of others," that is, with the blood of animal sacrifices which were only types and shadows of the true sacrifice to come.

In this present discussion the writer seems to imply that his Hebrew readers had questions with regard to the one sacrifice of Christ contrasted with the yearly repetition of the Levitical sacrifices. Consequently, he proceeds to demonstrate the incongruity of a repeated sacrifice on the part of Jesus Christ: "For then must he often have suffered since the foundation of the world." If, indeed, He offered an exact copy of the Levitical system, His death and resurrection would have to be constantly repeated since the beginning of time, for our Lord's atoning death did not merely cover sinners in the present and the future, it also, of necessity, looked backward and covered all the sins of all time from the fall of Adam until the end of time. This thought of Christ's death covering sins under the old covenant has already been mentioned in 9:15. Through His death He provided "redemption of the transgressions *that were* under the first testament."

His death is here presented in a very personal and emotional sense as having "suffered." From this word in the original (Greek *pascho*) we draw the terms "paschal" and "passion" in relation to the closing events of our Lord's earthly life, especially the events from His institution of the Lord's Supper, as He celebrated the Passover, until His death and burial. Note the variation of terms used for Christ's accomplishment at Calvary. It is referred to as blood, death, sacrifice, and suffering. Though the terms are similar in meaning, the variety presents the broadness of all that was involved (Lenski 317).

From the obvious absurdity of requiring the repeated offering of Christ, the writer turns to what is true: "But now once in the end of the world hath he appeared to put away sin by the sacrifice of himself." "But now" presents, by contrast of the inferior to that which is vastly superior, just as it did in 8:6. Once (Greek *hapax*) stands in contrast with the annual repetition of the Levitical sacrifices on the Day of Atonement, the same thought mentioned already in v. 12 (see also 7:27 and 10:10).

Furthermore, the timing of His death was not coincidental: it has taken place "in the end of the world": literally, "at the consummation of the ages." The terminology bears the same significance as "in these last days" (1:2). It refers to the period of the new covenant (8:6-13), when the old covenant has been set aside because of the arrival of Messiah and the completion of His earthly ministry. Paul expressed the same thought when he said, "When the fulness of the time was come, God sent forth his Son, made of a woman, made under the law" (Gal. 4:4).

All of history has found its fulfillment, from God's point of view, in the coming of Jesus Christ to this earth for His redemptive ministry culminating at Calvary. It is at this point in history that he has "appeared." This verb covers Christ's ministry from beginning to end, from incarnation to ascension, treating His entire earthly ministry as His "appearance." This corresponds to the declaration in Jn. 1:14, "The Word was made flesh, and dwelt among us." The purpose of His appearance was "to put away" (Greek *athetesis*) sin, which literally means "not placing" or "not putting" something. By implication this means "the removal" of something, or, in legal situations, "the annulling" of something. The only other place it is used in this epistle is in 7:18 where it refers to the "disannulling of the commandment going before." When applied to sin, as in this context, it points to the removal of sin itself from the repentant sinner as well as the debt to God which it has created. Through Jesus Christ, God refuses to place the debt of sin on our account and in fact removes the taint of sin from our lives. "If any man *be* in Christ, *he is* a new creature" (2 Cor. 5:17).

The means of this removal of sin was "by the sacrifice of himself." This stands in obvious contrast to the "blood of others" in v. 25, which the Levitical high priest offered on the Day of Atonement. That was good for the time but ineffective for eternity. Jesus Christ was both the priest and the sacrifice, both the offerer and the victim. John the Baptist summed it up well when he called attention to the approaching Messiah by exclaiming, "Behold the Lamb of God, which taketh away the sin of the world" (Jn. 1:29).

In vv. 27, 28 the writer makes a comparison between two things that are true of mankind in general, and those same two things as they are applied to Jesus Christ, the perfect man, the second Adam. Perhaps he is also further ridiculing the thought, mentioned in vv. 25, 26, of Christ repeating His sacrifice, as the Levitical priests did each year on the Day of Atonement. He offers, "And as it is appointed unto men once to die, but after this the judgment." Man's appointment for death is derived from the decree of a sovereign, all-powerful, all-knowing God. God predetermined man's fate prior to the fall when He promised, with regard to the forbidden tree, "In the day that thou eatest thereof thou shalt surely die" (Gen. 2:17). Though the primary application was to spiritual death as separation from God, the secondary application involved physical death. Thus, the Lord declared to Adam, after the fall, "In the sweat of thy face shalt thou eat bread, till thou return unto the ground; for out of it wast thou taken: for dust thou *art*, and unto dust shalt thou return" (Gen. 3:19).

Moses drove this truth home in Gen. 5 with the repeated phrase, "And he died." In like manner, Paul pointed to the result when he declared, "Wherefore, as by one man sin entered into the world, and death by sin; and so death passed upon all men, for that all have sinned" (Rom. 5:12). James adds, "And sin, when it is finished, bringeth forth death" (Jas. 1:15).

This appointment of man "once to die" is a general principle which does not preclude exceptions. Enoch did not die (Gen. 5:24; Heb. 11:5); neither did Elijah (2 Kings 2:11, 12); and there will, in fact, be a whole generation of Christians who will not die at the end of time (1 Th. 4:17; 1 Cor. 15:51, 52) but will rather "be caught up . . . to meet the Lord in the air." But unless the Lord intervenes the general rule will prevail.

We will all die, "but after this the judgment." In this passage "judgment" (Greek *krisis*) refers to the act or process of judging, not to the result or issue of judgment—the sentence (Greek *krima*), which appears in Heb. 6:2. No specifics are given about this judgment. It includes the appointment of all men with God, whether wicked or righteous (see Jn. 5:28, 29). If the judgment of the wicked and the righteous occur at different times in God's ultimate eschatological plan, that is not under consideration in this simple declaration. Sooner or later death comes to all (with the exceptions mentioned above) and the next event on the calendar is judgment.

Some religions speak of reincarnation where men have a second chance at living; and some, even in the broader Christian world (Roman Catholics, for example), embrace the idea of a purgatory after death where sins are purged over a period of time in preparation for Heaven. But the Bible contains no such teachings. For each one there is death, then judgment. For those who live by faith in Christ, there is absolutely no reason for concern, because our sins are under the blood; but for those who have not embraced the Savior, the urgent need to prepare for eternity cannot be overstressed (see Jn. 3:18, 19, 36). The idea of judgment is introduced here and further advanced in 10:26, 27.

What is true of men in general—that there is death, then judgment—is also true of Jesus Christ, the perfect man, though there are some variations in the fulfillment. The writer brings us to the comparison. He declares, So Christ was once offered to bear the sins of many. Our Lord's atoning sacrifice at Calvary satisfies the death parallel. Other than those unique exceptions like Lazarus, men generally die only once. In like manner Christ was once offered. The passive voice in no way contradicts the voluntariness of the sacrifice (Jn. 10:17, 18). Jesus was both the priest and the sacrifice.

Christ (Greek *ho christos*) is used with the definite article in the original, in contrast with v. 24, to place additional emphasis on His Messianic office ("The Christ," or "The Messiah"). This also calls greater attention to the fact that the writer is drawing from Isaiah's description of the Suffering Messianic Servant. In similar words, he prophesied, "He shall bear their iniquities" and "He bare the sin of many" (Is. 53:11, 12). Thus, the purpose of Christ's offering of Himself was to bear the sins of many. The picture of Jesus' bearing (Greek *anaphero*) our sins presents them as a heavy weight which has been lifted, an oppressive burden which has been removed.

On the ancient Day of Atonement, to which the writer often refers in this epistle, a second goat was selected according to God's instructions, called the scapegoat (Lev. 16:10). After the first goat was slain for the sins of the people, the high priest laid his hands on this goat and symbolically prayed the sins of Israel onto his head. Then a person selected for this specific purpose took the goat far into the wilderness with this declaration from the Lord, "The goat shall bear upon him all their iniquities" (Lev. 16:22).

Bearing the sins "of many" directly reflects the wording of Is. 53:12; thus it probably calls special attention toward the benefit of His death for Israel (Lenski 320), but it also may be a Hebraic way of referring to all (Hagner 149; see also Mk. 10:45). It certainly is not meant to contradict other clear statements in the New Testament, including those of this writer, which teach that Jesus' death was for everyone without exception (Jn. 3:16; 2 Cor. 5:14, 15; 1 Tim. 2:6; Heb. 2:9; 1 Jn. 2:2).

The second part of this declaration is parallel to the judgment mentioned for men in general in v. 27, but with an interesting and joyful variation as it is specifically applied to Jesus Christ: "And unto them that look for him shall he appear the second time without sin unto salvation." When the writer presents the return of Christ as to "them that look for him," he does not mean to suggest that the Second Coming will have no effect upon the unbelievers of this world. He is simply stressing the joyous aspects of Christ's return for believers. The pertinent question is, "Will Jesus find us watching?"

On the other side, the Apostle John spoke of "the resurrection of life" and "the resurrection of damnation" (Jn. 5:28, 29), and later he prophesied about Christ's return, "Behold, he cometh with clouds; and every eye shall see him, and they *also* which pierced him" (Rev. 1:7). Still, believers rejoice in the promise that he shall "appear the second time." Many Christians view Christ's return for His own and His return to judge the wicked as actually occurring at different times, but that must come from other Scripture and is not stated here. Note that there are three different appearances of Christ mentioned in these closing verses of chapter 9: (1) In the past He appeared on this earth "to put away sin by the sacrifice of himself" (v. 26); (2) In the present He has ascended to the Father's right hand "to appear in the presence of God for us" (v. 24); (3) In the future "he shall appear the second time without sin unto salvation" (v. 28).

But the purpose of His Second Coming will be entirely different from the first. This time His coming will be "without sin": that is, not to deal with sin, the primary purpose of His first coming. NIV translates, "not to bear sin." Then, positively, the Second Coming will be "unto salvation," that is, for the purpose of providing eternal deliverance for those who believe in Him. In the N.T. believers occupy three positions with regard to salvation: (1) At some point in the past, when we initially trusted Christ as our Savior, we were saved, and we received the gift of eternal life (Jn. 1:11, 12; 3:16; Eph. 2:8, 9; Rom. 10:13). (2) At the present time, and throughout our existence on this earth, we are being saved; that is, the Holy Spirit is still in the process of bringing us into conformity with the perfect image of Jesus Christ (see Heb. 10:14; Eph. 4:13). (3) In the future, we will be saved in the most complete sense of the word, when all of our hopes become a reality by the power of Jesus Christ (Heb. 9:28; 1 Jn. 3:2).

Summary (9:1-28)

In the latter part of chapter 8 the writer introduced the idea of the new covenant by quoting Jer. 31:31-34. Now in chapter 9 we find five contrasts between the old covenant and the new covenant. The first contrast with the old covenant is *in relation to the tabernacle and its furniture*. We come first into "the sanctuary" or The Holy Place where the candlestick or lampstand and the table of showbread were located. Then we proceed into "the Holiest of all," that is, The Holy of Holies, to which is attached "the golden censer." This apparently refers to the golden altar of incense, which in the O.T. account is listed with the furniture in the Holy Place. Here also is the Ark of the Covenant with its contents from the time of Moses: the golden pot of manna, Aaron's rod that budded, and the tables of the covenant. The contrast is completed with a reference to "the cherubims of glory" which shaded the mercy seat, actually a pure gold cover for the Ark of the Covenant (9:1-5).

The second contrast with the old covenant is *in relation to tabernacle divisions and priestly access*. The O.T. priests ministered regularly, even daily, in the first room, the Holy Place. They burned incense on the golden altar, lit the seven-branched lampstand every evening and put out the flame and dressed the lamp again every morning. They replaced the twelve loaves of bread on the table, representing the twelve tribes of Israel, once each week on the Sabbath (Lev. 24:5-9). But into the second room, the Holy of Holies, only the high priest entered each year on the Day of Atonement with blood from the sacrificial bullock for himself and blood from the sacrificial goat for the congregation. There was a message from the Holy Spirit in this, that, as long as the tabernacle was divided into two rooms, direct access to God was not open to all people. That tabernacle with its divisions and sacrifices was merely an external picture of the greater tabernacle and the greater sacrifice which was to come (9:6-10).

The third contrast between the old covenant and the new is *in relation to a better tabernacle, sacrifice, and covenant.* In 9:1-10 the writer has stressed the details and purpose of the O.T. tabernacle and sacrifices, and how they pointed toward the promise of that which was so much better. In these verses he proceeds to describe this more perfect tabernacle, which is not man-made, and this more perfect sacrifice, which is nothing less than the blood of Christ which cleanses those who receive it by faith, not merely externally, but also internally, and not just temporarily, but permanently. Because of this, Jesus Christ has become the Mediator of a new covenant which brings us genuine forgiveness and an eternal inheritance which we will share with Him (9:11-15).

The fourth contrast is between the old and the new *in relation to the inauguration and dedication of the covenants.* Here the word *covenant* is naturally and practically converted, in the KJV, to its alternate meaning of "testament" or "will." Since there is an inheritance to be gained, a testament must be presented; but for that testament to become active or effective, the testator—the one who left the will—must die. This death, signified by the shedding of sacrificial blood, was seen under the old covenant when Moses inaugurated and dedicated the tabernacle and all its contents. This necessity of death, which called for the shedding of blood, is also confirmed by the whole sacrificial system under the old covenant, especially sacrifices that involved the forgiveness of sins (9:16-22). If such shedding of blood was necessary in the inauguration and dedication of the old covenant, it is natural to expect that the new covenant, which was designed to replace the old, would be inaugurated and dedicated with a much better sacrifice. That expectation was fulfilled in Christ's death on the cross and His victorious presentation of Himself for service as our High Priest at God's right hand.

The fifth contrast is between the old and the new *in relation to the permanence of the sacrifice.* Whereas that old covenant was confirmed by the repetition of annual sacrifices on the Day of Atonement, the one sacrifice of Jesus Christ is good for all time. In this sense the ministry of Christ, as the perfect man, parallels what is true of men in general. For men there are death and judgment, and for Christ there are His vicarious death and His return for eternal deliverance of those who believe in Him (9:23-28).

Application: Teaching and Preaching the Passage (9:1-28)

The writer points out that the tabernacle, along with its furnishings, served as "a figure for the time then present" (9:9). Some of the ways in which the articles of furniture which are named served as types of Christ and the new covenant are easy to see. (1) The candlestick or lampstand, which always burned throughout the night, pointed to Christ as the light of the world (Jn. 8:12; 9:5). (2) The table of showbread pointed to Christ as the bread of life (Jn. 6:48-51). (3) The golden altar, upon which sweet incense was burned daily, pointed to the sweet fellowship we have with both the Father and the Son through the redeeming work of Christ. (4) The Ark of the Covenant pointed to Christ as He fully met all the demands of the law, which sinful man had never been able to do (Mt. 5:17, 18; Jn. 8:46). (5) The mercy seat with its cherubim, between which the presence of God appeared, pointed to Christ as the means of our reconciliation who, through offering His sinless person in our behalf, covered the charges against us and made it possible for us to have fellowship with a Holy God (2 Cor. 5:21; Col. 2:13, 14).

The three items contained in the Ark of the Covenant, which the writer calls attention to, were preserved for Israel at God's command because each item communicated an important message to future generations. (1) The golden pot of manna spoke of God's provisions for Israel, both spiritual and physical, and reminded them, and us, that God always knows our needs and will see that they are met, whether naturally or supernaturally (Mt. 6:33). (2) Aaron's rod that budded reminded Israel of the importance of priestly authority and of the need to follow good spiritual leadership; and of God's intolerance for rebellion against His clear commands (see Num. 16, 17; also Heb. 13:17). (3) The tables of the covenant, from which the ark got its name, presented the demands of a Holy God and, ideally, brought people to realize that sinful man could not fully meet these demands, making necessary further provision for God's mercy (Acts 15:10; Gal. 3:16; Jas. 2:10-12).

In 9:8-10 there are three things that were imperfect about the old system: (1) *Access was limited.* Under the old covenant only the high priest appeared in God's presence in the Holy of Holies, and that only once a year on the Day of Atonement. What a change has taken place through the death, resurrection, and ascension of Jesus Christ (see 9:24; 10:19). (2) *Sacrifices were lacking.* The sacrifices of the O.T. were somewhat similar to the modern credit card system. The card allows you to take the item with you, but it in no way pays the debt. Old Testament sacrifices postponed God's judgment on personal sin, but the payment was merely external, not internal. It did not bring completeness "as pertaining to the conscience." (3) *The purification did not last.* Everything under the old covenant was only temporary. It all had to be constantly repeated, awaiting "the time of reformation" which came in the person of Jesus Christ, our eternal high priest.

From 9:11-14, when the reformation did come (v. 10), changes necessarily occurred throughout the entire old covenant. Three changes are mentioned in these verses. (1) There was now *a perfect tabernacle* (v. 11). That tabernacle was "heaven itself," the dwelling place of God which the earthly tabernacle always symbolized. (2) There was *a perfect sacrifice* (v. 12). The O.T. sacrifices would only allow the high priest to enter before God's presence in the earthly Holy of Holies, and that only once each year. Christ, by His own blood, has entered the real Holy of Holies with a redemption that never needs repeating. (3) There was *a perfect purification* (vv. 13, 14). The O.T. sacrifices only provided a temporary, external cleansing, but the blood of Christ has provided both eternal and internal cleansing, cleansing that purges our "conscience from dead works to serve the living God."

The writer likes to stress things that are eternal throughout the epistle. He likes this emphasis, no doubt, because it contrasts so dramatically with all the temporary things under the old covenant. Three of the six references are in chapter 9. He mentions: (1) eternal salvation (5:9); (2) eternal judgment (6:2); (3) eternal redemption (9:12); (4) the eternal Spirit (9:14); (5) an eternal inheritance (9:15); and (6) the eternal (everlasting) covenant (13:20).

In 9:15-17 our English Bible uses a different word, "testament" or will, to bring out the fullness of the meaning of the Greek word (*diatheke*) which has been translated as "covenant." Therefore, in realizing that God's covenant with us also has the characteristics of a will, it is good to think of the various applications of that idea. (1) *A will is totally one-sided.* The one making the will, the testator, has sovereign authority over every aspect of the will. (2) *A will is often made by someone who has great wealth to pass on, an inheritance.* In contrast to earthly wills, however, that can only benefit the recipients for a short period, we receive an "eternal inheritance." (3) In the case of a will, there are also *heirs who may number as few or as many as the testator desires*. In this case we have already been told that Jesus Christ tasted death "for every man" (2:9). (4) A will may very well specify *conditions which must be met* before the inheritance can be received. The one main condition in this will is personal faith in Jesus Christ (see 4:2, 3; 6:1; 10:38; 11:1). (5) A will also may specify *circumstances under which the inheritance is forfeited*, and the writer of Hebrews seems to do just that in issuing five distinct warnings throughout the epistle (see the outline), especially the warnings of the two classic apostasy passages in 6:4-6 and 10:26-31.

In 9:19-22 what Moses dedicated under the old covenant with the blood of animal sacrifices should also be dedicated under the new covenant on the basis of the blood of Jesus Christ. (1) *He sprinkled the book with blood.* In Moses' case that referred to the covenant of law, that sacred document which informed man of all the requirements of a Holy God. In the case of Christians, we have the entire Bible, the Old and the New Testaments, which tell the whole story, not only of the demands of law, but also of the gift of grace. (2) *He sprinkled the people*, the people of Israel who had a mixture of attitudes in relation to the Lord and His covenant. In the modern Christian society not everyone is genuine either. Both then and now, only those who have a living relationship with God receive the true benefits of the sprinkled blood. But their sacrifices had to be repeated, while our sacrifice, the shed blood of Christ, is good for all time. (3) *He sprinkled the* tabernacle. Under the old covenant, that was where God's presence was manifested under very limited circumstances. We, too, should dedicate the buildings where we worship, where the true church meets, where we can experience the presence of God on a continuing basis, to the honor and glory of Jesus Christ and to the winning of disciples to His kingdom.

In 9:24-28 the word "appear" is used three different times. In each case a different Greek word is translated and a different time element is emphasized: (1) Past: in one of these appearances our Lord provided redemption for us—"He appeared to put away sin by the sacrifice of himself" (v. 26). (2) Present: in another appearance He provides continuing mediation and intercession for us—

"now to appear in the presence of God for us" (v. 24). (3) Future: in the final appearance at His Second Coming He will provide eternal deliverance for us—"unto them that look for him shall he appear the second time without sin unto salvation" (v. 28).

e. In relation to a permanent sacrifice (10:1-18)

Though we have a new chapter in the epistle, the discussion is a continuation of what the writer has been emphasizing in the last part of chapter 9. In a broader sense, he is continuing his contrasts between the old and new covenants which he began in 9:1. He has pointed to the tabernacle and its furniture (9:1-5), the tabernacle divisions and priestly access (9:6-10), the better tabernacle, sacrifice, and covenant (9:11-15), the inauguration and dedication of the covenants (9:16-28); now, finally, he points to the contrast between the temporary sacrifices of the O.T. and the permanent sacrifice of the N.T. (10:1-18).

(1) Yearly repetition points to an inadequate sacrifice (10:1-4)

1 For the law having a shadow of good things to come, *and* not the very image of the things, can never with those sacrifices which they offered year by year continually make the comers thereunto perfect.
2 For then would they not have ceased to be offered? because that the worshippers once purged should have had no more conscience of sins.
3 But in those *sacrifices there is* a remembrance again *made* of sins every year.
4 For *it is* not possible that the blood of bulls and of goats should take away sins.

"For" indicates that the writer is continuing the subject under discussion in the last part of chapter 9. In 9:25-28 he had emphasized the once-for-all sacrifice of Jesus Christ in contrast with the repeated sacrifices of the Old Testament. There his point was made in connection with the inauguration and dedication of the new covenant. Here he stresses the fact that the very repetition of the O.T. sacrifices proves their ineffectiveness. "The law" would include the whole Mosaic system, with all its instructions, rules, and symbols, but the primary reference is to the Levitical sacrifices. In comparison with the new covenant and the coming of Jesus Christ, the law offered a mere "shadow" (Greek *skia*), a word used previously in 8:5. There he referred to the Levitical priests "who serve unto the example and shadow of heavenly things." Here the "shadow" is the Levitical sacrifices and what they represented.

There are at least three different opinions concerning the meaning of the word "shadow" in this context: (1) It may refer to the shadow cast by the actual substance (Lenski 322). A shadow is valuable because it stands as the symbol of the real thing, the proof that something better is near at hand. (2) It may refer to the rough sketch, the outline, which the artist uses as a guide in producing the final painting. The sketch is merely black and white, but the finished work of art adds all the color and the substance (Westcott 303). (3) It may refer to the plans drawn by an architect which, when in the hands of master carpenters, result in a beautiful building. Just as with our English word shadow, the Greek word is capable of any of these meanings in a given context, and each one of these serves to illustrate the point. But the idea of the sketch of an artist leading up to the full painting is probably preferred by more commentators.

The Levitical sacrifices under the law of Moses looked forward to "good things to come." These are good things "to come" from the standpoint of those who were living under the law, those under the old covenant. These things point toward the fulfillment of the law in the coming of Jesus Christ, especially with regard to His being the perfect sacrifice for sin, of which the animal sacrifices under the old covenant were merely typical. These good things were primarily realized in the earthly work of Christ; but, as Westcott (305) points out, there may be some aspects which await complete fulfillment in our Lord's future kingdom (see 13:14). The meaning of "something that is to come," "something that is about to happen," must always be determined by the context, by the perspective from which the observation is made. For example, in 2:5 "the world to come" refers to the world which God was about to create, over which He placed Adam and his descendants; in 9:11 Christ as High Priest "of good things to come" refers primarily to the joys which we will experience with Christ in eternity, while the present passage refers to the fulfillment of the law in the ministry of Christ.

Thus, the law furnished only a shadow, a bare outline, a sketch, "not the very image of the things." "Image" (Greek *eikon* from which our English word "icon" is derived) refers to the visible manifestation of the real things, the real things as they appear, while "the things" refers to the real substance itself. The "image" was reality as manifested in the sacrifice of Jesus Christ, while the animal sacrifices under the law were only a poor shadow, a weak outline, of that reality.

Because of this the law "can never with those sacrifices which they offered year by year continually make the comers thereunto perfect." "Which they offered" is literally "which they are offering," furnishing yet another indication that the Temple was still standing and the Levitical sacrifices were still being made when Hebrews was written. "Year by year" indicates that the writer is primarily referring to the sacrifices of the Day of Atonement, as he did in 9:25, which occurred each year on the 10th day of the 7th month in the Hebrew calendar (Lev. 16:29, 30). This observance of the Day of Atonement not only occurred annually, on the same day each year, offering the same sacrifices each year, but it also occurred "continually": perpetually, year after year and generation after generation. The very fact of its regular and protracted repetition spoke volumes about the ineffectiveness of the sacrifices.

"The comers" are, literally, "those who are coming" for repentance, praise, and worship. These included both the high priest who made the offerings and the people of Israel for whom he made them. Those sacrifices on that remarkable day, as powerful and dramatic as they were to the Hebrew worshipers, could "never . . . make perfect" those who longed for peace and forgiveness, could never provide genuine pardon and purity of conscience (see 9:9) to meet the desired goal of those who came.

In v. 2 the writer stresses the simplicity of his point by asking "For then would they not have ceased to be offered?" The construction expects a positive answer to the rhetorical question: "Yes, those sacrifices would have ceased if they had provided true satisfaction and forgiveness in relation to sin." Their continual repetition proved their inefficacy in contrast to the eternal effectiveness of the one sacrifice of Jesus Christ. When Christ died, the Scripture record points out that the veil of the Temple was ripped open from the top to the bottom (Mt. 27:51), thus literally opening the way into the earthly Holy of Holies.

A powerful act of God through an earthquake brought those continuing and ineffectual sacrifices to a halt. Surely the unbelieving Jewish leaders must have repaired the damage, continuing in their feeble efforts to preserve the O.T. sacrifices for a period of time. But by another act of God's providence the Jewish Temple would be destroyed 40 years later in A.D. 70 by the Roman army. Since that time no sacrifices have been offered in Jewish worship, even by those who still, in rejection of Christ as their Messiah, claim to subscribe to the antiquated approach of the old covenant.

In the second clause of v. 2 the writer supplies the reason those O.T. sacrifices would have ceased had they been truly effective: "because that the worshippers once purged should have had no more conscience of sins." "Worshippers" suggests ongoing activity (Greek present tense), continuing to worship even when the sacrifice is permanently effective. In fact, worship (service) will take place even in the eternal state. John describes our experience in the Holy City, the New Jerusalem which he saw coming down from Heaven, in these words, "There shall be no more curse: but the throne of God and of the Lamb shall be in it; and his servants shall serve [worship—same Greek word] him" (Rev. 22:3).

"Once purged" (Greek *katharizo*) refers to a sacrifice that offers permanent cleansing, cleansing that never needs repeating. If such had been the case with the O.T. worshipers, then they "should have had no more conscience of sins." This is the single most telling characteristic of a sacrifice that is truly "perfect"; that is, the effect that it has on the consciousness of sin in the worshiper's heart and mind—a thought already mentioned in 9:9. Such genuine spiritual peace in the absence of self-condemnation comes only through the perfect sacrifice of God's Son, Jesus Christ (see Rom. 5:1; 8:1). The conclusion reached here, in relation to the sacrifices, is similar to that reached earlier in relation to the priesthood (7:11) and in relation to the covenant (8:7). The call for a new priesthood according to the order of Melchisedec argues for the passing of the old priesthood; the reference to a new covenant in Jeremiah suggests the passing of the old covenant, and the presence of the permanent sacrifice of Christ demands the abandonment of the old sacrificial system. But that conclusion in relation to the sacrifice of Christ awaits the discussion which begins in v. 5.

If, as the writer has just argued, the cessation of sacrifices attests to the effectiveness of those sacrifices, then the Levitical sacrifices were certainly not effective. He explains in v. 3: "But in those *sacrifices there is* a remembrance again *made* of sins every year." "But" (Greek *alla*) offers a strong contrast. The true situation, at least prior to the coming of Christ, was that there was a yearly continuation of the O.T. sacrifices on the Day of Atonement. Thus, instead of fully atoning for sins and effectively putting them aside, "a remembrance again" was made of personal and national sins each year, emphatically demonstrating that the sin problem had not been solved. This "remembrance" (Greek *anamnesis*) was not merely passive but an active recalling of the sinners' unpaid debt on an annual basis. Under the new covenant, when the sin problem has found permanent resolution in the sacrifice of Christ, not only does God not call our sins to our remembrance, He also does not remember them Himself (see 8:12 from Jer. 31:34).

In v. 4 the writer explains why the repetition of the O.T. sacrifices continued for so long, "For *it is* not possible that the blood of bulls and of goats should take away sins." "The blood of bulls and of goats" again recalls the sacrifices of the Day of Atonement, already mentioned in 9:12, 19. By their very nature those animals could not provide genuine atonement for sin, for their sacrifice was neither conscious nor voluntary. They could serve as types and symbols of the great sacrifice of Jesus Christ, but beyond that they were powerless. The verb "take away" (Greek *aphaireo*) views sin as something that needs to be removed to provide freedom of conscience and open access to God, a defiling stain that must be cleansed. The word is often used for the idea of forgiveness of sin in the Septuagint. The blood of animal sacrifices could not provide it.

(2) The psalmist points to an obedient sacrifice (10:5-10)

5 Wherefore when he cometh into the world, he saith, Sacrifice and offering thou wouldest not, but a body hast thou prepared me:
6 In burnt offerings and *sacrifices* for sin thou hast had no pleasure.
7 Then said I, Lo, I come (in the volume of the book it is written of me,) to do thy will, O God.
8 Above when he said, Sacrifice and offering and burnt offerings and *offering* for sin thou wouldest not, neither hadst pleasure *therein*; which are offered by the law;
9 Then said he, Lo, I come to do thy will, O God. He taketh away the first, that he may establish the second.
10 By the which will we are sanctified through the offering of the body of Jesus Christ once *for all*.

In 10:1-4 the writer has shown that the O.T. sacrifices were inadequate because they had to be repeated every year and because by their very nature, involving the blood of bulls and goats, they could not possibly atone for the sin and rebellion of humanity against a Holy God. Now in 10:5-10 he points to the sacrifice that did prove to be efficacious, the sacrifice of the obedient Son of God.

"Wherefore" (Greek *dio*) serves to highlight the contrast between the sacrifices that did not work and that one that did. "When he cometh into the world" is a specific reference to the birth of Christ, when the Son of God took upon Himself human flesh (Jn. 1:14). The

Gospel of John often associates this phrase with Christ's birth (see Jn. 6:14; 12:46; 16:28). In Jn. 18:37 Jesus responded to Pilate's question about being a king by declaring, "To this end was I born, and for this cause came I into the world, that I should bear witness unto the truth." The phrase may look at His total ministry, but without its beginning in His birth through the virgin Mary, the other parts of His ministry could not have been fulfilled.

At this point the writer puts the words of Ps. 40:6-8 into the mouth of Jesus the Messiah. But he has at least a twofold justification for doing so: the spirit of Christ was in David when he wrote these words concerning the coming of Messiah, and the seed of David was in Jesus Christ as He speaks these words through the writer of this epistle (see Rom. 1:3). Thus, we have the quotation with the writer's expression, "He saith." And what He said, through the inspired and prophetic words of the psalmist, is quite revealing: "Sacrifice and offering thou wouldest not." Several passages in the O.T. speak of God's dissatisfaction with sacrifices offered in a meaningless, ceremonial fashion (1 Sam. 15:22; Ps. 51:16, 17; Hos. 6:6; Is. 1:10-15; Jer. 7:21-23). In a similar declaration in Ps. 51:16, 17, the psalmist declares, "For thou desirest not sacrifice; else would I give *it*: thou delightest not in burnt offering. The sacrifices of God *are* a broken spirit: a broken and a contrite heart, O God, thou wilt not despise." This certainly does not mean that the sacrifices were not important, or that they were not a legitimate means of approach to God under the O.T. system. What it does mean is that, even in that era, sacrifices alone were useless.

The Messiah continues to speak, "But a body hast thou prepared me." This clause has caused a great deal of controversy. The reason for the dilemma is that the quotation from Ps. 40:6 seems to be totally different from what we read in our English O.T., which translates the Hebrew text. The same clause there reads, "Mine ears hast thou opened," or, as the margin reads, "Mine ears hast thou digged." Some have translated the Hebrew as, "Mine ears hast thou pierced" (NIV) and attempted an association with the ear-piercing of the submissive Hebrew slave (Ex. 21:6; Dt. 15:17), but this approach is rejected by most translators and commentators. The quotation recorded by the writer of Hebrews, as always, follows the Septuagint (LXX) reading.

At first the two different translations seem to have no similarity: the Septuagint, "A body hast thou prepared me," and the Hebrew, "Mine ears hast thou digged/opened." But when we read on in the quotation, we find that the primary thrust in both translations is about doing God's will, about fully and completely obeying the Lord. This ties the two approaches together. In following the Hebrew text, the ears have been cleared of all obstruction so that God's instructions may be clearly heard, received, and obeyed. In the Greek rendering a body has been prepared for carrying out the Lord's commandments to their fullest. The Septuagint reading, which our writer quotes, was most likely an interpretive paraphrase of the Hebrew text (Kistemaker 275; Lenski 328). In this case the Holy Spirit led our writer to use this quote from Ps. 40 because it applies so appropriately to the ultimate fulfillment of the words in the coming and ministry of Jesus Christ.

The ears hear God's instructions, but it is an obedient body that puts the instructions into practice.

In v. 6 Messiah continues to speak in the words of Ps. 40:6: "In burnt offerings and *sacrifices* for sin thou hast had no pleasure." Combined with the two words for Levitical offerings in the previous verse, these four terms give a broad summary of the different types of offerings in the Levitical system (Kistemaker 275; Hughes 397), described in detail in Leviticus 1—5. The prophets also often spoke of God's displeasure with sacrifices that were made without the accompaniment of obedient lives. Through Isaiah the Lord declared rather bluntly to Israel, "To what purpose *is* the multitude of your sacrifices unto me? saith the LORD: I am full of the burnt offerings of rams, and the fat of fed beasts; and I delight not in the blood of bullocks, or of lambs, or of he goats" (Is. 1:11). The context of such declarations always reveals that God's disappointment, even His wrath, was due to Israel's lack of obedience, not to the sacrifices in themselves which, of course, He had commanded. When King Saul attempted to cover his sin with an abundance of sacrifices, Samuel, as God's spokesman, thundered, "Hath the LORD *as great* delight in burnt offerings and sacrifices, as in obeying the voice of LORD? Behold, to obey *is* better than sacrifice, *and* to hearken than the fat of rams" (1 Sam. 15:22).

Now the Messiah-King speaks in the first person through the words of the psalmist: "Then said I, Lo, I come (in the volume of the book it is written of me,) to do thy will, O God." David originally spoke these words as an expression of his own desires. In the last part of Ps. 40:8, which our writer does not quote, David said, "Yea, thy law *is* within my heart." David was far above most men of his time in his spiritual relationship with God, as is clearly demonstrated by the psalms which he penned. The characteristic desire of his heart was, no doubt, to do God's will, notable failures and weaknesses admitted in this same Psalm: "Mine iniquities have taken hold upon me, so that I am not able to look up; they are more than the hairs of mine head" (Ps. 40:12). But the part of the psalm which Hebrews quotes is clearly Messianic: though David's basic desire was to obey God, that desire was only perfectly fulfilled in God's Son, Jesus Christ.

The Messiah-King's prevailing desire is "Lo, I come . . . to do thy will, O God." The expressions of His determination to do God's will occur throughout the Gospels, but especially in the Gospel of John: "For I came down from heaven, not to do mine own will, but the will of him that sent me" (Jn. 6:38; see also 4:34 and 8:29). For Him to be the perfect sacrifice, He must also be the obedient sacrifice. When the Jewish leaders accused Him of destroying the law of Moses because He did not follow their man-made rituals, he proclaimed, "I am not come to destroy, but to fulfil" (Mt. 5:17). That obedience was absolute, extending from the beginning of His life until the day of His death. Thus Paul observed that He "became obedient unto death, even the death of the cross" (Phil. 2:8).

Psalm 40:7 includes a parenthetical explanation: "In the volume of the book *it is* written of me." Perhaps David originally had in mind such prophecies as Dt. 17:14-20 which laid down guidelines concerning the future king of Israel, including making a copy of the law for himself, reading it regularly, and keeping "all the words of this law and these statutes, to do them." When given broader application to Messiah-King in this context, the reference includes all the Messianic prophecies throughout the five books of Moses (Gen. 3:15; 12:3; 49:10; Num. 24:17; Dt. 18:15, 18). "Volume" (Greek *kephalis*) properly refers to the highest point, the head of something (Yeager 327). It evidently referred to the small knobs on each end of the roll upon which the Scripture was stored in antiquity. In this case the smaller part evidently stands for the whole (in rhetoric a synecdoche or a metonymy), especially in the combined phrase, "The volume of the book."

"It is written" is the familiar expression of Biblical prophecy, meaning that it has been written and continues to stand as such (Greek perfect tense). Though the passage applies specifically to Jesus our Savior as the obedient sacrifice, such doing of His will is God's desire for all believers. Paul declared to the Roman Christians, "I beseech you therefore, brethren, by the mercies of God, that ye present your bodies a living sacrifice, holy, acceptable unto God, *which* is your reasonable service" (Rom. 12:1). We are truly saved through faith in the finished work of Christ, but "Faith, if it hath not works, is dead, being alone" (Jas. 2:17).

Now our writer turns to analysis: "Above when he said, Sacrifice and offering and burnt offerings and *offering* for sin thou wouldest not, neither hadst pleasure *therein*; which are offered by the law." By "above" (Greek *anoteron*) he does not mean, as we commonly say in writing, "As was said previously." He means, rather, to sum up "the first point" in the quotation from Ps. 40, that is, the negative point concerning God's displeasure with the animal sacrifices (Lenski 329; also NIV). He has put them all together in his abbreviated summary of the quotation. He acknowledges, however, that these are sacrifices "which are offered according to the law." The verb "which are offered," in reference to the Levitical sacrifices, is expressed in the present time, once again indicating that the sacrificial system was still being carried out when Hebrews was written.

The writer concedes, as his Hebrew audience knew, that the O.T. sacrifices were carried out at God's command. But in spite of this God was not satisfied with them for at least two reasons: (1) they were only types and shadows of the true sacrifice which was to come; and (2) they were often not offered by obedient worshipers, but only to meet formal and ceremonial requirements.

The analysis continues in v. 9: "Then said he, Lo, I come to do thy will, O God." The first point, the negative one, was God's displeasure with the sacrifices as they were offered by Israel; the second point, the positive point, is what God was pleased with: namely, the obedient sacrifice of Jesus Christ. Often in the N.T. the redemption of man is connected with the will of God. The inheritance which we have obtained in Jesus Christ was predestinated "according to the purpose of him who worketh all things after the counsel of his own will" (Eph. 1:11). God "will have all men to be saved, and to come unto the knowledge of the truth" (1 Tim. 2:4). God "is longsuffering to us-ward, not willing that any should perish, but that all should come to repentance" (2 Pt. 3:9; see also Eph. 1:5, 9).

The writer has enumerated the two main points from Ps. 40: first, the animal sacrifices of the O.T. with which God was not pleased; and, second, the obedient sacrifice of Jesus Christ, the Messiah-King, with which He was very well pleased (Mt. 3:17; 12:18; 17:5). The conclusion should be obvious to the Jewish readers: "He taketh away the first, that he may establish the second." The O.T. sacrificial system has been annulled, declared invalid (see also 7:11; 8:7, 13); the obedient sacrifice of Christ has been established as the only way of salvation for both Jews and Gentiles, indeed for all mankind (Jn. 14:6; Acts 4:12).

In v. 10 the writer gives his conclusion on the basis of the quotation from Ps. 40:6-8, "By the which will we are sanctified through the offering of the body of Jesus Christ once *for all*." "By the which will" means in connection with the will of God and included in the will of God as one of its most important aspects. "Will" refers us back to the same word in v. 9 from the quotation of Ps. 40:8: God's will that made Christ our perfect sacrifice, "obedient unto death, even the death of the cross" (Phil. 2:8). "We are sanctified" refers to an action that was completed in the past but with results that continue (Greek perfect tense). Theologians sometimes refer to this as initial sanctification. In the order of salvation, it occurs at the same time as justification (Rom. 3:24-28); but, where justification emphasizes our new position in Christ, this aspect of sanctification emphasizes the practical result, the cleansing effect of the work of redemption (2 Cor. 5:17; see also Jn. 17:19; Acts 20:32; 26:18; 1 Cor. 1:2).

We often think of sanctification in three phases: (1) *initial* sanctification which stands complete in Jesus Christ, but also serves as the basis of our continuing sanctification; (2) *progressive* sanctification, the process of growing in grace and gradually becoming more conformed to the image of Christ, a process which continues throughout our Christian lives (Heb. 2:11; 10:14; Eph. 4:11-13; 2 Pet. 3:18); and (3) *final* sanctification, which will not take place until we meet Christ, when our conformity to His spiritual image is finally complete (1 Jn. 3:2).

The means of this sanctification, this justification, was "through the offering of the body of Jesus Christ." The word "body" takes us back to the quotation from Ps. 40:6 as it reads in the Septuagint "A body hast thou prepared for me" (v. 5). It was the incarnation of the eternal Son of God, when the Word became flesh (Jn. 1:14), that made our redemption possible. Other aspects of His life on earth were also important, especially His perfect obedience and certainly His vicarious death, but without the incarnation there would have been no body that should bear our sins on the cross, that should suffer and die in our place.

Commentators disagree about the application of "once for all" (Greek *ephapax*). Some think that it goes with "we are sanctified," emphasizing that our initial sanctification or justification cannot be repeated (Lenski 331; Lunemann 366). Others think that it must apply to "the offering of the body of Christ" (Barnes 228; Kistemaker 277; Hughes 399), while Westcott (312) thinks that it goes with the whole sentence. The same word is used in 7:27 to refer to Christ's offering up Himself, and in 9:28 the more common word (Greek *hapax*) is used in the same way. This tends to support referring it to the offering of Christ here, but Westcott's explanation allows for both meanings, and there is something attractive about that. In any case, it is certain from other passages that initial sanctification or justification cannot be repeated. If salvation should ever be forfeited through final apostasy from Christ, a repeat experience would not be available (see 6:4-6; 10:26-31).

The writer combines both our Lord's human name and His official title (elsewhere only in 13:8, 21) in speaking about the offering of His body. It was "Jesus Christ," the Son of God, yes, but it was "Jesus Christ" in His total humanity who gave Himself for us.

(3) Christ's position points to a sufficient sacrifice (10:11-14)

11 And every priest standeth daily ministering and offering oftentimes the same sacrifices, which can never take away sins:
12 But this man, after he had offered one sacrifice for sins for ever, sat down on the right hand of God;
13 From henceforth expecting till his enemies be made his footstool.
14 For by one offering he hath perfected for ever them that are sanctified.

The writer confirms the finished work of Christ, in contrast to that of the Levitical priests, by emphasizing His present position at God's right hand. No repetition of His sacrifice will ever be needed. He will instead maintain His present position until He claims total victory at His Second Coming. Verse 11 reminds the Jewish readers of the tediousness and the uselessness of the efforts of the Levitical priests: "And every priest standeth daily ministering and offering oftentimes the same sacrifices." "And" demonstrates that he is continuing the subject at hand, the superiority of the sacrifice of Christ in contrast with the weakness and inefficacy of the Levitical offerings.

The work of "every priest" is involved, not just that of the high priest who performed the offerings of the Day of Atonement. This includes the whole gamut of Levitical services throughout the Jewish year. As the priests multiplied, they were divided into 24 different courses, each one taking his turn of service according to his appointment (1 Chr. 24:1-19; Lk. 1:5). That service is performed as the Jewish priest "standeth," clearly indicating that his work was not finished (see Dt. 10:8; 18:7). No performance of priestly duties was ever done from a seated position.

The priest's "ministering and offering" were, in many cases, performed "daily." The law required both a morning and an evening sacrifice (Num. 28:2-8), special offerings every Sabbath (Num. 28:9, 10), a variety of offerings for individuals as they approached the tabernacle with different needs on a daily basis, as well as all the sacrifices in connection with the Jewish holy days. The seven-branched lampstand also had to be dressed and refilled each morning, the lamps had to be lit each evening, and sweet incense was burned on the altar as these duties were performed (Ex. 30:7, 8). There were many other services and sacrifices too numerous to mention.

As the priest followed this ritual, he was "offering oftentimes the same sacrifices." The writer stresses the frequency and the redundancy under the Levitical system. Five different animals are mentioned as sacrifices under various circumstances: a bullock, a goat, a lamb, a turtledove, and a pigeon. In spite of this river of blood which flowed from the brazen altar of the tabernacle and Temple, that blood from those sacrifices "can never take away sins." "Take away" (Greek *periaireo*) views sin as a garment which is wrapped around its victims. Through regular and prolonged practice, they have woven for themselves a deadly robe, and the sacrifices that they offered were powerless to remove those old garments and to provide them with the garments of righteousness they needed.

The writer has set up vv. 11, 12 so that they provide a balanced contrast (Greek *men/de* clauses), with almost every part of v. 11 providing a contrast with a corresponding part in v. 12. (Such contrasts can often be translated "on the one hand; on the other hand.") The contrast is emphasized in v. 12: "But this man, after he had offered one sacrifice for sins for ever, sat down on the right hand of God." There are at least four contrasts here: (1) "Every priest" in v. 11 contrasts with "this man" in v. 12. (2) The repeated sacrifices contrast with the "one sacrifice" by Jesus Christ. (3) The fact that those sacrifices could "never take away sins" contrasts with this "one sacrifice for sins for ever." (4) The O.T. priestly position of "standing," indicating the unfinished aspect of their work, contrasts with the work of this man who "sat down," indicating that His work was now complete.

Indeed, "this man," Jesus Christ, the only-begotten Son of God, stands in contrast to the O.T. priest in many ways. Though Christ was a man, as they were, He was not a sinner. He had no need to make an offering for Himself. Furthermore, He needs no successor to carry on unfinished work; the sacrificial aspect of His work is complete. The "one sacrifice for sins" which He made has been defined several times, last in v. 10 where our writer pointed to "the offering of the body of Jesus Christ."

"Forever" grammatically can go with "one sacrifice for sins" or with the statement that this man "sat down" after completing His sacrifice. Because of this, Kent (192) avoids taking a position either way, indicating that both ideas are theologically possible. Lenski (333) feels strongly that "for ever," or "in perpetuity" as he translates it, should apply to Christ's seated position at God's right hand, emphasizing the continuation of His priestly ministry for us today; Westcott (315) points out that this and similar descriptions in Hebrews always refer to the permanent effectiveness of the offering of Christ (see 7:27; 9:12, 25-28; 10:10, 14). It seems best to go with this consistency and read, "One sacrifice for sins for ever."

The statement that He "sat down" after completing His sacrifice clearly stresses the finality of His work, the perpetual efficacy of His offering. This position of seated authority "on the right hand of God" is also mentioned, with some variation, in 1:3 ("on the right hand of the Majesty on high"); 8:1 ("on the right hand of the throne of the Majesty in the heavens"); and 12:2 ("at the right hand of the throne of God"); see also Eph. 1:20; Rev. 3:21; 4:9-11. When He took this position, of course, He did not cease to be our High Priest. The sacrificial aspect of His priesthood was complete, but the intercessory part of His ministry was just beginning. That important side of His ministry, which receives emphasis in this epistle, was pointed out earlier (see 2:18; 4:14-16; 7:25).

Without designating any specific time limits, in v. 13 the writer points out how long and with what attitude our Lord will keep this exalted position as our intercessory priest: "From henceforth expecting till his enemies be made his footstool." The Scripture points out that the exact time of our Lord's return is known only by the Father (see Mt. 24:36; Acts 1:7). Thus Jesus Christ is content, "expecting" (Greek *ekdechomai*) that time, as Paul waited expectantly for Timothy and Silas at Athens (Acts 17:16), or as the farmer eagerly awaits the harvest (Jas. 5:7).

That time will not come "till his enemies be made his footstool." The enemies of Christ include the devil, death (2:14; 1 Cor. 15:26), and all those who refuse Him as their Savior (Mt. 12:30; Ps. 2:1-3; Acts 4:25-27). The basis of our Lord's exalted position at God's right hand comes from Ps. 110:1, which the writer quoted earlier (1:13) in the context of his discussion of the superiority of Christ to angels. Paul describes in more detail this time of victory at the return of Christ when all enemies have been put under His feet (see 1 Cor. 15:24-28). While we look with eager expectation for His return (9:28), He also looks with anticipation, from His position of exalted authority, to the defeat of His last enemy and to His return in glory (Rev. 20:10-15).

In v. 14 the writer sums up his discussion in vv. 11-13, concisely contrasting the O.T. sacrifices with that of Jesus Christ: "For by one offering he hath perfected for ever them that are sanctified." "For" introduces the reason why Christ will continue to occupy His exalted position at the Father's right hand until the end of time. "By one offering" stands in sharp contrast with the many offerings offered daily, weekly, monthly, and annually under the Levitical system. Their ineffectiveness was proclaimed by the necessity of repetition, while the efficacy of Christ's offering, the offering of His own body (v. 10), is emphasized in the total satisfaction which it brings on the part of both God and man.

By this one offering our Lord "hath perfected for ever" those who come to Him by faith. This theme of perfection runs throughout this epistle. It appears in verb form in 2:10; 5:9; 7:19, 28; 9:9; 10:1, 14; 11:40; 12:23; and in noun form in 6:1; 7:11; and 12:2; and in adjective form in 5:14 and 9:11. Perfection, as our writer uses it, means completeness in relation to a specific goal: in this case, the goal of providing full atonement for sins and, by doing so, providing also complete reconciliation with a Holy God. This has been fully accomplished through the death and resurrection of Jesus Christ. "He hath perfected" points to completed action with continuing results (Greek perfect tense). The perfection referred to here is the same as justification in other passages (see Lk. 18:14; Acts 13:39; Rom. 4:25; 3:24; 5:1; etc.), and it is also the same as the sanctification referred to in v. 10 ("By the which will we are sanctified").

"For ever" should be taken in the most absolute sense. There will never be a need for this one offering to be repeated. Its effects are good for all time. The objects whom he has perfected, has justified by faith, are "them that are sanctified." "To sanctify" in the N.T. means "to set apart," "to make holy." It is most appropriate that those who are "in Christ" by faith become like Him, conformed to His image (Rom. 8:28, 29). One of the most common ways of referring to believers in the N.T. is as "saints," or "holy ones" (1 Cor. 1:2; 2 Cor. 1:1; Eph. 1:1; etc.)

The phrase used here can be translated, "Those who are being sanctified" (Greek present tense). Here sanctification refers to the process, which is guided in our lives by the word and the Holy Spirit, of making us more and more like Jesus Christ (see Jn. 17:17; Eph. 4:13; 2 Pet. 3:18). (See the more detailed discussion in the comments on v. 10.) In this verse, then, the writer deals with both justification or initial sanctification, a once for all accomplishment, and progressive sanctification, which continues throughout our Christian lives until the process finally comes to completion when we meet Christ (1 Jn. 3:2).

(4) Remission of sins points to a finished sacrifice (10:15-18)

15 *Whereof* the Holy Ghost also is a witness to us: for after that he had said before,
16 This *is* the covenant that I will make with them after those days, saith the Lord, I will put my laws into their hearts, and in their minds will I write them;
17 And their sins and iniquities will I remember no more.
18 Now where remission of these *is, there is* no more offering for sin.

The law said that two witnesses were needed to substantiate something as being true (Dt. 19:15). The first witness in this context was the words of Christ from Ps. 40:6-8, quoted in vv. 5-7. Now the writer reminds us of a second witness who was called to the stand earlier, so to speak. This was the witness of "the Holy Ghost" or the Holy Spirit in the words of Jer. 31:33, 34, which he cited in greater detail in 8:8-12. There he quoted Jer. 31:31-34, but here only two of those verses are needed to make the point, and even those in abbreviated form. This quotation from Jeremiah "also is a witness to us."

The writer has already emphasized the Holy Spirit as the ultimate author of Scripture in his earlier quotation of Ps. 95:7-11 in 3:7-11. At the same time, this does not prevent him from recognizing the human author of that psalm as David (see 4:7). Every word of Scripture was brought to us by the pen of a man, but every word of Scripture was also exactly what God wanted to say, and it was, thus, the witness of the Holy Spirit. In fact, the writer also pointed out that the tabernacle and its divisions served as a testimony from the Holy Spirit with regard to access to God (9:8).

The observation, "For after that he had said before," is meant to divide the quotation into point one and point two. The first point, a portion only of Jer. 31:33 (v. 16), concerns the *spiritual character* of the new covenant: "This is the covenant that I will make with them after those days, saith the Lord, I will put my laws into their hearts, and in their minds will I write them." For further details about this quotation, see the discussion of 8:10, above. In v. 17 the writer makes his second point about the new covenant by quoting the last part of Jer. 31:34. The point here is the *spiritual result* of the covenant: "And their sins and iniquities will I remember no more." For further commentary on this quotation, see the discussion of 8:12.

The first covenant did not free the conscience of the worshipers from the guilt of sin; thus, they continued offering those sacrifices on a regular basis (see v. 3). But the blood of Christ truly removes the guilt of sin, so that genuine forgiveness can be experienced by those who come to Him by faith.

On the basis of this reminder of the quotation from Jeremiah, the writer offers his conclusion in v. 18, "Now where remission of these is, *there* is no more offering for sin." "Remission" (Greek *aphesis*) has already been mentioned in 9:22. In connection with sin, as in this context, the word denotes a leaving, a departure, a removal, of the sin. In particular, it looks on sin as a debt that cannot be paid, but God's attitude of remission or forgiveness dismisses the debt, completely removing it from the books. The same word is used in this connection in Mt. 18:27, 32 (see also Mt. 9:2).

When such a debt has been dismissed, or as in this case has been fully paid, there is then "no more offering for sin." The writer has made clear to his Jewish readers why the Levitical sacrifices are no longer needed. To return to those sacrifices after having embraced the once-for-all offering of Jesus Christ would be to abandon that which is complete—that which meets all goals concerning our relationship with a holy God—for that which was imperfect and incomplete from the beginning. Such action, even in the face of increasing persecution for Christians, would certainly be illogical. However, far worse consequences than that are involved for those who willfully abandon Christ. Those consequences will be outlined in detail in 10:26-31.

4. Fourth warning: against neglecting the new way to God through Jesus Christ (10:19-39)

In the O.T. only the high priest of Israel, Aaron and his descendants, could enter the Holy of Holies of the tabernacle and the later temples, and even then only on the Day of Atonement when they made animal sacrifices for themselves as well as the people of Israel. But a wonderful change has taken place through Jesus Christ. No wonder the writer characterizes our position in Christ as a new and living way and severely warns of the consequences of turning from the finished work of Christ. Paul challenged the Galatians in what seems to have been a similar situation: "But now, after that ye have known God, or rather are known of God, how turn ye again to the weak and beggarly elements, whereunto ye desire again to be in bondage?" (Gal. 4:9). These Hebrew Christians must grasp hold of this new and living way and follow it through to its victorious conclusion.

a. The basis of the new and living way (10:19-21)

19 Having therefore, brethren, boldness to enter into the holiest by the blood of Jesus,
20 By a new and living way, which he hath consecrated for us, through the veil, that is to say, his flesh;
21 And *having* an high priest over the house of God.

The old way of entering the earthly Holy of Holies on the basis of animal blood had severe limitations: (1) only one man could enter, the Levitical high priest; (2) even he could enter only once a year on the Day of Atonement; (3) he could not enter without the blood of animals; (4) since the offering was ineffective, it had to be repeated every year. This new way removes all these limitations. The writer reminds these Hebrew Christians of the tremendous advantage they have: "Having therefore, brethren, boldness to enter." "Therefore" connects his encouragement for dependence on the High Priesthood of Christ with the arguments he has just made, especially the finished work of our Lord based on the fact that He "sat down on the right hand of God" (v. 12). By that He has brought in the new covenant where our "sins and iniquities" are remembered no more (v. 17). "Brethren" serves to personalize the admonition (as also in 3:1, 12; 13:22), as well as to emphasize the family relationship in Christ, that the benefits of this new way are shared by all.

"Boldness" (Greek *parresia*) refers to frankness, courage, confidence, or fearlessness, especially in the presence of persons of high rank (Bauer 630). Here it refers to the assurance that believers can have in their free access to the throne of God—the ease of approach that we enjoy in Christ. The same word appears three other times in Hebrews where it is twice translated "confidence" (3:6; 10:35) and once as an adverb, "boldly" (4:16). Such confidence in approaching God was largely absent under the old covenant; at the very best it was manifested only by certain heroes of the faith who had a unique relationship with God (i.e. certain prophets, David in the Psalms, etc.).

"Having" (Greek present tense) indicates that this boldness, this confidence, in our approach to God is an attitude that we can possess at all times, not just on some special occasion. As believers we possess this boldness or confidence "to enter into the holiest by the blood of Jesus." "To enter" emphasizes access into the presence of God and is parallel to the word "way" in v. 20. The veil has been removed, and the entrance ever stands open for us (Mt. 27:51). This entrance is "into the holiest" (see 9:8), here obviously referring to the true Holy of Holies which is "heaven itself" (9:24). Though this free access to the heavenly Holy of Holies is available to all who are "brethren," all who have trusted Christ as their Savior, it can only be attained "by the blood of Jesus." It is not just the death of Christ that saves us; it is His "blood," voluntarily shed in full payment for our sins, that saves us and opens the way to God for us (see also 9:12, 14; 10:29; 12:24; 13:12, 20). Furthermore, it is the blood of "Jesus," the name His mother and father gave Him at the command of the angel (Mt. 1:21), stressing His true humanity in living and dying for us.

This bold entrance into the heavenly Holy of Holies is available to us "by a new and living way." "New" (Greek *prosphatos*) means "freshly slaughtered," then, "new" or "recent." The writer seems to have chosen a special word for "new" in light of the fact that this entrance into God's presence is made possible "by the blood of Jesus" (Yeager 340). This way into God's presence is not only "new"; it is also living, described thus because: (1) it gives life for those who come to Christ; (2) it is permanent and abiding, a way that will never change (Barnes 233); (3) perhaps most of all, it is "living" because this way is centered in the person of the living and resurrected Christ who is Himself "the way, the truth, and the life" (Jn. 14:6). Jesus Christ is our personal road to Heaven, sufficiently able to bear the weight of all those who choose to travel through Him (Lenski 344; Kent 198). As indicated earlier, the word way is parallel to the word translated "to enter into" (lit. "an entrance") in v. 19. In other words, if we have an entrance into the heavenly Holy of Holies by the blood of Jesus, we also have "a new and living way" by that same blood.

This entrance into Heaven, this new and living way, "he hath consecrated for us." "Consecrated" (Greek aorist active of *egkainizo*) means "to bring in as new," "to begin" something. The writer presents it as a historical fact, a completed action (Greek aorist). Jesus Christ is the author, the creator, the engineer, of this new way to Heaven, the one that really works, and He did it for us. The blood of the animals offered by the O.T. high priest only gained entrance to the earthly Holy of Holies for himself, and that only on the annual Day of Atonement. The blood of Christ, on the other hand, has gained entrance into the heavenly Holy of Holies for all of us, and that on a continuous basis.

However, this entrance, this new and living way, is only "through the veil, that is to say, his flesh." The writer is simply drawing a parallel with the O.T. tabernacle. On the Day of Atonement the high priest parted the veil that separated the Holy Place from the Holy of Holies in order to present the blood of the animal sacrifices. The only way to reach that earthly Holy of Holies was through that veil. In like manner, the only way to reach the presence of God in the heavenly Holy of Holies is through the "veil" which is "the body of Jesus Christ" (see v. 10). When we celebrate the Lord's Supper, we take the bread as representing our Lord's flesh, His body, which was offered for us; and then we take the fruit of the vine as representing His blood which was shed for us (Mt. 26:26-28). Thus, here in close proximity, the writer has us coming into God's presence "by the blood of Jesus" as well as "through . . . his flesh." When we enter that heavenly Holy of Holies through the blood of Jesus by this new and living way, we find tremendous support in living the Christian life: "And *having* an high priest over the house of God" (v. 21). "And" introduces this fact as a second support, in addition to "having . . . boldness to enter the holiest," for going on with Christ to ultimate victory rather than retreating in the face of increasing persecution. Because of what Christ did on the cross, we should have no fear to go regularly into God's presence through faithful prayer and worship, and when we get there we find "an high priest"—literally, a "great priest" who is none other than Jesus Christ Himself.

The realm over which He ministers as our "Great High Priest" (see 4:14) is "the house of God." The Levitical high priest only served Israel, but the area of our Lord's ministry is universal. Indeed, He is in charge of His own house, "whose house are we, if we hold fast" (3:6). While on earth Jesus revealed to His immediate disciples this broader house. He explained, "And other sheep I have, which are not of this fold: them also I must bring, and they shall hear my voice; and there shall be one fold, *and* one shepherd" (Jn. 10:16). "These two advantages (access to God, and a great priest) should give constant encouragement for a continual approach to God" (Kent 199).

b. The duties of the new and living way (10:22-25)

In 10:19-21 the writer has given his Hebrew readers two supports for persisting in the new and living way which they have found in Jesus Christ. One is the free access which they now have into the very presence of God, the heavenly Holy of Holies, "by the blood of Jesus." The other is the mediation of Christ as their Great High Priest who is ever ready to lend divine support to face the trials and temptations of this life. However, though God will always give His support in the Christian life, and we could not even get started without it, He also expects cooperation from us. He will not save us in spite of ourselves nor will He take us "kicking and screaming" into His eternal kingdom. Free will does not stop at the door of salvation. Thus, in 10:22-25 the writer gives three different duties that need to be exercised by believers in moving toward a successful conclusion to our walk in Christ.

(1) The duty of true worship (10:22)

22 Let us draw near with a true heart in full assurance of faith, having our hearts sprinkled from an evil conscience, and our bodies washed with pure water.

All three of the duties outlined in vv. 22-24 are expressed in continuous action (Greek present tense). They are obligations of the Christian life which must have our constant attention.

Our first duty in sustaining our relationship with Jesus Christ as our Great High Priest is the duty of true worship. "Let us draw near" can be translated, "Let us keep on drawing near." The same word was used in 4:16 where we read, "Let us . . . come boldly unto the throne of grace." This same expression was often used in the Septuagint (LXX) in connection with Levitical worship, the act of reverently approaching God's presence for sacrifice, prayer, and adoration.

The admonition to keep on worshiping God is further defined by four qualifications. Two of them describe our spiritual attitude and the other two describe our spiritual condition. First, we are to worship God "with a true heart." "True" (Greek *alethinos*) means "genuine" or "sincere." It was used of the true tabernacle in 8:2. A true heart is opposed to a heart filled with hypocrisy, pretension, or deception. Jesus declared that God must be worshiped "in spirit and in truth" (Jn. 4:24). During the days just prior to Babylonian captivity God complained that "Judah has not turned to Me with her whole heart, but in pretense" (Jer. 3:10 NKJV). In his farewell address Joshua admonished Israel to "fear the LORD, and serve him in sincerity and in truth" (Jos. 24:14). Spiritually speaking, the heart is the seat of feelings, devotion, and commitment. Those who really love and serve God always do so "with a true heart."

Second, our worship is to be "in full assurance of faith." "Full assurance" (Greek *plerophoria*) refers to complete confidence, absolute trust, unhesitating certainty. It is our "faith" in Christ that produces this full assurance, the certainty that God will always do what He has promised and more. In a similar way the same word is used in 6:11 to refer to "the full assurance of hope."

Third, we must keep on coming to worship, "having our hearts sprinkled from an evil conscience," which expresses an action that is completed but with continuing result (Greek perfect tense). The writer is using figurative terminology to describe our conversion experience, our status as new creatures in Christ (2 Cor. 5:17), terminology right out of the Levitical system. In dedicating Aaron and his sons for priestly service, Moses was to sprinkle them with the blood of the sacrifices (Ex. 29:21; Lev. 8:30), and on the Day of Atonement the high priest was to take the blood "and sprinkle it upon the mercy seat" (Lev. 16:15). But that blood was for external cleansing only; it did not truly remove the guilt of sin inasmuch as it had to be regularly repeated. Here the writer refers to an atonement that is internal, where our hearts have been sprinkled "from an evil conscience." In an earlier context the writer pointed out that the gifts and sacrifices of the O.T. "could not make him that did the service perfect, as pertaining to the conscience" (9:9), but that the blood of Christ can and does "purge your conscience from dead works to serve the living God" (9:14). The conscience is the area of our minds where we have a sense of misery and guilt when we sin, or a sense of peace and joy when we experience release and forgiveness, when the weight of sin has been lifted. When sins are forgiven the "evil conscience" is removed and, like Paul, we can serve God "with pure conscience" (2 Tim. 1:3).

The fourth qualification for our continuing worship is, "Having . . . our bodies washed with pure water." Once again the language of the Levitical practice is evident. As the O.T. priest offered sacrifices on the brazen altar and sprinkled the blood on the mercy seat, so the priest also constantly washed himself at the brass laver in ceremonial purification from the defilement of sin (Ex. 30:19; 40:12; Lev. 8:6; 16:4, 24). Again, the words indicate a completed act with continuing results (Greek perfect tense). The washing under the law was only external. It had to be repeated as often as the sacrifices for sin were repeated. But this washing is "with pure water," the water of the Spirit (Tit. 3:5) and the Word (Eph. 5:26), and it never needs repeating (see Jn. 13:10).

Though admitting the internal emphasis of the spiritual condition described here, several commentators see a strong connection with water baptism (Westcott 322; Lenski 347; Hughes 412). Those who lean toward baptismal regeneration are inclined to find baptismal waters sloshing throughout the New Testament. Though there is no need to deny the figurative implications of cleansing in connection with Christian baptism (see Acts 22:16; 1 Pet. 3:21), there is also no need to see that connection in this context (Calvin 237; MacArthur 263; Kistemaker 288). These last two qualifications emphasize both the heart—the inside—and the body—the outside—of the believer. When we come to worship God, we should come as cleansed and forgiven in the whole man, for true worship must involve both body and soul.

(2) The duty of steadfastness (10:23)

23 Let us hold fast the profession of *our* faith without wavering; (for he *is* faithful that promised;)

Our second duty with regard to continuing our journey on the new and living way is the duty of steadfastness. Again the admonition is expressed in continuous action (Greek present tense). "Let us hold fast" might be translated, "Let us keep on holding fast." The same admonition is found in 4:14, though a different verb is used there (Greek *krateo*), basically a synonym for the one used here. Similar exhortations were also given in 3:6 and 3:14, using the same verb, though the tense of the admonition used there indicates completed action (Greek aorist tense), an admonition to grab hold and never turn loose. Here and in 4:14 our active participation in "holding fast" is emphasized.

What we are to keep holding fast is "the profession of our faith." As in 4:14, "profession" (Greek *homologia*) can also be translated "confession" (as in 1 Tim. 6:13). The word literally means "to speak alike" or "to agree." In this context, it means that what we say in relation to our faith is in line with what God says. We have stopped going our way, and are now going God's way, in action, attitude, and doctrine. The verb form of the same word is used in Rom. 10:9, 10, where belief in the heart and "confession" with the mouth are presented by the apostle Paul as the necessary components of salvation. Jesus Himself declared, "Whosoever therefore shall confess me before men, him will I confess also before my Father which is in heaven. But whosoever shall deny me before men, him will I also deny before my Father which is in heaven" (Mt. 10:32, 33).

The word translated "faith" (Greek *elpis*) is usually translated "hope" (see Heb. 3:6; 6:11, 18, 19; 7:19). Why "faith" was chosen as the translation here is not known; however, the two words are closely related—not just as first cousins, but, rather, as full-fledged sisters. Christian faith points to an attitude of trust in the person of Christ, and what the Scriptures teach about Him. Hope includes faith, but goes further to include an attitude of expectation and anticipation with reference to the promises of God (Kistemaker 289; Morris 413; Westcott 324). The writer frequently emphasizes the theme of hope in this epistle (see 3:6; 6:11, 18, 19; 7:19). Perhaps our translators used "faith" here rather than "hope" because of its more common association with "confession."

We are to keep on holding fast the confession of our "faith" or our "hope" "without wavering" (Greek *akline*), a word that appears only here in the N.T. and carries the idea of remaining erect or firm, unbending, like a strong oak tree in the midst of a storm. James uses a different figure, the figure of the sea, in his encouragement to pray, "But let him ask in faith, nothing wavering. For he that wavereth is like a wave of the sea driven with the wind and tossed" (Jas. 1:6), but he makes the same point.

Perhaps the writer's parenthetical conclusion of this exhortation explains his use of the word "hope," which relates so much to the promises of God. He reminds us, "For he *is* faithful that promised." Our faithfulness to the Lord should be enhanced by past examples and future promises of His faithfulness. With regard to temptation, Paul promises, "God *is* faithful, who will not suffer you to be tempted above that ye are able; but will with the temptation also make a way to escape, that ye may be able to bear *it*" (1 Cor. 10:13). With regard to sin in our lives, John declares, "If we confess our sins, he is faithful and just to forgive us *our* sins, and to cleanse us from all unrighteousness" (1 Jn. 1:9; see also 1 Cor. 1:9; 1 Th. 5:24; 2 Th. 3:3; 2 Tim. 2:13; 1 Pet. 4:19; Rev. 1:5; 3:14; 19:11). Note that we are reminded of God's faithfulness as we are approaching one of the most severe warnings in the epistle concerning the danger of apostasy. If we fail to hold fast to our confession of faith, and turn back into apostasy, it will not be because God failed us. It will be, rather, because we denied Him.

(3) The duty of mutual consideration (10:24, 25)

24 And let us consider one another to provoke unto love and to good works:
25 Not forsaking the assembling of ourselves together, as the manner of some *is*; but exhorting *one another*: and so much the more, as ye see the day approaching.

"And" connects this third duty, the duty of mutual consideration, with the two preceding and marks it as the final one in the series of exhortations which are designed to ensure the readers' continuation in the "new and living way" (v. 20). The writer admonishes, "Let us consider one another." There are many great aids which the Lord has given us for successfully sustaining the Christian walk: the keeping power of the Father and the Son (Jn. 10:28, 29), the indwelling of the Holy Spirit (Rom. 8:9-16), the penetration of the written word (Heb. 4:12). But along with these strategic helps we also have the mutual dependence of the Christian fellowship, the church of Jesus Christ. "Let us consider" is again expressed in continuous action (Greek present tense), "Let us keep on considering." The mutual consideration must be exercised on a constant basis.

"One another" clearly refers to our fellow believers. Our walk with Christ was never designed to be lived in isolation. The mutual encouragement that we give to one another in our life for Christ is of the utmost importance. Cain arrogantly responded to God's inquiry about the whereabouts of his brother, Abel, by asking, "*Am* I my brother's keeper?" (Gen. 4:9). The answer to that question among Christians is always, "Yes indeed, you are your brother's keeper." Paul admonished the Galatians, "Brethren, if a man be overtaken in a fault, ye which are spiritual, restore such an one in the spirit of meekness; considering thyself, lest thou also be tempted. Bear ye one another's burdens, and so fulfil the law of Christ" (Gal. 6:1, 2).

"To provoke" (Greek *eis paroxusmon*) seems, in light of the context, a bit harsh to some. The word appears only one other time in the N.T. in reference to the "sharp contention" which developed between Paul and Barnabas over taking John Mark on the second journey (Acts 15:39). A similar verb form is used in Acts 17:16 to refer to Paul's spirit "stirring" within him; and in 1 Corinthians 13:5 where Paul characterizes love as "not easily provoked." Since, in this context, we are to provoke one another "unto love and to good works," a positive thing, the newer translations use expressions like "to stir up," "stimulate," or "spur on." Each of these express the idea of the word, but there still seems to be something appropriate in saying "provoke." The truth of the matter is that our efforts with brothers and sisters to stimulate them, stir them up, and spur them on often results in their being provoked in a bad sense toward us before the good results finally come out through our compassionate persistence. But in most cases such brotherly concern results in the return of the drifter to "love," the right attitude, and to "good works," the right action. The Christian attitudes of faith and hope can be practiced in isolation, but love can only be exercised in the company of others (Hughes 105). "Good" (Greek *kalos*) is the broader term indicating "works" or deeds that are not only morally good, but also internally beautiful and externally appealing. Jesus used the same words in the Sermon on the Mount when He said, "Let your light so shine before men, that they may see your good *works*, and glorify your Father which is in heaven" (Mt. 5:16).

The exhortation in v. 25 concerning the Christian assembly is directly connected with the third admonition for mutual consideration (v. 24), but the writer probably also means to connect it with the other two duties of true worship (v. 22) and steadfastness (v. 23). Indeed, one of the most pertinent locations for the exercise of all three of these duties is in the individual assemblies of Christians—in this particular case, of Christian Jews. Thus the writer exhorts, "Not forsaking the assembling of ourselves together." There is no more appropriate place "to provoke one another to love and to good works" than in the weekly fellowship of believers!

"Forsaking" (Greek *egkataleipo*) is a strong word, indicating abandonment. Matthew used the same Greek word to translate our Lord's cry from the cross, "My God, my God, why hast thou *forsaken* me?" (Mt. 27:46). Perhaps the writer uses continuous action (Greek present tense) to suggest that this pernicious practice had been going on for some length of time with numerous participants. The word translated "assembling" (Greek *episunagoge*) is actually a noun rather than a verb; it emphasizes the act of assembling more than the place. The reference is to the local assemblies of Christians for prayer, praise, worship, reading, and exhortation, wherever they may meet, and not to the church as a whole, the universal church.

The word in the original is the same as that used for the synagogue, except that a prepositional prefix has been attached (Greek *epi*). Lenski (353) thinks that the addition serves to point out that the assembly, in each case, is in a particular location, "at" a certain place. In fact, the word normally translated "synagogue" (Greek *sunagoge*) is used to refer to the Christian "assembly" in Jas. 2:2. Many of the early Jewish Christians continued to worship in the synagogue (Lk. 6:6; Jn. 18:20; Acts 13:14; 18:4); it may be that some of those synagogues eventually became Christian churches because so many of their members became believers. With "ourselves" the writer includes himself in the number, and defines it as specifically Christian.

That the admonition is not merely speculative is seen in the observation, "As the manner of some is." "Manner" (Greek *ethos*) means "custom" or "habit." Some from the Christian community were already taking up this habit, this sad practice of abandoning the Christian assembly. Various reasons might have prevailed: (1) some were spiritually backslidden and needed a renewal of their faith; (2) some were withdrawing out of the fear of persecution for their faith in Christ; (3) some had abandoned the Christian assembly because "the care of this world, and the deceitfulness of riches" (Mt. 13:22) had lured them away (e.g. Demas in 2 Tim. 4:10); (4) some had come to feel spiritually superior to the congregation as a whole, considering that they no longer needed the fellowship or the instruction of the general assembly. Whatever the cause, it was a bad practice that would in all likelihood result in serious and potentially eternal consequences. Going to church does not make a person a Christian, but abandoning the church is almost always a sure sign of the presence of serious, spiritual problems in an individual's life. Even when serious problems in a local congregation exist, a spiritually mature person ought to help find a solution or, if that is not possible, to embrace a different congregation where fellowship, worship, and instruction can continue.

Instead of abandoning the Christian assembly, as some had, they ought to be "exhorting *one another*." "But" (Greek *alla*) here offers strong contrast to "forsaking" the local church. Continued mutual exhortation is what true believers must practice; if faithfully considered, the perceived problems will work themselves out. Though "*one another*" is not in the Greek text, the idea is correct and required in the context. "Exhorting" (Greek *parakaleo*) can also mean "entreat," "urge," "comfort," or "encourage." In this context, the exhortation or encouragement would be for persistence on the part of the Hebrew Christians in their worship, their steadfastness, and their mutual consideration of one another.

The writer adds, "And so much the more, as ye see the day approaching." "And so much the more" refers to faithfulness to the established meetings of the church, not to an unnecessary increase in the frequency of those meetings. Even more attention must be given to faithfulness in all these matters, our writer emphasizes, "as ye see the day approaching." Some commentators regard "the day" as a reference to the nearing of the time of the destruction of Jerusalem, which Jesus had prophesied in the Olivet Discourse (Mt. 24:2) almost 30 years earlier (Whedon 114; Pink 608; Barnes 238). Christ did suggest certain things to look for as that time draws near, declaring that it would occur before "this generation" has passed (Mt. 24:34). Others think "the day" has reference to both the destruction of Jerusalem as a type and the Second Coming of Christ as the ultimate fulfillment (Bruce 253; Alford 198). But most commentators see "that day" as specifically referring to the Second Coming, the end time when Christ will return for judgment (Hughes 105; Kent 203; Kistemaker 291; Westcott 325; Lenski 355).

The strongest argument for taking "the day" to mean the destruction of Jerusalem in A.D. 70 is that the writer was declaring these things only two to four years prior to that event. Surely warning signs were already on the horizon. But the argument for referring "the day" to the return of Christ is stronger. In the N.T. a reference to "that day" or "the day" is almost always to the Second Coming (see Mt. 7:22; 24:36; 25:13; 1 Cor. 3:13; 1 Th. 5:4; 2 Th. 1:10; 2 Tim. 1:12). Furthermore, 10:37 seems to confirm this interpretation, "For yet a little while, and he that shall come will come, and will not tarry." It is at the return of Christ that all believers will have to give account for their faithfulness, not at the destruction of Jerusalem, or any other intermediate judgment.

Though Lunemann subscribes to this latter view with regard to the meaning of "the day," he erroneously promotes the position that both our author and his readers mistakenly thought that the coming of Christ was quite near (375). Though the writer of Hebrews, like the other N.T. authors, certainly hoped for the soon return of Christ, they never made any attempt at date-setting or implied that they knew when His return would occur. Jesus made it clear to His disciples that the exact time of His return was unknown to everyone other than the Father, including Himself (Mt. 24:36; Mk. 13:32; Acts 1:6, 7). The writer is using simple logic: Whatever may be the date of Christ's return, each day that passes brings us nearer to that time; each generation should therefore give even greater diligence to the faithful assembly of the Christian brotherhood where we "provoke one another unto love and to good works."

c. The consequence of forsaking the new and living way (10:26-31)

In discussing Heb. 6:4-6 earlier, I iterated seven different views; the same seven positions will be taken by interpreters on this passage. (1) *They are professors of salvation, but not actual possessors*. They may have some of the characteristics of true Christians, but these people do not truly know Christ. (2) *They are "regenerate" but not "elect."* Though a genuine work of the Holy Spirit has taken place in their lives, they can and will fall away since they are not included among God's elect. (3) They are genuinely saved people who receive a serious warning about apostasy as a preventive measure, but the whole thing is *hypothetical* since other New Testament passages teach that a true Christian is eternally secure. (4) They are saved people, but the writer is not speaking about loss of salvation but about *loss of rewards*. (5) The sin of apostasy spoken of here involves *a special situation which could not be repeated today*. (6) They are saved people who are on the verge of apostasy, but *even if they proceed into apostasy, they could come back to God*. (7) They are saved people who are seriously backslidden in their spiritual lives; and, *if they continue to the point of apostasy they will be eternally lost since they have committed the sin against the Holy Ghost*.

The details of these different positions on the apostasy passages, and which commentators hold to each view, have already been given in the discussion of 6:4-6 and need not be repeated here. One commentator did confess to changing his position between his comments on chapter 6 and chapter 10. In commenting on chapter 6 Yeager (202) said that the writer was addressing true Christians who were in danger of loss of reward (view 4). But when he discusses chapter 10 (347: ten years later, he says), he has decided that the writer is addressing some readers who have not made a wholehearted commitment to Christ (view 1) and, though they came to understand the superiority of Christ's sacrifice, are now considering returning to the old system of shadow rather than substance, thus indicating that they have never been truly regenerate.

Pink also sends some mixed signals about the certainty of his position on these apostasy passages. His position seems to be that those who do commit apostasy, and he believes that some do, were never truly saved (604, 605). But, since he believes that the warning was also issued to genuine Christians in the Hebrew congregation, the passage must be taken as only hypothetical for them, God's means of preserving them from apostasy and guaranteeing that they are eternally secure (615). He further affirms this in his quotation from Barnes in connection with 10:38 (643), and Barnes clearly takes the hypothetical position.

It seems obvious that Hebrews 6:4-12 and 10:26-39 are very much parallel passages. This can be seen by the content as a whole, but especially by the similar approach that each passage takes to the subject of apostasy. In each passage there is: (1) a definition of apostasy from the standpoint of that passage; (2) a clear declaration of the result of apostasy; (3) an illustration to clarify the point; and (4) encouragement to avoid following the road that leads to apostasy.

In the present context the basis of the new and living way is "the blood of Jesus." The duties or practices which will enable us to continue on this new and living way are true worship, steadfastness, and mutual consideration. These may be exercised in a variety of ways, but they are especially carried out when Christians assemble for praise, worship, instruction, and mutual exhortation on the Lord's Day. Neglecting these practices, however, cannot be taken lightly. The severest consequences may develop for those who choose to ignore these duties of the new and living way. The ultimate danger is total and final apostasy from the Christian faith, and from that backward trek there is no return. None of these Hebrew Christians whom our writer is addressing are guilty of this sin at this point. If they were, there would be no reason for warning and admonishing them. It is for this cause that he describes this sin of apostasy in some detail in these verses.

(1) The definition (10:26a)

26a For if we sin wilfully after that we have received the knowledge of the truth.

"For" introduces this statement as an explanation of the dire consequences that may result for those who ignore the duties of the Christian faith. As defined in these words, apostasy involves three things. *First*, it involves habitual or continuous sinning. "If we sin" means, "If we continue sinning" (Greek present tense). This does not mean only an occasional sin but rather the practice of sin, sin as a way of life. Some of the early church fathers (as Chrysostom and Tertullian) thought the writer was saying that any sins after baptism could not be forgiven—a meaning that fits neither Scripture nor our experience. If that were true, none of us would be saved. John gladly announced, "If we confess our sins, he is faithful and just to forgive us *our* sins, and to cleanse us from all unrighteousness" (1 Jn. 1:9). Furthermore, John explained that he was writing to them "that ye sin not." But knowing that we all do sin, even as Christians, he added, "And if any man sin, we have an advocate with the Father, Jesus Christ the righteous" (1 Jn. 2:1). Though true Christians do sin, sin is the exception in their lives, not the practice (see also 1 Jn. 3:6, 9; 5:18). The original literally reads, "For, we sinning wilfully. . . ." Our translators correctly understand this construction (Greek participle) to be conditional, as do other translations. The writer is not saying that any of his readers had yet committed apostasy. He is merely warning them of the consequences should they choose that direction in their spiritual lives.

Second, apostasy involves sin committed as an act of rebellion against God. "Wilfully" (Greek *ekousios*) describes sin that is both voluntary and rebellious. The word stands first in the original, emphasizing its importance to the thought being expressed. Paul describes men who commit this type of sin as those "who knowing the judgment of God, that they which commit such things are worthy of death, not only do the same, but have pleasure in them that do them" (Rom. 1:32).

Apostasy, therefore, involves habitual rebellion against God and His known will. The writer often uses language and principles that come from the law, and so he does here. Under the law God made it clear that only sins which were committed in ignorance could be forgiven; that is, sins that were not acts of continual rebellion against God (Lev. 4:2; 5:15; Num. 15:25-29), sins caused by passion, impulse, and human weakness. Sins that were committed "presumptuously," or "with a high hand" could not be forgiven (Num. 15:30, 31).

The *third* element involved in defining apostasy is that it comes about "after that we have received the knowledge of the truth." This does not describe superficial believers who have only given intellectual assent to the truth. The acts of habitual rebellion against God which the writer has in mind are those committed "after coming to know" the truth. "We" indicates that the writer includes himself in this company of those who are subject to apostasy, and surely he considers himself a true believer.

"Have received" indicates completed action (Greek aorist tense), a definite point in the individual's life when the Gospel truth was assimilated. What they had received was "the knowledge of the truth." "Knowledge" (Greek *epignosis*) refers to full and complete knowledge, recognition, or understanding (Bauer 291). Paul uses the same word when he declares that God our Savior "will have all men to be saved, and to come unto the *knowledge* of the truth" (1 Tim. 2:4). Peter, using the verb form of the word to describe apostates, warns, "It had been better for them not *to have known* the way of righteousness, than, *after they have known it,* to turn from the holy commandment delivered unto them" (2 Pet. 2:21). These Hebrew Christians have obtained a full and complete knowledge "of the truth."

In the N.T. "the truth" refers primarily to the good news about Jesus Christ, His birth, life, death, resurrection, present position, and promised return. The Gospel of John especially emphasizes the true knowledge of Christ as "the truth." To his potential disciples Jesus declared, "If ye continue in my word, *then* are ye my disciples indeed; And ye shall know *the truth*, and *the truth* shall make you free" (Jn. 8:31, 32). To Thomas, who wanted to know how to follow Him, He declared, "I am the way, *the truth*, and the life; no man cometh unto the Father, but by me" (Jn. 14:6; emphasis added). In His final High Priestly prayer Jesus petitioned the Father, "Sanctify them through thy *truth*: thy word is *truth*" (Jn. 17:17).

(2) The result (10:26b, 27)

26b There remaineth no more sacrifice for sins,
27 But a certain fearful looking for of judgment and fiery indignation, which shall devour the adversaries.

Now that the writer has given a threefold definition of apostasy, he outlines the awful result. He announces the reason a true apostate cannot return to Christ or to Christianity: because "there remaineth no more sacrifice for sins." This statement is another strong reason to believe that the Hebrew recipients of the letter were considering a return to Judaism and the O.T. sacrificial system. If Jesus is the only way, and that way is abandoned, there can be no other provision. Such a person will have rejected the only sacrifice that can save. If the readers reasoned that the Levitical sacrifices had been good enough for earlier generations, they must remember that they were only effective as a picture of the true sacrifice of Christ which was to come. Now that that sacrifice has been made, the old types are invalid.

As mentioned in the discussion of chapter 6, that passage describes the psychological reason that apostasy is irremedial: "It is impossible . . . to renew them again unto repentance." This passage gives the soteriological reason "there remaineth no more sacrifice for sins." Apostasy takes a disastrous and eternal toll on both the mind and the soul of the person involved.

For the apostate, instead of redemption there is total and final rejection. Since no effective sacrifice remains, what is left for such a person? Nothing "but a certain fearful looking for of judgment and fiery indignation." "But" contrasts the terrible prospects of God's judgment with the merciful anticipation of forgiveness if an atoning sacrifice were available, but none remains. The fact that forgiveness is no longer possible may not immediately bring judgment, but rather the "fearful looking for of judgment." "Looking for" (Greek *ekdoche*) means "expectation" or "anticipation." "Certain" does not mean "sure," but it heightens or intensifies the fearful expectation of judgment (Bauer 820), a judgment that is so pervasive that it cannot be specifically defined (Westcott 329). "Judgment" (Greek *krisis*) refers to the act of judging, not the result.

The other thing that remains since no atoning sacrifice is available for the sin of apostasy is "fiery indignation," literally a "zeal of fire." The word "indignation" or "zeal" (Greek *zelos*) means "heat," and its translation depends on the context. It may refer to intense interest or concern (Rom. 10:2), "envy" where animosity is present (Acts 13:45), or "jealousy" in a love relationship (1 Cor. 11:2). Here it is the "heat" or "zeal" of fire, as associated with the expectation of judgment; thus, "fiery indignation" is an appropriate translation. Fire is often associated with judgment in Scripture (see Mt. 3:10, 12; Jn. 15:6), and so it is here. The judgment which the apostate anticipates is not immediate judgment—though elements of that may sometimes occur—but primarily final judgment which is to come (Barnes 240). Thus, in the absence of an effective, atoning sacrifice, only these two things remain: (1) a fearful expectation of the act of judging, and (2) fiery indignation or "the zeal of fire."

The judgment to which the writer refers is not meant for Christians. It is one, rather, "which shall devour the adversaries." There is a day coming when those who oppose God and His kingdom will be eaten up by His wrath, devoured by His judgment (2 Th. 1:4-10; Rev. 20:7-10). Though this is all that remains for apostates, they may not be aware of this because of their spiritual deadness (Rom. 1:28-32; Eph. 4:17-19; 1 Tim. 4:1, 2; Lenski 358; Barnes 840). All men should shrink from being identified as enemies of God. In light of such dismal prospects for apostates, these Hebrew Christians must speedily and decisively turn away from any consideration of abandoning Christ in order to return to the old, ineffective, animal sacrifices.

(3) The contrast (10:28, 29)

28 He that despised Moses' law died without mercy under two or three witnesses:
29 Of how much sorer punishment, suppose ye, shall he be thought worthy, who hath trodden under foot the Son of God, and hath counted the blood of the covenant, wherewith he was sanctified, an unholy thing, and hath done despite unto the Spirit of grace?

Following his definition and warning about apostasy in 6:4-6, the writer illustrated his point with a lesson from agriculture. Using the same pattern here, he first gives the definition and warning in 10:26, 27; then he explains further with an illustration from history in 10:28, 29. He points them to a truth with which they, as Hebrew Christians, would all be familiar: "He that despised Moses' law died without mercy under two or three witnesses." There were minor offenses against the law of Moses which did not demand capital punishment; these are not in mind here. "Despised" (Greek *atheteo*) can also mean "rejected" or "set aside." The writer has in mind nothing less than abandonment of the law for the purpose of embracing false gods—O.T. apostasy. Under "Moses' law" God had no toleration for spiritual infidelity.

The sin which the writer has in mind is described in some detail in Dt. 17:2-7. Under the law when a charge was made that an individual or individuals had gone after other gods, a careful investigation was made to ensure that the charges were true. If the charges proved true, there was only one option: the person "died" as punishment for his unspeakable sin and as an example for others who might be tempted. The death penalty for this and other grave violations under the law pointed to the accountability of the individual as well as the seriousness of the sin. "Died" is actually present tense in the original ("dies"), indicating a continuing principle under the law.

The criminal received death "without mercy." "Mercy" (Greek *oiktirmos*, not *eleos*) also means "compassion." When sins of this nature were committed under the law of Moses, there was little if any room for extenuating circumstances. According to Dt. 13:6-11 individual worshipers were to see that the punishment was carried out even if it involved the person's brother, son, daughter, wife, or close friend. But the law was also careful to make sure that the charges were true. Such charges had to be made "under two or three witnesses" (see Dt. 17:6, 7). They had to be able to give personal testimony as to the guilt of the condemned person, and they also had to begin the execution by throwing the first stones.

If the ultimate penalty of physical death was required for grave violations of the law of Moses, especially where apostasy was involved, what should we expect for equally serious violations of the new covenant under Jesus Christ? (Such an argument is called "from that which is less to that which is greater"; similar arguments can also be found in 2:2-4; 9:13, 14; 12:25, 26.) Thus the writer asks, "Of how much sorer punishment, suppose ye, shall he be thought worthy?" If the punishment for rejection of the law of Moses was bad, demanding physical death, then the punishment for abandoning Jesus Christ and His new covenant has to be worse, and that can only be spiritual death, eternal separation from God. "Punishment" (Greek *timoria*) is used only here in the New Testament. It describes punishment that is a result of divine retribution, the appropriate judgment of the wrath of God.

By saying, "Suppose ye," the writer is requesting the judgment of his readers. The conclusion is so obvious that all should be able to see it. Being "thought worthy" would normally be applied to rewards for good deeds; thus its use in the context of a logical demand for punishment for boundless evil makes it more emphatic. The adjective form of the word is used in a similar way by Felix in declaring that Paul had "nothing laid to his charge *worthy* of death or of bonds" (Acts 23:29). The idea, in this context, is that such people who are worthy of spiritual death have themselves earned that judgment through their abandonment of Christ, and they fully deserve that reward.

The writer describes the act of apostasy in three awful steps, each identifying a completed act (Greek aorist tense), not an activity in progress. In each case, the sin has been taken to its final conclusion. First, such an individual "hath trodden under foot the Son of God." To have "trodden under foot" any person is to reject that person in the most despicable manner. Jesus warned His disciples about casting their pearls before swine "lest they trample them under their feet" (Matt. 7:6). Such an act completely disregards the value of the person or the thing. The insolence of the crime is heightened even more, in this case, by the identity of the person treated in this way: none other than "the Son of God." That divine personage who has been exalted by His heavenly Father (see Phil. 2:9, 10) because of His atoning work for our sins has by this person been deposed from the throne of his heart to the lowest place possible. This amounts to an outright denial of the deity of Jesus Christ (Hughes 422).

Secondly, he "hath counted the blood of the covenant, wherewith he was sanctified, an unholy thing." The fact that he "hath counted" on the way to his conclusion means that he considered the subject, logically evaluated it in his own mind, and as a result formed his thesis. It was not a position that he drifted into without thinking. "The blood of the covenant" refers to the blood of Jesus Christ by which we enter the heavenly Holy of Holies (see 10:19). It is that new covenant which our Lord instituted on the night before He was crucified (Mt. 26:28), prophesied long ago by Jeremiah (Jer. 31:31-34; Heb. 8:7-12), in contrast with the old covenant under which the law of Moses was given.

But for this individual, this blood was not just soteriological; it was also personal. It was the blood "wherewith he was sanctified." A few commentators have tried to make "he was sanctified" refer to Christ, rather than to the apostate, using the terminology in some way to describe what Christ did on the cross (MacArthur 279; Hewitt 167), but this view is not worthy of consideration (Alford 202). Other commentators take a peculiar view about sanctification in this context in an attempt to maintain that these apostates were never saved. Kistemaker says,

> The sinner knows the Christian faith, for he was sanctified by the blood of the covenant. That is, at one time he professed his faith in Christ, listened to the preaching of the Word of God, and partook of the holy elements when he celebrated the Lord's Supper. But his faith was not an internal fulfillment. In word and deed he now repudiates his relationship to Christ's work (295).

Such a position is inconsistent with what this writer clearly meant in other places where he spoke about the sanctification of the believer. This is the same sanctification described in 10:10 and 2:11, which is initial sanctification, or justification as it is described from another perspective (Rom. 3:24-26). Sanctification is not a term applied by the writers of Scripture to unsaved people (Kent 206). This apostate who was once sanctified has come to consider our Lord's blood "an unholy thing." "Unholy" (Greek *koinos*) means common, ordinary, defiled. It depicts the blood of Christ as no different from the blood of sinners for whom He died, as no different from the thieves who died on either side. This person whose conscience had once been purged by the blood of Christ "from dead works to serve the living God" (9:14) has now rejected that blood as nothing better than that of any other man.

Thirdly, the apostate "hath done despite unto the Spirit of grace." The verb translated "hath done despite" (Greek *enubrizo*) means to insult or outrage someone by attitudes, actions, and words. The divine personage so insulted in this context is "the Spirit of grace," that is, the Holy Spirit who administers the grace of God in our hearts on the basis of the shed blood of Christ. The writer's earlier statement, "There remaineth no more sacrifice for sins" (10:26), has already placed the sin in the category of blaspheming the Holy Spirit, and the description given in the phrase used here leaves no question.

Remember that Jesus' warning about the sin against the Holy Spirit appears in two different contexts in the Gospels: once where the Pharisees and scribes, who as a whole were certainly not saved, charge Jesus with casting out demons by the power of Beelzebub, the prince of demons (Mt. 12:24-32; Mk. 3:22-30); and once to His followers in connection with the necessity of public confession for salvation (Lk. 12:8-10). Evidently Christ intended to include both saved and unsaved people in His warnings about the eternal consequences of this sin. But in all situations, whether saved or unsaved, it is a sin against light. The Pharisees willingly and persistently rejected the truth that was so clearly presented to them by the Son of God Himself. These Hebrew believers appear to be on the verge of refusing to confess Christ because of the threat of persecution and death. Such a severe warning must not be considered as merely "hypothetical," as the means that God uses to guarantee the doctrine of eternal security (Kent 207; Barnes 239). To take such a position robs the warning of all its power, like a judge who threatens the criminal with the death penalty, but announces ahead of time that he will never carry it out.

Hebrews 6:4-6 and 10:26-31 are unique passages in that so many commentators who reach for the same conclusion—the preservation of the doctrine of eternal security—also have such diverse opinions about the people in question. Some are absolutely sure they are saved (correctly, I believe), while others are just as certain, regardless of the characteristics outlined by the writer, that those in question could not possibly be saved, primarily because of what they think other passages say about eternal security. It seems to me that a better solution is to fully acknowledge the power and the impact of both sets of Scriptures. Some passages do indeed teach the security of the believer (Jn. 10:25-29; Rom. 8:28-39), and other passages warn about the clear danger of abandoning Christ through persistent rebellion which will ultimately result in eternal damnation (Lk. 12:8-10; 1 Cor. 9:24-27; Gal. 5:1-5; Heb. 6:4-6; 10:26-31; 2 Pet. 2:20-22; 1 Jn. 5:16, 17; Rev. 3:5). The passages which teach security never say that a believer could not, by his own free choice, become an unbeliever, and the passages which teach the possibility of apostasy never say that they are not addressed to Christians. Both passages should be taken at face value by the interpreters of Scripture. None of us would ever make it to Heaven without the keeping power of Christ, through His divine Priesthood, His written Word, and the indwelling Holy Spirit. But when He saved us He did not take away our free will; real choices remain for us throughout our Christian lives.

(4) The judgment (10:30, 31)

30 For we know him that hath said, Vengeance *belongeth* unto me, I will recompense, saith the Lord. And again, The Lord shall judge his people.
31 *It is* a fearful thing to fall into the hands of the living God.

The writer wants his audience to know that his warnings about God's judgment on those who persistently rebel against Him are not merely his opinion. He introduces his two affirming quotations from the O.T. with: "For we know him that hath said"; that is, this is the nature of the God whom we serve. We have a direct relationship with Him, and our behavior always brings an appropriate response on His part.

"Vengeance *belongeth* unto me, I will recompense, saith the Lord," is from Dt. 32:35, but the wording differs slightly from both the Hebrew text and the Septuagint, the latter from which the writer of Hebrews usually quotes. It is, however, identical to the same quotation in Rom. 12:19. Since the quotation is from the Song of Moses, which was frequently used in Hebrew worship, it is likely that the wording used here had become proverbial in the Hebrew synagogue and the N.T. church. When Paul quotes the passage in Romans, his purpose is to steer his readers away from a vengeful attitude, reminding them that judgment is God's business. In the present context our writer gives the quotation to assure his readers that God will, indeed, bring judgment on those who disobey. The quotation appropriately serves both situations.

"I will recompense" (Greek *antapodidomi*) is a compound verb which indicates that the judgment described is a payment from God in return for what is owed, a just reception of that which is due. If we come to the Father through His Son, Jesus Christ, we can freely enjoy His mercy and His grace; but if we choose to reject that mercy and grace through persistent rebellion against His will, we will face the severity of His justice and judgment. Our decision determines His response. The writer backs this up by quoting the very next verse, Dt. 32:36, "The Lord shall judge his people." The same words also occur in Ps. 135:14. Judging can result in punishment or reward, but the context here calls for punishment of the worst sort: eternal rejection for those who have become apostates from faith in Christ.

With these O.T. quotations as background, the writer gives his conclusion in v. 31: "It is a fearful thing to fall into the hands of the living God." The writer has already stressed the "fearful" aspects of God's judgment in v. 27. "To fall" indicates completed action, a final fall (Greek aorist tense). To fall into someone's hands means to come under that person's authority, to be totally subject to his will, usually for the purpose of discipline or judgment (Kent 208).

In this case, the apostate falls into the hands "of the living God." The writer mentions "the living God" four times in this epistle. Here and in 3:12 it is used negatively in warning about apostasy. In 9:14 and 12:22 it is used positively with regard to serving "the living God" and entering His city. Our God is alive; thus, He responds either in love or in wrath to our treatment of His Son and His Holy Spirit. His contrast with the gods of paganism is vividly described in connection with Elijah's contest with the prophets of Baal on Mt. Carmel (1 Kg. 18:21-39). Regardless of their frenzy, their dead god did not respond, but the God of Elijah responded so dramatically that, at least at that moment, the people bowed on their faces and cried, "The LORD, he is the God; the LORD, he is the God" (v. 39). It is to that same living God that we now relate. It is certainly appropriate to preach the love of God in order to win men to Christ, and the Scriptures (Jn. 3:16; 2 Cor. 5:14; etc.) abundantly attest to that approach; but it is also necessary to remind people of the judgment of God. Lenski, a Lutheran commentator, points out that some preachers hesitate to preach sermons that scare people. "But," he says, "by not frightening men into Heaven they fail to frighten them away from hell" (362). The Scripture has the right balance between reminders of the love of God and threats about the wrath of God, between the promise of Heaven and warnings about Hell. We should manifest that same balance in our preaching and teaching.

d. Encouragement to patience in the new and living way (10:32-39)

As in 6:9-12, again the writer turns from his warnings about apostasy to sincere encouragement toward their continuing progress in the new and living way. This is in no way meant to lessen the warnings or to suggest that they were only "hypothetical." God never seeks to preserve our faithfulness with deception or to ensure our security with meaningless threats. If God would not allow rebellious Israel to enter into His rest, neither will He allow Christians to enter that heavenly rest if they turn away from His Son in unbelief. In spite of the writer's sincere warning, however, he wants them to know that he has full confidence that all doubts will be dealt with and that they will all proceed with him in faith toward that heavenly city.

(1) By remembering past sacrifices (10:32-34)

32 But call to remembrance the former days, in which, after ye were illuminated, ye endured a great fight of afflictions;
33 Partly, whilst ye were made a gazingstock both by reproaches and afflictions; and partly, whilst ye became companions of them that were so used.
34 For ye had compassion of me in my bonds, and took joyfully the spoiling of your goods, knowing in yourselves that ye have in heaven a better and an enduring substance.

"But" introduces this closing section of chapter 10 as a contrast with the preceding section. There he has issued warnings and spoken of coming judgment for those who abandon Christ in order to return to Judaism. In contrast to that severe section, however, he now expresses his complete confidence in their perseverance. He first asks them to "call to remembrance the former days," expressed in continuous action (Greek present tense): "Keep calling to remembrance." This is something they must continue doing as persecution increases. The stress of difficult times can make us forget the good times that we have experienced. As Christians we cannot live in the past (Phil. 3:13, 14), but we can use the memories of past successes to give us strength to endure present struggles, especially when hope is even brighter for the future, as it always is with genuine Christians.

Identifying "the former days" is important in deciding the date and the destination of this book, as discussed in the introduction. If the epistle was written just a few years prior to A.D. 70, as seems likely, the sufferings of the early Christians in Palestine would have occurred too long ago (30 to 35 years earlier) to use this terminology. Furthermore, the statement in 12:4, that they had "not yet resisted unto blood," would not be fitting for Jewish Christians in Palestine after the death of Stephen. It also could not apply to Roman Christians much later than the autumn of A.D. 64 when severe persecution came on them through Nero and many died. If our contention is right, that the writer was addressing Jewish Christians in Rome, then the lighter persecution referred to here must have occurred in connection with Claudius' persecution of Jews in A.D. 49 (see Acts 18:2). If the epistle was written in early A.D. 64, about 15 years has passed, an appropriate length of time to refer to as "the former days." Lenski (364) wants to date the epistle in A.D. 66 or later, but the language of 12:4 seems to me to be a problem for this late date. These former days were "after ye were illuminated," that is, after the light of the Gospel had opened their spiritual eyes, after they were saved. It is the same word used to describe the Christians in 6:4 as "enlightened." Paul said to the Corinthians, "For God, who commanded the light to shine out of darkness, hath shined in our hearts" (2 Cor. 4:6). It is especially appropriate to say that a Christian has been "illuminated" or "enlightened."

The writer further describes these former days as days "in which . . . ye endured a great fight of afflictions." "Endured" speaks of a successful completion of the suffering in question (Greek aorist tense). The word (Greek *hupomeno*) means "to stay under," a proper description of those who do not flee persecution. "Fight" (Greek *athlesis*) is the word from which "athlete" comes, describing a "fight" which is a contest, a struggle. "Great" describes the intensity of the struggle, not necessarily its length. The great fight which they had endured during those earlier days was "of afflictions" (Greek *pathema*) or sufferings. Though the writer is probably not addressing Palestinian Christians, similar sufferings did take place in the early days of Christianity (see Acts 4:1-3; 5:17, 18; 6:9-14; 17:5-9; 18:12-17).

In those earlier days of their Christian experience these Hebrews had endured suffering in two different ways. These two different ways can be taken as the experience of two different groups among them; or as the group as a whole who had both of these experiences in their suffering for Christ; or, as is more likely, some overlapping of both.

The first way is referred to as, "partly, whilst ye were made a gazingstock both by reproaches and afflictions." Being "made a gazingstock" (Greek *theatrizo*) refers to the public exposure of persecution, even as taking place in the theater (you can see that in the original word), as some of the later persecution did. Here it may be merely figurative of the public way in which the suffering was carried out. Referring to the suffering of the apostles, Paul says that they had been "made a spectacle unto the world, and to angels, and to men" (1 Cor. 4:9). Their ministry was public, and their persecution was often public as well. This experience of the Hebrews is presented as occurring continuously over some length of time (Greek present tense).

This public exposure was "by reproaches and afflictions." "Reproaches" (Greek *oneidismos*) speaks of verbal abuse, of mocking and reviling. Peter says, "If ye be reproached for the name of Christ, happy are ye" (1 Pet. 4:14). "Afflictions" (Greek *thlipsis*) usually describes suffering of a more physical sort, including beatings and imprisonment. Paul told the Ephesian elders at Miletus that the Holy Spirit had informed him "that bonds and afflictions abide me" (Acts 20:23). The limitation that we must keep in mind from 12:4, that they had "not yet resisted unto blood," probably refers to martyrdom and not merely to the shedding of blood through beatings.

But their endurance of suffering had also occurred in a second way: "Partly, whilst ye became companions of them that were so used." The verb "became" (Greek aorist tense) indicates that their identification with the sufferers had been instantaneous and decisive, not that it had necessarily occurred only once (as Westcott 334). Having become "companions" (Greek *koinonos*) includes not only the idea of sympathizing with their misery but also sharing and fellowshipping with them, becoming real participants in their suffering. At the final judgment Jesus commended the sheep on

His right hand who had communed with Him and aided Him in His hunger, thirst, loneliness, nakedness, sickness, and bondage by communing with and aiding "one of the least of these my brethren" (Mt. 25:31-40).

Similarly, the readers of Hebrews had become companions of those who "were so used" (Greek *anastrepho*), that is, those whose lives were being lived in this manner, who were being treated like this (Bauer 61). These Hebrews could take special comfort from our Lord's Beatitude, "Blessed *are* they which are persecuted for righteousness' sake: for theirs is the kingdom of heaven. Blessed are ye, when *men* shall revile you, and persecute *you*, and shall say all manner of evil against you falsely, for my sake" (Mt. 5:10, 11).

In v. 34 the writer explains the suffering described in v. 33 in reverse order and in a bit more detail. First, he says, "For ye had compassion of me in my bonds." This is how they had become companions of those who were being persecuted. "For" introduces this statement as an explanation of what precedes. "Ye had compassion" speaks of the sympathy, the personal identification which the Hebrews openly displayed with those who were suffering persecution. It takes great courage to publicly identify oneself with those in prison, who may be awaiting execution. The writer makes the compassion personal: "of me in my bonds." Some manuscripts do not have the personal pronoun, and many have the word for "prisoners" (Greek *desmios*) rather than the word "bonds" (Greek *desmos*); see the translation in NIV and NASB; see also 13:3. In either case, the meaning is basically the same. Many Christians had languished in prisons during various periods of persecution, and these Hebrew believers had unashamedly come to their aid—a strong argument for the genuineness of their faith in Christ. The writer's inclusion of himself as one of those prisoners would make his knowledge even more direct and the commendation even more personal.

Furthermore, he explains how they had suffered "reproaches and afflictions": "And took joyfully the spoiling of your goods." Their "goods" were their physical possessions: furniture, equipment, livestock, even houses and land, etc., things which they owned that could be stolen or destroyed. "Spoiling" (Greek *harpage*) refers to the act of seizing or confiscating belongings, whether by vandals or by the official act of a government. The amazing thing is that they "took joyfully" such "reproaches and afflictions." This indicates that they had reason to expect such consequences, perhaps by their own previous experience or by information from other locations.

But the writer explains why they could maintain such an attitude in the face of personal financial ruin: "Knowing in yourselves that ye have in heaven a better and an enduring substance." "Knowing" (Greek *ginosko*) refers to knowledge which comes by personal experience (Westcott 334). It is difficult to defeat Christians who have this attitude toward what they have on this earth, but the reason they can be so serene under such circumstances is no secret. They know that they will "have in heaven a better and an enduring substance."

"Substance" (Greek *huparxis*) is the noun form of the word translated "goods" in the previous clause. Any possessions we may lose on this earth because of our faithfulness to Christ will be replaced in Heaven by something that is far "better," and one of the main reasons that it is better is that it is also "enduring" (Greek present participle of *meno*), abiding, continuing—indeed, eternal. The best of what we have on this earth wears out, but what we have in Heaven will last forever (see Mt. 6:19, 20; 19:27-29). Expressing these sentiments, Martin Luther wrote,

> Let goods and kindred go, This mortal life also;
> The body they may kill; God's truth abideth still,
> His kingdom is forever.
> ("A Mighty Fortress Is Our God," 1529)

(2) By remaining faithful until Christ's return (10:35-38)

35 Cast not away therefore your confidence, which hath great recompence of reward.
36 For ye have need of patience, that, after ye have done the will of God, ye might receive the promise.
37 For yet a little while, and he that shall come will come, and will not tarry.
38 Now the just shall live by faith: but if *any man* draw back, my soul shall have no pleasure in him.

The writer has encouraged his readers to patience in their Christian faith by remembering the past and the sufferings they have already experienced in the service of Christ. Now he points them toward the future to further enhance the encouragement they need during these stressful times. He admonishes them, "Cast not away therefore your confidence." "Confidence" (Greek *parresia*) refers to the boldness or the firm assurance that the Hebrews have already manifested in the promises of Christ. It is the same attitude to which the writer referred in 10:19 when he declared, "Having therefore, brethren, boldness to enter into the holiest by the blood of Jesus" (see also 3:6; 4:16). It is that confidence that looks forward to victory. "Cast not away" (Greek *apoballo*) means to abandon like a garment considered worthless, no longer useful (see Mk. 10:50). The verb tense indicates the finality of the action (Greek aorist tense). This is the negative side of the positive admonition in 3:6 where the writer says that we are God's house "if we hold fast the confidence and the rejoicing of hope firm unto the end" (see also 3:14). "Therefore" connects this admonition with what has just been said about their past sufferings for the cause of Christ. In light of the sufferings described in vv. 32-34, they must not consider abandoning Christ.

One of the primary reasons for not abandoning our confidence, our bold assurance in the promises of Christ, is because it is that "which hath great recompence of reward." "Recompence of reward" (Greek *misthapodosia*) comes from one word in the original which refers to a payment given back as something that is due (Lenski 367). It can point to just punishment for disobedience (as in 2:2) or to just reward for obedience (as here and in 11:26). The writer assures us that he is not speaking of some common repayment, some insignificant return. He refers, rather, to a "great" reward. Paul expresses the same idea when he says "that the sufferings of this present time *are* not worthy *to be compared* with the glory which shall be revealed in us" (Rom.

8:18). Though the Scriptures teach that there will be special rewards in addition to our salvation in return for dedicated service for Christ (see 1 Cor. 3:10-15), that is not what the writer means here (but see Morris 110). Salvation itself is a matter of grace, of totally unmerited favor.

Instead of casting away their confidence in light of the reward that awaits, the writer explains, "For ye have need of patience." "For" introduces the next statement as the preferred alternative to the abandonment of their confidence, boldness, or assurance. "Ye have need" (see 5:12) points to something that is absolutely essential, not just desirable. What they need is "patience" (Greek *hupomone*) or endurance, the characteristic of one who "stays under" the difficult circumstances he may be facing, who does not seek escape to an easier path. The writer has already used the verb form of the same word in v. 32 when he referred to the former days when they "endured a great fight of afflictions." They have already manifested the required attitude of patience in earlier days.

The result of such endurance will be that, "after ye have done the will of God, ye might receive the promise." "After ye have done" describes an act which is seen through to completion, a goal successfully attained (Greek effective aorist). In this case the object of completion is "the will of God," not His will in some narrow sense of obtaining a specific objective, as good as that might be (as Rom. 1:10; 1 Th. 4:3; 1 Pet. 2:15); but the will of God in its broadest sense, of remaining faithful to Him throughout our lives, seeking to grow in His grace and consistently obeying His teachings. One of our Lord's main purposes was to do God's will in His life (10:7-10); we should follow His example.

The ultimate purpose in faithfully pursuing God's will in this manner is that "ye might receive the promise." "Receive" (Greek *komizo*) goes beyond merely obtaining something in possession; it usually speaks of a reward which comes from the Lord, either a good reward which brings joy or a bad reward which brings judgment (see 2 Cor. 5:10; Eph. 6:8; Col. 3:25; 1 Pet. 1:9; 5:4; 2 Pet. 2:13). It refers to receiving the promise in one's own experience, receiving the fulfillment of the promise (Hughes 433). "The promise" which the Hebrews will receive as a reward for their patience, as well as all of us, is eternal life. In 9:15 he called it "the promise of eternal inheritance," and in 1 Jn. 2:25 we read, "This is the promise that he hath promised us, *even* eternal life" (see also 2 Tim. 1:1). The promise spoken of here is the same as the "great recompence of reward" mentioned in v. 35.

In v. 37 the writer points to the time when this promise—this great recompence of reward—will become a reality, using the language of the O.T.: "For yet a little while." The wording seems to be suggested by Is. 26:20 as it appears in the Septuagint. Isaiah's prophecy is in the context of the impending judgment of God on rebellious Judah inflicted by Nebuchadnezzar and the armies of Babylon. The Hebrew text says, "Hide thyself as it were *for a little moment*, until the indignation be overpast."

The rest of the verse is drawn from Hab. 2:3: "And he that shall come will come, and will not tarry." Writing 20 years or so before Babylon's first attack on Judah, the Lord gave the prophet a vision of His future deliverance after the period of judgment was past. The writer of Hebrews applies the wording to his readers' present situation and the promise of the return of Christ. "He that shall come" is, literally, "He who is coming." The promise of our Lord's coming is always current. From the human side, it can occur at any moment (Mt. 24:36-42; 25:13; 1 Cor. 15:51, 52; 1 Th. 5:1-6; 2 Pet. 1:10-14), but from the Father's side the time is certain (Mk. 13:32; Acts 1:7). However, one day soon the One who is coming "will come, and will not tarry." Using similar wording, Jesus promised, "Yet a little while, and the world seeth me no more; but ye see me: because I live, ye shall live also" (Jn. 14:19). Even during this time when He is away from us in physical presence, He promises to be with us in His spiritual presence and to empower us for Christian living through the Word and the indwelling Spirit.

Some may object that almost two thousand years seems like a long time, not just "a little while," but that is thinking from the human side, not from God's side. We must remember that the time of His return is a heavenly decision with heavenly reasoning. Peter points to this explanation when he says, "But, beloved, be not ignorant of this one thing, that one day *is* with the Lord as a thousand years, and a thousand years as one day" (2 Pet. 3:8). To an eternal God whose primary name is "I AM" (Ex. 3:14), two thousand years is not even a "drop in the bucket" of time. Some commentators think that there may be some immediate reference to the destruction of Jerusalem in A.D. 70, which would now be on the horizon (Pink 641), but the clearest application seems to be to the Second Coming of Christ.

But while we wait for God's permanent deliverance at the return of Christ, we must be busy in living for Him on this earth—as the writer emphasizes by quoting Hab. 2:4 as it reads in the Septuagint: "Now the just shall live by faith." "Now" (Greek *de*) or "but" offers a contrast between those who do have patience (v. 36) and those who don't. "The just" refers to positional justification or positional righteousness based on our identification with Jesus Christ. Some manuscripts read, "My just one," but "my" is not in the Hebrew text.

The future, "shall live," emphasizes the fact that the truly just man's faith extends from the present throughout the future to the end of his life: long term faith, not short term. He will live his life "by faith" (Greek *ek pisteos*); that is, faith is the basis of his spiritual life, the motivation from which he draws on a daily basis. Faith refers to his total trust in God and His promises through His Son, Jesus Christ. This part of Hab. 2:4 is also quoted in Rom. 1:17 to show that salvation by faith applies to everyone, whether Greeks or Barbarians, wise or unwise (see Rom. 1:14); and in Gal. 3:11 to show that men are saved by faith and kept saved by faith, not by the works of the law. Though believers do obey God's moral code, performing the works of the law by itself does not bring salvation.

The second part of Hab. 2:4, as it reads in the Septuagint, "But if *any man* draw back, my soul shall have no pleasure in him," has been transposed as compared with the Hebrew text; that is, this second phrase is actually the first phrase there. Furthermore, the Hebrew text reads, "Behold, his soul *which* is lifted up is not upright in him." Though the reading of the Septuagint is somewhat different, perhaps a paraphrase, it is still obvious that the Lord does not approve of a man's life apart from true faith in Him (Hughes 436).

The "*any man*" supplied by our translators refers back to "the just" one in the first clause and can as well be read, "But if he [the just man] draws back, my soul shall have no pleasure in him." In other words, it is the just man who both lives by faith and who has a potential for drawing back. The statement that the Lord "shall have no pleasure in him" who draws back is a negative way of saying that God will reject the apostate. It calls attention to the judgment with an intentional understatement (Lenski 371). Jesus Himself expressed the same principle in different ways. He declared, "He that shall endure unto the end, the same shall be saved" (Mt. 24:13), and "No man, having put his hand to the plough, and looking back, is fit for the kingdom of God" (Lk. 9:62).

(3) By positive identification with those who persevere (10:39)

39 But we are not of them who draw back unto perdition; but of them that believe to the saving of the soul.

Our writer ends his warning about apostasy on a positive note, just as he did in 6:9. Though he has seen some obvious dangers in their attitudes, he wants them to know that he has full confidence that their faith will continue and increase. He says, "But we are not of them." Just as he has included himself in the warnings (6:1; 10:26), now he enthusiastically includes himself in the statement of encouragement. "Them who draw back" are seen as a group to which "we who are faithful" do not belong, while "them that believe" are viewed as the group to which "we" do belong.

Those who draw back do so "unto perdition" (Greek *apoleia*) or "destruction," the only time the word is used in this epistle; it appears often in the N.T. as a designation for eternal punishment (Mt. 7:13; Jn. 17:12; Phil. 3:19; 2 Th. 2:3; 1 Tim. 6:9; 2 Pet. 3:7; Rev. 17:8). Those who believe, on the other hand, do so "to the saving of the soul." "Saving" (Greek *peripoiesis*) is not the usual word for salvation; it refers to the obtaining (of salvation), of claiming it as one's own possession (see 1 Th. 5:9). This is salvation in its final sense.

This latter group, the faithful Christians to whom "we" belong, will now be discussed in great detail. The statement introduces us to chapter 11, probably the most famous chapter in the epistle, which calls our attention to the great heroes of the faith who serve as examples and encouragement for our perseverance.

Summary (10:1-39)

In the first part of chapter 10 the writer continues to make contrasts between various aspects of the old covenant and the new covenant (10:1-18). The O.T. sacrifices were only shadows, pictures, or types of the true sacrifice which was to come. The very fact that they had to be repeated, especially those offered for the sins of the nation on the annual Day of Atonement, showed their ineffectiveness in making atonement for sin (10:1-4). In order to show that God had plans all along for the greater sacrifice of His Son, the writer quotes from Ps. 40:6-8 as it reads in the Septuagint. The quotation emphasized the coming of the Messiah in order to do God's perfect will in preparation for His perfect sacrifice. God gave Him a body, an intentional reference to the incarnation of Jesus Christ (10:5-10).

The O.T. priests always carried out their ministry in a standing position. This, along with the constant repetition of the sacrifices, demonstrated that their ministry was always incomplete, that the people needed something better. Jesus Christ provided that better sacrifice when He died on the cross for our sins and then sat down at God's right hand in Heaven. His sitting position speaks of the finality of His ministry. It demonstrates the meaning of His statement on the cross, "It is finished." Even so, though His atoning sacrifice never has to be repeated, His sanctifying work in our lives will continue as long as we live or until His victorious return (10:11-14).

To emphasize the distinctiveness of the new covenant, the writer returns to a portion of the quotation from Jer. 31:31-34 already given in 8:8-12. But this time he only quotes Jer. 31:33 and the last part of v. 34, referring authorship to the Holy Spirit rather than to Jeremiah. By quoting Jeremiah he wants to emphasize that the nature of the new covenant is internal, in contrast with the old covenant which was external; and that the new covenant brings permanent forgiveness of sins, in contrast with the old covenant which was constantly bringing them up again. Once forgiveness is complete, no further sacrifice is needed (10:15-18).

In the second part of the chapter, 10:19-39, the writer issues his fourth warning. He ties what he has to say in this warning to the new covenant, this "new and living way." The basis of this new and living way is the shed blood of Jesus Christ. Thus, spiritually speaking, we can go straight to Christ at the Father's right hand to seek His High Priestly help. We do that by going, as it were, through His crucified body into the heavenly Holy of Holies, much as the O.T. high priest entered the earthly Holy of Holies through the veil of the tabernacle (10:19-21).

If we would continue on the path of this new and living way, there are three duties to which we must faithfully adhere. First, we must eagerly pursue the true worship of God, getting closer to Him each day through justification and sanctification. Second, we must continue steadfast in our original confession of faith in Christ. Our faith, in fact, should gradually grow stronger, knowing that God's faithfulness to all His promises is always certain. Thirdly, we should constantly practice mutual consideration of our brothers and sisters in Christ. As Christians we must consider ourselves as our brother's keeper, even when our persistent concern is sometimes unappreciated.

Much of the practice of these duties of the new and living way is carried out when we meet together for worship, instruction, exhortation, and prayer; therefore, faithfulness in church attendance is absolutely essential (10:19-25). The urgency about practicing these duties is so important because the consequences of failing to do so are so severe. In fact, Christians who commit apostasy through acts of persistent rebellion against God's way will forfeit their salvation. Since they have continuously and stubbornly rejected the only sacrifice that can save, there is nowhere else to turn. Such a pitiful person has joined the side of the enemy, those who have never accepted Christ, and will share their eternal consequences.

When people broke the law of Moses, they were put to death physically; and when people break their covenant with Jesus Christ, God's Son, in the manner described, they are put to death spiritually. They become apostates with no hope of return (10:26-31). But, as in chapter 6, the writer follows his warning with strong encouragement for their perseverance in the faith. He reminds them of how committed to Christ they were in the early days of their faith, how they even suffered in various ways in behalf of the cause of Christ. The Lord rewards those who suffer for Him on this earth with heavenly blessings that are beyond all comparison. The Hebrews, therefore, need to continue to serve Christ faithfully. He will provide deliverance in just a little while when He returns to take us home to Heaven. If any man still chooses to abandon Christ after all these warnings, he must face the consequences; but the writer has confidence that these Hebrew Christians will not seriously consider that option (10:32-39).

Application: Teaching and Preaching the Passage

The tenth chapter of Hebrews is rich in preaching and teaching passages. In 10:1-4 there are some interesting observations about O.T. sacrifices: (1) *They served as shadows of the real thing.* The writer of Hebrews certainly does not paint the picture that the Levitical sacrifices had no purpose. They were very important for the time, and without them the O.T. worshiper could not be saved. But those sacrifices were acts of faith pointing forward to the coming of the true sacrifice in Jesus Christ: the "shadow" cast by the promise of His coming. To use a modern illustration, they were like a credit card that promises that the bill will be fully paid. (2) *They were imperfect with regard to the conscience of sinners.* Romans 5:1 says, "Therefore being justified by faith, we have peace with God through our Lord Jesus Christ." But the O.T. worshiper could not enjoy the sense of a fully settled peace with God. The sacrifices did temporarily settle the debt, but the next offering brought the subject up all over again. The conscience of the sinner was never totally eased with regard to the question of his sins. (3) *They were ineffective in relation to atonement.* The writer is blunt in this assessment: "It is not possible that the blood of bulls and of goats should take away sins." The O.T. makes some tremendous promises about the forgiveness of sins. They are buried in the depths of the sea (Mic. 7:19). They are removed from us as far as the east is from the west (Ps. 103:12). But these promises only find full validity in the coming of God's Son, Jesus Christ.

In 10:5-10 the writer draws some interesting points from his quotation of Ps. 40:6-8. As usual he quotes from the Septuagint, not the Hebrew text. In this we see: (1) *The body of Christ was essential for His Messianic ministry.* As powerful as our God is, He could not pay the price for our sins apart from becoming a man (see 2:9, 14). (2) *The body of Christ was His instrument of obedience.* God the Father did not give His Son a human body just so He could die for our sins, as important as that part of His ministry is. Of equal importance, He also gave Him a body to fully obey God's commandments. The Son of God in His earthly body had to be tested and proved. Only a perfect, obedient sacrifice could pay the penalty for disobedient sinners. (3) The body of Christ provided complete atonement forever. "We are sanctified" (v. 10) refers to initial sanctification, basically synonymous with justification. It pictures this sanctification or justification as an act that was completed in the past but with results that continue to the present (Greek perfect tense). Christ made the payment for our sins with His death on the cross at a specific point in time, but that payment is just as applicable today as it was the day of His crucifixion. In the same sense, it is effective in the life of each individual sinner from the moment we believe until we meet Christ through death or in His return.

In 10:11-14 the writer points out the significance of Christ's present position at God's right hand: (1) In contrast with the O.T. priests: they always ministered from a standing position; there were no seats in the O.T. tabernacle. The message communicated was that their ministry was never complete because the animal sacrifices did not settle the sin debt with God. Jesus, on the other hand, "sat down" after His sacrifice, indicating that the atonement was now complete. No further sacrifice needs to be made. (2) In expectation of a complete victory: the sin debt has been fully paid. Still, there are other aspects of our Lord's accomplished victory which await their final manifestation, especially His ultimate victory over death and Satan (see 1 Cor. 15:24-28; Rev. 20:10-15). (3) In carrying out permanent *justification and progressive sanctification* (10:14): the way this verse combines justification, which is a completed act, and progressive sanctification, which is a continuing process, is unique. "He has perfected" depicts an act that has been completed, but with continuing results (Greek perfect tense): as in our Lord's declaration from the cross in Jn. 19:30, "It is finished." The writer of Hebrews describes justification as applied to each individual. Christ's statement from the cross describes His act of atonement which made individual justification possible. But contrasted with justification, which is a finished work, the writer also mentions sanctification, which is a work in progress. The verse might be translated, "He has perfected forever those who are being sanctified." Justification deals with positional righteousness, while sanctification deals with practical righteousness. Progressive sanctification will be completed when we meet Christ (1 Jn. 3:2).

In 10:15-18 the writer reminds us of the new covenant prophesied in Jer. 31:31-34, already quoted in 8:8-12. Here, however, he quotes only portions of Jer. 31:33 and 34. We can draw from this that: (1) *The Holy Spirit is the author of all Scripture.* Even though the quotation is from Jeremiah, who is the human author of these words, they are at the same time the very words of God. This places even greater emphasis on their authority. (2) *Two aspects of the new covenant are emphasized: its nature and its effectiveness.* Its nature is seen in Jeremiah's description of the new covenant as internal, with the Lord putting His laws "into their hearts" and writing them "in their minds," in contrast with the law of Moses which was primarily external. Its *effectiveness* is seen in the emphasis on complete forgiveness of sins, so much so that God "will remember them no more." (3) *The implication about these truths from the new covenant is that there is no further need for Levitical sacrifices.* If Jeremiah was prophesying a new internal relationship with God through Jesus Christ and total forgiveness through the sacrifice of Christ, then O.T. sacrifices are no longer needed.

In 10:19-21 the writer describes our new position under the new covenant. (1) *Its location* allows us to enter the heavenly Holy of Holies to seek our Lord's help in living the Christian life. As Paul pointed out, God "hath raised *us* up together, and made *us* sit together in heavenly *places* in Christ Jesus" (Eph. 2:6). (2) *Its basis* is "by the blood of Jesus." (3) *Its name* is the "new and living way" in contrast with the old way which overflowed with death: dead laws, dead sacrifices, and dead priests. We serve Jesus Christ who is "the way, the truth, and the life" (Jn. 14:6). (4) *Its access* provides for us, as believer priests, to enter into the heavenly Holy of Holies through the sacrificed body of Christ. (5) *Its conclusion*, when we come into that heavenly Holy of Holies through prayer and worship, is that we have "an high priest over the house of God" to minister to our needs at any time.

In 10:22-25 three important duties are laid down which are designed to keep us on this new and living way. They are: (1) *The duty of true worship.* Unlike the Pharisees who were quite impressive in their external worship, but inside were "full of dead *men's* bones" (Mt. 23:27), God wants people to worship Him in true purity both inside and out (10:22). (2) *The duty of steadfastness.* God does not like a wavering faith, sometimes up and sometimes down. James says that such faith is "like a wave of the sea driven with the wind and tossed" (Jas. 1:6). God Himself is always faithful, and He expects the same from us (10:23). (3) *The duty of mutual consideration.* Unlike Cain, we are our brother's keeper (Gen. 4:9). Paul says, "Brethren, if a man be overtaken in a fault, ye which are spiritual, restore such an one in the spirit of meekness; considering thyself, lest thou also be tempted" (Gal. 6:1).

As a group, and as individuals, we must "provoke" (the pressing of brothers and sisters in their backslidden condition may sometimes seem unpleasant), "spur on" (NIV), "stimulate" (NASB), or "stir up" (NKJV) one another "to love and good works" (10:24, 25). Verse 25 is directly connected with v. 24, and likely is intended to go with the practice of all three duties of the new and living way mentioned here, for we carry out all these things in the Christian assembly, the regular meetings of the church, though their fulfillment may not be completely limited to this.

One of the texts that stand out in this chapter is 10:25. From it we can draw some admonitions concerning church attendance: (1) *The importance of church attendance.* Faithful attendance of the Christian assembly is important for several different reasons: (a) it is one of the main places where we carry out the duties described in vv. 22-24; (b) it should be a primary source for Biblical instruction that will help us keep on growing in the grace and knowledge of Jesus Christ (2 Pet. 3:18); (c) it is where the true fellowship of the Christian life can be best enjoyed (1 Jn. 3:14), and those who have no desire for this fellowship are likely not saved. (2) *The neglect of church attendance.* Though this does not change the seriousness of the problem, it is interesting to note that church attendance was a problem in the early church just as it is with us today. Going to church does not save one. But those who claim to be Christians, who are physically able, and do not faithfully attend church cannot, in my opinion, be spiritually healthy. Likewise, refraining from church attendance does not immediately make one an apostate, but it often leads to backsliding, and backsliding is the road that leads to apostasy. (3) *The increasing urgency of church attendance.* Paul declared, "All that will live godly in Christ Jesus shall suffer persecution. But evil men and seducers shall wax worse and worse, deceiving, and being deceived" (2 Tim. 3:12, 13). If times are going to get worse, and they always seem to do so, then Christians need each other's comfort and fellowship more than ever. When the writer says, "So much the more, as ye see the day approaching," he does not necessarily mean more frequent meetings of the church as much as increased faithfulness to the meetings that are already going on.

In 10:26-31 some important lessons can be drawn on the subject of apostasy: (1) *The definition.* Literally 10:26 reads, "For if we keep on sinning wilfully." On the basis of this verse, we can define apostasy as continuous rebellion against Christ by those who have genuinely known and experienced Christ. In this passage, at least, the writer seems to be talking about the apostasy of true Christians, one variety of the sin against the Holy Spirit (see Lk. 12:8-10). Other passages also indicate that certain categories of unsaved people may commit this sin (see Mt. 12:31, 32), but that is not what is being discussed here. (2) *The immediate result.* While Heb. 6:4-6 teaches the psychological result of apostasy (it is impossible to renew them to repentance), this passage teaches the soteriological result of apostasy (there is no more sacrifice for sins). Soteriology is the branch of theology which involves the doctrine of salvation. Since Christ is the only way to be saved, anyone who has experienced His salvation and has willfully abandoned Him has nowhere else to turn. (3) *The frame of mind.* The true apostate becomes a person without hope whose life is characterized by "a certain fearful looking for [expectation] of judgment and fiery indignation, which shall devour the adversaries" (10:27). A person who was once considered a friend of Jesus has now become His enemy. His fear of judgment may be manifested in total spiritual apathy toward all things spiritual. (4) *The eternal effect:* spiritual death. Those who committed serious violations of the law of Moses were put to death, providing that at least two or three witnesses could be found to testify against them. The writer says that the penalty for abandoning Christ and His teachings in our lives is much more severe. That can only be spiritual death—eternal separation from God, Jesus, His Son, all the people of God, and Heaven itself.

According to 10:29, those who commit the sin of apostasy, finally and completely turning away from salvation in Christ, are involved in three things: (1) *They have rejected none other than the Son of God.* (2) *They have considered the blood of Christ that saved them as nothing but common blood, nothing special at all.* (3) *They have insulted the Holy Spirit,* the member of the Trinity that, in this dispensation, is responsible for applying to us the salvation provided by Jesus' vicarious death on the cross.

Finally, in 10:32-39, the writer leaves a strong word of encouragement meant to change the backward drift of these Hebrew Christians. He admonishes them to: (1) *Remember the past.* They had already suffered for Christ in the early days of their Christian experience. Though they have not, at this point, resisted unto blood, they have suffered in other ways for the cause of Christ, have lovingly identified themselves with other suffering Christians, and have even had their property confiscated because of their stand for Christ. They have certainly gone too far to turn back now. (2) *Consider the reward for confidence* in Christ. Moses was willing to suffer for Christ rather than have the treasures of Egypt, as great as they were, because he saw that the reward for serving Christ was ultimately much greater (Heb. 11:25, 26). Paul said that the eternal reward for serving Christ was much greater than the paltry sufferings of this world, and that comparison was not even worthwhile (Rom. 8:18). (3) *Expect the promised return of Christ.* Suffering Christians in every generation have found hope and comfort in looking forward expectantly to the coming of Christ for final judgment and rewards. It may seem like we have been waiting a long time—and from the human side it has been almost 2,000 years—but from God's side it has been no time at all since our God is eternal (see 2 Pet. 3:8). One day soon the waiting will be over, and we will all be glad that we were found faithfully serving Him. (4) *Continue in faith and live.* With these words of encouragement the writer closes, emphasizing that saving faith is always continuing faith (see Jn. 8:31). In these closing words the writer quotes the famous text from Hab. 2:4 which later became the prime text of Martin Luther and the Protestant Reformation: "The just shall live by faith." This emphasis on the importance of persistent faith prepares us for chapter 11 and the O.T. heroes who serve as great examples of genuine and persevering faith.

IV. The Superiority of Faith Under the New Covenant (11:1—13:17)

Though faith has already been mentioned several times in Hebrews (4:2; 6:1, 12; 10:22, 23), the writer's quotation in 10:37, 38, from Hab. 2:3, 4, serves as an introduction to the theme of faith which will run throughout the rest of the epistle. In chapter 11 he illustrates faith from O.T. history; in chapter 12 we see faith progressing toward consummation; and in chapter 13 the writer closes with final admonitions for those who are living by faith.

A. Faith Illustrated from Old Testament History (11:1-40)

Salvation by faith as the only way to Heaven did not begin with the coming of God's Son, Jesus Christ. The writer has already demonstrated that fact with references to faith on the part of O.T. saints, particularly Abraham, Moses, and Joshua. He especially emphasized this idea by his quotation of Hab. 2:4, "The just shall live by his faith," in 10:38, the verse that became the key text of the Protestant Reformation because of its influence on Martin Luther, the German monk who became the father of the Protestant Reformation. But in chapter 11 the references to faith are multiplied (some 24 times throughout the chapter). It is certainly one of the most beautiful chapters in the N.T., both because of its eloquence and because of the power of its encouragement. The writer introduces us to great heroes of the faith from the Biblical record of Genesis, Exodus, Joshua, Judges, 1 Samuel, and 2 Samuel. By pointing to these O.T. heroes, he strongly emphasizes that justification by faith has been God's way of saving people from Adam to the present.

1. Faith defined for all time (11:1, 2)

1 Now faith is the substance of things hoped for, the evidence of things not seen.
2 For by it the elders obtained a good report.

"Now" (Greek *de*) shows the connection to 10:37-39. If the just can only live by faith, the writer feels that it is important to define faith and point to some key examples of those who manifested their faith even under difficult circumstances. Commentators debate as to whether what the writer says in v. 1 should be called a definition of faith (Hughes 440; Lenski 372) or merely a description of faith (Kent 216; Hewitt 171). Perhaps there are different ways in which the definition of a term can be given, but it seems to me that these words aptly serve as the best definition of faith anywhere in Scripture. We should grant, however, that the definition of faith given here is not an academic one but a working one. Its emphasis is more practical than intellectual.

"Faith is the substance of things hoped for." "Substance" (Greek *hupostasis*) literally means something that "stands under," thus giving support in whatever manner the context demands. We find a special use of the word in 1:3 where the writer points to the Son as "the express image of his *person*": "person" here refers to God's essence, what God is in reality, including all of His attributes. The usage here is more like 3:14 and 2 Cor. 9:4 and 11:17 where the idea of "confidence" or "assurance" stands out. Faith is the substance, the very foundation, of things hoped for because it gives us confident assurance that those things will come about. "Things hoped for" is expressed in continuous action (Greek present tense): "things which are being hoped for." Hope, which is belief accompanied by expectation, must ever be the attitude of God's people. The things hoped for are all of those promises which God has made which have not yet been realized: the bodily resurrection, Heaven, eternal life, etc.

The second line of the definition is classic parallelism, being essentially synonymous with the first line: faith is "the evidence of things not seen." "Evidence" (Greek *elegchos*) also appears in 2 Tim. 3:16 where it is translated "reproof." Thus, the word carries with it either the idea of "proof" or "evidence" or "reproof," for reproof is correction brought about by the presentation of proof or evidence of what is right. "Things not seen" (Greek present tense) is also in continuous action: "things not being seen." The things that matter most to believers are never visible, "for we walk by faith, not by sight" (2 Cor. 5:7). Paul connects these two ideas of things hoped for and things not seen when he says, "For we are saved by hope: but hope that is seen is not hope:

for what a man seeth, why doth he yet hope for? But if we hope for that we see not, *then* do we with patience wait for *it*" (Rom. 8:24, 25). Faith is not "a leap in the dark," as some skeptics have described it; it is, instead, sincere trust based on evidence and experience.

In v. 2 the writer connects this working definition with the evidence which he wants to point out in the rest of the chapter: "For by it the elders obtained a good report." "For" makes the connection with v. 1, presenting this verse and what follows as the explanation of the definition given. "By it" refers to the faith which the writer has defined. The term "elders" (Greek *presbuteros*) is used in Scripture in an official sense to refer to the leaders of Israel, both in Old and New Testament times (Ex. 3:16; Mt. 21:23) as well as to the leaders of the church (Acts 14:23; 1 Tim. 5:17; Tit. 1:5). It is sometimes used merely to describe those who are older in contrast to those who are younger (as in Lk. 15:25; 1 Tim. 5:1, 2). Here the word is used in a semi-official sense to refer to those in ancient times who stand out as examples of faith. It is through this faith, often under the most difficult circumstances, that they "obtained a good report:" that is, they received approving testimony from the Lord in that the circumstances of their life of faith were recorded in the Old Testament.

2. Specific examples of faith related (11:3-38)

In most of the rest of the chapter the writer gives brief accounts of O.T. heroes to demonstrate their faith. His purpose is to show these struggling Hebrew Christians that many believers, in as bad or worse circumstances than they were facing, had persevered in their faith with regard to the promises of God.

a. In the early days of Biblical history (11:3-7)

In vv. 3-7 the writer covers events from the earliest days of Biblical history which called for outstanding faith on the part of the participants. He wants his readers to know that God has demanded perseverance in faith from the beginning. He still expects the same from them, as well as from us today.

(1) Creation (11:3)

3 Through faith we understand that the worlds were framed by the word of God, so that things which are seen were not made of things which do appear.

Our writer starts where true faith must always start, with an acknowledgment of God as the Creator of all things. If a person can accept Genesis 1:1, "In the beginning God created the heaven and the earth," he will have no problem with anything else in Scripture. In like manner, if a person cannot accept that opening declaration of Scripture at face value, he may well have trouble with the rest of the Bible. Some think that an evolutionist can still be a Christian; if so, his faith about the rest of Scripture would have to be in stark contrast to his doubts about its opening statement. Here is the beginning of faith, and if a person is skeptical at this point, he will usually be skeptical about other important teachings: Biblical history in general, miracles, the person and work of Christ, especially His resurrection.

The Bible throughout holds the doctrine of creation, as it is taught in Gen. 1 and 2, to be of the highest importance. Thus, the writer says, "Through faith we understand that the worlds were framed by the word of God." This phrase, whether translated "through faith" or "by faith," is repeated some 21 times in this chapter. The Christian walk is one which is by faith from beginning to end, and even the testimony of the O.T. bears that out. Faith is the means, the prime instrument, that will take us successfully through the Christian life.

Though the other examples of faith in this chapter refer to some individual as the exhibitor of faith, that is not possible in this first case, for no human being was present at the beginning of creation. That is why the writer says, "We understand." All of us, including the writer, must accept by faith the fact that God created the world and everything in it. "Understand" does not mean that we fully comprehend creation with all of its scientific intricacies. It means, rather, that we accept creation by the direct hand of God as a reasoned and intelligent conclusion. Not only does this make the best sense, it is what the Scripture teaches. "The worlds" (Greek accusative plural of *aion*) is a translation of the same word used in 1:2. As there, it includes the idea of the visible universe, the *kosmos*, but it includes more than that. In the plural, as here, it literally means "the ages"; it is the world of both space and time, the world as it exists from beginning to end, for indeed God not only made the world, He also sustains it. Of course, whatever is true of God the Father is also true of God the Son (Jn. 1:3; Col. 1:16, 17; Heb. 1:2).

The verb translated "were framed" (Greek *katartizo*) is a broad word. In 10:5 it is translated "prepared," and in 13:21 "make perfect," in the sense of equipping us. In the context of creation, it refers to both bringing things into existence as well as to putting them in proper order. God saw His creation and declared that it was very good (Gen. 1:31). It met all the requirements of His strict design.

Furthermore, creation was accomplished "by the word of God." "Word" (Greek *hrema*) here refers to God's spoken word, His individual utterances which brought the universe and all its contents into existence. The first chapter of Genesis records eight separate utterances in the creation account, each one introduced by "And God said." These utterances brought about the creation of light, the firmament, sea and dry land, vegetation, the sun, moon, and stars, fish and fowl, animals, and finally man in His image. The writer uses the same word with regard to the work of the Son in creation in 1:3, but in that context it primarily refers to His sustaining power. The psalmist affirms God's creation by His spoken word when he says, "By the word of the LORD were the heavens made; and all the host of them by the breath of his mouth"; and "For he spake, and it was *done*; he commanded, and it stood fast" (Ps. 33:6, 9).

Now the writer gives us the result (Kent 218; Kistemaker 314): "So that things which are seen were not made of things which do appear." The universe is described as "things which are seen": literally, "that which is being seen" (Greek present tense and singular), things continuously visible to the eyes of man. The visible universe is viewed as a unit. "Were not made" (Greek perfect tense) presents a completed act with continuing results. God's creation of the universe was complete at the conclusion of the sixth day, but that universe with its living contents perpetuates itself to this day, but only "after their kind."

The visible universe was not made "of things which do appear" or "things which are appearing," are constantly visible (Greek present tense). This refers, of course, to material content and presents the doctrine of creation *ex nihilo*, that is, creation "out of nothing." For the universe in its origin, God had no preexisting material, and that was also evidently true for the rest of His creation as He brought His marvelous masterpiece into working order. For the physical part of man, his body, God did use preexisting material, "the dust of the ground"; but for his spiritual part, God "breathed into his nostrils the breath of life; and man became a living soul." Man is the only part of God's creation with a soul, in this sense, in God's own image.

Some translators and interpreters prefer to read the negative with "things which do appear" rather than with the verb "were made." Thus the RSV translates, for example, "So that what is seen was made out of things which do not appear." Many of the early church fathers translated in this manner. Most maintain that it is better, however, to take the negative with the verb (as Hughes 443; Kistemaker 315; Calvin 265; etc.), though the conclusion of the doctrine of creation out of nothing can be reached either way (Alford 210).

(2) Abel (11:4)

4 By faith Abel offered unto God a more excellent sacrifice than Cain, by which he obtained witness that he was righteous, God testifying of his gifts: and by it he being dead yet speaketh.

There are indications that Adam and Eve, after the fall, came to saving faith; we expect to see them in Heaven. When Cain was born, Eve, in thanksgiving, declared, "I have gotten a man from the LORD" (Gen. 4:1). When his third son was born, Adam named him Seth, which means "appointed," and declared, "For God . . . hath appointed me another seed instead of Abel" (4:25). But, unfortunately, the fall of Adam and Eve, the most catastrophic event in history, overshadowed their later faith. Consequently, the first person of faith to whom the writer directs our attention is Abel: "By faith Abel offered unto God a more excellent sacrifice than Cain." The writer is drawing from the historical account in Gen. 4:3-5. When they grew up, Cain became a farmer while Abel became a shepherd. Both were worthy occupations, one as entitled to God's approval as the other.

Abel, the younger brother, presented to God "a more excellent sacrifice than Cain." The majority of commentators say that Abel's sacrifice was "more excellent" because he offered it "by faith" (Lenski 382; Yeager 371; Hagner 184), for that reason and that alone. It would certainly seem that, from this brief account in Hebrews, we could not be dogmatic in going beyond this. Though not denying that the ultimate test of God's approval was Abel's faith, other interpreters have pointed to Moses' description of Abel's offering as "of the firstlings of his flock and of the fat thereof" (Gen. 4:4). The Scripture highlights the quality of Abel's offering, while no such remark is made about what Cain offered. Others have also emphasized that Abel's offering was a blood sacrifice, a qualification that God laid down for sin offerings later on (Lev. 17:11), a fact to which our writer has already referred in 9:22. Bruce notes, however, that there is no indication that this was a sin offering (285); at the same time there is no indication that it was *not* a sin offering. Both Cain and Abel were born after the fall; therefore, they were born in sin and needed atonement. It is also true that offerings other than the sin offering involved animal sacrifices (Gen. 8:20; 15:9, 10; Lev. 3:1-5). Alford (210) makes a good point when he notes that both the above reasons—the quality of Abel's offering as well as the fact that it was a blood sacrifice—may well have entered into the statement that it was offered by faith, but that cannot be drawn from what the writer of Hebrews has to say. Along this line, Kent (219) observes that, though Abel's offering was said to have been made by faith,

> Biblical faith is always based upon God's revelation. Thus it must be assumed that Abel's response was in direct obedience to the kind of offering God wanted . . . . This demands that the character of the gift cannot be disassociated from the heart of the offerer. Abel's offering proved something about Abel's heart that was not demonstrated by Cain's gift.

In the early chapters of Genesis some things must be assumed. Many things which God must have told Adam and Eve and their children about living and worshiping are obviously not recorded. It seems unlikely that Cain and Abel would present offerings to the Lord without instructions to do so. And if they had such instructions it might well be expected that details would be given about what God required, even to the point of specifying a blood sacrifice. In fact, Moses introduces the occasion of their offering by saying, "And in the process of time it came to pass" (Gen. 4:3), or, "It came to pass at the end of days." The statement implies a specified time for worship and sacrifice; thus instructions about the same would be indicated. MacArthur (299) feels strongly that God had given clear instructions about the type of offering which was to be brought, a blood sacrifice, and that Cain willfully disobeyed those instructions in preference for his own way. Taking that same position, Pink (659) points out that God had already given the basis for faith in the instructions to Adam and Eve after the tragic fall. To them He issued the first Gospel promise, the Protevangelium, when He pointed to the time when the seed of the woman would crush the serpent's head (Gen. 3:15). Furthermore, he implied the necessity of shedding blood to provide a proper covering when he supplied animal skins for their clothing (Gen. 3:21). Though further instructions were likely given, the basic content of the life of faith was already laid down.

With regard to the operation of faith, Paul declared, "So then faith *cometh* by hearing, and hearing by the word of God" (Rom. 10:17). For someone to offer a proper sacrifice by faith, divine revelation must exist containing the needed instructions. But we should also make clear that all the proper procedures could be followed, and the sacrifice still not be offered by faith (see Is. 1:10-20; Ps. 51:16, 17). Referring to Is. 29:13, Jesus described many in His own day as honoring God with their lips, while their heart was far from Him (Mk.

7:6). Whatever else may have been involved in Abel's "more excellent sacrifice," what made it most pleasing to God was that it was truly offered "by faith."

Concerning that display of faith, our writer explains further, "By which he obtained witness that he was righteous." The antecedent of "which" could be either the word "faith" or the word "sacrifice" (both are feminine in Greek). But it seems best to have it refer back to "faith" as the governing principle in the verse (the NIV actually supplies the word). By this act of faith "he obtained witness" (Greek *martureo*): that is, an outward testimony of his inward attitude became evident. It was a testimony "that he was righteous" (Greek *dikaios*), the same word used in 10:38 when the writer quoted Hab. 2:4, "The just [righteous] shall live by faith." Abel amply displayed that principle. Salvation is always by faith, for that is the only way to God. At the same time, however, that faith is outwardly demonstrated by obedience (see Mt. 25:34-40). Most of the other examples in this chapter will make that same point.

The writer goes on to say, "God testifying of his gifts." "Testifying" (Greek *martureo*) is from the same verb root as "he obtained witness." No greater testimony could ever be given about the validity of a person's faith than that given by God Himself, and such was the case with Abel. We get our word "martyr" from a noun form of the same root (see Rev. 2:13). A martyr is a special kind of witness or testimony who gives his life for his faith, and indeed Abel became the first martyr for faith in history.

"His gifts" are the sacrifices which Abel brought. The Scripture record says, "The LORD had respect unto Abel and to his offering: but unto Cain and to his offering he had not respect" (Gen. 4:4, 5). How that respect, that divine approval, was demonstrated is not explained, but it is obvious that it was clear to all parties. Ancient tradition says that God devoured the sacrifice by fire, as he did with Elijah on Mt. Carmel (1 Kg. 18), but there is no indication of that in Scripture.

The writer concludes, "And by it he being dead yet speaketh." "It" again refers back to Abel's "faith" at the beginning of the verse. Abel's act of faith still speaks clearly to us, even today, when we read the Scripture record which God led Moses to record. Further testimony of his righteousness is also found in Mt. 23:35 and 1 Jn. 3:12. An old saying goes, "Dead men tell no tales." That saying may have a point from one perspective, but it is not totally accurate. We all leave a message behind when we die, whether good or bad.

(3) Enoch (11:5, 6)

5 By faith Enoch was translated that he should not see death; and was not found, because God had translated him: for before his translation he had this testimony, that he pleased God.
6 But without faith *it is* impossible to please *him*: for he that cometh to God must believe that he is, and *that* he is a rewarder of them that diligently seek him.

In v. 5 we are introduced to our next example of those who lived by faith: "By faith Enoch was translated that he should not see death." The historical record is in Gen. 5:18-24. He was the son of Jared, who lived to be 962 years of age, and the father of Methuselah, who lived to be 969 years of age. In the midst of this longevity, Enoch's total life on this earth was only 365 years, summed up in one verse, "Enoch walked with God: and he *was* not; for God took him" (Gen. 5:24). Though Genesis does not specifically say that God took Enoch to Heaven, at least three things indicate that fact: (1) Enoch's short life span in contrast to others of this era; (2) the fact that the phrase, "And he died," is used for everyone else in this chapter, but not of Enoch; (3) the statement that, in the midst of his walking with God, "He *was* not; for God took him." This combination of things clearly indicates that what happened was exactly what the inspired commentary of Hebrews confirms.

Other than in this passage, Enoch is mentioned only in Luke's genealogy of Christ (Lk. 3:37) and in Jude 14 where he is cited as the seventh man from Adam. It is obvious that the writer of Hebrews wants to emphasize his supernatural removal or "translation" in that he uses the verb twice and the noun once. It is natural to see Enoch, and later Elijah (2 Kg. 2:11, 12), the two believers thus far in Biblical history to go to Heaven without dying, as types and illustrations of an entire generation who will experience a similar rapture at the end of time (1 Cor. 15:51, 52; 1 Th. 4:16, 17). Other commentators as far back as Tertullian in the third century have seen Enoch and Elijah as the two witnesses who are martyred in their stand against the Antichrist (Rev. 11:1-12). The reasoning is that since all must die (see Heb. 9:27) this is what Enoch and Elijah have been reserved for. The fallacy in that reasoning, as just pointed out, is that an entire generation of believers will be taken to Heaven without dying in the rapture at the end of time. It is probably better to see the two witnesses of Revelation as two spiritual leaders who actually live in that day, whenever it takes place, but those details are for Revelation, not Hebrews.

Quoting Gen. 5:24 from the Septuagint, as usual, the writer continues, "And was not found, because God had translated him." He "was not found" translates the Hebrew, "He *was* not." Perhaps the translators of the Greek version are suggesting that a search by family and friends might have occurred, as would be natural to assume, though the words do not have to be taken in that sense. Such a search did take place in the case of Elijah at the insistence of his students, the "sons of the prophets," though Elisha, his successor, discouraged it (2 Kg. 2:16-18). The reason Enoch could not be found was that "God had translated him," had removed him from the earthly sphere to the heavenly one.

The cause of his translation was that, "Before his translation he had this testimony, that he pleased God." The testimony of Enoch's faith in God was from his life "before his translation." For those who go to Heaven through death, or those who go in this unique manner through a supernatural rapture, their faith is manifested during life on earth. There is no intermediate state where second chances are given, no purgatory and no limbo. That "he had this testimony" (Greek perfect tense) indicates that the testimony of what happened to Enoch continues to stand, in the words of Scripture, for all time (Lenski 386). Though his life on earth is over, his testimony remains with us.

The record that Enoch left on the earth was "that he pleased God," the Septuagint translation of the Hebrew "walked with God." To walk with God means to have fellowship with Him, to truly enjoy His companionship and experience the fullness of His peace, as Adam and Eve did before the fall (Gen. 3:8). This type of relationship with God is always pleasing to Him.

The discussion of Enoch concludes with a general principle (v. 6): "But without faith *it is* impossible to please him." Genesis 5:18-24 never specifically says that Enoch had faith, but rather that he walked with God or pleased Him; but the writer wants us to know that absolutely no one can be pleasing to God, not Enoch and not us, without having a very direct and living faith in Him. To be more specific, "he that cometh to God must believe that he is." "For" introduces the statement as an explanation of what true faith is. "He that cometh," or "He that keeps on coming" (Greek present tense) "to God," has reference to genuine worship motivated by true faith. The writer used the same term in 7:25. "Must" (Greek *dei*) speaks of absolute necessity, that which cannot be logically or morally avoided. "Believe" (Greek aorist tense) emphasizes decisive commitment, unwavering certainty.

Those who would truly worship God must believe two things about Him. First, "they must believe that he is," that is, God's real existence. Some confused writers, claiming to be scholars and theologians, have identified themselves as "Christian atheists," an obvious oxymoron. Atheists (who dogmatically claim there is no God), and agnostics (who say they just don't know), cannot be Christians. Believing that God truly exists is the first step in genuine faith, and those who cannot qualify here may proceed no further.

But there are those who may meet this first demand who still fall short of genuine faith. The Deists (some of the founding fathers of our country subscribed to their views) claimed to believe in God, but they held that He was wholly transcendent. They said that He created the universe and the natural laws by which it functions, but that He has nothing to do with its everyday operation. Their man-made religion allowed no room for a personal relationship with God, and certainly none for eternal redemption through His blessed Son. Their religion was no better than atheism. James also addressed the problem of those who merely said, "I believe," with no outward evidence of their faith: "Thou believest that there is one God; thou doest well: the devils also believe, and tremble" (Jas. 2:19).

True faith, therefore, must include a second element: Those who worship Him must believe that "he is a rewarder of them that diligently seek him." "He is" (Greek *ginomai*) can also be translated, "He becomes," indicating that this second fact about God is the conclusion of a process, something that is true for those who follow through. "Rewarder" (Greek *misthapodotes*) has the same root as "recompence of reward" in 10:35 and 11:26. In those passages the writer refers to the reward itself, but here he refers to the agent who issues the reward, God Himself. There are passages that describe additional rewards for service and commitment (1 Cor. 3:11-15), but the reward meant here is eternal life, a living and abiding relationship with God.

God will become the rewarder of those "that diligently seek," who "continue to diligently seek" (Greek present tense), "him." The word (Greek *ekzeteo*) is always used to describe an intensive pursuit, a purposeful quest. It does not suggest that God is hard to find, but rather that He must be sought with the right attitude. Isaiah advised Judah, "Seek ye the LORD while he may be found, call ye upon him while he is near" (Is. 55:6). Paul also declared to the Athenians that God made of one blood all nations "that they should seek the Lord, if haply they might feel after him, and find him, though he be not far from every one of us" (Acts. 17:27). God can always be found by those who want to find Him.

(4) Noah (11:7)

7 By faith Noah, being warned of God of things not seen as yet, moved with fear, prepared an ark to the saving of his house; by the which he condemned the world, and became heir of the righteousness which is by faith.

Our writer proceeds in chronological order, as far as the Biblical record is concerned, to the example of the faith of Noah: "By faith Noah, being warned of God of things not seen as yet." "Being warned" (Greek *chrematizo*) is normally used in the N.T. of a divine communication that calls for action on the part of the one who receives it; thus it is often, but not always, in the form of a warning (Mt. 2:12, 22; Lk. 2:26; Acts 10:22). It appears in this sense in Heb. 8:5 and 12:26.

The warning itself is recorded in Gen. 6:13; Noah was warned by God "of things not seen as yet." Most commentators think that the writer is referring to the flood and the devastation it would bring. No one on earth had ever seen anything like the Lord was about to send in the universal flood (Barnes 261; Lunemann 402; Westcott 356; Yeager 319; Hughes 463). Some commentators, however, maintain that the phrase used here included the rain itself, that it had not rained at all up until the time of the flood (Kent 220; MacArthur 319; Pink 684). They base their view on Genesis 2:5 where the Scripture indicates that "the LORD God had not caused it to rain upon the earth, and *there was* not a man to till the ground." But the last phrase of that verse points to the reason why God had not caused it to rain in the very earliest days of creation, that is, because there was no one "to till the ground," no one to prune trees and bushes and to keep Eden from becoming a jungle. The implication is that, after there was a man to till the ground, God allowed the normal course of nature to begin, which would certainly include rain.

We do not know how long Noah lived after the time of creation, but it was at least several hundred years. Noah himself had already lived 600 years (Gen. 7:6) before the flood. It seems likely that the "things not seen as yet" is a broader reference to the flood and the worldwide destruction of everything on the earth. The phrase also harks back to the definition in v. 1, where faith is said to be "the evidence of things not seen."

Hearing this warning from God, Noah was "moved with fear:" that is, he was motivated to obedience by his deep respect for God and His Word. The verb form (Greek *eulabeomai*) only occurs here in the N.T., but the noun form appears in 5:7 (Jesus was heard in Gethsemane "in that he *feared*") and 12:28 (we are to "serve God acceptably with reverence and *godly fear*"). Noah was not afraid of God in the sense that he shrank from His presence; rather, he respected God and took His Word seriously.

Consequently, in obedience to divine instructions (Gen. 6:14-22), Noah "prepared an ark to the saving of his house." "Prepared" (Greek *kataskeuazo*) includes the construction of the ark and furnishing it according to all that God commanded. The word is also used in 3:3 ("he who hath builded"). The purpose of building the ark was for the saving of his house. The immediate reference is to the deliverance of Noah and his family from the flood; but the faith that motivated Noah, in obedience to God's command—to build the ark for the physical salvation of his family—was a sure indication of Noah's spiritual salvation and, most likely, the salvation of his entire household (Clarke 852). When the head of the house leads the way in trusting God and obeying His commandments, the rest of the family usually follows (see Jos. 24:15; Acts 16:31-33). Noah was, indeed, saved by faith, but it is important to note that saving faith always involves obedience to God's instructions. True faith never exists in a vacuum. James observes, "Faith, if it hath not works, is dead, being alone" (Jas. 2:17).

The writer adds, "By the which he condemned the world." "Which" could refer back to the ark and its preparation (Calvin 276; Westcott 356), but it is probably better to refer it back to Noah's faith at the beginning of the verse (Kent 222; Lenski 387), as we did in v. 4 with regard to the faith of Abel. Faith is, after all, the main principle which the writer is emphasizing, and Noah's act of faith included building the ark. In this manifestation of his faith which caused him to build the ark, Noah "condemned the world." "Condemned" is probably best taken as expressing continuous action (the Greek form can be imperfect or aorist). Then Noah "was condemning" the world (Westcott 357) over a period of 120 years as he built the ark (Gen. 6:3) and faithfully warned the people about God's coming judgment (2 Pet. 2:5; Lenski 389). The unbelieving world around us may feel condemned by our manifestations of faith (attending church, witnessing, giving, living right), as well as by more direct words which we may use to point them to Christ. Even when we try to witness for Christ with our lives and our words without being unnecessarily judgmental, our efforts are often resented, especially by those in open rebellion against God.

As a result of Noah's faith and its manifestation in building the ark and being a "preacher of righteousness" (2 Pet. 2:5), "He became heir of the righteousness which is by faith." When the writer says that Noah "became heir," he is not pointing so much to what he had received from his ancestors as to what he received from God, a more general use of the word "heir" (Rom. 4:13). Though some elements of the inheritance are already present, "heir" suggests complete fulfillment in the future (Kent 222). "The righteousness which is by faith" takes us back again to the theme suggested in 10:38, "The just shall live by faith." Righteousness connected with faith is usually positional righteousness, the righteousness which we have by being in Christ (Rom. 3:22; 2 Cor. 5:21). Though Noah lived long before the time of Christ, his legal standing before God was validated only by Christ's shed blood. Barnes points out correctly that Noah's faith was, of necessity, limited to the promise at hand, his trust and obedience with regard to God's command to build the ark and, by implication, to warn that generation of coming judgment. However, Barnes' more recent editor, Robert Frew (262), is rather harsh in his criticism of this point of view. He seems to think that Noah had a much greater knowledge of the person and coming of Christ than the Scripture record indicates, especially the knowledge that the ark in itself was a very specific type of Christ. As we look back on the record of Noah's ark and the universal flood, the idea is attractive and some excellent observations about the ark as a type of Christ can be made, but this does not mean that Noah himself saw this. It is best to maintain the principle of progressive revelation, which holds that God asks men to be responsible for faith in the promise only so far as it has been revealed to that point in history. Noah would likely have been familiar with the promise of Gen. 3:15—that the seed of the woman would one day crush the serpent's head—but no other details about Christ had yet been given. It is unfair to hold Noah responsible for details about Christ which we who have the blessings of completed revelation take for granted (see Heb. 1:1, 2).

b. Abraham and his family (11:8-19)

Though this chapter alludes to the faith of a number of O.T. heroes, the two that are given the most attention are Abraham and Moses, perhaps primarily because they would stand out in the minds of the Hebrew readers. From Noah the writer now turns his attention to Abraham.

(1) In his call and sojourn in Canaan (11:8-10)

8 By faith Abraham, when he was called to go out into a place which he should after receive for an inheritance, obeyed; and he went out, not knowing whither he went.
9 By faith he sojourned in the land of promise, as in a strange country, dwelling in tabernacles with Isaac and Jacob, the heirs with him of the same promise:
10 For he looked for a city which hath foundations, whose builder and maker *is* God.

Since Abraham is the father of all those who come to God by faith, whether Jews or Gentiles (Rom. 4:16), the writer gives extended attention to him as an example of living by faith. In v. 8 he says, "By faith Abraham, when he was called to go out into a place which he should after receive for an inheritance, obeyed." "When he was called" (Greek present tense) might be translated, "While he was being called": that is, while God was still in the process of calling him, Abraham proceeded to obey. The verb "obeyed" (Greek aorist tense) indicates a decisive act. His obedience was immediate, without any apparent hesitation. This does not mean that Abraham and his family left without any preparation for such a permanent move, but it does indicate that he did not waver in his reception of God's call.

Obeyed (Greek *hupaloooúo*) means "to hear under," that is, to hear in the sense of submitting to the one who has called. The call of Abraham (Gen. 12:1-3) originally took place while he still lived in Ur of the Chaldees (Acts 7:2). In that call God promised him three things:

(1) a land, fulfilled in the land of Canaan; (2) a great nation, fulfilled in the nation of Israel; and (3) to make him a blessing to all the world. The third part of the promise was the Messianic part. We do not know why his father Terah and his nephew Lot accompanied him when he left Ur to follow God's will. Perhaps his father needed his care because of his advanced age and his nephew because of his youth. Terah evidently remained an unbeliever until his death (see Jos. 24:2). It may have been his father's health that caused them to stop in Haran, some 600 miles up the Euphrates River from Ur. In any case, after his father's death, Abraham, his wife Sarah, and his nephew Lot moved on into Canaan, to the vicinity of Bethel and Hebron, about 400 miles southwest of Haran.

Thus at the age of 75 (Gen. 12:4), he finally arrived at the "place which he should after receive for an inheritance," which indicates that the fulfillment of the promise still looked toward the future. Because the place would fulfill the promise made in a covenant, it is called "an inheritance." The only part of the land that Abraham himself ever actually owned in Canaan was a burial plot for his family (Gen. 23:17-20). God revealed to Abraham that the promise about the land would be delayed for four generations while his descendants served in Egypt, and they would "come hither again: for the iniquity of the Amorites *is* not yet full" (Gen. 15:13-16).

Having received such a promise, Abraham "went out, not knowing whither he went." That "He went out" (Greek aorist tense) indicates a permanent departure. The final phrase in the verse enhances the demand for faith: Abraham departed from Ur, with no plans to return, "not knowing whither he went." "Not knowing" (Greek present tense) signifies that his ignorance about his destination continued for a time. "Whither he went" means "where he was going." Scripture never tells us how Abraham came to believe in the true God, but his faith certainly did not come from his father. It is obvious, however, that the light of true revelation that had been passed down from Noah and his three sons had not completely gone out, though it certainly must have been dim.

Once Abraham was in Canaan, "By faith he sojourned in the land of promise, as *in* a strange country." The contrast here is sharp and ironic. "He sojourned" (Greek *paroikeo*) means to live as a stranger and an alien; but he lived like this "in the land of promise"—the promise that God made in the Abrahamic Covenant (Gen. 12:1-3). The contrast is heightened even more when the writer adds, "As *in* a strange country."

Abraham manifested this in his lifestyle, "dwelling in tabernacles with Isaac and Jacob, the heirs with him of the same promise." This indicates the length of time that this lifestyle continued, for nearly three generations. "Tabernacles" (Greek *skene*) were tents, temporary structures that could be broken down and easily and quickly moved to another location. Abraham lived to be 175 years of age (Gen. 25:7) and so experienced his twin grandsons, Jacob and Esau, until they were about 15 years old (Gen. 25:26). Abraham, Isaac, and Jacob are all mentioned because the promise of the land was renewed to each of them (Gen. 12:1; 26:3; 28:13).

The promise was renewed to Isaac and Jacob because they were "heirs with him of the same promise." The only way any of these could be patient for such a long period of time is because they were living "by faith." Though these three patriarchs never experienced the complete fulfillment of the promise, they lived their lives in hope, in patient anticipation that the God whose timing is often much different from ours, will finally do what He has promised.

Three passages, in particular, emphasize the nature of their faith: (1) Abraham had to purchase a burial plot from Ephron, the Hittite, who lived among the sons of Heth, natives of Canaan (Gen. 23:4). (2) Isaac had difficulties with water rights with the herdsmen of Gerar (Gen. 26:17-33). (3) When Jacob returned with his family after his years with Laban, he had to purchase "a parcel of a field" from the children of Hamor in Shechem to put up his tent in Canaan (Gen. 33:18-20). In his notable sermon before he was martyred, Stephen emphasized the irony of Abraham's situation when he said about God, "He gave him none inheritance in it, no, *not so much as* to set his foot on: yet he promised that he would give it to him for a possession, and to his seed after him, when *as yet* he had no child" (Acts 7:5). If Abraham, Isaac, and Jacob could have this kind of enduring faith under such difficulties, surely the Christians being addressed in Hebrews could do the same. Indeed, even Abraham did not enjoy the godly heritage which this generation of believers had (Jos. 24:2; Rom. 9:4, 5).

The reason Abraham could endure as he did is explained in v. 10: "For he looked for a city which hath foundations, whose builder and maker *is* God." All those who have true faith look beyond the fulfillment of earthly promises, as good as they might be. Jesus reminded us of the wisdom of laying up treasures in Heaven where they are absolutely secure in contrast to the insecurity of earthly treasures. But He also added, "Where your treasure is, there will your heart be also" (Mt. 6:19-21). Abraham's heart was certainly focused on the city of God. Lot's experience in becoming absorbed in a city of this world was an additional reminder to Abraham that he was on the right track.

"For" introduces the statement in v. 10 as an explanation of v. 9, of why Abraham could be content though he never possessed the land of promise during his lifetime. "He looked for" (Greek imperfect tense) can be translated, "He was looking for," that is, his outlook for the eternal fulfillment of the promise continued throughout his life. What he kept looking for all of this time "was a city which hath foundations." The word "city" (Greek *polis*) has a definite article in the original: "the city," the one which God is preparing for all of His children. When Scripture describes Heaven as a city, it is emphasizing the fellowship which we will enjoy there, the joys of spiritual companionship with brothers and sisters in Christ from all ages.

Unlike the great cities of this world which in many cases perish with time (like Nineveh and Babylon), God's city "hath foundations," solid foundations which will stand forever. The reason is, its "builder and maker is God." "Builder" (Greek *teknites*) can refer to a craftsman, an artisan, or a designer. In this context, as a companion of the other word, it means a designer or an architect. "Maker" (Greek *demiourgos*) refers to the one who carries out the plans produced by the architect. God is both the designer and the builder of this eternal city.

Scripture frequently speaks of this city. Our writer later refers us to the city which God "hath prepared for them" (11:16), to "the city of the living God, the heavenly Jerusalem" (12:22), and to the "continuing city" which is "to come" (13:14). Paul spoke of the "Jerusalem which is above" (Gal. 4:26); and John, in his vision from Patmos, actually saw "that great city, the holy Jerusalem, descending out of heaven from God" (Rev. 21:9-14).

(2) In their reception of the promised seed (11:11, 12)

11 Through faith also Sara herself received strength to conceive seed, and was delivered of a child when she was past age, because she judged him faithful who had promised.
12 Therefore sprang there even of one, and him as good as dead, *so many* as the stars of the sky in multitude, and as the sand which is by the sea shore innumerable.

Abraham's faith in relation to the promised inheritance of the land was impressive. Now the writer turns to another important part of the Abrahamic Covenant, the promise of a seed, an heir. Though Sarah's faith seemed questionable at times, God gave her (as He often does with us) the benefit of the doubt, and the smallness of her faith was received and multiplied by God's grace. Jesus Himself indicated that possession of faith "as a grain of mustard seed" is enough to move a mountain. Thus the writer declares, "Through faith also Sara herself received strength to conceive seed." He points to "Sara also" as an important part of God's plan. Abraham's wife, too, was strategic in bringing to fruition the promise of the covenant, and God would grant her what was due.

The writer emphasizes "Sara herself" in anticipation of the surprise that readers familiar with the story might have about any attention called to Sarah's faith. But, though she did doubt with regard to the promised birth of the child, and even laughed to herself at the thought of the possibility of such a dream coming true for a woman who would be 90 by the time of the birth, she was apparently strengthened by the more vigorous and persistent faith of Abraham (Gen. 18:9-15). As a result, by the time the child was born, Sarah's faith also stands out. She joyfully declared, "God hath made me to laugh, *so that* all that hear will laugh with me. And she said, Who would have said unto Abraham, that Sarah should have given children suck? for I have born *him* a son in his old age" (Gen. 21:6, 7). As a result of God's promise, Sarah "received strength to conceive seed." Though Sarah's case is most unusual, no woman, regardless of her age, can bear children unless she has "received strength" from the Lord. When Rachel complained to Jacob about being barren, he angrily replied, "*Am* I in God's stead, who hath withheld from thee the fruit of the womb?" (Gen. 30:1, 2).

The words translated "to conceive seed" usually refer to the man's part in the conception of a child, referring to the placement of seed in the woman's womb. Perhaps the best suggestion about this is to take the sentence to mean that "Sarah received strength with regard to Abraham's placement of seed, and was delivered of a child" (See Kent 226; this takes the Greek *eis* to mean "with respect to" or "in reference to.")

As a result of God's miraculous blessing on Sarah, she "was delivered of a child when she was past age." Some of the older manuscripts do not contain the single word translated "was delivered of a child," but there is, of course, no question that this is exactly what occurred. The miracle was that it happened "when she was past age." The Lord delayed this aspect of the fulfillment of the Abrahamic Covenant for so long, both to test Abraham's faith in an unusual way as the father of the faithful and to show him, and us, that absolutely nothing is "too hard for the LORD" (Gen. 18:14).

Sarah, at the age of 90, was able to have this kind of faith "because she judged him faithful who had promised." The reminder that the birth of Isaac was a specific fulfillment of God's promise was especially emphasized at the time of his birth. Moses declared, "And the LORD visited Sarah *as he had said*, and the LORD did unto Sarah as *he had spoken*. For Sarah conceived, and bare Abraham a son in his old age, at the set time of which God had spoken to him" (Gen. 21:1, 2). Sarah's faith had almost a year to grow. She came to see, more than ever before, that God always does exactly what He says He will do.

The emphasis now shifts to Abraham (v. 12): "Therefore sprang there even of one, and him as good as dead." "Therefore" introduces the declaration of the ultimate result of the faith of Abraham, the "one" from whom there would come a seed more numerous than the stars. The miracle is emphasized even further: "And him as good as dead." The verb indicates a permanent situation that had developed (Greek perfect tense), obviously due to advanced age. Similarly, Paul says about both Abraham and Sarah, "And being not weak in faith, he considered not his own body now dead, when he was about an hundred years old, neither yet the deadness of Sarah's womb: He staggered not at the promise of God through unbelief; but was strong in faith, giving glory to God" (Rom. 4:19, 20).

Perhaps Abraham's deadness with regard to producing children involved his relationship to Sarah, the wife by whom the chosen seed was to come. After Sarah's death, Abraham would live on 40 more years (Gen. 25:7), marry Keturah (evidently a younger woman) and have six more sons (Gen. 25:1, 2; 1 Chr. 1:32). Or perhaps God rejuvenated that old man! Regardless, before his death Abraham sent the sons of Keturah away with gifts "unto the east country," evidently so there would be no conflict with Isaac, to whom he left everything (Gen. 25:5, 6). The point is that God blessed a man and a woman with faith so that from their one son God would bring a great nation as the stars of the sky in multitude, and as the sand which is by the sea shore innumerable. This latter description comes from Genesis 22:17 (see also Gen. 15:5; 32:12).

(3) In realizing that their citizenship was not of this world (11:13-16)

13 These all died in faith, not having received the promises, but having seen them afar off, and were persuaded of *them*, and embraced *them*, and confessed that they

were strangers and pilgrims on the earth.
14 For they that say such things declare plainly that they seek a country.
15 And truly, if they had been mindful of that *country* from whence they came out, they might have had opportunity to have returned.
16 But now they desire a better *country*, that is, an heavenly: wherefore God is not ashamed to be called their God: for he hath prepared for them a city.

These verses emphasize again, as in v. 10, that Abraham and his descendants looked beyond this world for the ultimate fulfillment of God's promise. Like many believers today, they were abundantly blessed on this earth with both spiritual and temporal rewards, but they realized that these things, as good as they are, do not last. They looked forward to a continuation of their fellowship with God and with those of like faith in the life that is to come.

"These all died in faith" refers back to Abraham, Sarah, Isaac, and Jacob, the four mentioned so far who were involved in the covenant of faith (Lunemann 408). "Died in faith" (Greek *kata pistin*) can also be translated, "died according to faith," referring both to the attitude in which they died and to their expectation in reference to the future. Their faith saw them all the way through this life and into the life to come. Indeed, they died, "Not having received the promises, but having seen them afar off." In reference to hope, which is closely related to faith, Paul said, "Hope that is seen is not hope: for what a man seeth, why doth he yet hope for?" (Rom. 8:24). When the promises that demand faith and hope are complete, then faith and hope will no longer be needed. But when these heroes of the faith passed to the other side, the promises which God made had not been completely fulfilled; thus they died earnestly looking for their fulfillment in the future. Even death could not quench their faith.

The word "promises" is plural because the Abrahamic Covenant was made up of different parts (Lenski 396). Since these patriarchs died "according to" faith because they had not yet received these promises, the writer gives in quick succession four things that emphasized their faith: (1) They had "seen them afar off." They were able to visualize them in the future. Jesus referred to this kind of faith when He said to the Jewish leaders, "Your father Abraham rejoiced to see my day: and he saw *it*, and was glad" (Jn. 8:56). (2) They "were persuaded of them." They were absolutely convinced that every promise would be fulfilled; they had no doubts. (3) They "embraced them." They drew each promise near to themselves, as one embraces a close relative or friend after a long absence. (4) They "confessed that they were strangers and pilgrims on the earth." Open confession of Christ is necessary for salvation (Mt. 10:32, 33; Rom. 10:9, 10). At the same time, those who would be friends with this world willingly position themselves as the enemies of Christ (Jas. 4:4; 1 Jn. 2:15-17). These two relationships cannot coexist. That the patriarchs were "strangers and pilgrims on the earth" reflects the language of Gen. 23:4 in the Septuagint. As believers, we must live our lives with the same attitude toward those promises that are still in the future, including the Second Coming, the resurrection, and eternal life in Heaven.

The writer points out something else that we can gather from this attitude of faith in the patriarchs: "For they that say such things declare plainly that they seek a country." "For" introduces the statement as an explanation of the last line of the previous verse. "Such things" refers back to the quotation from Gen. 23:4 to the effect that Abraham and his family were "strangers and pilgrims on the earth." All the verbal expressions in the verse indicate continuing action (Greek present tense), that their entire life was a pilgrimage, from beginning to end. Furthermore, this way of describing their lifestyle helps us apply the attitude to God's people in every age: we are all strangers and pilgrims in this world.

"Declare plainly" means that such people clearly claim their pilgrimage here without apologies or regrets. "Seek" (Greek *epizeteo*) is intensive, referring to arduous and dedicated pursuit. In reference to the perishable things of this world, Jesus said, "For after all these things do the Gentiles *seek*" (Mt. 6:32). As believers we should manifest the same intense pursuit of heavenly things. When the writer says that God's pilgrims are seeking a country (Greek *patris*), he means a homeland, a fatherland, the place where their citizenship can be permanently established.

In v. 10 Abraham was looking for a city; here in v. 14 he is seeking a country. Both terms are different ways of describing Heaven, the place of our eternal dwelling with God. When the writer calls Heaven a city, he is thinking of the fellowship, the close companionship which we will enjoy there; but when he calls it a country, he is speaking of citizenship, a real sense of belonging, a permanent place to settle down.

Since some of his readers were thinking about turning back from Christianity to return to Judaism in order to avoid persecution, the writer points out a parallel in the life of Abraham: "And truly, if they had been mindful of that *country* from whence they came out, they might have had opportunity to have returned." The sentence expresses a condition contrary to fact: "If they had been mindful"—but they were not. The action or attitude is continuous (Greek imperfect tense): if they kept looking back with longing pangs of homesickness to "that *country* from whence they came."

Abraham and his family had settled in Haran, in upper Mesopotamia, after they left Ur of the Chaldees, so that is apparently the country to which the writer is referring. If Abraham, and later Isaac and Jacob, had experienced such longing desires to go back home, "they might have had opportunity to have returned." In fact, two such opportunities are recorded in Genesis. When it was time for Isaac to have a wife, Abraham sent Eliezer of Damascus, his oldest and most trusted servant, back to Mesopotamia (Padan-aram) to seek one from Abraham's own family. But he gave strict instructions to the servant that, if the woman selected would not return to Isaac in Canaan, Isaac was by no means to be brought to her (Gen. 24:5, 6). Jacob also went back to the same place to get a wife, and in fact stayed for some 20 years while he acquired two wives, two concubines, and eleven children. But in spite of great pressure from Laban—his father-in-law and his mother's brother, he returned to Canaan to the earthly land of promise

(Gen. 31:17—33:20). God had reminded Jacob of his pledge at Bethel to return to his father's house (Gen. 28:10-22) and instructed him, "Now arise, get thee out from this land, and return unto the land of thy kindred" (Gen. 31:13). Abraham, Isaac, and Jacob did, indeed, have opportunities to return to their previous homeland, but they did not look back longingly to that place; therefore, they did not use such opportunities.

In this proclamation the free will of the patriarchs is emphasized. Even after we have started on our way to that heavenly land of promise, God does not coerce us. Like the Israelites during the exodus, many, after facing the difficulties of journeying through the wilderness, yearned for their former bondage in Egypt, conveniently forgetting their cries for God's help in those miserable conditions (Num. 11:4-6). Stephen said that they "in their hearts turned back again into Egypt" (Acts 7:39). Hebrews has already pointed out that God swore concerning them, "They shall not enter into my rest" (3:11). In like manner, backslidden Christians, or at least professing Christians, often look back with rose-colored glasses on the world they left behind, seriously considering a return.

The patriarchal fathers did not even consider such a return. The writer emphasizes, "But now they desire a better *country*, an heavenly," and thus completes the balanced contrast (Greek *men/de*). On the one hand, if they had longed for their old home, they could have returned, and indeed had abundant opportunity to do so. On the other hand, they looked eagerly toward their eternal home instead.

The writer allows us, as it were, to personally witness the faithfulness of the patriarchs by putting the declaration in the present tense, "But now they desire." "Now" enhances that emphasis. "Desire" (Greek *orego*) means "to stretch out," "to reach one's hand toward" something. Paul uses the word of the desire of a young man to be a bishop or a pastor (1 Tim. 3:1). Thus, the patriarchs enthusiastically stretched forward toward their eternal home. What they were reaching for was "a better *country*." The key word of the epistle, "better," comes up once again: the country they reached out for is better because it is "heavenly," a permanent dwelling, not a temporary one.

The Lord blesses those who yearn for such a heavenly home: "Wherefore God is not ashamed to be called their God." Since they were not ashamed to confess Him, He was not ashamed to confess them (Mt. 10:32, 33). The negative declaration demands more attention than the positive, but it is the same as saying, "I am glad to be your God" (Hughes 480). One of the common declarations of the O.T. was, "I am the God of Abraham, Isaac, and Jacob" (Gen. 28:13; Ex. 3:6, 15, 16; 4:5; 1 Kg. 18:36). In answering the Sadducees' skepticism about eternal life, Jesus used this statement, emphasizing the fact that God proudly claimed this identification, "I am" their God, even after they were dead. Then Jesus concluded, "God is not the God of the dead, but of the living" (Mt. 22:29-32). Those patriarchs obtained the promise that they had so persistently reached for.

The writer gives us proof that God was not ashamed of them, that He, in fact, rejoiced to be their God: "For he hath prepared for them a city." "He hath prepared" (Greek aorist active of *hetoimazo*) translates the same verb as the one Jesus used in Jn. 14:2, 3 when He said, "I go to *prepare* a place for you. And if I go and *prepare* a place for you, I will come again, and receive you unto myself; that where I am, *there* ye may be also." While Jesus said He was going to prepare a place for us, this passage indicates that the preparation is complete (Greek aorist tense). The two ideas are easily correlated, however, when we realize that the primary preparation that has to be done is from our side. God will always be ready for us whenever we are ready for Him. "For them" means for their benefit, their advantage, indeed, for their eternal enjoyment. (On Heaven as "a city" see v. 10.)

(4) In offering Isaac, the promised seed (11:17-19)

17 By faith Abraham, when he was tried, offered up Isaac: and he that had received the promises offered up his only begotten *son*.
18 Of whom it was said, That in Isaac shall thy seed be called:
19 Accounting that God *was* able to raise *him* up, even from the dead; from whence also he received him in a figure.

The writer moves now to the culminating act of faith in the life of Abraham, one that placed a greater emotional demand on him than anything else, the offering of Isaac: "By faith Abraham, when he was tried, offered up Isaac." The verb "offered" (Greek perfect tense) indicates that Abraham offered Isaac in his heart and will from the moment he received the commandment: he offered him and that offering stood. "When he was tried" (Greek present tense) can also be translated, "While he was being tried." The whole situation, from the time the command was given until the Lord provided the ram to take Isaac's place, was a process of testing that required a period of time, in fact a journey of three days (Gen. 22:4). The word itself can mean either to try or to test, or to tempt, a person. The trial or test becomes a temptation only when an evil outcome is intended. Thus we see the word in Mt. 4:1, "Then was Jesus led up of the Spirit into the *wilderness to be tempted* of the devil." It is in this sense that James states, "Let no man say when he is *tempted*, I am *tempted* of God: for God cannot be *tempted* with evil, neither *tempteth* he any man" (Jas. 1:13). In this light, in Genesis 22:1, with regard to the command to offer Isaac, it might be better to read, "God tested Abraham" (see NKJV; NASB; NIV), for the Lord's motives were certainly good in this context.

The irony of the commandment is further emphasized, "And he that had received the promises offered up his only begotten *son*." "The promises" are referred to in the plural to indicate the different parts of the Abrahamic Covenant as well as the several different occasions when they were reviewed. The Covenant called for a land, a great nation, and universal blessings for all mankind; but Isaac, Abraham's son, was the key to the fulfillment of all of these things. Even before his birth God had said, "My covenant will I establish with Isaac, which Sarah shall bear unto thee" (Gen. 17:21). The fact that Abraham "had received" (Greek aorist tense) the promises was a settled matter, a well established truth. The verb (Greek *anadechomai*) is emphatic, pointing to a willing and joyful taking up of the promises as his personal responsibility (Westcott 377).

This second reference, in v. 17, to the fact that Abraham "offered up" his son is expressed as continuous action (Greek imperfect tense): "He was offering up his son." While the first statement sees Isaac as offered in Abraham's heart from the beginning, this one views the actual process and puts us there on the scene to visualize Abraham's prolonged struggle.

The first irony in the dreadful commandment, therefore, was that the entire covenant was built around Isaac; the second irony is the fact that he was Abraham's "only begotten *son*" (Greek *monogenes*). The word doesn't mean that Isaac was his only son; he also had Ishmael and would later have more sons by Keturah. It means, rather, that Isaac was unique, the only one of his kind (Bruce 311). The same word is used to describe Jesus Christ in Jn. 3:16, 18, and 1 Jn. 4:9. It seems obvious, in fact, that Abraham's offering of Isaac serves as a type pointing toward the ultimate sacrifice of our Lord. What God asked of Abraham, as unreasonable as it may have seemed, was exactly what He would do in the offering of His only begotten Son to atone for our sins.

What we have been saying about Isaac's importance is now confirmed by the writer's quotation from Gen. 21:12, 18: "Of whom it was said, That in Isaac shall thy seed be called." Abraham was able to render such unquestioning obedience because he was placing the weight of responsibility on God Himself. It was God who had established the covenant and made Isaac the key to the whole thing; therefore, it was God's own name and reputation that was at stake. Abraham knew the Lord well enough to have full faith and confidence that He would come through.

In v. 19 the writer explains some of Abraham's reasoning in the midst of this awesome test: Abraham was "accounting that God *was* able to raise *him* [Isaac] up, even from the dead; from whence also he received him in a figure." "Accounting" (Greek *logizomai*) means reasoning, thinking, or considering and it indicates that Abraham's decision was immediate and conclusive (Greek aorist tense). He was able to obey this stern command without any apparent reservation because he believed in the ultimate manifestation of God's power, the power of the bodily resurrection. The adjective "able" (Greek *dunatos*) is used of God's power in a variety of connections. Jesus used it when He declared, "With God all things are *possible*" (Mt. 19:26), and Paul used it to describe Abraham as "being fully persuaded that, what he [God] had promised, he was *able* also to perform" (Rom. 4:21). It pictures God's power as without limits; in this context it applies even to the ability to raise Isaac from the dead.

Abraham's faith in God's power "to raise *him* up, even from the dead" is most impressive in light of the fact that so little revelation had been given at that point concerning the subject of the resurrection. Note that *him* is in italics, meaning that it is not in the original. "To raise up" (Greek present tense) is continuous action: Abraham believed that God was able "to be raising up," not just Isaac, but anyone, anytime, and anywhere (Alford 220). Abraham's faith in the resurrection could well have been drawn from his knowledge of God as the Creator of all things, for that information had certainly been passed down; and from Abraham's own experience of God's working in his life, especially in the birth of Isaac. Abraham's faith is especially displayed in Gen. 22:5 when he tells his two servants to stay with the donkey while he and Isaac go to worship and then he declares, "I and the lad will . . . come again to you." He was fully committed to sacrificing Isaac, but he was also fully committed to his strong faith in the resurrection. Job 19:25, 26 also gives us an early example of a strong O.T. belief in the bodily resurrection.

The writer adds, "From whence also he received him in a figure." "From whence" means "from the dead." "He received" (Greek *komizo*) refers to taking something and carrying it away as your own, reclaiming it as your possession. Abraham actually received Isaac back from the dead "in a figure" (Greek *parabole*), that is, figuratively speaking, though not literally (Hughes 484; Kistemaker 328). Most commentators refer this last clause to the offering of Isaac, to the fact that Isaac was "as good as dead" as far as Abraham was concerned. If God had not stopped him while the knife was in mid-air, Abraham would have literally sacrificed Isaac; therefore, when God brought the sacrifice to a halt, it was, in a manner of speaking, a resurrection (Gen. 22:9-12).

A few commentators have suggested that this last clause could refer to the birth of Isaac (Westcott 366) rather than to the sacrifice of Isaac. When the writer says that Abraham had received Isaac from the dead, figuratively speaking, he means that Isaac's birth was from two people who were as good as dead in regard to bearing children (see Heb. 11:11, 12; Rom. 4:19). Though that observation is true, it seems foreign to the context here; the verse is best referred to the offering of Isaac. Many commentators also feel that Abraham's offering of Isaac should be considered as a type of Christ's death and resurrection, whether on the basis of the phrase "in a figure" or "in a parable" (Bruce 312; Lenski 403; Hewitt 178), or on the basis of the statement and the account as a whole (Kent 232; Hagner 198; Hughes 484).

Three typical things, in particular, stand out in the account: (1) Abraham is a type of the loving father, (2) Isaac is a type of the submissive son, and (3) the ram is the substitute. Other commentators, however, like Kistemaker, oppose this idea altogether: "We ought to avoid making a writer say more than he intends to convey" (329). But the typical significance seems too obvious to ignore. Jesus might have been referring to this incident when he said, "Your father Abraham rejoiced to see my day: and he saw *it*, and was glad" (Jn. 8:56).

c. Isaac, Jacob, and Joseph (11:20-22)

20 By faith Isaac blessed Jacob and Esau concerning things to come.
21 By faith Jacob, when he was a dying, blessed both the sons of Joseph; and worshipped, *leaning* upon the top of his staff.
22 By faith Joseph, when he died, made mention of the departing of the children of Israel; and gave commandment concerning his bones.

The writer now turns in brief succession to the three immediate descendants of Abraham: Isaac, his son; Jacob, his grandson; and Joseph, his great-grandson. In each case he focuses on an act of faith at the close of their lives as a summary of their life of faith as a whole. This is sufficient to show that the line of Abraham's faith was being perpetuated.

In v. 20 the writer says, "By faith Isaac blessed Jacob and Esau concerning things to come." In patriarchal times there were two important things which the father normally passed along to his eldest son: the birthright, primarily emphasizing the physical inheritance; and the blessing, primarily emphasizing the spiritual inheritance. The birthright granted a double portion of the property to be inherited, while the blessing passed on the right of the head of house. God had spoken to Rebekah while she was carrying the twins, Jacob and Esau, when she prayed to Him about her sons. The Lord's instructions were clear, "Two nations *are* in thy womb, and two manner of people shall be separated from thy bowels; and *the one* people shall be stronger than *the other* people; and the elder shall serve the younger" (Gen. 25:23). Surely Rebekah shared this information with Isaac, but if she did he ignored God's instructions. Jacob, who was able to see the value of things over the long term, had already deceived Esau, who mostly valued the immediate, to sell his birthright for a bowl of pottage (Gen. 25:29-34). The writer of Hebrews refers to the granting of the second element, the blessing. Isaac's original intention was to give the blessing to Esau as the oldest of the two and the one that he personally preferred; but once again, with his mother's help, Jacob was able to plan a deception which resulted in Isaac blessing Jacob rather than Esau (Gen. 27:1-40).

Isaac's faith was manifested in his acknowledgment that the blessing on Jacob would stand, regardless of the deception, an apparent concession that this was God's will after all. Isaac declared, "I . . . have blessed him? yea, and he shall be blessed" (Gen. 27:33). The full account does not paint a great picture of Isaac's faith, but God's grace recognizes our lives of faith as a whole and His mercy ignores our occasional lapses. Isaac knew that the blessing related to "things to come," even things that would take place long after he and his sons were dead. Indeed, his blessing involved both "Jacob and Esau," though the major blessing was bestowed on Jacob as God had instructed. This story is an amazing account of the exercise of the free will of man in combination with the sovereignty of God. God's will is eventually accomplished in spite of the stubborn resistance of human beings, sometimes even by those who are God's own.

In v. 21 our writer proceeds to Jacob, the next patriarch: "By faith Jacob, when he was a dying, blessed both the sons of Joseph." The account is in Gen. 48:8-22. Jacob bestowed the blessing which he had received from Isaac on Joseph by placing it on Joseph's two sons, thus granting him a double portion (see Gen. 48:22). Jacob passed over Reuben, his firstborn son by Leah, because of his adultery with Jacob's concubine, Bilhah (Gen. 35:22; 49:3, 4). He chose Joseph, his firstborn son by Rachel, to receive the blessing.

Though the writer of Hebrews, probably for the sake of brevity, does not mention the details, Jacob's blessing of

Joseph's sons was both interesting and prophetic. Joseph lined his sons up before Jacob with Manasseh, the oldest, on Jacob's right to receive the greater blessing, and Ephraim on Jacob's left to receive the lesser blessing. When Jacob crossed his hands, placing his right hand on Ephraim's head and his left hand on Manasseh's head, Joseph attempted to correct him, but Jacob resisted, indicating that what he was doing was prophetic: Ephraim eventually gained ascendancy over Manasseh (see Gen. 48:20; Num. 26:34, 37), as Jacob had prophesied. Jacob also claimed Joseph's sons as his own (Gen. 48:5), thus prophetically pointing toward their position in giving names to two of the twelve tribes of Israel. Ephraim and Manasseh—though raised in Egypt by an Egyptian mother, Asenath (Gen. 46:20), an Egyptian priest's daughter—associated themselves with their father's people to the extent that their descendants left with Moses in the exodus (Num. 1:10).

After Jacob blessed Joseph's two sons, the writer adds, "And worshipped, *leaning* upon the top of his staff." The Genesis record actually notes this activity of Jacob prior to the blessing, in Gen. 47:31, in connection with the oath that Jacob asked of Joseph concerning his burial in Canaan. But Gen. 47:29—49:33 should be taken as a unit, so that what is said of Jacob's manner of worship can apply throughout the passage. In 47:29 Jacob realized that his death was near; in 48:1 he became ill; and in 49:33 he died.

The Hebrew text of Gen. 47:31 reads, "And Israel bowed himself upon the bed's head." The writer of Hebrews, as usual, quotes from the Septuagint, not from the Hebrew. The difference in the two is based on the vowel pointing in the Hebrew text to the final word. (The ancient Hebrew text had no vowels. One way the word is *matteh*, "staff"; another way it is *mittah*, "bed.") Thus, while the O.T. reads "bed," the Septuagint reads "staff." Either reading makes sense, though a number of commentators feel that the Septuagint preserves the older reading (Hughes 489; Lenski 405; Kent 233). Jacob's staff is mentioned on two different occasions in his travels, so it must have been an important item which he usually carried with him for protection, for an aid when he walked, and for other useful purposes (Gen. 32:10; 38:18, 25). In any case, Jacob prayed and worshiped the Lord, using his bed or his staff to hold him up in his weakened condition, as he made his final statements to Joseph and then to all his sons.

Many things could be pointed out about the faith of Joseph, but our writer chooses one special incident at the close of his life, just as he did with Isaac and Jacob. Indeed, one of the greatest commentaries on any man's faith is how he dies: "By faith Joseph, when he died, made mention of the departing of the children of Israel, and gave commandment concerning his bones." The dates of the patriarchs vary rather widely among commentators. According to Unger (607), Joseph died about 1778 B.C., over 300 years prior to the exodus. Whatever system of dating one chooses, Joseph made his request a long time before the event, and that makes his faith stand out even more. Joseph could have turned bitter toward his family, and especially toward his brothers who sold him into bondage. Many would have done so under similar circumstances. But Joseph saw God's hand in all the things that happened to him. When his brothers appeared before him again after the death of Jacob, fearing that Joseph might now take revenge, Joseph replied, "As for you, ye thought evil against me; *but* God meant it unto good, to bring to pass, as *it is* this day, to save much people alive" (Gen. 50:20).

The dreams that Joseph had experienced in his earlier life were revelations from God about these events that occurred in Egypt. Joseph's request just prior to his death brought to a grand conclusion a life that had been lived by faith. Joseph placed his brothers and their descendants under oath as he declared, "God will surely visit you, and ye shall carry up my bones from hence" (Gen. 50:25). His bones are a figure of speech for his body, for since he was embalmed, evidently according to the traditional Egyptian process of mummification, more than his bones would have been preserved (Gen. 50:26).

As part of the oral tradition the Israelites passed down from generation to generation, even as their pleasant experience in Egypt turned into bondage, they also passed down this request of Joseph. The Scripture record is careful to note that Moses honored the request at the time of the exodus (Ex. 13:19), and that, even after the death of Moses, Joshua saw that the oath and the request which had been made so long before was honored (Jos. 24:32). When Joseph looked forward by faith to the exodus from Egypt, there is no indication that God had given him any further revelation. The covenant promises which God had originally given to Abraham (Gen. 12:1-3), along with the additional revelation that his family would return from their place of affliction "in the fourth generation" (Gen. 15:13-16), was all that Joseph needed. Though he had become accustomed to the luxuries of Egypt, he never forgot his religious heritage, and God honored him for it by having our writer record his last request as a summation of his faith.

d. Moses (11:23-29)

The writer of Hebrews moves forward now from the faith of Joseph to the faith of Moses, to whom he dedicates attention only second to Abraham. His comments about Moses cover two periods: from Moses' birth until he fled to Midian, and during the exodus through the crossing of the Red Sea.

(1) From birth to his flight to Midian (11:23-26)

23 By faith Moses, when he was born, was hid three months of his parents, because they saw *he was* a proper child; and they were not afraid of the king's commandment.
24 By faith Moses, when he was come to years, refused to be called the son of Pharaoh's daughter;
25 Choosing rather to suffer affliction with the people of God, than to enjoy the pleasures of sin for a season;
26 Esteeming the reproach of Christ greater riches than the treasures in Egypt: for he had respect unto the recompence of the reward.

The first reference to the faith of Moses is really to the faith of his parents: "By faith Moses, when he was born, was hid three months of his parents." According to Ex. 6:20 their names were Amram and Jochebed, both descendants of Levi. They hid him for three months "because they saw *he was* a proper child"; the writer draws this information about Moses as an infant from Ex. 2:1, 2. Moses' parents hid him because Pharaoh had issued a nationwide edict for every son of the Hebrew slaves to be cast into the Nile River. The information in Exodus emphasizes the efforts of Moses' mother and sister in hiding the infant, but they obviously did so with Amram's approval.

His parents were willing to take this risk because they saw he was "a proper child." "Proper" (Greek *asteios*) means well-formed, of bodily grace and charm (Bauer 117). Stephen used the same word to describe Moses in Acts 7:20. Exodus 2:2 called Moses a "goodly *child*." There was something about Moses' demeanor and appearance, even as an infant, that impressed his parents in an unusual way. There is no indication that they had any kind of special revelation, but they were certainly aware of God's promise to Abraham that his descendants would return to Canaan in the fourth generation (Gen. 15:13-16).

Moses' parents hid him not only because he was a proper child, but also because "they were not afraid of the king's commandment," the one that gave orders for all male Hebrew babies to be thrown in the Nile River. They knew the risks that were involved—perhaps death for the entire family—but they were willing to take those risks because of the special feeling they had about Moses and because they believed that they served a sovereign God who was in control, who causes all things to "work together for good to them that love God, to them who are the called according to *his* purpose" (Rom. 8:28). They did this "by faith," and God wonderfully rewarded their faith with His faithfulness. When they could no longer hide the little baby, they carefully made a little ark or basket of reeds that grew by the Nile. They placed the baby in the basket and pushed it down river, in the direction where Pharaoh's daughter took her morning bath, with a fervent prayer that the Lord would do His work.

Calvin sees this act as a lapse in faith on the part of Moses' parents (293), but it is more accurate to see it as an act of ultimate trust in a sovereign God. We know, of course, that Pharaoh's daughter claimed the little Hebrew baby as her own and named him "Moses," because he had been drawn out of the river. Moses' sister, Miriam, who was watching all the time, brought his mother, whom Pharaoh's daughter paid to raise the baby in his early years (Ex. 2:3-10). Jochebed did such an excellent job in teaching Moses during those years that he never forgot who he really was or his purpose in life.

The good job which Moses' mother did in teaching him is reflected in v. 24. "By faith Moses, when he was come to years, refused to be called the son of Pharaoh's daughter." "When he was come to years" is literally "having become great"—referring to maturity of age. Moses was about 40 years old at this time (Acts 7:23) and "was learned in all the wisdom of the Egyptians, and was mighty in words and in deeds" (Acts 7:22).

Remembering well his mother's teaching, Moses "refused to be called the son of Pharaoh's daughter." "Refused" (Greek *arneomai*) means "to deny, disdain, repudiate, or disown" and indicates a definite and conclusive refusal (Greek aorist). The title, "son of

Pharaoh's daughter," carried high privileges in Egypt. One tradition suggests that Moses might have been next in line for the throne of Egypt. If Moses' act of refusal involved any verbal renunciation, that is not recorded. Though something like that may well have occurred, his refusal may have been solely in his willing association with the Hebrew slaves. Stephen observed that Moses "supposed his brethren would have understood how that God by his hand would deliver them: but they understood not" (Acts 7:25). Stephen's inspired evaluation of his motives gives a strong indication that Moses realized, at least at this point in his life, that God had a special calling for him. The rejection of his efforts by his own people, combined with his fear of Pharaoh, apparently disillusioned Moses for the time. It is evident, however, that God used the next 40 years of his life in the wilderness of Midian to give him further preparation for the great task that lay ahead.

Verse 25 emphasizes what was involved in Moses' refusal of the title which he had enjoyed for some 40 years: he was "choosing rather to suffer affliction with the people of God, than to enjoy the pleasures of sin for a season." Moses made this choice by faith, knowing full well the consequences. Some might ask, "Would it not have been better to hold on to his position of honor and use the political power and prestige that were his to gain help and freedom for his people with the approval of Pharaoh, even as Joseph did in an earlier time?" But the situation was not at all the same, and Joseph's descendants did not have the status that they had in his day. Moses, in fact, introduced this period by declaring, "Now there arose up a new king over Egypt, which knew not Joseph" (Ex. 1:8). This was an entirely new dynasty, likely the "new kingdom" of native Egyptian rulers after the Hyksos kings were driven out (Edersheim 32). The Hebrews were now slaves, performing the menial tasks that bolstered the prosperity which Egypt was experiencing. When Moses sided with the Hebrew slaves, he made a clear choice, and there was no turning back. The choice had to be made by faith because it made no sense in the eyes of this world. He willingly chose suffering and affliction with God's people instead of the wealth and comfort he had known as long as he could remember. The contrast could not be more extreme.

Moses chose such suffering rather than "to enjoy the pleasures of sin for a season." "To enjoy" (Greek *echo*) is literally to possess, to experience. Moses was not rejecting something he dreamed about, but something that was part of his life on a daily basis. The word "pleasures" (Greek *apolausis*) means "enjoyment." The word in itself does not imply wrongful pleasure. Paul uses the same term when he charges Timothy to remind those who are wealthy that it is God "who giveth us richly all things *to enjoy*" (1 Tim. 6:17). But in this context the word "sin" makes these pleasures forbidden. Scripture does not deny that there are certain enjoyments in sin, but such enjoyment always carries a qualification: it is only "for a season," temporary (Greek *proskairos*). Such pleasures often do not last long, even from the world's point of view; most of all, they never extend beyond this life. Jesus advised laying up "treasures in heaven, where neither moth nor rust doth corrupt, and where thieves do not break through nor steal" (Mt. 6:20).

The pleasures of "sin" which Moses rejected did not necessarily involve a life of indulgence and debauchery. God, in fact, never instructs all wealthy people to rid themselves of their wealth; instead, they are to be generous with it in helping proper causes and to put God first in their lives (1 Tim. 6:17-19). The reason that Moses' life in Egypt would have been a sinful choice was that it meant rejecting God's people, God's cause, and God's calling. Such a choice is always a sin, regardless how innocent the alternative.

The reason for Moses' choice is explained further in v. 26: Moses was "esteeming the reproach of Christ greater riches than the treasures in Egypt." "Esteeming" (Greek *hegeomai*) means "to consider or regard" and thus, in this context, to evaluate. The verb indicates a conclusion that had already been reached (Greek aorist tense). It was not a rash or impulsive decision on Moses' part; he had thought it over very well. The same word is used in 10:29 for those who "*counted* the blood of the covenant . . . an unholy thing," and in 11:11 it refers to Sarah who "*judged* him faithful who had promised."

"The reproach" (Greek *oneidismos*) of Christ refers to the reproaches which Christ Himself suffered, the reviling and rejection which He experienced. Moses, like all the patriarchs, looked far ahead of his time toward the Messianic promises that would be fulfilled in the future, that time when the seed of the woman whose heel had been bruised would triumphantly crush the serpent's head (Gen. 3:15). Paul, quoting from Ps. 69:9, observed, "For even Christ pleased not himself; but, as it is written, The reproaches of them that reproached thee fell on me" (Rom. 15:3). Jesus Christ was "despised and rejected of men; a man of sorrows, and acquainted with grief" (Is. 53:3). If we mean to be identified with Him, we must be willing to suffer the same. This same word appears again in 13:13: "Let us go forth therefore unto him without the camp, bearing his *reproach*."

Moses evaluated this reproach and concluded that it was "greater riches than the treasures in Egypt." Egypt was known for its treasures. The discovery of various tombs and temples from the days of the Pharaohs has given us a knowledge about that wealth. The tomb of Tutankhamen (discovered in 1922) has yielded much information about the vastness of these treasures. Because of his position as the son of Pharaoh's daughter, Moses stood to inherit large amounts of this wealth. All he had to do was continue to live as he had for the first 40 years of his life, to help keep the Hebrew slaves in their place, and to wait for time to open the door to many other opportunities on this earth. But when Moses made an honest comparison, there was no question in his mind what he should do.

Moses' faith helped him to take the long look, and when he did the choice was clear. If some should say, "Oh, Moses did not think about the reward; he just thought about spiritual things," they haven't read the whole passage. Though Moses' outlook truly was spiritual, he did, at the same time, consider the ultimate outcome of his investment: "For he had respect unto the recompence of the reward." Moses did, indeed, compare the ultimate returns in the two different lifestyles. The treasures of Egypt promised immediate enjoyment, the satisfaction of those desires that cater to the body almost without limitation; but, at the same time, they offered no hope for eternity.

The reproach of Christ, on the other hand, offered immediate rejection and suffering with a nation of slaves who would often refuse his leadership and curse his good intentions, but it promised eternal life, including limitless enjoyment of fellowship with God and His people. With regard to this subject Jesus declared, "Blessed are ye, when *men* shall revile you, and persecute *you*, and shall say all manner of evil against you falsely, for my sake. Rejoice, and be exceeding glad: for great *is* your reward in heaven" (Mt. 5:11, 12). Though the Scriptures do promise additional rewards for service (Mt. 10:42; 1 Cor. 3:12-15), the writer of Hebrews usually has in mind the primary reward of eternal life.

(2) During the exodus from Egypt (11:27-29)

27 By faith he forsook Egypt, not fearing the wrath of the king: for he endured, as seeing him who is invisible.
28 Through faith he kept the passover, and the sprinkling of blood, lest he that destroyed the firstborn should touch them.
29 By faith they passed through the Red sea as by dry *land*: which the Egyptians assaying to do were drowned.

The first part of our writer's comments about Moses concerned multiple facts: the first 40 years of his life in Egypt, his parent's faith during his infancy, his own faith in willingly siding with the Hebrew slaves in conscious rejection of his adopted people and the Egyptian hierarchy. In this second part of Moses' testimony, the writer points to Moses' return to Egypt to confront Pharaoh, which eventually led to the exodus and Moses' direction of Israel toward the Promised Land.

"By faith he forsook Egypt, not fearing the wrath of the king." There is some disagreement among commentators as to the time meant. Moses left Egypt on two different occasions: when he fled to Midian and when he led Israel out of Egypt in the exodus. Many interpreters, including most of the early church fathers, have maintained that the reference here is to Moses' initial departure from Egypt, when Moses fled from Pharaoh and dwelled in Midian (Delitzsch II:265; Lunemann 418; Alford 225; Hughes 498; Morris 127). They offer three arguments in support of this position: (1) Moses' departure during the exodus was not in defiance of Pharaoh, but with his permission. Though this may be true on the surface, it was a permission that was only grudgingly given, and from which the Pharaoh soon relented. The whole process of the ten plagues, judgments of God against Pharaoh and the gods of Egypt, were in defiance of what the king really wanted. (2) If the reference is to the exodus, there is a problem in chronology between v. 27 and v. 28 since the Passover actually occurred prior to the exodus. Though this is technically true, the Passover was really part and parcel of the departure, celebrated the night before Israel actually left Egypt the next day (Ex. 12). It was, in fact, celebrated with everyone fully dressed, even with their staff in their hand (Ex. 12:11), completely prepared to depart. (3) The verb "he forsook" is in the singular, referring only to Moses, not the nation as a whole. But it refers to Moses alone because that's whose faith the writer is discussing in this passage; indeed, it was Moses, even in the exodus, who led the nation out of Egypt. Without Moses there would have been no departure.

These arguments are not convincing against the more likely interpretation that Moses' forsaking of Egypt refers to the exodus, not the flight to Midian, as appears to be the view of most modern commentators (Calvin 297; Westcott 373; Lenski 411; Barnes 279; MacArthur 356; Kent 241; Kistemaker 339). "Forsook" (Greek aorist tense of *kataleipo*) refers to leaving something or someone behind, an abandonment and indicates a decisive act. Though a process may have led up to the decision, when it was made, it was made with finality.

When Moses forsook Egypt, he "was not fearing the wrath of the king." That observation does not seem to be in line with Moses' first departure into Midian. When his authority was challenged by a fellow Hebrew the day after he had killed the Egyptian taskmaster, the Bible says, "And Moses feared, and said, Surely this thing is known. Now when Pharaoh heard this thing, he sought to slay Moses. But Moses fled from the face of Pharaoh" (Ex. 2:14, 15). In other words, at that time Moses *did* fear the wrath of the king but not when he returned to Egypt after 40 years in the desert of Midian, for then he boldly confronted Pharaoh. There is nothing necessarily incongruous with faith for one to flee in order to avoid the threat of death, providing that no compromise of principle is involved (Jn. 7:1); even the earlier departure to Midian might therefore have been "in faith" in spite of the fear. But once Moses returned from Midian there was no fear, only faith. Throughout the entire process of the ten plagues, Moses did not flinch. God had warned Moses that He would harden Pharaoh's heart so that the entire weight of His judgments might fall on Egypt (Ex. 4:21), for they were not just judgments against Pharaoh, but also against all the gods of Egypt (Ex. 12:12). The wrath of the king came to a peak when, just prior to the tenth plague, the death of the firstborn, Pharaoh angrily declared, "Get thee from me, take heed to thyself, see my face no more; for in *that* day thou seest my face thou shalt die" (Ex. 10:28).

The writer says, "For he endured, as seeing him who is invisible." "Endured" (Greek *kartereo*) means to stand firm or steadfast, to be strong in persisting in a certain direction (Yeager 406). It is complementary to the endurance which remains under a burden, even as the level of stress increases (Greek *hupomeno* in 10:32), and to that endurance that waits long for the fulfillment of a promise (Greek *makrothumeo* in 6:15).

Moses was able to stand firm in the midst of Pharaoh's vacillations during the plagues because he kept "seeing him who is invisible." This statement is paradoxical. How can a person see someone who is invisible? But that is precisely what Moses was noted for, perhaps above all else, in his very personal relationship with God. When the Lord appeared to Moses at the tabernacle in the visible manifestation of the cloudy pillar, the Scripture says, "The LORD spake unto Moses face to face, as a man speaketh unto his friend" (Ex. 33:11). Moses was not satisfied even with this, and asked for a further demonstration of

God's glory (Ex. 33:18-23). But even in the days prior to that special experience, Moses was already practicing seeing the invisible as he confronted the greatest ruler in all the world and challenged him to let God's people go. Though the vision was not quite as literal as he would later experience, it was nevertheless very real because he saw God "by faith." Seeing by faith Him who is invisible was the cause of Moses' successful endurance in his prolonged contest with Pharaoh.

Indeed, Moses' forsaking of Egypt was a process which culminated in a final act, the actual departure which we call "the exodus." In v. 28 the writer points to the great event which marked the climax: "Through faith he kept the passover." "Through faith" and "by faith" translate the same word in the original, and thus have the same meaning in each usage throughout the chapter, indicating that faith is the means, the instrument, through which the specified action is taken. "He kept" (Greek *poieo*) literally means "to make" or "to do"; thus, Moses "did it" in the sense of carrying it out, celebrating it, and in this case instituting it. Though all Israel kept or celebrated the initial Passover, the writer legitimately refers to Moses as the one who brought God's instructions to Israel and led in the celebration itself.

As God instructed, the Passover would be celebrated in Israel as a memorial of this night until Jesus used it to introduce the Lord's Supper the night before He was crucified. The word translated "Passover" (Greek *pascha*) is derived from the Hebrew word *pesah*, referring to an act of passing over (Bruce 324). When the blood of the lamb was applied to the doorposts of a home, as God instructed, He promised, "When I see the blood, I will pass over you" (Ex. 12:13). It seems obvious that the Passover was a clear type of Christ, for what God did with Israel in sparing each home from the judgment of the death of the firstborn He also does with us, as individuals, when the sacrificial blood of Jesus Christ is applied to us through faith. Paul declared, "For even Christ our passover is sacrificed for us" (1 Cor. 5:7).

"He kept" has two objects, both "the passover," and "the sprinkling of blood," referring to the blood of the Passover lamb that was sprinkled on the doorposts over and on each side of the entrance to the house (Ex. 12:7). The word "sprinkling" (Greek *proschusis*) is used only here in the New Testament. The application of the blood is specifically mentioned because it was strategic to avoiding God's judgment (Ex. 12:23).

Each home was required to apply the blood "lest he that destroyed the firstborn should touch them." "He that destroyed" might be translated, "The one who was destroying" or simply, "the destroyer": such is his purpose and office, at least in that setting. The destroyer is viewed as "the angel of the LORD" in 1 Chr. 21:12 when the Lord judged David for numbering Israel. The destruction of "the firstborn" was unlimited, including male and female of both man and beasts, from the highest in the land to the most humble—except for those who were covered by the blood. The implication is that the judgment also fell on Israelites who refused to believe and obey. The purpose of instituting the Passover and the sprinkling of the blood was so that the destroying angel and his judgment should not "touch them," that it should not fall upon them as well.

Verse 29 speaks of the last act of faith led by Moses: "By faith they passed through the Red sea as by dry *land*." "They" points back to "them" in v. 28, referring to Moses and all the believing Israelites. This colossal miracle is recorded in Ex. 14:19-29. "They passed through" dramatically pictures exactly what Moses described in Ex. 14:16. The exact place where this crossing occurred is not known today, but this does not take away from the significance of the miracle. The miracle was so complete that the Israelites evidently did not get their feet wet: they crossed as if on "dry *land*." As with several of the miracles throughout the ten plagues and the exodus, God used a natural force, "a strong east wind" (Ex. 14:21), to part the waters of the Red Sea; but that in no way lessens the miracle, for God was in complete control of this wind, fully determining when it started and when it stopped. The scene must have been awesome. Moses indicates that there was a wall of water on the left and the right as they passed through the sea (Ex. 14:22), and that the waters "stood upright as an heap" and that they actually "congealed in the heart of the sea" (Ex. 15:8).

Just as in the celebration of the Passover, there were certainly many Israelites who did not truly believe. That unbelief would become exceedingly clear in days and months to come as they traveled through the wilderness (see Heb. 3:16, 17). In the modern church, as in the exodus, the genuine faith of some brings many of God's gracious benefits to all who are part of the external church. Paul mentions this principle when he instructs a believing wife to stay with her unsaved husband, or vice versa, saying, "For the unbelieving husband is sanctified by the wife, and the unbelieving wife is sanctified by the husband" (1 Cor. 7:14). Some of the general benefits of grace may be extended to those who are just along for the ride. But such benefits must not be allowed to lure the unsaved in the external church to a state of comfort that ultimately results in their eternal damnation. Thus Paul admonishes, "Examine yourselves, whether ye be in the faith; prove your own selves. Know ye not your own selves, how that Jesus Christ is in you, except ye be reprobates?" (2 Cor. 13:5).

Concerning the crossing of the Red Sea, the writer further observes, "Which the Egyptians assaying to do were drowned." The antecedent of "which" is the word "sea" in the preceding clause (Westcott 375; Kistemaker 346), not the whole preceding clause as Yeager (409) suggests, though that is the practical outcome. "Assaying" is literally "making an attempt." We might render, "When the Egyptians attempted the same, they were drowned" (see NIV; NASB). "Were drowned" (Greek *katapino*) indicates that "they were drunk down" by the waters of the sea: that is, the sea devoured them and thus they were drowned.

The failed attempt of the Egyptians to do what the Israelites had done successfully illustrates an important principle: just as faith without works is dead, so works without faith is dead also. Paul says, "So then faith *cometh* by hearing, and hearing by the word of God" (Rom. 10:17). The Egyptians had no promise from God's Word; therefore, they could have no genuine faith (Lenski 413), thus, they were subjects of God's judgment rather than His mercy. This victorious crossing of the Red Sea is celebrated in the Song of Moses in Ex. 15:1-19.

e. In the fall of Jericho: Joshua and Rahab (11:30, 31)

30 By faith the walls of Jericho fell down, after they were compassed about seven days.
31 By faith the harlot Rahab perished not with them that believed not, when she had received the spies with peace.

Our writer skips the entire wilderness period in retracing the journey of faith. Though there were instances of faith during this time—as in the minority report of Joshua and Caleb among the twelve spies of Canaan (Num. 13:30; 14:6-10), and Moses' leadership in receiving the law and instructions for the tabernacle at Sinai (Ex. 20-30) and in his intimate communication with God (Ex. 33)—yet unfortunately it was also a time of disappointing rebellion on the part of the nation as a whole. Indeed, this is the theme of the book of Numbers, which records some ten different rebellions on the part of the nation of Israel. The writer has already called attention to this period as an example of unbelief and disobedience to be avoided at all costs (3:7-19). Therefore, he finds his final examples of faith in the fall of Jericho as a new generation of Israelites entered the Promised Land.

Though the writer could certainly have isolated the faith of Joshua in the fall of Jericho, as the courageous successor of Moses, he chooses to emphasize the obedience of the nation as a whole in this strange approach to conquering an enemy fortress: "By faith the walls of Jericho fell down." Joshua's faith for the victory at Jericho had been emboldened by the appearance of the man with the drawn sword (Jos. 5:13-15), an apparent Christophany. Jericho was one of the great walled cities of Canaan about which the unbelieving spies had testified (Num. 13:28), perhaps the most fortified of all.

Though the inhabitants of Canaan were alarmed at the news of the miraculous crossing of the Jordan (Jos. 5:1), the people of Jericho must have felt secure inside the great walls that completely surrounded the city. The normal method of conquering a walled city in those days was to lay siege against it, to completely surround it so that no people or supplies could go in or come out (see 2 Chr. 32:9, 10). That could, of course, be a rather long process. With two to three million people making up the nation of Israel, there was no time for such normal methods of warfare. Instead the walls of this ancient city fell "after they were compassed about seven days."

Scholars have long speculated about some natural cause for the collapse of the great walls of Jericho. Indeed, God could have used some natural cause, such as an earthquake, to accomplish His purpose. He certainly did that several times in the ten plagues on Egypt and in the crossing of the Red Sea (Ex. 9:22; 10:13; 14:21). Even so, it was still the direct work of God to cause the walls to fall at just the right time and under just the right circumstances. When Jesus calmed the storm on the Sea of Galilee, His disciples marveled, saying, "What manner of man is this, that even the winds and the sea obey him!" (Mt. 8:27). Since our God is the creator of all things, He is completely unlimited as to His method of accomplishing a miracle like this.

The instructions about how to bring the walls of Jericho down are given in Jos. 6:1-5. Once each day, for six days, seven priests led the men of war in a march around the city, carrying the Ark of the Covenant at the head of the procession and blowing loudly on trumpets made from rams' horns. Imagine what those who were viewing the procedure from within Jericho must have thought! Perhaps their initial fear of these Israelites because of the information they had received was replaced by a feeling of uneasy security. But on the seventh day the priests and the men of war marched around the city seven times, as instructed, and at the end of the final round, they blew loudly on the rams' horns and "all the people" shouted as loudly as they could. Just as God had promised, the walls of Jericho fell flat (Jos. 6:20, 21). Thus the triumphal victory at Jericho became the key to conquering the major sections of the land of Canaan.

In concluding the individual accounts of faith, the writer selects, under the guidance of the Holy Spirit, what may seem to some a strange choice: "By faith the harlot Rahab perished not with them that believed not." There are at least four things that make her faith unique. First was her moral character. Barnes mentions those who have been so troubled that a harlot is used as an example of faith that they have attempted to find some other meaning of the word. Some have said that the Hebrew word for "harlot" could mean "hostess," suggesting that she kept an inn and put up guests overnight. Others have suggested that the word should be taken in a spiritual sense, that her idolatrous way of life branded her as a harlot. But such attempts are unlikely and unnecessary. Rahab serves as a tremendous example of the fact that no sin, other than the sin against the Holy Spirit, places a person beyond the reach of God's grace. Jesus Himself declared to the self-righteous scribes and Pharisees, "The publicans and the harlots go into the kingdom of God before you" (Mt. 21:31). Jesus evidently reached many women from that walk of life, including the woman who washed Jesus' feet as He dined in the home of a Pharisee (Lk. 7:36-50). After all, He did not come to "call the righteous, but sinners to repentance" (Mt. 9:13).

The second thing about Rahab is that she was a non-Israelite, a Gentile—a Gentile under a curse, at that! God delayed the possession of Canaan for Abraham and his descendants for four generations until "the iniquity of the Amorites" should become full (Gen. 15:16). Now that time had come, and God promised to drive out the various Canaanite tribes so Israel could possess the land (Ex. 33:2; 34:11).

Third, the basis of Rahab's faith was small: she had heard about the miraculous crossing of the Red Sea, which was 40 years earlier, and the more recent victories which the Lord had given the Israelites over Sihon and Og, the two Amorite kings on the eastern side of Jordan. She said, "I know that the LORD hath given you the land." She also explained that she believed in the God of Israel because "he is God in heaven above, and in earth beneath" (Jos. 2:9-11). Rahab's expression of faith was quite strong for one who had so little to go on. The rest of the people of Jericho had the same information that Rahab did; yet they chose not to believe. By her act of faith she separated herself from "them that believed not." While the writer of Hebrews emphasizes that she acted because of her faith, James points out that Rahab's action proved the genuineness of her faith (Jas. 2:25). The two truths are compatible and essential.

Fourth, Rahab's act of faith was imperfect. Rahab escaped God's judgment on the unbelieving inhabitants of Jericho because "she had received the spies with peace": that is, she had welcomed them as friends and treated them with kindness and hospitality. Rahab's act of faith has often been criticized because she lied about the two spies, claiming that they had just left her house and gone out the gates of the city, when she was actually hiding them on her roof (Jos. 2:1-7). Without attempting to justify the lie, it should at least be noted that she did not face a normal situation. She was hiding enemy spies during a time of war. Regardless, God is willing to work with an imperfect faith; if not, many of us would not be Christians. In the account in Joshua, the Lord makes no attempt to condone her lie, though there is no direct condemnation of it either. The writer of Hebrews commends her faith in receiving the spies without any qualification. The Scripture reminds us that Joshua fulfilled the promise made to Rahab and her family by sending the two spies she had saved to deliver her; and when the book of Joshua was written it was recorded that, "she dwelleth in Israel *even* unto this day" (Jos. 6:22-25).

The Gospel of Matthew reveals another reason, perhaps the best reason of all, that so much attention is given to the faith of Rahab. Rahab was the mother of Boaz, who married Ruth the Moabite, who bore Obed, the father of Jesse, the father of David the king (Mt. 1:5). In other words, Rahab was King David's great-great-grandmother and thus in the direct human line of Jesus Christ.

f. Others too numerous to relate (11:32-38)

Up to this point the writer has named specific heroes of faith, in each case giving some information about each person's act or acts of faith. He has gone far enough in Israel's history to make his point that the life of faith carries abundant and eternal rewards; therefore, these Hebrews must not consider turning from their faith regardless of the persecution that may threaten them. In the rest of the chapter he summarizes other personalities and acts of faith which could be considered, first dealing with those who found deliverance through faith in this life, and then those whose deliverance was primarily in the life that is to come.

(1) Many who experienced earthly victory (11:32-35a)

32 And what shall I more say? for the time would fail me to tell of Gedeon, and *of* Barak, and *of* Samson, and *of* Jephthae; of David also, and Samuel, and *of* the prophets:
33 Who through faith subdued kingdoms, wrought righteousness, obtained promises, stopped the mouths of lions,
34 Quenched the violence of fire, escaped the edge of the sword, out of weakness were made strong, waxed valiant in fight, turned to flight the armies of the aliens.
35a Women received their dead raised to life again.

The writer feels that he has gone far enough to make his point that the life of faith produces rich rewards. The Hebrew Christians who make up his audience have a rich ancestry of heroes who have lived by faith. "And what shall I more say?" means, "What is the need to go on any further?" The point could be illustrated with many other examples, but extending the subject unnecessarily might lose the readers' attention and defeat his purpose. It would be well for preachers to follow the writer's example.

To show that he could go further, he makes reference to other possible examples of faith: "For the time would fail me to tell of Gedeon, and of Barak, and of Samson, and of Jephthae; of David also, and Samuel, and of the prophets." The names that he chooses to mention are not in chronological order. They come from both the theocracy and the monarchy. Five of the six men mentioned are judges; the first four are dealt with in the book of Judges. Gideon delivered Israel from the Midianites with the help of his 300 dedicated men (Jg. 7); Barak from the Canaanites with the support of his co-judge Deborah and the heroic actions of Jael, the wife of Heber the Kenite (Jg. 4); Samson from the Philistines (Jg. 14-16); and Jephthah from the Ammonites (Jg. 11). Some commentators have expressed surprise that Jephthah is included as a hero of the faith when he offered his own daughter as a human sacrifice in fulfillment of a rash vow (see Jg. 11:31). Though there is not space here for a full discussion of this problem, I recommend the extensive attention which Keil and Delitzsch give to the subject (II:388-395). I agree with their conclusion that Jephthah dedicated his daughter to lifelong virginity, which was, in a spiritual sense, a burnt offering to the Lord.

David, as the second king of Israel, represents the monarchy; and Samuel, who was before David, is perhaps listed last because he served during both the theocracy and the monarchy, as an introduction to the prophets. The story of Samuel is in 1 Samuel 1—25, and the story of David extends from 1 Samuel 16 through all of 2 Samuel to his death in 1 Kg. 2:10. Though David's faith was certainly not perfect, his trust in the Lord is evident throughout his life, both in his acts of faith before and after he became the king of Israel and in his composition of the Psalms which reveal so much about his heart. Samuel was a prophet, priest, and judge; therefore, he serves as an appropriate conclusion to the list of names since he connects, by right of his offices, all of these together. Samuel's dedication to God is clear from the time he became an apprentice to Eli through his introduction of the monarchy in anointing both Saul and David as kings of Israel.

In vv. 33-35a the writer names actions of faith in Israel's history without attaching them to any name. Some of the acts are recognizable as applying to specific individuals, while others could apply to more than one person. First is that there were some "who through faith subdued kingdoms." "Through faith" (Greek *dia pisteos*) is different here in the original from the form used throughout the chapter (Greek *pistei*). Though the meaning is the same, the change in form marks a new approach. Though all the statements in v. 33 do not necessarily refer to the individuals named in v. 32, some certainly do; but the characteristics are meant to be applied to Israel's broader history as well, men like those named who exhibited acts of faith in their lives. All of the judges mentioned "subdued kingdoms," and David was especially blessed by the Lord in extending the borders of Israel from Egypt to the Euphrates River (2 Sam. 8:3).

They "wrought righteousness:" that is, they used their successful conquests to extend what is right and just rather than for evil purposes (2 Sam. 8:15).

Some, by faith, "obtained promises." The expression, "He obtained the promise" has already been used of Abraham in reference to the birth of Isaac. The phrase is meant to apply to both the reception and the fulfillment of the promises of God, and these Hebrew Christians had lived to see the fulfillment of the greatest promise of all, the coming of the seed of the woman who had crushed the serpent's head (Gen. 3:15; Jn. 12:31, 32).

Some, by faith, "stopped the mouths of lions." Samson stopped the roar of a young lion when he killed the beast with his bare hands in the vineyards of Timnath (Jg. 14:5, 6). David stopped the mouth of both a lion and a bear when he killed them to retrieve one of his sheep (1 Sam. 17:34). Daniel, when cast into the lions' den, testified to King Darius, "My God hath sent his angel, and hath shut the lions' mouths, that they have not hurt me" (Dan. 6:22).

Our writer continues in this same fashion in v. 34. Some unspecified heroes of the faith "quenched the violence of fire." This would certainly include the experience of Shadrach, Meshach, and Abednego, the three young men of Judah who were brought with Daniel to Babylon, who were thrown by Nebuchadnezzar into the fiery furnace because they refused to bow to his image. When they were brought out of the fire, all the witnesses, including Nebuchadnezzar, "saw these men, upon whose bodies the fire had no power, nor was an hair of their head singed, neither were their coats changed, nor the smell of fire had passed on them" (Dan. 3:27).

By faith some "escaped the edge of the sword." Moses named his second son Eliezer, "My God a helper," because the Lord "delivered me from the sword of Pharaoh" (Ex. 18:4). David praised the Lord who delivered "his servant from the hurtful sword" (Ps. 144:10), no doubt especially during the time he fled from Saul. Furthermore, the prophet Elijah was threatened with the sword by Jezebel (1 Kg. 19:1, 2); and Elisha was under the threat of death from both the king of Syria (2 Kg. 6:13, 14) and the king of Israel (2 Kg. 6:30, 31).

Various persons of faith "out of weakness were made strong." Such was the case with Moses who led a nation of slaves to depart from Egypt against the resistance of the most powerful king on earth (Ex. 5—14); with Gideon who brought victory to Israel by God and 300 men (Jg. 7); and with Samson who, in spite of his blindness, killed more Philistines at his death than during his lifetime (Jg. 16). Paul prayed three times for the removal of some physical malady, but God answered, "My grace is sufficient for thee: for my strength is made perfect in weakness" (2 Cor. 12:9). When we perceive ourselves as strong, we may not depend on God; but when we fully realize our weaknesses against the wiles and strength of Satan, we are more likely to rely completely on the Lord through whom we will always gain the victory.

Through faith some "waxed valiant in fight." Joshua led Israel in conquering major portions of the land of Canaan. Though God was with them and gave them the victory, they still had to do their part. David too, in order to establish his kingdom, had to fight many battles. God never indicates that Christians are to be pacifists. Jesus' instructions about non-resistance in the Sermon on the Mount were given primarily in regard to personal relationships (Mt. 5:38-42). Free nations sometimes have to fight to preserve that freedom. In relation to government, Jesus said, "Render therefore unto Caesar the things which are Caesar's; and unto God the things that are God's" (Mt. 22:21).

As a result of their becoming courageous in war, they "turned to flight the armies of the aliens." All of those who fought victorious battles for God's cause experienced the joy of seeing the enemy retreat. Abraham conquered Chedorlaomer and the kings of the East and brought back Lot and the people of Sodom (Gen. 14). Moses successfully fought off the attack of Amalek with the help of Aaron and Hur in keeping his hands held high (Ex. 17). Joshua led Israel to victory in numerous battles in conquering Canaan. All the judges put aliens to flight, and so did David and many of the later kings of Israel and Judah. But the spiritual application should also be obvious. If we would experience spiritual victory, we must recognize that we are in a war, and that the enemy is strong. Paul admonishes us to put on the whole armor of God (Eph. 6:10-18), and he challenges Timothy to "war a good warfare" (1 Tim. 1:18). Though Satan and his forces are strong and intimidating, we have the assurance that we can "overcome them: because greater is he that is in you, than he that is in the world" (1 Jn. 4:4).

The first statement in v. 35 gives the final description of those who have experienced earthly victory: Through faith "women received their dead raised to life again." In the O.T. we have two examples of this. Elijah raised the poor widow of Zarephath's son (1 Kg. 17:17-24), and Elisha raised the son of the wealthy woman of Shunem (2 Kg. 4:18-37). In the first case the widow lived outside of Israel in a city of Sidon (see Lk. 4:25, 26), while in the latter case the woman lived in Israel. In the N.T. two of Jesus' resurrections were directly for women: the widow of Nain's son (Lk. 7:11-15) and Lazarus for Mary and Martha (Jn. 11:34-44). In Acts 9:36-41 Luke tells about the resurrection of Tabitha, or Dorcas, by Peter for the widows of Joppa. The writer emphasizes women receiving their dead by resurrection probably because the majority of the six accounts are for women. Women, especially in ancient days, would be viewed as being in greater dependence and in need of such help.

(2) Many who experienced earthly defeat, but eternal victory (11:35b-38)

35b And others were tortured, not accepting deliverance; that they might obtain a better resurrection:
36 And others had trial of *cruel* mockings and scourgings, yea, moreover of bonds and imprisonment:
37 They were stoned, they were sawn asunder, were tempted, were slain with the sword: they wandered about in sheepskins and

goatskins; being destitute, afflicted, tormented;
38 (Of whom the world was not worthy:) they wandered in deserts, and *in* mountains, and *in* dens and caves of the earth.

In the middle of v. 35 the writer's summation takes a sudden turn. Up to this point he has stressed those who were delivered from death that they might live for a further period of time in even greater ministry for the Lord. Such deliverance is wonderful and miraculous; for it the Lord should be greatly praised. But the writer wants his readers to know that faith does not always lead to immediate deliverance, that those who experience severe suffering and even die in their faith are just as blessed, and in some ways even more so. When he says "and others," he uses the word for "others" (Greek *allos*) that indicates others of the same quality or kind; they are just as righteous, just as holy, just as dedicated as the group just discussed. Our sovereign God determines whether we are delivered from suffering and death or experience it to the fullest extent. The latter has been the lot of many believers down through the years. Paul declared, "It is required in stewards, that a man be found faithful" (1 Cor. 4:2). God will do His part, and He expects us to do our part, whatever the conclusion of the matter.

Among these "others" who were heroes of faith, some "were tortured, not accepting deliverance." "Were tortured" (Greek *tumpanizo*) originally refers to suffering inflicted by means of a frame or a wheel to which the body was fastened by the extremities and stretched to the point of excruciating pain; then the victim was executed by being beaten with clubs. The writer may have reference here to examples of this type of suffering recorded in some of the Apocryphal books. One case involved a devout man of the Maccabean line named Eleazar (2 Maccabees 6:18, 19, 28); another involved a mother and her seven sons (2 Maccabees 7:1ff.; 4 Maccabees 8:1ff.).

Those who died under such awful circumstances were "not accepting deliverance," that is, the deliverance they could have had had they renounced their stand and their faith in God. They did not accept such deliverance so "that they might obtain a better resurrection," that is, than the one they would have experienced if they had been raised from the dead at that time, like those in the first part of v. 35. Those in the first group who received miraculous deliverance in the various situations described certainly had reason to rejoice. But one unfortunate thing in each of those cases is that they would one day have to face death again. Their resurrection was to this life. Those who are martyred for God's cause, on the other hand, begin immediately to experience the bliss of eternal life. Their concerns about death are over forever, and at the resurrection of the last day they will receive an incorruptible body.

A pastor in communist Romania, when threatened with death by a soldier, held himself erect and declared, "Sir, do you not know what will happen if you kill me? I will go straight to glory. Sir, you cannot threaten me with glory!" The writer is not suggesting that those who die for Christ will receive a better resurrection than those who live for Him, but that they will receive a better resurrection than the one they would have received by denying their faith and, thus, receiving earthly deliverance (Hughes 512; Barnes 287). The resurrection to eternal life can never be taken away.

Though the O.T. did not reveal as much about the resurrection and eternal life as the N.T., it certainly appears clear that O.T. believers were looking forward with hope to the future, even beyond the end of this life. When challenged about the doctrine of the resurrection by the Sadducees, Jesus replied with interesting evidence. He pointed out that God said in the O.T., "I *am* . . . the God of Abraham, the God of Isaac, and the God of Jacob" (Ex. 3:6). Then He observed, "God is not the God of the dead, but of the living" (Mt. 22:32). When God spoke those words to Moses, the patriarchs had long since departed this life; but according to Jesus they were more alive afterward than ever before. Perhaps Jesus also had this in mind when he said, "Your father Abraham rejoiced to see my day: and he saw *it*, and was glad" (Jn. 8:56).

Among those who lived by faith, "others had trial of cruel mockings and scourgings." "Others" (Greek *heteros*) points to a group different from the martyrs mentioned in v. 35. These did not die, at least not immediately, but prolonged suffering can create a trial worse than death. "Had trial" (Greek *peiran elabon*) could be translated, "received a trial" or "experienced" these things. The suffering is expressed in two pairs, two sets of things that often accompany each other: "mockings and scourgings," and "bonds and imprisonment." Jesus Himself predicted that His enemies would "deliver him to the Gentiles to mock, and to scourge" (Mt. 20:19). That prophecy was fulfilled when Pilate had Him scourged and then He was mocked by the soldiers and then by different groups in the crowd as He hung on the cross (Mt. 27:26, 29, 39-44). Scourging involved being beaten with a long leather whip, usually with the ends embedded with bone or metal fragments. Each lash of the whip drew both flesh and blood. Victims often died under the scourging alone. The mocking added psychological suffering to physical suffering.

"Yea, moreover" (Greek *eti de*) in this context means, "On top of this." The words are used to connect the first pair with the second pair, and the implication is that "bonds and imprisonment" followed the mockings and the scourgings; "trial" goes with all four words. One trial included all four things. Jeremiah, as a result of his faithful prophecies concerning God's judgment on Judah, was beaten and placed in stocks as well as being mocked (Jer. 20:2, 7, 8); another time he was beaten and put in prison (Jer. 37:15; 38:6). After Herod Agrippa I had James killed with a sword, he also put Peter in prison and bound him with chains (Acts 12:1-6). Such has been the lot of many saints of God down through the ages.

The list of heroes of faith continues: "They were stoned." Stoning was the primary form of capital punishment under the law of Moses (Lev. 20:27; Dt. 17:2-5). It was often used against those who had been falsely charged as well, especially as Israel drifted away from God. Such was the fate of Naboth at the hands of Jezebel (1 Kg. 9-14), and Zechariah the priest, the son of Jehoiada (2 Chr. 24:17-22; Mt. 23:35), as a result of a conspiracy by King Joash of Judah. Stephen, the first martyr of the church, was stoned by the Jewish leaders (Acts 7:54-60), and Paul was stoned and left for dead at Lystra (Acts 14:19, 20).

"They were sawn asunder." This awful method of execution, which involved cutting the body through with a saw, was sometimes used against captives of war (2 Sam. 12:31; 1 Chr. 20:3; Keil & Delitzsch II:395). Jewish tradition, in connection with 2 Kg. 21:6, indicates that Isaiah died in this manner.

Some "were tempted" or put to the test, likely meaning that they were pressured to renounce their faith prior to their execution (Kent 253).

Some "were slain with the sword." This was the fate of numerous prophets of Jehovah under Jezebel (1 Kg. 18:4; 19:10), and of the priestly city of Nob at the hands of Doeg the Edomite (1 Sam. 22:17-19), and of Urijah the prophet at the hands of Jehoiakim (Jer. 26:20-23). James, the brother of John, became the first apostolic martyr of the church in this manner (Acts 12:1, 2).

Even those who escaped death faced a dismal situation: "They wandered about in sheepskins and goatskins" because they were without home, shelter, and proper clothing. The best they could do for clothing was animal skins which they had prepared for themselves. "They wandered" (Greek aorist active of *perierchomai*) can also be translated, "They went about." This looks back on the entire event as a historical fact (Greek effective aorist) though it actually occurred over a period of time. The last three characterizations apparently go closely with the preceding and indicate continuous action (Greek present participles). They were constantly "being destitute," lacking the most basic necessities of food, water, and clothing. They were continuously "afflicted" and "tormented" by the severe circumstances around them and by those who opposed them. Constantly on the run, they had no comfort or peace day or night.

Before he continues, the writer expresses his admiration and elevation for these heroes of the faith: "Of whom the world was not worthy." When Paul related the story of his salvation to the Jewish leaders, and told of his call to minister to the Gentiles, they angrily rejected his message and declared, "It is not fit that he should live" (Acts 22:22). Such has often been the case with the skeptics and unbelievers of this world. Many would just as soon rid the world of all Christians, by whatever means they may use. The righteousness of Christians presents a clear contrast to the wickedness of this world, and as in Noah's day (11:7) the wicked stand condemned by the example of those of faith. This world is not worthy of them.

The description of the tragic circumstances of many of faith's heroes resumes: "They wandered in deserts, and *in* mountains, and *in* dens and caves of the earth." "They wandered" expresses continuous action (Greek present tense) and actually completes the thought of "they wandered" in v. 37, though a different word is used. The same word is used to refer to the lost sheep going astray (Mt. 18:12) as well as the apostasy of the ancient Israelites who do always err in their heart (Heb. 3:10). But the writer has no error in mind here; these were wandering about because there was no other option. Their situation was unstable; they were God's saints whose ultimate home would be in Heaven but who had no permanent place on this earth.

Our Lord Himself experienced this homelessness in His life on this earth as part of His being tested in all points as we are, yet without sin (Lk. 9:58; Heb.

4:15). David endured this type of circumstance when he was fleeing from Saul (1 Sam. 22:1; 24:1-3). Obadiah hid prophets in a cave to protect them from the wrath of Jezebel (1 Kg. 18:4, 13). Elijah sought refuge in a cave when he was fleeing, in fear and discouragement, from the wicked wife of Ahab (1 Kg. 19:9). Perhaps at a date a little later than this writing, Christians hid in the catacombs of Rome, ancient cemeteries underneath the city. Such perilous situations often result when Christians become a small minority in a society. But our Lord warned us of times like this when He said, "Ye shall be hated of all *men* for my name's sake: but he that shall endure unto the end, the same shall be saved" (Mk. 13:13). Believers must never give in to the temptation to escape suffering by renouncing Christ. A few more years of comfort here can never replace the joys of Heaven that await those who continue to be faithful until God calls them home.

3. The connection of their faith with ours (11:39, 40)

39 And these all, having obtained a good report through faith, received not the promise:
40 God having provided some better thing for us, that they without us should not be made perfect.

The writer closes this chapter concerning the heroes of faith with a reminder that we continue in the great heritage which they passed down to us. "These all" refers back to the entire list enumerated in the chapter, from creation to wanderers in the deserts and caves of the earth. "Having obtained a good report" is concessive (Greek circumstantial participle), meaning "Although all of these have obtained a good report through faith, they *still* did not receive the promise." They obtained their good report or their good testimony by the acts of faith which they performed and by the record of those acts which was included in Scripture. The writer has summed up the report, but it has been drawn, by and large, from the pages of the Old Testament. In spite of their faithfulness, they "received not the promise." "Received" (Greek *komizo*) refers to receiving something to be carried away as your own (see also 10:36; 11:13, 19). Though they experienced many blessings in their life of faith, these O.T. saints did not receive "the promise," that is, the ultimate promise of the Messiah. The promise had been given to them as early as Gen. 3:15. Many other passages after that included the terms of the Abrahamic Covenant (Gen. 12:3); promises to the tribe of Judah (Gen. 49:10); prediction of a prophet like Moses (Dt. 18:15, 18); the Davidic Covenant (2 Sam. 7); Isaiah's Suffering Servant (Is. 53). But these O.T. heroes were not able to carry it away for themselves; they did not live to see the promise fulfilled. In 10:36 "the promise" is that of the return of Christ and the reward we will receive when we go to be with Him. In 11:13 "the promises" refer to the various aspects of the Abrahamic Covenant, which, of course, included the promise of the coming Messiah in whom all the families of the earth would be blessed (Gen. 12:3). It is to that promise that the writer points here in v. 39.

In v. 40 the writer gives the reason these O.T. saints did not receive the promise: "God having provided some better thing for us." The word translated "having provided" (Greek *problepo*) literally means "to see before" and refers to God's providential foreknowledge. God was able to make such provisions as described here because He saw all of history from beginning to end before creation. We are all part of His great plan. Jesus died for all men, and every person who has ever lived or ever will live could be saved through the drawing power of God in the Holy Spirit; at the same time God knows beforehand who will accept Christ and who will reject Him. Some have a problem in coordinating this view of divine sovereignty and human free will, but we believe this is what Scripture teaches.

God is so certain about who will be saved that our names have been "written in the book of life from the foundation of the world" (Rev. 17:8). He "provided," He "saw beforehand" those who would come to Christ in the O.T. dispensation, and those who would come in the N.T. dispensation; He also saw and provided for the earthly life, death, and resurrection of His Son, which made salvation possible. Furthermore, according to Peter, one of the main reasons He has delayed the return of Christ as long as He has is that He is "longsuffering to us-ward, not willing that any should perish, but that all should come to repentance" (2 Pet. 3:9). But one day soon the last one will come in, and our Lord will split the skies to receive to Himself those who have been faithful. If we have confessed Him in this world, He will confess us before the Heavenly Father (Mt. 10:32, 33).

In His great plan God provided "some better thing for us," an emphasis carried throughout the book. This is the twelfth time (of thirteen) that the word "better" is used in the epistle. The writer has referred to Christ as being better than angels, a better hope, a better covenant, better promises, better sacrifices, a better substance, a better country, and a better resurrection. Now, the better thing which He has provided for us is "that they without us should not be made perfect." After Jesus died on the cross, the sin debt of all the O.T. saints was paid in full. Until then, they were "saved on credit," so to speak; but with Jesus' death and resurrection the slate was cleared. God could have called a halt to redemptive history at that point, and have taken on to Heaven those who had been saved in the past, and were now dead, and His disciples that were then living. But He wanted to include us as well, those in the church dispensation.

"Made perfect" (Greek *teleioo*) refers to the completion of God's salvation plan for the ages, the fulfillment of the promises that He has made to the redeemed on the basis of the life, death, resurrection, and exaltation of Jesus Christ (Kent 256; Calvin 310; Alford 234; Morris 132; Kistemaker 359). From the cross Jesus cried "It is finished," using a verb form closely related to that used here (Greek *teleo*). The verb indicates that the plan of redemption is complete, and remains complete for the rest of human history (Greek perfect tense). What Christ did on the cross for the plan of redemption as a whole He also does for us individually when we become believers in Christ. In 10:14 the writer already declared, "For by one offering he hath perfected for ever them that are [being] sanctified."

It is true, however, that the full manifestation of this perfection, this redemption in all of its ramifications, awaits the Second Coming of Christ (Westcott

382; Kent 256; Lenski 422; Rom. 8:18-24; Heb. 10:36, 37). Making things perfect is another of the ideas which the writer has repeated throughout the epistle (2:10; 5:9; 6:1; 7:11, 19; 9:9, 11; 10:1). This closing remark of chapter 11 places N.T. saints on a high plain. A representative honor roll of O.T. saints has just been called, and we learn, to the glory of God, that they cannot be made complete without us. What joy, what delight to know that we who serve Christ by faith are included in that number!

Summary (11:1-40)

If the just shall live by faith—as the writer concluded in 10:38 by quoting from Hab. 2:4—then his readers need to truly know what genuine faith is and have some well-known examples to look to in their great time of need. He starts off by giving a concise, working definition of faith in 11:1: in essence, faith gives reality to those things which cannot be seen. Then he points to examples of faith from the past, beginning with the earliest days of Biblical history. All the scientific investigations in the world cannot tell us how the universe was created. This is a place where faith is absolutely essential since there were no eyewitnesses. We must accept the Biblical account that the universe was created, simply and completely, by the direct Word of God. Abel proved his faith by the sacrifice which he offered, and Enoch by his close walk with God—so close, in fact, that he went on to Heaven without dying. Faith involves more than merely believing in God; one must also have a personal relationship with Him. Noah showed his faith in building the ark in response to God's command.

By faith Abraham answered God's call to leave Ur and go to Canaan, though he and Isaac and Jacob never actually had a permanent home there. Indeed, they were looking beyond an earthly home to their heavenly home. Sarah, Abraham's wife, also trusted God in bearing a son, Isaac, in her old age, and from him came a great nation. Abraham and his immediate descendants continued to live by faith even though the Promised Land would never be theirs during their lifetime, for they were in search of a better country and a better city. Abraham's greatest trial was when God asked him to offer his only son, Isaac, as a sacrifice. Though God stopped Abraham before the sacrifice could be completed, he really sacrificed his son in his heart. Figuratively, Abraham received Isaac back, as though he had returned from the dead. Isaac demonstrated his faith when he blessed Jacob, Jacob when he blessed Joseph's two sons, and Joseph when he asked that his body be taken to Canaan when his people returned there.

Moses had faithful parents who allowed him to be raised by Pharaoh's daughter, but Moses remembered the early lessons that his mother taught him so well that he chose to identify himself with a nation of slaves rather than the unlimited wealth of Egypt. Moses by faith courageously confronted Pharaoh until God broke his resistance in the tenth and final plague, the death of the firstborn, from which Israel was protected by the application of the blood of the passover lamb. Moses' final act of faith, as noted in Hebrews, was leading Israel through the Red Sea. After Moses died, Joshua, who had been his assistant, led

Israel in conquering Jericho, and in that wicked and idolatrous city Rahab manifested her faith by hiding the spies of Israel.

Many more examples of people who lived by faith in the O.T. could be cited, but these are enough to prove the point. Many heroes of faith enjoyed great victories through faith, but some endured great hardship: in many cases, hardship which led to physical death. It is God's sovereignty which determines who enjoys the victories and who endures the hardship. Such people have left an excellent testimony for us when our faith, like theirs, is tried. But the most wonderful thing of all is that they could not be complete without us since salvation by faith could only become a reality through the fulfillment of God's ultimate promise in the atoning work of Christ.

Application: Teaching and Preaching the Passage

Following his quotation from Hab. 2:4 in 10:38, the writer, in chapter 11, gives numerous examples directly from the pages of the O.T. of those who did, indeed, live their lives by faith. On the basis of the working definition of faith given in 11:1, and its development in the chapter, at least five points can be made: (1) Faith is needed only when all of God's promises have not been fulfilled. (2) Faith only requires believing a promise to the extent that it has been developed up to that time. (3) Faith makes it possible to treat promises which have not been fulfilled as though they had already been fulfilled. (4) Faith is the only evidence we need when God's revelation or God's promises cannot be put to the test. (5) Faith is not "a leap in the dark," but rather trust in God for the future because He has proved Himself faithful in the past.

When the writer starts pointing to examples of faith, he starts with creation. Through the rest of the chapter he points to individual examples of faith, but he cannot do that here since no human witnesses are available. Creation is one event of history for which we must totally take God's Word, but it is also a crucial turning point in establishing the reality of faith in our lives. If we can accept Gen. 1:1 we can easily believe anything else in Scripture, no matter how contrary to normal experience that thing may seem. A God who can create the universe by His direct word can do anything else that He may need or want to do (11:3).

A teaching or preaching outline which could be used for 11:4-7 is as follows: (1) Abel demonstrated his faith by his worship. (2) Enoch demonstrated his faith by his walk. (3) Noah demonstrated his faith by his work.

Hebrews 11:6 deserves some special attention when teaching this chapter. The statement there is tied to the observation that Enoch "pleased God" in his life. But the writer wants us to know that there may be more to a faith that truly pleases God than some may think. Faith in God must manifest itself in at least two ways. *First*, a man must truly believe that God exists, and his faith in God's existence must be defined by the Scripture, not by his own whims and imagination. Some want to make the idea of God vague and subjective, but, according to Scripture, God is objective and His attributes are clearly defined. His existence is real and is manifested in three distinct, co-equal and co-eternal personalities. *Second*, a man must also believe that God rewards those who come to Him by faith. God is a social being, and we are made in His image. He longs for our fellowship, evidently one of the primary reasons for which He made man. But that fellowship can only exist through faith. Amos asked, "Can two walk together, except they be agreed?" (Amos 3:3). The answer is, "Absolutely not!" Unbelievers cannot go to Heaven. They would not be happy there anyway, for they would be completely out of place.

In 11:8-19 Abraham's faith was manifested in several different ways: (1) in his unique call to follow the Lord's guidance (v. 8); (2) in the paradox of "sojourning [dwelling in temporary dwellings] in the land of promise" (vv. 9, 10); (3) in the miraculous birth of Isaac (vv. 11, 12; including Sarah's faith as well); (4) in his persistence in faith throughout his lifetime, even though some of the promises were unfulfilled (v. 13; including Isaac and Jacob as well); (5) in looking forward even beyond the earthly promises, along with a stubborn refusal to look back on what he had left behind (vv. 14-16); (6) in his willing obedience in sacrificing Isaac, the son of the promise (vv. 17-19).

Notice also that Abraham saw Heaven as: (1) a city where fellowship would abound (vv. 10, 16), but also (2) as a country where his citizenship would be permanent (vv. 14-16).

The idea of Abraham's offering of Isaac as a type of Christ could be pursued from vv. 17-19 in company with the historical account in Gen. 22:1-19. Three major points can be made: (1) Abraham represents the loving father willing to offer his only son (see Jn. 3:16). (2) Isaac represents the obedient son, willing to be sacrificed if that is necessary (see Jn. 10:15-18; Mt. 26:39-44). (3) The ram caught in the bush represents Christ as our substitute (2 Cor. 5:21).

The faith of Abraham's three immediate descendants deserves emphasis: (1) Isaac in blessing Jacob over Esau, in spite of his personal prejudice (see Gen. 27:1-40); (2) Jacob in blessing the two sons of Joseph near the end of his life in Egypt (Gen. 48:1-22); (3) Joseph in his request that his bones (his body) be carried back to Canaan when Israel would return years later (Gen. 50:22-26; Ex. 13:19; Jos. 24:32).

Faith was demonstrated in the story of Moses in several different ways: (1) in his parents' courageous protection of the baby Moses against the wrath of Pharaoh (v. 23); (2) in Moses' own rejection of the wealth of Egypt in preference for the greater riches of Christ, which would come through his identification with a nation of slaves (vv. 25, 26); (3) in his courageous challenge of the Pharaoh of Egypt, the most powerful ruler in the world, culminating in the death of the firstborn and the celebration of the Passover (vv. 27, 28); (4) in his leading the nation of Israel through the Red Sea on dry ground (v. 29). Though we can certainly use Moses in the fourth point above, it is interesting to notice that the writer of Hebrews places the emphasis in both v. 29 (the crossing of the Red Sea) and v. 30 (the fall of Jericho) on the faith of the nation of Israel ("they") rather than on the leadership of Moses and Joshua.

The last personal act of faith which our writer identifies by name is the faith of Rahab. She stands as a beautiful example of the worst of sinners, and ultimately that includes all of us, saved by grace. She was saved by faith: (1) in spite of her moral weaknesses (Rahab, the harlot); (2) in spite of her Gentile ancestry (a native Canaanite); (3) in spite of her religious background (idolatry); (4) in spite of her lack of divine revelation (some, but not much); (5) in spite of personal danger in hiding the spies of Israel.

But her salvation by faith propelled her to wonderful blessings and great heights: (1) in the salvation of herself and her whole family (Jos. 6:22, 23); (2) in her becoming an adopted member of God's covenant people (Jos. 6:25); (3) in her marriage to Salmon, a native Israelite (Mt. 1:5); (4) in becoming the mother of Boaz, who married Ruth (Mt. 1:5); (5) in becoming the great-great-grandmother of King David (Mt. 1:5, 6); (6) in being included in the earthly genealogy of Jesus Christ (Mt. 1:5, 6).

The enumeration of the experiences of faith in 11:33-38 is partially drawn from the heroes mentioned but not discussed in v. 32. Some of the acts of faith are identifiable, either from the Scripture record itself or from Jewish tradition. The primary contrast which needs to be emphasized is between: (1) those whose faith brought deliverance and victory (vv. 33-35a), and (2) those whose faith saw them through defeat, suffering, and death (vv. 35b-38). The word "others" in v. 35b should be stressed (Greek *allos*), indicating others of the same kind, whose faith was just as great as those in the first group, but for whom our sovereign God willed a different outcome. In either case, faith always brings deliverance, either in this world or from this world.

The writer closes this great chapter, the faith chapter, by emphasizing the unity between the saints of the O.T., whose record he has just been reviewing, and those of the New Testament. We join them in enjoying the fulfillment of God's ultimate promise in the life, death, resurrection, and exaltation of His Son, and with them we still look forward to the joy of eternal life in Heaven when Christ returns to complete His plan for the ages (11:39, 40).

B. Faith Progressing Toward Consummation (12:1-29)

In chapter 12 the writer continues to emphasize the character and importance of faith to his Hebrew readers. He shows how faith will carry us all the way through if we continue to maintain it. He does so by pointing to Jesus as both the source and the example of our faith (12:1-4), by stressing the importance of divine discipline as a means of Christian growth (12:5-13), by using Esau as an example of those who fail to establish long-term priorities (12:14-17), and finally by issuing his fifth warning in the epistle with regard to the severe consequences of turning away from Christ (12:18-29).

1. Jesus as our source and our example (12:1-4)

1 Wherefore seeing we also are compassed about with so great a cloud of witnesses, let us lay aside every weight, and the sin which doth so easily beset *us*, and let us run with patience the race that is set before us,
2 Looking unto Jesus the author and finisher of *our* faith; who for the joy that was set before him endured the cross, despising the shame, and is set down at the right hand of the throne of God.
3 For consider him that endured such contradiction of sinners

against himself, lest ye be wearied and faint in your minds.
4 Ye have not yet resisted unto blood, striving against sin.

"Wherefore" (Greek *toigaroun*) in v. 1 calls our attention back to the witnesses the writer has enumerated in chapter 11. What he is about to say must be connected with what he has said there. His next statement lays down a cause for faithfulness in the Christian life: "Seeing [since] we also are compassed about with so great a cloud of witnesses." The writer does not mean to suggest that the O.T. saints were "also" surrounded by witnesses, but that we "also," like the heroes of the faith in chapter 11, must endure the Christian race before us.

Before he admonishes us about running the race, he points to two things by way of preparation; one is an *attitude* and the other is an *action*. With regard to attitude, we need to recognize that we have for our benefit "so great a cloud of witnesses." These witnesses to a life of faith from the O.T. are represented as "a cloud" because of the large number, the mass, of them; in a sense they "hang over" us. They include all the saints from the pages of the O.T., of which chapter 11 only presented a selection (see 11:32), as well as the great number of believers in the church era, those in the N.T. and since, about whose faith we also have much information.

These witnesses are "compassed about" (Greek *perikeimai*) us, surrounding us like a large crowd in an amphitheater or sports arena. But the picture does not mean that we should think of the saints who have passed on as personally witnessing our successes and failures on earth (Lenski 424). The saints who are in Heaven evidently give their full attention to what is going on there (Lk. 16:23, 25; 2 Cor. 5:8; Rev. 14:13), especially their rest in the Lord, though there is some indication that good news about spiritual things on earth is shared with the inhabitants of Heaven (Lk. 15:7, 10). But the depiction of the crowd of witnesses in the amphitheater is there nevertheless (Barnes 292; Westcott 391; Kent 257; Kistemaker 366; Hughes 519) and serves to enhance the picture of the Christian life as a race. The scene must, of course, be interpreted figuratively.

In addition to our attitude in acknowledging these witnesses we must also take preparatory action: "Let us lay aside every weight, and the sin which doth so easily beset *us*." "Lay aside" (Greek aorist tense) is viewed as completed action, something that needs to be taken care of once and for all as the race begins. "Every weight" refers to every hindrance present in our lives that would keep us from living our best for Christ. It will include things that in themselves might not be sinful, but if they hinder us from doing our best for God, they should be surrendered. For a young person, it might be someone who does not share an outlook about doing God's will, or choices about college and career. For an adult it might be a job that is interfering with service to God, or friends pulling in the wrong direction. The Greek runner, dressed as lightly as possible, desired to have nothing that would burden him in the race. Christians should be that eager to rid themselves of all hindrances in their race for the Lord.

We should also lay aside "the sin which doth so easily beset *us*." "Easily beset" (Greek *euperistatos*) is an adjective describing "the sin" as "that which stands around [us] with ease." In this context it refers to that sin with which we are most bothered. Though all sin is to be avoided, for most if not all of us there is at least one sin that gives us more trouble than anything else, and each of us knows better than anyone else what that sin is. It must be put aside if we would live victoriously for Christ.

Having prepared for the race in both attitude and action, "Let us run with patience the race that is set before us." "Let us run" (Greek present tense) is in continuous action: the race will go on throughout the Christian life. It is not a sprint, but a marathon. This is further indicated by the phrase, "With patience" (Greek *hupomone*), that attitude which "keeps us under the load" (see also 10:36), which perseveres until the end.

The word translated "race" (Greek *agon*) includes various athletic events. It refers to a "fight" in 1 Tim. 6:12 and 2 Tim. 4:7. In this passage it is clearly a race since it is used with the word "run." It always speaks of a struggle, a contest, an effort which demands total commitment. The race is "set before us." The past is under the blood. Mistakes or sins in our Christian lives must be set aside, after appropriate repentance, to look onward to successful accomplishments in the future. Even successes must not be dwelt upon to the extent that the continuing race is hindered. When we get to Heaven there will be abundant time for rejoicing.

The writer continues with the picture of the race in v. 2: "Looking unto Jesus the author and finisher of *our* faith." As the runner runs his race, he must constantly keep his mind and, when he gets close enough, his eye on the finish line, the goal for which he is reaching. Even so the Christian must always be "looking unto Jesus." "Looking" (Greek *aphorao*) means "to look away," to fix one's eyes on something at a distance with a concentrated gaze. The Lord's human name, "Jesus," views Him in His humanity and suffering on the cross; and in that humanity He is the appropriate object of our concentrated gaze.

He is the "author" (Greek *archegos*), the Leader, the Originator, of our faith. In this capacity He both sets an example of faith, in His own implicit trust in the Father (Jn. 5:19; 8:28; 11:41, 42; 14:10), and empowers our faith through the Holy Spirit (Kent 258; Westcott 395; Hughes 522). But He is also the "finisher" (Greek *teleiotes*) of our faith. He will lead and empower us all the way through. Lenski (426) does not agree that Jesus is our example in faith; he thinks the idea should be limited to His being the Originator, the Cause, of our faith; but the meaning of the word and the statements in the Gospels about Jesus' trust in the Father apparently justify the broader approach.

Furthermore, "*our* faith" is "the faith" (definite article in Greek). The article connects us back to faith as defined in 11:1: that is the faith he speaks about. If we keep our eyes on Him, He will lead us all the way. When Peter was invited to walk to Jesus on the water, he did well until he took his eyes off the Lord and looked down instead at the turbulent sea (Mt. 14:28-31). We too must keep our eyes on Jesus to the finish. Paul observed that "he which hath begun a good work in you will perform *it* until the day of Jesus Christ" (Phil. 1:6).

The writer further describes Jesus as the one "who for the joy that was set before him endured the cross, despising the shame." The preposition translated for (Greek *anti*) often means "instead of" in the New Testament. When Jesus spoke of a son asking a father for a fish, he asked, "Will he for [instead of] a fish give him a serpent?" (Lk. 11:11); or the Son of man came "to give his life a ransom for [instead of] many" (Mt. 20:28). Some commentators, including some of the early church fathers (Cyril of Alexandria, Gregory of Nazianzus), and the Syriac Peshitta, have taken this as the meaning in this passage (see Hughes 523). If so, the writer is saying that Jesus endured the cross "instead of" the joy that was set before Him: that is, the joys of Heaven which He had experienced from all eternity prior to the incarnation. He gave up the joys of Heaven in order to come to a cruel world that rejected Him and nailed Him to a tree. That is basically the same truth taught in Phil. 2:7, 8.

But most commentators take "for" here in the sense of "in exchange for" (the preposition is used in a similar way in v. 16): in order to obtain the joy that was "set before him," the joy of the blessed issue of redemption as it applies to us as well as the joy of His exalted position at the Father's right hand (Westcott 395; Lenski 426; Hughes 522).

This was the reason He "endured the cross." "Endured" (Greek *hupomeno*) is the verb form of the noun used in v. 1. As we are asked to run the race "with patience," endurance, to remain under the burden until it is finished, so our Lord "endured," stayed under the burden of the cross, until He fully accomplished the plan of redemption (see also Phil. 2:8).

Because of His love for us, Christ was willing to do that even though He was "despising the shame." Death on a cross was so despicable that Roman law forbade a Roman citizen to be executed in this manner. The Jewish law said, "Cursed *is every* one that hangeth on a tree" (Gal. 3:13; Dt. 21:23). Jesus willingly bore that curse for us. But for Jesus, the shame was greatly multiplied in regard to the special nature of His death. That is why He shrank so from "this cup" in His agony in Gethsemane (Mt. 26:39). The innocent Son of God, who knew no sin, had all the sins of all the world placed upon Him (2 Cor. 5:21; 1 Pet. 3:18), and as a result the Heavenly Father forsook Him (Mt. 27:46; Ps. 22:1). The cross still separates men. To those who refuse Christ, it is foolishness, but to those who believe it is "Christ the power of God, and the wisdom of God" (1 Cor. 1:18, 23, 24). Now comes "the joy that was set before him": He "is set down at the right hand of the throne of God." This is His position of glorification from which He now ministers as our High Priest according to the order of Melchisedec (see chapter 7; also 1:3, 13; 8:1; 10:12). The verb translated "is set" (Greek perfect tense) indicates that Christ has taken this position and remains there.

Christ is not only the "author and finisher" of our faith; in v. 3 He is also our example in suffering: "For consider him that endured such contradiction of sinners against himself." "For" introduces v. 3 as an additional reason to look to Jesus. In v. 2 the admonition to keep looking to Jesus as the author and finisher of our faith is in continuous action, as is the exhortation to keep running at the end of v. 1. But here the admonition to "consider" Christ as our example in suffering calls for a decisive act (Greek aorist tense) that must be taken to heart throughout the rest of the race, a careful estimate of comparing one thing to another that must never be forgotten (Westcott 397). Here we are glancing back at our Lord's record on earth, but in v. 2 we are looking ahead to the promises of the future.

Some commentators would make Christ's suffering and death on the cross *only* an example, one who is to be admired for His simple and sacrificial way of life. Such views must be completely rejected as belonging to those who would dethrone Christ and rob Christianity of its power and its promise of eternal life. Even so, in addition to being our vicarious sacrifice who has graciously provided salvation for us, He is also our example to be followed in every respect that men can follow Him. The writer refers to Him as our model in suffering. If the general bears the brunt of the battle, the soldiers can follow.

We are to consider "him that endured"; the endurance is finished, but the results continue (Greek perfect tense). Patience or endurance has drawn special attention in these first three verses. We must keep running the race "with patience" (endurance) in v. 1, Jesus "endured" the cross in v. 2, and now He has "endured" suffering in v. 3. What he specifically endured was "such contradiction of sinners against himself." The contradiction (Greek *antilogia*) literally refers to the act of "speaking against" some person or thing, but it includes the ideas of opposition, hostility, and rebellion of all kinds, not just in spoken form. Jesus suffered opposition throughout His earthly life.

At Jesus' birth Herod the Great tried to exterminate Him. During His three-year ministry He was increasingly opposed by the Jewish leaders, whether scribes, Pharisees, Sadducees, or Herodians. Though these groups disagreed about many things, they came together in their opposition against Jesus. Following God's purpose (Jn. 19:10, 11), that opposition finally appeared to be victorious when these leaders succeeded in pressuring Pontius Pilate, the Roman procurator, to order Jesus' crucifixion. Even on the cross they mockingly challenged Him to come down and save Himself if He was really who He claimed to be.

Through all of this Jesus' hostile opponents acted as "sinners" of the worst sort. Early in His ministry, He told His followers, many of whom considered the Pharisees the embodiment of religion as they knew it, "Except your righteousness shall exceed *the righteousness* of the scribes and Pharisees, ye shall in no case enter into the kingdom of heaven" (Mt. 5:20). If our Lord could keep going toward His goal in spite of such hostility, then surely these Hebrew Christians can endure the opposition they are facing at the present time.

The reasons the writer wants them to take Jesus' sufferings into careful consideration is, "lest ye be wearied and faint in your minds." "Be wearied" (Greek *kamno*) refers to becoming tired by exertion, succumbing to a state of exhaustion; in Jas. 5:15 it refers to being sick. "Faint" (Greek *ekluo*) is a near synonym, referring to becoming weary or slack, giving out; it is used in Mt. 15:32 when Jesus expressed a desire to feed the multitudes "lest they *faint* in the way," and in Gal. 6:9 where Paul promises his readers, "In due season we shall reap, if we *faint* not." In this context the latter word describes the process of becoming slack and the former word expresses the resulting state of exhaustion. Aristotle used both words for runners who relaxed and collapsed after they had crossed the finish line (Morris 135).

The word translated "minds" (Greek *psuche*) is usually translated "soul," including the five other places it appears in Hebrews (4:12; 6:19; 10:38, 39; 13:17). But the soul is the sum total of a man's inner being, a combination of both heart and mind, of emotions and intellect. The writer does not want his readers, in the face of persecution, to become heart sick, to lose spirit and quit the race.

Another thing that should make the Hebrews take heart in their suffering, at least for the time, is that it has not gone as far as it could go: "Ye have not yet resisted unto blood, striving against sin." The word translated, "Ye have resisted" (Greek *antikathistemi*) means "to stand against" something, "to stand in opposition." This is often the case for Christians: in following the teachings of our Lord, we are going in a direction opposite to that of the world around us. When the Jewish Sanhedrin ordered the apostles not to speak any more in the name of Jesus, Peter had to answer, "We ought to obey God rather than men" (Acts 5:29). In normal times Christians are instructed to obey civil authority (Mt. 22:21; Rom. 13); but when civil authority issues commands that are contrary to those of God, the choice has already been made for us.

"Unto blood," of course, means "unto death." The writer might have had in mind the phrase "unto death" with regard to the death of Christ in Phil. 2:8. That the first readers of Hebrews had not yet been martyred is significant in determining the place and the time of the writing of Hebrews (see introduction). It makes it unlikely that the epistle could have been written in Palestine since Stephen was martyred about A.D. 34, and it could not have been written in Rome after A.D. 64 when the Neronian persecution of the church broke out. We note, however, the "not yet": they had no promise that death would not be their lot, and it eventually was. If our Lord suffered unto death, so can we, but for this group the sufferings had not yet reached that point.

Their resistance was in "striving against sin." "Striving" refers to "fighting against" something, "agonizing against" it. The word (Greek *antagonizomi*) has the same root as the word for "race" in v. 1. The athletic emphasis is still present. The writer indicates that their struggle is "against sin," not against sinners. Perhaps he does this to allow for the broadness of their resistance, for their struggle was not only against sinners without but also against sin within (Alford 240).

2. Divine discipline a means of Christian growth (12:5-13)

Verse 4 acts as a connecting link between the thought of vv. 1-3 concerning running our race for the Lord and keeping our eyes on Jesus and the thought of vv. 5-13 which pictures Christian suffering as God's means of discipline. It serves both as a conclusion to the first subject and as an introduction to the second. The writer seeks to encourage the Hebrews by helping them look at the persecution they were facing from the right perspective.

a. It confirms that one is a true son of God (12:5-8)

5 And ye have forgotten the exhortation which speaketh unto you as unto children, My son, despise not thou the chastening of the Lord, nor faint when thou art rebuked of him:
6 For whom the Lord loveth he chasteneth, and scourgeth every son whom he receiveth.
7 If ye endure chastening, God dealeth with you as with sons; for what son is he whom the father chasteneth not?
8 But if ye be without chastisement, whereof all are partakers, then are ye bastards, and not sons.

Some commentators suggest taking v. 5 as a question: "Have ye forgotten?" (Hughes 136; Barnes 298). Viewing the statement as a question lightens the weight of the accusation, but it also robs it of some of its potency. It seems just as well to leave it as it is. "Ye have forgotten" (Greek perfect tense) indicates a past act with continuing results. The message in this passage had not just slipped their minds; they had completely put it aside, giving it no consideration. They were indicating by their extreme discouragement in suffering that they had lost sight of this aspect of God's discipline.

The writer refers to the Scripture he is about to quote as "the exhortation" (Greek *paraklesis*), which can also mean comfort, consolation, or encouragement. The Scripture quoted "exhorts" in that it calls for a certain attitude to be adopted or a certain action to be taken, but it also "encourages" in helping the readers to see things in the right light. It brings a positive point of view to a negative situation. The same word is translated "exhortation" in 13:22 and "consolation" in 6:18.

This Scripture, like all Scripture, "speaketh unto you," which personifies the Scripture because it is none other than the Word of God. When we read the Bible, it is just as if God was speaking to us personally. Thus, James admonishes, "Be ye doers of the word, and not hearers only" (Jas. 1:22). But this passage speaks to believers in a special light, "as unto children." When taken as a whole, the Scripture addresses many different needs. Some parts involve admonitions and warnings to the unsaved of many different varieties, while other parts are specifically designed for the encouragement and motivation of believers. The passage he is about to quote is the latter.

"My son, despise not thou the chastening of the Lord, nor faint when thou art rebuked of him": the quotation here and in the next verse is from Pr. 3:11, 12 (see also Job 5:17). Solomon addressed these words to his own son with regard to the struggles of life which God allows to come our way. Writing under inspiration, he spoke also to all of God's children. The admonition is, "Despise not"; the construction may simply indicate a habit that is forbidden, or it may (as seems likely here) indicate action that was already happening and needed to be stopped (Greek negative present imperative). Either way, men despise God's discipline when they fail to recognize that it is from God, that it is designed for a purpose, and when they think or speak disparagingly of it (Barnes 298).

"Chastening" (Greek *paideia*) refers to the whole education of a child, both positive and negative, acts meant for instruction and those meant for correction. Since our English word "chastening" primarily refers to correction, some of the newer translations use the word "discipline" (NIV; NASB) because it carries with it this broader connotation. The experiences of suffering and affliction in our lives are not always intended for correction, though some may be (see 1 Cor. 11:27-34). Others, however, are for our spiritual education, to help us grow in the Lord or to depend more upon Him (Job 42; 1 Cor. 12:7-9).

"Nor faint when thou art rebuked of him." This admonition also may indicate something that is already happening and needs to cease: "Stop fainting." There is a certain breed of goats that habitually faint when frightened. Christians must not be like that. God will allow sufferings to come in all our lives. We must have the right attitude toward them and we must not want to quit when we are "rebuked of him." Some parents never tell their children, "No!" They are hesitant to deny them any desire. But our God is the perfect parent. He treats us as we ought to be treated.

"For whom the Lord loveth he chasteneth." These Hebrew Christians need to see their suffering in a positive light. Some might have expressed doubts about God's love in allowing them to experience affliction. The writer wants them to see that such suffering is, in itself, a sign that God does love them. Discipline indicates the presence of a parental relationship. God is our Father, and we are His sons and daughters. Because of that He "scourgeth every son whom he receiveth." The Hebrew text reads, "Even as a father the son *in whom* he delighteth," but the meaning is basically the same. The writer of Hebrews, as always, quotes from the Septuagint.

There is much debate today about corporal punishment, which is certainly not the only kind of discipline or correction that parents should exercise. But if we would follow God's example, that possibility should not be eliminated. It must always, of course, be administered with no hint of abuse. We should, no doubt, have some variety in our discipline, just as God does. Some things work better for one child, and other things for another; some methods are better at one time, and others at another. The hard tasks assigned by loving parents may be correctional or they may be educational. The writer has already pointed out that our Lord learned "obedience by the things which he suffered" (5:8). If He who needed no correction benefitted from the discipline of suffering, then it is certainly to our benefit who need both education and correction.

In v. 7 the writer applies the lesson from his quotation of Pr. 3:11, 12. He says, "If ye endure chastening, God dealeth with you as with sons; for what son is he whom the father chasteneth not?" Instead of "if" (Greek *ei*), many manuscripts have the preposition (Greek *eis*) that means (among other things) "with reference to." The verb "endure" (Greek *hupomeno*) can be an imperative (NIV; Morris 137; Kistemaker 376) or an indicative (NASB; Lenski 435; Westcott 434). Consequently, we might render "With reference to chastening keep on enduring" or "You are enduring with reference to chastening." Since a pattern for exhortations and commands has already been set in the preceding verses of this section (vv. 1, 3), it seems best to me to take it as a command, but the final meaning is the same regardless: we are to keep on enduring in a time of chastening because "God dealeth with you as with sons."

He "dealeth" with us, treats us, like sons when He allows us to experience suffering. Rather than being a sign of the absence of God's care, as some might have been thinking, God's discipline is a sure indication of the presence and depth of His care. The writer asks, "For what son is he whom the father chasteneth not?" The answer to the rhetorical question is: "There are not any fathers—good fathers, at least—who do not appropriately discipline their children." Paul reveals something very important about such discipline: he says that "God *is* faithful, who will not suffer you to be tempted above that ye are able; but will with the temptation also make a way to escape, that ye may be able to bear *it*" (1 Cor. 10:13).

We should be concerned, as professing Christians, if no discipline ever comes our way: "But if ye be without chastisement, whereof all are partakers, then are ye bastards, and not sons." "But" (Greek *de*) introduces a contrast to the previous situation, a life for Christ that includes suffering viewed as God's discipline. The "if" used in this sentence (Greek *ei*) expresses a situation assumed true for the sake of showing what it means when it is true. It is applicable to any individual or group who never experience chastisement, a sure sign that they are not God's children. God does not discipline those who are not His children. Believers have often been bothered by seeing wicked men who appear never to get their due, never to reap ill consequences from their sin. Job lamented that, while he suffered greatly under the hand of God, his wicked neighbors seemed never to face judgment (Job 21:7-13). What the writer is saying here provides an answer to Job's question. They are not God's children; therefore, He does not discipline them. When wicked men suffer, and they sometimes do, it is not God's discipline, for that is only for His children. Paul said to Timothy, "Some men's sins are open beforehand, going before to judgment; and some *men* they follow after" (1 Tim. 5:24); and Peter explains, "The Lord knoweth how to deliver the godly out of temptations, and to reserve the unjust unto the day of judgment to be punished" (2 Pet. 2:9).

When the writer says, in relation to discipline, "whereof all are partakers," he means "all" true believers, all those who are the sons of God through the new birth. The verb "are" (Greek perfect tense *ginomai*) means "have become." It indicates a past act with continuing results. God's children have come to be in a position to experience His discipline. To those who never experience God's discipline, the writer says, "then are ye bastards, and not sons." "Bastards" (Greek *nothos*) are illegitimate children who have no right of inheritance in the spiritual realm; they claim to have a son relationship to God, but there is no basis or evidence for their claim. Scripture indicates that there will be those who apparently even fooled themselves about their relationship with Christ. Some who claim to have prophesied, cast out demons, and worked miracles in His name will hear Him say, "I never knew you: depart from me, ye that work iniquity" (Mt. 7:22, 23). Thus Paul admonishes, "Examine yourselves, whether ye be in the faith" (2 Cor.

13:5). True Christianity will bear up under periodic reexamination.

b. It is better than what our earthly parents gave us (12:9, 10)

9 Furthermore we have had fathers of our flesh which corrected *us,* and we gave *them* reverence: shall we not much rather be in subjection unto the Father of spirits, and live?
10 For they verily for a few days chastened *us* after their own pleasure; but he for *our* profit, that *we* might be partakers of his holiness.

"Furthermore" (Greek *eita*) in v. 9 is used to introduce a new argument. In vv. 5-8 our writer has maintained that discipline is a sign of sonship, a sign that we are under the active care and guidance of God. But now he argues that God's discipline is better than that of our earthly parents and produces a more noble outcome. In the previous section he argued that the presence of divine discipline indicates that we are *now* true believers, real sons of God; here he warns about the importance of a proper attitude toward chastisement if we would *continue* to be sons of God. The contrast is from the less to the greater: in this case, earthly fathers in contrast to the Heavenly Father. This method of contrast is seen several times in the epistle (2:2, 3; 9:14; 10:29; 12:25).

The first part of the contrast is, "We have had fathers of our flesh which corrected *us*, and we gave *them* reverence." "Fathers of our flesh" simply means our earthly fathers in contrast to our Heavenly Father. "We have had"—literally, "We were having" (Greek imperfect tense)—presents such fathers over an extended period of time in our past. Such fathers had the responsibility of our discipline over some length of time as we grew to maturity. Now, as adults, we are no longer under that discipline, though we still respect them for that role whether they are alive or dead. (The term "fathers" is not meant to eliminate the proper participation of mothers in the discipline of children, but that is not relevant to the point here.) "Which corrected" is actually a noun, not a verb: literally, "we have had fathers of our flesh (as) correctors/discipliners"; it has the same root as "chastening" in v. 5.

God placed our parents in this position "and we gave *them* reverence" or respect. This verb matches the first one, "We were having," and so we might translate, "We were reverencing [respecting] them," over this same extended period of time. We made it a practice to acknowledge their proper authority and our position, as children, in relation to them.

In the second part of the contrast, our writer asks, "Shall we not much rather be in subjection unto the Father of spirits?" Our earthly parents were not always perfect in their discipline; therefore, we had "rather" have the discipline of our Heavenly Father; furthermore, if there were good reasons to reverence our earthly father, there are much greater reasons for submitting to our Heavenly Father. "Be in subjection" (Greek *hupotasso*) is stronger than the word used for reverencing our earthly fathers in the first clause; it calls for absolute submission without any qualification (Westcott 402).

God is, after all, the "Father of spirits." The terminology may be drawn from Num. 16:22 and 27:16. "Spirits" should be understood in its broadest sense. God is the Father, the Creator and Source, of all spiritual beings: the spirits or souls of men, whether in the body or out, and the angelic spirits, as well as the new spiritual life which we have when we are born again (Jn. 3:3, 5) and receive the Holy Spirit to dwell in us (Rom. 8:9).

Some have tried to use this phrase as a proof text for the direct creation of the spirit or soul in each individual (Creationism) (Barnes 300; Delitzsch II:318), as opposed to the view that the soul or spirit is passed only through the parents in the conception of the child (Traducianism); but such a fine distinction seems beyond the purpose of this passage. In fact, it is doubtful that the Scriptures address this problem anywhere. They clearly teach that both physical and spiritual elements are passed from parents to children (Rom. 5:12; 1 Cor. 15:22), but how this is done is not discussed (Hughes 531; Lenski 436; Kent 263).

Not only are we to subject ourselves gladly to the Father of spirits, we also do this so that we shall live. Both verbs, "We shall be in subjection" and "We shall live," are expressed in the future tense, but both the subjection and the living starts now and extends into eternity. The implication is also very much present that if we do not submit to His discipline, we will not live. If properly understood and received, this discipline is viewed as an aid for the continuation of our life in Christ (Lenski 438; Clarke 861). Those who have no faith or who abandon the faith will perish, will be eternally separated from God in Hell; but those who continue in the faith will experience the glorious blessings of eternal life. Those who rebel against God's discipline do so to their eternal detriment.

The writer continues (v. 10) the contrast between the discipline of our earthly fathers and that of the Heavenly Father: "For they verily for a few days chastened *us* after their own pleasure; but he for *our* profit, that *we* might be partakers of his holiness." "For" introduces this verse as carrying the thought of v. 9 further. The discipline of our earthly parents was only "for a few days," usually at least the first 18 years of our lives, with various methods of discipline used as we grew older. But in contrast with our eternal relationship with the Father, our disciplinary relationship with our parents was brief.

"They chastened us," or "They were chastening us" (Greek imperfect tense) over some period of time in the past. But it was "after their own pleasure," according to their own thinking, as it seemed good to them. In other words, they did as they pleased with regard to our discipline. Some, no doubt, did better than others. Some were more conscientious than others. But they all made mistakes because they, without exception, were frail human beings subject to the weaknesses of the flesh: sometimes too tired, sometimes too angry, sometimes too concerned about other things to do their best in discipline.

But our earthly parents' discipline is in sharp contrast with that of our Heavenly Father: "he for *our* profit." This expression indicates a movement in the ultimate direction of our profit or benefit. As with God's command to Abraham to offer Isaac, what the possible benefit could be did not at first appear; but when the test was complete it became perhaps the greatest point of victory in his life. The same was true with the sufferings of Job. God's discipline is always just right, not too harsh, but also not too light. He promises never to allow His children "to be tempted [tried, tested] above that ye are able; but will with the temptation also make a way to escape, that ye may be able to bear *it*" (1 Cor. 10:13).

The ultimate benefit that God has in mind for all of us is "that *we* might be partakers of his holiness": literally, "for the purpose of sharing in "His holiness." "Holiness" in the context of suffering, as here, refers to moral or behavioral holiness, the culmination of progressive sanctification (Bruce 359; Kent 264; see also Heb. 2:11; 10:14). Peter made the same point to another group of suffering Christians when he said, "But as he which hath called you is holy, so be ye holy in all manner of conversation [behavior, conduct]; Because it is written, Be ye holy; for I am holy" (1 Pet. 1:15, 16; Lev. 19:2).

c. It produces good results in the end (12:11-13)

11 Now no chastening for the present seemeth to be joyous, but grievous: nevertheless afterward it yieldeth the peaceable fruit of righteousness unto them which are exercised thereby.
12 Wherefore lift up the hands which hang down, and the feeble knees;
13 And make straight paths for your feet, lest that which is lame be turned out of the way; but let it rather be healed.

This is the third point that the writer has made explaining how divine discipline is a means of Christian growth. Here he shows how God's discipline, when it is received with the right attitude, produces outstanding results. He first observes the typical human reaction to discipline: "Now no chastening for the present seemeth to be joyous." In their immaturity, children cannot be given a choice about their discipline, especially whether to receive it. In like manner, God does not normally ask for our input with regard to His discipline (but see 1 Sam. 24:10-14), and that is as it should be. The Scripture says, "Tribulation worketh patience" (Rom. 5:3), but we should not pray, "Lord, I need patience, would you please send tribulation my way." That should be left completely in God's hands.

The contrast emphasized in the verse (Greek *men/de* clauses) is in the time element; on the one hand, receiving no discipline "for the present seemeth to be joyous," but, on the other hand "afterward" it produces grand results and we are glad we received it. In the short run, instead of rejoicing over discipline, it appears to be "grievous." We may very well weep and complain, but that is not the long look.

When we receive God's discipline in the right way, "it yieldeth the peaceable fruit of righteousness." "Yieldeth" (Greek *apodidomi*) means that it pays back what is due; it gives back the desired result. "Fruit of righteousness" means "the fruit which is righteousness" (Greek genitive of apposition), and the righteousness is behavioral, not positional, the practical righteousness that comes through progressive sanctification. The fruit is "peaceable" because it brings a settled calmness to the soul when the discipline is past (Jas. 3:18). When a student takes a test on a hard subject, he may have feelings of struggle and turmoil during the time of testing; but when it is over, and he feels that he has done well, he experiences peace, contentment, and satisfaction. He is not only glad that the test is over; he is also glad that he took it.

But this good fruit of divine discipline is only "unto them which are exercised thereby." If these Hebrew believers decide to abandon Christ and return to Judaism in order to escape persecution, the beneficial results will not come about. In fact, even if they do not go so far as to abandon Christ, but do not endure suffering with the right attitude, the right trust in the Lord, the discipline will not produce its intended result. "Are exercised" (Greek perfect tense) indicates that the results continue after the exercise is over. The writer still carries on the athletic emphasis that he initiated at the beginning of the chapter (see 5:14 also). Only those who fully experience the "exercise" of divine discipline will reap its benefits (see Acts 5:41). Even when the suffering is inflicted at the hands of wicked men, it is still viewed as divine discipline because our sovereign God is in control. And we should also remember that Jesus indicated that in some cases the reward may not be realized until we meet the Lord in Heaven (Mt. 5:10-12).

In vv. 12, 13 the writer closes this section on divine discipline with encouragement based on the words of Scripture: "Wherefore lift up the hands which hang down, and the feeble knees." "Wherefore" indicates that he is making his conclusion about God's discipline based on the arguments that he has made. The admonition is drawn from Is. 35:3. "Hands which hang down" and "feeble knees" picture a discouraged, defeated person. In light of his explanation about the long-term benefits of divine discipline, these Hebrew Christians need to take heart, to reflect a new attitude of encouragement in their bodily posture.

With this positive attitude of encouragement he admonishes, "Make straight paths for your feet," perhaps reflecting the words of Pr. 4:25-27. The "straight" (Greek *orthos*) path is one that is level, with all obstacles removed which might interfere with our Christian progress in the new and living way which Christ inaugurated for us (10:20). "Make" (Greek present tense) calls for continuous effort to keep the path open for unimpeded travel on our way to Heaven: "Keep on making." John the Baptist did this for Jesus. He fulfilled the prophecy of Is. 40:3, "The voice of one crying in the wilderness, Prepare ye the way of the Lord, make his paths straight" (Mt. 3:3). What John did for Jesus we, too, must do, through the help of the Word and the Spirit.

This effort must be kept up in our Christian lives "lest that which is lame be turned out of the way." Mature Christians are to keep the road clear for those who are immature (Gal. 6:1). Jesus strongly warned against offending "one of these little ones," creating a stumbling block that would hinder them on their way to Heaven. The verb "be turned out of the way" (Greek *ektrepo*) can mean, in this context, "be dislocated" (Bauer 246), referring to the further weakening of the "lame limb" (see NIV; NASB; Barnes 303). We must not create stumbling blocks for the "lame," the spiritually immature; we should "let it rather be healed." By taking God's discipline in the right manner, the lame members of the congregation, which may include all of us to some extent, will reap the good benefits which have been discussed and will proceed directly and successfully on their road to Heaven. Such correction will result in a return to the straight and level way, and the crippled limb which was thrown out of joint will be healed.

3. A proper attitude develops good priorities (12:14-17)

Attitudes in our lives, by and large, govern our actions. If we would succeed in the Christian life, we must develop positive attitudes that promote progress and avoid negative attitudes that tend to turn us back. In these verses the writer points to attitudes to be pursued as well as those to be avoided, and he emphasizes Esau's bad example in making such choices.

a. To pursue peace and holiness and avoid bitterness (12:14, 15)

14 Follow peace with all *men*, and holiness, without which no man shall see the Lord:
15 Looking diligently lest any man fail of the grace of God; lest any root of bitterness springing up trouble *you*, and thereby many be defiled.

The writer admonishes a persistent pursuit of both peace and holiness, "Keep on following" or "Keep on pursuing": both words refer to a desirable state which can only be obtained with continuous effort throughout the Christian life. Some commentators think that "peace with all *men*" is primarily applicable to those within the church (Kent 266; Lenski 442). As such the admonition is parallel to Rom. 14:19 instead of Rom. 12:18. But it seems to me that it should be taken in its broader sense (including Rom. 14:19 and Rom. 12:18; Barnes 303). One of the main problems with which the Hebrew Christians would have to deal was their attitude toward their persecutors. Even with them they must strive to have peace, without any hint of compromise of Christian principles, of course. Peter admonished another group of suffering Christians to make sure that their suffering was not deserved, for God will not reward that kind (1 Pet. 2:12-23; 4:12-16).

The "holiness" mentioned here refers to progressive sanctification, the practical or behavioral holiness in our lives which reflects the positional holiness which we have in Christ by faith. There is a definite article in front of the word in the original ("the holiness"), probably referring us back to the holiness of Christ mentioned in v. 10 (Kent 266). Though His holiness is absolute, and ours is very much relative, the goal of the Christian life is to become more and more like Him until the process is complete at His return (1 Jn. 3:2). Jesus Himself admonished us to pursue both peace and purity in the midst of persecution in the Sermon on the Mount (Mt. 5:8-12).

Concerning holiness, the writer adds, "Without which no man shall see the Lord." Someone may ask, "Is the writer suggesting human works as the means of salvation?" The answer is, No; he is suggesting the works of the professed believer as the evidence of his salvation (Jas. 2:20-25). Our works do not save us (Tit. 3:5), nor do they keep us saved (Gal. 3:2, 3), but they do provide a primary verification that our salvation is genuine. In the well-known passage in

Eph. 2:8, 9, Paul declares that salvation is a gift of God, not a work of man, that comes only "by grace . . . through faith." But he also adds that "we are his workmanship, created in Crhist Jesus unto good works, which God hath before ordained that we should walk in them" (Eph. 2:10). If there is no evidence of true holiness in a person's life, then there is also no evidence that he is in Christ.

The writer views such examination of our behavior (toward both those outside and inside the church) essential because eternal consequences may very well develop if these things are ignored: "Looking diligently lest any man fail of the grace of God." "Looking diligently" (Greek *episkopeo*) refers to overseeing something, looking intensely at it with an attitude of care and concern. The very same verb form is used in only one other place, where Peter admonishes the elders, the church leaders, "Feed the flock of God which is among you, *taking the oversight thereof*" (1 Pet. 5:2). The noun form of the same word (Greek *episkopos*) is used to denote the overseer, bishop, or pastor in the church, the one whose duty was to take care of the church of God, even as a shepherd takes care of his sheep (Acts 20:28; 1 Tim. 3:2; Tit. 1:7). The admonition to look diligently calls for continuous examination. Though God will call bishops or pastors to lead the church in this kind of oversight, it is God's will that all Christians share in that responsibility, for we are our brothers' keepers (Gen. 4:9; Gal. 6:1-3).

In this context the purpose of the intense oversight or examination is "lest any man fail of the grace of God." The word translated "fail" (Greek *hustereo*) means "to fall short of" some goal, to stop without finishing a stated end. The continuous action (Greek present tense) suggests that the failure is gradual, that it does not happen overnight. To come short of "the grace of God" is to abandon it, to turn from God's grace, the only source of salvation, to some other way of life. In like manner Paul begged some at Corinth not to receive "the grace of God in vain" (2 Cor. 6:1), and to the Galatians he warned that those who turned back to the law for salvation have "fallen from grace" (Gal. 5:4).

It seems obvious that this passage is referring to the sin of apostasy, as much so as in the other apostasy passages in Hebrews (6:4-6; 10:26-31). For those who hold to the doctrine of unconditional security, the explanation will be the same as on the other passages. Kent (267) maintains that such a person was never saved. He says,

> The reference is to those who may have made a beginning in the Christian community, but may through fear of persecution or faintheartedness in suffering be tempted to defect and thus fall short of true salvation. They would be shut out of the blessings provided by God's saving grace, and demonstrate to all that they really had never been made new creatures in Christ.

Yeager, on the other hand, seems just as sure that such a person is truly a child of God, but has become backslidden and will thus cause problems within the congregation and lose his rewards, but not become apostate (447). Barnes, who takes the warning as hypothetical, indicates that they were apparently saved, but that the writer never says that they can actually fall from grace (304); such a warning is merely God's means of preventing apostasy.

The writer of Hebrews, however, exhibits no such concerns about unconditional security. He strongly implies that he is speaking about saved people, and that if they continue in this wrong direction they will not enjoy the blessings of grace in eternity. He is taking the same position as in the other apostasy passages in the epistle. In 6:4-6 the apostates could not come back to Christ because there was no more repentance; in 10:26-31 there was no more sacrifice; here there is no more grace (see also 3:12). The writer is consistent in his message to apostates.

Falling short of God's grace bears eternal consequences for the individual, but the writer is also concerned about the effect on the church as a whole. They should keep looking diligently "lest any root of bitterness springing up trouble *you,* and thereby many be defiled." The language seems to be an allusion to Dt. 29:18 in the Septuagint. The "root" of bitterness "springing up" is horticultural language. As in the process of the sprouting of a plant, the growth of this root of bitterness is gradual. It may start as a small complaint, a slight dissatisfaction, but like a small ivy plant at the root of a tree it will soon engulf and destroy if allowed to grow unhindered. Parallel to the progressive growth of this root of bitterness is the possibility that it will "trouble" (Greek present tense) *you*, that it will keep on troubling you as long as it is allowed to grow in your midst, "and thereby many" will be "defiled." The disease is contagious. All that can be done to prevent its occurrence must be put into action. Once it sets in, it can spread rapidly. One of our old sayings warns, "One rotten apple will spoil a whole barrel." Paul used a similar proverb, "A little leaven leaveneth the whole lump" (1 Cor. 5:6). The smallest evidence of bitterness in a believer's life must be rooted out before it can take hold. Devotion to the constant pursuit of peace and holiness (v. 14) will slow the growth of that root of bitterness and eventually eliminate it.

b. To note the tragic example of Esau (12:16, 17)

16 Lest there *be* any fornicator, or profane person, as Esau, who for one morsel of meat sold his birthright.
17 For ye know how that afterward, when he would have inherited the blessing, he was rejected: for he found no place of repentance, though he sought it carefully with tears.

We deal with vv. 16 and 17 separately for convenience, and in fact a separate point is being made. But v. 16 is actually the third object of "looking diligently" in v. 15. The Hebrews were to look diligently to prevent anyone from falling short of God's grace, from allowing a root of bitterness to grow in their hearts, and from anyone like Esau developing in the congregation.

They are to keep on looking diligently "lest there *be* any fornicator, or profane person, as Esau." Many commentators think that the word fornicator does not apply to Esau since they can find no direct characterization of him in this light in the O.T. (Westcott 407; Bruce 366). But it seems very unnatural in the construction to try to separate the designations, taking the first as independent of the second, though they are connected by "or." It is much more natural to take both "fornicator" and "profane" as describing Esau (so Barnes 305; Lenski 447; Morris 540; Delitzsch II:333). The writer probably sees Esau as a fornicator with regard to his disappointing marriages to at least two wives of Canaanite descent and to the daughter of Ishmael (Gen. 26:34, 35; 28:8, 9; 36:1-3). Concerning the Canaanite marriages as recorded in Genesis, Keil and Delitzsch observe, "Esau by these marriages furnished another proof how thoroughly his heart was set upon earthly things" (II:272). The fornication to which the writer refers, if it is especially meant as a description of these unadvised marriages of Esau, would include both literal and spiritual fornication (see the idea in Jas. 4:4). The fact that these women of Canaan worshiped idols and served pagan gods seemed to make no difference to him.

The writer also describes Esau as "profane" (Greek *bebelos*), meaning that he was totally secular, earth-bound, worldly. This description pairs up remarkably with his identification as a fornicator. Esau was totally in love with this world and the pleasures that it offers, and as a result he had no control over his physical desires. The women of Canaan were, no doubt, physically beautiful, sexually appealing. Since Esau apparently did not consider spiritual values in the choices he made, he did not hesitate to marry such women. Jewish writers contemporary with this epistle and later give abundant testimony to Esau's immorality and worldliness.

The writer observes the sad result of Esau's way of thinking and living: "who for one morsel of meat sold his birthright." He is referring to the account in Gen. 25:29-34. Though Jacob and Esau were twins, with Esau born first, the two boys were as different as day and night. As they grew, Esau became a man of the fields and the woods, an outdoorsman, a great hunter, a man who lived for his appetites. Jacob, on the other hand, was industrious; he saw the importance of planning for the long term. Knowing full well his brother's shortcomings, Jacob prepared a big pot of what we might call vegetable soup, aromatic to the smell and delicious to the taste. Coming home empty-handed, the brave hunter was famished, and under pressure from Jacob he willingly traded his birthright, his advantage as the first born, for a bowl of the soup.

"Meat" (Greek *brosis*) refers to food of any kind. It was only a "morsel of meat," a small amount, only one meal. For such a paltry amount, Esau "sold his birthright," he gave it up by means of such a meager trade. For anyone who has any sense of value, or who has any amount of restraint on the physical appetites, the trade makes no sense. But to Esau, with his warped reasoning, it made perfectly good sense. He was so hungry that he felt he would die without some food immediately; what good is an inheritance to a dead man (Gen. 25:32)?

The writer follows the story further: "For ye know how that afterward, when he would have inherited the blessing, he was rejected." He introduces the continuation with, "For ye know." These Hebrew Christians were well read in the O.T., so they were familiar with the story. In the patriarchal system, the inheritance consisted of both a birthright—representing at least a double portion of the physical inheritance—and a blessing—representing spiritual and family leadership. Esau had given up the birthright in his foolish trade with Jacob, perhaps when they were 20 to 30 years of age.

This second incident occurred at least 40 years "afterward" (see Gen. 26:34). Esau thought that his opportunity had arrived. At the age of about 100, Isaac felt that death might be near, especially because of his deteriorating health and blindness. Therefore, he called Esau in as his oldest son, and his favorite (Gen. 25:28), with the determination to grant him the blessing after he had eaten of Esau's freshly killed and prepared venison. This is the occasion, according to our writer, "when he would have inherited the blessing." Esau must have been elated as he went out to enjoy his greatest hunting trip ever. Having overheard Isaac's plan, however, Rebekah and Jacob conspired to deceive Isaac. With his bare arms and neck covered with animal skins to mimic Esau's hairy body, wearing Esau's woodsy odor and bearing the quickly prepared goat meat, Jacob duped blind Isaac into bestowing on him the blessing.

Two unknown factors might help us in evaluating this situation: (1) Did Rebekah share with Isaac God's revelation, when she was carrying the twins, that the older would serve the younger, that Jacob rather than Esau was God's chosen heir (Gen. 25:20-23)? (2) Did Isaac know about the agreement that Esau and Jacob had made about the birthright? The answer to neither of the questions is given in Scripture. Surely Rebekah told her husband about this important revelation from God that would so affect the future nation of Israel! If she did, that makes Isaac's attempt to give the blessing to Esau, in spite of God's revelation, nothing less than an act of rebellion. It may be less likely that Jacob or Esau told him about the trading of the birthright, both being embarrassed about the incident for different reasons. But the episode is another clear sign that God is in control. His sovereign will will be accomplished regardless of human interference.

Though we cannot condone Jacob's deception in either the birthright or the blessing (after all his name meant "heel-catcher," by implication "deceiver"), both incidents show how Jacob gave priority to that which is highly valued over the long term, not that which lasts only for a moment. The implication that Isaac had learned about God's revelation to Rebekah is seen in the fact that he placed his stamp of approval on Jacob's receiving the blessing, in spite of his deception. When Isaac became aware of the ruse on the arrival of Esau, he said, "I have eaten of all before thou camest, and have blessed him? yea, *and* he shall be blessed" (Gen. 27:33). When Esau made his pitiful plea to Isaac, our writer observes, "He was rejected." Though some physical blessings were granted to Esau, the primary blessing was gone, and gone forever.

The writer continues, "For he found no place of repentance, though he sought it carefully with tears." The "repentance" (Greek *metanoia*), the change of mind which Esau found no place for, was his own (Delitzsch II:336; Westcott 407; Lenski 447), not Isaac's (Lunemann 453). Esau could not repent because Isaac would not allow it, just as the apostate cannot repent (Heb. 6:4-6) because God will not allow it. The Genesis account said that Esau, when he heard about the deception, "cried with a great and exceeding bitter cry" (27:34); and when he continued to beg for at least some small blessing, Scripture says that "he lifted up his voice, and wept" (Gen. 27:38). But all the begging and weeping did not bring back the birthright and the blessing.

Commentators disagree widely over how to apply this passage. Kent (267) and others who deny the possibility of apostasy of anyone truly saved think that it has no application in relation to salvation. Even Lenski, who does believe that the main apostasy passages teach the real possibility of apostasy for true believers, nevertheless does not think that this passage has any reference to apostasy. He thinks that it is simply saying that some things that happen in the Christian congregation cannot be changed, that the effects of bad attitudes and bad behavior do damage that cannot be undone (447). Westcott, who also holds that Hebrews teaches the possibility of apostasy for believers, does not make himself clear on the application of this passage (407). Other commentators who believe that Hebrews teaches apostasy as a real possibility, but who maintain that apostates, in all cases, were never saved, argue that the passage does clearly and aptly apply to the sin of apostasy as they see it (Bruce 366; Morris 540).

Barnes, who holds to the hypothetical position on the apostasy passages, does say, however, "This passage, therefore, is in accordance with the doctrine more than once stated before in this epistle, that if a Christian should really apostatize it would be impossible that he should be saved" (307).

Perhaps one of the main reasons that those who believe that Hebrews teaches the possibility of apostasy of true Christians hesitate to apply this passage to that subject is the statement in v. 17 that Esau "found no place of repentance, though he sought it carefully with tears." They are rightly bothered by the picture of an apostate begging to be taken back by the Lord, but being refused. Three facts are against this occurring: (1) Jesus said, "Him that cometh to me I will in no wise cast out." This statement does not seem to be in line with someone genuinely wanting to repent, but being refused by the Lord. (2) Hebrews 6:4-6 says, "*It is* impossible . . . to renew them again unto repentance" who have fallen away into apostasy. This passage implies that apostates will have no desire to repent. (3) If apostasy is one form of the sin against the Holy Spirit, as I believe it is, apostates cannot repent because the Spirit has been taken from them. God is always the instrument of repentance and salvation (Jn. 6:44).

I believe that there is a solution that will take care of these objections. These verses about Esau are an illustration, a parable, if you please. As with all parables, one should center on the main point and avoid pressing all the details into some kind of doctrinal teaching. The main point of this illustration about Esau is that bad spiritual choices can be made in our lives which cannot be corrected. It is, indeed, possible for Christians to go beyond the point of repentance, just as Esau made bad choices about the birthright and the blessing which could not be corrected. Since this is a parable or an illustration, however, not all the details in the story can be doctrinally applied. Esau's bad choices about the birthright and the blessing are not the same as personal salvation choices. A story about a nonsalvation circumstance is being used to illustrate a salvation truth. Esau's seeking for a place of repentance, in context, was only in relation to obtaining the blessing; therefore, his seeking it carefully with tears was in relation to that too, not to repentance with regard to salvation (Delitzsch II:337).

Even so, these Hebrew Christians should take note: The spiritual decision which some were considering—to abandon Christ and return to Judaism to avoid persecution—would prove to be a drastic choice. They must put that kind of thinking aside before going any further toward such a foolish solution. Such a decision would take them to the point where the cry, "Too late, too late," would apply to them.

One other thing might help alleviate this problem. When the writer says in the last clause that Esau "found no place of repentance, though he sought it carefully with tears," the "it" may not refer back to "repentance" (but see Alford 249), but rather to "the blessing" mentioned earlier in the verse, especially in light of Gen. 27:34, 38 (Bruce 368; Calvin 328; Westcott 409). But the meaning is basically the same either way. If "it" does refer to repentance, the repentance that Esau was seeking was being able to secure the blessing after it had been given to Jacob (Hagner 223; Hughes 541). Thus, both possible antecedents are involved either way.

4. Fifth warning: against the more severe consequences of departing from Mt. Zion (12:18-29)

The writer issues his fifth and final warning in 12:18-29. He bases this warning on a contrast between the awesome scene of Mt. Sinai, where the law of Moses was given, the even more terrible scene of Mt. Zion, representing the place where Jesus died and rose again, where the new covenant was instituted.

a. The threat to Israel at ancient Sinai (12:18-21)

18 For ye are not come unto the mount that might be touched, and that burned with fire, nor unto blackness, and darkness, and tempest,
19 And the sound of a trumpet, and the voice of words; which *voice* they that heard intreated that the word should not be spoken to them any more:
20 (For they could not endure that which was commanded, And if so much as a beast touch the mountain, it shall be stoned, or thrust through with a dart:
21 And so terrible was the sight, *that* Moses said, I exceedingly fear and quake:)

The contrast which our writer presents in this section is that between the old covenant and the new covenant, one he has emphasized throughout the epistle. In 2:1-3 it was a contrast between the word spoken by angels and that which was first spoken by the Lord. In 3:5, 6 the contrast was between Moses as a servant and Christ as a Son. In 7:11—8:5, the temporary Levitical priesthood was contrasted with the permanent priesthood of Christ according to the order of Melchisedec. In 8:6-13 the writer contrasted the old covenant and the new. In 9:1-11 he contrasted the old tabernacle and the new. In 9:12—10:18 he contrasted the ineffective sacrifice of bulls and goats and the eternally effective sacrifice of Jesus Christ. Here that comparison and contrast is made again with Mt. Sinai (though the name itself is not mentioned) representing the law and Mt. Zion representing the new covenant. The language which the writer uses in vv. 18-21 is drawn from Ex. 19:11-25; 20:18-21; Dt. 4:10-15, 32-36; and 5:32, 33. He does not quote these passages directly, but he uses the language of the passages.

Verses 18-24 form one long sentence contrasting the old covenant and the new. The writer says, "For ye are not come unto the mount that might be touched," referring to Mt. Sinai, of course, where the law was given to Moses. "Ye are not come" indicates that they did not come to remain at Sinai (Lenski 450). Their forefathers did indeed come to Sinai, as recorded in the O.T., but he never meant for them to stay there physically or spiritually. The law served a purpose in its time, but now that the new covenant has arrived they must not return to Sinai.

It was a mountain "that might be touched," in contrast to the spiritual Mt. Zion which cannot be touched. One mountain symbolized a covenant which stressed *externals*, things that are *visible*, the other mountain symbolized a covenant that stresses what is *internal* and *invisible* (Calvin 331; Lenski 452). Though it was, indeed, a real mountain that might be touched, they were, nevertheless, forbidden to touch it (Ex. 19:12, 13), as the writer will point out in v. 20. Moses and Aaron did touch the mountain, and came up on it to receive the commandments (Ex. 19:20-25), but the people were not to touch it. The holy place where the law was given was off limits to them.

Nor have the Hebrews come to that Sinai which "burned with fire" (Ex. 19:18; Dt. 4:11, 15), "nor unto blackness, and darkness, and tempest" (Dt. 4:11; Ex. 19:18), which continues to describe the scene at Sinai. Furthermore, they have also not come to "the sound of a trumpet" (Ex. 19:16; 20:18), "and the voice of words" (Ex. 19:19; Dt. 4:12; 5:22); "which voice they that heard intreated that the word should not be spoken to them any more" (Ex. 20:18, 19; Dt. 5:25-27). The language paints a scene of dread and fear throughout. What a joy to know that, through the incarnation of God's Son, Jesus Christ, we rejoice in the Gospel message He left with us and long to be near Him and hear His voice once more.

In vv. 20, 21 the writer adds a further, parenthetical explanation of the scene at Sinai: "For they could not endure that which was commanded." This is an extension of his observation about God's voice in v. 19 and still reflects Ex. 20:18, 19 and Dt. 5:25-27. "And if so much as a beast touch the mountain, it shall be stoned, or thrust through with a dart" (Ex. 19:12, 13). "And so terrible was the sight, *that* Moses said, I exceedingly fear and quake": The punctuation indicates that the sentence has not ended, and in fact goes on through v. 24. Though these exact words spoken by Moses are not recorded in the O.T., Kent (211) suggests three possibilities. (1) The quotation may reflect an extrabiblical Jewish tradition with which our writer was familiar. We do see other places in the N.T. where such sources are acknowledged. (2) The quotation may summarize several different passages which reflect the understandable attitude of Moses on that occasion. See Dt. 9:19, for example, and compare Acts 7:32.

(3) The Scripture does say that, when the awesome display took place on Sinai on the third day after Moses had come down from the mountain, that "all the people that *was* in the camp trembled" (Ex. 19:16), and Moses was apparently among them at this point.

b. The awesome position of the New Testament believer (12:22-24)

22 But ye are come unto mount Sion, and unto the city of the living God, the heavenly Jerusalem, and to an innumerable company of angels,
23 To the general assembly and church of the firstborn, which are written in heaven, and to God the Judge of all, and to the spirits of just men made perfect,
24 And to Jesus the mediator of the new covenant, and to the blood of sprinkling, that speaketh better things than *that of* Abel.

Our writer now depicts an equally dynamic scene with regard to Mt. Zion. This mountain or ridge was also a literal place within the boundaries of the city of Jerusalem. It was originally a fortress without the ancient city of Jerusalem when David took it from the Jebusites, and he designated it "the city of David" (2 Sam. 5:6-9). It was often used in the O.T. to represent the broader city of Jerusalem itself (Ps. 126:1; Is. 1:26, 27). But the writer is using it here in a figurative sense to symbolize the new covenant, with its heavenly counterparts, in pointed contrast with Mt. Sinai, which symbolized the old covenant.

It appears that there are seven phrases or descriptions used by the writer to describe both Sinai and Zion (Hughes 545). "But" (Greek *alla*) introduces a strong contrast between earthly Sinai and heavenly Zion. "Ye are come" (Greek perfect tense) "unto mount Sion" indicates that we have come here to stay. Our arrival at Zion will only be perfected when the temporal aspects of the new covenant become eternal. It offers a foretaste of glory divine. In contrast, we have not come to Sinai (same verb negated in v. 18). It was only a stop along the way. The law was added because of sin. It was only the schoolmaster to bring us to Christ.

This is not, however, earthly Zion. We have rather come to "the city of the living God, the heavenly Jerusalem." It is the city that Abraham was looking for in his journey through the earthly land of promise (11:10, 16), and the city to come for which we are still seeking in our earthly journey (13:14). It is the "Jerusalem which is above . . . which is the mother of us all" (Gal. 4:26), as well as that great city, the holy Jerusalem which John saw "descending out of heaven from God" in his vision of the events of the last days (Rev. 21:2, 10).

The writer uses the phrase "the living God" several times. He warns the Hebrews about "departing from the living God" (3:12), encourages them, with purged consciences, "to serve the living God" (9:14), and urges them to avoid falling "into the hands of the living God" (10:31). "The heavenly Jerusalem" is, indeed, His city, as well as ours to share with Him, for in it we, as believers, will fully experience eternal life in His presence. Because He is the living God, we will live also.

We have also come "to an innumerable company of angels." The word translated "an innumerable company"

(Greek *murias*) literally means "ten thousand," but it is used figuratively in Scripture to represent a very large number, not exactly defined (Bauer 529), myriads of angels. Angels did their work at Sinai, as well, where they were evidently mediators of the law (Acts 7:53; Gal. 3:19), but here they aid in bringing the redemptive work of Christ to its ultimate conclusion. Angels ministered to our Lord in His earthly work (Mt. 4:11; Lk. 22:43), aided in the ministry of the early church (Acts 5:19; 8:26; 10:3; 12:7; 27:23), and continue to promote God's cause in the world today (Mt. 18:10; Heb. 13:2). They will accompany Christ at His return (Mt. 13:42, 49; 16:27; 24:30, 31; 25:31; 2 Th. 1:7), and will lead in witnessing God's judgment and praising His name in Heaven (Dan. 7:10; Rev. 5:11; 7:11). Revelation 5:11, in particular, seems to picture a very similar scene when John says, "I heard the voice of many angels round about the throne . . . and the number of them was ten thousand times ten thousand, and thousands of thousands."

Most commentators feel that the phrase, "the general assembly" goes better with this description of the angels rather than with the church in the next phrase, as in the KJV. If so, we would read, "to an innumerable company of angels in festal assembly," a celebratory gathering like that pictured in Rev. 5:11 (so NIV; see also Job 1:6; Hughes 545; Lenski 456; Barnes 310; Calvin 333; Bruce 375; Westcott 414, Delitzsch II:349). As the above references show, Christians do not worship angels, but we do share with them, both now and in eternity, in praising our Lord for His perfection of the plan of redemption.

Furthermore, we have come "to the general assembly and church of the firstborn." If the "general assembly" does go with the reference to the church (NASB; Henry VI:959; Lunemann 462), it emphasizes the fact that the writer is alluding to the church universal, whether gathered figuratively on earth or literally in Heaven. "Church" (Greek *ekklesia*), referring to "those who are called out" of the world for God's special purposes, is used only one other time in Hebrews. In 2:12 the writer quotes Ps. 22:22, "I will declare thy name unto my brethren, in the midst of the church will I sing praise unto thee." These words are prophetically placed in the mouth of Messiah, the Son of David, as He testifies to His willing identification with His brethren. In the O.T. setting the "church" would be the "congregation" of Israel, and that is the translation in the O.T. passage. Though the N.T. church did not begin until the day of Pentecost (Acts 2), when the Holy Spirit descended as had been promised, God's people who are saved by faith have existed since the time of the fall.

The church here is the church "of the firstborn." In Hebrew tradition the firstborn son received a double portion of the inheritance (Joseph through his sons Ephraim and Manasseh, for example), or in some cases basically all the inheritance (Isaac from Abraham). The firstborn received very special treatment, and it seems likely that our writer uses the term in this sense. In the O.T. Israel was God's firstborn (Ex. 4:22, 23); and now, in the NT, the church, individually and collectively, is God's firstborn through Jesus Christ.

Commentators debate whether this is referring to the universal church in Heaven, or the church which is still on earth. Some think that it is a reference to saints who are already present with the Lord in Heaven, whether primarily believers under the old covenant (Lunemann 463; Calvin 334)—whose example of faith was emphasized in chapter 11—or early believers in the N.T. church, including martyrs like Stephen and James, the brother of John (Conybeare and Howson 816), or both (Henry VI:959). Two things weigh heavily against this interpretation. The first is the next phrase, "Which are written in heaven." "Which are written" (Greek perfect tense) emphasizes the completion of the act with continuing results. The names were written in the past, through God's foreknowledge and predestination (Rom. 8:28; Rev. 17:8), and they will stand written through all time unless, because of apostasy, their names should be blotted out (Ex. 32:32, 33; Rev. 3:5; see Lenski 458). It does not seem likely that this observation about their names being written in Heaven would be made about people who are already there. Furthermore, the same thing is said, precisely, about living believers when Jesus admonishes the 70 disciples to rejoice that their names "are written in heaven" (Lk. 10:20). There it is clearly a reference to the church still on earth, and it is likely that our writer has the same connotation in mind (see also Dan. 12:1; Phil. 4:3; Rev. 21:27).

The second reason that this probably refers to the church on earth is that the church in Heaven is clearly emphasized in the later description, "To the spirits of just men made perfect." The word "church" occurs only twice in the Gospels: the first to the universal church (Mt. 16:18), and the second to the local church (Mt. 18:17). Here in Hebrews the writer is observing that this local congregation of Hebrew Christians, who are being persecuted, has come, in their life for Christ, to the church universal, the church now living, witnessing, and praying for them all over the world.

They have also come "to God the Judge of all." Some suggest that, because of the order of the words in the original, we should read, "To the Judge, the God of all" (Kent 273), but the meaning is basically the same either way. Our sovereign God is in complete charge of ultimate judgment, both now and in eternity. In His office as Judge, he both vindicates and rewards (1 Cor. 3:10-15; 2 Th. 1:4-10). If the readers are thinking of escaping persecution through abandoning Christ and returning to Judaism, they must know that they will bring upon themselves wrath and judgment that are much more severe than anything they might suffer at the hands of men.

Furthermore, they have come also "to the spirits of just men made perfect." These are "spirits" because they are no longer in their earthly bodies; they are "absent from the body, and . . . present with the Lord" (2 Cor. 5:8). At the resurrection they will receive new bodies (2 Cor. 5:1-9), incorruptible bodies no longer subject to age or decay because death has been "swallowed up in victory" (1 Cor. 15:51-57). But here they are viewed in the intermediate state anxiously but joyously awaiting the coming of that great day. They are "just men" from the viewpoint of their relation with Jesus Christ on earth (10:38). They have lived the life of faith and are now enjoying their rest and reward in the presence of Christ. That they have been "made perfect" (Greek perfect tense) indicates a completed act with continuing result or status. Their state of perfection or completeness will now last forever. They already had perfect standing on earth through their position in Jesus Christ (10:14), now they have claimed the total perfection they have been reaching for by their presence with Christ in glory (6:1). They are now like Him, because they "see him as he is" (1 Jn. 3:2). This group includes the just men and women under both covenants. We are divided by the cross on earth, but we are united by the cross in Heaven.

They have also come "to Jesus the mediator of the new covenant." Throughout this epistle the writer often emphasizes "Jesus" (Jehovah will save), the human name of our Lord, to stress the importance of the incarnation in His redemptive work (see 2:9; 4:14; 6:20; 7:22; 10:19; 12:2). From eternity He has been our God (Jn. 1:1). All things were made by Him (Jn. 1:3). But only in His incarnation has He become our Savior (Jn. 1:14). It is through His humanity, and on the basis of His redemptive work, that He is able to serve as "mediator" (Greek *mesites*), one who comes between two parties who stand in need of reconciliation. The two parties involved in redemptive mediation are a holy and offended God and rebellious and offending mankind. In earthly mediation the art of negotiation is often involved. In this mediation, however, there is no room for negotiation. The supreme price for sin must be paid, and only our Lord can make that payment.

In 8:6 He was presented as "the mediator of a *better covenant*, which was established upon better promises," but here as the mediator of "the new covenant." The word "new" is different from the word previously used by the writer for the new covenant (8:8, 13; 9:15). The word used there (Greek *kainos*) means new in relation to quality or substance. It is, indeed, a new covenant because it is a better covenant with better promises. The word here (Greek *neos*) means new with regard to time, the recentness of its existence (Westcott 417). These Hebrew Christians must realize that the old covenant mediated by Moses is no longer valid. This newly established covenant through Jesus Christ is their only effective means for reaching God. They must not consider turning away from it, regardless of how severe the persecution may become.

Finally, they have come "to the blood of sprinkling, that speaketh better things than *that* of Abel." "The blood of sprinkling" is, of course, the blood of Christ, which the writer refers to in the language of various special O.T. offerings—especially that of the Day of Atonement when the blood of the sacrifice was sprinkled on the mercy seat inside the Holy of Holies (see 9:19-22; 10:22). But the effectiveness of that blood only lasted for one year, because it had to be repeated when the next Day of Atonement came around. In remarkable contrast, the blood of Christ is good for all time, never needing repetition.

This blood also "speaketh better things than *that* of Abel." Our writer is, no doubt, recalling his earlier reference to Abel as one of the heroes of faith from the O.T. who left his witness in his obedient sacrifice, and through it, "he being dead yet speaketh" (11:4). But the blood of Jesus our Savior speaks louder. It speaks of "better things" because Abel's blood served as only a witness of faith; our Lord's blood serves as the very basis of faith for people of all ages, both those under the old covenant and those under the new. Furthermore, this voice "speaketh" (Greek present tense) continually; it is ever there for those who would listen. There was a voice at Sinai which was awesome and threatening, one which made those present want to run away. But there was a more powerful voice at Calvary, a voice which makes us want to draw near through faith in Jesus Christ.

c. The solemn consequences for those who turn away from Christ (12:25-29)

The writer reminds his Hebrew readers of all they have as Christians, what encouragement they have concerning the promise of Heaven, those who have already gone there, the help of angels, the church around us, and most of all the mediation of our Lord who died for us. In light of this reminder, they have every reason to remain steadfast in the face of whatever persecution may come their way. But should they still consider abandoning Christ, they need one more reminder of the severe consequences.

(1) Warning about God's final revelation (12:25-27)

25 See that ye refuse not him that speaketh. For if they escaped not who refused him that spake on earth, much more *shall not* we *escape*, if we turn away from him that *speaketh* from heaven:
26 Whose voice then shook the earth: but now he hath promised, saying, Yet once more I shake not the earth only, but also heaven.
27 And this *word*, Yet once more, signifieth the removing of those things that are shaken, as of things that are made, that those things which cannot be shaken may remain.

On the basis of what has been said, the writer issues his solemn warning, "See that ye refuse not him that speaketh." "Him that speaketh," or "the one who is speaking," refers back to v. 24, to Jesus the Mediator whose blood speaks much better things than that of Abel. As there, it is in continuous action (Greek present tense). He continues to speak through this epistle and the rest of the New Testament. Likewise, the admonition "see" (Greek present tense) calls for continuous concern about this matter, "Keep on taking heed," "Keep on watching." (The same word was used for a similar warning at the beginning of 3:12.) They should continue to take heed lest they "refuse" the one who is speaking. The verb indicates a definite decision (Greek aorist tense), a pointed departure from the faith they had embraced. In Lk. 14:18 the same word is used by those who turned down the privileged invitation to the great supper. Luke says, "They all with one *consent* began *to make excuse*." What an insult to turn down such a special invitation! But these Hebrew Christians are considering just that.

The writer again compares the *lesser* to the *greater*, as he does several times in the epistle (2:2, 3; 9:14; 10:29; 12:9): "For if they escaped not who refused him that spake on earth, much more *shall not* we *escape*, if we turn away from him that *speaketh* from heaven." "For" is causal, introducing the statement which follows as a justification for the warning at the front of the verse. Those "who refused him that spake on earth" were the Israelites at Sinai. Their act of refusal was not in their fear of and shrinking from God's voice at Sinai, but in their construction of the golden calf when Moses was communicating with

God on the mountain. Their fearful shrinking might have said something about their inner faith, but it was their act of disobedience that brought God's wrath and punishment (see Ex. 32:25-29). Thus "they escaped not" for their sin at Sinai. God "spake on earth" in giving the law in that He met with Moses on Sinai and the ordinances that He gave him there specifically applied to Israel for life on this earth. "Him that spake" (Greek *chrematizo*) refers to a divine message or communication, whether positive or negative. It is used in 11:7 when Noah was *warned of God* about the coming flood.

Now the writer makes his contrast: "Much more *shall not* we *escape*, if we turn away from him that *speaketh* from heaven." Those who were guilty of capital disobedience under the law of Moses, like those who built the golden calf, paid with their lives (Ex. 32). Those who continuously rebel against "him that *speaketh* from heaven"—with the Gospel message of redemption centered in God's Son who came down from Heaven—will face a more severe punishment, even spiritual death and eternal separation from God (see 10:29). Note that the writer, by using "we," includes himself in the warning. It is perhaps a sympathetic identification because of his great care and concern for his readers, but it also shows how seriously he takes the warning. The same judgment applies to all.

"If we turn away" (Greek present tense) from him is expressed in continuous action, "If we keep turning away from him." The implication is that the action has already started (Westcott 418). Their backsliding has not reached the point of apostasy, but their attitude needs to be corrected before it results in that dire consequence. The abbreviated nature of the last clause in the original, as indicated by the five words in italics in our English Bible (v. 25), adds to the emphasis of the declaration. The words supplied are appropriate to the context.

In v. 26 the writer continues the thought from the first part of v. 25, with the warning about refusal and rebellion as somewhat of a parenthesis: "whose voice then shook the earth." "Voice" refers back to "him that speaketh" in the beginning of the previous verse. It was the voice of God which originally spoke from Sinai, but it is that same voice which speaks to the church today through the Gospel. At the very beginning of the epistle, the writer explained that God spoke, under the old covenant, "unto the fathers by the prophets," but that He has "in these last days spoken unto us by *his* Son" (1:1, 2). It was God's voice in both places, and in both places the voice demands respect and obedience. But this voice from Heaven under the new covenant is God's final word.

The writer continues, "But now he hath promised, saying, Yet once more I shake not the earth only, but also heaven." The quotation is from Hag. 2:6 in the Septuagint, with some minor variations. "But" introduces the promise quoted as in contrast with the shaking that occurred at Sinai. That shaking (Ex. 19:18) was only local, both geographically limited to that area and nationally limited to Israel. But this shaking prophesied by Haggai will be universal. "Now" further contrasts that dispensation—represented by Sinai—with this dispensation—represented by Zion. "He hath promised" presents the promise as having been made in the past, as indicated by the quotation from Haggai, but still standing in the present (Greek perfect tense). Although the quotation seems to involve a catastrophic prediction, it is still viewed as a promise to God's people since it points toward the victory of God's cause and the permanence of His kingdom.

In the context of the quotation from Haggai, the contrast is also with Sinai, when Israel "came out of Egypt" (Hag. 2:5). Haggai was delivering God's Word to Zerubbabel, the appointed governor of Judah, and Joshua, the high priest, with regard to the restoration Temple. Though the prospects of the new Temple did not look great, God looked ahead to a future Temple which would be even more glorious and would bring nations together around a common goal (Hag. 2:7). In the context of Haggai, Zerubbabel seems to stand as a type of Christ (Hag. 2:23). Just as in Haggai, the voice that shook Sinai is in contrast ("yet once more") with a shaking that will be universal: "I shake not the earth only, but also heaven." Commentators disagree widely about how our writer means this quotation to be applied. Some take Haggai's prophecy of the shaking of both the earth and Heaven to have been figuratively fulfilled in the Gospel of Christ and its power to change both individuals and societies all over the world (Calvin 337; Henry VI:960; Pink 1070; Whedon 140; Barnes 313). Many commentators, however, do not feel that a figurative fulfillment does justice to the prophecy. The shaking at Sinai was literal, and they feel that the prophecy calls for a parallel fulfillment in a literal manner in connection with the events prophesied at the end of time (Kent 273; Lunemann 467; Morris 144; MacArthur 417; Westcott 419; Lenski 463; Alford 257; Bruce 382). Other commentators think the fulfillment is to be seen primarily in our Lord's first coming and in the universal spread of the Gospel, but they also see a secondary fulfillment in the complete arrival of God's kingdom at the end of time (Kistemaker 398; Clarke 863).

I would suggest a fourth approach as a distinct possibility: that the primary fulfillment is in the climactic events of this dispensation in connection with the return of Christ, which are so graphically prophesied in other passages of Scripture; but that secondary implications are also seen with regard to our Lord's first coming, which did, indeed, bring the removal of the Jewish sacrificial system, the Levitical priesthood, and all obligation to the ceremonial law. Hughes (558) and Westcott (421) seem to subscribe to this approach. Even Kent, who emphasizes the fulfillment of the prophecy at the end of time (the eschatological approach), admits that there may be some inference here "that the author already regards the last days as upon them" (276).

Several passages depict a grand and universal earthquake at the end of time, accompanied by phenomenal convulsions of the heavens (Mt. 24:29; 2 Pet. 3:10-13; Rev. 6:12-14). This removal of Heaven and earth as we now know them is to be combined with the appearance of a new Heaven and a new earth which cannot be destroyed (Is. 65:17-25; 2 Pet. 3:13; Rev. 21:1-3). This is, no doubt, Haggai's primary meaning and our writer's primary application. Even so, there may be some figurative fulfillment with regard to the tremendous changes brought about by the first coming of Christ and the spread of the Gospel. The implications of such a figurative application would certainly fit in with the point that the writer is making here. Some of them are considering returning to the Jewish sacrifices and priesthood along with the law given at Sinai, but our writer suggests that those things have been shaken by the appearance of Christ and the Gospel to the point of their final removal. They were never intended to be permanent, and the upheaval caused by the power of the Gospel has taken them away.

Such a double fulfillment of prophecy is frequently seen in Scripture, whether denoted as a partial and complete fulfillment, a figurative and a literal fulfillment, or by some other appropriate terminology. A good example would be Peter's application of Jl. 2:28-32 to the unique events that occurred on the Day of Pentecost when the Holy Spirit descended upon the church. Along with the earthly phenomena that accompanied the reception of the Spirit, the prophecy also calls for "wonders in heaven above, and signs in the earth beneath; blood, and fire, and vapour of smoke: The sun shall be turned into darkness, and the moon into blood, before that great and notable day of the Lord come" (Acts 2:16-21). Without Peter's inspired application, perhaps we would apply this prophecy only to the Second Coming; but as it is, we usually suggest that the literal fulfillment of the entire passage awaits the end of time. I am suggesting that same possibility with the prophecy from Haggai.

The writer continues (v. 26) with his application of the prophecy: "And this *word*, Yet once more, signifieth the removing of those things that are shaken, as of things that are made, that those things which cannot be shaken may remain."

This *word*—the phrase "Yet once more"—is from the quotation of Hag. 2:6. The writer uses a device that he has used before, selecting a text from an O.T. passage he has quoted and preaching on it, so to speak. In chapter 2 he quoted Ps. 8:5-7 and isolated the phrase "made a little lower than the angels" and applied it to the incarnation of Christ (2:9). In chapter 3 he quoted Ps. 95:7-11 and isolated the word "today," driving home the urgency of strong and immediate commitment (3:13, 15). In chapter 8 he quoted from Jer. 31:31-34 and isolated the word "new" in relation to the establishment of the covenant of gospel and the passing of the covenant of law (8:13). Now from Haggai 2:6 he isolates the phrase, "Yet once more," and emphasizes the finality of what God is doing and will do in the church. This grand shaking which Haggai has predicted will be the final one.

This proclamation "signifieth the removing of those things that are shaken." The word "signifieth" (Greek *deloo*) means that which demonstrates, shows forth the truth that he states (compare 9:8). "Removing" (Greek *metathesis*) does not call for complete destruction or obliteration of the thing removed, but rather a change to the extent defined. The word is used in 7:12 concerning the *change* of priesthood and law as being replaced by a new priesthood and new commandments and in 11:5 it is used of the *translation* of Enoch from earth to Heaven without dying.

Even so one day the earth as we know it will pass away, but it will evidently be replaced by a renewed earth and Heaven which appear to have some relationship to the one where we now live (Is. 65:17-25; 2 Pet. 3:12, 13). In

Rev. 21:1-5 John sees the new heavens and the new earth, as well as the holy city, the new Jerusalem, "coming down from God out of heaven." The fact that there is "no more sea" in this new order of things also seems to indicate some re-creation of this present earth. In Rom. 8:18-23 Paul indicates the redemption of creation itself, along with those who are saved, at the end of time. He says, "Because the creature [creation] itself also shall be delivered from the bondage of corruption into the glorious liberty of the children of God" (Rom. 8:21).

What is to be removed, or changed, are "those things that are shaken" or "are being shaken" (Greek present tense), indicating that the shaking is already in progress (Westcott 420). This again implies some application of the beginning of Haggai's prophecy, in a figurative sense, to the tremendous upheaval involved in the change which the readers had experienced between the old dispensation and the new.

Those of us who did not live during that time cannot possibly imagine how great that upheaval must have been. But these Hebrew Christians must not even consider going back to those temporary ordinances, for that which is permanent has come about through the life, death, resurrection, and ascension of Jesus Christ. Though that change has already started, it will only find its perfect accomplishment at the return of Christ and the cataclysmic events of the end times.

The removal of the things that are being shaken will take place "as of things that are made." The reference is to God's completion of the original creation and to His continuing control of it (Greek perfect tense). The God who made the material universe, and all that is in it, can bring it to a conclusion and change it to meet the goals of His eternal plan. The writer earlier quoted Ps. 102:25-27 in contrasting God's permanence with the temporariness of His creation, "They shall perish; but thou remainest; and they all shall wax old as doth a garment; and as a vesture shalt thou fold them up, and they shall be changed: but thou art the same, and thy years shall not fail" (Heb. 1:11, 12).

The purpose for the removal of those things which are being shaken is "that those things which cannot be shaken may remain." This statement goes along with the idea discussed above that the final judgments may leave the basis of the universe intact. The earth in particular will be renewed to its Edenic status or better. Revelation 21:1-5 pictures the new Jerusalem coming down from Heaven to what is apparently this earth re-created. For the extra room needed to accommodate the saved of all ages, there will be no more sea, more than tripling the land space available. But that which cannot be shaken refers to far more than just material things. It refers, especially, to the persistence of faith under stress, and in particular to the faith of the readers of this epistle. Neither the severe shaking of persecution nor the literal shaking of end-time events will be able to destroy the faith of those who keep their eyes on Jesus. As Paul said to Timothy, "He is able to keep that which I have committed unto him against that day" (2 Tim. 1:12).

(2) Admonition concerning God's coming kingdom (12:28, 29)

28 Wherefore we receiving a kingdom which cannot be moved, let us have grace, whereby we may serve

God acceptably with reverence and godly fear:
29 For our God *is* a consuming fire.

On the basis of this final shaking which will take place and to some extent is already taking place, the writer points his readers to personal application: "Wherefore we receiving a kingdom which cannot be moved." "Wherefore" introduces us to a conclusion based on what has been said in the previous verse. Since God is already in the process of shaking up this world so that what can be shaken is passing away, we are, therefore "receiving a kingdom." The phrase should be taken as causal: "*because* we are receiving a kingdom."

The idea of the kingdom may have been implanted in the writer's mind from Hag. 2:21-23, the companion passage to that quoted in v. 26 (Bruce 383). The Lord says to Zerubbabel, the governor of Judah, "I will shake the heavens and the earth; And I will overthrow the throne of kingdoms, and I will destroy the strength of the kingdoms of the heathen . . . In that day, saith the LORD of hosts, will I take thee, O Zerubbabel, my servant . . . and will make thee as a signet: for I have chosen thee, saith the LORD of hosts."

The process of receiving the kingdom was instituted with the beginning of the gospel dispensation. John the Baptist, Jesus Himself, and His disciples all preached that the kingdom was at hand (Mt. 3:2; 4:17; 10:7). Jesus gave to Peter "the keys of the kingdom of heaven," evidently referring to his introduction of the Gospel to the Jews at Pentecost (Acts 2) and later to the Gentiles through Cornelius, the Roman centurion (Acts 10). We enter the kingdom through the new birth (Jn. 3:3, 5), and through that experience God "hath delivered us from the power of darkness, and hath translated *us* into the kingdom of his dear Son" (Col. 1:13; see also Acts 20:25; Rom. 14:17; 1 Cor. 4:20).

But the complete realization of the kingdom is still future. We pray in the Lord's prayer, "Thy kingdom come. Thy will be done in earth, as *it is* in heaven" (Mt. 6:10); and "many shall come from the east and west, and shall sit down with Abraham, and Isaac, and Jacob, in the kingdom of heaven" (Mt. 8:11). When Jesus instituted the Lord's Supper, and ate the Passover with His disciples, He said, "I will not any more eat thereof, until it be fulfilled in the kingdom of God" (Lk. 22:16). Jesus will "judge the quick and the dead at his appearing and his kingdom" (2 Tim. 4:1), and at that time the kingdoms of this world will "become *the kingdoms* of our Lord, and of his Christ; and he shall reign for ever and ever" (Rev. 11:15).

This kingdom will survive God's final shaking at the end of time because it is a kingdom "which cannot be moved" (Greek *asaleutos*). Luke uses the same word to describe the bow of Paul's ship which ran aground on the trip to Rome. In spite of the winds and waves which assaulted the stern, the bow "remained *unmoveable*" (Acts 27:41). This final kingdom includes that "city which hath foundations, whose builder and maker *is* God" (11:10) which Abraham looked for all of his life. When all that is temporary collapses, this kingdom will not only stand, it will develop into its perfect manifestation in connection with the return of Christ. At that time "the saints of the most High shall take the kingdom, and possess the kingdom for ever, even for ever and ever" (Dan. 7:18).

Because they are receiving a kingdom which cannot be moved, the writer admonishes his readers, as well as himself, "Let us have grace, whereby we may serve God acceptably." "Grace" refers to God's unmerited favor; it may also, in a context like this include the ideas of strength, fortitude, and perseverance to do what needs to be done with the help of God (see Lk. 2:40; Acts 4:33). If so, the readers are being exhorted to constantly depend on the grace and strength of God to bolster their faithful service to God, even in the face of persecution (Barnes 314). But the phrase used here in the original—literally, "to be having grace"—often refers to giving thanks, having gratitude toward someone or for something (see Lk. 17:9; 1 Tim. 1:12; 2 Tim. 1:3). Many commentators think that we should understand it that way here (Alford 260; Westcott 421; Kistemaker 401). In that case we might render, "Let us keep on being thankful" (NIV; NASB).

Having an attitude of thanksgiving is viewed as a primary way by which "we may serve God acceptably." "Serve" (Greek present tense of *latreuo*), which means to worship God here, is viewed as a continuous activity. Our service or worship of God must be offered continuously with graditude if it is to be rendered "acceptably" (Greek *euarestos*): that is, in a manner that pleases Him. The writer qualifies acceptable worship with two further descriptions. It should be given "with reverence and godly fear." The words translated "reverence" (Greek *eulabeia*) and "godly fear" (Greek *deos*) are basically synonyms. The first word is used only here and in 5:7 where he says that Christ's prayer in Gethsemane "was heard in that he *feared*." The verb form is used in 11:7 to refer to Noah's building the ark, "moved with *fear*." The latter word is found nowhere else in the New Testament. Our constant service and worship to God will only prove acceptable if they are given with our greatest respect, fully recognizing who God is and who we are.

Serving God with this attitude of thanksgiving and reverence is appropriate, "For our God *is* a consuming fire." The words seem to come directly from Dt. 4:24, though Ex. 24:17 says almost the same thing. In the first passage Moses reminds Israel of God's nature in warning them against worshiping graven images; and in the latter phrase he uses the terminology to describe God's presence on top of Sinai. It obviously refers to the fierceness of God's judgment. It applies to both believers and unbelievers: to believers so they will stay right, and to unbelievers so they will get right. God is also merciful, longsuffering, and forgiving, and it is the same God in both cases. Our belief and behavior will determine which side of God we see, and the Hebrews must keep that in mind as they face increasing persecution. The writer used similar words earlier when he warned the Hebrews about continuing to "sin wilfully after that we have received the knowledge of the truth" (10:26). There he concluded, "*It is* a fearful thing to fall into the hands of the living God" (10:31).

Summary (12:1-29)

In chapter 11 the writer has called the attention of his Hebrew readers to a number of the great heroes of the faith in the O.T. who persevered under the most difficult circumstances. He starts chapter 12 by driving home the example of those witnesses of faith, and pictures them as spectators in the athletic arena rooting on the runners on the track of life below. He doesn't mean to suggest by this that those who have gone on to Heaven actually observe what is happening on the earth, but he does mean that they have left a powerful witness in the pages of the O.T., of which the writer has given only a sample. Christians are to lay aside absolutely anything that will keep them from running life's race with top effort and endurance, whether that be merely a hindrance or an actual sin. They are to keep their eyes fixed on Jesus who, because of what He did on the cross, both started them on the race and will meet them rejoicing at the finish line. He also serves as the greatest example in suffering since He endured far more than any of them (12:1-4).

They must see persecution for their faith in Christ as part of God's discipline in their lives. It confirms that they are truly sons of God, for if they experienced no suffering at all it would indicate that they are not what they claim to be since the Lord disciplines only those whom He loves. God also is a better disciplinarian than our earthly parents. Their discipline may at times be too harsh, and at other times too light; but God's discipline is always just right, specifically designed to make us more like Him. Since the Lord's discipline ultimately produces good fruit, the Hebrews need to manifest a more positive attitude in their Christian living, both inwardly and outwardly (12:5-13).

Such an attitude will promote peace and holiness in their lives and will prevent backsliding and bitterness which will affect both them and others in the church as well. Those who refuse the help of God's grace may fall into various kinds of sin, and finally abandon the faith and become totally secular like Esau, who lost both the patriarchal birthright and blessing with no way to get them back (12:14-17).

The writer issues the fifth and final warning in the epistle by pointing to the severe consequences of abandoning the new covenant represented by Mt. Zion, the heavenly Jerusalem. They need to be reminded of the story of Moses' reception of the law at Sinai and the dreadful results if even a beast touched that flaming and quaking mountain where God met Moses. But they must know that there is no comparison between those awful repercussions and what should be expected if they should abandon the new covenant, represented figuratively by Mt. Zion, the heavenly Jerusalem. God shook Sinai with only earthly results, but one day soon—indeed, the process has already started—He will shake both earth and Heaven so violently that only that which finds its foundation in Christ will stand. Those who come through this final earthquake at the end of time will participate in God's eternal kingdom which already finds its beginnings in the Gospel of Christ. All must realize, however, both believers and unbelievers, that God is the supreme and final judge (12:18-29).

Application: Teaching and Preaching the Passage

In light of the motivation for faith that the writer has given to his readers in the example of O.T. heroes, he now challenges them to proceed vigorously in moving forward for Christ, with no consideration for retreat. He does this at the beginning of chapter 12 by presenting the Christian life as running a race, like the athletes did in the Greek and Roman contests of that day (12:1-4). We run this race for Christ: (1) *By taking advantage of the home crowd* (v. 1). The O.T. saints presented in chapter 11 are pictured as the spectators in the grandstand, rooting us forward in our race. The writer in no way, by this interesting comparison, means to suggest that departed saints actually see what is happening on this earth. There is no Scriptural basis for that. He wants us, rather, to visualize their example of faith from the pages of the O.T. as an encouragement for progress, as spectators in the grandstands would in a literal race. (2) *By getting rid of every hindrance* (v. 1). A runner in a real race dresses as lightly as possible. Some of the ancient Greek runners ran naked. We too in this race for Christ must discard all excess baggage: both things that may not be sinful in themselves, only hindrances that hold us back ("every weight"), as well as those things which are actually sinful, our pet sins with which we constantly struggle ("the sin which doth so easily beset us"). (3) *By keeping our eyes on the goal* (v. 2). Every game has a goal, a method of scoring to determine who is to be the ultimate winner. There is a goal to put the ball through in basketball, a hit to be made in baseball, a touchdown in football, a puck or ball to be driven through the goal in hockey or soccer, or a finish line to be crossed in running a race. Paul declared, "Know ye not that they which run in a race run all, but one receiveth the prize? So run, that ye may obtain" (1 Cor. 9:24). The most wonderful thing about this race for Christ is that we can all receive the prize. There is something about keeping one's eyes on the goal that makes him run harder and have greater determination for endurance. Peter did fine in walking the stormy waters of Galilee, just like his master, until he took his eyes off Jesus and focused on the danger around him (Mt. 14:28-31). We, too, are to keep our eyes focused on Jesus as both the Author, the Originator, and the Finisher of our faith, the One who will keep us all the way through and take us home to Heaven if we will trust in Him. He died on the cross to make our salvation possible, and He sits at God's right hand to intercede for us all the way through.

The writer wants his Hebrew readers to view the persecution they are experiencing as God's discipline; for, although men may be administering it, it is God who is in control. To understand and benefit from God's discipline he emphasizes several things for consideration (12:5-13): (1) *The presence of discipline demonstrates God's love* (vv. 5-7). Proverbs 3:11, 12 reminds us that discipline is a sign that God cares, that we really are sons and daughters of God (2 Tim. 3:12). As a general practice we do not discipline other people's children; therefore, the fact that God allows His discipline in our lives shows a living relationship. We must realize that discipline is for our benefit, not for our detriment. (2) *The absence of discipline demonstrates that salvation is not genuine, that profession of faith is empty* (v. 8). The wording is strong and it needs to be: "Then are ye bastards, and not sons." Jesus Himself said, "Woe unto you, when all men shall speak well of you! for so did their fathers to the false prophets" (Lk. 6:26). No suffering, no persecution, no discipline in our lives indicates no real relationship with God. (3) *The perfection of discipline in the hand of God* (vv. 9, 10a). As good parents we discipline our children, and we experienced the same under the loving watchcare of our own parents, but none of us are perfect parents. If we are honest, all earthly parents will have to admit some mistakes. But discipline in God's hand is always just right, never too harsh, never too light, never without proper control. (4) *The purpose of discipline is "that we might be partakers of his holiness"* (vv. 10b, 11). God's ultimate desire is for us to be like Him (Rom. 8:28, 29): though the perfection of that image will not come until we actually meet Him (1 Jn. 3:2), discipline—which includes all ranges of spiritual education in our lives, including persecution and suffering—brings that goal into gradual reality. It "yieldeth the peaceable fruit of righteousness" in our lives. (5) *The joy of discipline can only be realized by contemplating the ultimate result* (vv. 12, 13). The writer mixes the language of Is. 35:3 and Pr. 4:25-27 to encourage their glad reflection on God's discipline, both inwardly and outwardly. A spirit that groans and complains under discipline is not a good testimony to immature believers or to those who don't know Christ at all.

This subject of discipline is so important that the writer takes it a step further (12:14-17). God's discipline, when rightly received, helps develop the right sense of priorities concerning: (1) *What we should pursue* (v. 14). The pursuit must be continuous to be effective, "Keep on pursuing." With men we pursue peace, a harmonious relationship. Paul said, "If it be possible, as much as lieth in you, live peaceably with all men" (Rom. 12:18). With God we pursue holiness. Though the emphasis is probably on behavioral holiness—that which is visible in our lives—it is based on positional holiness—that which we have by faith in Christ. It is not possible to live even relatively holy lives without truly knowing Him who is absolutely holy, who gave Himself for us (2 Cor. 5:21). (2) *What we should avoid* (vs. 15-17). There are four different actions and attitudes which we must avoid with regard to the priorities of discipline. *First*, we must avoid abandoning God's grace (v. 15a). We must keep on "looking diligently lest any man fail of the grace of God." There is no reason to lighten the harshness of this warning. He is not speaking of a temporary failure to rely on God's grace, but of a permanent failure (see also Gal. 5:4). *Second*, we must not allow the development of an attitude of bitterness (v. 15b). Like a root from a noxious plant, it will produce the most unpleasant fruit in our lives. *Third*, we must always steer clear of sexual immorality, both in our thought lives and in our outward conduct (v. 16a). With regard to such need for self-discipline, Paul says, "Put ye on the Lord Jesus Christ, and make not provision for the flesh, to *fulfil* the lusts *thereof*" (Rom. 13:14). If we would avoid inappropriate sexual behavior, we must first avoid inappropriate thoughts and inappropriate situations. *Fourth*, we must avoid the development of a secular, materialistic lifestyle as manifested by Esau (vv. 16, 17).

Esau was a prime example of one whose priorities were grossly misplaced; unfortunately, he represents the exact attitude and behavior of many in our modern world. He made a *foolish decision* to sell his highly valued birthright for a bowl of soup. He sacrificed that which was permanent on the altar of the immediate. He set himself up for *future rejection* when he, in God's providence, was denied the blessing also; and the sad result was *fruitless regret*, with no opportunity or power to change the dismal outcome. Esau, in a parabolic sense, represents those who willingly place themselves in a situation where they find "no place of repentance," where they are beyond the limits of the Spirit and grace of God, where it is, for all eternity, too late.

In order to see the great contrasts between the two covenants, the old and the new, our writer depicts them in the form of two mountains from the pages of O.T. history (12:18-24). First, he points to Mt. Sinai as representing the covenant of law (vs. 18-21). *With regard to its earthly nature*, it was a mountain "that might be touched." It represented that which was only external and temporary. *With regard to its awful display*, he graphically pictured the scene described in Exodus 19 which caused such dread and fear on the part of Israel. *With regard to the distant relationship,* it was in all things the opposite of the new covenant. In Jesus Christ we can "come boldly to the throne of grace," but under the old covenant even Moses said, "I exceedingly fear and quake."

Then the writer points to Mt. Zion as representing the new covenant (vv. 22-24), using seven descriptions. Though there does not seem to be any particular design in the writer's order, we can organize his description into three broad categories. First, he points to *what we have in Heaven*. There we will find: (1) a permanent home, "the city of the living God, the heavenly Jerusalem," the city with foundations which Abraham had been looking for; (2) a universal Judge, "God the Judge of all," both believers and unbelievers; (3) the departed saints, "the spirits of just men made perfect," those who have finally reached that goal in Heaven for which we all are aiming. Second, he points to *what we have on earth,* "the general assembly and church of the firstborn, which are written in heaven," the universal church of all ages. Third, he points to *what we have in between*. We have: (1) the help of angels, "an innumerable company" of them to aid us and deliver us in our work for Christ; (2) the intercession of "Jesus the mediator of the new covenant," the only person in the universe who could bring together a holy God and sinful men; (3) "the blood of sprinkling, that speaketh better things than *that* of Abel." Abel's innocent blood, shed in jealousy and anger by his own brother, Cain, spoke clearly of his fervent faith in God's commandments (see 11:4); but the blood of Jesus, the virgin born Son of God, was "sprinkled," poured out, like the blood of the Passover lamb or the sacrifice of the Day of Atonement. The blood of the O.T. sacrifices only covered the individual worshiper, and even that only temporarily and ineffectually, while the blood of Christ covers all the sins of all the world for all time (see 2:9; 1 Jn. 2:2; 1 Tim. 4:10).

In light of the power of this new covenant, the writer reemphasizes the dire consequences of rejecting it and its author, Jesus Christ (12:25-29). First, he makes *a comparison with the old covenant,* and the consequences of rejecting it, much as he has already done in 10:29. That was when God was speaking on the earth, from the smoking heights of Sinai; but this new covenant is wrapped up in God's revelation from Heaven in the person of His Son, Jesus Christ (see 1:1, 2). Second, he asks for *contemplation of God's last great earthquake,* when, as prophesied in Hag. 2:6, He shakes both heaven and earth to permanently separate what is genuine from what is only pretense (Rev. 6:12-17; 16:16-21). Third, his warning is issued in *consideration of the permanent kingdom* which will come into full realization at the end of time (Mt. 13:26-43, 45-50; 24:31-46), which, according to some, will include or follow a thousand-year reign of Christ (Rev. 20:1-6). This kingdom is already partially manifested in the reign of believers in Christ during the church age.

C. Final Admonitions for Those Who Are Living by Faith (13:1-25)

Chapter 13 serves as somewhat of an appendix to the main body of the epistle to the Hebrews. It is composed of advice of a general nature regarding their relation to one another within the Christian community and to their spiritual separation from the world around them, even under the continuing threat of persecution. The work then closes with some personal requests along with an assurance that the writer will likely visit them soon.

1. Attitudes and actions that reflect the teachings of Christ (13:1-9)

Those who are Christians must closely reflect the teachings and the example of Christ in their own lives. In doing so they will demonstrate their love for one another, not just in words, but also in conduct. Husbands and wives must be faithful to one another, as they are to Christ, and they must avoid the entrapment of materialism. Though leaders will come and go as time passes, Christ Himself will always be the same.

a. Brotherly love and hospitality (13:1, 2)

1 Let brotherly love continue.
2 Be not forgetful to entertain strangers: for thereby some have entertained angels unawares.

Christians living under persecution and the threat of even greater danger, even death, may tend to turn their attention inward, to become self-centered in light of the circumstances. These Hebrew believers must not let that happen. If they have ever needed each other, the need is greater now. God never intended for His children to live in isolation. We are, indeed, a family. Thus the writer admonishes, "Let brotherly love continue." "Brotherly love" (Greek *philadelphia*) refers to expressions of kindness which are demonstrated in the Christian community by words, feelings, and actions. Jesus indicated its importance when He declared, "By this shall all *men* know that ye are my disciples, if ye have love one to another" (Jn. 13:35). Love for one another is so much the badge of our Christianity that John observes, "We know that we have passed from death unto life, because we love the brethren. He that loveth not *his* brother abideth in death" (1 Jn. 3:14). If our Lord was not ashamed to call us brethren, and act on that relationship (2:11-14), then we should likewise not be ashamed to do the same with regard to our brothers and sisters in Christ. "Let brotherly love continue" (Greek present tense), means "Let it keep on continuing" or "keep on abiding." The demand for the continuation of this important attitude indicates some degree of slackness. This local congregation must notice what is happening and make necessary corrections.

Verse 2 points to one primary way in which brotherly love is manifested: "Be not forgetful to entertain strangers." The admonition may indicate that they had already been forgetting: "Stop forgetting" (Greek present tense prohibition). Under the stress of persecution, it is easy for attention to turn inward, to a person's own needs and those of his family. But the Christian family is always broader than that, a truth we must never forget. "Entertain strangers" (Greek *philoxenia*) literally refers to "the love of strangers." The word "hospitality" is our English equivalent. God often instructed Israel about kindness toward strangers because they "were strangers in the land of Egypt" (Ex. 22:21; 23:9; Lev. 19:34; Dt. 10:19). Though we should no doubt be open and generous toward strangers in general, the writer especially has in mind strangers who are fellow Christians. Such openness would be even more important in times of persecution when suffering Christians might often need a place to stay and food to eat.

With regard to properly using our gifts, Paul uses the same word when he admonishes the Roman church to be "given to hospitality" (Rom. 12:13). Bishops or pastors must always be "given to hospitality" (see 1 Tim. 3:2; Tit. 1:8) as should desolate widows who are helped by and help the church (1 Tim. 5:10). Peter urges Christians to exercise hospitality "without grudging" or complaining (1 Pet. 4:9).

As encouragement for hospitality, the writer observes, "For thereby some have entertained angels unawares." The antecedent of "thereby"—literally, "through this"—is the word translated "to entertain strangers," or hospitality. Through generous and voluntary acts of hospitality "some have entertained angels unawares." An angel (Greek *angelos*) is a "messenger," and it can be applied to anyone who serves as a messenger of God, whether human or supernatural. The word is used to refer to John the Baptist as God's "messenger" in Mk. 1:2, quoting the prophecy of Mal. 3:1. These humble believers were completely unaware that their service was anything special (see Mt. 25:38, 40). But the writer says that only "some" have done this, not many, indicating that the number may be relatively small. It seems obvious that he has in mind the experiences of Abraham (Gen. 18:1-33) and Lot (Gen. 19:1-3) who were most hospitable toward visitors whom they thought to be human "strangers" (so Hughes 563; Delitzsch II:369). As their relationship developed, it became evident that they were dealing with God (probably a Christophany, an appearance of Christ in pre-incarnate form) and His angels. Manoah and his wife, the father and mother of Samson, had a similar experience of giving hospitality to an angel disguised as "a man of God" (Jg. 13:1-16). Though the writer is certainly not suggesting that we should show hospitality just in case the stranger might be an angel in the supernatural sense (Lenski 468; Morris 146), he is also not closing the door to that possibility. But his primary point is that surprising blessings can come from the generous act of "entertaining strangers" (Kent 278; Bruce 391).

b. Suffering believers (13:3)

3 Remember them that are in bonds, as bound with them; *and* them which suffer adversity, as being yourselves also in the body.

The writer turns to an extended form of hospitality. We should love strangers who come seeking our help, especially those who are brothers and sisters in Christ; but we should also take our hospitality to those who are unable to come to us. "Remember" (Greek present tense) is expressed in continuous action, "Keep on remembering." "Them that are in bonds" refers specifically to those who are imprisoned, who are bound for the cause of Christ. Though a jail or prison ministry is an excellent way to witness to the lost and to carry out the great commission, that is not what the writer primarily has in mind in this context. In the first century those who openly and boldly confessed Christ often suffered imprisonment. In earlier days some from this congregation had ministered to the writer himself when he was in bonds (see 10:34). To "remember" those in such circumstances means more than just to think about them, or even just to pray for them; it means to visit them and help them in any way possible (see Mt. 25:36; Phil. 2:25; 2 Tim. 1:16, 17; 4:11-13, 21). If we can do nothing but pray for them, then we should fervently do that; in the case of Peter such praying by the church, even with some weakness of faith, resulted in his deliverance (see Acts 12:3-19).

We should remember such prisoners for Christ "as bound with them." In comparing the members of the church to the members of the body, Paul observes, "Whether one member suffer, all the members suffer with it" (1 Cor. 12:26). In the Sermon on the Mount Jesus said, "Whatsoever ye would that men should do to you, do ye even so to them" (Mt. 7:12).

But the writer broadens his compassion: we must also remember "them which suffer adversity." This would, no doubt, include those who are in prison for their faith, but it would also involve those who are in the midst of suffering and afflictions of other kinds. The same verb is used in 11:37 to refer to believers who were being "tormented," subjected to evil treatment of the worst sort. It would also include natural sufferings brought on by the difficult circumstances of life.

They should remember those who are suffering for Christ "as being yourselves also in the body." As long as we are in this world, living in a physical body as we all do, we, too, could be subjected to the same kind of suffering. With regard to those who err spiritually, Paul admonishes us to seek to "restore such an one in the spirit of meekness; considering thyself, lest thou also be tempted" (Gal. 6:1). This is all part of carrying out the Golden Rule, as mentioned above. Calvin wants to apply the word "body" to the church, of which we are all members (341), but it is best to take it, with most commentators, as interpreted above (Kent 279; Westcott 431; Lenski 470). There is no definite article before the word in the original; thus, we might translate "in body" rather than "in the body."

c. Christian marriage (13:4)

4 Marriage *is* honourable in all, and the bed undefiled: but whoremongers and adulterers God will judge.

The writer moves from the broadest of social concerns for Christians—the need for kindness and hospitality toward suffering believers—to that which is more narrow, the sanctity of marriage within the church. Three different things are controversial about the form of this verse: (1) Should the verb supplied (no verb is expressed in the original) be a declaration ("is"), as in the KJV, or should it be an admonition ("Let it be"), as in the NIV and NASB? (2) Should "in all" be interpreted as neuter, "in all respects," or as masculine, "among all" people or all classes? (3) Should we take "but" (Greek *de*) as the correct reading, as in the KJV, or "for" (Greek *gar*), as in the NIV and NASB, following the oldest manuscripts? Regardless of how we settle these three questions, the meaning of the verse is basically the same.

Most commentators favor taking the first statement as an admonition, as hortatory: "Let marriage be honorable in all," etc. The writer is issuing an appeal to the Hebrew congregation about protecting the sanctity of marriage in light of prevalent problems (Kent 279; Bruce 387; Hughes 566; Westcott 431). Perhaps the strongest argument for understanding the verse as an admonition rather than a declaration, is that v. 5 demands this form. Delitzsch points to a possible solution when he suggests taking it as a declaration with the tone of an admonition (II:372). Either way the meaning stands.

In the early days of Christianity, marriage was being assaulted from two sides. There was, first, a growing movement toward asceticism or monasticism which taught that celibacy, the state of being unmarried, promoted personal holiness better than being married. Paul warned against false teachers who would forbid marriage and promote dietary restrictions as a false means of attaining holiness (1 Tim. 4:3-5). In contrast to such false teachers our writer recommends and elevates marriage in the highest manner. There were also those who disregarded God's demands of sexual purity, both before and after marriage, and the declaration or admonition of this verse may be especially pointed in that direction.

Whether admonition or declaration, then, the writer wants his readers to know that "marriage *is* honourable" and to protect it in that light. God ordained it for the original pair in Eden (Gen. 2:24), blessed it with our Lord's first miracle in Cana of Galilee (Jn. 2:1-11), and reaffirmed its intended permanence against the liberal teachings of Jewish rabbis like Hillel (Mt. 19:3-9). Though He himself did not marry, He was of all men unique, devoted totally to the single purpose of redemption, with His eyes constantly set on Jerusalem (Lk. 9:51-53). But He never suggested in any way that celibacy was to be preferred over marriage, indicating only that for some rare people God gave the gift of celibacy so that they might have no other concerns in this life than serving God (Mt. 19:10-12; compare 1 Cor. 7:1-9). Even in this case the purpose is for more intense service, not for some elevated idea of holiness.

"In all" can be interpreted as neuter, "in all respects," "in every way," or as masculine, "among all" people or classes of people. It is difficult to decide this issue since both are true in light of the total teaching of Scripture on the subject of marriage. Taking the neuter places more emphasis on the moral question (Lenski 471), and taking the masculine places more emphasis on the ascetic problem (Hughes 565), but the verse may well address both situations.

If marriage is honorable and blessed of God, then also is "the bed undefiled" and to be kept that way. "Bed" (Greek *koite*) refers to the marriage "bed," to sexual union. God blessed the sexual relationship between a man and a woman within the bonds of marriage. In ancient Eden, prior to the fall, Adam and Eve had no sense of guilt with regard to their spiritual, emotional, and physical relationship (see Gen. 2:25). Guilt came only with sin. But within the bonds of marriage that same innocent and beautiful relationship can still be enjoyed. There is absolutely no stain, no defilement, to the sexual relationship of a husband and wife in the bonds of marriage.

As in our day, however, even then there were those who had no regard for God's strict limitations on sexual relations. The writer warns, "But whoremongers and adulterers God will judge." "But" (Greek *de*) introduces the warning as a contrast to the stated sanctity and beauty of marriage expressed in the first clause. The reading "for" (Greek *gar*), which appears in a number of manuscripts, introduces this statement as a cause for preserving the sanctity of marriage. The result is the same either way. "Whoremongers" (Greek *pornos*) refer to those who practice sexual promiscuity before marriage, while "adulterers" (Greek *moichos*) points to those who are sexually unfaithful to their marriage vows. The world around us often refuses to pass judgment on such sins, even encouraging their practice in many ways. We can be sure that God has not changed His mind. The seventh commandment which He issued from Sinai (Ex. 20:14) was reemphasized and clarified by Jesus (Mt. 5:27, 28) and still stands for us today. If we disregard it, we will pay, often here and now, but certainly in eternity: "God will judge" (see 10:30; 1 Th. 4:3-7).

d. Provision of material needs (vv. 5, 6)

5 *Let your* conversation *be* without covetousness; *and be* content with such things as ye have: for he hath said, I will never leave thee, nor forsake thee.
6 So that we may boldly say, The Lord *is* my helper, and I will not fear what man shall do unto me.

Prohibitions against sexual immorality and covetousness often go together in Scripture. Both have to do with self-control. The seventh commandment prohibits adultery and the eighth commandment prohibits stealing, while the tenth commandment prohibits covetousness in its broadest sense. In like manner Paul admonishes the Ephesians, "But fornication, and all uncleanness, or covetousness, let it not be once named among you, as becometh saints" (Eph. 5:3).

"Conversation" (Greek *tropos*) refers to one's "manner of life," "conduct," or "behavior." "Without covetousness" (Greek *aphilarguros*) literally means "not a lover of silver," not one whose life is controlled by the desire for wealth and possessions. Jesus gave the parable of the rich farmer, whose plans for laying up even greater earthly wealth were interrupted by God's final call, to warn His disciples against covetousness (Lk. 12:15-21). Paul advises Timothy to warn the Christians at Ephesus against allowing the pursuit of wealth to control them, and he reminds them, "The love of money is the root of all [kinds of] evil: which while some coveted after, they have erred from the faith, and pierced themselves through with many sorrows" (1 Tim. 6:10).

One of the primary ways to keep the desire for wealth under control is to "*be* content with such things as ye have." Those who have no desire to add "stuff" to their inventory, who are perfectly satisfied when their daily needs are met, are not likely to be troubled by covetousness. Thus, from Roman imprisonment Paul declared, "I have learned, in whatsoever state I am, *therewith* to be content" (Phil. 4:11; see also 1 Tim. 6:6). Like that rich farmer in Jesus' parable, some never seem to have enough, and their lives are totally dominated by the effort to secure more possessions that will one day be burned up (2 Pet. 3:11).

Since some of them had been financially ruined by those who had persecuted them (10:34), they might now be tempted to regain that wealth with the sacrifice of their devotion to Christ. They must not allow that to happen. To counter this attitude, the writer reminds them of God's promises about His provisions, "For he hath said, I will never leave thee, nor forsake thee." "He hath said" (Greek perfect tense) emphasizes that God spoke in the past and His Word still stands. The words seem to be drawn from God's promise to Moses (Dt. 31:6, 8) and to Joshua (Jos. 1:5). David communicated the same promise from the Lord to his son, Solomon, in preparing him to build the Temple in Jerusalem (1 Chr. 28:20). It appears to have been a promise that was repeated so often in Hebrew worship that it took on a proverbial form with the final wording being slightly different from its original form. Though leaving and forsaking are similar in meaning, the latter is the result of the first. The combination presents the idea of complete abandonment (see Mt. 27:46).

In v. 6 the writer adds a positive promise to the negative one, introduced by "So that we may boldly say." Though the promise that the Lord will not abandon us in our time of trial is great, the promise that He will meet all of our needs is even greater. The quotation is from Ps. 118:6: "The Lord *is* my helper, and I will not fear what man shall do unto me." In times of trial and suffering, the Lord will be with us and will see that every need is met to enable us to endure the test. No wonder Psalm 118 was Martin Luther's favorite (Lenski 472). Like these Hebrews, he, too, victoriously endured great opposition, but only by the grace and the help of the Lord. God's promise is better than any other guarantee, because His promise never fails.

e. Respect for Christian leaders and an unchanging Christ (13:7, 8)

7 Remember them which have the rule over you, who have spoken unto you the word of God: whose faith follow, considering the end of *their* conversation.
8 Jesus Christ the same yesterday, and to day, and for ever.

Spiritual leaders are very important in any congregation. They usually set the tone of the worship services and provide motivation for the growth of the church, spiritually and numerically, individually and collectively. The writer acknowledges this importance by mentioning the leaders of this congregation three times in chapter 13. Here he points to the past leaders, and in vv. 17, 24 he mentions the present leaders: "Remember them which have the rule over you." "Remember" (Greek present tense) is expressed in continuous action, "Keep on remembering." The ministry of past leaders must not be forgotten, both out of respect for them and their sacrifices and because of the impact of their teaching and example. "Them which have the rule over you" might also be translated, "Those who *were* leading you." (The Greek participle used here can be in any time context.) Other things in the verse indicate that their leadership was in the past; see below.

Some church leaders have used passages like this to promote themselves as kings in their congregation, as "dictators" whose authority must never be questioned on any matter, whether spiritual or personal. Though Scripture certainly does teach a proper and necessary authority for pastors and church leaders, it does not teach an obnoxious authoritarianism with regard to all matters, both great and small.

The word used in this verse and in vv. 17, 24 (Greek *hegeomai*) points to one who rules by leading, who clearly shows the way in both word and conduct. Scripture presents the pastor in the role of the shepherd who both feeds his flock ("pastor") and protects them from the enemy ("bishop," "overseer"). Paul stated this rather powerfully when he exhorted the Ephesian elders, "Take heed therefore unto yourselves, and to all the flock, over the which the Holy Ghost hath made you overseers, to feed the church of God, which he hath purchased with his own blood" (Acts 20:28). Peter, in like manner, advised the elders to whom he wrote to "feed the flock of God which is among you, taking the oversight *thereof* . . . neither as being lords over *God's* heritage, but being ensamples to the flock" (1 Pet. 5:2, 3). John also warned against an absolute authoritarian like Diotrephes "who loveth to have the preeminence among them," and thus refused to open up his congregation to John or his traveling missionaries (3 Jn. 9, 10). As pastors we are not building a personal empire but we are rather God's servants in bringing His kingdom to fulfillment.

The former leaders which this congregation was to keep remembering were those "who have spoken unto you the word of God." The verb "have spoken" (Greek aorist indicative), indicates that the writer has past leaders in mind, those who first communicated to them "the word of God," the Scriptures, God's recorded revelation. That is to be the primary content of the preaching and teaching of every pastor. Paul said to Timothy, as a young pastor, "Preach the word" (2 Tim. 4:2), and that advice still stands. The "Word" consisted of the Old Testament which God spoke "in time past unto the fathers by the prophets," and the New Testament, in which God "hath in these last days spoken unto us by his Son" (1:1, 2). When this congregation was founded, the New Testament was still in the process of being written; but the Gospel, whether in spoken or written form, had clearly been communicated to them. Perhaps the writer already referred to some of these earlier preachers when he pointed out that the Gospel was first "spoken by the Lord, and was confirmed unto us by them that heard *him*" (2:3).

The writer continues to point his readers to these past leaders; he admonishes: "Whose faith follow, considering the end of *their* conversation." These past leaders are to be remembered not only for their faithful preaching and teaching of God's Word, but also for the example of faith which they left behind. Follow (Greek present tense of *mimmeomai*) is expressed in continuous action. Our word "mimic" is derived from this word. We might translate, "Keep on following," or "Keep on mimicking" their faith.

The reason that we are to follow their faith so closely is because we are considering the end of their conversation. The act of considering (Greek present tense of *anatheoreo*), of carefully examining, must also be constant. The end (Greek *ekbasis*) refers to the issue, the conclusion, the outcome of these leaders' lives of faith. Conversation (Greek *anastrophe*) has nothing to do with speech—but is old English usage which is no longer current; it means one's manner of life, conduct, or behavior. It is similar in meaning to the word translated "conversation" in v. 5. The writer is asking the Hebrews to constantly and closely consider the way the lives of these past leaders turned out and thus to emulate their example of faith as closely as possible.

Many early church fathers and modern commentators think the writer is referring to Christian martyrs Stephen, James, the brother of John, and even Peter and Paul (see Lenski 464; Westcott 434; Lunemann 477). But this is not a necessary conclusion, though the language does seem to point to leaders whose lives have reached a conclusion through death. Like the heroes of chapter 11, they have "died in faith," but there is nothing to clearly define them as martyrs (Kent 281; Bruce 395).

As great as these leaders were, one outcome is that their lives have ended. Even among Christians, leadership is constantly changing. It is often frustrating in the Christian world, locally, nationally, and internationally, that leadership must always be renewed. In this light the writer reminds us of someone who does not change. In v. 8 he points us bluntly and forcefully to "Jesus Christ the same yesterday, and to day, and for ever." He does not refer to Him as the eternal Son of God through whom all things were made (Jn. 1:3), but as "Jesus Christ," the incarnate Son, the Word when he became flesh (Jn. 1:14). The eternal Son did not become "Jesus" until He was born of the virgin Mary and was so named by His parents (Mt. 1:21). The name "Jesus" emphasizes His humanity and the name "Christ" emphasizes the fulfillment of prophecy in His life as "the Anointed One" of Israel, the Messiah, the great Prophet, Priest, and King.

In this context, then, "yesterday" refers, not to eternity past, but to the time when their leaders first preached the Word to them. "To day" is the time when they were then living and the writer was writing these words. And "for ever" is all time henceforth (Delitzsch II:380; Lenski 477). Kistemaker (415) suggests that "yesterday" refers to our Lord's mediatorial ministry on earth, "to day" to His priestly ministry in Heaven, and "for ever" to the time when we will actually be in His presence. Once the eternal Son became Jesus Christ the incarnate Son, He remains "the same," and will do so throughout all time to come. As long as our Lord tarries, leaders will come and go, and their faith should be emulated, but our Savior Himself ever remains the same to provide continuity and encouragement for our Christian faith!

f. Doctrinal steadfastness (13:9)

9 Be not carried about with divers and strange doctrines. For *it is* a good thing that the heart be established with grace; not with meats, which have not profited them that have been occupied therein.

In contrast with the stability found in Jesus Christ, both personally and doctrinally, there is always the constant threat of false teaching and false teachers. Thus the writer admonishes, "Be not carried about with divers and strange doctrines." "Be not carried about" (Greek present tense prohibition) may, once again, imply "Stop being carried about." Apparently the original readers had made no definite choices, but were beginning to experience the influence of false teaching. The verb used (Greek *paraphero*) refers to being carried or borne along away from the right path and thus in the wrong direction. Paul warned the Ephesians against being "carried about with every wind of doctrine" (Eph. 4:14), where a similar word is used.

These Hebrews were in danger of being carried about "with divers and strange doctrines" or teachings. False teachings are "divers" (Greek *poikilos*) because they come in all varieties of shades and hues (the word means "multi-colored"); and they are "strange" (Greek *xenos*) because they are contrary to what is normally taught. In the church we can have variety and creativity with regard to methods and procedures, but there is no room for variety in content. That has been settled by our affirmation of Scripture as our only source of doctrine and practice, and our commitment to the unchanging Christ of Scripture.

The writer points to one particular variety of false teaching which was threatening these Hebrew Christians at the moment: "For *it is* a good thing that the heart be established with grace; not with meats." The primary question in understanding this statement is what the writer means by "meats." He is obviously making a contrast between the new covenant—which finds its basis in God's grace, in a work of His life-changing power in our hearts—and the old covenant, which was built primarily on external observances. "Meats" (Greek *broma*) refers to foods of all kinds, not just to the flesh of animals. As we think of Scripture as a whole, several possibilities come to mind. (1) Paul goes into a rather thorough discussion of whether Christians should eat food that had been offered to idols (see 1 Cor. 8), but that question seems foreign to the present context. (2) There appears to have been a growing tendency in N.T. times toward false teaching concerning abstinence from certain foods (Col. 1:16-23; 1 Tim. 4:3). This may have included adherence to the teachings of the law with regard to clean and unclean meats (Delitzsch II:382; Kent 282). But the idea of abstinence, for whatever reason, does not fit the present context. (3) Therefore, some commentators think it better to see the reference to participation in eating foods, not to abstinence. Such would be the case with the eating of certain meals in connection with the keeping of the law and the sacrificial system (see Ex. 12:8; Lev. 19:5-7; 22:29, 30). This would include the eating of the passover lamb and other ceremonial meals in connection with the sacrifices (Hughes 573; Lunemann 479; Lenski 481). The reference back to the O.T. tabernacle in the next verse would favor this last meaning of the word "meats." All the ceremonial meals, along with the sacrifices, were only types. It is the highest kind of insult to the antitype, the fulfillment of the type, to turn back to that which was only representative when the real thing is present.

There may be some sense in which the writer had in mind all matters pertaining to food, whether abstinence or participation, which took them away from Christ and pointed back to the law. Paul declared, "For the kingdom of God is not meat and drink; but righteousness, and peace, and joy in the Holy Ghost" (Rom. 14:17). Our writer earlier referred to the old covenant which was characterized by "meats and drinks, and divers washings, and carnal ordinances, imposed *on them* until the time of reformation" (9:10).

The heart of sinful man finds no permanence, no foundation, no anchor, in such practices. Instead, the heart is "established with grace," and grace and salvation by law do not mix (Gal. 2:21). That the heart is established and strengthened by grace is "a good thing" (Greek *kalos*), beautiful in its effectiveness both inside and outside of the believer. Grace is used here in its broadest sense, referring both to the saving grace of God as well as to His continuing grace that gives us strength for the Christian life.

But these meats, these foods, which point directly back to the law, "have not profited them that have been occupied therein." "Them that have been occupied" is, literally, "Those who are walking." As in many other places in Scripture, a "walk" refers to a way of life, and the continuous action (Greek present tense) refers to a lengthy period of participation. The sacrificial meals, or (if preferred) clean and unclean foods scrupulously observed, "have not profited them," have not yielded permanent spiritual benefits whether in reference to O.T. people who so lived or to the Hebrews under the new covenant who may be considering returning to the old practices. A clear line must be drawn, the attitudes and practices of these Hebrew Christians must demonstrate without question a full dedication to Jesus Christ and the new covenant.

2. Willingness to stand with Christ against opposition (13:10-16)

In these verses the writer makes clear that the Hebrews must be willing to separate themselves from the practices of the old covenant and fully and completely embrace Christ. Those O.T. sacrifices and ceremonies were only types. They must be completely laid aside in full deference to our Lord who came not to destroy the law but to fulfill it (Mt. 5:17). The law served a legitimate purpose for its time, but that time is now past.

a. The Old Testament sin offering: a type of Christ (13:10, 11)

10 We have an altar, whereof they have no right to eat which serve the tabernacle.

11 For the bodies of those beasts, whose blood is brought into the sanctuary by the high priest for sin, are burned without the camp.

Two rather diverse opinions are held by Bible believing interpreters with regard to the meaning of v. 10. Probably the majority think that the first phrase, "We have an altar," refers to Christians. In this case the "altar" is the cross of Christ, the place of our Lord's supreme sacrifice (Hughes 574; Westcott 437; Kistemaker 417; Delitzsch II:384; Lunemann 481; Barnes 321; Bruce 399). This way, the word "altar" stands in purposeful contrast with the brazen altar where animals were sacrificed in the O.T. tabernacle.

As a reason for this usage, it may be that non-Christian Hebrews had complained to the Christians about the absence of an altar in their worship, that visible sign that was so obvious in the tabernacle of Moses and in the later temples. If so, the writer answers that we *do* have such an altar, though not a visible one; it is the altar of the cross and the supreme sacrifice of Christ.

At this altar "they have no right to eat which serve the tabernacle." According to the view suggested above, those who "serve the tabernacle" included both the priests making the sacrifices as well as the people worshiping at the tabernacle. Anyone still committed to the Levitical sacrifices cannot avail themselves of the sacrifice of Christ. One cannot continue to embrace the type and at the same time enjoy the benefits of the antitype. That "they have no right to eat" means that those still participating in Jewish worship cannot participate in the benefit of the cross, the Christian's "altar." Jesus said, "Except ye eat the flesh of the Son of man, and drink his blood, ye have no life in you" (Jn. 6:53). Some interpreters, especially Roman Catholic and Greek Orthodox scholars, take this more specifically as meaning that they cannot participate in the Eucharist, the Lord's Supper, which does indeed symbolize the sacrifice of Christ. But there is no hint of that meaning here, and most commentators reject that idea.

The interpretation given above is certainly in line with the thrust of Hebrews as a whole, and the only problem that leaves any doubt about this approach is how v. 10 fits in with v. 11. It appears that the writer, by his use of the word "for" at the beginning of v. 11, is introducing an explanation of what he has said in v. 10. Because of this some interpreters think that, when the writer says, "We have an altar," he means "we who are in the Hebrew culture," not Jews as Christians but Jews *as Jews*. In this case the altar meant was the one in the O.T. tabernacle. And "they have no right to eat which serve the tabernacle" refers to the fact that the Levitical priests could take a portion of various sacrifices for themselves and their families to eat (Lev. 7:28-33) with God's permission and blessing, but certain other sacrifices which were sin offerings could not be eaten at all (see Leviticus 4 in reference to the sin offerings for the high priest, the whole congregation, a ruler, or one of the common people). Such was particularly true of the sacrifices for the sins of the priest and the people on the Day of Atonement (Lev. 16), the day that has been emphasized so often in this epistle (5:3; 7:27; 9:7, 25; 10:1-3).

From these sacrifices neither the priests nor the people had any right, permission, or authority to eat (so Kent 382; MacArthur 440). As mentioned above, the appeal of this interpretation is the natural connection of v. 11 as an explanation why those who serve the tabernacle had no right to eat of certain sacrifices. With either approach the ultimate point that the writer is making is made clear in v. 13: the Hebrew Christians must be willing to stand boldly with Christ outside the camp of traditional Judaism.

Thus the writer explains in v. 11, "For the bodies of those beasts, whose blood is brought into the sanctuary by the high priest for sin, are burned without the camp." These are obviously the sacrifices offered for the priest and the people on the annual Day of Atonement (Lev. 16). Other offerings could be eaten, and spiritual fellowship could be experienced in connection with the meal, especially with the Passover (see Ex. 12; Num. 9). But this was not the case with sacrifices designated as sin offerings. After the blood of these sacrifices was sprinkled within the veil, the remaining carcasses of the animals were taken outside the camp of Israel and burned with fire.

If, then, the altar in v. 10 is taken to represent Christ and the cross, and those who have no right to eat are the Jewish priests and worshipers, then v. 11 should be seen as introducing a different consideration, and the word translated "for" (Greek *gar*) might be rendered "moreover" (Barnes 321). (The NIV just begins a new paragraph without translating the preposition at all.) If however, the altar is that in the tabernacle, and those who have no right to eat are the ministering priests, then v. 11 is an explanation why they have no right to eat: because the sacrifice is the sin offering of the Day of Atonement which must be burned without the camp.

b. Jesus: the fulfillment of the sin offering (13:12-14)

12 Wherefore Jesus also, that he might sanctify the people with his own blood, suffered without the gate.
13 Let us go forth therefore unto him without the camp, bearing his reproach.
14 For here have we no continuing city, but we seek one to come.

The Jewish leaders rashly accused Jesus of destroying the law of Moses. On this subject He declared, "Think not that I am come to destroy the law, or the prophets: I am not come to destroy, but to fulfil" (Mt. 5:17). Jesus fulfilled the entire Levitical sacrificial system, thus making further animal sacrifices completely unnecessary. Early in Jesus' ministry, John the Baptist had announced, "Behold the Lamb of God, which taketh away the sin of the world" (Jn. 1:29). When the Jewish leaders asked Pilate, the Roman procurator or governor, to order the legs of the three who were crucified to be broken to hasten their deaths, the soldiers did not break the legs of Jesus because He was already dead. John observes that this occurred to fulfill a prophecy, "A bone of him shall not be broken" (Jn. 19:36), a prophetic word from the instructions for the Passover lamb (Ex. 12:46).

Now the writer of Hebrews points out that Christ also fulfilled the sin offering of the O.T., especially the sin offering of the Day of Atonement: "Wherefore Jesus also, that he might sanctify the people with his own blood, suffered without the gate." "Wherefore" indicates the connection with v. 11. There the O.T. sin offering of the Day of

Atonement was explained; now in v. 12 the writer shows how Jesus became the fulfillment, the type perfected in the antitype. Our Lord became the sin offering also, but unlike that ancient offering, His will never need repetition. The only person who has ever lived on this earth completely free from sin actually became the sin offering for us that we might stand righteous before God in Him (2 Cor. 5:21).

Our Lord became the eternal fulfillment of the sin offering "that he might sanctify the people with his own blood." "Sanctify," in this context (and as often in Hebrews), probably points to initial sanctification, the supernatural cleansing and setting apart which occurs in connection with justification (Greek ingressive aorist). The writer has mentioned God's act of sanctifying us, of making us holy in Christ throughout the epistle (see 2:11; 9:13, 14; 10:10, 14; 12:14). Some of the references are to initial sanctification, as here, and some are to progressive sanctification, the lifelong process of becoming like Christ through the Spirit and the Word.

"The people" especially points to Israel as God's chosen nation, but it ultimately includes all who trust Christ and become, through His special adoption, the sons and daughters of God. Jesus' sanctifying act was not with the blood of bulls and goats, as in the sacrifices of the Day of Atonement, but rather "with his own blood" (see 9:12; 10:19; 12:24).

In perfect fulfillment of the sin offering of the Day of Atonement, down to the last detail, Jesus also "suffered without the gate." The Gospels do not give enough information about the place of crucifixion to identify it with certainty. We know that it was called "(place of) a skull," *Golgotha* in Hebrew (Mt. 27:33), and *Kranion* in Greek. Our English Bible uses the Latin equivalent, *Calvary*, to translate the Greek word in Lk. 23:33, giving us the most commonly used name for the place of crucifixion. We know that it was located near a main road (Mt. 27:39; Mk. 15:29), and that there was a garden tomb nearby (Jn. 19:41, 42). We also know that it was located outside the walls of the city of Jerusalem because of the description used in getting there (they "went forth"; Jn. 19:17), because condemned criminals were always executed "outside the camp" (see Lev. 24:11-16; Num. 15:32-35; Jos. 7:24-26; Acts 7:58), and most of all because the writer of Hebrews tells us this when the location would have been common knowledge. The traditional location is at the Church of the Holy Sepulcher, which is well within the walls of today's city. A more likely location is called "Gordon's Calvary." Since the walls have been destroyed and rebuilt more than once, we have no way of knowing with certainty the exact location, nor is that important for our purposes.

Though the writer wants us to know that Christ fulfilled the sin offering of the O.T. for the purpose of eternal redemption, he has another equally important point to make on the basis of this historical lesson. He exhorts his readers, "Let us go forth therefore unto him without the camp, bearing his reproach." "Let us go forth" (Greek present tense) is expressed in continuous action, "Let us keep on going forth." Our effort to identify ourselves with Christ must be constant, for the appeal of the world is strong. It is always easier to run with the crowd, to fit in with the world, to adopt the most popular position, and to avoid conflict. But there is a serious problem with this attitude and practice. One cannot be a true Christian and do this.

The world will hate us because it hated Christ (Jn. 15:18). Those who live godly in Christ Jesus will suffer persecution (2 Tim. 3:12). A man who truly loves God cannot love the world and what it offers (1 Jn. 2:15-17), for no man can serve two masters (Mt. 6:24). If we would stand with Christ, we must come out from among them and be separate (2 Cor. 6:17). After Aaron and the Israelites made the golden calf at Sinai, Moses called for a time of separation. He stood at the gate and asked, "Who is on the LORD's side? *let him come* unto me" (Ex. 32:26). Then he erected the tabernacle on the outside of the camp, not in its usual position at the center of the tribal arrangements. The Scripture says, "And it came to pass, *that* every one which sought the LORD went out unto the tabernacle of the congregation, which *was* without the camp" (Ex. 33:7).

In like manner we as believers must be willing to stand with Christ "without the camp, bearing his reproach," Moses chose "the reproach of Christ" in preference to the treasures of Egypt because he saw that it resulted in greater riches in the long run (11:26). Simon of Cyrene was the first one to literally bear the reproach of Christ's cross (Lk. 23:26); and, judging by Mark's listing his sons Alexander and Rufus (Mk. 15:21), Simon probably became a true disciple of Jesus Christ.

There will always be a stigma to the preaching of the cross. Paul observed that "the preaching of the cross is to them that perish foolishness; but unto us which are saved it is the power of God" (1 Cor. 1:18). The way of least resistance is the broad road that leads to Hell, and it is always well traveled; but the road to Heaven is always narrow and difficult, and the travelers, relatively speaking, are scarce (Mt. 7:13, 14). Without apology, our Lord demands total commitment (Rom. 12:1). He gave everything for us, and He asks for our absolute faithfulness in return. Family and friends cannot come before Him (Lk. 14:26). A person who is not willing to take up his cross and follow Christ cannot be His disciple (Lk. 14:27). A person who loves the world and courts its approval will never be a lasting servant of Christ (2 Tim. 4:10).

The reason Christians should be willing to take their stand with Christ "without the camp" and joyfully bear His reproach is clear: "For here have we no continuing city." Abraham looked for a city whose builder and maker was God; and, though part of God's covenant with him referred to the earthly land of Canaan, he realized that the Lord had more in mind than that, for He had "prepared for them a city" (11:10, 16). Even the earthly Jerusalem with all its attraction for Jews and Christians has not been a "continuing city." It was destroyed by Nebuchadnezzar and the Babylonian armies in 586 B.C., then again by Roman General Titus and his legions in A.D. 70. The cities of this world, regardless of the status they may attain, will not endure.

"But we seek one to come." The writer has already pointed out that those who trust in Christ have "come unto mount Sion, and unto the city of the living God, the heavenly Jerusalem" (12:22). We recognize that no earthly promises or wealth can endure, but the promises of Christ and the riches of Christ are good for all time. The city we are seeking is not uncertain; the original has a definite article: "*the* one which is coming." The promise of it and the preparation of it are in the hands of our Lord (Jn. 14:1-3). Thomas, always the skeptic, questioned Jesus about directions to this prepared place. Jesus' answer was simple and direct, "I am the way, the truth, and the life: no man cometh unto the Father, but by me" (Jn. 14:6). One who knows Christ will get to that eternal city.

Though the ultimate fulfillment of God's promises awaits eternity, this does not mean that Christians on this earth have nothing worthwhile to do. Our remaining here is for a very important purpose. When Christ went back to Heaven, He gave us the Great Commission, instructing us to make disciples of all nations, and promising to be with us as we obey (Mt. 28:18-20). Since He has gone away to receive a kingdom, He commanded us as His representatives, "Occupy till I come": that is, "Do my business," "Bring in the best return on my investment in you." We are to be both the salt of the earth and the light of the world (Mt. 5:13, 14). Even so, we yearn for that city which is to come.

c. Appropriate Christian sacrifices (13:15, 16)

15 By him therefore let us offer the sacrifice of praise to God continually, that is, the fruit of *our* lips giving thanks to his name.
16 But to do good and to communicate forget not: for with such sacrifices God is well pleased.

The supreme sacrifice of Christ on the cross brought an end to the Levitical system for all time. But appropriate sacrifices should still be made to God for those who would maintain a vibrant relationship with Him. In vv. 15, 16 the writer mentions three of the primary sacrifices that we still need to make: the sacrifice of praise, the sacrifice of good works, and the sacrifice of sharing. He says, "By him therefore let us offer the sacrifice of praise to God continually." "By him" (Greek *dia autou*) means "through him" who stands as our only Mediator (1 Tim. 2:5), who "ever liveth to make intercession for" us (7:25). "Therefore" connects this with what has just been said about our Lord Jesus suffering "without the gate" for us. We should be willing to suffer with Him to whatever extent He deems necessary and continue to offer these appropriate sacrifices through Him.

"Let us offer" (Greek present tense) is expressed in continuous action, "Let us keep on offering." The verb used is the same as in 7:27 in reference to the offering of sacrifices by the high priest on the Day of Atonement, referring to offering something up to God. Though those sacrifices are no longer needed, the sacrifices which the writer admonishes here are always appropriate. They are, in fact, the necessary manifestation of a heart which is truly in love with God.

This first offering is "the sacrifice of praise to God." The phrase used here may reflect Ps. 54:6 where the psalmist exclaims, "I will freely sacrifice unto thee: I will praise thy name, O LORD; for *it is* good." Old Testament believers voluntarily offered a peace offering through which they gave praise and thanks to God for the joy of reconciliation through the shedding of blood (Lev. 7:11, 12). If such was appropriate for that temporary reconciliation under the Levitical system, how much more for the permanent reconciliation which we enjoy in Christ. But those sacrifices were only rendered periodically or annually; the sacrifice of praise is to be offered "continually." To the believer it should become as routine as breathing, the natural outpouring of a grateful heart to the Lord.

The writer further defines this sacrifice so as to avoid any misunderstanding: it is "the fruit of *our* lips giving thanks to his name." The words in this phrase reflect Hos. 14:2 where Israel promises, in return for God's forgiveness and acceptance, to "render the calves of our lips," with the word "calves" standing for "sacrifices" (Hughes 584). Thanksgiving and praise are referred to as "fruit" because they are the natural production of a heart which loves God. "Giving thanks" (Greek *homologeo*) is commonly rendered elsewhere "confessing" (Mt. 10:32; Rom. 10:9, 10; 1 Jn. 1:9). We give thanks to God for what He has done for us in Jesus Christ by openly, publicly, and unashamedly confessing "his name."

Our confession and thanksgiving must be specific. God's name speaks of His personal identity, His character. As our name identifies us, even more does God's name identify Him. Because the god of pantheism merges with his creation, he becomes subjective and impersonal. Because the god of deism is totally transcendent, he is unsympathetic, uninvolved, and unidentifiable. In emphatic contrast, our God is personal and objective, and His name is worthy of our full attention and confession.

The second and third spiritual sacrifices are mentioned in v. 16: "But to do good and to communicate forget not." The writer's presentation of these spiritual sacrifices in vv. 15, 16 implies that they were rendering praise to God, and this they must continue; but of the two companion matters in v. 16, "to do good and to communicate," they had apparently been more neglectful. This conclusion can be drawn from the use of "but" (Greek *de*) to point up the contrast between v. 15—what they were doing well—and v. 16—what they were not doing so well. This is confirmed by the admonition, "Forget not" (Greek present tense prohibition), which might be translated, "Stop forgetting" (Hughes 584). Full confession of Christ must be manifested both by the praise of our lips and by the performance of our deeds. Praise without performance becomes empty and hypocritical.

The word translated "to do good" (Greek *eupoiia*) does not occur elsewhere in the New Testament. It refers to all acts of love shown toward others, especially toward fellow believers. Paul uses similar terminology when he admonishes, "Let us not be weary in well doing: for in due season we shall reap, if we faint not. As we have therefore opportunity, let us do good unto all *men*, especially unto them who are of the household of faith" (Gal. 6:9, 10); and Peter pointed out to Cornelius and his household that Jesus of Nazareth "went about doing good" (Acts 10:38).

They must also stop forgetting "to communicate" (Greek *koinonia*), that is, to be sharing with one another. The two action nouns translated "to do good and to communicate" are united under one article, indicating that they should be taken together. The act of communication, of sharing with those in need, is a specific kind of doing good. Paul uses this same word (*koinonia*) with regard to sharing in a material way when he mentions that those of Macedonia and Achaia had made "a certain *contribution* for the poor saints which are at Jerusalem" (Rom. 15:26), and when he commends the Corinthians for their "liberal *distribution* unto them, and unto all men" (2 Cor. 9:13).

Most commentators understand the word to mean sharing materially in this context (Hughes 584; Westcott 444; Kistemaker 424; etc.). The root meaning of the word refers to association, communion, or fellowship (Bauer 438). John says, "If we walk in the light, as he is in the light, we have *fellowship* one with another, and the blood of Jesus Christ his Son cleanseth us from all sin" (1 Jn. 1:7). Lenski (488) thinks that the word should be restricted to that meaning here, that the writer is referring to the communion of hearts, not of earthly goods. He associates it with the writer's earlier warning against "forsaking the assembling of ourselves together" (10:25). But the context seems to demand that we at least include the idea of communion of material wealth, of sharing in the needs of others. Perhaps Kent's solution is best in taking the word in its broadest sense to include both communion of hearts and communion of goods (288). James condemned those who promised to pray for the needs of poor brothers or sisters but refused to give materially to meet those needs (Jas. 2:15, 16); and John, in like manner, pointed toward helping brothers or sisters in need as a test of the presence or absence of the love of God in an individual (1 Jn. 3:17).

The writer commends the appropriateness of doing good and communicating: "For with such sacrifices God is well pleased." "Such sacrifices" refer directly back to those mentioned in v. 16, but they would naturally include "the sacrifice of praise to God" which was already pointed out in v. 15. Christians must separate themselves completely from the Levitical system of sacrifices, for Jesus Christ has come as the "better sacrifice" who has provided complete and permanent atonement for sins. But the sacrifices mentioned in these verses will always remain appropriate; God is well pleased with them (see 11:5, 6; also 12:28; 13:21).

d. Submission to church leaders (13:17)

17 Obey them that have the rule over you, and submit yourselves: for they watch for your souls, as they that must give account, that they may do it with joy, and not with grief: for that *is* unprofitable for you.

This admonition finds its logical connection with v. 7. There the writer referred to the past leaders, those who originally delivered God's Word to them and who had apparently died. They are to remember them and follow the courageous example of their faith. Now, new spiritual leaders have taken their place. When we have experienced good leaders in the church, we often feel that no one can possibly take their place, but that is not true. We must never refuse the leadership of a new pastor, or other church leaders, because of an emotional attachment to the past. The church must continue. Elderly and retired leaders will go to their reward, but Jesus Christ is "the same yesterday, and to day, and for ever" (13:8).

Concerning the present leaders the writer says, "Obey them that have the rule over you, and submit yourselves." "Obey" covers our response to our leaders when we agree with their decisions and "submit" covers occasions when we may disagree (Lenski 489), or when their instructions may initially appear to be harsh. The word translated "obey" (Greek *peitho*) is not the word for absolute obedience (Greek *hupakouo*), as this writer has used in 5:9 and 11:8 with reference to obeying God. This word refers rather to obedience that results from persuasion, and that persuasion would come as the pastor faithfully teaches and preaches the Word of God. Spiritual leaders should be given the benefit of the doubt. Those who want to question every decision that a pastor makes and every direction that he takes become hindrances to the church's progress.

The writer's instructions imply that the leadership among these Hebrew Christians was still good. Any wavering with regard to faith in Christ was apparently among the laity. In a similar way Paul instructed the Thessalonians "to know them which labour among you, and are over you in the Lord, and admonish you; And to esteem them very highly in love for their work's sake" (1 Th. 5:12, 13). Such passages, however, must not be taken in an absolute sense. Concerning the spiritual leader, Yeager (482) says, "He has the moral right to expect obedience, even when he is wrong, because he alone is charged by God with the responsibility of standing guard over the spiritual welfare of the souls of his parishioners." I believe this is going too far. Such a position implies that we, as individuals, have no direct responsibility to God, which is certainly in error (see Lk. 12:20, 21; 1 Cor. 3:5-17). It almost makes the pastor our high priest, who personally stands between us and God when actually there is only "one mediator between God and men, the man Christ Jesus" (1 Tim. 2:5). The Lord never asks us to surrender our consciences to any man. Calvin observes, "But it ought at the same time to be noticed that the Apostle speaks only of those who faithfully performed their office; for they who have nothing but the title, nay, who use the title of pastors for the purpose of destroying the Church, deserve but little reverence and still less confidence" (352).

To suggest that there is little if any problem with bad pastoral leadership is to ignore the history of the church. The pastor's primary authority comes from preaching the Word (v. 7; 2 Tim. 4:2), and only when he faithfully does so are those in the church bound under God's command to obey and submit to that authority. The Bible itself is ultimately the sole authority of faith and practice, and when anyone attempts to lead us contrary to the Word, whether church (Mt. 23:2, 3; 3 Jn. 9-11) or civil leader (Acts 4:19; 5:29), we have a responsibility to refuse to follow. Though Peter was an apostle before him, Paul refused to follow his bigoted example in separating from Gentiles and rebuked him for his actions (Gal. 2:11-17).

The reason we must obey and submit to faithful leaders is because "they watch for your souls, as they that must give account." The writer draws from the picture of the watchman in the O.T. (Is. 62:6; Jer. 6:17; Ezek. 3:17; 33:7). God said to Ezekiel, "Son of man, I have made thee a watchman unto the house of Israel: therefore hear the word at my mouth, and give them warning from me." He went on to remind Ezekiel of his own accountability if he failed to warn his people of God's coming judgment (Ezek. 3:17-19). Hughes (586) thinks that "souls" (Greek *psuche*) here should be taken as a reference to the whole person, and thus, translated "you" (see the NIV). Though that usage is probably legitimate in some passages (see Acts 2:41, 43; 3:23; 7:14; 27:37; 1 Pet. 3:20), the more narrow spiritual meaning seems appropriate here since the accountability of spiritual leaders is primarily with regard to the spiritual welfare of the church.

We are to obey and submit to our spiritual leaders so that, when they give account to God, "they may do it with joy, and not with grief." Spiritual leaders give account immediately when they pray to God for their congregation and ultimately when they stand before Him at the judgment seat of Christ (2 Cor. 5:10, 11). Paul thought of the Philippians as his "joy and crown," but he did not have the same estimate of some in the church at Corinth (1 Cor. 3:1-3) as he addressed their many problems in his first epistle to them, or of those at Galatia who had been so influenced by the Judaizers (Gal. 3:1-4). In like manner, John told his constituents, "I have no greater joy than to hear that my children walk in truth" (3 Jn. 4), but he rebuked Diotrephes for his self-serving leadership and warned, "I will remember his deeds which he doeth" (3 Jn. 9, 10).

Christians should not want their pastor to give a bad report to God in their prayers and in their ultimate appearance before God because "that is unprofitable for you." Of course, the writer does not mean to suggest that God does not keep His own account of our lives, that He is dependent on our pastor for spiritual information about us, for there are too many Scriptures that contradict that idea. What he does imply, however, is that God honors, in a very special way, the prayers and opinions of those who are faithful leaders. It is not in our best interest, both in this world and in the world to come, to maliciously oppose the leadership of God's choice servants.

Conclusion (13:18-25)

The writer begins his concluding remarks in v. 18. He asks his readers to pray for him, and in turn, he makes a special prayer for them and for their spiritual maturity. He closes by admonishing them to take his epistle seriously, to expect a visit from him and Timothy soon, and to give a special greeting to their leaders and the church as a whole.

A. Prayer for The Writer (13:18, 19)

18 Pray for us: for we trust we have a good conscience, in all things willing to live honestly.
19 But I beseech *you* the rather to do this, that I may be restored to you the sooner.

In spite of the severe warnings the writer has issued throughout this epistle, he still has confidence in the congregation as a whole. He manifests this confidence by a request, "Pray for us," that is "Keep on praying for us" (Greek present tense). He asks a continuing interest in their faithful prayers that the Lord will supply his needs and give him strength. But his request is for more than himself; it is "for us." Some think this is an editorial plural, merely a manner of speech when the writer only has himself in mind (Bruce 409; Yeager 483). It seems more likely, however, that the plural is to be taken literally, including both the writer and the company traveling with him

(Hughes 587; Lenski 492). Verse 23 suggests the potential presence of Timothy, and others may be with him as well (compare Col. 4:3; 1 Th. 5:25; 2 Th. 3:1). Though the writer is probably not Paul, as discussed in the introduction, he was almost always accompanied by helpers, and our present writer would likely be no different.

The writer's request for prayer is based on the integrity of his life, the consistency of his conduct: "For we trust we have a good conscience, in all things willing to live honestly." The observation may suggest that he fears that some of the readers might question his motives or his compassion when they hear the stern warnings of the epistle. He wants them to know that he stands firmly behind what he has said, that he has "a good conscience" about it. Though we are not certain about his identity, the readers certainly were. Because they know him well, they know that he is "in all things willing to live honestly." "In all things" means "in every respect." It includes his entire manner of life, both as a preacher and as a person. His willingness refers not merely to a wish but to an intense desire that permeates his being. "Honestly" (Greek *kalos*) refers to a way of life that is "good" both inwardly and outwardly, a lifestyle that is appealing in both intent and appearance, an honorable way of living in every respect (see NIV; NASB).

Paul said to the Thessalonians, "For our gospel came not unto you in word only, but also in power, and in the Holy Ghost, and in much assurance; as ye know what manner of men we were among you for your sake" (1 Th. 1:5; see also 2 Tim. 3:10). The readers of Hebrews might not take the strong words of this epistle well from a stranger, but they should receive it and heed it in light of their knowledge of the writer and of his proven concern for them.

When they pray for him, the writer has something specific which he wants them to ask: "But I beseech *you* the rather to do this, that I may be restored to you the sooner." "But" (Greek *de*) is used here to emphasize a specific appeal, not to make a contrast. The word translated "the rather" (Greek *perissoteros*) is placed emphatically at the front of the clause in the original and is meant to intensify the verb, "I beseech you." We might read, "I beseech you very earnestly" (see the same word in 2:1). This is a matter about which he has deep concern, and he firmly believes that their prayers can make a difference. He exhorts them earnestly "to do this," referring back to his request for their prayers in the previous verse. Although his request for prayer was in continuous action, desiring that they constantly pray for him, the infinitive here, "to do this," is expressed in completed action (Greek aorist tense), emphasizing the fact that he wants immediate attention given to the matter. His desire is that they begin praying for this request right away.

The specific request is "that I may be restored to you the sooner." Some think that the writer's request to "be restored" to them indicates that he was in prison at the time of writing. That does not seem likely, however; he does not specifically say that, and he mentions Timothy's imprisonment in such a way in v. 23 as to imply that his situation was not the same.

There are three things that we can deduce from the request: (1) that the writer had been previously in the company of his readers; (2) that he is now in a different location, probably some distance away; and (3) that he wants to come to them soon, but is presently hindered from doing that (Hughes 587; Delitzsch II:397). Paul expressed a similar confidence in prayers for restoration in his brief letter to Philemon (v. 22), though on that occasion the writer was in prison.

Through their prayers the writer believes that he will "be restored to you the sooner." Our sovereign God, who knows all things, has nevertheless ordained that many things be accomplished in His kingdom through prayer. Our Lord instructed us, "Ask, and it shall be given you; seek, and ye shall find; knock, and it shall be opened unto you" (Mt. 7:7). There is great power in prayer, and our writer shows that he has full confidence in it.

B. Prayer for The Readers (13:20, 21)

20 Now the God of peace, that brought again from the dead our Lord Jesus, that great shepherd of the sheep, through the blood of the everlasting covenant,
21 Make you perfect in every good work to do his will, working in you that which is wellpleasing in his sight, through Jesus Christ; to whom *be* glory for ever and ever. Amen.

Having requested prayer from his readers, especially for his soon return to them, the writer now leaves them with a prayer that reflects themes which have permeated his epistle, a prayer addressed to "the God of peace." Paul also makes a closing prayer for the Thessalonians in the name of "the very God of peace" (1 Th. 5:23). Both writers prefer to use "peace" in its broadest sense in that God is the ultimate source of all true peace. He makes peace possible between sinful man and a holy God through the death and resurrection of His Son. Paul declared, "Therefore being justified by faith, we have peace with God through our Lord Jesus Christ" (Rom. 5:1). This is soteriological peace. But peace in this context also includes that calmness of attitude and action which is only possible through our constant trust in God through Jesus Christ.

In one of our Lord's greatest invitations, he exclaimed, "Come unto me, all *ye* that labour and are heavy laden, and I will give you rest" (Mt. 11:28). This is that practical peace and rest which Christians can enjoy even in the midst of struggle and persecution, situations which these Hebrews were facing at the time. It refers to the "gospel of peace" with which our feet are shod (Eph. 6:15) and the peace we enjoy "through the blood of his cross" (Col. 1:20); but it also includes "the peace of God, which passeth all understanding" which will keep our "hearts and minds through Christ Jesus" (Phil. 4:7).

It is the God of peace "that brought again from the dead our Lord Jesus, that great shepherd of the sheep." This is the only time that the resurrection is directly referred to in this epistle. The writer's usual approach is to move from the humiliation of Christ to His exaltation at God's right hand, but of course the fact of the resurrection is always implied in such a transition. The resurrection of Christ demonstrates God's approval of the efficacy of His death. Without the resurrection Christianity is powerless, no more than a grand scheme which leaves it in no higher position than all the other religions of the world. If the resurrection is not a fact, Paul declared, "Let us eat and drink; for to morrow we die" (1 Cor. 15:32).

In his sermon at Pentecost, when the N.T. church was founded, Peter concluded, "This Jesus hath God raised up, whereof we all are witnesses" (Acts 2:32), and it is to the subject of the resurrection that the disciples primarily gave their witness in the spread of the Gospel as recorded throughout the book of Acts. In one of the greatest salvation verses in the N.T., Paul declared, "That if thou shalt confess with thy mouth the Lord Jesus, and shalt believe in thine heart that God hath raised him from the dead, thou shalt be saved" (Rom. 10:9).

The God of peace brought up from the dead "our Lord Jesus." He is "Lord" because He is our sovereign God, our supreme ruler, the Jehovah of the O.T., and as such we submit all that we have and all that we are to His guidance. But He is also "Jesus," the Word who became flesh and dwelt among us (Jn. 1:14), the One who can be "touched with the feeling of our infirmities," who was "in all points tempted like as *we are, yet* without sin" (Heb. 4:15). And He is "Our" Lord Jesus, both the writer's and his readers', both then and now.

The entire tone of this epistle is pastoral; thus the writer presents our Lord as "that great shepherd of the sheep." The wording of the original makes the phrase even more emphatic: "the shepherd of the sheep, the great one." In 4:14 He is our "great high priest," and here He is our "great shepherd." The idea of Messiah as a shepherd is emphasized in the O.T. (see Is. 40:11; 63:11; Ezek. 34:23), and the Lord Himself is presented as our Shepherd (Ps. 23). Jesus rightfully and boldly claimed this identity and pointed to the ultimate outcome when He said, "I am the good shepherd: the good shepherd giveth his life for the sheep" (Jn. 10:11).

The role of the primary leader of a N.T. church is based on the role of a shepherd. He is presented as an elder, spiritually mature enough to be able to minister to others. He is presented as a pastor, always conscious of his need to feed the sheep. And he is presented as a bishop, an overseer, ever responsible to guard the sheep against the attack of wolves (see Acts 20:17, 28; 1 Tim. 3:1-7; Tit. 1:5-9). As lost sheep we have all returned to Jesus Christ, "the Shepherd and Bishop" of our souls (1 Pet. 2:25); and one day all of the pastors, the under-shepherds, will have to give account "when the chief Shepherd shall appear" (1 Pet. 5:4).

God has brought our great Shepherd from the dead "through the blood of the everlasting covenant," the new covenant which our writer has discussed in 8:8-13 on the basis of his quotation of Jer. 31:31-34. Some think that this particular wording refers back to Zech. 9:11, but it may also be connected with our Lord's own declaration when he instituted the Lord's Supper (Lenski 493). He said, "This is my blood of the new testament, which is shed for many for the remission of sins" (Mt. 26:28). On the basis of, or in connection with that new covenant which involved the shedding of His blood, our Lord's resurrection took place.

The new covenant is also "the everlasting covenant." "Everlasting" (Greek *aionios*) is translated in every other occurrence in the epistle by the word "eternal." The writer has referred to "eternal salvation" (5:9), "eternal judgment" (6:2), "eternal redemption" (9:12), the "eternal Spirit" (9:14), our "eternal inheritance" (9:15) and, finally to the eternal or "everlasting covenant" here. This covenant is everlasting both because it was formed in eternity by the God whose most descriptive name is "I AM" (Ex. 3:14) and because its existence is eternal; its effectiveness will never cease (Barnes 325).

The writer presents the body of his request to God: that the God of peace will "make you perfect in every good work to do his will." "Make you perfect" (Greek *katartizo*) means "to put in order," "restore," "complete," or "prepare" (Bauer 417). The same word was used in 10:5 in the quotation from Ps. 40:6, "A body hast thou *prepared* me," and in 11:3, "Through faith we understand that the worlds *were framed* by the word of God." In this context it is a request for God to supply that which is lacking so that which is desired may be accomplished. In a similar way Paul prayed that he might be with the Thessalonians to "*perfect* that which is lacking in your faith" (1 Th. 3:10), and to the Ephesians he spoke of various offices in the church which were given to them "for the *perfecting* of the saints, for the work of the ministry, for the edifying of the body of Christ" (Eph. 4:12).

The writer wants God to make his readers complete "in every good work." Many manuscripts do not include the word "work" (Greek *ergon*), which would leave us to translate "in every good thing." Some manuscripts include both "work" and "word," after the pattern of 2 Th. 2:17. But "work" is broad enough to include all the writer might have intended. "Good" (Greek *agathos*) refers to that which is intrinsically good, good from its very foundation.

The purpose for our completion is "to do his will," indicating decisive commitment (Greek aorist tense). Jesus Himself set this example for us. He declared, "I seek not mine own will, but the will of the Father which hath sent me" (Jn. 5:30; see also Jn. 6:38). In his quotation from Ps. 40:8, the writer has already pointed out that Messiah's purpose was "to do thy will, O God" (10:7). If we would become conformed to His image (Rom. 8:29), then that must also be our ultimate goal. God's will is primarily expressed in His Word. To do His will we must know and obey His Word. The writer's prayer to God goes further; as he wants them to be complete in everything to do God's will, he knows that can only happen if God is "working in you that which is wellpleasing in his sight." Just as our salvation must come from God's work in us (Jn. 3:3-8; Eph. 2:8, 9; Tit. 3:5), so also must every subsequent accomplishment which would please Him, for without Him we can do nothing (2 Cor. 5:17, 18). While our commitment to do His will is presented in completed action, His "working" in us (Greek present tense) is presented as continuous action. Paul presents this same idea of the cooperative effort between God and man when he says to the Philippians, "Work out your own salvation with fear and trembling. For it is God which worketh in you both to will and to do of *his* good pleasure" (Phil. 2:12, 13). Though salvation comes solely by God's work through our faith in Christ, yet "we are his workmanship, created in Christ Jesus unto good works, which God hath before ordained that we should walk in them" (Eph. 2:10).

When we allow God to work thus in our lives, that then will produce "that which is wellpleasing in his sight." Faith in His person and obedience to His Word are always "wellpleasing" (Greek *euarestos*) to God. Using a different word with a similar meaning, God the Father approved of Christ at His baptism with the words, "This is my beloved Son, in whom I am well pleased" (Mt. 3:17). Using the verb form of the same word, our writer has spoken of Enoch's walk of faith as pleasing to God (11:5, 6), as well as the sacrifices of praising God, doing good, and sharing (13:15, 16).

This completing work of God in our lives, for which the writer prays, is to be accomplished "through Jesus Christ." Jesus is the Mediator through whom God does all of His work under the new covenant. Such an exalted thought causes our writer to launch into a doxology, a written exclamation of praise that might be called "shouting in print": "To whom *be* glory for ever and ever." Since "Jesus Christ" is the nearest antecedent, and because His exaltation has been the theme of the epistle, it seems best to apply the doxology to Him (so Barnes 326; Calvin 357; MacArthur 451; Kistemaker 434; Lunemann 493; Kent 294). A number of commentators, however, think it refers back to "God" in v. 20 as the main subject in the sentence (so Alford 272; Delitzsch II:401; Bruce 412; Westcott 449). Since the application grammatically could go either way, Morris (156) finds it impossible to decide and thinks that the writer may have intended us to apply the doxology both ways. This doxology points to the exaltation of Christ "for ever and ever:" literally, "unto the ages of the ages," an idiomatic way of expressing time without end. The glorification of our Lord will go "on and on." "Amen" is a Hebraism both emphasizing and affirming the truth of the statement (Lenski 495). It is frequently used in doxologies. It is interesting to note that Christ permeates the prayer by being presented in five different ways: (1) His resurrection; (2) His role as the Great Shepherd; (3) His blood; (4) His mediatorial help—"through Jesus Christ"; and (5) His exaltation.

C. Closing Admonitions (13:22-25)

22 And I beseech you, brethren, suffer the word of exhortation: for I have written a letter unto you in few words.
23 Know ye that *our* brother Timothy is set at liberty; with whom, if he come shortly, I will see you.
24 Salute all them that have the rule over you, and all the saints. They of Italy salute you.
25 Grace *be* with you all. Amen.

The writer concludes his composition with elements that are more characteristic of an epistle than what we saw at the beginning. Some features have made it more like a prolonged sermon, but for that matter all the N.T. epistles bear homiletic traits. In the conclusion, however, the identifying aspects of a letter stand out more clearly. He refers to the writing of a letter (v. 22); he mentions a planned visit to them in the near future (v. 23); he gives personal greetings to the leaders and to the church in general, and gives special stress to a greeting from a group which obviously bears some direct relationship to this congregation (v. 24). Then he closes with an abbreviated benediction (v. 25).

"And I beseech you, brethren, suffer the word of exhortation." This is the first time that the writer refers to himself in the singular, emphasizing his desire to be even more personal with them in his conclusion. "I beseech" (Greek *parakaleo*) literally means "to call to one's side" with the idea of giving assistance. In a given context it may also mean "to exhort," "to encourage," "to comfort," or "to request or entreat." Though the latter meaning stands out here, as in v. 19, it almost always carries an element of "encouraging" or "exhorting." This is the fourth time the writer has addressed his recipients as "brethren" (see also 3:1, 12; 10:19), indicating his strong feeling that his readers have a genuine relationship with the Lord and thus with him in the bonds of Jesus Christ who is Himself not ashamed to call us brethren (2:11).

The writer requests that they "suffer the word of exhortation." "Suffer" (Greek *anechomai*) means to "permit, endure, or bear with" something or someone. It is often used of persons (Mt. 17:17; 2 Cor. 11:1), but here the appeal is to "bear with" "the word of exhortation," referring to the letter he is now drawing to a conclusion. He asks for ongoing endurance (Greek present tense) so that they may fully consider the important admonitions in the letter. "Exhortation" (Greek *paraklesis*) is the noun form of the verb translated "I beseech" at the beginning of the clause. It also appears in 6:18 ("consolation") and 12:5. It carries the same ideas as the verb form, and here the meanings "exhortation" and "encouragement" merge. This same phrase is used in Acts 13:15 when the rulers of the synagogue in Antioch of Pisidia wanted to know if Paul and his company had "any word of exhortation" for their Sabbath assembly. There it obviously refers to a spoken sermon, thus adding to the characterization of Hebrews as a written sermon.

The reason the writer wants his readers to bear with his word of exhortation or encouragement is "For I have written a letter unto you in few words." He uses completed action (Greek aorist tense), because the composition is basically complete and when they read it, it will be. Some modern-day letter writers might question our author's characterization of this document of some 13 chapters as a letter "in a few words," but we must allow for three considerations. First, he is not speaking of a modern business letter which is often brief and addresses one particular point. He has written a more personal letter with diverse ramifications on one primary theme. His warnings are urgent and in some cases extended. Second, and most significantly, he means that he has been much more brief in writing this letter than he would have been if he could address them in person. He has given them a sufficient basis, in written form, for turning from their leanings toward apostasy back to a vibrant and growing faith in Christ. Still, he hopes to visit them soon in person when he can go into much greater detail. Third, since this letter is also a sermon, as sermons go the document is not excessively long. It can easily be read aloud, as his recipients would have done, in less than an hour. Peter, using a similar word, also spoke of the brevity of his first epistle (1 Pet. 5:12).

In v. 23 the writer returns to his desire to visit this Hebrew congregation in person, but he also introduces another factor: "Know *ye* that *our* brother Timothy is set at liberty." The verb "know ye" can be taken as an imperative or as an indicative, "You know." If imperative, the writer is giving them news; if indicative he is reminding them of something they already know. All translators have taken it as an imperative, and there is no need to change that. He wants them to understand this good news about Timothy.

The good news is "that *our* brother Timothy is set at liberty." Though "our" (Greek *humon*) is supplied by our translators (indicated by italics) because it does not appear in the Received Text, it is found in many of the ancient manuscripts and the context certainly calls for it. It seems obvious that the writer, whoever he might have been, was very close to Timothy. Though Paul occasionally referred to Timothy in his known epistles as "our brother" (2 Cor. 1:1; Col. 1:1; 1 Th. 3:2; Philem. 1), he also often used more endearing terminology for him: "my beloved son" (1 Cor. 4:17), "*my* own son" (1 Tim. 1:2), "son Timothy" (1 Tim. 1:18), "*my* dearly beloved son" (2 Tim. 1:2). Consequently, the terminology alone cannot settle the question of authorship. Timothy also had a close relationship with other prominent N.T. figures who could be candidates for the authorship of Hebrews (Barnabas, Luke, Silas, etc.). He had evidently enjoyed a previous connection with this congregation, and it would be good news for them to learn that he "is set at liberty."

Though this imprisonment is not recorded in the N.T., such an experience was quite common for Christians in the first century, as Acts and the epistles of Paul clearly show. Paul, by the way, never uses the word here translated "has been set at liberty" in his known epistles, but Luke uses it frequently both in his Gospel and in the book of Acts. Though the word is used for other types of liberation, it is used frequently in the same sense as here, "to set at liberty" from arrest or imprisonment (Lk. 23:16, 17, 18; Acts 3:13; 4:21; 5:40; 16:35, 36; 17:9; 26:32; 28:18). Lenski, contrary to most commentators, holds that the word refers to Timothy's being away on a mission rather than being freed from prison (498).

Concerning Timothy's release from imprisonment, the writer says, "With whom, if he come shortly, I will see you." Perhaps both the writer and Timothy had ministered to this congregation together. What a joy it would be for both of these great men of God to be able to visit the Hebrews in their distress so that they might provide the same kind of warning and encouragement that the writer has given in his letter!

"If he come shortly" is a conditional statement (Greek third class); the writer is making no assumption as to when or whether this will occur, though it is a reasonable possibility. The implication is that Timothy is presently in another location, likely some distance away, and though the writer is not certain of his soon arrival he has reason to expect that it may happen. The writer has already requested prayer for his speedy restoration to them (v. 19), and the fact about Timothy that he has revealed here should give them even greater motivation for their petitions. His promise is, "I will see you:" he evidently plans to see them soon whether accompanied by Timothy or not. Especially in light of v. 19, there is reason to believe that he will come to them alone if Timothy does not arrive in the allotted time.

As he brings the epistle to a close, in v. 24 the writer has a final word of greeting for the church leaders in particular and for the whole church in general: "Salute all them that have the rule over you." Most of Paul's epistles close with similar salutations, though none are exactly like this one. (The longest list is in Romans 16.) The writer has placed great emphasis on the need to respect and submit to the church leaders. In v. 7 he asked them to remember their original leaders and follow their example. In v. 17 he commanded them to obey and submit to their leaders as the watchmen of their souls who must give account. Now he emphasizes the importance of the church leaders by giving a special greeting to all them "that have the rule over you." Such a three-fold emphasis on heeding the church leaders seems to indicate that this was a major part of the Hebrews' problem. The leaders were still preaching the right message and leading them in the right direction, but there had been a tendency on the part of some to ignore their leadership and take things into their own hands.

The salutation adds, "And [to] all the saints." The letter is not merely to some special segment of the church, but to the church as a whole. Since the church is a body, if one member suffers, all the members suffer with it (1 Cor. 12:26). As everyone knows who is a student of the N.T., the word "saint" (Greek *hagios*) is synonymous with "disciple" or "Christian." It is never intended to designate some super Christian, one who is head and shoulders above all the rest. As saints of God we are set apart and made holy only in Jesus Christ, on the basis of His shed blood.

A Roman Catholic pope recently died, and some of his promoters carried signs saying, "Sainthood Immediately." My thought was, If he wasn't a saint already, it's too late now. We are not saints because of what we have done, but rather because of what Christ has done. The text of the N.T. never refers to any individual as a saint, so as to give one a special spiritual status over others. Even the designation of the Scripture writers as St. Matthew, St. Luke, St. Paul, etc., is never found in the text of Scripture. All Christians stand as saints together, made holy as part of the body of Christ, and He alone is the Head.

A special group who were evidently in the presence of the writer passes on their greeting, "They of Italy salute you." The wording in the original literally means "those from Italy." Thus it may refer to Christians who were from Italy and were still there, whether in Rome or some other location in Italy. Many of the early church fathers took this position. This would indicate that the writer was presently located in Italy and was sending greetings to his recipients from his fellow church members. But the phrase may equally refer to those who were originally from Italy but were now located in some other part of the world away from their home country. To me this seems to be the more natural way of understanding the phrase. If this is correct, the implication would be that the Hebrew church to whom he was writing was likely located in Italy, perhaps in Rome, and that the writer was himself presently located in some other part of the empire. Since both methods of expression seem to be present in the N.T. (see Acts 17:13 as an example of the first approach and Acts 21:27 as an example of the second), we must admit that this statement cannot settle the question of destination or origin for certain.

The writer brings his letter to a close with a benediction, "Grace *be* with you all." All of Paul's letters have benedictions, some quite similar to this one, but only Tit. 3:15 agrees exactly. Though such benedictions were traditional at the conclusion of letters, we must still take the words as full of meaning. The "grace" that he wishes upon all his recipients includes all the broadness of meaning attached to the virtue throughout the epistle. It refers to that grace, that unmerited favor, which is the very basis of our salvation through the death of Christ (2:9), which also keeps us saved through our continued faith in Him (12:15), which gives us strength for Christian living (4:16; 13:9) and makes us thankful for all that we have in Jesus Christ (12:28).

The writer has said what needs to be said about the superiority of Christ above all things and of Christians' need to keep trusting in Him until we go to meet Him or He returns for us. May God give us the grace to read and heed the grand message of this epistle. "Amen."

Summary (13:1-25)

In this closing chapter the writer brings together some final and concluding admonitions for those who are living by faith. First, he discusses attitudes and actions that often reflect the teachings of Christ (13:1-9). Under the stress of increasing persecution Christians can forget to exercise brotherly love. They must remember that this is one of the primary characteristics of the Christian family. Even in hard times they must be open and hospitable toward those passing through, remembering that they may need the same demonstration of kindness from their brothers. Every stranger is God's messenger offering an opportunity for ministry in the name of Christ.

Faithfulness must also be exercised internally in the Christian home. Regardless of the practices of the world around us, Christians must be loyal to their marriage commitments, knowing that God will judge those who disobey. They must restrain themselves from inordinate attraction to material things since such attraction demonstrates a lack of trust in God's promises for the necessary provisions of life.

They should always cherish the memory of their original leaders who have now passed from the scene and show their love by their commitment to their example. Though it is often frustrating that leaders come and go, we can always take consolation that Jesus Christ is the same, and He will guide the new leaders just as He did the old ones. Thus, they must not waver in their commitment to God's grace, remembering its effectiveness for life in contrast with the formalism of the old covenant.

The writer then challenges his readers to be willing to stand firm with Christ against the increasing opposition they are experiencing (13:10-16). Just as the sin offering of the O.T. was taken outside the camp of Israel to be burned, even so Jesus Christ, as the fulfillment of that sin offering, was literally crucified outside the walls of ancient Jerusalem. We must take His actions not only as the full payment for our sins, but also as furnishing us an example of personal separation from all compromise. Like Abraham of old, we are still looking for a city, and that city with eternal foundations cannot be found on this earth as we now know it. Though we no longer offer animal sacrifices as they did in O.T. times, the sacrifices of praise to God, doing what is right, and sharing with one another are always appropriate.

The epistle concludes with some important observations (13:18-25). The writer asks them to keep praying for him in spite of the strong but necessary warnings and admonitions he has written to them. He especially desires their prayers concerning a planned visit when he can explain his concerns in greater detail. He in turn prays for special blessings on them from the God of peace through the risen and ruling Savior, Jesus Christ, particularly that they may continue to be fully prepared and equipped to do God's will in every possible way. Such a thought about God's work in Jesus Christ calls forth a doxology: to whom be glory forever and ever.

They must be especially patient in considering this letter and applying its admonitions in their lives. The writer hopes to visit them soon, along with Brother Timothy, to give them even more personal encouragement to follow on with Christ. He communicates special greetings to their leaders, and to the church as a whole, both from himself and the Italian believers who are with him. Finally, he wants God's grace, with all of its broad meaning, to guide every one of them.

Application: Teaching and Preaching the Passage

The writer knows what a strain hard times in the Christian life can place on relationships within the church. Thus he admonishes, "Let brotherly love continue" (13:1). This text offers an opportunity for preaching and instruction on the subject of *brotherly love*. (1) *It is based on a family relationship.* If our Lord is not ashamed to call us brothers (2:11), and became like us in taking upon Himself "flesh and blood" (2:14), then we certainly must not be ashamed of each other in the great family of Christ. Even within a local church there may be different social levels, but that must never be reflected in personal relationships within the congregation. We must always acknowledge the family relationship in our love for one another. (2) *It should be continuous.* The writer does not say that this church had stopped demonstrating brotherly love, but he does say, "Let brotherly love continue." He knows that there is a natural tendency in fallen man for love to wane. The manifestation of brotherly love must have no gaps. (3) *It must be encouraged.* Though we are, indeed, new creatures in Christ (2 Cor. 5:17), and have the Holy Spirit dwelling within us (Rom. 8:9-11), we still must struggle against the fallen nature. Thus, even things that ought to come naturally to us must be encouraged as part of our mutual concern for one another. (4) *It stands as a sign.* It is a sign of our uniqueness to the unsaved world around us (Jn. 13:35), our badge of faith, as well as a sign to us and to our fellow church members of our true conversion (1 Jn. 3:14). (5) *It has hindrances.* There are many stumbling blocks in the way of the continuous manifestation of brotherly love, and this point could easily become a sermon in itself. Only a few such considerations are: pride, a divisive spirit, a lack of patience, and even the strain of persecution. (6) *It has various manifestations.* Some of these can be seen in vv. 2, 3. They include hospitality, especially toward those who may be fleeing persecution, and visiting and ministering to those who are bound or afflicted for the cause of Christ. Other manifestations could be added.

The writer points to the *importance of Christian* marriage (v. 4). On the basis of this verse we can look at least at three things about the subject. (1) Its *commendation*. Marriage between a man and a woman, and only between a man and a woman, has been commended since the beginning of time. Though God knew what He was going to do all along, for didactic purposes He had Adam to intelligently survey all the animals in His lower creation. As Adam named them according to their characteristics, it became very obvious that there was no suitable companion for him among the group. Thus, God formed Eve from Adam's own side and presented her to him in the first marriage ceremony (Gen. 2:18-25). (2) *Its purpose*. God's purpose for marriage is social, because it is not good for us to be alone throughout our lives. It is spiritual because we can pray for and encourage one another in our mutual service for Christ. The formation of the home, with the husband as the loving head and the wife as the submissive mate, also teaches a constant lesson with regard to Christ and His church (Eph. 5). Its purpose is also physical, as the text clearly shows. There is nothing evil about the sexual relationship between a man and a woman in marriage. It is, in fact, one of the most beautiful manifestations of love that can be experienced. The marriage bed is undefiled, but there is severe judgment for those who would betray this sacred commitment. (3) *Its permanence*. God never intended for marriage to be a trial relationship. It has been God's will from the beginning of time for one man and one woman to remain faithful to each other until death parts them. Jesus Himself emphatically confirmed that in answering the Pharisees' question about why Moses allowed divorce. God made provisions for divorce through Moses "because of the hardness of your hearts," Jesus said, but then He declared, "From the beginning it was not so" (Mt. 19:3-9). God meant marriage to be a permanent commitment.

Christians must be careful to *avoid a covetous lifestyle* (vv. 5, 6). It is such an important sin to be avoided that the Lord emphasized it in the tenth commandment, "Thou shalt not covet." One of the reasons it is so important is that it affects several of the other commandments as well. Several things can be pointed out about covetousness. (1) *Its definition*. Covetousness refers to an unholy and uncontrolled desire for wealth and possessions. To want something because one truly needs it, and to seek after it by legitimate means is not covetousness. The desire for acquisition becomes a sin when it gains control of one's life and causes neglect of other matters that deserve priority. (2) *Its power.* Satan recognized the forceful appeal of wealth and possessions in making the second temptation of Christ his offer of the kingdoms of this world (Lk. 4:5-8). For our Lord it was an offer to bypass the cross, but for us the devil would make similar offers to cause us to bypass spiritual priorities. Paul lamented the powerful effects of covetousness when he declared, "Demas hath forsaken me, having loved this present world" (2 Tim. 4:10). (3) *Its manifestations*. Covetousness can take a wide variety of forms in our lives. It may show itself in the goals we set for our lives, the kind of friends we make, and the relationships we cultivate. It is especially demonstrated in our attitude toward material things and our contentment or lack thereof with regard to our lot in life. Paul indicated that he was in control of covetousness in his life when he said, "I have learned, in whatsoever state I am, *therewith* to be content" (Phil. 4:11). But notice that even he said he had "learned" this, suggesting perhaps that this had not always been his attitude. (4) *Its dangers.* Covetousness can cause us to take wrong directions in our lives (as Demas), to fail to be thankful for the good blessings that we have, to neglect depending on God for all of our needs (Mt. 6:33; also vv. 5, 6 in this passage), and to make choices that may affect our eternal destiny.

Our writer presents something of a contrast between the original human leaders of this church and the Savior Himself (vv. 7, 8). As to *the original leaders,* he points out: (1) *Their authority.* "Them which have the rule over you" could also be translated, "Those who were leading you." Effective leadership demands that people follow. Here he evidently refers to the leaders of the past, now dead; but their memories of them and their gratitude for their work should make them even more submissive to God's will and to the leaders who have replaced them. (2) *Their preaching.* The primary authority of spiritual leaders in the church comes from their faithful preaching and teaching of the Word of God. Though we have a great appreciation for all preachers of God's Word, no doubt the one who first presented to us the good news about Christ has a special place in our memories. May it always be so! (3) *Their example.* Of course, there is more to a preacher than his preaching. The way he lives is also extremely important. The qualifications for a pastor in 1 Tim. 3:1-7 have much to say about the kind of person he is, his family relationships, his habits, and his spiritual maturity. The original leaders of this church had been faithful both in preaching the Word and living by faith to the end. (4) *Their departure.* Unfortunately, like the priests of the O.T. (7:23), the preachers of the church pass too quickly from their scene of service. This sometimes can be frustrating to the laity, and that is why our writer makes the contrast in v. 8, "*Jesus Christ* the same yesterday, and to day, and for ever." The complete absence of verbs in the verse makes the contrast even more dramatic. "Yesterday" emphasizes our Lord's incarnation and earthly ministry, now complete (2:9, 14). "To day" points to His present ministry of intercession at the right hand of God in Heaven (7:25). "For ever" takes us forward to the promise of His return and the joys that await us in that eternal city which John saw coming down (10:36, 37; 12:22; Rev. 21:1-4).

The writer also challenges his readers about their *stability of doctrine.* If Christ is always the same, then His followers must not demonstrate their instability in being carried about by various whims of false teachers, a problem with which some were apparently struggling (v. 9). In order to settle any doubts along this line, they must: (1) pledge themselves to the strength of grace which has proven itself again and again; and (2) firmly avoid the deceptions of law which did not produce desirable effects even when it was valid (see also Acts 15:10, 11; Gal. 3:1-6; 4:9-11).

In contrast to the ineffective altar under the old covenant, the writer speaks about a *Christian altar* and its beneficial characteristics (13:10-14). Though there is some controversy about how to interpret this passage, several things seem to stand out clearly about this altar. (1) *It is spiritual, not physical.* Though a place to pray at the front of a church building is both convenient and appropriate, we must be careful not to overdo its emphasis. Christians can pray anywhere and at any time. Under the old covenant there was a physical altar and a physical temple, but under the Christian dispensation the body of each individual believer "is the temple of the Holy Ghost" (1 Cor. 6:19), and our altar is the altar of our heart. Wherever a Christian bows in prayer, praise, and worship a holy altar is created. (2) *It leaves no room for compromise* (v. 10). Those who worship at the Christian altar must make a choice. There can be no room for a mixture of law and gospel (Gal. 5:1-4). These Hebrew Christians cannot have it both ways. (3) *It is based on the supreme sacrifice of Christ* (v. 12). The sacrifices of the sin offering on the Day of Atonement were burned outside the camp of Israel, symbolically indicating the separation of the sin and the sinner. But that sin offering would have to be repeated the next year, and every year after that until the coming of Christ. Jesus Christ demonstrated His fulfillment of that O.T. sin offering by being crucified outside the walls of Jerusalem, and His sacrifice never needs repeating. (4) *It demands separation on the part of all who worship there.* The writer uses the reference to Christ's death outside the walls of Jerusalem for a double purpose: both to point out His fulfillment of the sin offering of the Day of Atonement, and to challenge us to a life of willing separation from all that would take us away from fully serving Him. There was great reproach in Christ's death on the cross, the reproach of the law (Gal. 3:13) as well as the reproach of men (Mt. 27:29-49). That reproach is still present for those who would boldly take their stand for Christ (Lk. 9:23; 1 Cor. 1:17-24; Gal. 2:20).

Though we no longer offer animal sacrifices because of Christ's full and sufficient death on the cross, there are some appropriate *Christian sacrifices* which need to be offered on a regular basis (vv. 15, 16). They are: (1) *the sacrifice of praise to God*; (2) *the sacrifice of doing right and living right* in all the situations we face; (3) *the sacrifice of sharing anything that we may have,* whether wealth, abilities, or service, to help others along in their advancement in the kingdom of God. What a wonderful attitude existed, at least for a brief period of time, in the early church! They came to the place where none of them said "that ought of the things which he possessed was his own" (Acts 4:32). These are sacrifices that are made with our lips, with our lives, and with our attitudes.

The writer mentions again the *church leaders of this congregation* (v. 17). While v. 7 called their attention to leaders of the past who had passed from the scene, this verse exhorts them concerning present leaders. *First*, he emphasizes the church's responsibility to them. (a) *We are to render obedience to them* as a result of the pastor's effective persuasion (the original word, *peitho*, implies this). Such obedience indicates agreement between pastor and church members. (b) *We must also "submit" to them.* This suggests compliance in the face of disagreement or uncertainty. Church leaders should be given the benefit of the doubt. Their authority is not absolute, for only God and His Word stand in that position, but their good leadership must be followed for the church to be effective. *Second*, he emphasizes their responsibility to the church. (a) *As church leaders they must lead.* The phrase translated, "Them that have the rule over you," can also be translated, "Those who are leading you." Pastors do not rule as kings, but they lead as shepherds. Those in the congregation are not their subjects but their sheep. As the word also implies (Greek present tense of *hegeomai*), the leadership must be continuous, even as the obedience and submission is continuous. (b) *Church leaders must also diligently watch the flock* to ward off the attacks of the enemy. They accomplish a major part of their watching by faithfully preaching God's Word, both in warning against false teachers and in feeding the sheep toward spiritual maturity. In the O.T. God warned the spiritual watchmen of Israel to deliver their souls by crying aloud as the enemy approached. If the watchman fails to cry out, he is responsible. If he cries out and the recipients disregard the warning, they must bear the responsibility (Ezek. 33:7-9). (c) *Church leaders must give account.* They do so immediately as they pray for their congregation, and they do so ultimately as they appear at the Judgment Seat of Christ (2 Cor. 5:10). Though God certainly keeps His own record of His people, it is to our benefit for our spiritual leaders to be able to speak well of us both to God and to man.

In bringing the letter to a close, the writer emphasizes *the importance of prayer* (vv. 18-21). In requesting continual prayer for himself from these Hebrew Christians, He points to *his clear conscience,* apparently about the contents of the letter, and to *his clean living* in every area. His primary request concerns his desire to visit them again soon so that he might teach them more personally and in even greater detail. *He also prays for the church* and the struggles they were experiencing *in the name of "the God of peace."* He places special emphasis on *the work of Christ* with regard to His resurrection, His role as the Great Shepherd, His shed blood, His role as Mediator, and His position of eternal exaltation. His *primary request for them is that God will make them perfect,* will supply all that is lacking spiritually in their lives, to enable them to do His will fully with the power and the strength that only He can give.

The *concluding admonitions* call for: (1) *patient consideration of the letter* (v. 22); (2) *planned visit to the church* (v. 23); and (3) *pointed salutations for the people* (v. 24).

BIBLIOGRAPHY: WORKS CITED IN THIS COMMENTARY

Books (cited by author's last name)

Alford, Henry, "Prolegomena & Hebrews" (vol. IV in *Alford's Greek Testament,* Guardian Press, 1857).

Archer, Gleason L. Jr., *The Epistle to the Hebrews in Shield Bible Study Series* (Baker, 1957).

Arminius, James, *The Works of James Arminius* (vol. 1, Baker, 1996; from edition printed in 1825).

Ashby, Stephen M., "A Reformed Arminian View" (in *Four Views on Eternal Security*, ed. Matthew Pinson, Zondervan, 2002).

Barnes, Albert, *Hebrews* (*Barnes' Notes on the New Testament,* edited by Robert Frew, Baker, 1949).

Bauer, Walter, *Griechisch-Deutsches Worterbuch zu den Schriften des Neuen Testaments und der ubrigen urchristlichen Literatur,* trans. and adapted by William F. Arndt and Wilbur F. Gingrich as *A Greek-English Lexicon of the New Testament and Other Early Christian Literature* (U. of Chicago Press, 1957).

Bengel, John Albert, *Romans to Revelation* (vol. 2 in *Bengel's New Testament Commentary,* Kregel, 1981).

Brown, John, *An Exposition of the Epistle to the Hebrews* (1862 edition, reprinted by Banner of Truth, 1961).

Bruce, F. F., *The Epistle to the Hebrews* (Eerdmans, 1964).

Calvin, John, *Commentary on Hebrews* (*Calvin's Commentaries,* orig. published in 1549; reprinted by Baker, 1981).

Carter, Charles W., *Hebrews to Revelation* (vol. 6 in *The Wesleyan Bible Commentary,* Eerdmans, 1966).

Clarke, Adam, *Clarke's Commentary on The New Testament* (J. Fagan & Sons, 1826).

Conybeare, W. J. & Howson, J. S., *The Life and Epistles of St. Paul* (Eerdmans, reprinted 1974).

Crowson, Milton, *The Epistle to the Hebrews* (Randall House, 1974).

Delitzsch, Franz, *Commentary on The Epistle to the Hebrews* (vols. 1, 2, T & T. Clark, 1871; reprinted by Klock & Klock, 1978).

Dods, Marcus, *The Epistle to the Hebrews* (vol. 4 in *The Expositor's Greek Testament,* Eerdmans, 1976).

Draper, James T. Jr., *Hebrews: The Life that Pleases God* (Tyndale, n.d.).

Edersheim, Alford, *Bible History Old Testament* (Eerdmans, 1890, reprinted 1972).

Edwards, Thomas Charles, *Hebrews* (vol. 6 of *The Expositor's Bible: Ephesians to Revelation;* J. Little & Ives, 1890).

Ellingworth, Paul, *The Epistle to the Hebrews: A Commentary on the Greek Text* (Eerdmans, 1993).

Erdman, Charles R., *The Epistle to the Hebrews* (in *Commentaries on the New Testament Books,* Westminster, 1946).
Gaebelein, A. C., *Philippians to Hebrews* (vol. 3 in *The Annotated Bible: The New Testament;* Our Hope Publishers, 1917).
Gill, John, *Romans to Revelation* (vol. 6 in *Gill's Commentary;* originally published in 1854; reprinted by Baker, 1980).
Gouge, William, *Commentary on Hebrews* (orig. published 1866; reprinted by Kregel, 1980).
Guthrie, Donald, *The Letter to the Hebrews* (TNTC, Inter-Varsity/Eerdmans, 1983).
Guthrie, George H., *Hebrews* (in *The NIV Application Commentary,* Zondervan, 1998).
Hagner, Donald A., *Hebrews* (NIBC, Hendrickson, 1983).
Henrichsen, Walter A., *After the Sacrifice* (Zondervan, 1979).
Henry, Matthew, *Matthew Henry's Commentary on the Whole Bible,* vol. 6, Acts to Revelation; Matthew Henry's comments on Hebrews recorded posthumously by William Tong (Fleming H. Revell, n.d.).
Hewit, Thomas, *The Epistle to the Hebrews* (TNTC, Eerdmans, 1960).
Hiebert, D. Edmond, *The Non-Pauline Epistles* (vol. 3 of *New Testament Introduction,* Moody, 1977).
Hughes, Philip Edgcumbe, *Commentary on the Epistle to the Hebrews* (Eerdmans, 1977).
Ironside, H. A., *Hebrews* (Loizeaux, 1932).
Jamieson, Robert, Fausset, A. R., Brown, David, *Matthew to Revelation* (vol. 3 in *A Commentary on the Old and New Testaments*, orig. pub. 1875, reprinted by Eerdmans, 1982).
Jensen, Irving L., *Hebrews: A Self-Study Guide* (Moody, 1970).
Josephus, Flavius, *Josephus' Complete Works* (Kregel, 1969; from edition published in 1867).
Keil, C. F. & Delitzsch, F, *Commentary on The Old Testament: The Pentateuch* (Eerdmans, reprinted 1975).
Kent, Homer A. Jr., *The Epistle to the Hebrews* (Baker, 1972).
Kistemaker, Simon J., *Exposition of the Epistle to the Hebrews* (NTC, Baker, 1984).
Lane, William, *Hebrews: A Call to Commitment* (Hendrickson, 1985).
Lange, John Peter, *Thessalonians—Hebrews* (vol. 22 in *Commentary on the Holy Scriptures,* orig. pub. 1868, reprinted by Zondervan, n.d.).
Lenski, R. C. H., *The Interpretation of the Epistle to the Hebrews and the Epistle of James* (Augsburg, 1966).
Lunemann, Gottlieb, *Critical and Exegetical Handbook to the Epistle to the Hebrews* (T. & T. Clark, 1882).
MacArthur, John F., *Hebrews* (in *The MacArthur New Testament Commentary,* Moody, 1983).
Meyer, F. B., *The Way Into the Holiest: Expositions of the Epistle to the Hebrews* (Revell, n.d.).

Moffatt, James, *A Critical and Exegetical Commentary on the Epistle to the Hebrews,* (ICC, T. & T. Clark, 1924).
Morgan, G. Campbell, *God's Last Word to Man: Studies in Hebrews* (Baker, 1974).
Morris, Leon, *Hebrews* (in *The Expositor's Bible Commentary,* vol. 12; Hebrews—Revelation, ed. Frank Gaebelein, Zondervan, 1981).
Moulton, W. F., *Ephesians to Revelation* (vol. 8 in *Ellicott's Commentary on the Whole Bible,* Zondervan, n.d.).
Murray, Andrew, *The Holiest of All: An Exposition of the Epistle to the Hebrews,* Revell, n.d.).
Newell, William R., *Hebrews Verse By Verse* (Moody, 1947).
Owen, John, *An Exposition of the Epistle to the Hebrews* (vol. 6: 6:1 to 7:28; orig. pub. in 1855, reprinted by Baker, 1980).
Pentecost, J. Dwight, *The Words and Works of Jesus Christ* (Zondervan, 1981).
Pettingill, William L., *Into the Holiest: Simple Studies in the Epistle to the Hebrews* (Van Kampen, 1939).
Picirilli, Robert E., *Grace, Faith, Free Will* (Randall House, 2002).
Pink, Arthur W., *An Exposition of Hebrews* (Baker, 1954).
Ridout, S., *Lectures on the Epistle to the Hebrews* (Loizeaux, 1903).
Robinson, Theodore H., *The Epistle to the Hebrews* (in *The Moffatt New Testament Commentary,* Harper, 1933).
Roddy, Clarence S., *The Epistle to the Hebrews* (Baker, 1962).
Saphir, Adolph, *The Epistle to the Hebrews: An Exposition* (Loizeaux, 1946).
Schneider, Johannes, *The Letter to the Hebrews* (Eerdmans, 1957).
Seiss, Joseph Augustus, *Lectures on Hebrews* (Baker, 1954).
Stedman, Ray C., *Hebrews* (*The IMP Commentary Series,* Intervarsity, 1992).
Theissen, Henry Clarence, *Introduction to the New Testament* (Eerdmans, 1943).
Thomas, W. H. Griffith, *Hebrews: A Devotional Commentary* (Eerdmans, 1961).
Trapp, John, *Trapp's Commentary on the New Testament* (Zondervan, 1958; reprinted from 1865 edition).
Turner, George Allen, *The New and Living Way* (Bethany Fellowship, 1975).
Unger, Merrill F., *Unger's Bible Dictionary* (Moody, 1966).
Westcott, Brooke Foss, *The Epistle to the Hebrews* (Eerdmans, 1889).
Whedon, D. D., *Titus-Revelation* (vol. 5 in *Commentary on the New Testament,* Hunt & Eaton, 1880).
Wiersbe, Warren W., *Be Confident* (Victor, 1982).
Wiley, H. Orton, *The Epistle to the Hebrews* (Beacon Hill, 1959).Wuest, Kenneth S., *Hebrews in the Greek New Testament* (Eerdmans, 1955).
Yeager, Randolph O., *Titus, Philemon, Hebrews, James 1:1—3:18* (vol. 16 in *The Renaissance New Testament,* Pelican, 1985).